Lecture Notes in Computer Science 16189

The series Lecture Notes in Computer Science (LNCS), including its subseries Lecture Notes in Artificial Intelligence (LNAI) and Lecture Notes in Bioinformatics (LNBI), has established itself as a medium for the publication of new developments in computer science and information technology research, teaching, and education.

LNCS enjoys close cooperation with the computer science R & D community, the series counts many renowned academics among its volume editors and paper authors, and collaborates with prestigious societies. Its mission is to serve this international community by providing an invaluable service, mainly focused on the publication of conference and workshop proceedings and postproceedings. LNCS commenced publication in 1973.

Dominik Bork · Roman Lukyanenko ·
Shazia Sadiq · Ladjel Bellatreche · Oscar Pastor
Editors

Conceptual Modeling

44th International Conference, ER 2025
Poitiers, France, October 20–23, 2025
Proceedings

Springer

Editors
Dominik Bork
TU Wien
Vienna, Austria

Roman Lukyanenko
University of Virginia
Charlottesville, VA, USA

Shazia Sadiq
The University of Queensland
Brisbane, QLD, Australia

Ladjel Bellatreche
ISAE-ENSMA
Poitiers, France

Oscar Pastor
Universidad Politécnica de Valencia
Valencia, Spain

ISSN 0302-9743 ISSN 1611-3349 (electronic)
Lecture Notes in Computer Science
ISBN 978-3-032-08622-8 ISBN 978-3-032-08623-5 (eBook)
https://doi.org/10.1007/978-3-032-08623-5

This Springer imprint is published by the registered company Springer Nature Switzerland AG
The registered company address is: Gewerbestrasse 11, 6330 Cham, Switzerland

Preface

This volume of the Lecture Notes in Computer Science series contains the proceedings of the 44th International Conference on Conceptual Modeling – ER 2025, held in Poitiers, France, during October 20–23, 2025.

The "City of a hundred bell towers," Poitiers is a world-renowned gem of art and culture. Poitiers made significant marks on the course of world history, celebrated for its Romanesque architecture and famous for the Battle of Poitiers in 732. Today, its winding streets, imposing churches, and charming squares are seamlessly interwoven with modernity. A bustling technology hub, Poitiers is a leader in education and innovation. ISAE-ENSMA is a driver of aeronautical and space excellence for the mobility of the future. It addresses industrial and societal challenges by providing high-level scientific and technological expertise to lead complex research and technology projects. Futuroscope, just outside the city, is a unique technology-driven theme park that combines immersive attractions with cutting-edge multimedia and virtual reality experiences. ISAE-ENSMA (École Nationale Supérieure de Mécanique et d'Aérotechnique) was the venue for ER 2025, while Futuroscope was the scene of the social event, making ER even more alluring.

The ER Conference, with a nearly half-century tradition of nurturing high-end research in the field of conceptual modeling, is evolving to embrace the rapidly expanding landscape of artificial intelligence and digitalization everywhere. The theme of this year's ER was "Building Trust Through Conceptual Modeling."

Building trust in digital ecosystems has gained heightened importance in an increasingly contested world. This year's theme focused on the important role conceptual modeling plays in creating systems that are trustworthy, inclusive, and transparent. With this theme, we encouraged the conceptual modeling community to deliberate on how traditional modeling principles and frameworks can contribute and adapt to new advancements in AI, data ecosystems, and autonomous platforms while upholding ethical standards and fostering trust in digital innovations.

While seeking to facilitate a brighter tomorrow with trustworthy digital technologies, ER 2025 also embraced traditional conceptual modeling topics, including data and process modeling, goal modeling, theoretical foundations of modeling, and more. It also welcomed industry and vision papers, reflecting the conference's commitment to both theoretical advancements and practical applications.

ER 2025 received a total of 109 paper submissions for the main conference. The double-blind review began with three submissions being desk-rejected by the program co-chairs for being incomplete or outside the conference's scope. The remaining 106 submissions underwent independent evaluations by at least three Program Committee (PC) members, followed by a detailed discussion phase moderated by a senior PC member who provided a meta-review summarizing and explaining recommendations to the authors. PC co-chairs reviewed all recommendations, sought revisions of reviews and meta-reviews, and made the final decisions.

Ultimately, 22 submissions were accepted based on their novelty and contributions to advancing the state of the art, with 17 directly accepted and five conditionally accepted pending minor revisions verified by the senior PC member or the PC Chairs acting as shepherd. This rigorous process culminated in an acceptance rate of 20.75%. Additionally, some submissions were offered a fast-track to the ER Forum, which four author teams accepted.

The main conference included sessions on Research papers, Keynotes, Tutorials, Panels, the Forum for short visionary papers, Industry papers, Posters, and Demos. The three invited keynote presentations were "Some Implications of Agential Realism for Conceptual Modeling" by Ron Weber, Emeritus Professor, Monash University, Australia; Emeritus Professor, The University of Queensland, Australia; and laureate of the 2025 ER Peter Chen Award; "A Modeler's Trials and Tribulations - Defeats, Successes and Open Issues" by Heinrich C. Mayr, Emeritus Professor, Alpen-Adria University of Klagenfurt, Austria and laureate of the 2024 ER Peter Chen Award; and "The bumpy road of data and AI transformation - How conceptual models help address wicked problems" by Professor Christine Legner, University of Lausanne, Switzerland.

On behalf of our community, we extend our gratitude to the keynote speakers for sharing their invaluable insights into the evolution of conceptual modeling research over the past 44 years and its future.

We thank the authors for submitting their work to ER 2025, the Program Committees for their dedication and expertise in writing and handling the reviews, and the Organizing Committee for flawlessly managing promotion, submissions, and communication to bring ER 2025 to life and ensure its success.

September 2025

Dominik Bork
Roman Lukyanenko
Shazia Sadiq
Ladjel Bellatreche
Oscar Pastor

Organization

General Chairs

Ladjel Bellatreche	ISAE-ENSMA, France
Oscar Pastor	Universidad Politécnica de Valencia, Spain

Program Co-chairs

Shazia Sadiq	University of Queensland, Australia
Dominik Bork	TU Wien, Austria
Roman Lukyanenko	University of Virginia, USA

Forum Chairs

Stéphane Jean	University of Poitiers, France
Hongzhi Wang	Harbin Institute of Technology, China

Posters and Demos Chairs

Jeffrey Parsons	Memorial University, Canada
Hui Ma	Victoria University of Wellington, New Zealand

Tutorial Chairs

Veda Storey	Georgia State University, USA
Sihem Amer-Yahia	IMAG, France

Panel Chairs

Hasan Yasar	CMU SEI, USA
Boualem Benatallah	Dublin City University, Ireland

Doctoral Consortium Chairs

João Paulo A. Almeida	Federal University of Espírito Santo, Brazil
Isabelle Comyn-Wattiau	ESSEC Business School, Cergy-Pontoise, France
Geert Poels	Ghent University, Belgium

Workshop Chairs

Anna Bernasconi	Politécnico di Milano, Italy
Sergio de Cesare	University of Westminster, UK
Claudenir Morais Fonseca	University of Twente, The Netherlands

CEUR Proceedings Chair

Patrick Marcel	University of Orléans, France

Publicity Chair

Selma Khouri	École Nationale Supérieure d'Informatique, Algeria

Industrial Track Chairs

Thomas Polacsek	ONERA, France
Kamalakar Karlapalem	IIIT Hyderabad, India

Proceedings Chair

Amin Mesmoudi	University of Poitiers, France

Web and Social Media Chair

Mickaël Baron	ISAE-ENSMA, France

Senior Program Committee

Jacky Akoka	CEDRIC-CNAM & IMT-TEM, France
João Paulo A. Almeida	Federal University of Espírito Santo, Brazil
Paolo Atzeni	Università Roma Tre, Italy
José Borbinha	INESC-ID, IST, Universidade de Lisboa, Portugal
Stefano Ceri	Politecnico di Milano, Italy
Isabelle Comyn-Wattiau	ESSEC Business School, France
Gill Dobbie	University of Auckland, New Zealand
Aldo Gangemi	Università di Bologna, Italy
Nicola Guarino	ISTC-CNR, Italy
Giancarlo Guizzardi	University of Twente, The Netherlands
Manfred Jeusfeld	University of Skövde, Sweden
Paul Johannesson	Stockholm University, Sweden
Kamalakar Karlapalem	IIIT Hyderabad, India
Alberto Laender	Federal University of Minas Gerais, Brazil
Steve Liddle	Brigham Young University, USA
Sebastian Link	University of Auckland, New Zealand
Wolfgang Maass	Saarland University, Germany
Heinrich C. Mayr	Alpen-Adria-Universität Klagenfurt, Austria
John Mylopoulos	University of Ottawa, Canada
José Palazzo M. de Oliveira	Federal University of Rio Grande do Sul, Brazil
Jeffrey Parsons	Memorial University of Newfoundland, Canada
Henderik A. Proper	TU Wien, Austria
Jolita Ralyté	University of Geneva, Switzerland
Iris Reinhartz-Berger	University of Haifa, Israel
Stefanie Rinderle-Ma	Technical University of Munich, Germany
Colette Rolland	Université Paris 1 Panthéon-Sorbonne, France
Pnina Soffer	University of Haifa, Israel
Veda Storey	Georgia State University, USA
Stefan Strecker	University of Hagen, Germany
Bernhard Thalheim	Christian-Albrechts-Universität zu Kiel, Germany
Juan Trujillo	Universidad de Alicante, Spain
Gerd Wagner	Brandenburg University of Technology at Cottbus, Germany
Barbara Weber	University of St. Gallen, Switzerland

Program Committee

Mara Abel	Federal University of Rio Grande do Sul, Brazil
João Araújo	Universidade NOVA de Lisboa, Portugal
David Aveiro	University of Madeira, Portugal
Wolf-Tilo Balke	TU Braunschweig, Germany
Monalessa Barcellos	Federal University of Espírito Santo, Brazil
Anna Bernasconi	Politecnico di Milano, Italy
Devis Bianchini	University of Brescia, Italy
Sandro Bimonte	INRAE, France
Luiz Olavo B. Da Silva Santos	University of Twente, The Netherlands
Shawn Bowers	Gonzaga University, USA
Robert Andrei Buchmann	Babeş-Bolyai University of Cluj Napoca, Romania
Lola Burgueño	University of Málaga, Spain
Jordi Cabot	Luxembourg Inst. of Science and Technology, Luxembourg
Diego Calvanese	Free University of Bozen-Bolzano, Italy
Cinzia Cappiello	Politecnico di Milano, Italy
Arturo Castellanos	William & Mary, USA
Luca Cernuzzi	Universidad Católica "Nuestra Señora de la Asunción", Paraguay
Suphamit Chittayasothorn	King Mongkut's Institute of Technology Ladkrabang, Thailand
Loek Cleophas	TU Eindhoven; and Stellenbosch University, The Netherlands
Sergio de Cesare	University of Westminster, UK
Vadim Ermolayev	Ukrainian Catholic University, Ukraine
Rik Eshuis	Eindhoven University of Technology, The Netherlands
Luís Ferreira Pires	University of Twente, The Netherlands
Peter Fettke	German Research Center for Artificial Intelligence (DFKI) and Saarland University, Germany
Hans-Georg Fill	University of Fribourg, Switzerland
Marco Franceschetti	University of St. Gallen, Switzerland
Enrico Franconi	Free University of Bozen-Bolzano, Italy
Mattia Fumagalli	Free University of Bozen-Bolzano, Italy
Frederik Gailly	Ghent University, Belgium
Faiez Gargouri	University of Sfax, Tunisia
Philippe Giabbanelli	Old Dominion University, USA
Asif Gill	University of Technology Sydney, Australia

Cesar Gonzalez-Perez	Incipit CSIC, Spain
Jaap Gordijn	Vrije Universiteit Amsterdam, The Netherlands
Guido Governatori	Independent researcher, Australia
Georg Grossmann	University of South Australia, Australia
Esther Guerra	Universidad Autónoma de Madrid, Spain
Sergio Guerreiro	INESC-ID/Instituto Superior Técnico, Portugal
Renata Guizzardi	University of Twente, The Netherlands
Simon Hacks	Stockholm University, Sweden
Hyoil Han	Illinois State University, USA
Sven Hartmann	Clausthal University of Technology, Germany
Martin Henkel	Stockholm University, Sweden
Felix Härer	FHNW University of Applied Sciences and Arts Basel, Switzerland
Marta Indulska	University of Queensland, Australia
Shareeful Islam	Anglia Ruskin University, UK
Araz Jabbari	Université Laval, Canada
Marite Kirikova	Riga Technical University, Latvia
Stefan Klikovits	Johannes Kepler University Linz, Austria
Agnes Koschmider	Kiel University, Germany
Thomas Kühne	Victoria University of Wellington, New Zealand
Vinay Kulkarni	Tata Consultancy Services Research, India
Julius Köpke	Alpen-Adria-Universität Klagenfurt, Austria
Tong Li	Beijing University of Technology, China
Sotirios Liaskos	York University, Canada
Sergio Lifschitz	Pontifical Catholic University of Rio de Janeiro, Brazil
Jim Logan	Dassault Systèmes, USA
Claudenir M. Fonseca	University of Twente, The Netherlands
Hui Ma	Victoria University of Wellington, New Zealand
Maria Luiza Machado Campos	Federal University of Rio de Janeiro, Brazil
Beatriz Marín	Universitat Politècnica de València, Spain
Wolfgang Mayer	University of South Australia, Australia
Massimo Mecella	Sapienza University of Rome, Italy
Judith Michael	RWTH Aachen University, Germany
João Moreira	University of Twente, The Netherlands
Haralambos Mouratidis	University of Essex, UK
Júlio César Nardi	Federal Institute of Espírito Santo, Brazil
Bernd Neumayr	Johannes Kepler University Linz, Austria
Selmin Nurcan	Université Paris 1 Panthéon – Sorbonne, France
Leo Obrst	MITRE, USA
José Oliveira	Aeronautics Institute of Technology, Brazil
Andreas L. Opdahl	University of Bergen, Norway

Elda Paja	IT University of Copenhagen, Denmark
Robert Pergl	Czech Technical University in Prague, Czechia
Barbara Pernici	Politecnico di Milano, Italy
Geert Poels	Ghent University, Belgium
Fabio Porto	National Laboratory of Scientific Computation, Brazil
Tiago Sales	University of Twente, The Netherlands
Luise Pufahl	TU Munich, Germany
Christoph Quix	Hochschule Niederrhein University of Applied Sciences, Germany
Manfred Reichert	University of Ulm, Germany
Hajo A. Reijers	Utrecht University, The Netherlands
Ben Roelens	Open Universiteit, Ghent University, The Netherlands
Michael Rosemann	Queensland University of Technology, Australia
Kristina Rosenthal	Hochschule Niederrhein University of Applied Sciences, Germany
Marcela Ruiz	Zurich University of Applied Sciences, Switzerland
Bernhard Rumpe	RWTH Aachen University, Germany
Maribel Yasmina Santos	University of Minho, Portugal
Estefania Serral	KU Leuven, Belgium
Samira Si-Said Cherfi	Conservatoire National des Arts et Métiers, France
Tijs Slaats	University of Copenhagen, Denmark
Monique Snoeck	KU Leuven, Belgium
Vítor E. Silva Souza	Federal University of Espírito Santo, Brazil
Markus Stumptner	University of South Australia, Australia
Arnon Sturm	Ben-Gurion University of the Negev, Israel
Angelo Susi	Fondazione Bruno Kessler, Italy
Panos Vassiliadis	University of Ioannina, Greece
Yves Wautelet	Katholieke Universiteit Leuven, Belgium
Hans Weigand	Tilburg University, The Netherlands
Mathias Weske	HPI, University of Potsdam, Germany
Manuel Wimmer	Johannes Kepler University Linz, Austria
Andreas Wortmann	University of Stuttgart, Germany
Robert Wrembel	Poznań University of Technology, Poland
Hasan Yasar	Carnegie Mellon University, USA
Apostolos Zarras	University of Ioannina, Greece

Steering Committee

Chair

Giancarlo Guizzardi — University of Twente, The Netherlands

Vice Chair

Jolita Ralyte — University of Geneva, Switzerland

Treasurer

Stephen W. Liddle — Brigham Young University, USA

Emeritus

Peter P. Chen

Steering Committee Members

João Paulo A. Almeida
Peter P. Chen
Isabelle Comyn-Wattiau
Ulrich Frank
Giancarlo Guizzardi
Jennifer Horkoff
Paul Johannesson
Gerti Kappel
Kamal Karlapalem
Alberto Laender
Stephen W. Liddle
Tok Wang Ling
Sebastian Link
Hui Ma
Wolfgang Maaß
Heinrich Mayr
Jeffrey Parsons
Oscar Pastor
Jolita Ralyte
Sudha Ram
Motoshi Saeki
Vítor Estêvão Silva Souza
Il-Yeol Song
Veda Storey
Juan Carlos Trujillo
Carson Woo
Eric Yu

Additional Reviewers

Greta Adamo
Milda Aleknonyte-Resch
Faten Atigui
Leon Bein
Daniel Borcard
Marcel Bühlmann
Ana Costa
Juan de Lara

Mauro Sérgio dos Santos Moura
Karamjit Kaur
Maximilian König
Suhwan Lee
Arvid Lepsien
Roman Lukyanenko
Adrian Costin Marin
Michael McCain
Bruno Menezes
Gabriela Moraes
David M. Negrin
Thomas Ricardo Pathe
Janik Rapp
Alejandro Reina
Elena Romanenko
Suman Roychoudhury
Anjo Seidel
Matt Selway
Henrik Thillmann
Jan Martijn van der Werf
Sebastian Will
Felipe Xavier

Keynote Summary

A Modeler's Trials and Tribulations: Defeats, Successes and Open Issues

Heinrich C. Mayr

Alpen-Adria-Universität, Klagenfurt, Austria
heinrich.mayr@aau.at

It is undisputed that modeling is an essential part of the development of systems and thus also of information systems. Programming in particular is a modeling discipline, because computer programs are nothing more than prescriptive models of processes.

The body of knowledge on modeling is rich and difficult to grasp. First attempts to provide access to this jungle propose a systematic characterization of research contributions along a taxonomy and supported by LLM-based tools. The focus is on "conceptual modeling," which has been explicitly discussed and researched since the 1970s. Despite decades of effort, however, there is still no generally accepted theory of conceptual modeling and hardly any standards. We even lack a community agreement on the definition of what a concept model is, although there are a number of proposals, some of which are even frequently cited.

Regardless of this, many methods, modeling languages, and tools for conceptual modeling and model-based systems engineering were introduced, highly praised, and then forgotten. Most of them came with the aim of providing support in system development, business process design, and complex data management. Measured against this objective, the results of all efforts are sobering, at least as far as small and medium-sized development companies are concerned. For them, modeling usually consists of drawing diagrams, recently with the help of LLM-based tools. Many developers struggle with the abstraction that comes with modeling, and managers are put off by the time required, "which the customer does not pay for". This stands in sharp contrast to other engineering disciplines, where development without systematic modeling is unthinkable.

Since the early 1970s, I have been involved in research and practice in (conceptual) modeling, sometimes successfully, sometimes with dismal failures. In this keynote speech, I will report on some earlier and some more recent findings and experiences and take the liberty of making recommendations for future work in our field. This includes discussing fundamental principles (in particular the concept of model), specifying the meaning of models, deepening the understanding of abstraction, and more.

Some Implications of Agential Realism for Conceptual Modeling

Ron Weber[1,2]

[1] Monash University, Melbourne, VIC, 3800 Australia
ron.weber@monash.edu
[2] The University of Queensland, Brisbane, QLD, 4072 Australia

Agential realism is a highly cited, iconoclastic philosophy proposed by Karen Barad about the nature of the world [2]. It has roots in quantum theory, science and technology studies, and feminist studies. It conceives ontology, epistemology, and ethics as intertwined, entangled, mutually implicated, co-constituted fields. Accordingly, it is a philosophy that Barad characterizes as a singular, unitary ethico-onto-epistemology.

The fundamental ontological unit in Barad's agential realism is her notion of "phenomena." Contrary to the ontologies that underpin much conceptual modeling research and practice, phenomena are not entities, nor objects, nor things with intrinsic and mutual properties or relationships and attributes. Instead, phenomena are "intra-acting agencies" in the world—elementary forces that are somehow present in the world. These agencies "intra-act" with each other rather than interact because, within phenomena, only indeterminate entities with indeterminate properties and indeterminate causal structures exist. Barad characterizes phenomena as "primitive relations"—relations that do not have pre-existing relata.

The entities and their properties and causal structures within phenomena become determinate only when something called an "agential cut" occurs. An agential cut is enacted by "material-discursive practices"—practices that involve material objects as well as verbal and non-verbal communications. These practices may include both humans (e.g., information system users and conceptual modelers) and non-humans (e.g., information technologies and inventory items) as they bring worlds into existence via agential cuts. These somewhat strange and perhaps counterintuitive ideas derive in part from quantum theory (e.g., the notions of superposition and indeterminacy with quantum objects) and feminist theory (e.g., an expanded notion of discourse and the range of and power afforded to discursive practices among humans and non-humans).

Agential realism has had most impact on several fields in the humanities and social sciences. It has had less impact on fields in the physical, life, engineering, and design sciences. In the information systems field, however, agential realism underpins extensive work on the concept of sociomateriality (e.g., [3]), whereby information technologies and their users are conceived as co-constituted, entangled wholes rather than separate things that interact. In the computer science field, agential realism has recently been used by human-computer interface developers to inform their design practices (e.g., [5]).

What are the implications of agential realism for the conceptual-modeling field? To address this question, in my presentation, I will frame conceptual-modeling activities using the lens of agential realism. Based on this framing, I will consider five substantive challenges that the philosophy poses for the ways we currently do our work as conceptual modelers. I will discuss the nature of these challenges, their implications for conceptual modeling, and how we might address them in our research and practice. Hopefully, the merits (or lack thereof) of an agential-realism framing of conceptual modeling can then be better assessed.

The first challenge that agential realism poses for the conceptual-modeling field is that it eschews the notion that an independent reality exists and that this reality can be discovered with the "right" apparatuses (e.g., high-quality user-requirements elicitation methods or insightful use-cases). The implication is that any belief we might have as conceptual-modeling professionals that we can discover a single, correct domain that we can then model is misplaced. Reality, which entails knowing the semantics of a domain, only materializes when "measurement" occurs. Moreover, the resulting reality is specific to and entangled with the specific measurements that are done. What, therefore, are we doing when we develop conceptual models of a domain—creating realities, or representing realities, or both? How do we deal with the recognition that multiple realities exist, which are the outcomes of multiple agential cuts in which the users of information systems (or software products or services) and we, as conceptual modelers, are entangled?

The second challenge that agential realism poses for the conceptual-modeling field is that it eschews the notion that a faithful representation of reality can be constructed. On the one hand, an independent reality does not exist under agential realism (as per the first challenge above). Instead, depending on the agential cuts that are enacted, different realities will materialize. On the other hand, even if an independent reality existed, representations are also constructed via material-discursive practices. Depending on the agents entangled in these material-discursive practices, different representations will materialize, all of which purportedly faithfully represent the focal domain. Moreover, because material-discursive practices are constantly unfolding and enfolding, the verisimilitude of representations that are enacted will be ephemeral. If, as agential realism implies, representations are always tenuous, what are the implications for the information systems (or software products or services) that we build which are based on them?

The third challenge that agential realism poses for the conceptual-modeling field is that even if we acknowledge the importance of context when eliciting information requirements to build a conceptual model, our understanding of what is meant by context is likely to be impoverished. In agential realism, context must be understood as the many entanglements that underpin the material-discursive practices that enact an agential cut. For instance, for ourselves as conceptual modelers, context encompasses the conceptual-modeling approaches we use, our commitment to a particular ontological theory, the hardware and software technologies we use in our organizations, our prior education, training, and experience, the incentives we face in our organisation, the layout of our workspace, the norms of professional organizations to which we belong, our social and economic views, how we feel on the day we develop a conceptual model, and so on. For the users of an information system (or software product or service), similar considerations apply. When we build conceptual models, clearly, we cannot consider all aspects of context. Does agential realism provide pointers to those aspects of context that are likely to be important to our conceptual-modeling work? Or must we develop our own guidelines for surfacing which aspects of context are likely to be important?

The fourth challenge that agential realism poses for the conceptual-modeling field is that we, as conceptual modelers, need to understand more deeply the ways in which we are entangled in the material-discursive practices that lead to the development of a conceptual model. Absent an understanding of agential realism, our awareness of these entanglements is probably limited (as per the third challenge above). Most likely, our awareness will be confined primarily to proximate, overt things—for instance, the organizations in which we work, the individuals who will use the information systems (or software products or services) that we build, and the information technology tools that we employ to undertake our conceptual modeling work. But inevitably our entanglements are more extensive, opaque, and nuanced. Moreover, some of these entanglements might be especially important to the conceptual-modeling work we undertake. For instance, our education, training, experience, and organizational context may have inculcated us in ways that lead us to build conceptual models which inform the development of information systems that reinforce a particular socio-economic or organizational hegemony or entrap users via the addictive behaviors they evoke.

The fifth challenge that agential realism poses for the conceptual-modeling field is that we need to better understand the ethical implications of the conceptual models we develop. The agential cuts we make when we develop conceptual models are deeply entangled with matters of ethics because the conceptual models we build materialize some worlds and foreclose other worlds. Often, we do not understand or even contemplate the consequent intra-actions that will or will not unfold. For instance, we may not realize that the worlds we have materialized in our conceptual models will facilitate surreptitious surveillance of individuals or the worlds we have foreclosed will mask important social changes that occur via disparate shifts in wealth and power. This agential-realism challenge becomes more salient with generative artificial intelligence systems as we try to understand the worlds that might unfold through using these systems and the worlds that potentially will dissipate and disappear. It also becomes more salient as we seek to build systems that are trustworthy, fair, inclusive, and transparent.

Whether agential realism proves to be a philosophy that over the long run is robust and useful is still unclear. While it has many zealous advocates (e.g., [1]), others contest some of its important tenets (e.g., [4, 6]). These differences aside, in some ways, an important benefit of using agential realism to reflect on conceptual modeling is that it gives us a different "voice" and lens to re-consider matters that perhaps we already know about. For instance, we know that we are unlikely to find a situation where information system users hold a unanimous view about the semantics of a domain, and we know that the work we undertake sometimes has important ethical implications. Nonetheless, agential realism gives us a new lexicon and some new ways to reflect on these matters. Potentially, the outcome could be a changed discourse that leads to higher-quality, more ethically informed conceptual-modeling research and practice.

References

1. Atkinson, P., Delamont, S., Cernat, A., Sakshaug, J.W., Williams, R.A.: SAGE Research Methods Foundations. SAGE Publications Ltd (2021)
2. Barad, K.: Meeting the Universe Halfway: Quantum Physics and the Entanglement of Matter and Meaning. Duke University Press (2007)
3. Cecez-Kecmanovic, D., Galliers, R.D., Henfridsson, O., Newell, S., Vidgen, R.: The sociomateriality of information systems. MIS Q. **38**(3), 809–830 (2014)
4. Faye, J., Jaksland, R.: Barad, Bohr, and quantum mechanics. Synthese **199**(3), 8231–8255 (2021)
5. Rajcic, N., Rodriguez, M.T.L., McCormack, J.: Towards a diffractive analysis of prompt-based generative AI. In: Mueller, F.F., et al. (eds.) Proceedings of the CHI Conference on Human Factors in Computing Systems, CHI 2024, Honolulu, HI, USA, 11–16 May 2024. pp. 844:1–844:15. ACM (2024). https://doi.org/10.1145/3613904.3641971
6. Weber, R.A.: A critique of agential realism. Commun. Assoc. Inf. Syst. **57**, 11 (2025), https://aisel.aisnet.org/cais/vol57/iss1/11

The Bumpy Road of Data and AI Transformation: How Conceptual Models Help Address Wicked Problems

Christine Legner

Faculty of Business and Economics (HEC), University of Lausanne, 1015 Lausanne, Switzerland
christine.legner@unil.ch

Over the past years, many organizations have significantly ramped up their investments in data, analytics and artificial intelligence (AI), a trend further accelerated by the rapid rise of Generative AI. They aspire to become data- and AI-driven enterprises that continuously and systematically use data (from internal and external sources) and AI to inform decision-making and improve operational efficiencies, products, services, and customer experience. According to McKinsey's Global Survey on the State of AI [1], 78% of organizations use AI in at least one business function in 2024, a notable increase from 55% in the previous year. Despite these advances, most organizations have yet to fully embed data and AI into the core of their business and (re)design their business processes and system landscapes for large-scale data and AI use. While becoming "data-driven" remains a north star for many, only 37% consider themselves truly data-driven [2]. Transforming an organization's approach to data and AI is a bumpy journey marked by numerous challenges. The complexity arises not only from making appropriate technology choices, designing data platforms and architectures, and developing trustworthy AI-based systems, but equally from reshaping organizational practices and developing the capabilities and skillsets needed for large-scale data and AI adoption.

These transformations are fraught with so-called *"wicked problems"* that are complex, difficult to understand and define, have no single correct solution, and involve multiple stakeholders with different worldviews and diverging interests [3]. Because of their ill-defined nature, these problems cannot be addressed by solely employing analytical methods, but involve exploring multiple solutions, testing and iterating, and co-creating solutions with stakeholders, therefore providing a fertile ground for contributions from the conceptual modeling research community.

In our research at the Competence Center Corporate Data Quality (CC CDQ), we have been collaborating with experts from multinational companies for two decades to co-innovate and jointly develop concepts, methods, and tools in the field of data management [4]. Following the design science paradigm, our research encompasses analysis (exploration of the problem space, leading to problem identification and the definition of requirements), design (development of the solution space via the iterative design and development of artifacts), demonstration and evaluation (via expert evaluation and situational instantiations). Among the key artifacts developed in this research, conceptual models have proven to be an effective means of addressing critical challenges in data – and increasingly AI – transformations, yielding several important insights:

- A key challenge lies in *the inherent complexity of data and AI transformations*, where organizations struggle to understand the overall scope and boundaries, assess their current situation and articulate a clear target state and roadmap. Frameworks in the form of capability or maturity models are popular among practitioners because they synthesize expert knowledge and provide guidance in transformation journeys. Today, only a few – among them the CDQ Data Excellence Model – have been designed following academic principles and grounded in a solid knowledge base [4].
- The *lack of transparency and trust in data*, together with persistent data silos, represents another key challenge in data and AI transformations. While data cataloguing and metamodels contribute to making data FAIR (findable, accessible, interoperable and reusable), a semantic layer establishes a shared data understanding and ensures consistent use within and across organizational boundaries. Conceptual models have historically been central to organizing enterprise data [5], but need to evolve to cope with the massive amounts of largely unstructured data originating from heterogeneous sources that feed AI and agentic systems. Yet, most companies lack the skills and resources to create semantic models, opening opportunities for industry-level and academic initiatives to establish domain-specific vocabularies and ontologies.
- Moving from narrowly defined pilots to *scalable data and AI-based solutions* that effectively support large user communities in their routines represents another major challenge. Designing such solutions requires understanding the broader business context, accounting for real-life constraints and incorporating multiple stakeholder views. Conceptual models can serve as boundary objects in this process, though an important trade-off exists between their complexity and usability. Taking a more pragmatic and accessible form, canvases – as visual inquiry tools – are effectively supporting cross-functional teams, composed of business users data and AI experts, and IT specialists, for example in data product design [6].
- Driven by rapid technology advances and emerging AI use cases, companies must fundamentally *redesign their existing architectures and platforms to enable data- and AI-driven innovation*. In this process, architecture blueprints are needed that outline the required components and layers, including the shift from on-premise to cloud infrastructures and their configuration in federated approaches.

In conclusion, conceptual models are currently underused in data and AI transformations, but they can play a key role in tackling their inherent wicked problems – specifically through (1) capability and maturity models, which guide organizations in their data and AI transformation journeys; (2) (meta)data and semantic models to enable consistent interpretation and use of data; (3) canvases and other visual inquiry tools, which facilitate the collaborative design of data and AI-based solutions; and (4) reference models, which facilitate the development of modern enterprise data platforms and trustworthy AI applications.

References

1. Singla, A., Sukharevsky, A., Yee, L., Chui, M., Hall, B.: The State of AI: HOW Organizations are Rewiring to Capture Value. McKinsey & Company (2025). https://www.mckinsey.com/capabilities/quantumblack/our-insights/the-state-of-ai#/
2. Davenport, T., Bean, R.: Five Trends in AI and Data Science for 2025. MIT Sloan Management Review (2025). https://sloanreview.mit.edu/article/five-trends-in-ai-and-data-science-for-2025/
3. Rittel, H., Webber, M.: Dilemmas in a general theory of planning. Policy Sci. **4**(2), 155–169 (1973)
4. Legner, C., Pentek, T., Otto, B.: Accumulating design knowledge with reference models: insights from 12 years' research into data management. J. Assoc. Inf. Syst. **21**, 3 (2020)
5. Storey, V., Song, I.-Y.: Big data technologies and management: what conceptual modeling can do. Data Knowl. Eng. **108**, 50-67 (2017)
6. Hasan, R., Finkel, B., Legner, C.: The data product canvas: designing data products for sustained value from enterprise data. Inf. Syst. J. (2025)

References

1. Singla, A., Sukharevsky, A., Yee, L., Chui, M., Hall, B.: The State of AI ...

Contents

Data and Process Modeling

Knowledge Graphs and Graph Databases

Applications of Conceptual Modeling

Modeling for Safeguarding

Interactive Repair of Inconsistencies in Conceptual Models

Juan Antonio Gómez-Gutiérrez(✉) and Robert Clarisó

Universitat Oberta de Catalunya, Barcelona, Spain
{juanto,rclariso}@uoc.edu

Abstract. Conceptual models, such as UML class diagrams annotated with OCL invariants, can contain inconsistencies—such as contradictory constraints—that prevent the construction of any valid system instance. Resolving these issues requires more than automatic detection or correction: it demands a deep understanding of the domain, as improper modifications may lead to unintended behavior or violate domain semantics. Existing approaches tend to focus on inconsistency detection, localization, or limited forms of automated repair, offering little support for domain experts who must interpret complex faults and reason about suitable corrections.

This paper presents an approach to assist conceptual modelers in understanding and repairing inconsistencies in UML/OCL models. This approach is based on the use of object diagrams to instantiate the model and make inconsistencies tangible. These instances serve as a diagnostic aid, allowing users to explore the implications of conflicting constraints and to evaluate multiple candidate repairs interactively. The approach is implemented in a tool integrated into the UML Specification Environment (USE), which guides users through fault analysis, helps identify root causes, and supports the assessment of alternative repairs through model exploration.

Keywords: UML · OCL · class diagram · verification · integrity constraint · conceptual model debugging · OCL optimization

1 Introduction

Developing software that fully meets its requirements is challenging. UML diagrams [31] support this process by offering high-level system descriptions useful for communication, documentation, verification, testing, and code generation. UML class diagrams capture structural aspects graphically, while the Object Constraint Language (OCL) [30] allows the specification of textual constraints, such as class invariants and operation pre/post-conditions.

Complex software systems may include a large collection integrity constraints. While designers typically define those constraints one by one, the interactions among them can become problematic. For instance, it is possible to define

D. Bork et al. (Eds.): ER 2025, LNCS 16189, pp. 3–23, 2026.
https://doi.org/10.1007/978-3-032-08623-5_1

a set of conflicting integrity constraints that, considered as a whole, cannot be satisfied simultaneously. A software system containing *inconsistencies* such as this one would not be usable in practice.

Diagnosing why a UML class diagram is unsatisfiable is complex. Model finders are not very informative, simply stating that it not possible to synthesize a satisfying instantiation but without explaining why. Recent model finders include facilities for *fault localization* (identifying the subset of constraints that are in conflict) [32,34,37,50–53] or *automated repair* (proposing changes to existing constraints that avoid the inconsistency) [5,10,15,39,49,55,56]. However, some conflicts require a deep understanding of the problem domain in order to propose meaningful and correct fixes. Thus, it is not feasible to perform this task without the intervention of human experts.

In this paper, we propose an *interactive* system for verifying, validating, and repairing UML class diagrams with OCL constraints. Verification is guided by instantiations that reflect valid scenarios, helping experts determine whether constraints are met. Using satisfiability, fault localization, and automated repair, designers can identify violations, explore fixes (by adjusting scenarios or modifying models), and backtrack if needed. The system is implemented as an extension to the UML Specification Environment (USE) [17].

To support automated repair, it is essential to reduce the number of alternatives shown to experts. Therefore, potential fixes are analyzed to eliminate redundant or semantically equivalent repairs through simplification and normalization of OCL expressions.

Paper Organization. The rest of the paper is organized as follows. Section 2 presents related work on verification, debugging and repairing software models. Section 3 discusses the proposed interactive verification methodology. Then, Sect. 4 presents a tool implementing this methodology, its most relevant features and the feedback provided to the user. Section 5 presents the experimental results. Finally, Sect. 6 describes our conclusions and outlines future work.

2 Related Work

2.1 Correctness of Conceptual Models

Static software models capture structural aspects of a system. UML class diagrams [31] define its *conceptual model*, a set of classes, attributes, operations, and relationships that encode domain and business logic. Alloy [24] offers a similar capability via a textual notation with formal semantics and automated analysis.

UML class diagrams include basic *integrity constraints*, such as association multiplicities and the `unique` modifier. More complex constraints can be expressed using the Object Constraint Language (OCL) [30], which allows specifying *class invariants* and operation *pre- and post-conditions*.

A model must be *correct* to be usable. A basic requirement is *well-formedness*, ensuring syntactic validity—*e.g.*, UML forbids cyclic inheritance.

More semantic correctness notions fall under *consistency*. This includes *vertical, horizontal/multi-view*, and *evolution consistency* [15,16,48], often focused on use-declaration compatibility.

This paper addresses *intra-model consistency*, where a single UML model annotated with OCL is *satisfiable* if an instance exists fulfilling all constraints [7, 12,37]. Stronger variants include *finite* [8] and *weak/strong satisfiability* [19].

2.2 Verification of Software Models

Many works have considered the formal verification of UML class diagrams annotated with OCL constraints. The fundamental property being checked in UML/OCL verification is *satisfiability*. Model finders should be capable of checking whether a valid instance that fulfills all integrity constraints can be constructed. If the class diagram is satisfiable, then the model finder should produce an example instance as a *witness* of this satisfiability.

Overall, these approaches operate by translating the UML/OCL model to a formal notation with a *model finder* capable of checking properties. Then, the model finder's response is expressed in terms of the original UML/OCL model (as an instance of the class diagram) to provide meaningful feedback. The choice of underlying formalism dictates the *efficiency* of the analysis as well as its *expressiveness*, *i.e.*, the set of UML/OCL constructs that are supported by the translation and verification.

Some examples of formalisms and model finders used to analyze UML/OCL models are: SAT ([35], USE [25], MVM [18], EFinder [40]), query containment (AuRUS [37]), SAT-modulo theories (PLEDGE [46], OCL2MSFOL [12]), heuristic search ([1], PLEDGE [46]), constraint logic programming (EMFtoCSP [20], UMLtoCSP [7]), term rewriting (mOdCL [13], ITP/OCL [11]), ... In contrast, the Alloy notation comes with a built-in analyzer. For this reason, some approaches verify UML/OCL models by translating them into Alloy [2,28]. Meanwhile, other methods consider the use of graph-based notations to describe domain models and propose specific graph-based model finders such as VIATRA [41,43]. The verification of UML/OCL class diagrams is an undecidable problem. Some techniques to deal with this limitation include: *bounded verification*, that is, searching for instances within a finite search space defined a priori [7,20,25,35]; defining a decidable subset for UML/OCL [36]; using incomplete methods that may fail to terminate or may provide inconclusive answers [51]; or relying on *interactive* verification, where user assistance may be required to guide the theorem prover [6,45].

Some research directions in model verification consider, among other topics, the scalability of model finding [44], the expressiveness of modeling notations [29, 42] or the quality (realism and diversity) of model finder instances [41,46]. In this work, we are more concerned with the quality and usefulness of the feedback provided to the domain experts and, above all, helping the user in an interactive verification that allows him to do and undo actions on the instance in a guided and simple way.

2.3 Model Debugging

When a model is found to be inconsistent, some solvers provide features for *fault-localization*: identifying which specific model elements are involved in the fault. This process is also called *model debugging* or *diagnosis*.

In the case of well-formedness or multi-view consistency it is possible to quickly identify which parts of the model cause the consistency problem [14]. However, this analysis is more complex in the case of intra-model consistency. Two dual approaches [3] have been proposed to tackle this problem:

- Computing the smallest set of unsatisfiable constraints in a model, called *Minimal Unsatisfiable Core* (MUC) or *Minimal Unsatisfiable Subsets* (MUS). This method has the advantage of pinpointing the location of errors within the model.
- Computing the largest set of satisfiable constraints in a model, called *Maximal Satisfiable Subset* (MSS). This method has the advantage of providing an instance that satisfies most of the constraints of the model, and which can be used as a starting point to understand why the remaining constraint cannot be satisfied.

The problem of computing MUSes/MSSes has been widely studied in several areas such as boolean satisfiability (SAT) [27], SAT Modulo Theories (SMT) [9], constraint satisfaction problems [21], entity-relationship models [22,23], database queries [38] and relational logic (Alloy) [47,54,57]. Notice that a single model can contain more than one MUS. Most verification techniques focus on *finding one* MUS while a few others aim to *enumerate all* MUSes [4,26].

In the context of UML/OCL models, previous works such as AuRUS [37] or [32–34,50] have considered the computation of unsatisfiable cores in OCL specifications, using algorithms from query containment and SAT solvers, respectively. Meanwhile, others such as MaxUSE [51,53] or its evolution QMaxUSE [52] explore the computation of maximal satisfiable sets using max-satisfiability capabilities provided by SMT solvers. In this paper, in addition to compute MSSes/-MUSes, we aim to use them to provide actionable feedback to domain experts.

2.4 Model Repair

A final set of techniques aim to generate *repairs*, *i.e.*, small (or even minimal) changes to a model that fix a particular fault. This task is manageable when repairing well-formedness or multi-view inconsistencies [15], as fixes may consist on renaming wrong references or adding missing declarations. However, checking intra-model consistency is more complex and requires different methods.

Some of these approaches have targeted Alloy specifications [5,49,55,56] and UML/OCL class diagrams [10]. As a drawback, the catalog of strategies to generate candidate fixes (mutation operators) has to be established a priori and, in some cases, additional predicates to validate the fix must be defined.

The synthesis of candidate repairs is usually syntax-driven, and as a result it may generate complex expressions that are (a) hard to understand by a human reader and (b) inefficient to evaluate, as they include unnecessary calculations. As a result, some works have considered the simplification of such repairs to improve their readability and efficiency [39]. In this paper, we will introduce new types of optimizations and normalizations in order to detect semantically equivalent mutants.

A challenge of model repair is that fixing a fault may require domain-specific knowledge. That is, a change in the UML/OCL model such as rewriting an invariant may eliminate an inconsistency but produce a constraint that is non-sensical in the context of the domain. Moreover, fixing a fault may require performing several changes in different parts of the diagram, as the fixes may cause other inconsistencies due to interactions with other model elements. As a result, *automated* model repair has its limitations and it may be necessary to include domain experts in the model repair process. Thus, our approach aims to help modelers locate, understand and fix faults. That is, it does not assume that the model is almost correct and can be fixed with small updates as other previous works.

3 Verification and Validation Methodology

Our approach aims to assist modelers in identifying, locating, understanding and fixing consistency issues in conceptual models described as UML class diagrams annotated with OCL constraints. The outcome of this approach is a set of changes to the UML class diagram (multiplicities) and OCL constraints (class invariants) that will make it possible to populate the conceptual model while satisfying all integrity constraints simultaneously.

3.1 Motivating Example

The example conceptual model from Fig. 1 will be used as a running example. This model describes the information system of an e-commerce service, capturing information about products, customers and their orders. The system includes several integrity constraints in order to regulate the product stock (including lower and upper bounds) as well as the amounts of items that can be charged in each order.

Unknown to the modelers, the set of constraints in this model does not reflect their intent. For instance, it is not possible to instantiate using less than 5 objects per class. We can detect this defect by means of model finders such as the model analyzer plug-in provided by USE [25] or a max satisfiability solver [18]. Those solvers would report that it is not possible to build an instantiation of the model satisfying all the integrity constraints simultaneously. However, they would not provide insights on the reasons that motivate this problem or help modelers explore potential fixes.

3.2 Overview of the Methodology

The key feature of our methodology is the use of instantiations of UML class diagrams to drive the analysis of inconsistencies. Let us assume that a class diagram CD that is modeling a particular domain is inconsistent. In this scenario,

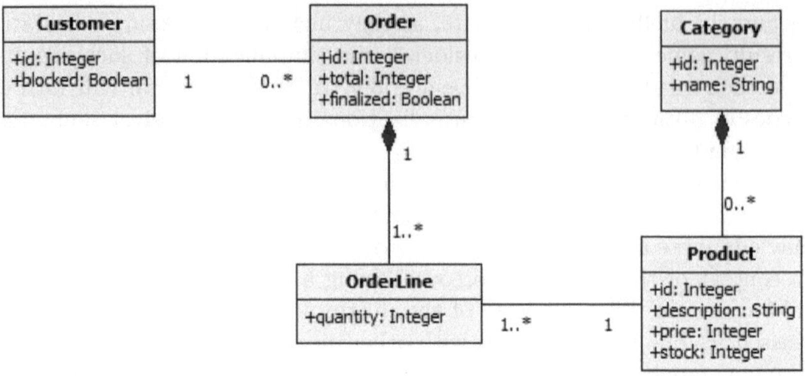


```
context Product inv sufficientStock:
    self.stock =
       OrderLine.allInstances()
       →select(ol | ol.product = self and not ol.order.finalized)
       →collect(ol | ol.quantity)→sum()
context Product inv stockLimits:
    self.stock >= 5 and self.stock <= 10
context OrderLine inv singleProductOrders:
    self.quantity = 1
```

Fig. 1. Example conceptual model: (top) class diagram and (bottom) OCL invariants.

CD has no valid instantiations, as each potential instantiation would violate one or more integrity constraints. However, the domain expert knows that there are indeed valid instantiations in the real domain and proposes an instantiation of *CD* that *should* be valid. Then, to solve the inconsistency we need to: (a) identify which integrity constraints are being violated by this particular instantiation; and (b) rewrite each of them in a way that preserves the domain logic and makes these constraints satisfiable for this particular instantiation. In other word, this instantiation becomes the *goal* of our repair process.

This methodology can be divided into a set of activities that need to be carried out in order to successfully repair an inconsistent class diagram:

1. **Consistency checking**: Decide whether a UML/OCL diagram is consistent.
2. **Diagnosis**: Identify the unsatisfiable core, the minimal subsets of constraints involved in the inconsistency, as well as sample instantiations that satisfy the maximum number of constraints in the model.
3. **Validation**: Create, visualize and modify instantiations using a graphical user interface, as well as to evaluate the validity of the model constraints in the context of that instantiation.
4. **Guided interactive repair:** Propose potential fixes to the identified inconsistencies, both in terms of graphical constraints in the class diagram (such as multiplicities) or textual constraints (such as OCL invariants); evaluate

the suitability of those candidate fixes; and backtrack if a previous decision in the repair process if is deemed inadequate.

Steps 1 and 2 have been considered by previous work, as previously described in Sects. 2.2 (step 1) and Sect. 2.3 (step 2), including our previous work [7,18]. In this paper, we extend these previous works to include steps 3 (validation) and 4 (guided interactive repair) in order to allow modelers to understand the causes of inconsistencies and find potential ways to repair them. Moreover, we evaluate optimizations to reduce the number of candidate fixes that need to be presented to the modeler. This method is implemented in a tool called MVM, an extension of the UML Specification Environment (USE) [17] that integrates steps 1 to 4 in a cohesive way.

3.3 Workflow

Figure 2 depicts the overall verification flow in this methodology. The first two steps (consistency checking and diagnosis) detect inconsistencies by searching for an instantiation that satisfies all integrity constraints simultaneously. In inconsistent models, model finders are not capable of creating such instantiation, notifying the lack of such instantiations (for SAT based solvers) or providing an instantiation that satisfies as many constraints as possible (for max-SAT based solvers).

Once this inconsistency has been identified, the repair process proceeds in the following way:

1. The modeler identifies a target potential instantiation of the UML class diagram that, according to this domain knowledge, is a viable instantiation that should satisfy all the constraints in the model. Modelers can create it from scratch or use the sample instantiations previously computed by the max-SAT model finder.
2. The tool highlights all the multiplicities and textual constraints that are not satisfied in this specific instantiation. For each of them, the tool proposes a potential candidate fix:
   - For multiplicities, the modeler can update the multiplicity, if it turns out it is incorrect; or he/she can update the instantiation (if he/she realizes that the instantiation is not correct according to the domain) by adding or removing objects and links. The tool suggests the required changes and implements them according to the modeler's instructions.
   - For textual invariants, the tool proposes mutations of the original constraint that are *weaker*, *i.e.*, less restrictive. Mutants are generated according to the weakening rules proposed in [10] and evaluated to select those that satisfy the integrity constraints.

   A challenge of this syntax-driven mutation process is that it includes many alternative rules to generate mutants. As a result, it can produce many candidates that differ syntactically but are semantically equivalent, *e.g.*,

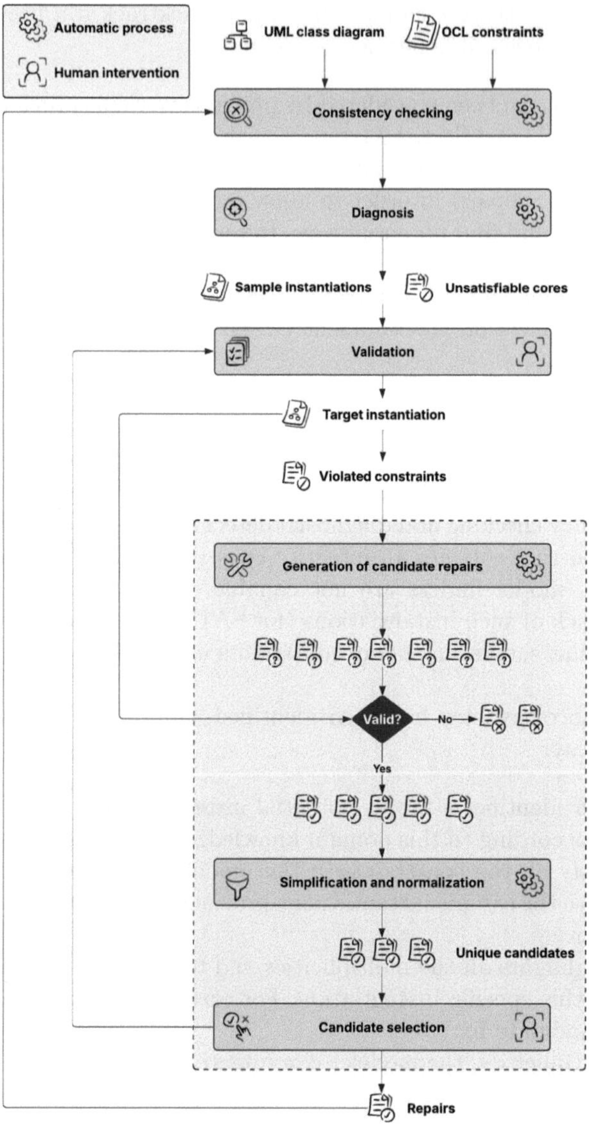

Fig. 2. Workflow of the methodology.

due to the existence of constant subexpressions or logical equivalences between subexpressions. To address this issue, we perform an optimization and normalization step on these OCL expressions to simplify them and improve the detection of duplicate mutants. This optimization has two benefits: first, it makes the overall process more efficient (duplicates are removed and only evaluated once); and second, it reduces the number of

alternatives presented to users, making the selection of suitable candidates easier.
3. The tool records the changes applied by the modeler and allows them to backtrack and changes their decisions at any time, if it turns out that some previous decision was incorrect.
4. At any point, the modeler may decide that the instantiation being used is inadequate and modify it to continue the analysis using a different one.
5. This process continues until the changes introduced by the modeler make the model consistent.

Following this procedure, a modeler can gain an understanding of the reasons why the set of constraints in the model is inconsistent and iteratively explore candidate repairs until the model becomes consistent. As previously described, the process is guided by the use of an instantiation of the diagram, that guides the repair process.

Some steps in this verification and validation methodology require the domain knowledge provided by the human expert, *e.g.*, selecting a suitable instantiation in step (a). However, some activities in steps (b)–(e) can be automated or at least tool-assisted. In the following section, we present the tool MVM that supports domain experts in the application of this methodology.

4 Tool Implementation

In this section, we describe how the verification methodology presented in Sect. 3 can be carried out using the features of MVM[1]. Revisiting the inconsistent model used as a motivating example (Fig. 1), we will illustrate how our approach would assist a modeler to understand and repair this inconsistency.

4.1 Creating and Exploring Instantiations

The starting point of our methodology consists in crafting an instantiation that, according to the domain expert, should be a legal instantiation of our conceptual model. Using this target instantiation as a guide, we will introduce changes to the graphical and textual constraints in the conceptual model until the target instantiation satisfies all of them.

Figure 3 shows the user interface provided by MVM to create, modify and inspect instantiations. It allows creating, modifying and deleting its objects and attribute values (top) as well as the links between objects (center). It also reports which association multiplicities and invariants are currently satisfied (bottom). There are several ways to use this features to create the initial instantiation that will guide the repair process:

– The modeler can create the objects in the instantiation manually one by one, using the commands in the top of the screen, and then add links manually.

[1] The tool MVM is available for download at https://github.com/juanto2021/MVM.

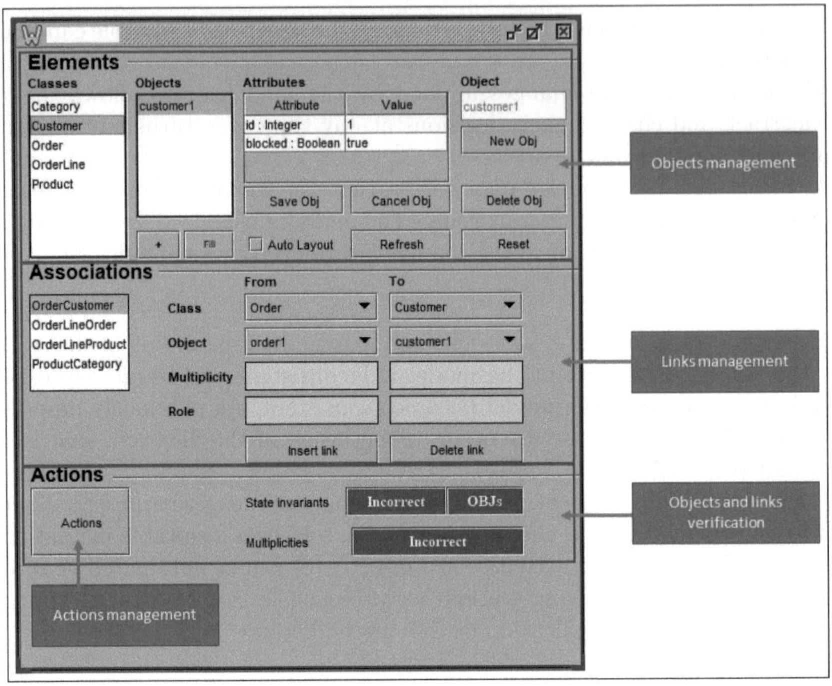

Fig. 3. Creating and exploring instantiations.

- The modeler can use a "quick creation" option (the "Fill" button on the top) to populate each class and association with one object (with suitable attribute values) and link respectively. This can be useful to facilitate populating large conceptual models, avoiding repetitive work.
- Finally, it is possible to replay a list of actions (from the "Actions" button) that was used in a previous session to recreate that instantiation.

A sample instance of the class diagram created in this way would look like the object diagram in Fig. 4. In MVM, this object diagram is shown alongside the main window to facilitate crafting the initial instance. An auto-layout is automatically applied to make the model easier to understand. In the case of our e-commerce motivating example, the modeler has created this particular instance using her domain knowledge, because it captures an scenario that she knows should be valid.

4.2 Checking and Fixing Graphical Constraints

The following step of our verification and validation methodology consists in identifying potential faulty constraints, either graphical or textual. In this Section, we will start by considering graphical constraints, *i.e.*, the multiplicities of association ends.

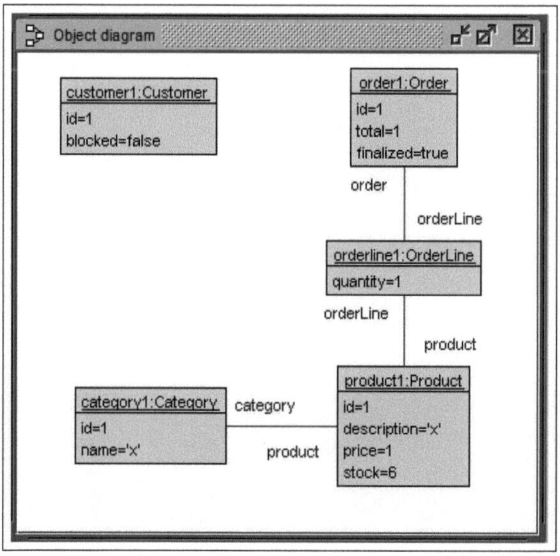

Fig. 4. Sample instantiation of our motivating example.

For this purpose, MVM reports the multiplicity constraints that are not satisfied in our target instance (Fig. 5), displaying the current links (top), explaining why the multiplicity is not satisfied (center) and proposing solutions to fix the problem (bottom). Candidate fixes for multiplicities can consist of creating or deleting links, creating or deleting objects or updating multiplicities. The modeler can select the desired fix and MVM will apply it, either modifying the object diagram or the multiplicity in the class diagram.

It should be noted that, when it comes to repair actions, which actions are adequate and which are inadequate entirely depends on the characteristics of the domain being modeled. This is why the domain knowledge of a human expert is required in order to make the right call. MVM provides assistance by identifying constraints that are not satisfied, proposing tentative repairs and implementing the selected one.

4.3 Checking and Fixing Textual Integrity Constraints

In addition to fixing problems with graphical constraints, we also need to analyze potential problems regarding the textual constraints, *i.e.*, OCL class invariants. MVM offers a dedicated user interface to inspect the satisfiability of the invariants on each of the existing objects, as shown in Fig. 6. In this view we can filter which invariants are not satisfied and, for each one, identify which specific objects are not fulfilling its body. For these objects, there are two possible outcomes:

- The modeler may conclude that the invariant seems correct in this scenario as the object should not fulfill the invariant body. In this case, the modeler can

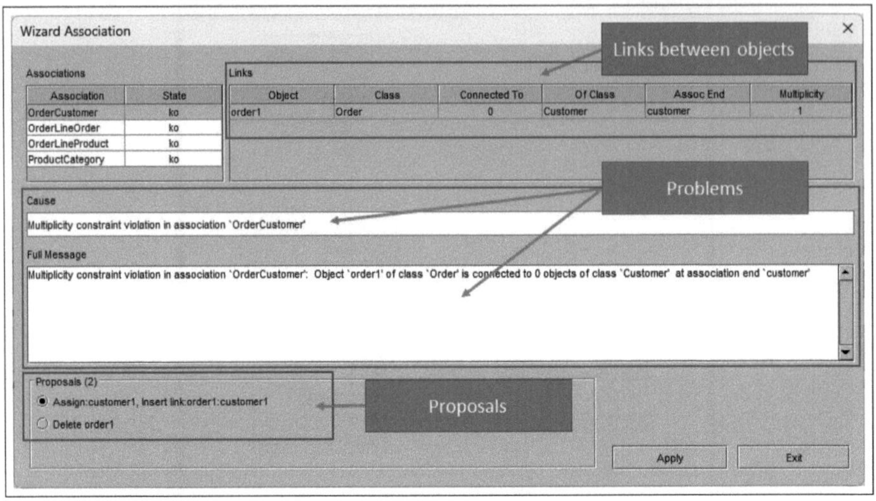

Fig. 5. Assessing and fixing multiplicity constraints in associations.

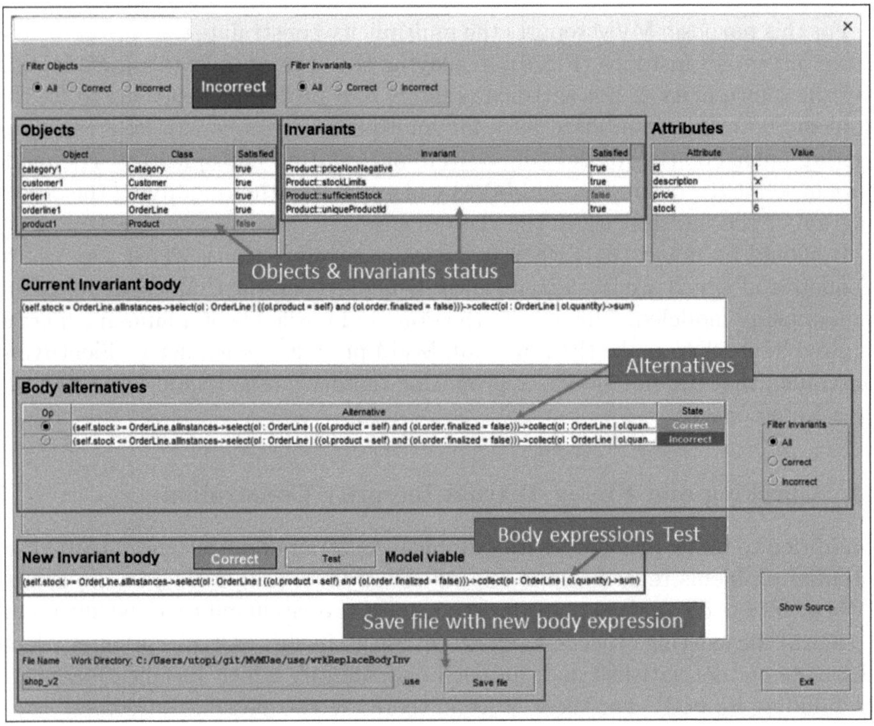

Fig. 6. Assessing and fixing OCL invariants.

go back to editing the object diagram, introducing changes until obtaining a new object diagram that represents an instantiation that should be valid, and which therefore illustrates the problem in the invariant.
- The modeler may conclude that the invariant is incorrect and should be fixed. Here, MVM will suggest potential candidate fixes computed by *weakening* the invariant that is currently not being satisfied. The modeler can select one of the potential fixes or provide her own. The new invariant will replace the old one, and the verification methodology will continue from this point if there are any other constraints that need to be fixed.

A limitation of the use of *weakening* to generate candidate fixes is the implicit assumption that the correct invariant is somehow related to the existing invariant. That is, it assumes the original invariant is *almost* correct and can be repaired by applying simple changes to the original one. While this assumption may not hold in all cases, it is employed by almost all automated repair approaches. If the modeler realizes that a complete rewrite of the invariant is necessary, MVM lets the modeler define this new invariant from scratch.

In our running example, MVM complains that constraint `sufficientStock` is not being satisfied in this current scenario. This constraint, depicted in Fig. 1 (bottom), is specifying that we should have sufficient stock to deliver all non-finalized orders. Why is it not being satisfied in this case? The reason is an error in the definition of the constraint: it requires the stock to match exactly the amount required to deliver the pending orders (using `=`). In Fig. 6 (section "Body alternatives"), MVM suggests a weaker invariant which uses `>=`, which considers that the quantity required by pending orders should be a lower bound of the stock. That is, there is no problem in having extra stock, while keeping insufficient stock should be forbidden.

4.4 Optimizing Candidate Repairs

The weakening process generates a very large number of candidates fixes. Unfortunately, many of them may be semantically equivalent. These duplicates makes the verification process slower and add unwanted noise to the candidate selection process. Thus, after applying the weakening, candidate mutants are optimized and normalized as a means to detect and prune semantically equivalent mutants. This optimization simplifies expressions such as boolean (`not`, `and`, `or`, `xor`, `implies`), arithmetic (sum, product, division, ...), conditionals, collection operators and iterators.

To this end, it takes advantage of constant operators by performing *constant folding*, *i.e.*, computing the result of operations with constant expressions, *e.g.*, `7 + 5` can be replaced by 12. Moreover, it applies *mathematical identities* whenever possible to simplify expressions, such `X or X` being equivalent to `X`. Finally, it considers properties of iterators and collection operators, such as `X->including(Y)->isEmpty()` being always `false` or `not X->isEmpty()` being equivalent to `X->notEmpty()`.

Table 1. Examples of optimized expressions.

Original Expression	Optimized Expression
`true and ((self.stock - 1) <= 10)`	`self.stock <= 11`
`(self.stock >= 5) and true`	`self.stock >= 5`
`self.orderLine->exists(ol1 : OrderLine, ol2 : OrderLine | (false implies (ol1.product <> ol2.product)))`	`self.orderLine->notEmpty`
`false implies ((self.blocked implies false) and (false implies self.blocked))`	`true`
`(self.stock - 1) <= (6000 + 4000)`	`self.stock <= 10001`

Table 2. Pruning redundant candidates: number of candidate fixes for each invariant (as generated by weakening) and number of unique fixes after optimization and normalization (with % of removed candidates).

Initial invariant	Candidates	Unique	Pruned %
`Category.allInstances->forAll(c : Category | ((c <> self) implies (c.name <> self.name)))`	25	5	80%
`Order.allInstances->forAll(o : Order | ((o <> self) implies (o.id <> self.id)))`	25	5	80%
`Product.allInstances->forAll(p : Product | ((p <> self) implies (p.id <> self.id)))`	25	5	80%
`self.orderLine->forAll(ol1, ol2 : OrderLine | ((ol1 <> ol2) implies (ol1.product <> ol2.product)))`	25	9	64%
`((self.stock >= 5) and (self.stock <= 10))`	24	12	50%
`(not self.blocked implies self.order->notEmpty)`	6	2	67%
`(self.order->notEmpty implies (self.blocked = false))`	4	2	50%

These optimizations are applied recursively, which can lead to complex invariants becoming significantly simplified. For instance, let us consider the following constraint suggested as a candidate repair:

```
Category.allInstances->exists(c:Category| c.name = c.name) implies false
```

First of all, considering that the second operand of `implies` is the constant `false`, the entire expression is equivalent to:

```
not Category.allInstances->exists(c:Category| c.name = c.name)
```

The query inside the existential quantifier can be replaced by `true`, as both operands of the equality are exactly the same expression.

```
not Category.allInstances->exists(c:Category| true)
```

An existential quantifier requiring an element that satisfies the query `true` is equivalent to requesting the collection to be non-empty.

Table 3. Class diagrams used in the experiments.

Id	Model	Classes	Assoc	Attrib	Inv	Sat?
M01	AcademicManagementSystem	6	5	17	30	Y
M02	AirlineReservationSystem	8	7	31	40	N
M03	CarModeling	10	8	23	48	Y
M04	FileAndUserManagement	10	8	30	46	Y
M05	HotelManagement	8	6	29	39	Y
M06	LibraryManagement	6	6	28	27	Y
M07	RailwayTicketSystem	6	5	17	23	N
M08	RestaurantManagement	6	6	11	22	N
M09	SchoolManagement	6	7	18	24	Y
M10	SeminarSystem	4	4	15	18	N
M11	TestResultsSystem	7	7	17	24	N

```
not Category.allInstances->notEmpty()
```

Considering the semantics of `not` and `notEmpty`, this expression can be rewritten as:

```
Category.allInstances->isEmpty()
```

Table 1 shows additional examples of these optimizations of OCL constraints. In order to illustrate the effectiveness of these optimizations in the generation and evaluation of candidates, Table 2 shows some data from our motivating example. Sample OCL invariants from the running example are presented, with the number of candidate repairs generated by weakening and the number of unique invariants remaining after the optimization phase. Notice that, in our motivating example from Fig. 1, these optimizations are able to prune between 50–80% of the proposed candidates, facilitating the task of the domain expert.

5 Experiments

In order to assess our methodology, we have analyzed a collection of conceptual models for different domains[2], gathered from example libraries of modeling tools such as Visual Paradigm, Creately and Boardmix. Each model was rewritten to follow the USE syntax, and more integrity constraints were added to increase their complexity and coverage of OCL constructs. Table 3 summarizes the main features of these models: the domain represented in the model, the number of classes and associations, the number of attributes and the number of invariants.

[2] Dataset available at https://doi.org/10.5281/zenodo.16881354.

Only 6 of these models were initially determined to be satisfiable by a bounded satisfiability solver. Given that our approach targets unsatisfiability problems, additional constraints were added to satisfiable models in order to make them unsatisfiable. The new constraints either contradicted a single invariant or a pair of other invariants in the model.

Table 4 reports the results of the analysis of these examples: the number of mutants that were proposed as candidate fixes by the weakening algorithm, the number of mutants left after optimization and the number of mutants discarded because they were not satisfied by the target instantiation. Globally, our method reduced the number of candidates to be considered by the designer by half and produced almost always feasible candidate fixes (almost 97% of the times).

On the other hand, we report the number of Minimal Unsatisfiable Subsets (MUS), which provides an estimation on the number of independent consistency faults in each model. We also report the time (in seconds) required to generate an initial target instance and the time needed to generate all initial target instances. Execution times report the average time for 3 executions. Notice that our approach is fast (less than one second) to compute a first instantiation that satisfies some but not all constraints in the model and can be used as the target instantiation to generate potential repairs. This can be done even for examples where the satisfiability analysis takes a long time. For instance, model M06 requires attributes values and class populations outside the scope of the bounded satisfiability solver, making the solver's search exhaustive. Even in this worst case scenario, our approach was able to provide rapid feedback that could be used to diagnose the problem.

Table 4. Experimental results.

		Opt.		Correct			Solver time	
Id	Mutants	#	%	#	%	MUS	First(sec)	All(sec)
M01	94	92	97.87	92	100.00	1	0.035	15
M02	205	125	60.98	122	97.60	1	0.048	97
M03	172	142	82.56	133	93.66	5	0.063	548
M04	174	130	74.71	116	89.23	2	0.063	471
M05	176	124	70.45	123	99.19	3	0.056	227
M06	1365	403	29.52	400	99.26	1	0.445	1063
M07	44	42	95.45	39	92.86	1	0.024	4
M08	391	223	57.03	222	99.55	2	0.020	10
M09	392	199	50.77	188	94.47	1	0.036	28
M10	199	106	53.27	101	95.28	1	0.187	120
M11	275	165	60.00	158	95.76	2	0.069	42
Global			50.22		96.83			

6 Conclusions

We have presented an approach to diagnose and fix consistency errors in UML class diagrams annotated with OCL constraints. This approach is guided by a target instantiation, selected by a domain expert, which is used to identify inappropriate integrity constraints and propose candidate repairs. Tool support facilitates the creation of target instances and the exploration of candidate fixes, and constraint optimization reduces the number of repairs to be reviewed.

As future work, we plan to refine the algorithm used to synthesize potential fixes to OCL constraints in order to suggest better repairs. We will also provide mechanisms to rank potential fixes from most to least promising. Furthermore, we plan to assess the usability of the tool by means of a user evaluation. Moreover, we will work on generating natural language explanations of the causes of inconsistencies and the repair actions needed to fix them.

Acknowledgements. This work has been partially funded by Agencia Estatal de Investigación (MCIN/AEI/10.13039/501100011033) and FEDER under project SE4GenAI (PID2023-147592OB-I00).

References

1. Ali, S., Zohaib Iqbal, M., Arcuri, A., Briand, L.C.: Generating test data from OCL constraints with search techniques. IEEE Trans. Software Eng. **39**(10), 1376–1402 (2013). https://doi.org/10.1109/TSE.2013.17
2. Anastasakis, K., Bordbar, B., Georg, G., Ray, I.: UML2Alloy: a challenging model transformation. In: Engels, G., Opdyke, B., Schmidt, D.C., Weil, F. (eds.) MODELS 2007. LNCS, vol. 4735, pp. 436–450. Springer, Heidelberg (2007). https://doi.org/10.1007/978-3-540-75209-7_30
3. Bailey, J., Stuckey, P.J.: Discovery of minimal unsatisfiable subsets of constraints using hitting set dualization. In: Hermenegildo, M.V., Cabeza, D. (eds.) PADL 2005. LNCS, vol. 3350, pp. 174–186. Springer, Heidelberg (2005). https://doi.org/10.1007/978-3-540-30557-614
4. Clavel, M., Egea, M.: ITP/OCL: a rewriting-based validation tool for UML+OCL static class diagrams. In: Johnson, M., Vene, V. (eds.) AMAST 2006. LNCS, vol. 4019, pp. 368–373. Springer, Heidelberg (2006). https://doi.org/10.1007/11784180_28
5. Brida, S.G., et al.: Bounded exhaustive search of Alloy specification repairs. In: International Conference on Software Engineering (ICSE), ICSE 2021, pp. 1135–1147. IEEE (2021)
6. Brucker, A.D., Wolff, B.: HOL-OCL: a formal proof environment for UML/OCL. In: Fiadeiro, J.L., Inverardi, P. (eds.) FASE 2008. LNCS, vol. 4961, pp. 97–100. Springer, Heidelberg (2008). https://doi.org/10.1007/978-3-540-78743-3_8. https://www.scopus.com/inward/record.uri?eid=2-s2.0-47249144817&doi=10.1007%2f978-3-540-78743-3_8&partnerID=40&md5=3d9dac3d08ff2a5bdae1293d10912067
7. Cabot, J., Clarisó, R., Riera, D.: On the verification of UML/OCL class diagrams using constraint programming. J. Syst. Softw. **93**, 1–23 (2014)

8. Cadoli, M., Calvanese, D., De Giacomo, G., Mancini, T.: Finite satisfiability of UML class diagrams by constraint programming. In: CSP Techniques with Immediate Application (CSPIA), vol. 2, pp. 2–16 (2004)
9. Cimatti, A., Griggio, A., Sebastiani, R.: Computing small unsatisfiable cores in satisfiability modulo theories. J. Artif. Intell. Res. **40**(1), 701–728 (2011)
10. Clarisó, R., Cabot, J.: Fixing defects in integrity constraints via constraint mutation. In: International Conference on the Quality of Information and Communications Technology (QUATIC), pp. 74–82. IEEE (2018)
11. Clavel, M., Egea, M.: ITP/OCL: a rewriting-based validation tool for UML + OCL static class diagrams. In: International Conference on Algebraic Methodology and Software Technology (AMAST). LNCS, vol. 4019, pp. 368–373. Springer, Cham (2006)
12. Dania, C., Clavel, M.: OCL2MSFOL: a mapping to many-sorted first-order logic for efficiently checking the satisfiability of OCL constraints. In: International Conference on Model Driven Engineering Languages and Systems (MODELS), pp. 65–75. ACM Press, New York, NY, USA (2016). https://doi.org/10.1145/2976767.2976774
13. Durán, F., Roldán, M., Moreno, A., Álvarez, J.M.: Dynamic validation of Maude prototypes of UML models. In: Iida, S., Meseguer, J., Ogata, K. (eds.) Specification, Algebra, and Software. LNCS, vol. 8373, pp. 212–228. Springer, Heidelberg (2014). https://doi.org/10.1007/978-3-642-54624-2_11
14. Egyed, A.: Instant consistency checking for the UML. In: International Conference on Software Engineering (ICSE), ICSE 2006, pp. 381–390. ACM, New York, NY, USA (2006). https://doi.org/10.1145/1134285.1134339
15. Egyed, A.: Fixing inconsistencies in UML design models. In: International Conference on Software Engineering (ICSE), pp. 292–301. IEEE (2007). https://doi.org/10.1109/ICSE.2007.38
16. Egyed, A., Letier, E., Finkelstein, A.: Generating and evaluating choices for fixing inconsistencies in UML design models. In: International Conference on Automated Software Engineering (ASE), pp. 99–108. IEEE (2008). https://doi.org/10.1109/ASE.2008.20
17. Gogolla, M., Büttner, F., Richters, M.: USE: a UML-based specification environment for validating UML and OCL. Sci. Comput. Program. **69**, 27–34 (2007). https://doi.org/10.1016/j.scico.2007.01.013
18. Gómez-Gutiérrez, J.A., Clarisó, R., Cabot, J.: A tool for debugging unsatisfiable integrity constraints in UML/OCL class diagrams. In: Augusto, A., Gill, A., Bork, D., Nurcan, S., Reinhartz-Berger, I., Schmidt, R. (eds.) Enterprise, Business-Process and Information Systems Modeling, pp. 267–275. Springer, Cham (2022). https://doi.org/10.1007/978-3-031-07475-2_18
19. González, C.A., Cabot, J.: Formal verification of static software models in MDE: a systematic review. Inf. Softw. Technol. **56**(8), 821–838 (2014)
20. González, C.A., Büttner, F., Clarisó, R., Cabot, J.: EMFtoCSP: a tool for the lightweight verification of EMF models. In: International Workshop on Formal Methods in Software Engineering: Rigorous and Agile Approaches (FormSERA), pp. 44–50 (2012). https://doi.org/10.1109/FormSERA.2012.6229788
21. Grégoire, E., Mazure, B., Piette, C.: On finding minimally unsatisfiable cores of CSP. Int. J. Artif. Intell. Tools **17**(4), 745–763 (2008)
22. Hartmann, S.: Coping with inconsistent constraint specifications. In: Kunii, H.S., Jajodia, S., Sølvberg, A. (eds.) ER 2001. LNCS, vol. 2224, pp. 241–255. Springer, Heidelberg (2001). https://doi.org/10.1007/3-540-45581-7_19

23. Hartmann, S.: Soft constraints and heuristic constraint correction in entity-relationship modelling. In: Bertossi, L., Katona, G.O.H., Schewe, K.-D., Thalheim, B. (eds.) SiD 2001. LNCS, vol. 2582, pp. 82–99. Springer, Heidelberg (2003). https://doi.org/10.1007/3-540-36596-6_5
24. Jackson, D.: Software Abstractions: Logic, Language, and Analysis. MIT Press (2012)
25. Kuhlmann, M., Hamann, L., Gogolla, M.: Extensive validation of OCL models by integrating SAT solving into USE. In: Bishop, J., Vallecillo, A. (eds.) TOOLS 2011. LNCS, vol. 6705, pp. 290–306. Springer, Heidelberg (2011). https://doi.org/10.1007/978-3-642-21952-8_21
26. Liffiton, M.H., Previti, A., Malik, A., Marques-Silva, J.: Fast, flexible MUS enumeration. Constraints **21**(2), 223–250 (2016)
27. Lynce, I., Marques-Silva, J.: On computing minimum unsatisfiable cores. In: International Symposium on Theory and Applications of Satisfiability Testing (SAT), pp. 305–310 (2004)
28. Maoz, S., Ringert, J.O., Rumpe, B.: CD2Alloy: class diagrams analysis using alloy revisited. In: Whittle, J., Clark, T., Kühne, T. (eds.) MODELS 2011. LNCS, vol. 6981, pp. 592–607. Springer, Heidelberg (2011). https://doi.org/10.1007/978-3-642-24485-8_44
29. Milicevic, A., Near, J.P., Kang, E., Jackson, D.: Alloy*: a general-purpose higher-order relational constraint solver. Formal Methods Syst. Des. **55**(1), 1–32 (2019)
30. OMG: Object Constraint Language specification (version 2.4). https://www.omg.org/spec/OCL/2.4/
31. OMG: Unified Modeling Language specification (version 2.5.1). https://www.omg.org/spec/UML/2.5.1
32. Przigoda, N., Soeken, M., Wille, R., Drechsler, R.: Verifying the structure and behavior in UML/OCL models using satisfiability solvers. IET Cyber-Phys. Syst. Theory Appl. **1**(1), 49–59 (2016)
33. Przigoda, N., Wille, R., Drechsler, R.: Contradiction analysis for inconsistent formal models. In: International Symposium on Design and Diagnostics of Electronic Circuits & Systems (DDECS), pp. 171–176. IEEE (2015). https://doi.org/10.1109/DDECS.2015.52
34. Przigoda, N., Wille, R., Drechsler, R.: Analyzing inconsistencies in UML/OCL models. J. Circuits Syst. Comput. **25**(03), 1640021 (2016)
35. Przigoda, N., Wille, R., Przigoda, J., Drechsler, R.: Automated Validation & Verification of UML/OCL Models Using Satisfiability Solvers. Springer, Cham (2018). https://doi.org/10.1007/978-3-319-72814-8
36. Queralt, A., Artale, A., Calvanese, D., Teniente, E.: OCL-lite: finite reasoning on UML/OCL conceptual schemas. Data Knowl. Eng. **73**, 1–22 (2012). https://doi.org/10.1016/j.datak.2011.09.004
37. Rull, G., Farré, C., Queralt, A., Teniente, E., Urpí, T.: AuRUS: explaining the validation of UML/OCL conceptual schemas. Soft. Syst. Model. **14**(2), 953–980 (2013). https://doi.org/10.1007/s10270-013-0350-8
38. Rull, G., Farré, C., Teniente, E., Urpí, T.: Computing explanations for unlively queries in databases. In: ACM Conference on Information and Knowledge Management (CIKM), p. 955. ACM Press, New York, NY, USA (2007). https://doi.org/10.1145/1321440.1321584
39. Cuadrado, J.S.: Optimising OCL synthesized code. In: Pierantonio, A., Trujillo, S. (eds.) ECMFA 2018. LNCS, vol. 10890, pp. 28–45. Springer, Cham (2018). https://doi.org/10.1007/978-3-319-92997-2_3

40. Sánchez Cuadrado, J., Gogolla, M.: Model finding in the EMF ecosystem. J. Object Technol. **19**(2), 10:1–21 (2020). https://doi.org/10.5381/JOT.2020.19.2.A10
41. Semeráth, O., et al.: Automated generation of consistent, diverse and structurally realistic graph models. Softw. Syst. Model. **20**(5), 1713–1734 (2021). https://doi.org/10.1007/s10270-021-00884-z
42. Semeráth, O., Babikian, A.A., Li, A., Marussy, K., Varró, D.: Automated generation of consistent models with structural and attribute constraints. In: Syriani, E., Sahraoui, H.A., de Lara, J., Abrahão, S. (eds.) International Conference on Model Driven Engineering Languages and Systems (MODELS), pp. 187–199. ACM (2020). https://doi.org/10.1145/3365438.3410962
43. Semeráth, O., Nagy, A.S., Varró, D.: A graph solver for the automated generation of consistent domain-specific models. In: International Conference on Software Engineering (ICSE), pp. 969–980 (2018)
44. Shaikh, A., Clarisó, R., Wiil, U.K., Memon, N.: Verification-driven slicing of UML/OCL models. In: International Conference on Automated Software Engineering (ASE), pp. 185–194. ACM, New York, NY, USA (2010). https://doi.org/10.1145/1858996.1859038
45. Snook, C., Savicks, V., Butler, M.: Verification of UML models by translation to UML-B. In: Aichernig, B.K., de Boer, F.S., Bonsangue, M.M. (eds.) FMCO 2010. LNCS, vol. 6957, pp. 251–266. Springer, Heidelberg (2011). https://doi.org/10.1007/978-3-642-25271-6_13
46. Soltana, G., Sabetzadeh, M., Briand, L.C.: Practical constraint solving for generating system test data. ACM Trans. Softw. Eng. Methodol. (TOSEM) **29**(2), 1–48 (2020)
47. Torlak, E., Chang, F.S.-H., Jackson, D.: Finding minimal unsatisfiable cores of declarative specifications. In: Cuellar, J., Maibaum, T., Sere, K. (eds.) FM 2008. LNCS, vol. 5014, pp. 326–341. Springer, Heidelberg (2008). https://doi.org/10.1007/978-3-540-68237-0_23
48. Straeten, R., Mens, T., Simmonds, J., Jonckers, V.: Using description logic to maintain consistency between UML models. In: Stevens, P., Whittle, J., Booch, G. (eds.) UML 2003. LNCS, vol. 2863, pp. 326–340. Springer, Heidelberg (2003). https://doi.org/10.1007/978-3-540-45221-8_28
49. Wang, K., Sullivan, A., Khurshid, S.: Automated model repair for Alloy. In: International Conference on Automated Software Engineering (ASE), pp. 577–588. IEEE (2018)
50. Wille, R., Soeken, M., Drechsler, R.: Debugging of inconsistent UML/OCL models. In: Design, Automation & Test in Europe Conference & Exhibition (DATE), pp. 1078–1083. IEEE (2012). https://doi.org/10.1109/DATE.2012.6176655
51. Wu, H.: MaxUSE: a tool for finding achievable constraints and conflicts for inconsistent UML class diagrams. In: Polikarpova, N., Schneider, S. (eds.) IFM 2017. LNCS, vol. 10510, pp. 348–356. Springer, Cham (2017). https://doi.org/10.1007/978-3-319-66845-1_23
52. Wu, H.: QMaxUSE: a query-based verification tool for UML class diagrams with OCL invariants. In: FASE 2022. LNCS, vol. 13241, pp. 310–317. Springer, Cham (2022). https://doi.org/10.1007/978-3-030-99429-7_17
53. Wu, H., Farrell, M.: A formal approach to finding inconsistencies in a metamodel. Softw. Syst. Model. **20**(4), 1271–1298 (2021). https://doi.org/10.1007/s10270-020-00849-8
54. Zhang, C., et al.: AlloyMax: bringing maximum satisfaction to relational specifications. In: ACM Joint Meeting on European Software Engineering Conference and

Symposium on the Foundations of Software Engineering (ESEC-FSE), pp. 155–167 (2021)
55. Zheng, G., Bagheri, H., Nguyen, T.: Debugging declarative models in Alloy. In: International Conference on Software Maintenance and Evolution (ICSME), pp. 844–848. IEEE (2020)
56. Zheng, G., et al.: ATR: template-based repair for Alloy specifications. In: International Symposium on Software Testing and Analysis (ISSTA), pp. 666–677. ACM, New York, NY, USA (2022). https://doi.org/10.1145/3533767.3534369
57. Zheng, G., et al.: Flack: counterexample-guided fault localization for Alloy models. In: International Conference on Software Engineering (ICSE), pp. 637–648. IEEE Press (2021). https://doi.org/10.1109/ICSE43902.2021.00065

Rethinking Learning: The Role of Unlearning in Generative AI-Based Conceptual Modeling

Shahnewaz Karim Sakib[1], Stephen W. Liddle[2], Christopher J. Lynch[3], Ameeta Agrawal[4], and Philippe J. Giabbanelli[3(✉)]

[1] Department of Computer Science and Engineering, University of Tennessee at Chattanooga, Chattanooga, TN, USA
shahnewazkarim-sakib@utc.edu

[2] Brigham Young University, Provo, UT, USA
liddle@byu.edu

[3] Virginia Modeling, Analysis, and Simulation Center (VMASC), Old Dominion University, Norfolk, VA, USA
{cjlynch,pgiabban}@odu.edu

[4] Department of Computer Science, Portland State University, Portland, OR, USA
ameeta@pdx.edu

Abstract. Generative AI models such as ChatGPT, Claude, and Gemini are increasingly used in conceptual modeling tasks to create, combine, or assess models. To improve performance, the emphasis has been to further guide the AI through prompt engineering or data (e.g., fine-tuning, retrieval augmented generation). In other words, when AI does not perform satisfactorily in a conceptual modeling task, the dominant approach is to do 'more'. In this paper, we examine the potential for an under-explored approach: *cutting* rather than *augmenting* the AI by deleting or canceling out the data that causes AI models to under-perform. We identify research themes in unlearning that can be applied to the field of conceptual modeling. In particular, this vision paper examines two research questions: what should be unlearned to improve conceptual modeling performances (e.g., identifying data that causes issues in causal representation or terminological consistency) and how to unlearn (e.g., whether to do it approximately or completely, whether we have access to the AI model).

Keywords: AI Assistants · Forgetting · Large Language Models · Unlearning

1 Introduction

Generative AI models such as ChatGPT, Claude, and Gemini have been used for a multitude of conceptual modeling tasks, including generating models from text (e.g., white papers, academic articles, scenario description by experts) [33,37,57],

D. Bork et al. (Eds.): ER 2025, LNCS 16189, pp. 24–44, 2026.
https://doi.org/10.1007/978-3-032-08623-5_2

comparing and combining models of sub-systems to achieve a more comprehensive perspective [3,23,29,66], or assessing conceptual models [27]. As the use of generative AI for conceptual modeling is maturing, we are witnessing the emergence of systematic reviews (e.g., for enterprise modeling [27]) and the transition from academic empirical studies to industrial applications [55]. Most of these works have focused on improving performance through prompt engineering, for instance by defining tasks or providing examples (so-called "few-shot learning"). Recent works have also used Retrieval Augmented Generation (RAG) to further guide AI. This approach simplifies the prompt by 'offloading' information to a database that can be queried, thus providing contextually relevant cases instead of generic examples [6]. The use of an external, queriable database also emulates experts to provide contextual information [53].

Throughout these studies, AI assistants are *enhanced with more knowledge* to provide better results. Instead of continuously adding information, our study posits that *conceptual modeling can benefit from trimming detrimental elements from the AI.* These are complementary views: aligning the AI's outputs more closely with desired outcomes can be obtained either through the dominant paradigm of accumulation or, as we suggest, through reduction.

Unlearning, the subject of this paper, can be considered to be a form of design by subtraction. The notion of "design by subtraction" has been studied in many fields such as engineering and architecture [1,38]. Embodied in the aphorism "less is more," design by subtraction aims to improve a design not by adding something more, but rather by taking something away. Humans have a strong cognitive bias toward adding rather than subtracting even in the presence of incentives and prompts to look for subtractions to solve a problem or make an improvement [1,38]. Part of the issue for humans is that additions are visible, whereas subtractions are invisible and it is harder for us to value what is missing. Yet across a wide variety of disciplines, we understand intuitively that a smaller or simpler design can be superior. A skilled editor improves clarity by trimming unnecessary words, software engineers refactor code into shorter and better organized expressions, and hollow cement blocks reduce material use without sacrificing structural integrity. Across these examples, innovations that subtract constitute legitimate and useful enhancements. In contrast, the development of LLMs has emphasized aggregating data, so much that experts worry about running out of human-generated content on which to train future LLMs [72].

The philosophy of design by subtraction suggests that we should consider not only what else we can add, but very purposefully we should study what we could remove. Consider the following situation. A modeler asks ChatGPT to turn a written scenario into a model, using SysML as domain-specific language. The AI uses the data it has encountered involving SysML, which may include online posts from novice learners who may struggle to differentiate between the various SysML diagram types (e.g., use case diagrams, activity diagrams, sequence diagrams) or produce cluttered diagrams that are hard to maintain instead of the selective models created by seasoned experts. As a result, ChatGPT produces a model that may be cluttered and use the wrong diagram type. Since LLMs like ChatGPT are trained with as much data as possible, it is expected that they contain samples with incorrect conceptual models. Having such samples is not necessarily a problem: exposing the LLM to negative examples during pre-training can enhance performance, *as long as the LLM knows that they are negative examples.* But when the LLM interprets bad cases as good conceptual models, then we have a problem. Forgetting *in order to improve performance* thus needs a fine comb rather than a mass removal of data, as inadvertently deleting negative examples could be detrimental. When modelers realize from the LLM outputs that bad instances are incorrectly seen as a desirable target, they may remove such instances and (partially) re-train, or attempt to steer the LLM away from issues in its knowledge model through expanded prompts (e.g., to teach best practices in SysML or proper use of each diagram type) or by 'diluting' the bad practices within an additional set of curated models. This situation exemplifies that there are many options available to modelers.

To foster the use of unlearning in conceptual modeling and identify key research questions for the conceptual modeling community, our vision paper explores two interrelated questions:

- *What* should be unlearned? Studies in healthcare focus on patient confidentiality, but unlearning in conceptual modeling is about improving performance by forgetting undesirable training data. Defining what is 'undesirable' is important and complex.
- *How* should we unlearn? Several options have emerged in the recent literature, but not all of them may be available to modelers (e.g., whether they use AI-as-a-service through a provider or can modify a local neural network). Trade-offs are of particular interest, since unlearning is about *mitigating* the impact of problematic data.

The remainder of this paper is organized as follows. In Sect. 3, we examine *what* should be unlearned to improve conceptual modeling. These choices inform *how* we unlearn in Sect. 4, where we emphasize the potential and open research questions for approximate unlearning in conceptual modeling. We conclude this vision paper with a brief summary of open research problems.

2 Background: Improving LLMs for Conceptual Modeling

2.1 Using LLMs for Conceptual Modeling

The history of AI and conceptual modeling goes much deeper than just LLMs. Knowledge representation is one of the foundational fields that contributed to the development of conceptual modeling [68]. But the public release of ChatGPT in November 2022 inspired much new activity as researchers studied how to apply practical, accessible LLMs to the domain of conceptual modeling.

Cámara *et al.* [8] studied whether LLMs could be used to generate conceptual models with sufficient quality. While they noted significant progress and indeed encouraged everyone to actively use LLMs, they found that unlike the state of LLMs generating code with a high degree of success, the performance of ChatGPT for generating software models was much more limited. They observed both syntactic and semantic deficiencies, together with too much inconsistency in the responses and scalability problems. Nevertheless, they saw a role for LLMs in helping generate and evolve models of software, allowing designers to interact with them through natural language, and potentially explore alternatives and adapt to changing requirements more efficiently than could be done otherwise. They encouraged educators to use LLMs proactively and to teach their students how to use and critically evaluate their use of LLMs. They also called for the community to *make "more (correct) software models" available in public repositories so LLMs can learn better* how to support the software modeling task.

Fill *et al.* conducted experiments in using LLMs to generate conceptual models [16]. They noted that a breakthrough of ChatGPT was its ability to filter out harmful responses. Their experiments with generating ER, BPMN, UML, and HERAKLIT diagrams led to the conclusion that large portions of such diagrams could be generated successfully, but that *human intervention is still needed to correct problems in generated models.* They also observed that improvement was noticeable from GPT-3 to GPT-4 and recommended that researchers always use the latest version of the available tools since they are improving so rapidly.

Chen *et al.* [11] examined whether LLMs can effectively perform fully automated domain modeling, concluding that GPT-4 was superior to other tested models and LLMs did a better job at some domain modeling tasks than others. Specifically, generating appropriate relationships was more difficult than generating classes or attributes. In their experiment, zero-shot prompting yielded better results than few-shot or chain-of-thought approaches. Given the overall results, they concluded that state-of-the-art LLMs are not yet ready to support fully automated domain modeling; human supervision is still required. Prokop *et al.* [53] agree with this perspective and conclude that LLMs can still make useful contributions with appropriate supervision.

Caution is warranted in our use of AI, and that is true for conceptual modeling as well. In a keynote address at the ER2023 conference, Saba demonstrated and emphasized that LLMs make stochastic predictions; they do not "think" or "understand" *per se* [56]. Sometimes LLMs hallucinate and produce poor results for other reasons. And even though recent generative AI products from OpenAI, Anthropic, and Google are labeled "reasoning" models, they still are not actually "reasoning" in the anthropomorphic sense; rather, they are integrating additional techniques with LLM models, like dividing problems into multiple steps and using chain-of-thought prompting together with reinforcement learning.

Prompt engineering and the incorporation of advanced techniques like retrieval augmented generation (RAG) will continue to be topics of major interest, both for LLMs generally and for the use of LLMs in conceptual modeling specifically. An example is the "tree-of-thoughts" approach that shows promise by decomposing the complex modeling process into sub-tasks and then combining sub-task results into a larger response [65].

2.2 Unlearning: From Healthcare to Conceptual Modeling

Legislation in several jurisdictions (e.g., GDPR in Europe) supports the 'right to be forgotten;' thus there is a legally compelling argument to process data withdrawal requests in relation to AI models. A model may also have been inadvertently trained on sensitive patient information (e.g., medical records) that violate privacy laws (e.g., HIPAA) thus unlearning would ensure compliance. Medical knowledge and best practices issued by leading academic societies change, and medical professionals are legally bound to provide care that meets the current standard of medical practice; unlearning thus prevents a model from recommending outdated medical treatments to professionals. The situation is different when it comes to conceptual modeling: novice modelers are not actively seeking for their 'bad models' to be removed from AI, and there are no severe legal consequences if AI drafts a conceptual model that does not meet current standards. This may explain why unlearning has received less attention in the conceptual modeling community than in the fields where it addresses a legal requirement.

Given these legal frameworks, *unlearning* is well-established in areas such as healthcare [59], particularly in medical imaging, where it provides a crucial mechanism to ensure compliance with data privacy regulations [2,15,20,50]. A systematic evaluation of unlearning algorithms in the medical imaging domain demonstrated effectiveness for specific scenarios, but generalizability remained a challenge [50]. In addition, some approaches to unlearning can present security risks since adversaries can manipulate a model through unlearning interfaces and reconstruct sensitive information that was intended to be forgotten [31]. The use of unlearning techniques from fields like healthcare has yet to be explored for supporting design-by-subtraction in conceptual modeling.

3 What to Unlearn

Unlearning is motivated by the need to fix shortcomings in the use of an LLM for conceptual modeling. This implies two sub-tasks: *identifying* when the LLM provides an unsatisfactory output, and *tracing* this error back to the data. *Given the current evidence base*, this section covers six types of mistakes and provides evidence of state-of-the-art LLMs (DeepSeek R1, Mistral's LeChat, Grok 3, GPT-4, Claude 3.7, Llama 4) making at least one of these conceptual modeling mistakes. Each issue is exemplified and illustrated in our online supplementary material available at doi.org/10.5281/zenodo.15531297, where mistakes are highlighted in the output. The importance and demonstrated existence of these issues give us practical targets on what to unlearn, using techniques described in Sect. 4. As the list of issues was derived from the collective experience of the five authors, there are potentially other issues that remain undetected or unreported. Note that issues depend on the LLM as they make different mistakes.

Many additional challenges in conceptual modeling and expectations for modeling practices are familiar to practitioners [22], such as beginners conflating conceptual, logical, and physical layers in data modeling, or misapplying model facets across development phases in software engineering. However, these issues are not consistently documented in the literature. Because our goal is to provide evidence-based guidance, we limit our overview to problems that are supported by published studies, allowing readers to consult additional sources as needed.

In particular, we emphasize that conceptual modeling with LLMs often involves the translation of structured or semi-structured text into graph-based abstractions. As such, many of the errors discussed in this section are not merely internal failures of structure or logic, but mismatches between the model and the source text. These functional misalignments arise when a conceptual model fails to capture the logic, dependencies, or causal relationships described in the input. If a graph omits key mechanisms, reverses dependencies, or introduces spurious links, it may lead decision makers to draw incorrect conclusions about system behavior, assumptions, or interventions. Ensuring alignment between the text and the generated structure is therefore essential—not only for technical accuracy, but also for maintaining trust in the model's outputs.

3.1 Temporal Representation

Temporal representations are a central role in dynamic systems modeling and errors can occur when events are assigned inconsistent or mismatched time units, or when the ordering of events is misrepresented [61,67]. These can arise from uncertainties in temporal expressions such as ambiguous time-related phrases, conversions between calendar systems, or adjustments over short, intermediate, or long time frames [74]. Models that mismatch daily vs. weekly timescales, or that invert event sequences, can hinder stakeholder understanding or lead to incorrect decisions [61]. Recent analyses of LLM-generated narratives demonstrate how even subtle temporal inconsistencies—such as reversed event ordering or vague time markers can disrupt the interpretability and accuracy of system descriptions [46]. These issues extend to conceptual models and graphs derived from such texts. Online supplementary material **S1** exemplifies this issue as `DeepSeek R1` incorrectly captures temporal aspects of a short scenario. Temporal conflicts can often be detected through the presence of inconsistent time units, non-monotonic time references, or reversals in expected event orderings.

3.2 Task Structure

Task structure issues arise when complex or branched processes are overly simplified or improperly flattened into linear chains. This problem can be observed among practitioners (despite extensive training or the expectations of using a model for high-stake decisions), as people tend to "(un)consciously reduce complexity in order to prevent information overload and to reduce mental effort" [71], thus ignoring structures such as feedback loops or multiple paths between two concepts. In the case of LLMs, these errors can be caused by (over-)training on procedural corpora that encode knowledge in sequential form, such as manuals or recipes. This matters because many real-world processes involve branching, looping, or recursive behaviors that cannot be captured by a simple sequence.

Without accurate task structure, a model will fail to represent parallel operations, dependencies, or decision points critical to operational and organizational workflows. Online supplementary material **S2** exemplifies this issue as `Mistral's LeChat` incorrectly captures parallelism and dependencies in a short scenario. Structural analysis can identify anomalies such as the presence of unconditional branches, excessive nesting levels, and multiple graph entry and exit points [4].

3.3 Semantic Ambiguity and Node Specificity

Semantic ambiguity and low node specificity occur when node labels are vague, generic, or context-free [19]. Labels such as 'activities' or 'tasks' [47] fail to convey clearly measurable underlying concepts. Such ambiguous labels increase cognitive load through unnecessary repetition and reduce the interpretability of the model. Conceptual clarity is necessary for validation, explanation, and reuse of the model in new settings. Semantic ambiguity can be harder to trace directly to the LLM unless it is asked to generate or elaborate conceptual models on its own, where vagueness is a symptom of its *failure to ground meaning.* As illustrated in online supplementary material **S3**, `Grok 3` created a conceptual model of personal growth that includes ambiguous labels such as 'integration' (of what?), 'intentional exploration' (what is being explored?), and 'personal transformation' (a placeholder for anything). Detection methods can flag nodes with high lexical ambiguity, overuse of placeholder tokens, or repeated label forms across conceptually distinct nodes. These issues parallel findings from semantic consistency benchmarks such as BECEL, which show that pretrained language models often fail to maintain stable outputs for semantically equivalent inputs, indicating difficulty with precise meaning capture in structure-aware settings [35].

3.4 Causal Representation

Causal representation issues occur when LLMs generate undirected or incorrectly directed edges between nodes that imply causal relationships. These issues often arise from datasets that collapse causality into co-occurrence. This matters because causal models conceptualized from a real system, or real data, are used to infer outcomes, simulate interventions, and understand propagation effects that should structurally represent the real system [5]. A lack of causal directionality can produce models that violate user expectations or mislead decision-making. As shown in online supplementary material **S4** using `GPT-4-turbo`, correlation is mistaken for causation in thinking that green space availability decreases air pollution (e.g., as vegetation absorbs pollutants), whereas they are determined by shared causes (e.g., urban planning, population density). Detecting this problem includes assessing edge directionality, identifying reversed cause-effect pairs, and comparing against known causal templates or domain-specific rules [28].

3.5 Terminological Consistency

Terminological inconsistency emerges when synonyms or paraphrased concepts are treated as distinct nodes in a model. This can result in node duplication or fragmented clusters that reduce model cohesion. For instance, online supplementary material **S5** with `Claude 3.7 Sonnet` shows that the LLM expanded a model of team dynamics by creating related concepts in opposite framing (communication breakdown, willingness to voice concerns) and by creating separate paths for different expressions of the same coordination failure (reduced collaboration, task duplication). Such inconsistencies impair both human interpretability and machine reasoning. A single concept split across multiple labels may lead to undercounting, disconnection, or redundant model fragments. LLMs frequently distribute probability mass across surface forms representing the same concept, leading to token-level competition and terminological fragmentation in output structures [62]. Detection methods include ontology-based semantic similarity [60], synonym and antonym detection [21,70], or the use of structural information when concepts originate from different conceptual models [18].

3.6 Structural Cohesiveness

Structural cohesiveness refers to whether there are disconnected components, that is, sub-parts of the models that cannot be reached from the rest (including single floating states). While some situations call for one connected model, others are best represented as a collection of separate models [73]. On the one hand, LLMs may fail to create a connected model when needed: as noted in recent surveys, linearization-based approaches often produce fragmented or ill-formed graphs unless augmented by graph-aware architectures or alignment mechanisms [36]. On the other hand, LLMs may exhibit a training bias toward well-structured outputs since reinforcement learning from human feedback can penalize disconnected or incomplete responses. An example of prioritizing connectivity at the expense of accuracy is provided in online supplementary material **S6**, where `Llama 4` connects unrelated infrastructures by using broad conceptual bridges, such as connecting tunnel ventilation systems to railroad monitoring, or bus tire pressure monitoring to stormwater management. A simple graph connectivity test can check for structural cohesiveness, but subject-matter experts should decide whether a specific situation calls for a single connected model or a set.

4 How to Unlearn

As LLMs are now used in conjunction with other tools, unlearning could be achieved elsewhere in the system. For example, if the LLM is paired with reasoning tools, the tools could act as a filter to 'forget' undesirable LLM ideas. In a similar manner, we could block LLM outputs when the issues listed in Sect. 3 are detected (e.g., if the model contains synonyms among concepts) and simply re-run the prompt to generate a different output, given the inherent variability of LLMs. However, filtering and re-running provides no *guarantee* that the next results will be better. In contrast, LLM unlearning *removes the influence of undesired data and associated model capabilities without compromising the model's overall utility* beyond the intended scope of unlearning.

The task of unlearning specific concepts in LLMs has gained significant attention due to its importance in mitigating undesirable model behaviors, such as generating harmful, private, or incorrect information [10,34,43,44,79]. A seemingly easy approach to unlearning would be to retrain the model from scratch after removing the problematic training data. For example, modelers may realize that the output includes ambiguous concept names (see Sect. 3.3), thus they can apply detection methods to identify and then remove such instances from the training set and then rebuild the LLM. However, this is impractical: modelers cannot afford the immense computational cost associated with re-training a model of ChatGPT's capability from scratch. Instead, recent research has explored more efficient methods for concept removal and targeted forgetting.

This section focuses on practical approaches to unlearn in conceptual modeling. First, we clarify an important distinction between two classes of techniques: *exact machine unlearning* that involve (partial) re-training and *approximate machine unlearning*, which we posit to be more applicable for our research community and summarize in Table 1.

4.1 Exact Machine Unlearning

While re-training an entire system may not be computationally feasible, the system can be *modular*. That is, we can have an *ensemble* of models, each trained on a subset of the data. The hope is that deletions (e.g., conceptual models with vague labels or inconsistent time units) would affect only some of the subsets, thus reducing the need for re-training. The Sharded, Isolated, Sliced, and Aggregated (SISA) technique [7] uses this idea by dividing the training data into shards, which are further divided into slices (Fig. 1). While re-training or removing only the shards affected by unlearning requests is efficient, there are three issues.

First, it can inadvertently impact fairness [80]. For example, a deletion may occur in a shard that heavily represents novice learners, as they may be more prone to creating conceptual models with issues such as semantic ambiguity. As a result, the model's ability to treat this group fairly may degrade, and it can become harder to generate conceptual models of novices—which are important learning artifacts when teaching best practices.

Second, minority group data—often sparse to begin with—can be disproportionately affected [39] because it is already concentrated in fewer shards, whereas majority group data is more evenly distributed across shards so its influence persists after unlearning. For instance, Giles *et al.* [24] created models from scientists and from aboriginal communities regarding diabetes. While the most important concepts for scientists included body weight and physical activity, the main ones for communities were the relationships with land and others. These concepts may be flagged as semantically ambiguous and if the shard containing this data is affected, unlearning would erase the perspectives of aboriginal communities. As a result, the retrained LLM would create conceptual models that default to the dominant trends from the majority group and reinforce existing biases.

Lastly, although SISA is less costly than retraining the whole model, retraining a whole shard may not be computationally feasible. In particular, if unlearning requests accumulate, then SISA scales poorly. To address this issue, the more scalable Sequence-aware Sharded Sliced Training (S^3T) [14] minimizes retraining to only the necessary components of the model while ensuring exact unlearning. Instead of retraining entire shards, S^3T first isolates the specific parameters most affected by the data to be unlearned, ensuring that modifications remain localized. It then applies low-rank adaptation (LoRA) to fine-tune only a subset of model parameters, drastically reducing computational requirements compared to full retraining. Finally, layer deactivation ensures that erased data do not leave residual influence in the model while preserving its overall structure.

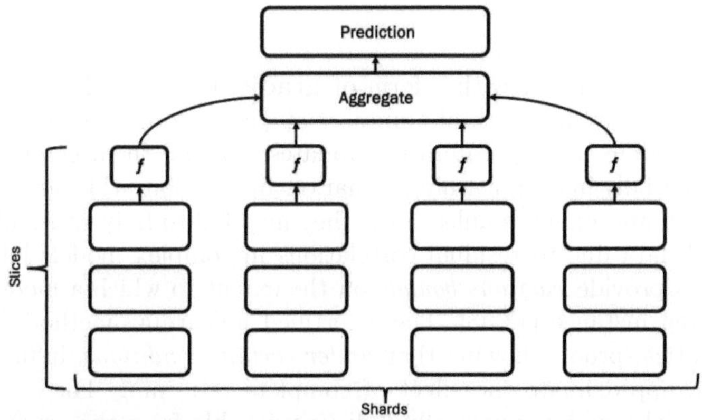

Fig. 1. The SISA training framework splits data horizontally into shards, and each shard is further split vertically into slices. Each slice is used to train a local model f, capturing only the data in that slice. These local models are then aggregated to form a single, global predictor, from which final predictions are generated.

4.2 Fundamentals of Approximate Machine Unlearning

The requirement to retrain (parts of) a model for every data deletion request can make exact unlearning computationally prohibitive [78], especially for deep learning models with millions or even billions of parameters [14]. In addition, many proposed unlearning mechanisms require maintaining additional checkpoints or shadow models to facilitate selective data removal [49], which significantly increases storage and memory overhead. Given these limitations, approximate unlearning techniques are an attractive alternative that seek to *mitigate* the impact of deleted instances by approximating the model parameters.

In the traditional training of neural networks, *gradient descent* minimizes a loss function by adjusting the model parameters in the direction of negative gradients. When unlearning a data point, the idea is to approximate the inverse effect: *estimating* the influence that a particular data point had on the gradient

Table 1. Comparison of Machine Unlearning Approaches for Conceptual Modeling

Category	Forgetting Focus	Technique Style	Pros	Cons
Gradient Ascent	Specific data instances	Inverse-like gradient updates	Simple; instance-level	Can destabilize model
Differential Privacy	Training-time influence limitation	Noise added to training gradients	Avoids entanglement early	Not retroactive; weak edits
Preference Optimization	Undesired outputs (e.g., bad answers)	Learn to prefer alternate responses	Targeted response control	Traces may persist internally
Data-Centric	Corrupt data (instances/classes)	Balanced forgetting and retaining loss	Maintains task consistency	Needs careful data partitioning
Model-Centric	Explicit concepts or facts	Edit internal weights or subspaces	High factual precision	Can disrupt nearby concepts

descent, and countering it with a form of **gradient ascent**. Early approaches such as the adaptive approach of Gupta *et al.* [26] and the "Descent-to-Delete" method [51] require multiple iterative updates, making them computationally intensive, especially in deep learning scenarios. In addition, while gradient-based techniques can approximate unlearning, they may fail to fully erase all traces of the removed data due to residual correlations in complex models [69]. Recent developments provide *rigorous bounds* on the extent to which a model has forgotten a given instance [42,48]. These certified unlearning methods are based on mathematical proofs showing that *under certain conditions*, influence-based updates can approximate the effect of complete retraining. For example, the retrained model may be empirically indistinguishable from the original one, or we can prove that its outputs are within some distance of the original model (e.g., the conceptual models differ by a bounded amount in graph edit distance). However, the theoretical conditions that allow these guarantees can break down when changing the LLM to forget just one instance triggers unexpected changes in other parts of the LLM (i.e., highly non-convex loss landscapes). In sum, conceptual modeling can use gradient methods when the problem is *localized* (e.g., one bad scenario-to-model translation, a specific fact is error-prone), when the model has been *fine-tuned* (to limit rippling consequences from removing one data point), and the certified method provides a quantified margin that is *interpretable* for the conceptual modeling task (e.g., missing at most one concept).

Since not all cases for conceptual modeling fit these three specific conditions, other methods will have to be considered. To avoid the risk of pulling one data point and seeing the whole model crumble, **Differential privacy** (DP)-based unlearning techniques take a different approach: they add a controlled amount of noise during the training process, which limits the influence of any single data point. When unlearning is requested, instead of removing the data and retraining the model, we can adjust the noise distribution to reduce the model's dependence on that particular instance. Neel *et al.* [51] integrated DP principles into gradient descent, showing that models trained with controlled noise can approximate unlearning by adjusting or recalibrating the noise distribution post hoc. Although these methods *reduce* individual influence, the critical examination of Suriyakumar *et al.* [69] showed that *they do not fully eliminate all traces of a data point* in deep models. Although this approach ensures from the start that each data point has limited influence, preventing entanglement problems through noise comes at the expense of a small degradation in conceptual models. Consequently, this method can be used in early exploratory settings for conceptual modeling (e.g., to generate hypotheses or prompt discussions in an educational context), but we do not recommend it if the conceptual models must be semantically faithful (e.g., DP may distort causality in critical relationships) or if the LLM was already trained without DP (like most mainstream LLMs).

While DP was originally designed for privacy-sensitive settings, the philosophy of forgetting for conceptual modeling is to consider some LLM outputs as *undesirable* rather than as privacy-sensitive, which would be a stronger requirement. Thus, it would be sufficient to *discourage* certain responses, such as generating conceptual models with inconsistent terminology. **Preference Optimization** is not about erasing training data but about forcing the model to stop showing a particular behavior. This technique fine-tunes the model using a dataset with preference feedback in the form of ⟨input x_i, preferred response y_i^+, unfavored response y_i^-⟩. The original response (y_i^-) is considered undesirable, and the model is optimized to prefer y_i^+, effectively replacing the learned knowledge. Variants include Direct Preference Optimization (DPO) which maximizes the log-likelihood ratio between preferred and unfavored responses while keeping the model's distribution close to its original state [54] and Negative Preference Optimization (NPO) which focuses on minimizing the likelihood of the unfavored response, discarding the favored response altogether [81]. Since this approach relies on curated examples of correct and incorrect conceptual model outputs, it can be *labor-intensive*. Furthermore, if preferences are ambiguous (e.g., aspects of a conceptual model that are very application or person dependent), then fine-tuning may inadvertently reinforce the wrong behavior.

4.3 Data and Model-Centric Unlearning

While exact and approximate unlearning methods focus on removing the influence of training data either through exact retraining or through behavioral or statistical approximations, they have limitations for conceptual modeling. Exact unlearning is computationally prohibitive for large language models, while approximate methods may leave residual traces or affect other parts of the LLM. Recent work address these challenges with two alternatives: data-centric and model-centric unlearning. **Data-centric methods** intervene at the level of training data influence, often combining selective gradient updates and optimization strategies to *suppress specific examples while preserving the rest.* In contrast, **model-centric methods** directly target the learned parameters or internal representations to *remove specific facts or concepts.* These two alternative categories can be used in both exact and approximate settings and offer more direct control over what is forgotten and how, which corrects LLMs for conceptual modeling while minimizing unintended negative impacts to the LLM.

While several works have recently offered data-centric unlearning methods, they do not all apply to conceptual modeling. For example, methods such as the Guided Loss-Increasing [13] and others [25,32] are designed for computer vision, where tasks involve *dense continuous* feature spaces (e.g., image embeddings) and well-defined semantic distances between images. In contrast, conceptual modeling involves discrete, interpretable elements (e.g., entities and relationships) organized as structured symbolic representations, not as feature vectors in a latent space. Several methods can address specific needs relevant to conceptual modeling, for instance by making a model forget an entire category such as a group of related entities or relationships. These methods first identify what parts of the data influenced the model's internal decision-making (i.e., post-hoc bottleneck models) and then weaken that influence by carefully designed synthetic examples (i.e., targeted data poisoning) [9] or influence functions [12,77]. While these techniques are potentially powerful, they are not plug-and-play: precise control requires a *clear understanding of what must be forgotten*. Also, since we cannot revisit the training data for a pre-trained LLM, forgetting is most applicable for *adjusting the training data used by the modeler during fine-tuning*.

Instead of revisiting training examples (that are either unavailable to a modeler or limited to fine-tuning), model-centric methods edit or erase internal representations as a direct intervention on the model itself. That is, a modeler *must be able to download the LLM's weights* instead of accessing the LLM through an API or web portal. While popular LLMs such as GPT 3.5 and GPT-4 cannot be downloaded, model-centric unlearning can be performed on LLMs such as GPT-J (a derivative of GPT-3), LLaMA 3, Mistral 7B, Phi-2, or the DeepSeek family of LLMs including the recent DeepSeek 67B with strong reasoning performance.

In a similar manner to data-centric methods, not all methods for model-centric unlearning can be applied to conceptual modeling. For example, while some methods state that they unlearn a 'concept', it is in the context of vision models where the concept (e.g., 'nudity') is associated to images [41]. One of the most applicable techniques for unlearning in conceptual modeling is the `UNLEARN` algorithm [45]. It erases specific factual associations embedded in the LLM, such as 'Poitiers is the location of ER25'. For example, if the LLM generates a conceptual graph from a medical scenario by incorrectly associating 'headache' with a treatment rather than a symptom, `UNLEARN` can erase that false association without disrupting the rest of the model's medical knowledge. `UNLEARN` identifies the subnetwork (subspace of weights) encoding the target knowledge and selectively erases it, while using a complementary mechanism to preserve closely related knowledge. Empirically, `UNLEARN` achieves about 96% forgetting of the target knowledge with minimal impact (within 2–11% performance drop) on similar topics. This significantly outperforms naive fine-tuning baselines, and the same approach can be run in reverse to add knowledge, highlighting its dual nature.

4.4 Theoretical Insights Into Unlearning for Conceptual Modeling

Given the plethora of techniques that can be empirically evaluated to perform unlearning, conceptual modelers face two questions: what limits can I run into regardless of the approach that I use? How do I know if it really worked?

Consider the most likely scenario for conceptual modelers: the LLM is already trained, a subset of the data must be forgotten, but we do not have access to the original training data. We only have the LLM and the data to unlearn. To set expectations, Foster *et al.* frame the unlearning problem in terms of information gain [17] by quantifying the information content of a specific sample as the change in a model's predictions when the sample is seen versus unseen. Using this insight, they show that *unlearning can be approximated without access to the full training set, which is valuable for conceptual modelers, who typically work with pre-trained LLMs and must correct specific misbehaviors* (e.g., an incorrect mapping from narrative to graph) without full retraining. While the authors do not impose a hard limit on what can be unlearned, they clarify that *there is a trade-off*: if the data point to forget contributed heavily to the model's decision-making, removing it without full retraining becomes increasingly difficult. This provides a theoretical lower bound: the more a point changed the model's predictions, the harder it will be to erase it without destabilizing the rest of the model.

To verify whether unlearning has been correctly performed, the Proof of Unlearning (PoUL) framework [75] proposes three audit mechanisms. *Membership auditing* detects whether there is still a memorized, unwanted mapping. For example, is the model still using a specific undesirable narrative-to-graph example to guide its output? *Consistency auditing* goes further, by checking whether the LLM is just suppressing one specific case or has corrected the conceptual generalization. This is important because many unlearning methods conceal undesirable facts instead of removing them: as these facts remain embedded in the model's latent space, they can be triggered under certain conditions [63]. To appreciate this subtlety, consider the following situation. We are using an LLM to convert legal narratives into conceptual models. During fine-tuning, the LLM mistakenly associates "the defendant filled a motion" with the model Motion $\xrightarrow{\text{filed\_by}}$ Plaintiff, which incorrectly says plaintiff instead of defendant. To know whether the unlearning method worked, we consider (i) a retrained model that was never exposed to the faulty example and (ii) the LLM where unlearning was used to remove the faulty training. We can feed both models with an input that was not part of the data, involves the same underlying concepts, and is semantically close enough to reveal whether the 'fixed' model still generalizes incorrectly. For example, "the defendant submitted a request to dismiss the charges" should create Request $\xrightarrow{\text{submitted\_by}}$ Defendent in both models. Finally, *confidence auditing* assesses whether the LLM becomes less confident in its predictions on the data it was supposed to forget. This is useful given that several unlearning methods aim to weaken particular structural associations (e.g., 'A symptom is treated' vs. 'A symptom is experienced').

5 Discussion

5.1 Forgetting as a Foundation for Better Conceptual Modeling

In the words of Saint-Exupéry, "it seems that perfection is finally attained not when there is no longer anything to add, but when there is no longer anything to take away" [58]. Taking away from LLMs has been studied primarily in vision and general NLP tasks, in particular under the motivation of legal compliance for fields such as healthcare. In contrast, unlearning has not yet been applied to LLMs that transform, compare, or maintain conceptual models. By organizing unlearning methods and clarifying their applicability to conceptual modeling, this paper posits that LLMs can better support conceptual modeling if we *remove* issues, along with offering guidance on when, how, and why to apply forgetting.

Beyond the detection and correction of technical modeling errors, a deeper challenge lies in recognizing that many potential avenues for failure are not simply errors in how LLMs generate conceptual models. Instead, these errors reflect how the LLMs learned about systems in the first place. These LLMs are trained on massive amounts of text, and that text often includes inconsistent, informal, or even conflicting ways of explaining how things work. If we want AI systems to help build useful models, attention must be given to the underlying patterns and assumptions picked up during training. Then, we must be willing to assist the AI systems in forgetting the learned components that do not belong.

An important area for future unlearning involves how models represent entities and the logic connecting them. Sometimes, AI systems collapse distinct people, organizations, or ideas into a single point in the model, leading to errors that may not be obvious at first glance but ultimately confuse or contradict the logic of the system. Helping models forget incorrect combinations requires rethinking how models treat roles and relationships across different parts of a graph. This connects closely to research on logic graphs and entity typing, where understanding who or what plays which role is key to build trustworthy models.

Another crucial direction involves the logic comprising a model's structure. Even if a graph appears complete or well-aligned with its text description, it can still fail to follow the intended decision-making process or rules of a domain. These failures are often harder to detect because they involve how the pieces work together, not just whether the pieces are present. Forgetting flawed logical patterns, such as misleading shortcuts or template-driven flows, will require new tools for checking whether models truly capture the reasoning we expect. Similarly, improving how AI handles model documentation, including handling tabular completeness in tables and matrices, is essential. These components can be incomplete or oversimplified in generated models or lose sight of the relationships between tabular observations and their corresponding column features. Yet, these are key for interpreting, validating, and reusing the results. Forgetting bad habits in table generation will mean building better connections between unstructured text and structured representations, especially for technical and domain-specific content.

5.2 Adding and Forgetting as Part of Ongoing Maintenance

Although we focus on unlearning, it *complements* widely used methods to improve LLM performance for conceptual modeling, such as prompt engineering. There are situations in which errors would not be resolved solely by unlearning. For instance, consider the task of text-to-model in which the LLM uses its knowledge base to create a conceptual model from a narrative, including implicit or missing links. On the one hand, the World Health Organization recently and unequivocally stated that "when it comes to alcohol consumption, there is no safe amount that does not affect health; [...] risks start from the first drop" [76]. On the other hand, as shown in online supplementary material **S7**, GPT holds the old competing belief that alcohol is good for health. Debunking the myths about moderate drinking solely by *removing* these ideas from GPT would then leave it in a neutral state as it would not *know* how to connect drinking and health. Removing should thus followed by adding the more recent evidence base.

As the evidence base and the world around us keep changing, we need to build AI systems that efficiently integrate new knowledge over time. This means that AI systems cannot function solely as large knowledge ingestion engines: they must also deliberately remove or suppress outdated knowledge. As a result, we posit that going forward, LLMs would not be retrofitted after training, with modelers discovering issues and manually triggering an unlearning algorithm. Rather, unlearning would be built into the AI training process. Conceptual modeling demands not just correct outputs, but consistency, interpretability, and maintenance of structured knowledge. LLMs that can 'forget with intention' (correcting concept mappings, removing deprecated ontology structures, or updating role associations) would transform how conceptual models are managed.

We encourage conceptual modeling researchers to view unlearning as a routine *knowledge hygiene practice*, similar to cleaning up terminologies or correcting domain misconceptions. Just as quality control techniques help identify and remedy issues in conceptual models [40,52], emerging unlearning techniques offer the ability to identify and remedy issues in LLMs.

To support ongoing maintenance of LLMs for conceptual modeling (e.g., when narratives change, policies are updated, ontologies evolve), several emerging techniques allow LLMs to forget specific knowledge *over time*, not just once [64]. For example, under 'selective amnesia' [30], models can forget without needing access to the full training set, an important feature for conceptual modelers working with pre-trained LLMs. However, most current methods are primarily designed for vision or diffusion models rather than the text-based LLMs used in conceptual modeling. Selective amnesia, for instance, applies incremental updates that cause a model to lose the ability to generate specific visual concepts (e.g., a particular celebrity). While such approaches show that continual forgetting is feasible, new tools and benchmarks with known modeling errors are needed to increase practical value for the conceptual modeling community.

Disclosure of Interests. The authors have no competing interests to declare that are relevant to the content of this article.

References

1. Adams, G.S., Converse, B.A., Hales, A.H., Klotz, L.: People systematically overlook subtractive changes. Nature **592**(7853), 258–261 (2021). https://doi.org/10.1038/s41586-021-03380-y
2. Alvandi, A.O.: Machine unlearning in digitalized healthcare arena a comprehensive exploration (2024)
3. Amini, R., Norouzi, S.S., Hitzler, P., Amini, R.: Towards complex ontology alignment using large language models. arXiv:2404.10329 (2024)
4. Balci, O.: Verification, validation, and testing. Handb. Simulat. **10**(8), 335–393 (1998)
5. Barlas, Y.: Multiple tests for validation of system dynamics type of simulation models. Eur. J. Oper. Res. **42**(1), 59–87 (1989)
6. Baumann, N., et al.: Combining retrieval-augmented generation and few-shot learning for model synthesis of uncommon dsls. In: Modellierung 2024 Satellite Events, pp. 10–18420. Gesellschaft für Informatik eV (2024)
7. Bourtoule, L., et al.: Machine unlearning. In: 2021 IEEE Symposium on Security and Privacy (SP), pp. 141–159. IEEE (2021)
8. Cámara, J., Troya, J., Burgueño, L., Vallecillo, A.: On the assessment of generative AI in modeling tasks: an experience report with chatGPT and UML. Softw. Syst. Model. **22**(3), 781–793 (2023)
9. Chang, W., Zhu, T., Xu, H., Liu, W., Zhou, W.: Class machine unlearning for complex data via concepts inference and data poisoning. arXiv preprint arXiv:2405.15662 (2024)
10. Chen, J., Yang, D.: Unlearn what you want to forget: efficient unlearning for llms. arXiv preprint arXiv:2310.20150 (2023)
11. Chen, K., Yang, Y., Chen, B., López, J.A.H., Mussbacher, G., Varró, D.: Automated domain modeling with large language models: a comparative study. In: 26th ACM/IEEE International Conference on Model Driven Engineering Languages and Systems, MODELS 2023, Västerås, Sweden, 1–6 October 2023, pp. 162–172. IEEE (2023). https://doi.org/10.1109/MODELS58315.2023.00037
12. Cheng, J., Dasoulas, G., He, H., Agarwal, C., Zitnik, M.: Gnndelete: a general strategy for unlearning in graph neural networks. In: International Conference on Learning Representations (ICLR) (2023)
13. Choi, D., Choi, S., Lee, E., Seo, J., Na, D.: Towards efficient machine unlearning with data augmentation: guided loss-increasing (gli) to prevent the catastrophic model utility drop. In: Proceedings of the IEEE/CVF Conference on Computer Vision and Pattern Recognition, pp. 93–102 (2024)
14. Chowdhury, S.B.R., Choromanski, K.M., Sehanobish, A., Dubey, K.A., Chaturvedi, S.: Towards scalable exact machine unlearning using parameter-efficient fine-tuning. In: Neurips Safe Generative AI Workshop 2024
15. Deng, Z., Luo, L., Chen, H.: Enable the right to be forgotten with federated client unlearning in medical imaging. arXiv preprint arXiv:2407.02356 (2024)
16. Fill, H.G., Fettke, P., Köpke, J.: Conceptual modeling and large language models: impressions from first experiments with chatGPT. Enterp. Model. Inf. Syst. Arch. (EMISAJ) **18**, 1–15 (2023)

17. Foster, J., Fogarty, K., Schoepf, S., Dugue, Z., Öztireli, C., Brintrup, A.: An information theoretic approach to machine unlearning. arXiv preprint arXiv:2402.01401 (2024)
18. Freund, A.J., Giabbanelli, P.J.: Automatically combining conceptual models using semantic and structural information. In: 2021 Annual Modeling and Simulation Conference (ANNSIM), pp. 1–12. IEEE (2021)
19. Gao, B.B., Xing, C., Xie, C.W., Wu, J., Geng, X.: Deep label distribution learning with label ambiguity. IEEE Trans. Image Process. **26**(6), 2825–2838 (2017)
20. Ge, L.: Erasing memories: implementing client unlearning in medical image analysis. In: International Conference on Image Processing and Artificial Intelligence (ICIPAl 2024), vol. 13213, pp. 955–960. SPIE (2024)
21. Giabbanelli, P., Witkowicz, N.: Generative AI for systems thinking: can a gpt question-answering system turn text into the causal maps produced by human readers? In: Proceedings of the 57th Hawaii International Conference on System Sciences (HICSS), pp. 7540–7549. University of Hawai'i at Mānoa (2024). https://hdl.handle.net/10125/107291
22. Giabbanelli, P.J., Voinov, A.A., Castellani, B., Törnberg, P.: Ideal, best, and emerging practices in creating artificial societies. In: 2019 Spring Simulation Conference (SpringSim), pp. 1–12. IEEE (2019)
23. Giglou, H.B., D'Souza, J., Auer, S.: Llms4om: matching ontologies with large language models. arXiv:2404.10317 (2024)
24. Giles, B.G., Findlay, C.S., Haas, G., LaFrance, B., Laughing, W., Pembleton, S.: Integrating conventional science and aboriginal perspectives on diabetes using fuzzy cognitive maps. Soc. Sci. Med. **64**(3), 562–576 (2007)
25. Goel, S., Prabhu, A., Torr, P., Kumaraguru, P., Sanyal, A.: Corrective machine unlearning. Trans. Mach. Learn. Res. (2024). https://openreview.net/forum?id=v8enu4jP9B
26. Gupta, V., Jung, C., Neel, S., Roth, A., Sharifi-Malvajerdi, S., Waites, C.: Adaptive machine unlearning. Adv. Neural. Inf. Process. Syst. **34**, 16319–16330 (2021)
27. Gutschmidt, A., Nast, B.: Assessing model quality using large language models. In: IFIP Working Conference on The Practice of Enterprise Modeling, pp. 105–122. Springer, Heidelberg (2024). https://doi.org/10.1007/978-3-031-77908-4_7
28. Guyon, I., Goudet, O., Kalainathan, D.: Evaluation methods of cause-effect pairs. In: Cause Effect Pairs in Machine Learning, pp. 27–99 (2019)
29. He, Y., Chen, J., Dong, H., Horrocks, I.: Exploring large language models for ontology alignment. arXiv:2309.07172 (2023)
30. Heng, A., Soh, H.: Selective amnesia: a continual learning approach to forgetting in deep generative models. Adv. Neural. Inf. Process. Syst. **36**, 17170–17194 (2023)
31. Hu, H., Wang, S., Dong, T., Xue, M.: Learn what you want to unlearn: unlearning inversion attacks against machine unlearning. In: 2024 IEEE Symposium on Security and Privacy (SP), pp. 3257–3275. IEEE (2024)
32. Huang, Z., et al.: Unified gradient-based machine unlearning with remain geometry enhancement. In: Globerson, A., et al. (eds.) Advances in Neural Information Processing Systems, vol. 37, pp. 26377–26414. Curran Associates, Inc. (2024)
33. Jalali, M.S., Akhavan, A.: Integrating AI language models in qualitative research: replicating interview data analysis with chatGPT. Syst. Dyn. Rev. (2024)
34. Jang, J., et al.: Knowledge unlearning for mitigating privacy risks in language models. arXiv preprint arXiv:2210.01504 (2022)
35. Jang, M., Kwon, D.S., Lukasiewicz, T.: Becel: benchmark for consistency evaluation of language models. In: Proceedings of the 29th International Conference on Computational Linguistics, pp. 3680–3696 (2022)

36. Jin, B., Liu, G., Han, C., Jiang, M., Ji, H., Han, J.: Large language models on graphs: a comprehensive survey. IEEE Trans. Knowl. Data Eng. (2024)
37. Klievtsova, N., Mangler, J., Kampik, T., Benzin, J.V., Rinderle-Ma, S.: How can generative AI empower domain experts in creating process models? In: Wirtschaftsinformatik, vol. 66 (2024)
38. Klotz, L.: Subtract: The Untapped Science of Less. Flatiron Books, New York (2021)
39. Koch, K., Soll, M.: No matter how you slice it: machine unlearning with sisa comes at the expense of minority classes. In: 2023 IEEE Conference on Secure and Trustworthy Machine Learning (SaTML), pp. 622–637. IEEE (2023)
40. Köhler, J., Munn, K., Rüegg, A., Skusa, A., Smith, B.: Quality control for terms and definitions in ontologies and taxonomies. BMC Bioinf. **7**, 1–12 (2006)
41. Li, J., et al.: Single image unlearning: efficient machine unlearning in multimodal large language models. Adv. Neural. Inf. Process. Syst. **37**, 35414–35453 (2024)
42. Liu, J., Lou, J., Qin, Z., Ren, K.: Certified minimax unlearning with generalization rates and deletion capacity. Adv. Neural. Inf. Process. Syst. **36** (2024)
43. Liu, S., et al.: Rethinking machine unlearning for large language models. Nat. Mach. Intell. 1–14 (2025)
44. Liu, Z., Dou, G., Tan, Z., Tian, Y., Jiang, M.: Towards safer large language models through machine unlearning. arXiv preprint arXiv:2402.10058 (2024)
45. Lizzo, T., Heck, L.: UNLEARN efficient removal of knowledge in large language models. In: Chiruzzo, L., Ritter, A., Wang, L. (eds.) Findings of the Association for Computational Linguistics: NAACL 2025, pp. 7257–7268. Association for Computational Linguistics, Albuquerque (2025). https://aclanthology.org/2025.findings-naacl.405/
46. Lynch, C., et al.: Ai-generated messaging for life events using structured prompts: a comparative study of GPT with human experts and machine learning. TechRxiv (2025). https://doi.org/10.36227/techrxiv.174123588.85605769/v1
47. Mendling, J., Reijers, H.A., Recker, J.: Activity labeling in process modeling: empirical insights and recommendations. Inf. Syst. **35**(4), 467–482 (2010)
48. Mu, S., Klabjan, D.: Rewind-to-delete: certified machine unlearning for nonconvex functions. arXiv preprint arXiv:2409.09778 (2024)
49. Muresanu, A., Thudi, A., Zhang, M.R., Papernot, N.: Unlearnable algorithms for in-context learning. arXiv preprint arXiv:2402.00751 (2024)
50. Nasirigerdeh, R., Razmi, N., Schnabel, J.A., Rueckert, D., Kaissis, G.: Machine unlearning for medical imaging. arXiv preprint arXiv:2407.07539 (2024)
51. Neel, S., Roth, A., Sharifi-Malvajerdi, S.: Descent-to-delete: gradient-based methods for machine unlearning. In: Algorithmic Learning Theory, pp. 931–962. PMLR (2021)
52. Nelson, H.J., Poels, G., Genero, M., Piattini, M.: A conceptual modeling quality framework. Softw. Qual. J. **20**, 201–228 (2012)
53. Prokop, D., Stenchlák, Š., Škoda, P., Klímek, J., Nečaský, M.: Enhancing domain modeling with pre-trained large language models: an automated assistant for domain modelers. In: International Conference on Conceptual Modeling, pp. 235–253. Springer, Heidelberg (2024). https://doi.org/10.1007/978-3-031-75872-0_13
54. Rafailov, R., Sharma, A., Mitchell, E., Manning, C.D., Ermon, S., Finn, C.: Direct preference optimization: your language model is secretly a reward model. Adv. Neural. Inf. Process. Syst. **36**, 53728–53741 (2023)
55. Reitemeyer, B., Fill, H.G.: Applying large language models in knowledge graph-based enterprise modeling: challenges and opportunities. arXiv preprint arXiv:2501.03566 (2025)

56. Saba, W.S.: Stochastic llms do not understand language: towards symbolic, explainable and ontologically based llms. In: Almeida, J.P.A., Borbinha, J., Guizzardi, G., Link, S., Zdravkovic, J. (eds.) Conceptual Modeling - 42nd International Conference, ER 2023, Lisbon, Portugal, November 6-9, 2023, Proceedings. Lecture Notes in Computer Science, vol. 14320, pp. 3–19. Springer, Heidelberg (2023). https://doi.org/10.1007/978-3-031-47262-6_1
57. Saeedizade, M.J., Blomqvist, E.: Navigating ontology development with large language models. In: European Semantic Web Conference, pp. 143–161. Springer, Heidelberg (2024)
58. de Saint-Exupéry, A.: Terre des hommes. Gallimard, Paris (1939)
59. Sakib, S.K., Xie, M.: Machine unlearning in digital healthcare: addressing technical and ethical challenges. In: Proceedings of the AAAI Symposium Series, vol. 4, pp. 319–322 (2024)
60. Sánchez, D., Batet, M., Isern, D., Valls, A.: Ontology-based semantic similarity: a new feature-based approach. Expert Syst. Appl. **39**(9), 7718–7728 (2012)
61. Senge, P.M., Forrester, J.W.: Tests for building confidence in system dynamics models. Syst. Dyn. TIMS Stud. Manag. Sci. **14**(14), 209–228 (1980)
62. Shani, C., Vreeken, J., Shahaf, D.: Towards concept-aware large language models. arXiv preprint arXiv:2311.01866 (2023). https://doi.org/10.48550/arXiv.2311.01866
63. Sharma, A.S., Sarkar, N., Chundawat, V., Mali, A.A., Mandal, M.: Unlearning or concealment? A critical analysis and evaluation metrics for unlearning in diffusion models. arXiv preprint arXiv:2409.05668 (2024)
64. Shibata, T., Irie, G., Ikami, D., Mitsuzumi, Y.: Learning with selective forgetting. In: IJCAI, vol. 2, p. 6 (2021)
65. Silva, J., Ma, Q., Cabot, J., Kelsen, P., Proper, H.A.: Application of the tree-of-thoughts framework to llm-enabled domain modeling. In: Maass, W., Han, H., Yasar, H., Multari, N.J. (eds.) Conceptual Modeling - 43rd International Conference, ER 2024, Pittsburgh, PA, USA, 28–31 October 2024, Proceedings. Lecture Notes in Computer Science, vol. 15238, pp. 94–111. Springer, Heidelberg (2024). https://doi.org/10.1007/978-3-031-75872-0_6
66. Snijder, L.L., Smit, Q.T., de Boer, M.H.: Advancing ontology alignment in the labor market: combining large language models with domain knowledge. In: Proceedings of the AAAI Symposium Series, vol. 3, pp. 253–262 (2024)
67. Sterman, J.: System Dynamics: Systems Thinking and Modeling for a Complex World. McGraw-Hill Higher Education, New York (2000)
68. Storey, V.C., Trujillo, J., Liddle, S.W.: Research on conceptual modeling: themes, topics, and introduction to the special issue. Data Knowl. Eng. **98**, 1–7 (2015). https://doi.org/10.1016/J.DATAK.2015.07.002
69. Suriyakumar, V., Wilson, A.C.: Algorithms that approximate data removal: new results and limitations. Adv. Neural. Inf. Process. Syst. **35**, 18892–18903 (2022)
70. Thießen, F., D'Souza, J., Stocker, M.: Probing large language models for scientific synonyms. In: SEMANTiCS 2023 EU: 19th International Conference on Semantic Systems. vol. 3510. CEUR Workshop Proceedings, Leipzig (2023). https://ceur-ws.org/Vol-3510/paper_nlp_2.pdf
71. Vennix, J.A.M.: Individual and organizational problem construction. In: Group Model Building, pp. 9–41. John Wiley and Sons (1996)
72. Villalobos, P., Ho, A., Sevilla, J., Besiroglu, T., Heim, L., Hobbhahn, M.: Will we run out of data? Limits of llm scaling based on human-generated data (2024). https://arxiv.org/abs/2211.04325

73. Wang, B., Giabbanelli, P.J.: Identifying informative features to evaluate student knowledge as causal maps. Int. J. Artif. Intell. Educ. **34**(2), 301–331 (2024)
74. Wang, Y., Zhao, Y.: TRAM: benchmarking temporal reasoning for large language models. arXiv preprint arXiv:2310.00835 (2023)
75. Weng, J., Yao, S., Du, Y., Huang, J., Weng, J., Wang, C.: Proof of unlearning: definitions and instantiation. IEEE Trans. Inf. Forensics Secur. **19**, 3309–3323 (2024)
76. World Health organization: no level of alcohol consumption is safe for our health (2022). https://www.who.int/europe/news-room/04-01-2023-no-level-of-alcohol-consumption-is-safe-for-our-health
77. Wu, J., Yang, Y., Qian, Y., Sui, Y., Wang, X., He, X.: Gif: a general graph unlearning strategy via influence function. In: Proceedings of the ACM Web Conference 2023, pp. 651–661 (2023)
78. Yan, H., Li, X., Guo, Z., Li, H., Li, F., Lin, X.: Arcane: an efficient architecture for exact machine unlearning (2022
79. Yao, Y., Xu, X., Liu, Y.: Large language model unlearning. Adv. Neural. Inf. Process. Syst. **37**, 105425–105475 (2025)
80. Zhang, D., et al.: To be forgotten or to be fair: unveiling fairness implications of machine unlearning methods. AI Ethics **4**(1), 83–93 (2024)
81. Zhang, R., Lin, L., Bai, Y., Mei, S.: Negative preference optimization: from catastrophic collapse to effective unlearning. arXiv preprint arXiv:2404.05868 (2024)

ModelFed: A Federated Protocol for Collaborative Cross-Platform Modeling

Iván Alfonso[1](✉) and Jordi Cabot[1,2]

[1] Luxembourg Institute of Science and Technology, Esch-sur-Alzette, Luxembourg
{ivan.alfonso,jordi.cabot}@list.lu
[2] University of Luxembourg, Esch-sur-Alzette, Luxembourg

Abstract. Modeling is inherently a collaborative process, involving multiple stakeholders with different expertise and technical levels, often using a myriad of modeling tools, each one tailored to their individual profiles. This poses a major interoperability challenge, even more when we want this collaboration to happen in real-time and without relying on a centralized node. Indeed, a centralized architecture introduces scalability, privacy and reliability concerns.

In this sense, this paper presents ModelFed, a federated protocol for real-time collaboration across heterogeneous and distributed modeling platforms. ModelFed, currently focused on data models but extendable to others, enables participant platforms to maintain their own data, policies, and model representations while synchronizing changes efficiently. We evaluate our approach in a multi-platform modeling environment, demonstrating consistent model synchronization and practical efficiency for distributed stakeholders.

Keywords: Collaborative modeling · cross-platform · model federation

1 Introduction

Information systems development is naturally a collaborative activity involving various stakeholders working together to build a system [19]. This is also true for approaches like Model-Driven Engineering (MDE), where conceptual models serve as the foundation for designing, using, analyzing, and transforming models during the software development process. Indeed, in conceptual modeling, multiple stakeholders with diverse knowledge and expertise (from the development team to non-technical stakeholders and domain experts) often must contribute collaboratively to defining the system-to-be.

Although this need is recognized in many modeling methods and frameworks, that support collaborative modeling, they typically require all actors to use the same tool. This greatly limits the collaboration by imposing restrictions on all actors (not only on the tool to be used, but also on the modeling language and even the syntax), forcing all participants to learn those even if, due to their profile, each participant would prefer to use a different tool and language [12].

D. Bork et al. (Eds.): ER 2025, LNCS 16189, pp. 45–62, 2026.
https://doi.org/10.1007/978-3-032-08623-5_3

Beyond cross-platform modeling, an ideal collaboration environment should also be not only distributed but fully decentralized. As solutions relying on a central server introduce single failure points, hamper scalability, and raise privacy and control concerns for participants.

This paper proposes such a collaborative modeling architecture. Our approach is inspired by the concept of Fediverse [17], an interconnected and decentralized ecosystem of social platforms. In Fediverse, independent platforms can interact with each other, enabling users to communicate and share content. One of its key advantages is that each platform retains control over its own data and infrastructure, improving privacy, data ownership, and security [17]. The Fediverse primarily ensures interoperability between platforms by using the ActivityPub[1] protocol, which enables the federation of independent servers and reduces dependence on large social media companies. However, while ActivityPub defines general purpose activities (such as *Create*, *Update*, and *Delete*), it lacks domain-specific semantics required for collaborative modeling, such as representing model elements (e.g. classes and relationships).

With a vision similar to ActivityPub and the Fediverse, but focused on model federation, we propose ModelFed and Modelverse, a decentralized ecosystem that enables collaborative modeling across different platforms. ModelFed, the protocol that enables platforms to communicate, extends ActivityPub by introducing new concepts tailored to modeling collaboration, particularly for the creation and maintenance of structural models. Modelverse adopts a federated architecture, where modeling platforms maintain their own data and policies but synchronize changes via a shared protocol, eliminating the need for a central server while ensuring interoperability.

The remainder of this paper is structured as follows. Section 2 establishes foundational concepts and background. Section 3 introduces our running example, which illustrates key concepts throughout the paper. We then present our core contributions: Section 4 details the Modelverse ecosystem, Sect. 5 describes the ModelFed vocabulary extension, and Sect. 6 explains the runtime implementation. Tool support and prototyping are discussed in Sect. 7, followed by experimental validation in Sect. 8. Section 9 examines the extensibility of the protocol for new domains. Finally, Sect. 10 reviews related work, and Sect. 11 concludes with future directions.

2 Background

2.1 Federated Systems

The term federation in software and systems engineering refers to the collaboration between multiple systems, databases, services, or platforms without requiring centralization of all data or resources in a single location [25]. Federated systems share information, resources, or functionalities in a coordinated manner while maintaining their autonomy.

[1] https://www.w3.org/TR/activitypub/.

The main advantages of federated systems are their interoperability, as they enable seamless communication and synchronized information sharing; scalability, achieved through resource decentralization, which avoids reliance on a single point of failure; security, since each system can store and protect sensitive information locally, minimizing exposure risks; and autonomy, as systems maintain their independence while collaborating within the federated framework [5].

2.2 Fediverse and ActivityPub

The Fediverse is a very popular example of a federated system in which a federated network of interconnected servers is used for social networking and content publishing. Each server operates independently, but communicates with others using a shared protocol called ActivityPub. As a federated system, there is no central corporation, platform, back-end, or website that coordinates and controls all activity. Instead, users can interact on servers (following, sharing, and messaging) regardless of which platform or provider they use.

ActivityPub is the protocol that enables communication between social networks in the Fediverse. Established by the World Wide Web Consortium (W3C), it facilitates interoperability by defining two decentralized APIs: (1) client-to-server API, which enables interactions between users and platforms, and (2) server-to-server API, which specifies the procedures that servers follow to federate or distribute activities across different servers.

The data format and vocabulary of ActivityPub are based on ActivityStreams[2], a standardized JSON-LD[3] based format used to represent social activities and interactions in a structured manner. The core concepts defined in this vocabulary include:

- Activities: Actions that may happen, are happening, or have already occurred. Common activity types include Create, Block, Delete, Like, and Update.
- Objects: The specific entities involved in an activity, such as Article, Note, Image, Video, or Place.
- Actors: The entities performing activities, such as Person, Organization, or Application.

In ActivityPub, all objects (including actors and activities) have a unique global identifier (URI).

The following sections present Modelverse and ModelFed, our federated architecture for collaborative modeling, inspired by the decentralization principles of the Fediverse and ActivityPub.

3 Running Example

As a running example, imagine a collaboration scenario aimed at creating a common model to formalize the Digital Product Passport (DPP) initiative, part

[2] https://www.w3.org/TR/activitystreams-core/.
[3] https://www.w3.org/TR/json-ld11/.

of the Ecodesign for Sustainable Products Regulation (ESPR) by the European Commission [10]. The development of a DPP model involves concepts and knowledge from various areas, making it an ideal case for exploring collaborative modeling among stakeholders with diverse profiles.

A DPP aims to manage, collect, and share crucial information about products throughout their lifecycle to promote product sustainability and circularity. Its goals include accelerating the transition to a circular economy, improving material and energy efficiency, extending product lifetime, and optimizing design, manufacturing, usage, and end-of-life processes [29].

According to the ESPR agreement, between 2026 and 2033, the European Union is expected to adopt the DPP for several product categories, such as textiles, batteries, electronic devices, and others. However, the design of a structural or data model for the DPP requires foundational knowledge from several sectors and user profiles, depending on the product category. Our running example focuses on designing a general DPP data model that could serve as a foundation for more specialized areas. Specifically, we identify three key areas, each covered by a distinct user profile:

- Materials: Modeling the composition of products, including raw materials, recycled materials, hazardous substances, etc. This part of the model must be lead by a materials scientist.
- Manufacturing and supply chain: Representing manufacturing processes, carbon footprint, certifications, production standards, and supply chain traceability. This knowledge can be provided by an industrial engineer with experience in manufacturing and logistics.
- Knowledge and management of DPP: Review the overall structure of the DPP data model, ensure consistency, and manage collaboration between various industry experts. This includes knowledge of the DPP regulations, data governance, and interoperability requirements. An IT expert or DPP data manager can fulfill this role, acting as a DPP model administrator.

To help these profiles efficiently collaborate together, they require a collaborative space where each can use its own tool to describe the parts of the model relevant to them. Additionally, they should only see the parts of the model that they need to see to avoid information overload and prevent unauthorized changes.

In the next sections, we will see how a Modelverse provides the right environment to support this type of complex cross-platform distributed modeling scenarios.

4 Modelverse

We call Modelverse the federated ecosystem of distributed modeling platforms interconnected through ModelFed, a protocol specifically designed for collaborative modeling.

Unlike centralized solutions, Modelverse enables decentralized collaboration by allowing multiple users to concurrently edit shared models without relying on a central server. Changes propagate in real-time across platforms, ensuring runtime synchronization while maintaining platform autonomy as each modeling tool preserves its own internal representation of the model while adhering to the federation protocol.

To illustrate this, Fig. 1 depicts our running scenario from Sect. 3 as a potential Modelverse configuration, where three platforms joined the Modelverse and talk to each other via the ModelFed protocol. In this scenario, users collaboratively design the model at runtime, using different notation: the *Admin* and the *Industrial engineer* work graphically, while the *Materials scientist* interacts through a tabular view. This heterogeneity is naturally supported by Modelverse, where each platform manages its own concrete syntax and user interface for model representation. Additionally, platforms can store and maintain their local representation of the complete model or specific portions, depending on the user's needs. This local storage is not dictated by the ModelFed protocol and can follow the platform's own architectural choices (e.g., SQL/NoSQL databases, in-memory caching, or external storage solutions), as long as the platform complies with ModelFed's synchronization interface.

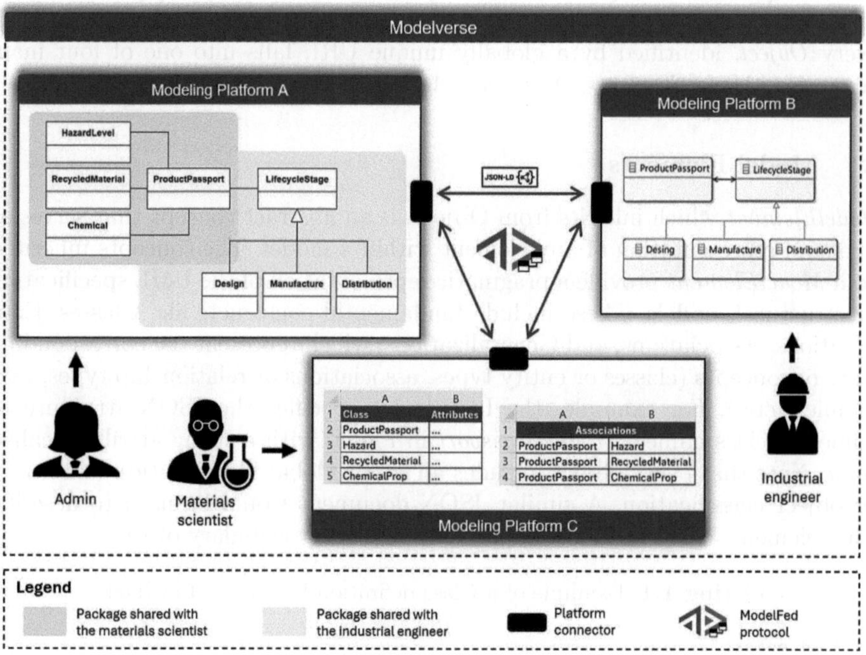

Fig. 1. Collaborative modeling in Modelverse.

The realization of a Modelverse scenario requires two key elements: (1) a standardized vocabulary to ensure semantic interoperability of modeling activities, and (2) the implementation of the ModelFed protocol based on this vocabulary. Section 5 details the vocabulary design and its modeling-specific concepts, while Sect. 6 describes the protocol's technical implementation.

5 ModelFed Vocabulary

As illustrated in the Modelverse schema (Fig. 1), platform-to-platform communication is based on JSON-LD messages structured using the ModelFed vocabulary, an extension of the ActivityStreams vocabulary[4].

The ModelFed vocabulary enables semantic interoperability by supporting: (1) the representation of structural model elements (e.g., classes, attributes, relationships), (2) modeling-specific activities (e.g., Create, Update, Clone), and (3) access control through actor and grant definitions.

Without loss of generality (see Sect. 9, our vocabulary focuses on defining a JSON-LD syntax for structural conceptual models, drawing inspiration from the UML specification [21], as it is widely adopted in modeling practice.

Figure 2 illustrates the core concepts and relationships of the ModelFed Vocabulary, emphasizing its extension points from the ActivityStreams foundation[5]. At its core, we find the *Object* concept, defined as an entity of any kind. Every *Object*, identified by a globally unique URI, falls into one of four main categories (*ModelElements*, *Activities*, *Actors*, and *Grants*) discussed below.

5.1 Model Elements

ModelElement which inherits from Object, is an abstract concept that serves as a general representation of any element within a model. The concepts inherited from *ModelElement* provide a pragmatic representation of the UML specification for structural models. These include fundamental constructs like Classes, Enumerations, Associations, and Generalizations, which represent the corresponding types of concepts (classes or entity types, associations or relationship types, taxonomies, etc.). For example, the Listing 1.1 specifies the JSON structure to define the class named *ProductPassport* in Fig. 1, with a string attribute called *name*. Note that every object includes an *id* for global identification and a *type* for object classification. A similar JSON document would be used to describe other elements of our DPP example, following the vocabulary of Fig. 2

Listing 1.1. Example of a Class definition based on ModelFed

```
{
  "@context": [
    "https://www.w3.org/ns/activitystreams",
    "https://besser-pearl.github.io/ModelFed/ns/modelfed.jsonld"
  ],
```

[4] https://www.w3.org/TR/activitystreams-vocabulary/.

[5] ModelFed vocabulary specification available at https://modelfed.readthedocs.io.

```
  "type": "Class",
  "id": "https://platformA.com/classes/product_passport",
  "name": "ProductPassport",
  "attributes": [
    {
      "type": "Property",
      "id": "https://platformA.com/properties/name",
      "name": "name",
      "elementType": "str"
    }
  ]
}
```

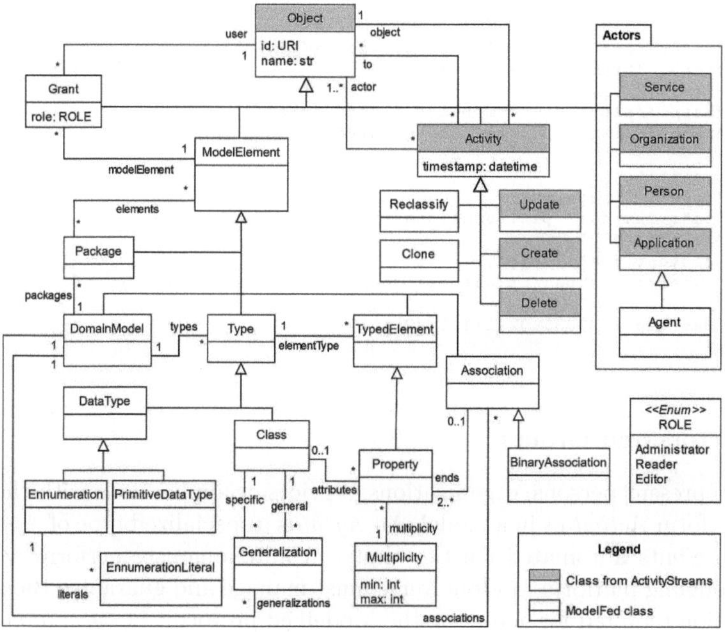

Fig. 2. The ModelFed vocabulary as an ActivityStreams extension.

5.2 Activities

Activities are among the most important concepts in Modelverse, as they allow the specification of actions performed on any *Object*. An *Activity*, serialized as a JSON-LD object, constitutes the primary payload exchanged during interactions between platforms.

ModelFed defines or reuses five activities: Create, Update, Delete, Reclassify (to change the classification of a *ModelElement*), and Clone (to create an identical copy of a *ModelElement*). Each *Activity* links one *Object* (on which the action is performed), one or more *Actors* who execute the action, and a list of *Actors* to federate the activity (relation named *to* in the diagram).

The JSON structure in Listing 1.2 represents an activity to create an attribute (*Property* object) named *UID* for the class *ProductPassport*, identified by the URI in the *owner* field. This action is performed by the *Admin* actor and is federated with the *Materials scientist* and the *Industrial engineer*. Finally, the *timestamp* field indicates the date and time of creation, which should be automatically calculated by the actor platform server.

Listing 1.2. Example of a *Create* activity based on ModelFed

```
{
  "@context": [
    "https://www.w3.org/ns/activitystreams",
    "https://besser-pearl.github.io/ModelFed/ns/modelfed.jsonld"
  ],
  "type": "Create",
  "id": "http://platformA.com/activities/a1c2t3",
  "actor": "https://platformA.com/admin/",
  "to": [
    "http://platformB.com/materialsscientist/",
    "http://platformC.com/industrialeng/"
  ],
  "object": {
    "type": "Property",
    "id": "https://platformA.com/properties/uid",
    "name": "UID",
    "elementType": "str",
    "owner": "https://platformA.com/classes/product_passport"
  },
  "timestamp": "2025-02-11T15:42:45Z"
}
```

5.3 Actors and Grants

Actors represent persons, organizations, services or applications with the capacity to perform *Activities* in a model. An *Agent* is a specialized type of *Application* that represents automated entities that can autonomously perform activities. Each modeling platform in Modelverse must manage and guarantee the minimal information required for actors by the ModelFed protocol: *id*, *type*, *name*, *inbox*, and *outbox*. In particular, the *inbox* and *outbox* are communication endpoints for the activity distribution. Federation is implemented through direct actor-to-actor interactions using these endpoints: *inbox* receives activities shared by other actors, while *outbox* publishes activities to be shared with others. For example, when the *Material scientist* creates the *Hazard* class, the activity is first sent to the *Material scientist's outbox*, and then delivered to the *Admin's inbox*.

The *Grant* concept governs access control and permissions. It specifies which actors are authorized to perform certain types of activity on specific model elements. As depicted in Fig. 2, a *Grant* specifies the *Actor* involved (*user* relationship), a *ModelElement*, and a role. Three role types are defined: *Administrator* with full control (including grant creation), *Editor* with read/write access (excluding deletion), and *Reader* with read-only access.

For instance, in our DPP running example, the *Admin* assigns editor permissions to the *Materials scientist* and *Industrial engineer* for distinct model packages, ensuring that each user interacts only with relevant components. Any change in the *LifecycleStage* class will be federated only between the *Admin* and the *Materials scientist*, while changes in the *ProductPassport* class will be shared with everyone, as it belongs to both packages where all users have valid *Grants*.

6 Runtime Implementation of ModelFed

The integration of modeling platforms within the Modelverse is mediated by a *Platform connector* (as shown in Fig. 1), which orchestrates bidirectional synchronization of modeling activities. Figure 3 details the connector's architecture, specifying the core components required for implementation:

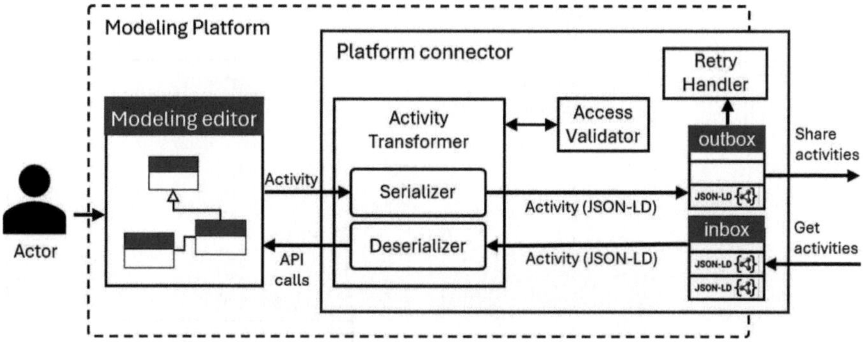

Fig. 3. Platform connector architecture

The **inbox** and **outbox** endpoints are RESTful services that handle the exchange of activities between platforms. The inbox accepts ModelFed activities in JSON-LD format, while the outbox uses the same format to queue outgoing activities for the federated nodes.

The **Activity Transformer** consists of two main components: the *Serializer*, which converts platform-specific events (e.g., "ClassCreated") into standardized ModelFed activities by mapping them to ModelFed vocabulary terms, adding metadata (such as actor and timestamp), and generating valid JSON-LD using the ModelFed @context; and the *Deserializer*, which performs the inverse operation by resolving JSON-LD contexts and translating the activities into platform-specific API calls to recreate the original actions.

The **Access Validator** performs mandatory authorization checks during both the serialization and deserialization phases. It checks the actor's *Grants* against the target model elements, applies role-based policies (e.g., editors can modify but not delete), and rejects any unauthorized activities.

Finally, to handle delivery failures, the Platform Connector can include a **Retry Handler**. This component ensures reliability by queuing failed activities and retrying delivery with an exponential backoff policy. If delivery still fails after a set number of attempts, the system logs the error and notifies the user. This fault-tolerant approach follows established distributed system practices [24].

To illustrate the activity federation process and the orchestration of the key components involved, Fig. 4 presents a sequence diagram based on the DPP scenario from Sect. 3. In this scenario, the user *Admin* has already created a domain model and assigned editor permissions to the *Materials Scientist.*

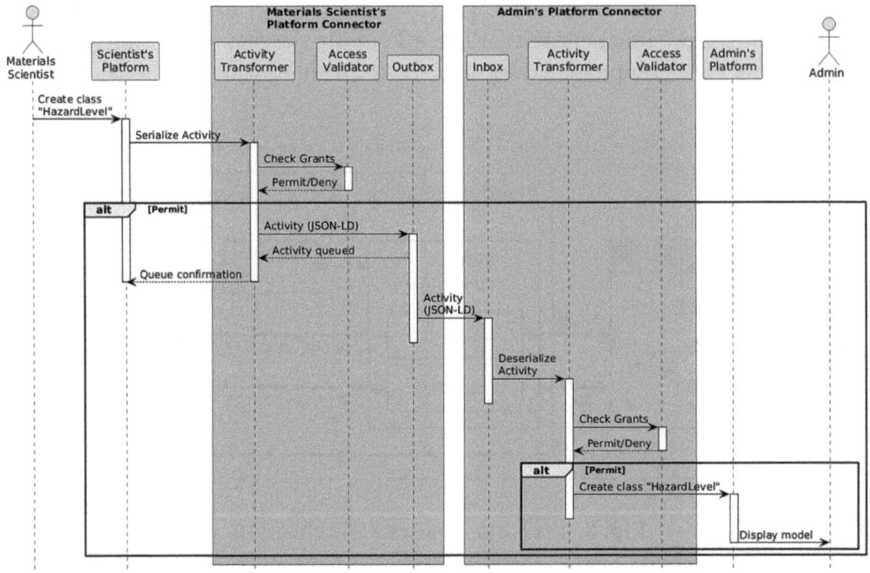

Fig. 4. Modelverse sequence diagram: *HazardLevel* class creation

The process begins when the *Materials Scientist* creates a *HazardLevel* class. This event triggers the platform to send an activity to the *Activity Transformer* for serialization. The transformer first delegates authorization to the *Access Validator*, which checks the actor's *Grants* against both the target model element (*HazardLevel* class or its owner domain model) and the requested operation (*Create*). Upon successful validation, the transformer serializes the activity in ModelFed's JSON-LD format and queues it in the *Outbox* for asynchronous distribution. This design ensures non-blocking user interaction by decoupling the *Materials Scientist* modeling tasks from the background federation subprocesses.

On the *Admin* side, once the message is received on the *Inbox*, it is sent to the *Activity Transformer* for deserialization. Before this, however, a second permission check is performed (this time on the recipient's side). This dual-authorization mechanism (enforced on both the actor and recipient servers) ensures that activities are executed only when the actor is authorized to perform them. If the activity passes this check, it is replicated on *Admin's Platform* via the corresponding API calls, allowing the Admin to view the updated model.

7 Tool Support

To facilitate the adoption of ModelFed, we provide a comprehensive set of open-source resources, including docs, vocabulary definitions, and a prototype.

The official documentation describes the protocol architecture, message formats, vocabulary structure, and implementation guidelines. It is available online[6] as a practical reference for developers and researchers.

Moreover, we have released a proof-of-concept prototype that supports and connects two modeling platforms via Python-based connectors: one for BESSER [1], a low-code modeling platform based on UML, and another for PyEcore [27], an MDE framework compatible with the EMF Java implementation. We configured web servers for each platform using FastAPI and implemented the endpoints required by the ModelFed protocol (e.g., outbox and inbox activities for users). These connectors handle inbox/outbox communication, interpret JSON-based modeling activities, reproduce them within each platform (e.g., creating or updating a class), and coordinate activity federation.

The prototype is available in a public repository[7]. The ModelFed vocabulary, which extends ActivityStreams with modeling-specific concepts, is defined using JSON-LD. The vocabulary context is publicly accessible[8] and can be extended as needed to support other modeling domains. Also, following the examples in the repo, it is easy to add support for additional platforms.

8 Validation

This section evaluates ModelFed via two experiments involving two modeling platforms. The goal is to assess the interoperability, consistency, and efficiency of the protocol. In particular, we want to address the following questions:

- RQ1 (interoperability): Does ModelFed enable an effective model federation across heterogeneous modeling platforms?
- RQ2 (consistency): Are the federated models correct and coherent across platforms after modeling collaboration?
- RQ3 (efficiency): What is the performance impact of using the federation protocol under different collaboration loads?

The evaluation uses the prototype presented in Sect. 7, and tests the DPP scenario discussed in Sect. 3. All experimental artifacts, including test scenarios, collected data, and experiment results are available[9]. For both experiments, we deployed separate web servers (BESSER or PyEcore) for each actor on a single machine with 32 GB of RAM, an Intel(R) Core(TM) i7-1280P processor, and Windows 11 to simulate collaborative modeling.

[6] https://modelfed.readthedocs.io.
[7] https://github.com/BESSER-PEARL/ModelFed.
[8] https://besser-pearl.github.io/ModelFed/ns/modelfed.jsonld.
[9] https://github.com/BESSER-PEARL/ModelFed/tree/main/validation.

8.1 Experiment 1: Evaluating the Consistency of ModelFed

Our first experiment consisted of recreating the DPP modeling scenario. To do so, we defined 50 modeling activities to build a simplified DPP domain model inspired by the ISO 59040 standard [14][10] and assign the activities to our three different actors: the *Admin*, who creates the domain model, packages, and grants access to other users (interacting through the BESSER platform); the *Materials Scientist*, who defines the aspects of the model related to material composition and hazardous substances (using the PyEcore platform); and the *Industrial Engineer*, who models the stages of product life (also using the PyEcore platform).

First, we used a Python script to simulate the actions of the three actors on their respective servers, with each activity performed every 100 ms. Figure 5 presents the final federated model as viewed by the *Admin* user in the BESSER modeling platform. All 50 activities were properly processed by their corresponding servers, federated as intended, and handled by the platform connector. Specifically, 11 activities were performed by the *Admin* and federated with the other two users; 17 activities by the *Material Scientist* were federated only with the *Admin*; and 22 activities by the *Industrial Engineer* were federated with the *Admin*. We verified that the activities were federated or shared correctly by checking the outbox and inbox of each user.

After this first initial experiment, we permuted the order of the actions and repeated the test to confirm proper processing of the actions and consistency of the global model. In total, we tested eight different sequences, randomly reordering the activities while adhering to a set of basic rules to avoid logical errors. For instance, the first activity must always be the creation of the Domain Model, and an attribute cannot be created before its owning class exists. We chose eight sequences, as in our opinion, they are representative enough to cover a variety of execution orders, allowing us to discard potential consistency issues.

In these tests, we also mixed the activities of the three actors instead of keeping them grouped, simulating a more realistic scenario where users work concurrently. Finally, we analyzed the eight resulting models and confirmed that all were identical, containing the same model elements.

This experiment demonstrates that the ModelFed protocol enables interoperability (**RQ1**) and supports effective model federation (**RQ2**) between BESSER and PyEcore. Synchronization between both platforms was achieved by implementing technological connectors, and the federation of activities remained consistent after several attempts. However, as discussed in Sect. 6, this requires that each participant platform properly implements the protocol.

8.2 Experiment 2: Performance Analysis

The objective of the second experiment was to evaluate the performance of a modeling platform under stress using the ModelFed protocol. We designed a

[10] Note the goal of the experiment is not to create an ideal DPP model, but to create one collaboratively; the model itself is just a possibility based on a standard description.

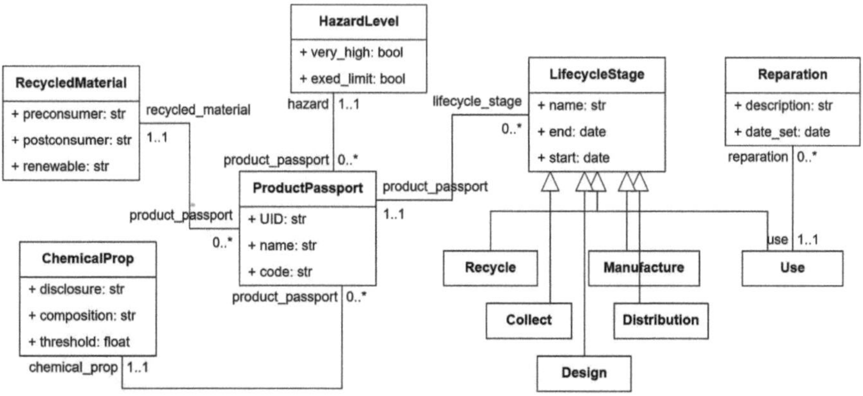

Fig. 5. Federated DPP Model in the BESSER Platform

scenario in which an admin user creates a model and executes *Create* activities for classes that are federated with multiple users. To simulate this, we ran a series of tests, gradually increasing the number of modeling activities and the number of federated users (from 5, 10, and to 20 federated users). For each user, we deployed a separate web server instance on the same machine We used JMeter to configure the test plan and collected metrics such as processing time (the time taken to process and deliver activities), error percentage (the proportion of failed requests), and throughput (the number of successfully completed requests per second), among others.

The average processing times for different numbers of activities (ranging from 10 to 300) are presented in Fig. 6. As shown, the processing time increases with a higher number of activities and users to federate. The response time remains below 500 ms for up to 50 concurrent activities with 20 users, while for 10 and 5 users, the processing time is significantly lower. It is important to note that, in a real-world scenario, executing 50 concurrent activities may not be typical. In all three cases (5, 10, and 20 users), when the number of activities reaches 250, some errors occurred, and some activities were not processed due to server overload (the server was unable to handle the volume of requests). This explains why the response time decreases at this point (failed requests are handled more quickly). Again, unless the participants are AI Agents, this volume of modeling activities is not realistic, so we do not see this as an issue.

Based on these results, we argue that the response time remains acceptable, and therefore our approach is scalable, answering **RQ3**.

9 Extending ModelFed

For the sake of simplicity, until now we have focused on the use of ModelFed to implement collaborative modeling on structural conceptual models. However, ModelFed can be used to collaborate on all types of models by just defining the corresponding vocabulary as described in Sect. 5.

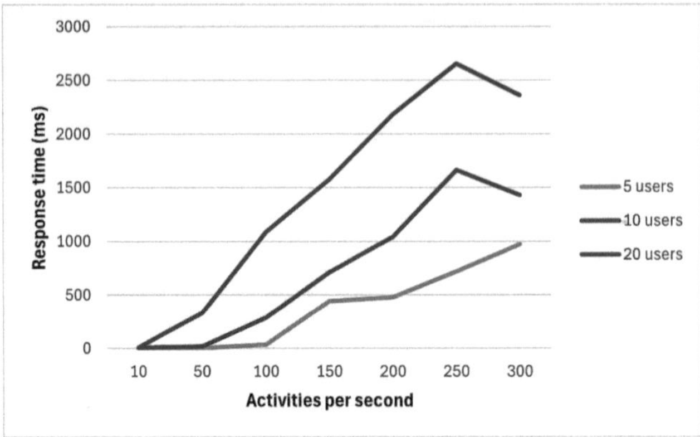

Fig. 6. Response time vs. number of activities varying federated user load

As an example, we define a minimal extension to support the specification of object models [21], which can be used to model relevant scenarios of the system, expressed as instances of classes defined in the structural model. Figure 7 models this extension by introducing two new concepts: *Instance*, which represents instances of a class (e.g., instances of the *ProductPassport* class), and *AttributeLink*, which represents instances of a class attributes (such as *UID* or *name*). Note that in this case, the extension is created on top of the vocabulary we created so far, but we could create a brand new vocabulary if needed, e.g. to represent state machines or any other type of dynamic model.

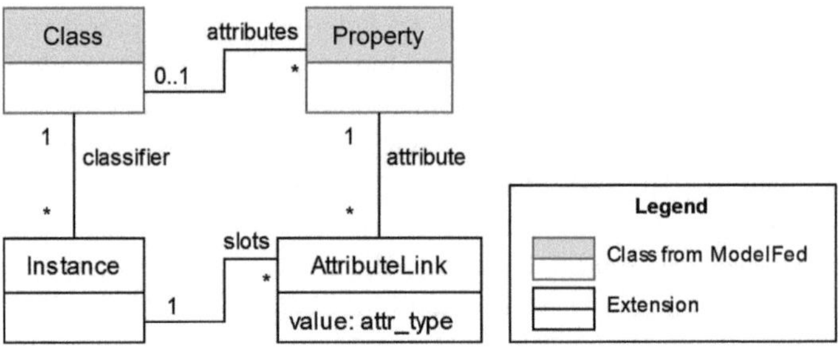

Fig. 7. ModelFed extension to enable object specification

Once this extension is modeled with JSON-LD, following the approach used in ActivityStreams (see Section *ModelElements*) we can automatically collaborate and exchange partial specifications of object models across the actors of our system. An example is shown in Listing 1.3, where the object model is an instance of our DPP running example. Note that the context in line 4 corresponds to the new vocabulary extension, and it must be available and accessible to guarantee interoperability and automatic validation. This is key to understanding how to correctly map the concepts. The rest of the listing (lines 6âĂŞ20) defines an *Instance* of the *ProductPassport* class with slots (attribute values) being *name* and *UID*, with values "Battery_AAA" and "A1B2C3", respectively.

Listing 1.3. Example of object definition extending ModelFed

```
1 {
2     "@context": [
3       "https://www.modelverse.com/ns/modelverse",
4       "https://your-domain.org/ns/object_modeling.jsonld"
5     ],
6     "type": "Instance",
7     "id": "http://platformA.com/productpassport/12345",
8     "classifier": "https://platformA.com/classes/product_passport",
9     "slots": [
10      {
11        "type": "AttributeLink",
12        "attribute": "https://platformA.com/properties/name",
13        "value": "Battery_AAA"
14      },
15      {
16        "type": "AttributeLink",
17        "attribute": "https://platformA.com/properties/uid",
18        "value": "A1B2C3"
19      }
20    ]
21 }
```

It is worth highlighting that, since the JSON-LD format ensures that properties without a defined context are ignored, existing platforms in the Modelverse can continue to operate without errors, even if they do not support the new modeling extensions. This facilitates cross-platform collaboration when not all the tools connected in the Modelverse understand all types of models.

10 Related Work

Many approaches have addressed collaborative modeling, though mostly focusing on a single preexisting framework or platform. Some are based on EMF (e.g., Sirius [9], MONDO [6], and Collaboro [15]), others rely on MPS (e.g., Modelix [20]), or other standalone solutions (e.g., WebGME [26], FlexiSketch [30], and MetaEdit [18]). Despite their benefits, they cannot be used as part of cross-platform interoperability scenarios without ad-hoc extensions.

A few approaches focus on the synchronization and federation of models across different platforms. Nevertheless, their main goal is data consistency, transformation and exchange among the platforms, more than the support for interactive collaboration features. Examples of tools in this category are NAOMI [8], which enables definition of model dependencies for change propagation, Reactive Links [23], which synchronizes primitive properties through explicit linkages, or OpenFlexo [13], which provides a dedicated language to define model mappings. Beyond the lack of real-time modeling, they lack support for essential collaborative features (such as fine-grained access control) and rely on centralized architectures for model integration.

Closer to ModelFed goals, Parsafix [28], DesignSpace [7], and BUMBLE-CE [2] also target cross-platform collaborative modeling. Parsafix relies on a central component that acts as an intermediary to synchronize model changes between two specific platforms. There is no support to add additional platforms. DesignSpace is also centralized, storing models as graphs that can be modified via tool adapters. Although DesignSpace offers a mechanism to control access by marking a model as public or private, it is not possible to share specific parts of a model with specific users. Similarly, BUMBLE-CEalso adopts a centralized architecture, where models are maintained in a central inventory, and modeling activities are coordinated through an inventory controller using platform-specific plugins. Also, similar to previous tools, BUMBLE-CE lacks support for fine-grained model sharing.

Finally, we remark that ModelFed has taken inspiration from several ActivityPub extensions developed to support federation in other domains. For example, BookWyrm [4] for social reading communities, Pixelfed [22] for photo sharing networks, and ForgeFed [11] to federate software project hosting activities across software forge platforms. These extensions demonstrate the protocol's extensibility, but they focus on domains outside of modeling.

To sum up, and to the best of our knowledge, our approach is the first to propose a federated architecture that enables collaborative cross-platform modeling without relying on a central server for model synchronization.

11 Conclusion

We presented ModelFed, a federated protocol that enables real-time collaboration across heterogeneous modeling platforms. To demonstrate its feasibility, we developed a prototype integrating two distinct modeling platforms and validated the whole approach in a collaborative modeling scenario, showing that ModelFed can synchronize activities both consistently and efficiently.

As further work, we plan to extend both the ModelFed protocol and its implementation. Regarding the protocol, our goal is to add more sophisticated traceability and conflict resolution mechanisms beyond the current timestamp-based ordering, e.g. via Conflict-free Replicated Data Type (CRDT). Existing work based on the use of Natural Language Processing (NLP) techniques to suggest semantically similar model concepts across different models [3,16] could also be useful here. Implementation efforts will focus on three directions: expanding support for other platforms (platform connectors), enhancing reliability through delivery failure handling and cryptographic signature verification, and developing an AI-assisted connector to automate JSON-LD serialization, validation, and consistency checking. This intelligent component will reduce the integration barrier for new modeling platforms joining Modelverse.

Acknowledgments. This work is supported by the Luxembourg National Research Fund (FNR) PEARL program, grant agreement 16544475.

References

1. Alfonso, I., et al.: Building BESSER: an open-source low-code platform. In: van der Aa, H., Bork, D., Schmidt, R., Sturm, A. (eds.) BPMDS EMMSAD 2024 2024. LNBIP, vol. 511, pp. 203–212. Springer, Cham (2024). https://doi.org/10.1007/978-3-031-61007-3_16
2. Aslam, K., Chen, Y., Butt, M., Malavolta, I.: Cross-platform real-time collaborative modeling: an architecture and a prototype implementation via EMF.Cloud. IEEE Access **11**, 49241–49260 (2023)
3. Aydemir, F.B., Dalpiaz, F.: Supporting collaborative modeling via natural language processing. In: Dobbie, G., Frank, U., Kappel, G., Liddle, S.W., Mayr, H.C. (eds.) ER 2020. LNCS, vol. 12400, pp. 223–238. Springer, Cham (2020). https://doi.org/10.1007/978-3-030-62522-1_16
4. BookWyrm Project: Bookwyrm (2025). https://bookwyrm.social/. Accessed 13 Aug 2025
5. Busse, S., Kutsche, R.D., Leser, U., Weber, H.: Federated information systems: concepts, terminology and architectures. Forschungsberichte des Fachbereichs Informatik **99**(9), 1–38 (1999)
6. Debreceni, C., Bergmann, G., Búr, M., Ráth, I., Varró, D.: The MONDO collaboration framework: secure collaborative modeling over existing version control systems. In: Proceedings of the 2017 11th Joint Meeting on Foundations of Software Engineering, pp. 984–988 (2017)
7. Demuth, A., Riedl-Ehrenleitner, M., Nöhrer, A., Hehenberger, P., Zeman, K., Egyed, A.: DesignSpace: an infrastructure for multi-user/multi-tool engineering. In: Proceedings of the 30th Annual ACM Symposium on Applied Computing, pp. 1486–1491 (2015)
8. Denton, T., Jones, E., Srinivasan, S., Owens, K., Buskens, R.W.: NAOMI – an experimental platform for multi–modeling. In: Czarnecki, K., Ober, I., Bruel, J.-M., Uhl, A., Völter, M. (eds.) MODELS 2008. LNCS, vol. 5301, pp. 143–157. Springer, Heidelberg (2008). https://doi.org/10.1007/978-3-540-87875-9_10
9. Eclipse Foundation: Eclipse Sirius (2025). https://eclipse.dev/sirius. Accessed 13 Aug 2025
10. European Commission: Proposal for an Ecodesign for sustainable products regulation (2022). https://environment.ec.europa.eu/publications/proposal-ecodesign-sustainable-products-regulation_en. Accessed 3 Apr 2025
11. ForgeFed Project: Forgefed (2025). https://forgefed.org/. Accessed 13 Aug 2025
12. Franzago, M., Di Ruscio, D., Malavolta, I., Muccini, H.: Collaborative model-driven software engineering: a classification framework and a research map. IEEE Trans. Software Eng. **44**(12), 1146–1175 (2017)
13. Golra, F.R., Beugnard, A., Dagnat, F., Guerin, S., Guychard, C.: Addressing modularity for heterogeneous multi-model systems using model federation. In: Companion Proceedings of the 15th International Conference on Modularity, pp. 206–211 (2016)
14. International Organization for Standardization: ISO 59040:2025, Circular economy—Product circularity data sheet (2025). https://www.iso.org/standard/82339.html. iSO Standard
15. Izquierdo, J.L.C., Cabot, J.: Collaboro: a collaborative (meta) modeling tool. PeerJ Comput. Sci. **2**, e84 (2016)
16. Köse, S.G., Aydemir, F.B.: Automated glossary extraction from collaborative requirements models. In: 2021 IEEE 29th International Requirements Engineering Conference Workshops (REW), pp. 11–15. IEEE (2021)

17. Cava, L., Greco, S., Tagarelli, A.: Understanding the growth of the Fediverse through the lens of mastodon. Appli. Netw. Sci. **6**, 1–35 (2021)
18. MetaCase: Metaedit+ (2025). https://www.metacase.com/products.html. Accessed 13 Aug 2025
19. Mistrík, I., Grundy, J., Van der Hoek, A., Whitehead, J.: Collaborative software engineering: challenges and prospects. In: Mistrík, I., Grundy, J., Hoek, A., Whitehead, J. (eds.) Collaborative Software Engineering. Springer, Heidelberg (2010). https://doi.org/10.1007/978-3-642-10294-3_19
20. Modelix Project: Modelix (2025). https://modelix.org. Accessed 13 Aug 2025
21. Object Management Group: OMG Unified Modeling Language (UML)—version 2.5.1 (2017). https://www.omg.org/spec/UML/2.5.1. oMG Specification
22. PixelFed Project: Pixelfed (2025). https://pixelfed.org/. Accessed 13 Aug 2025
23. Raţiu, C.C., Assunção, W.K., Herac, E., Haas, R., Lauwerys, C., Egyed, A.: Using reactive links to propagate changes across engineering models. Softw. Syst. Model., 1–27 (2024)
24. Shahid, M.A., Islam, N., Alam, M.M., Mazliham, M., Musa, S.: Towards resilient method: an exhaustive survey of fault tolerance methods in the cloud computing environment. Comput. Sci. Rev. **40**, 100398 (2021)
25. Sheth, A.P., Larson, J.A.: Federated database systems for managing distributed, heterogeneous, and autonomous databases. ACM Comput. Surv. (CSUR) **22**(3), 183–236 (1990)
26. Vanderbilt University: Webgme (2025). https://webgme.org. Accessed 13 Aug 2025
27. Vincent Aranega: PyEcore (2025). https://github.com/pyecore/pyecore. Accessed 13 Aug 2025
28. Voogd, S.N., Aslam, K., Van Gool, L., Theelen, B., Malavolta, I.: Real-time collaborative modeling across language workbenches–a case on JetBrains MPS and eclipse Spoofax. In: 2021 ACM/IEEE International Conference on Model Driven Engineering Languages and Systems Companion (MODELS-C), pp. 16–26. IEEE (2021)
29. Walden, J., Steinbrecher, A., Marinkovic, M.: Digital product passports as enabler of the circular economy. Chem. Ing. Tec. **93**(11), 1717–1727 (2021)
30. Wüest, D., Seyff, N., Glinz, M.: FlexiSketch team: collaborative sketching and notation creation on the fly. In: 2015 IEEE/ACM 37th IEEE International Conference on Software Engineering, vol. 2, pp. 685–688. IEEE (2015)

Ontological Modeling

Group Modelling as Discourse: Games, Play, Ontologies and the Emergence of Shared Understandings

Max Willis[1(✉)], Greta Adamo[2], and Giancarlo Guizzardi[3]

[1] Universitat Politècnica de València, Valencia, Spain
maxwillismax@gmail.com
[2] Free University of Bozen-Bolzano, Bolzano, Italy
Greta.Adamo@unibz.it
[3] Semantics, Cybersecurity and Services, University of Twente, Enschede, The Netherlands
g.guizzardi@utwente.nl

Abstract. Participatory practices rely on group discussions to elicit information and shared understandings about systems under consideration, often employing representations such as conceptual models to help make sense of complexity. However the semantics of such models are often unclear, and a lack of participation in their creation can negatively impact their sense-making potentials. Ontologies can aid in multi-stakeholder engagements through semantic alignment, yet these can be difficult to learn and apply, adding more complexity to participation activities. This paper attends to these challenges by incorporating aspects of game and play to mediate expertise discourses through shared, cooperative, and playful experiences. It presents an exploratory case study of game-based group modelling using ontology-based models, reporting on two purpose-built group modelling games and their deployment in a conference workshop. The analysis of workshop outcomes examines in-game modelling, individual models, and corresponding model pairs, using qualitative discourse analysis techniques. Supplementary pre- and post-experience questionnaires and ethnographic observations elaborate the advantage of combining modelling, ontologies and games to foster and visualise shared understandings. This research sets a baseline for the study and development of participatory, ontology-based group modelling, and the examination of conceptual models as texts in multi-modal discourse analysis.

Keywords: Participatory sense-making · Ontologies · Game and play · Group modelling · Multi-modal discourse analysis

1 Introduction

Participatory and collaborative practices are pillars of open and democratic science, and policy-making [62], especially in complex and critical sectors, such

D. Bork et al. (Eds.): ER 2025, LNCS 16189, pp. 65–84, 2026.
https://doi.org/10.1007/978-3-032-08623-5_4

as social-environmental sustainability [43] and risk assessment [4]. Indeed participation is a prerequisite to ensure local, global, and equitable inclusion in knowledge co-production, the transdisciplinary engagement that concerns delicate and sometimes life-threatening matters [4,48,61]. Sense-making and the formation of shared understandings among interested parties are at the center of co-production strategies [6,45], thus the development of adequate research tools for such interactions, their facilitation, data collection and evaluation are critical for successful implementation [65]. A large body of literature is dedicated to participatory knowledge representation, for instance in conceptual modelling (e.g. Enterprise and Business Process Modelling [19,28,53]), ontology engineering [15,34,47], with an even larger corpus in environmental and social-ecological systems sciences (e.g. [6,65]). However, there is a prevailing lack of information on how the practices described deal with the mediation of pluralistic discourses and dialogues during co-design and associated group activities, which are often configured as challenging social spaces [36], particularly in transdisciplinary settings where redress of existing power imbalances is required for the inclusion of all participants' voices [61].

The study presented in this paper emerges from the recognition of ontologies and ontology-based formalisations as compelling tools for the explicit definition of shared meanings, for communication, and consensus-building [25,44,64]. As practices of formal disambiguation and conceptual alignment, ontologies would seem well-disposed to the tasks of co-design for knowledge representation. Nevertheless, ontologies can pose limitations in participatory contexts, including (*a*) a steep, time consuming, and often discouraging learning curve for beginners and (*b*) the potential imposition of top-down views driven by knowledge engineers with stakeholders in tow as information providers. Those claims are supported by relevant literature, e.g. [15,26,37,47], and the authors' personal experiences. Additionally, (*c*) the current lack of in-depth human-centric research on *how* ontologies encourage consensus and foster shared understandings can bring further uncertainty to the use of ontologies in group activities.

This research addresses these limitations by integrating ontologies with aspects of game, play, and group modelling to structure unambiguous communication in *participatory sense-making* [14], and by paying close attention to the discourse, dialogue, and intersubjective engagements that are central to collaborative enterprise [68]. We present two purpose-built group modelling games, (i) *Type Token*, a game grounded on the top-level ontology *Unified Foundational Ontology* (UFO) [27] that aims at making ontological notions accessible for beginners, and (ii) *Risk Response*, an adversarial discourse game on risk and human responses, both of which revolve around the creation of ontology-based conceptual models through rule-based interactions. The co-design of these game artefacts was initiated by the first authors, and we report here on their gameplay during a conference workshop, as an exploratory case study. An evaluation is presented via *multi-modal discourse analyses* [51] that examines group models, pre- and post-experience questionnaires, photographs of gameplay, group debriefs and observations of participant interactions. The main contributions of this research are ($C1$) the introduction of gameful experiences to guide participatory sense-making using ontologies and ($C2$) a new perspective on analysis of ontology-based group modelling as discourse, which allows to trace uptake of ontological notions in emergent shared understandings.

The article is structured as follows: Section 2 introduces background knowledge, Sect. 3 explains the research design, Sect. 4 and 5 outline results and offer critical reflections. While Sect. 6 discuss the efficacy and utility of the research, Sect. 7 provides contextualised related works, finally Sect. 8 concludes the paper.

2 Background Notions

Participatory sense-making [14] is the shared construction, appreciation, and modification of meanings through social situations that involve discussion and embodied interpersonal experiences [20]. Design for participatory sense-making involves the development of artefacts, such as narrative texts, models, and games, to reinforce intersubjective engagement and drive pluralistic discourse [68]. So-called gameful interactions [57] can be particularly useful for participatory sense-making [69], and games have long been used to facilitate group activities, from sustainable development research [17] to Requirements Engineering [13]. The utility of games in participatory practices leverages the social contract that agreeing to play a game entails, as participants signal their availability and interest to engage in cooperative behavior [57]. Game mechanisms of rule-based interaction, turn taking and role-play can drive intersubjective engagement, re-frame power imbalances in communication and incite inclusive participation [68], which are especially important in outlining socio-technical systems which have existential impact on people's lives, for example AI-driven information applications used to inform sustainable development policy [49].

Participatory processes and sense-making are grounded in *discourse*, the use of spoken and written language in a social context, and *dialogue*, the sequentially evolving communication between and among actors [8]. Dialogue is necessary in the development of intersubjectivity [23], the connection between participant identities in interaction, and the maintenance of dialogue is an act of social coordination [54]. *Discourse analysis* (DA) offers a range of insights into the communication acts and development of mutual grounds [51] at the heart of participatory sense-making. DA brings to light *dialogic syntax*, the analysis of linguistic structures such as resonance, the iterative re-elaboration of speech partners' utterances [16], and *discursive psychology*, [67], naturalistic text interactions and texts' relations to participant actions and goals. Critical Discourse Analysis [63] further examines the structures of power and control conveyed by the rules and norms of verbal communication, attention to which aids in balancing expert and non-expert voices [56,61]. Over many decades of practice in cognitive linguistics, social psychology and Human-computer Interaction (HCI), *multi-modal discourse analysis* [12,39] has expanded the definition of discourse, and what constitutes text beyond spoken and written language, to include any symbolic representation or embodied communication that contributes to the sense-making of a subject, as well as their *intertextual* relations, i.e. similar or differentiated semantic properties [51]. Although related to multi-modal interaction analysis in HCI [60], and Conversation Analysis [58], multi-modal discourse analysis refers specifically to techniques for examination and evaluation of the discursive properties of textual artefacts which are extended to include gameplay interactions, embodied communications and co-created models in addition to written and spoken language.

A type of participatory sense-making involves a family of practices we refer to as *group modelling*,[1] which belong to a range of disciplines, from computer science and information systems (see e.g. [28,53]) to sustainability sciences and policy-making [6,61,65], and development research [17]. In group modelling, knowledge is elicited through multi-party discussions that strive for mutual learning and problem solving, subsequently modelled using a variety of analog and computational tools [65]. It exploits well-known social science and HCI approaches to engage stakeholders, gather information, and collectively design artefacts. *Facilitation*, a central aspect of group modelling, can involve the use of diagrams, pictures, the ever-popular sticky notes, digital interfaces, and games [65], yet all facilitation is not created equal. Its democratic and inclusive enactment requires expertise, experience and tacit knowledge derived from trial and error, and the mediation of the chosen modelling activity, which can include *qualitative* (e.g. causal loops diagrams and simple conceptual models), *semi-quantitative* (e.g. fuzzy cognitive maps), and/or *quantitative* representations (e.g. agent-based modelling) [65]. Frequently outcomes from guided group tasks are modelled by an expert modeller, such as in companion modelling [17], bringing into question the level of actual stakeholder participation in the modelling life-cycle [33].

3 Research Design

The **goal** of this exploratory case study is to evaluate gameful approaches for group modelling, and examine the structuring of unambiguous communication through the introduction of ontological notions. It follows Constructive Design Research protocols [35] and builds on previous research experiences, literature reviews, community discussions, and evolving design intuitions to create artefacts, enact interventions with them, and interrogate the outcomes for insights. This Section describes the research context and artefacts (Sect. 3.1), data collection, and evaluation approaches (Sect. 3.2).

3.1 In-the-Wild Deployment and Research Artefacts

The artefacts and activities of this study emerged from several preliminary investigations by the authors of ontology-based interaction design [69] and use of participant-authored models as interaction analysis tools [72]. These informed

[1] For a terminological discussion on participatory, collaborative and group model building see [66].

the design of the two group modelling games described in the following, and their in-the-wild deployment at the *1st Playing with Meanings* (PwM) workshop, part of the *Joint Ontology Workshops* (JOWO 2024) held at the *14th International Conference on Formal Ontology in Information Systems* (FOIS2024) conference held in Enschede, Netherlands.

The workshop setting was predominantly interactive and took place in two sessions facilitated by two authors. In the first session, participants played the foundational ontology *Type Token*, and in the second, the adversarial discourse and group modelling *Risk Response*. Figure 1 depicts the two games in action. Conference attendees could join one, or both sessions, and were asked to sign an informed consent document which acknowledged that records of their participation would be included in the study. Preflight and post-experience questionnaires were provided, with a followup questionnaire after three months. Consent form and questionnaires can be found in the additional materials: https://drive.google.com/drive/folders/1C76kH9o1_7HUs6rAFHNM82yhjjZkTLC6.

Fig. 1. *Type Token* (left) and *Risk Response* (right) group models.

Type Token. This session was initiated with a presentation of the project and a primer on participatory sense-making, and continued with gameplay of *Type Token*, which introduces salient UFO concepts [27]. UFO comprises a theory of types, with finer-grained ontological distinctions among types of types. For example, it distinguishes between: *kinds* (types that capture essential properties shared by their instances and that provide a uniform principle of identity for these instances, e.g. Bird); *subkinds* (static specializations of kinds; e.g. Waterfowl); *roles* (dynamic and relational specifications of kinds, e.g. Laying Hen); *phases* (dynamic but non-relational specializations of kinds, e.g. Chick); *categories* (union types that classify instances of multiple kinds, e.g. Raptor for the union of Hawk and Falcon); *collectives* (types whose instances are mereologically complex entities composed of multiple members, e.g. a Flock of birds). The game's objective is to introduce players to aforementioned UFO distinctions by modelling taxonomic structures with printed cards; an initial card starts the model, and in successive turns, players must add ontologically coherent phrases, vertically or horizontally building on card sequences, i.e. *threads*, that have previously been played. Special cards allow players to overcome of impasse, when no card in play can be added to the model, in which case a player can trade their cards with new ones from the deck, take cards from another player, or clean up the model and start anew. A detailed description of the game, its cards, rules and gameplay is available in [70]. The gameplay session lasted approximately 60 min, and wrapped up with a short debrief.

Risk Response. In the second session, participants played *Risk Response*, the adversarial discourse game that has its origins in an ontological unpacking of the Intergovernmental Panel on Climate Change (IPCC) definitions of climate change risks [1], extended with concepts from United Nations Disaster Risk Reduction (UNDRR) risk profiles and with cybersecurity and socio-technical systems concepts. Game time was also approximately 60 min. The goal of *Risk Response* is to stimulate discussion and group modelling, and unfolds as players form two teams: Team Risk must propose a risk, and Team Humanity must devise a plausible response. A discussion phase using a Futures Cone diagram (see additional materials, adapted from [22]), then ensues to decide a winner. Is Team Risk's proposal overwhelming, or will Team Humanity's response overcome? In Level I conversational play, risks and responses are discussed and debated vocally. In Level II group modelling play, teams create conceptual models to describe and argue for their proposals. As each team describes their Risk or Response, they draw a model following a reference model, for which blank A3 paper and several colors of marker are provided. The game is described in detail in [71].

Group modelling task employed reference models to guide and ground the model created by group's participants: the first round of gameplay followed the largely UFO-based *social-ecological systems (SESs) integrated model* [2,3], that represents components such as *governance*, *natural*, *human-made resource*, *plan*, and *ecosystem service*, and their relations. The model and several of its patterns were made available as A2 and A3 printouts, as was the Futures Cone diagram. For the second round, the *Common Ontology of Value and Risk* (COVER) [52] served as reference model, with accompanying printed A3 model patterns extracted from that ontology. COVER is a UFO extension that deals with elements of risk and value, for example *vulnerability*, *object at risk*, *value object*, and *threat event*. White A3 paper and four colors of sharpie markers were provided for the group modelling. This session also concluded with a debrief, and participants were directed towards the post-experience questionnaire.

3.2 Data Collection Methods and Evaluation Strategy

A variety of data was collected before, during, and after the workshop for analysis. The modalities, i.e. types of data analysed, are listed in Table 1 and include:

a pre-flight questionnaire (**PreQ**), the *Type Token* and *Risk Response* collaborative models (**TT, RR**), post-experience (directly following) and post-post-experience (after three months) questionnaires (**PostQs**), photographic evidence (**Photo**), and supplemental group debrief feedbacks and ethnographic observations (**EObs**).

Table 1. Multi-modal discourse analysis dimensions.

	Modality					
		Coll. modelling				
Meta-function	**PreQ**	**TT**	**RR**	**PostQs**	**EObs**	**Photo**
IDEATION [IDEA]	+	+	+	+	-	+
INTERPERSONAL [INTERP]	-	+	+	+	+	+
COMPOSITIONAL [COMP]	-	+	+	-	+	+

Multi-modal discourse analysis [12] was chosen as the evaluation method for its utility in elucidating intersubjective engagement in participant-authored texts and game-based interactions [68], and allowance for coincident examination of graphical and textual aspects of conceptual models created during gameplay. In discourse analysis, data is annotated using [CODES] that correspond to particular linguistic forms and useage; coded words, phrases and passages are scrutinized within and between modalities, i.e. intertextual analysis. Through this process complementary intersemiotic relations, the ways that different modes of expression complement each other in their production and conveyance of meanings [51] are identified, such as markers of participants' intersubjective engagement [23], and the articulation of similar, or differentiated meanings, i.e. signs of common ground [20]. We follow a revised framework for Halliday's *Systemic Functional Linguistics* [29], after [51], to isolate three textual meta-functions: IDEATION [IDEA] (what is represented in a text/image), INTERPERSONAL [INTERP] (use of semantics in action and social contexts), and COMPOSITIONAL [COMP] (structure of visual and textual elements). Table 1 summarises (i) the **modalities** and (ii) the discourse **meta-functions** under analysis, wherein the symbols + and - specify the presence/absence of the meta-function within each modality. Additional codes used in the analysis, which can be found at "workshop_data_and_analysis" are as follows:

- SYNTACTIC RESONANCES [RES], or dialogic resonances, mark the repetition, use and reuse of language to introduce and maintain conversation topics [16]; these are signs of emergent intersubjectivity, i.e. participants' engagement with one another's perspectives [46].
- INTERSUBJECTIVE REPAIR [REP], or repair-after-next-turn, is the use of language structures, also by third-parties, to redress misunderstandings and breakdowns of intersubjectivity [23,54] in sequential communication.

- Repair can demarcate DISAGREEMENT [DISAG] being handled in consensus, or in an agonistic sense (see [68]), absorbed in pluralistic discourse; it denotes the overlapping of individual understandings, or dynamic understanding [41].
- EMBODIMENT [EMB] is a reference to physical, gestural and bodily objects that form part of a discourse [67], including interactional displays and the use of space and material artefacts, positioning, gaze, laughter, and non-verbal language; these provide reinforcement cues towards agreement/disagreement.
- SEQUENTIAL ELABORATION [SEQ] is the turn-based unfolding of discourse, wherein meanings evolve and are elaborated from what is expressed before, and after a participant's communicative action; indicates emergence of shared understandings, i.e. ideational, and at times compositional, cohesion [51].

4 Results

This section reports on participant demographics and the multi-modal discourse analysis of the group models (spreadsheet available in the additional materials, see the README for assistance in navigating the files). A total of twenty-five (25) participants joined the workshop, fifteen (15) of whom completed the questionnaires. The majority claimed Millennial age, with 3 Gen. Z, and one Gen. X, with 8 males and 6 females and one who "prefer not to say" their gender. Only 3 respondents declared to have middling to no expertise with ontologies, most considering themselves to be advanced or near to, 5 stated having none or beginner level experience with conceptual modelling, and the rest claiming between intermediate and expert experience. While most of the surveyed subjects had never played research games, all regularly engage in gaming, many quite frequently, predominantly role-playing games, board- and card games, with between 3 and 5 players.

4.1 *Type Token* Group Models

This session was attended by 17 participants arranged in 3 groups, *A* (4 players), *B* (8 players), and *C* (5 players). We examined models that were on the tables at the final stage of the session. *Group A* created a model using 24 cards that had two main threads, the [IDEA] elaborating a UFO *Category* of *Object* and a third thread of artefacts with associated tokens, e.g. *Dog mummy*. They used 5 UFO types and 11 specialised classes. *Group B* constructed a model using 37 cards, with four main threads [COMP], two of which were modelled in multiple directions, two branching clusters with numerous instances, two outliers, and several clusters of instances around a class. *Group C* used 11 cards to create a model with two ontological interpretations of *Dog* [IDEA]: as an actual animal instantiating UFO *Subkind*, with two instances, and as an artefact, i.e. a *Dog-Sculpture* with multiple instances. A transversal row of cards ([COMP]), extended the *Sculpture* card, with *Print*, *Photograph*, and *Painting*, signaling that these are types that are siblings of the type *Sculpture* as common specialisations of the same super-type.

Ontological assumptions across the group models were for the most part coherent, showing development of shared understandings via sequential elaboration [SEQ], even if the ontological structures were not always correct. For example, *Group B* modelled correctly that *Dog* and *Cat* are both *Subkind* of an *Animal* class, but also that *Species* is a *Kind* belonging to the *Animal* class, and it subsumes *Lupullella sp.*, *Canis familiaris*, as well as *Cat* [IDEA]. *Groups A* and *C* both sequentially elaborated [SEQ] a secondary thread of artefact classes, e.g. *Print*, *Image*, *Photo* and *Box*, many with associated tokens, that diverged from their main game model. These threads were not elaborated with UFO meta-type cards, yet were correctly populated with subkinds and instances. Both groups accepted this transversal modelling practice, and in concerted efforts of repair [REP], players further elaborated them during subsequent turns [SEQ]. In *Group C* the artefact classes appeared in a horizontal row within the main model, while in *Group A* an *Object* card placed above eventually brought their secondary thread into alignment with the main model [REP]. At one point in *Group C*, a *Photograph* class card had been added, with a instance photo of a mixed breed dog, either as meta-play or as another compound class *DogPhotograph*. This was removed from the model [DISAG], and became the source of extended debate. *Group B*'s model also included meta-level play as a token of *Sleeping cat* is placed below the class *Image*, yet this gameplay was agreed by the group.

When the *Type Token* B deck was introduced, *Groups A* and *B* immediately added it to their gameplay, while *Group C* ignored it and continued on their initial model. At several points, when it appeared this group was having difficulty, the facilitators suggested they should feel free to start again, to which several group members replied [Oh No! We are having fun!] and one explained that argumentation and disagreements is something that all of them, and indeed most of the community present at the conference, enthusiastically engages in [DISAG]. See Table 2 for more details.

4.2 *Risk Response* Group Models

Seventeen (17) participants played *Risk Response*, forming three groups, *A* (5 players), *B* (7 players), and *C* (5 players) each of them divided into *Team Risk* and *Team Humanity*. The groups were instructed to create models during the gameplay following, in the first round, the SESs integrated model, and in the second, COVER. Instructions on how to model were left purposefully vague, viz. to model their risks and responses using elements from the reference model, which resulted in a diversity of group modelling practices. Table 2 provides precise account of the elements captured in the group models [IDEA].

In the first round, both *Group A*' teams produced models *à la* UML mimicking the SESs integrated model [COMP]. Team Risk built their first model using 5 elements, correctly connected by 5 relations from the SES reference model, while proposing 6 new entities, e.g. *farmer* and *food production*. Team Humanity used 4 elements and 1 type of relation repeated three times from the reference model [RES], plus 5 new elements. *Group A* did not model in the second round using COVER, yet engaged in a personal discussion on the risks and possible

Table 2. Group modelling results breakdown.

	Type Token		
	Group A	*Group B*	*Group C*
#of players	4	8	5
#of cards	24 (tot.), 1 in play, one uncertain	37	11
Type of cards	6 instances (+ 1 in play) 5 UFO entities (+ 1 uncertain) 11 specialised cards	14 instances 7 UFO entities 17 specialised cards	5 instances 1 UFO entities 7 specialised cards
#of thread [COMP]	3	4	3
Type of INTERP	REP	REP	REP,DISAG
Meta-play	+	-	+/-
	Risk Response		
# of players	5	7	5
Ref. model	*SES integrated model*		
Team Risk:			
Ref. model element	actor,activity,plan, social actor,resource	natural resource,actor human-made resource	natural resource,government organisation,actor human-made resource
Ref. model relation	performed by,affects, is_a recognized by,relevant for	affects,is_a	is_a
New element	protect habitat,habitat habitat loss,State of the Netherlands farmer,food production	habitat,reservoir lakes,water scarcity	farmers,income, population,crops food insecurity,rain/water feed people,drought,flood short bouts of heavy rain,impact reduced crop production
New relation	-	-	-
Team Humanity:			
Ref. model element	human-made resource,activity organisation, natural resource	-	governance
Ref. model relation	recognizes (3)	is_a	-
New model element	empty building,urban farming intention to preserve company,natural habitat	FOIS,servers,robots (defend) Internet of Things,GIS Earth Observation,byproduct integrating ontologies creating a super-AI dune technology,material science destroy fashion industry destroy capitalism	regulate the prices,technology external trade partners economy,replace crops investments in new markets
New model relation	has,uses,exploits	defend,located in utilizes,enables	-
Ref. model	*COVER*		
Team Risk:			
Ref. model element	-	(risk)event,risk enabler vulnerability,loss situation object at risk	value subject,value experience value event,value enabler trigger event,impact event intention,impactful outcome
Ref. model relation	-	is_a	participates in (2),causes(2) impacts (2),inheres in, is_a
New model element	-	mad hacking skills passwords are not quantum safe password secure software 2.53 cracking password software released	humans,Russian space weapon hits a sat. Kessler Effect! satellites explode! communication (global),navigation weather satellites space travel,espionage GPS fails No new sat. launched due to space debris
New model relation	-		brings about
Team Humanity:			
Ref. model element	-	risk event	-
Ref. model relation	-	-	-
New model element	-	systems isolation massive hacking systems!	mitigation,space clean solutions to current problems future tech,old tech,EWS Engage SM to employ spy
New model relation	-	-	-

response to the impending loss of indigenous languages [IDEA]. *Group B*'s Team Risk, in their first modelling session, used 3 elements and 2 relations from the SESs reference model, and invented 4 new elements. Team Humanity's response model used none of the reference model's elements, and invented numerous entities, e.g. *servers* and *byproduct*, using lines in place of *is_a* relations. While the compositional structure of both teams diverge from the reference framework [COMP], Team Risk produced an organised representation, instead Team Humanity's model is rather disorganised; the dissonance continues in the second round models using COVER, which offer few discernible resonances [RES].

Group C, in their SESs integrated model, produced a schematic textual description of risk and response scenarios [COMP], naming 4 elements from the reference model and exclusively using *is_a* relations. The response description used entirely invented classes and no relations. In their COVER models, *Group C* risk model directly reflected the COVER pattern [COMP], with main elements named and labelled with proper relations. *Group C*'s response model elaborated mitigation solutions from an explicit futures perspective, differentiating between *old tech* and *future tech*, with examples of yet-to-be discovered technologies [IDEA]. This explicit notion of potential future technologies shows the intertextual relations with the Futures Cone [22].

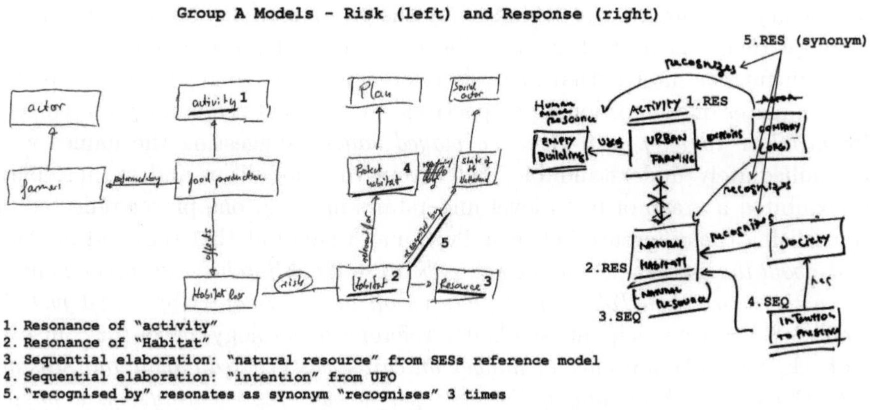

Fig. 2. Intertextual relations of Group A *Risk Response* models.

An examination of the models as discourse uncovers intertextual semiotic traces between them, and in the following we focus on specific instances which demonstrate the percolation of concepts from the reference ontologies in particapants' sense-making. For example, in *Group A*'s *Risk Response* models (see Fig. 2) multiple resonances can be identified as parts of the risk model are mimicked in the response model [RES], directly, as with the entities *activity* and *habitat*, and as synonyms, in the reuse of the *recognized by* relation from the risk model, as *recognizes* in the response. These resonances reflect the game's framing of the textual exchange, wherein the second team was prompted for a response.

Examples of sequential elaboration [SEQ], however, depict the mediation effect of the ontology and emergent shared understandings, such as where Team Humanity further specifies *habitat* with its superclass *natural resource* following the reference SESs integrated model, renaming it accordingly *natural habitat*, and their elaboration of the concept *protect habitat* as *intention to preserve*, drawing from the UFO assumptions [27] found in the SES model, i.e. *social actor* is a *actor*, and has *intentions*. In another profound intertextual relation from the second round, the COVER-inspired risk model of *Group B* depicts several empty boxes connected with unlabelled relations, all correctly placed as in COVER. Similarly, *Group C* modelled several blank COVER entities, correctly labelled, but unpopulated. The compositional structure ([COMP]) of both models and their ontological commitments ([IDEA]) are expressed by mimicking the structure of the ontology, even if the understanding of each element is not articulated.

5 Critical Reflections and Limitations

The following offers some critical reflections on (i) *the utility of our gameful approach*, and (ii) *the analysis of group models as discourse* and their potential to guide, and study, emergent shared understandings using ontologies.

The Gameful Approach. As evidenced by the group model analysis, participants in groups took quickly to the *Type Token* and the reference ontology concepts, although further intertextual analysis referencing participant responses to the questionnaires offer additional perspectives. Respondents commonly stated they "*learned how to play only after we played some.*" suggesting the games were not immediately understandable. Yet across the modalities and groups, players exhibited a grasp of meta-level understandings, e.g. one player reflected on internalising the difference between Type and Token but that they did not "[...] *think about the answer during the game, because the difference was already apparent in the sense that Tokens had pictures on the cards and Types had just the names.*" Several participants explicitly referenced ontology-driven discourse in feedback, e.g. "*The presence of images on cards was debated during our session, 'à la Duchamp': discussing if the card per se was representing e.g. a puppydog, or a photo of a puppydog, or a physical support reproducing a photo of a puppydog...*", and most engaged in participatory sense-making with the ontologies, at least for the duration of gameplay. For some this engagement extended beyond, with one suggesting after three months that playing *Type Token* had some influence on their thinking during study or working practice, and "*that the opinion or perceptions of type token can differ and it is important to discuss it.*" Many players reported learning, e.g. about UFO subkind, and discussing the ontological topics of Sortals, Rigidity, and Phase, and while several agreed that *Type Token* helped to understand foundational ontologies, some were less convinced that it provided better understanding of UFO. Of 10 participants who answered the question "When there was misunderstanding or a dispute in the game, how was this resolved?," all chose the answer "*Together we as players decided what was correct/acceptable,*" although three also selected the answer about having searched online, three said that a more expert player explained, and one stated that their group moved on without proper resolution. All 6 participants who responded to a multiple choice question about their participation during gameplay felt that their voices and perspectives were valued during discussions. Overall the analysis supports the notion that gameful approaches have the potentials to assist in introducing complex ontological structures, concepts and relations, while mediating pluralist discourse in participatory settings.

Group Modelling as Discourse. Examination of the group models provides evidence of the uptake of ontological concepts, and conceptual alignment within and between groups, yet also reveals some challenges. For example the models from *Risk Response* varied widely, even though a majority of players reported having some experience with conceptual modelling; the models were for the most part coherent, but not always ontologically correct. Although they were quite agile at creating elements and drawing relations, many were less able to label those relations, hence stricter rules and clearer instructions on what, and how to model, may be necessary. The *Risk Response* models contain many instances of participants' sharing understandings with, and without agreement. Sequential elaborations of concepts between the group models provide some sense that consensus was reached, even if group understanding did not always comply with the ontologies. However the various parallel occurrences of both agreement and disagreement in, and between group models, and during modelling activities, suggest that ontologies not only facilitate consensus, but also flexibly accommodating for a plurality of understandings. Yet, there remains a challenging negotiation between the need to ease people into ontologies, and the structured representation of their thinking as group models, while ensuring that abstract notions are correctly understood and interpreted.

Limitations. The main limitations of this study regard facilitation, target audience, and participation itself. In retrospect two facilitators were insufficient to engage participants, record, and report; at least a third facilitator would be required to take photos and observation notes. In addition, participants were rather few in number, and all had pre-existing interest in ontologies, which likely influenced their positive engagement. A more comprehensive study involving a more diverse group of expert and non-expert members, from different communities would be needed to claim the games' utility for ontology learning. Finally, engagement with the questionnaires was patchy, and future facilitation should leverage the situation's momentary social contract to prompt attendees into completing the surveys *during* the workshop.

6 Efficacy and Utility of the Research

Games and playful experiences are acknowledged tools for managing group interactions and structuring discourse in knowledge co-production. Their potential for guiding social learning has been leveraged for decades to gather knowledge and inform stakeholders in systems analysis, management and design [32]. Simulation games play an important role in the elaboration of socio-ecological systems concepts [10], working with people at the community level both to understand local and traditional perspectives, and to guide understandings of sustainability, conservation and risk outcomes [55]. In information sciences, such as in Requirements Engineering, games offer tools to negotiate expertise discourses [56], wherein informal, playful situations bring together various expert, and non-expert, opinions, perspectives and tacit knowledge to build a more complete understanding of a system under consideration [13]. However the empirical study of such games is complicated by the multilayered overlapping of experience, information, social interaction and learning which combine in games (see [42]). While acknowledging that proving the efficacy of game and play approaches is a valid and interesting area of study, this study makes no claims as to the superiority of game and play techniques over other stakeholder engagement or learning strategies, and eschew analysis of the learning potentials of our games. Rather we deploy games for their collaborative, discursive functions, the shared social experience and connection between players [57] that games provide, and examine aspects of participatory sense-making from within game-based experiences. The particular focus of this research is on the uptake and mediating influence of ontologies, communicated and shared through collaborative creation of conceptual models, which is supported by the discourse analysis. The rule-based interactions of the proposed two games provide a lattice upon which discussions can build, and the onus is more on the procedures of group modelling [65] in navigating a plurality of perspectives that arise in multi-stakeholder engagements. Participant feedback does suggest that less expert participants, and less vocal participants, are afforded opportunity to add to discussions during gameplay, and as in Type Token, actually engage in modelling practices which are often dominated by more experienced modellers [33].

In social-ecological systems, risk, and sustainability research, the inclusion of pluralistic perspectives from e.g. academia, business, government, civil society and local communities, provides a richer description of the components of a system and how they interact [48]. Equally useful for enterprise modelling [28,53], the game-based participatory process can integrate the management perspectives of how an organisation *should be structured* with those of line managers, employees and even customers on how it functions *in practice*. In software engineering, the use of multi-stakeholder game and play interactions is well established (see e.g. [9]) and extends to the design of how future information systems *can be* configured, for example in AGILE development [50] and requirements elicitation [40], looking beyond which components and processes are necessary, to address understandability, accessibility and the user experience of proposed systems. Throughout these practices is infused an attention to mediating discourses among experts and non-scientific stakeholders, wherein the use and co-creation of conceptual models becomes a form of communication [21] to co-produce knowledge, outlining, examining and defining systems that accommodate a plurality of needs and intentions.

7 Related Works

Despite the proliferation of participatory modelling techniques in fields such as environmental science [66], we were unable to retrieve empirical studies combining ontologies, group modelling, game and play. Practices such as risk and vulnerability assessment [4] strongly focus on developing models with stakeholders, but seemingly without formal semantics. Literature on disaster risk games abounds, typically reporting on simulations and role-play for multi-party information sharing [55], yet few concrete ontology games exist, notable experiments being *Play-a-LOD* (www.pldn.nl/wiki/Play-a-LOD), a game to learn Linked Data triples and rules, and one for mapping of greenhouse data using the Semantic Sensor Network Ontology (SOSA/SSN) [11].

The combination of games and group modelling is a recurrent theme in information sciences literature, as Bakhanova et al. [5] report on potential uses of games for participatory modelling, yet beyond seminal investigations of role-play and model sketching with stakeholders by Bousquet et al. [7], and the use of a game for knowledge elicitation in *Companion Modelling* [17], in-game modelling has few precedents. The crossover of models, games and simulations has been widely examined, for example games for business process modelling [38], service design [30] enterprise modelling (see [31]) and agent based modelling [59]. However few examples of games can be found which facilitate collaborative creation of models as a game mechanic, and the bulk of this research is on modelling game mechanics, interactions or genres, and applying specific models to create games, often in educational contexts. A promising team-based game does exist for ontology and modelling discussions on cultural heritage information using the CIDOC Conceptual Reference Model [26]. This has evolved into a digital edition, however that appears not to enact group modelling, but single-player learning. Unfortunately, the evaluation of the aforementioned games, is limited to either domain-specific functionalities, or reporting on post-experience questionnaires, and lacks at the moment concrete evidence of learning outcomes. In sum, the cross-chatter between ontology, risk, and modelling communities on the need for new forms of engagement and learning has not (yet) translated into a substantial body of research.

Though it does not specifically concern game-based or group modelling, one notable related work approaches modelling and discourse analysis by examining ontology, argumentation and agency [24]. However in our study we do not employ video or audio surveillance necessary to record players' in-game argumentative or rhetorical strategies, to preserve the intended relaxed play experience, and attenuate ethical challenges regarding personal data protection [18].

8 Concluding Remarks

This paper presents an empirical research that combines game, play and ontology-based group modelling. An exploratory study evaluates two group modelling games, *Type Token* based on a foundational ontology and *Risk Response* that can deploy various frameworks for risk and response discussions. Multimodal discourse analysis is applied to a collection of models and texts generated before, during and after the workshop, and provides evidence of (i) the utility of the gameful approach to foster intersubjective engagement and pluralistic discourse using ontology-based formulations, and (ii) the uptake of ontological notions from reference models and their structuring of participatory sensemaking. Future works on the gameful approach to ontology-based participatory sensemaking include a multi-player game for another top-level ontology to play with relations, and an update to *Risk Response* that adds compound risks and their analysis.

Acknowledgments. We gratefully acknowledge the support of EG2401 "Fondo sviluppo e nuovi progetti."

References

1. Adamo, G., Sperotto, A., Fumagalli, M., Mosca, A., Sales, T.P., Guizzardi, G.: Unpacking the semantics of risk in climate change discourses. In: Trojahn, C., Porello, D., Barcelos, P.P.F. (eds.) Formal Ontology in Information Systems - Proceedings of the 14th International Conference (FOIS 2024), Enschede, The Netherlands, July 2024. Frontiers in Artificial Intelligence and Applications, vol. 394, pp. 163–177. IOS Press (2024). https://doi.org/10.3233/FAIA241303
2. Adamo, G., Willis, M.: Conceptual integration for social-ecological systems - an ontological approach. In: Guizzardi, R., Ralyté, J., Franch, X. (eds.) RCIS 2022. LNBIP, vol. 446, pp. 321–337. Springer, Cham (2022). https://doi.org/10.1007/978-3-031-05760-1_19
3. Adamo, G., Willis, M.: The omnipresent role of technology in social-ecological systems - ontological discussion and updated integrated framework. In: Nurcan, S., Opdahl, A.L., Mouratidis, H., Tsohou, A. (eds.) RCIS 2023. LNBIP, vol. 476, pp. 87–102. Springer, Cham (2023). https://doi.org/10.1007/978-3-031-33080-3_6
4. André, K., et al.: Improving stakeholder engagement in climate change risk assessments: insights from six co-production initiatives in Europe. Front. Clim. **5**, 1120421 (2023)
5. Bakhanova, E., Garcia, J.A., Raffe, W.L., Voinov, A.: Targeting social learning and engagement: what serious games and gamification can offer to participatory modeling. Environ. Model. Softw. **134**, 104846 (2020)
6. Biggs, R., De Vos, A., Preiser, R., Clements, H., Maciejewski, K., Schlüter, M.: The Routledge Handbook of Research Methods for Social-Ecological Systems. Taylor & Francis (2021)
7. Bousquet, F., Barreteau, O., d'Aquino, P., Etienne, M., Boissau, S., Aubert, S.: Multi-agent systems and role games: collective learning processes for ecosystem management. In: Complexity and Ecosystem Management, pp. 248–285. Edward Elgar Publishing (2002)
8. Brennan, S.E., Kuhlen, A.K., Charoy, J.: Discourse and dialogue. In: StevensV Handbook of Experimental Psychology and Cognitive Neuroscience, Language and Thought, vol. 3 (2018)

9. Bucchiarone, A., Cooper, K.M., Lin, D., Melcer, E.F., Sung, K.: Games and software engineering: engineering fun, inspiration, and motivation. ACM SIGSOFT Softw. Eng. Notes **48**(1), 85–89 (2023)
10. Cardenas, J., Janssen, M., Bousquet, F.: "Dynamics of rules and resources: three new field experiments on water, forests and fisheries" 1. In: Handbook on Experimental Economics and the Environment (2013). https://doi.org/10.4337/9781781009079.00020
11. Chen, G.: Serious Game Prototype for mapping Greenhouse Data to the Semantic Sensor Network Ontology. B.S. thesis, University of Twente (2024)
12. Constantinou, O.: Multimodal discourse analysis: media, modes and technologies. J. Socioling. **9**(4), 602 (2005)
13. Dalpiaz, F., Cooper, K.M.: Games for requirements engineers: analysis and directions. IEEE Softw. **37**(1), 50–59 (2018)
14. De Jaegher, H., Di Paolo, E.: Participatory sense-making. Phenomenol. Cogn. Sci. **6**(4), 485–507 (2007)
15. Dimitrova, V., Denaux, R., Hart, G., Dolbear, C., Holt, I., Cohn, A.G.: Involving domain experts in authoring OWL ontologies. In: Sheth, A., et al. (eds.) ISWC 2008. LNCS, vol. 5318, pp. 1–16. Springer, Heidelberg (2008). https://doi.org/10.1007/978-3-540-88564-1_1
16. Du Bois, J.W.: Towards a dialogic syntax. Cogn. Linguist. **25**(3), 359–410 (2014)
17. Étienne, M.: Companion Modelling: A Participatory Approach to Support Sustainable Development. Springer, Dordrecht (2013). https://doi.org/10.1007/978-94-017-8557-0
18. Everri, M., Heitmayer, M., Yamin-Slotkus, P., Lahlou, S.: Ethical challenges of using video for qualitative research and ethnography. In: Challenges and Solutions in Ethnographic Research, p. 68 (2020)
19. Forster, S., Pinggera, J., Weber, B.: Collaborative business process modeling. In: EMISA 2012–Der Mensch im Zentrum der Modellierung, pp. 81–94. Gesellschaft für Informatik eV (2012)
20. Fuchs, T., De Jaegher, H.: Enactive intersubjectivity: participatory sense-making and mutual incorporation. Phenomenol. Cogn. Sci. **8**(4), 465–486 (2009)
21. Fumagalli, M., Guizzardi, G.: Philosophical reflections on conceptual modeling as communication. Data Knowl. Eng., 102453 (2025)
22. Gall, T., Vallet, F., Yannou, B.: How to visualise futures studies concepts: revision of the futures cone. Futures **143**, 103024 (2022)
23. Gillespie, A., Cornish, F.: Intersubjectivity: towards a dialogical analysis. J. Theory Soc. Behav. **40**(1), 19–46 (2010)
24. Gonzalez-Perez, C., Pereira-Fariña, M., Calderón-Cerrato, B., Martín-Rodilla, P.: IAT/ML: a metamodel and modelling approach for discourse analysis. Softw. Syst. Model. **23**(5), 1157–1181 (2024). https://doi.org/10.1007/S10270-024-01208-7
25. Guarino, N., Oberle, D., Staab, S.: What is an ontology? In: Staab, S., Studer, R. (eds.) Handbook on Ontologies. IHIS, pp. 1–17. Springer, Heidelberg (2009). https://doi.org/10.1007/978-3-540-92673-3_0
26. Guillem, A., Bruseker, G.: The CIDOC CRM game: a serious game approach to ontology learning. In: 26th International CIPA Symposium 2017, vol. 42, pp. 317–323 (2017)
27. Guizzardi, G., Benevides, A.B., Fonseca, C.M., Porello, D., Almeida, J.P.A., Sales, T.P.: UFO: unified foundational ontology. Appl. Ontol. **17**(1), 167–210 (2022)
28. Gutschmidt, A.: Advantages and limitations of experiments for researching participatory enterprise modeling and recommendations for their implementation. In:

Barn, B.S., Sandkuhl, K. (eds.) 15th IFIP WG 8.1 Working Conference, PoEM 2022. LNBIP, vol. 456, pp. 216–231. Springer, Cham (2022). https://doi.org/10.1007/978-3-031-21488-2_14
29. Halliday, M.A.K., et al.: Language as social semiotic (1978)
30. Hannula, O., Harviainen, J.T.: Efficiently inefficient: service design games as innovation tools. In: Service Design Geographies. Proceedings of the ServDes. 2016 Conference, vol. 125, pp. 241–252. Linköping University Electronic Press (2016)
31. Hoppenbrouwers, S., Wilmont, I.: Focused conceptualisation: framing questioning and answering in model-oriented dialogue games. In: van Bommel, P., Hoppenbrouwers, S., Overbeek, S., Proper, E., Barjis, J. (eds.) PoEM 2010. LNBIP, vol. 68, pp. 190–204. Springer, Heidelberg (2010). https://doi.org/10.1007/978-3-642-16782-9_14
32. Janssen, M.A., Falk, T., Meinzen-Dick, R., Vollan, B.: Using games for social learning to promote self-governance. Current Opin. Environ. Sustain. **62**, 101289 (2023)
33. Jonsson, A., Andersson, L., Alkan-Olsson, J., Arheimer, B.: How participatory can participatory modeling be? Degrees of influence of stakeholder and expert perspectives in six dimensions of participatory modeling. Water Sci. Technol. **56**(1), 207–214 (2007)
34. Kingsun, M., Myers, T., Hardy, D.: C-DOM: a structured co-design framework methodology for ontology design and development. In: Proceedings of the Australasian Computer Science Week Multiconference, pp. 1–10 (2018)
35. Koskinen, I., Zimmerman, J., Binder, T., Redstrom, J., Wensveen, S.: Design research through practice: from the lab, field, and showroom (2011)
36. Kothari, U., Cooke, B.: Participatory Development: Power, Knowledge and Social Control. Zed Books, United Kingdom (2001)
37. Kotis, K., Vouros, G.A.: Human-centered ontology engineering: the HCOME methodology. KAIS **10**, 109–131 (2006)
38. Machado Leitao, T., Lima Navarro, L.L., Florido Cameira, R., Silva, E.R.: Serious games in business process management: a systematic literature review. Bus. Process. Manag. J. **27**(3), 685–721 (2021)
39. Malinverni, L., Guiard, J.M., Parés, N.: Towards methods for evaluating and communicating participatory design: a multimodal approach. Int. J. Hum Comput Stud. **94**, 53–63 (2016). https://doi.org/10.1016/J.IJHCS.2016.03.004
40. Marcelino-Jesus, E., Sarraipa, J., Agostinho, C., Jardim-Goncalves, R.: The use of serious games in requirements engineering. In: Mertins, K., Jardim-Gonçalves, R., Popplewell, K., Mendonça, J.P. (eds.) Enterprise Interoperability VII. PIC, vol. 8, pp. 263–274. Springer, Cham (2016). https://doi.org/10.1007/978-3-319-30957-6_21
41. Matusov, E.: Intersubjectivity without agreement. Mind Cult. Act. **3**(1), 25–45 (1996)
42. Mayer, I., et al.: The research and evaluation of serious games: toward a comprehensive methodology. Br. J. Edu. Technol. **45**(3), 502–527 (2014)
43. United Nations: Stakeholder engagement and the 2030 agenda: a practical guide. Technical report, United Nations (2020)
44. Neuhaus, F., Hastings, J.: Ontology development is consensus creation, not (merely) representation. Appl. Ontol. **17**, 495–513 (2022)
45. Newell, B.: Simple models, powerful ideas: towards effective integrative practice. Glob. Environ. Chang. **22**(3), 776–783 (2012)
46. Nir, B., Zima, E.: The power of engagement: stance-taking, dialogic resonance and the construction of intersubjectivity. Funct. Lang. **24**(1), 3–15 (2017)

47. Norris, E., Hastings, J., Marques, M.M., Mutlu, A.N.F., Zink, S., Michie, S.: Why and how to engage expert stakeholders in ontology development: insights from social and behavioural sciences. J. Biomed. Semant. **12**, 1–8 (2021)
48. Norström, A.V., et al.: Principles for knowledge co-production in sustainability research. Nat. Sustain. **3**(3), 182–190 (2020)
49. Ozmen Garibay, O., et al.: Six human-centered artificial intelligence grand challenges. Int. J. Hum.-Comput. Interact. **39**(3), 391–437 (2023)
50. Przybyłek, A., Zakrzewski, M.: Adopting collaborative games into agile requirements engineering (2018)
51. Royce, T.D.: Intersemiotic complementarity: a framework for multimodal discourse analysis. In: New Directions in the Analysis of Multimodal Discourse, pp. 63–109 (2007)
52. Sales, T.P., Baião, F., Guizzardi, G., Almeida, J.P.A., Guarino, N., Mylopoulos, J.: The common ontology of value and risk. In: Trujillo, J.C., et al. (eds.) ER 2018. LNCS, vol. 11157, pp. 121–135. Springer, Cham (2018). https://doi.org/10.1007/978-3-030-00847-5_11
53. Sandkuhl, K., Seigerroth, U.: Participative or conventional enterprise modelling? Multiple-case analysis on decision criteria. In: ECIS 2020 (2020)
54. Schegloff, E.A.: Repair after next turn: the last structurally provided defense of intersubjectivity in conversation. Am. J. Sociol. **97**(5), 1295–1345 (1992). https://doi.org/10.1086/229903
55. Solinska-Nowak, A., et al.: An overview of serious games for disaster risk management-prospects and limitations for informing actions to arrest increasing risk. Int. J. Disaster Risk Reduction **31**, 1013–1029 (2018)
56. Sprain, L., Reinig, L.: Citizens speaking as experts: expertise discourse in deliberative forums. Environ. Commun. **12**(3), 357–369 (2018)
57. Stenros, J.: Behind Games: Playful Mindsets and Transformative Practices, pp. 201–222 (2014)
58. Stivers, T., Sidnell, J.: Introduction: Multimodal Interaction (2005)
59. Szczepanska, T., et al.: GAM on! Six ways to explore social complexity by combining games and agent-based models. Int. J. Soc. Res. Methodol. **25**(4), 541–555 (2022)
60. Turk, M.: Multimodal interaction: a review. Pattern Recogn. Lett. **36**, 189–195 (2014)
61. Turnhout, E., Metze, T., Wyborn, C., Klenk, N., Louder, E.: The politics of co-production: participation, power, and transformation. Current Opin. Environ. Sustain, **42**, 15–21 (2020)
62. UNESCO: Unesco recommendation on open science. Technical report, United Nations (2023)
63. Van Dijk, T.A.: Critical discourse analysis. In: The Handbook of Discourse Analysis, pp. 466–485 (2015)
64. Verdonck, M., Gailly, F., Pergl, R., Guizzardi, G., Martins, B., Pastor, O.: Comparing traditional conceptual modeling with ontology-driven conceptual modeling: an empirical study. Inf. Syst. **81**, 92–103 (2019)
65. Voinov, A., et al.: Tools and methods in participatory modeling: selecting the right tool for the job. Environ. Model. Softw. **109**, 232–255 (2018)
66. Voinov, A., et al.: Modelling with stakeholders-next generation. Environ. Model. Softw. **77**, 196–220 (2016)
67. Wiggins, S., Potter, J.: Discursive psychology. In: The Sage Handbook of Qualitative Research in Psychology, pp. 73–90 (2008)

68. Willis, M.: On agonism and design: dialogues between theory and practice (2019)
69. Willis, M., Adamo, G.: Ontology-based interaction design for social-ecological systems research. In: Araújo, J., de la Vara, J.L., Santos, M.Y., Assar, S. (eds.) RCIS 2024, pp. 74–82. Springer, Cham (2024). https://doi.org/10.1007/978-3-031-59468-7_9
70. Willis, M., Adamo, G.: Type token: a competitive, collaborative modeling game for ontology education and development. In: 9th IEEE/ACM International Workshop on Games and Software Engineering, GAS@ICSE 2025, Ottawa, ON, Canada, 29 April 2025, pp. 17–24. IEEE (2025). https://doi.org/10.1109/GAS66647.2025.00008
71. Willis, M., Adamo, G., Sperotto, A.: Risk response - an adversarial discourse game and group modelling tool. In: Grabis, J., Vos, T.E.J., Escalona, M.J., Pastor, O. (eds.) RCIS 2025, Part I. LNBIP, vol. 547, pp. 156–172. Springer, Cham (2025). https://doi.org/10.1007/978-3-031-92474-3_10
72. Willis, M., Angeli, A., Zancanaro, M.: Experience probes: immersion and reflection between reality and virtuality. In: Bernhaupt, R., Dalvi, G., Joshi, A., Balkrishan, D.K., O'Neill, J., Winckler, M. (eds.) INTERACT 2017. LNCS, vol. 10516, pp. 253–262. Springer, Cham (2017). https://doi.org/10.1007/978-3-319-68059-0_16

Creon: A Capability Reference Ontology for the Analysis and Design of Systems Capabilities

Rodrigo F. Calhau[1,2,3](✉), João Paulo A. Almeida[2], Raquel Hoffmann[3], and Giancarlo Guizzardi[4]

[1] LEDS Research Group, Federal Institute of Espírito Santo, Vitoria, Brazil
calhau@ifes.edu.br

[2] Ontology and Conceptual Modeling Research Group (NEMO), Federal University of Espírito Santo, Vitoria, Brazil
jpalmeida@ieee.org

[3] System Design and Management Graduate School, Keio University, Minato City, Japan
raquel.hoffmann@keio.jp

[4] Semantics, Cybersecurity and Services, University of Twente, Enschede, The Netherlands
g.guizzardi@utwente.nl

Abstract. Enabling system-wide capabilities is a key aspiration of systems engineering. It comes as no surprise then that a number of system modeling techniques have turned their attention to the analysis and design of capabilities. Despite that, these tasks have remained challenging due to the interactive and emergent nature of capabilities, as evidenced by the cases of agility, resilience, adaptability and security. Modeling capabilities requires a proper understanding of capability-related concepts and also how capabilities interact and emerge. To address these challenges, this paper proposes a capability reference ontology (*Creon*) grounded in system science, emergence explanations, and disposition theories. The ontology aims to enhance the modeling of emergent capabilities and capability relationships in systems engineering. By leveraging concepts from the Unified Foundational Ontology (UFO), *Creon* supports a comprehensive representation of capabilities. We illustrate the use of the ontology in a transportation context, and present some implications for system capability modeling.

Keywords: capabilities · dispositions · emergence · ontologies · systems modeling

1 Introduction

Providing desired system-wide capabilities while avoiding other undesirable properties, such as vulnerabilities, is a primary objective of system engineering (i.e., developing, designing, maintaining, or creating systems). To facilitate

D. Bork et al. (Eds.): ER 2025, LNCS 16189, pp. 85–105, 2026.
https://doi.org/10.1007/978-3-032-08623-5_5

the understanding of system capabilities, they have been modeled in different ways in different fields. E.g., system (functional and non-functional) capabilities have been modeled directly or indirectly through descriptions of system requirements, often employing notations such as UML [47] and SysML [54] (e.g., using requirements and use case diagrams) or notations from the Enterprise Architecture (EA) area, such as ArchiMate [58] and Unified Architecture Framework (UAF) [35] (which have explicit 'capability' constructs).

While these notations are used to articulate descriptions of 'capabilities' in different ways, they lack an explicit foundation for capabilities. This is especially the case for how capabilities interact and how they emerge or are implemented. E.g., system-wide capabilities like security, resilience, and scalability are the result of complicated combinations of elements. A resilient system does not always have resilient components, be they hardware or software. In this case, resilience can result from flexible and adaptable components. Hence, modeling these system-wide capabilities requires a foundation that can account for how they emerge from the capabilities of the various system components.

Such a foundation can be provided by establishing the semantics of language constructs in terms of a well-founded ontology. Ontologies can improve conceptual modeling's expressiveness and domain appropriateness in terms of representing system aspects[1]. Moreover, they have proven helpful in the computing field, according to [21], for formalizing the semantics of different kinds of artifacts. Many ontologies have been proposed to explain system aspects in distinct fields, including, but not limited to, business capabilities [5,49], competences [14], vulnerabilities [46,49], and system functions and qualities [23]. Ontologies about capabilities of different types of systems have been proposed, such as systems-of-systems [18], enterprise systems [44], engineered systems [4], cyber-physical systems (CPS) [16,24,60], manufacturing systems [25,28,51]; among others [31]. Nevertheless, they tend to have a narrow understanding of capability concepts and concentrate on addressing technological and practical problems associated to a particular domain, thus neglecting other fundamental aspects such as dealing with the phenomena of capability interaction and emergence.

We attempt to fill this gap in this paper by using notions from system science [1,8,9,11], emergence explanations [27,40,45,55], and disposition theories [7,19,38,41]. This effort is complementary to our early work [13], in which we approached the structural aspects of systems that make emergence possible (components, connections, and constraints), but in which we did not approach capabilities and their relationships explicitly. It is also complementary to [12], where we addressed the emergence of organizational capabilities from personal competences grounded on disposition theories (e.g., [7,19]), but in which we did not propose a general ontology for capabilities and their context. In this paper, we focus on such a reference ontology. Our proposed reference model is based on the Unified Foundational Ontology (UFO) and represented using the OntoUML modeling language [21]. We follow the SABiO approach [2] and assess the ontol-

[1] Following [21], by 'ontology' we do not mean a description logic specification but a theory articulating domain distinctions as a result of an ontological analysis process.

ogy by showing how it address the competency questions, as well as illustrating its instantiation in a number of cases, including its use in modeling a particular organizational domain. We discuss the implications of the proposed ontology to the conceptual modeling of capabilities. The remainder of this paper is structured as follows: Sect. 2 presents an overview of the literature related to capabilities and UFO; Sect. 3 presents the main result of this work, the Capability Reference Ontology (*Creon*); Sect. 4 discuss some implications of the ontology to capability representation; Sect. 5 discusses related work, and Sect. 6 concludes with our final remarks.

2 Background

In this section, we address some relevant capability-related concepts. We also address the notion of disposition, which is key to our account of capabilities. In the end, we also briefly review the foundational base we use to ground *Creon*.

2.1 Capabilities

Generally speaking, capabilities are abilities, with the a widely accepted definition referring to capability as an ability to accomplish a certain outcome [39]. Ability, in its turn, is often described as a propensity of behavior or as a type of dispositional aspect that permits an individual (usually an agent) to perform an action, whether or not it has value [32]. Maier [32] defines the notion of ability more specifically as the "power that relates an agent to an action" [32]. Ability, then, is a potentiality associated with both an action and a bearer. In light of this definition, what sets abilities apart from capabilities? The value factor, or the intended outcomes, is one of the primary differences. Ability descriptions are typically more general and do not state the desirable performance-related outcomes, results, or accomplishments. On the other hand, capabilities have a teleological component that is connected to an individual's purpose [31].

E.g, in EA and systems engineering areas, capabilities are defined as the "ability to do something *useful*" (our emphasis) [33,34,37]; in IS as "ability to achieve a *desired* effect" (our emphasis); and, in the military field, it is defined as "ability to achieve a *determined military objective*" (again, our emphasis) [3]; As illustrated, a teleological aspect is present in capability definitions in distinct areas. Many of these definitions were studied by Tell [56], who generalized a definition for capability. The author defines a capability as the possibility of achieving specific results with regard to specific source entities and stakeholders.

Martin et al. [36] conducted a systematic literature review on the concept of capability in the field of system-of-systems and EA. A total of 77 works were considered in the research, aimed at gaining a better understanding of the definitions in the area as well as frameworks and guidelines. As the authors detail, most of the works come from the defense sector and define capability essentially as having the same meaning presented above, i.e., as the "power or ability to achieve some result". Based on these definitions, a set of keywords was identified and classified into four groups: (i) ability, power, and capacity; (ii) effects; (iii) patterns, and conditions; and (iv) task, mission, function, and action. In a similar way, Loucopoulos & Kavakli [31] states that capabilities integrate four key perspectives within an enterprise: (i) *teleological* perspective, which justifies the existence of capabilities; (ii) *operational* perspective, which deals with the use and implementation of capabilities; (iii) *service* perspective, which connects capabilities to the value they deliver to stakeholders; and (iv) *context* perspective, which ties capabilities to their specific situation and environment.

Martin et al. [36] also identifies common characteristics to the definitions of capabilities, such as: (i) *composition*: capabilities have sub-capabilities; (ii) *abstract nature*: capabilities describe "what" (but some can include "how"); (iii) *boundaries*: defined through measurement and desired effects; (iv) *measurement*: capabilities can have performance metrics, i.e., they can be gradable; (v) *directional view*: capabilities can be seen vertically (functional area) or horizontally (cross-cutting functions); (vi) *evolution*: capabilities can evolve regarding time; (vii) *engineering*: capabilities can be engineered through iterative, incremental, feedback-based processes.

Capabilities as Dispositions. We adopt the notion of *disposition* to account for capabilities. This notion has been the subject of study in the ontology and philosophical literature, with applications in various fields. Capabilities can be viewed as dispositions of a special type, which can bring insight into how to conceptualize and represent them. Dispositions typically encompass characteristics such as propensities, affordances, capacities, potentials, tendencies, and powers. These characteristics are generally similar in that they give their bearers the possibility to exhibit a particular behavior or produce a particular outcome in specific circumstances. While specific circumstances may be required for dispositions to manifest, they may also fail to do so even in the right circumstances. When they manifest, it is because they are triggered (activated) by a situation (context). As a result, they are manifested in terms of the occurrence of certain events [38,41]. A classical example is the case of the magnet's disposition to attract ferrous objects. When a magnet o_1 is close to one such object o_2 (situation/circumstance), the attraction disposition d_1 of o_1 is manifested together with the disposition d_2 of being attracted within o_2. In any case, even if the disposition d_1 is manifested or has never manifested – e.g., in case o_1 has never been near a ferrous object – the magnet o_1 has this disposition. In other words, o_1 possesses d_1, independent of d_1's manifestations or lack thereof. Dispositions and their manifestation through events are strongly associated [7,19]. Complex actions can be interpreted as the outcome of the "combination" of various dispositions. This includes interactions as *triggering*, *preventing*, *complementarily activating*, and *mutually activating* [7,19]. As explained in [41], dispositions can be "combined' to form new dispositions, e.g., by adding dispositions together (yield a new added resultant disposition) or by subtracting them (reducing the resultant disposition). Dispositions cannot always be combined as a simple sum (using "additive composition"). In such cases, it is necessary to have a systemic, "nonlinear" understanding of these dispositions and their interactions (ibid.).

Capability and Emergence. Emergence in systems science is the phenomenon where a system exhibits characteristics or actions that its constituent parts would not possess on their own [9]. Emergent powers (dispositions) must be associated with a certain uniqueness [41]. In addition, they need to be independent with respect to the "emergent base" [42]. Bunge [9,10] divides aspects of the system into emergent and resultant. Aspects of a system that can be broken down, clarified, or reduced to aspects of its constituent parts are known as *resultant aspects*. For instance, the simple sum of the weightÂăof a system's constituent parts determines the system's overall weight. Emergent aspects, as opposed to resultant aspects, do not exist by themselves in the disconnected components. E.g., the flotation capacity of a ship cannot be reduced to flotation capacities of its constituent parts (by itself, a random section of a steel hull typically cannot float). The emergent aspects supervene on the aspects of the parts [45]. Some authors [27,40] add that emergent aspects are also the outcome of system restrictions, which both restrict them and allow for the emergence of novel traits. Juarrero [27] provides an example of this by showing how the knee joint limits the movements of the femur and tibia, which helps the walking ability to develop. Similarly, emergent aspects are a direct result of the connections between the components [55]. E.g., the manner in which molecules of carbon are linked is what separates diamond from graphite. These variations give rise to unique emergent characteristics, such as the conductivity of electricity in graphite and transparency in diamonds.

2.2 Ontological Baseline

Here, we use a portion of the UFO foundational ontology [20], which defines a system of domain-independent categories and their ties, to more accurately account for capability-related phenomena. Conceptualizations of phenomena of interest can be expressed using the domain-independent categories and their relationships defined by UFO. Theories from Formal Ontology, Philosophical Logics, Philosophy of Language, Linguistics, and Cognitive Psychology have all been incorporated into the development of UFO [21]. The used fragment encompasses the first two fundamental ontological categories: those of *individuals* (specific things, such as John, Mary, Saturn, and The Beatles) and those of *types* (concepts, universals, such as Person, Planet, and Music Band). There are two types of individuals: concrete and abstract. Concrete individuals are divided into *situations*, *endurants*, and *events* (also known as perdurants).

Events are things that take place in time, such as tasks, activities, and processes. Events can be atomic or complex and are causally related. In addition, endurants, including their aspects, can be created, altered, or terminated by events [22]. *Endurants* are individuals that endure over time while maintaining their identity (i.e., people, organizations, cars, contracts). Endurants are classified into *objects* and *aspects*. An endurant that is regarded as existentially independent is called an *object* (e.g., John's car). *Functional complexes* are objects formed by components that carry out different functional roles with respect to the whole. An *aspect* is a reified characteristic that is existentially dependent on another endurant (referred to as its bearer). Aspects have their own lifecycle and can be created, destroyed, or undergo other qualitative changes over time (as much as objects).

We are particularly interested in the UFO concept of *dispositions.* Aspects known as *dispositions* can be made observable by the occurrence of *events* (perhaps the actions of agents, like Anna speaking English). Dispositions are said to be "activated" by *situations* where they might manifest, such as when a magnet is near ferrous material, or when Anna is requested to bring up the subject of a meeting. As endurants, they are able to experience changes over time and undergo qualitative transformations [20]. Situations circumscribe a portion of the world that can be understood as a whole, with objects exhibiting certain properties and standing in certain relations (e.g., John being two meters apart from Mary; Mary being 1.8 m tall; John being married to Mary; Mary having Dengue Fever; John having a Heart that once belonged to Paul).

We are modeling our reference ontology using OntoUML as a language that incorporates the UFO distinctions and axiomatization [21], thus supporting the construction of models that are ontologically well-founded according to UFO. From a syntactical point of view, OntoUML is a UML profile that uses stereotypes (and colors) to incorporate the fundamental distinctions put forth by UFO. There are a number of UFO-compliant core ontologies created with OntoUML. One that is particularly relevant for this work is the Disposition Interaction and Emergence Core Ontology (Disc-O).[2] This ontology uses several theories of dispositions and emergence to make explicit how dispositions interact and emerge, including relations of reciprocity [19,41], complementarity [41], enabling and disabling [7], changing [41], among others.

3 The Capability Reference Ontology (*Creon*)

This section presents the proposed capability ontology. This ontology was built following the Systematic Approach for Building Ontologies (SABiO) [2]. This approach starts by identifying the main purpose of the ontology, which is to support the modeling of capabilities, particularly the modeling of capability interaction. For this purpose, a number of requirements were elaborated. In summary, the ontology must consider: (i) the concept of capability (and related concepts) in a general sense; (ii) the different relations between capabilities; (iii) the different types of capabilities. Based on these requirements, the main competency questions (CQ)[3] were formulated, including: What differentiates capabilities from dispositions of other types? How can capabilities be classified? How can they be interrelated? How do interrelated capabilities manifest? How do capabilities emerge?[4]

---

[2] http://purl.org/disc.

[3] The list of all competency questions are available at: https://purl.org/creon/cq/.

[4] Note that, in a novel reference ontology such as *Creon*, competency questions and research questions coincide to a certain extent. Ultimately, these questions are

Based on this, the key concepts related to each ontology were identified: capability, capable object, capability context, capability manifestation, capability output, capability outcome, capability type, capability phase, and capability-bound role. In addition to the main concepts, the ontology engineering approach also outlines the key relationships between them, such as the interaction between capabilities (based on disposition theories), emergence relationships, and part-whole relationships. Finally, the more technical aspects were addressed. The ontology is modeled using OntoUML and transformed into an OWL implementation (based on the UFO implementation called gUFO), shared using FAIR principles [59][5]. The ontology is divided into three components: (i) *capability core concepts sub-ontology*, (ii) *capability manifestation sub-ontology*; and, (iii) *capability type sub-ontology.*

Capability Core Sub-ontology. Based on the distinctions presented in Sect. 2, we consider capabilities to be dispositions distinguished by the *beneficial* impact they may cause (to a subject) when they manifest. E.g., the disposition to sell is beneficial to both the supplier and the customer, the disposition to walk is beneficial to its bearer, and the disposition of a bus to carry passengers is beneficial to them. Dispositions that do not have this beneficial aspect, such as vulnerabilities, can generate undesirable impacts when manifested (e.g., the fragility of a vase).

Some dispositions may have this beneficial impact by their nature, such as the capability to walk, which is basically always beneficial to its bearer. However, others may have beneficial or negative impacts (even at the same time) depending on the context (or perspective) and subject. E.g., the cutting disposition of a knife may have positive or negative impacts, since it may be useful for cooking but may injure a person. Thus, we consider the capability type to have rigid and anti-rigid aspects [21], i.e., there are dispositions that are necessarily capabilities, and other dispositions that are capabilities only in certain contexts and with respect to certain agent's intentions (goals).

Figure 1 presents a fragment of the proposed ontology. It shows "Capability" as a subtype of "Disposition". "Capability" is considered a *«mixin»*, as it applies necessarily to some of its instances and contingently to others.

Capabilities inhere in *capable objects.* Capable objects include agents, non-agentive objects, functional complexes (as systems of any kind), and also "simple" (or atomic) objects. Examples include people, animals, teams, organizations, software, and other engineered systems such as electronic and mechanical devices. Objects may be capable at a given time but may cease to be so at another time. Such distinctions are represented in Fig. 1. As illustrated, "Capable Object" is a subtype of "Object" (from UFO). Capable objects are characterized by one or more capabilities; that is, an object must have at least one capability to be considered an instance of "Capable Object". "Capable Object" is represented as

addressed by the ontology artifact, as it embodies the knowledge uncovered through research.

[5] http://purl.org/creon.

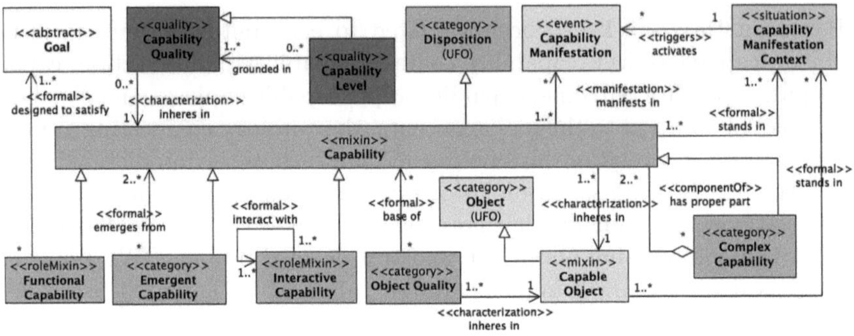

Fig. 1. Capability Ontology - Core Concepts

a *«mixin»*, once more, given that there objects that bear capabilities essentially and others only contingently.

By "benefiting" a capability subject, we mean that when a capability c_1 manifests through the event m_1, it generates an outcome o_1 that positively impacts the capability subject s_1 (according to its intention i_1). Dispositions that are designed with an explicit connection to a *goal* (i.e., to the propositional content of agents' intentions) are termed *Functional Capabilities.*

The benefit brought by capabilities is always associated with their manifestation. In this context, the degree or level at which a capability benefits the capability subject may vary depending on different aspects that characterize such capability and its level (graduation or degree of development). E.g., a wooden stool has the capability to support a user sitting on it. This capability is based on the strength of the wood and the shape of the stool. The stool's capability can be fragile or very resistant, depending on the stool's strength. Or, another example, the capability of software developer (or even a company) can be at the beginner or advanced level. The capability level can evolve with time. This means that the value assigned to the capability level of an individual can change (can increase or decrease). E.g., a knife may become dull due to the time it has been used but it can become sharper if sharpened. Hence, as shown in Fig. 1 capabilities are characterized by a *capability level*, which corresponds to the degree to which such a capability benefits the capability subject. Based on UFO, "Capability Level" is a *«quality»* kind, and is associated with a *quality value*, which can vary over time. Capabilities can also have other qualities. E.g., the capability of an organization to produce a product can be measured by the quality "products produced per day"; the stool's capability can have different qualities, such as the "maximum weight" it can support. This aspect is represented in Fig. 1 as a *capability quality*, which characterizes capabilities. Capability qualities can also "ground" a specific capability level as, e.g., the maximum output of translating 20 texts a day associated to a Dutch translation capability corresponds to an intermediate level of that capability, while having a maximum output of 100 texts a day corresponds to have that same capability at an advanced level. A capability quality q_1 grounds a capability level l_1 only if q_1 and l_1 are inherent to the same capability c.

Being dispositions, capabilities can also be composed of other capabilities (including other dispositions); *emergent capabilities* can also "emerge from" other capabilities (including other dispositions); and, finally, *interactive capabilities* can also "interact with" other capabilities, including other dispositions. Regarding the interaction between capabilities, we use the term "interacts with" as an abstract supertype to these interactive relations between capabilities. These relations (omitted in the figure) include relations of reciprocity, complementarity, enabling and disabling, changing, among others, in line with the disposition ontology, *Disc-O*[6].

Capabilities (like other dispositions) are typically grounded in some qualities called the "base" of those dispositions. E.g., the water solubility of sugar is grounded on some qualities of the sugar (its crystalline structure), or the electrical conductivity of a wire is grounded on some qualities of material constituting the wire (e.g., a copper wire is constituted by copper which has a large quantity of dissociable electrons in its outer electron shell). In Fig. 1, this is represented by a *«formal»* relation between a capability inhering in a "Capable Object" and a quality inhering in that very same object that serves as a base for that capability. Thus, object quality q is only the basis of capability c if q and c characterize the same object o.

Capability Manifestation Sub-ontology. Since capabilities are *dispositions*, a capability may be manifested in *capability manifestations*. These are events in which the capability is manifested. As a disposition, a capability is activated by a *capability manifestation context*. This context corresponds to the physical and temporal context, including all conditions and needed objects (i.e., resources), called here *enabler objects*. So, for this reason, a capability manifestation context is a *«situation»*.

These enabler objects are objects that play the role of supporting the capable object. The enabler object (which may also be a capable object) has dispositions that interact with the capabilities of the capable object, enabling it to manifest its capabilities. Examples of enabler objects supporting capable objects include a paintbrush supporting a painter, a car supporting a driver, or hardware infrastructure supporting a software development company. In all these examples, the dispositions of the enabler objects are essential for the manifestation of the capable objects' capabilities. In these cases, the dispositions of enabler objects and capable object interact in order to manifest together. Objects can act as an enabler object at one point in time and then stop being one at another. Moreover, objects are enablers to other objects. Enabler object has a role-like nature being an anti-rigid (contingent) and relational type. So, "Enabler Object" is represented as a *«roleMixin»* of objects in Fig. 2.

In addition to *enabler objects*, there are also objects that can serve as inputs in the manifestation of a capability, represented as *capability manifestation input*. Unlike enabler objects, these inputs are not connected to the capable object, and

[6] http://purl.org/disc.

do not play a specific role regarding it (i.e., as a component of a system). Instead, they just play a *historical role* in participating in the "capability manifestation" event, being in many cases destroyed in it. Inputs are "raw materials" necessary for the capability manifestation, and include items that "flow" as information carriers, matter, or energy. Examples are the data files necessary for a processing software to work, the energy needed for a blender to manifest its capability of mixing, and the water and coffee powder needed for the coffee machine to manifest its capability to produce coffee. Figure 2 depicts these ontological distinctions.

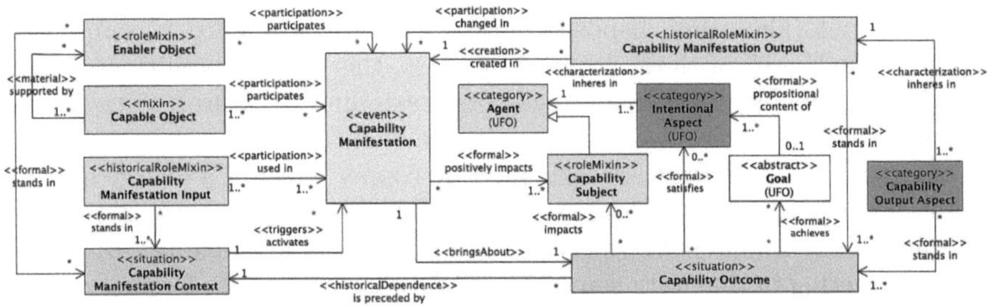

Fig. 2. Capability Ontology - Capability Manifestation

Due to the teleological nature of capabilities (and their potential benefits to a subject), one of the most important aspects related to capabilities is their outcomes. Outcomes include different types of results, outputs, effects, and impacts generated by the manifestation of the capability. This aspect is not only related to a specific output (i.e., a product) but also to the entire situation generated, which includes qualitative aspects (related to the perception of the subject), temporal aspects (when the result was generated), how it was generated, and also aspects related to the outputs (qualities and dispositions). We summarize all these results to capability subject (beneficial or not) through the concept of *capability outcome*. Based on UFO, a *capability outcome* is also considered a *«situation»* that brings benefits to the capability subject, as depicted in Fig. 2.

The manifestation of a capability can also produce (or change) a *capability manifestation output*. Some of these outputs represent "desired" results for the capability subject (not all of them, e.g., residues, waste, and by-products). In this context, the output represents a "historical role" related to the participation (creation or change) of an object in the capability manifestation event. Furthermore, the output of a manifestation can have different aspects (represented as *capability output aspect*), including dispositions and capabilities, which satisfy the capability subject. E.g., the software development capability of a team or company is primarily characterized by generating software (output) that is functional, usable and safe (output aspects) for a client (capability subject).

The capability subject is an agent that can be, e.g., just a person or an entire organization. As an agent, the capability subject performs actions and can even be a capable object. As an agent, it has intentional aspects such as intentions, beliefs and desires. As previously explained, the capability subject may be impacted (mainly positively) by the manifestation of a capability. This impact occurs based on the intentions of such capability subject but also due to qualitative changes the subject may suffer. E.g., a medication may have a positive impact on a patient by reducing a headache, but it may also have negative impacts (side effects) on the patient as well (even at same time); or it can also have no effect at all. Capability subjects, because they are agents, can even share the same goal (propositional content of one or more intentions), that can also be satisfied by the capability manifestation. Figure 2 represents what was discussed above. As depicted, a "Capability Subject" is a «roleMixin» played by an *agent* (from UFO). As agents, capability subjects have *intentional aspects* (from UFO), including *intentions* (omitted in the figure) whose contents are *goals* (from UFO). When a capability is manifested, it generates a capability outcome (possibly with capability outputs), which positively impacts one or more capability subjects. Such an impact is represented by the «formal» relationship in which a capability outcome "positively impacts" the capability subject. Such a positive impact occurs together with the satisfaction of (one or more) intentions of the capability subjects, represented by the («formal») "satisfies" relationship. As a consequence, a capability outcome can also "achieve" (none or more) goals. As depicted, in addition to impacting through an outcome, the manifestation of a capability can also positively impact the capability subject directly. This is represented by the («formal») "positively impacts" relationship.

The model of Fig. 2 is subject to a number of important constraints: a capability manifestation *m* of a capability *c* is only activated by a capability manifestation context *cx* if *c* stands in *cx*; an enabler object *r* only participates in a capability manifestation *m* along with a capable object *o* if the enabler object *r* supports *o*; a capability manifestation input *ci* only participates in a capability manifestation *m* activated by a capability manifestation context *co* if the input *ci* stands in *co*; an enabler object *or* only participates in a capability manifestation *m* activated by a capability manifestation context *co* if the resource *r* stands in *co*; a capability manifestation output *o*, created or altered by the capability manifestation *m*, necessarily participates in the capability outcome *oc* generated by the manifestation *m*.

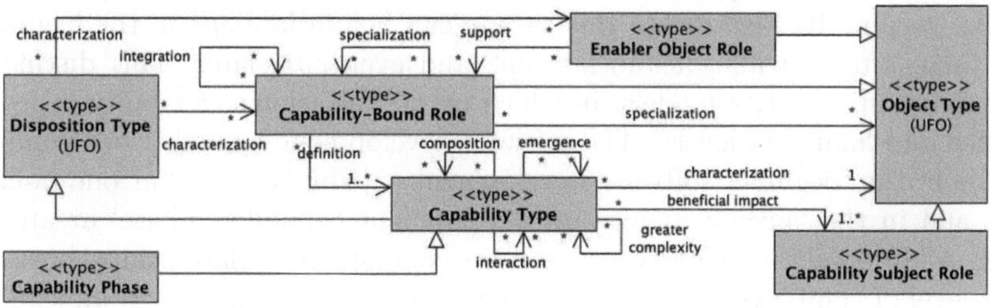

Fig. 3. Capability Type (Sub) Ontology

Capability Type Sub-ontology. When we say that a capability may cause a beneficial impact, this is a potentiality, even independently of the capability's manifestation. Thus, to determine whether a disposition d would be a capability or not, sometimes it is also considered the type level, that is, whether the disposition d instantiates some capability type t. Figure 3 illustrates the sub-ontology of capability type. As depicted, "Capability Type" is a subclass of "Disposition Type" (from UFO). Therefore, it inherits relationships of interaction, emergence, and composition; the manifestation relationship with event types; and the activation relationship with situation types. Like disposition types, capability types can also be classified by level and function.

What this (sub)ontology adds is the concept of the *capability subject role*, *capability-bound role*, *enabler object role*, and the concept of the *capability phase*. A *capability subject role* corresponds to the roles of objects positively impacted by a capability. This aspect is represented by "beneficial impact" relation between *capability type* and *capability subject role.* A *capability-bound role* corresponds to the roles that capable objects can perform. As depicted in Fig. 3, these roles are defined by capability types through a *characterization* relationship. This means that a capable object o can only instantiate a capability-bound role r if it has capabilities $c_1 ... c_n$ which instantiate the capability type t which characterize the correspondent capability-bound role r. Moreover, capability-bound roles have *integration* relations among them which means that capable objects that instantiate them can interact among them (according to their interactive capabilities). In this case, this means that, capable objects that perform capability-bound roles related by interaction relations should also interact. In fact, this is a condition for the capable object to instantiate the capability-bound role, besides that the capable object possesses the required capability types for that role. E.g., an object $o1$ can only instantiate a capability-bound role $cr1$, which is defined by capability types $ct1, ct2, \ldots, ctn$, if: the object $o1$ possesses capabilities $c1, c2, \ldots, cn$ that instantiate $ct1, ct2, \ldots, ctn$; if the capability-bound role $cr1$ has an interaction relationship with the capability-bound role $cr2$ this means that $o1$ should interact with $o2$, a capable object that instantiates $cr2$.

Enabler object role corresponds to the distinct roles an object can perform supporting a capable object. Moreover, the *capability phase* corresponds to the various "development levels" or "complexity levels" that capabilities can have. E.g., a capability type ct has three capability phases $cp1$, $cp2$, and $cp3$. This means that a capability c, instance of ct, can instantiate distinct phases during its life, keeping its identity. In this case, c can instantiate $cp1$ in the beginning and then, after a while, instantiate $cp2$ and even $cp3$, later. This distinction is common in maturity models, in which an organization's capability types are divided into "maturity levels". The software development capability of a company can be in the 'beginner software development capability phase' at one point in time and in the 'advanced software development capability phase' at another time. Additionally, capability types have comparative relationships based on their level of complexity, represented by the relationship "greater complexity".

Capability Phase not only represents stages of evolution of a capability, but also other modes of functioning and manifestation of it. E.g., due to technical problems, an automatic car may have problems avoiding obstacles in some situations. Thus, e.g., such a capability may instantiate a "malfunctioning" capability phase or even an "inactive" one. Capability Phases also classify the states of a capability. E.g., the moving capability of a car can be "not manifesting" or "manifesting", if the car is stationary or moving.

Ontology Evaluation. For the verification of the proposed ontology, each of the competence questions is mapped to the corresponding concepts and to the relationships between such concepts of the ontology, generating a traceability table[7], as suggested in [2]. *Creon* is validated through instantiation in distinct scenarios and comparison with the capability modeling metamodel's constructs, especially in the EA context. Main sources from the capability literature for *Creon* include [3,17,26,33,34,37,39,48,52,53,56,57]. As suggested in [2], we create ontology instantiation tables related to real situations (with distinct types of capable objects, such as simple objects, agents, complex systems, etc.)[8] In order to demonstrate the applicability of the ontology for conceptual modeling, we use it in a concrete modeling task, using the Uber scenario, as presented in the sequel.

Uber is a digital ride-hailing platform that forms an ecosystem composed of numerous passengers and drivers, the latter operating with their own vehicles. The interactions among these human agents, physical artifacts, and the Uber software system gives rise to system-level dispositions such as ride-hailing capability. Figure 4 illustrates this case using OntoUML, showing how the *passenger transportation capability* emerges from the combination of other capabilities. As depicted, *driving capability* (of the driver) and the car's *being driven capability* contribute to the emergence of the *passenger transportation capability.* In this case, *driving capability* and *being driven capability* are reciprocal, since they need each other to manifest.

The *passenger transport capability* is enabled by the *ride coordination capability* of the *ride coordinator system* (performed by the Uber software system). In this case, the Uber software system enables the meeting between the passenger and the driver, providing the necessary information, as well as helping with navigation. The emergent capability of *passenger transportation* is reciprocal to the *passenger's being transported susceptibility.* These reciprocal relationships reflect the mutual dependencies between these dispositions. The figure also highlights certain vulnerabilities: the *car's susceptibility to breaking* can disable its *"being driven capability"* and prevent the transportation of the passenger. The *Uber software system's susceptibility to fail* (due to technical issues) may disable its *capability to coordinate rides.*

In this context, as depicted, the passenger is the *capability subject*, and the driver in this context is a *capable object*, characterized by the *capability to drive.* As illustrated in Fig. 4, the *passenger transportation* capability is manifested

[7] https://purl.org/creon/cq/.
[8] URL of the instantiation table: https://purl.org/creon/validation.

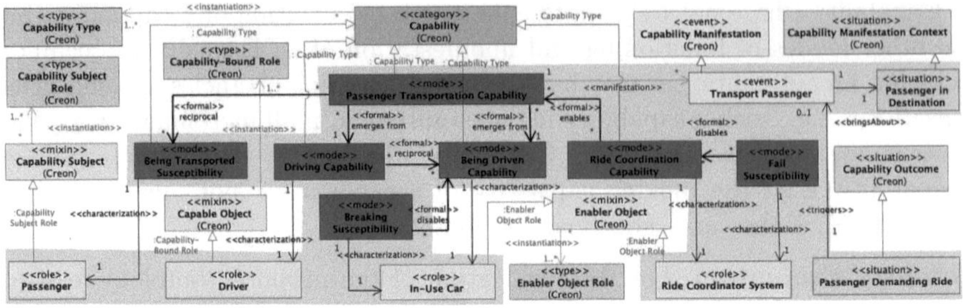

Fig. 4. Ontology Validation: Uber's Scenario

through the event *"transport passenger"*, which constitutes a *capability manifestation.* This event is triggered by a situation—a *capability context*—in which the passenger is located at an origin point and wishes to reach a destination (named *passenger demanding ride* situation). In order to transport the passenger to the desired location, the driver must know the originating point, who the passenger is, and the intended address. This information, in this case, is considered a *capability manifestation input* (not depicted).

As a result of the action of transporting the passenger to their destination, a new situation is brought about: the *"passenger being at the destination location"*. This situation, as it results from a capability manifestation, is classified as a *capability outcome*, since it satisfies the intentions of the passenger (capability subject). An important aspect of this example is that both the *car* and the *Uber software system* work as *enabler objects* in this scenario (in addition to also being *capable objects* as well), as they support the driver (the *capable object*) in the passenger transport process. Notably, the distinction between *capable object* and *enabler object* is dependent on the perspective adopted in the analysis of a given scenario.

4 Implications for the Analysis and Design of System Capabilities

The proposed distinctions can support a better understanding of how capabilities of distinct nature (from people, hardware, software, etc.) interact and contribute to the emergence of IS and organizational capabilities in distinct platform implementations, such as CPS and IoT. One implication of the ontology includes the redesign of modeling notations. Concerning this, the ontology can be used to improve, e.g., requirement models in software and system engineering areas. Requirements generally represent the desired (functional and non-functional) capabilities, i.e., those capabilities are required for achieving stakeholders' goals (and must interact for this). Like capabilities, requirements are often structured hierarchically, decomposed into different levels, and related to allow traceability. Considering that a system's requirements generally refer to capabilities, the relationships between the capabilities proposed in this study could be applied to improve the modeling of required capabilities, improving traceability, design, and implementation of the capabilities.

The same idea is also applicable to use case diagrams. They also essentially represent the functional capabilities of systems. *Creon*, in this case, can also improve how to decompose use cases and how to relate them. In fact, as dispositions (capabilities) integrate structural and behavioral aspects, the proposed ontology can contribute to supporting the modeling of behavioral aspects as well. Widely used notations such as UML and SysML incorporate the concept of "behavioral features" such as *operations* and *methods*. Methods and operations are similar to the concept of disposition (and also capability), as they represent characteristics that are manifested through actions, using inputs, and generating outputs. However, modeling operations in such notations is often simplistic and does not consider how these operations can interact, be combined, or form other operations. *Creon* can support the development of contributions along this line. It can underpin relationships between operations, especially in the context of emergence, improve the modeling of interactive diagrams (e.g., sequence diagrams), and improve the understanding of the behavior resulting from these operations' interactions.

Creon can also be used to define the temporal order of activities and tasks in behavioral diagrams, such as activity diagrams and sequence diagrams (UML/SysML). The flow of activities is essentially a manifestation of the capabilities of these actors. Consequently, the way the activities flow unfolds depends on the relationships between the dispositions and capabilities of the actors involved. E.g., if one capability enables another, this will be reflected as sequential actions in the activity flow. By representing dispositions and capabilities and their relations, it would be possible to infer, validate, verify, or even support the construction of these behavioral diagrams.

The distinctions proposed in the capabilities ontology can also impact the structural modeling of Information Systems (IS). In this context, a connection between entities or components of the IS can only exist if they have interactive capabilities that allow their interaction, that is, if their capabilities are related. In this way, capability models based on the proposed distinctions can help in the elaboration, validation, and verification of structural models of different types in the IS context.

5 Related Work

Related works that use foundational ontologies in the context of EA modeling include [6,43,50]. Both use UFO to perform ontological analysis of ArchiMate's constructs. For instance, the work approached by Azevedo et al. [6] conducts an ontological analysis of capability, but it concentrates on strategic elements. In this ontological analysis, which we adopt and expand upon in the current work, the authors briefly address the definition of capability. The author suggests using ArchiMate to enhance Enterprise Modeling as an application, even permitting the language to represent capabilities. Nevertheless, no capability ontology was put forth in that work. In addition, the ontological analysis did not take capability relationships into account.

The work presented in [28] presents a capability ontology within the context of the manufacturing industry, seeking to provide a conceptual framework for understanding and representing organizational capabilities. Furthermore, it emphasizes that capabilities are related not only to people's individual skills but also to resources of different types. However, capabilities there are not considered as possibly complex entities. Although they have specific restrictions and properties, the phenomena of emergence or interaction between capabilities within that ontology are not addressed. Similarly, the work proposed in [31] also contributes in this sense by proposing a business capabilities ontology. In that ontology, capabilities are subdivided into internal and external, reflecting their relationship with business processes and services. These capabilities are defined as a combination of abilities and capacities. The work [31] emphasizes that capabilities are complex entities, susceptible to being composed of others. A fundamental aspect therein is the way in which capabilities are related and interconnected. They are connected through collaborative relationships. Despite considering elements such as context, outputs, relationships between capabilities, and their composition, the phenomenon of emergence is not considered. The interactions between the capabilities are also not refined into sub-relationships as we do here.

The work of [30] contributes to the understanding of organizational capabilities by presenting a conceptual model that connects capabilities to the organization's objectives and metrics. Among the related works, this one stands out for its consideration of the types of capabilities, including some important classifications, such as the distinction between primary capability and enabling capability. Furthermore, the work introduces the idea of a relationship of influence between capabilities, recognizing that these capabilities do not exist in isolation, but dynamically interact with each other in the organization. However, like previous works, this research does not delve into the different types of relationships between capabilities, nor does it consider the phenomenon of emergence, which plays a crucial role in understanding organizational dynamics.

The proposal shown in [15] also offers a contribution in this area by proposing an ontology that addresses the concepts of function, behavior, and capability. It provides an understanding of the capabilities inherent to artifacts and their relationship with the functions performed by these artifacts. Therefore, one of its main contributions is representing the interconnection between the capabilities and functions of artifacts. Although the work offers a well-founded understanding of capabilities, it does not explore how these capabilities interact and influence each other. Furthermore, the emergence and composition of capabilities, that is, how capabilities can be combined to form more complex capabilities, are also not comprehensively addressed there.

The ontology proposed in [25] proposes a capability ontology in the context of manufacturing resources. An important feature of that ontology is allowing capabilities to be combined with each other. Furthermore, capabilities are

Table 1. Related Works Comparison

RELATED WORKS	Interaction	Composition	Cap. Type	Obj. Quality	Manifestation
Köcher et at. [28]				X	X
Loucopoulos et al. [31]	O	X			
Kudryavtsev et al. [30]	O		X		
Järvenpää et al. [25]		X			X
Koutsopoulos et al. [29]	X				X
Compagno et al. [15]				X	O

related to a specific context (workspace). Another relevant aspect is the relationship between capabilities, which is established through inputs and outputs. However, despite the introduction of the concept of combined capability, the phenomenon of emergence was also not considered there. Moreover, the relationships between capabilities are refined into more specific relationships as we do here. Table 1 summarizes the comparison with the related works mentioned above. Each column represents an aspect compared above that the related work satisfies totally (X) or partially (O). As shown, no related work addresses the emergence phenomenon but just the composition.

6 Final Remarks

In this paper, we propose *Creon*, a reference ontology for capabilities. Key concepts associated with capability, including capability manifestation, output, outcome, level, capability types, and so forth, were defined by the ontology. To explain their emergence and interaction, *Creon* drew on system science and disposition theory. Based on UFO distinctions, this ontology was proposed using the OntoUML notation. An illustration in the context of transportation was used to demonstrate the application of the ontology. We discussed capability interaction and the emergence, and demonstrated how these aspects contribute to the manifestation of behaviors. Furthermore, we conducted an analysis of the different concepts of capability found in the literature, specifically those pertaining to tasks in capability modeling in the context of ISs, in order to establish the requirements for our methodology.

Concerning future works, the evolution of capability over time is a topic that we intend to further elaborate on. This is possible in these foundations given that capabilities are endurants and can change qualitatively while maintaining their identity. This was explored partially with the capability level concept, but it is important to further explain how complex capabilities alter their composition and relationships. Using the system ontology to support system capability representation for particular system types related to IS context would be a significant future endeavor. For these kinds of systems in the IS context, the relationships between dispositions (and also capabilities) that are discussed in this work can be made more specific. In complex contexts involving various types of systems, such as system-of-systems, cyber-physical systems, or digital twins, an extension of ontology can be useful for describing system capabilities and digital requirements. Finally, we plan to look into how ontology can help with pattern recognition methods that find capability emergence patterns in ISs and organizational data, particularly in intricate network models.

Acknowledgments. This study was financed in part by the Coordenação de Aperfeiçoamento de Pessoal de Nível Superior – Brasil (CAPES) – Finance Code 001, CNPq (443130/2023-0, 313412/2023-5), FAPES (129/2021-P:2021-GL60J, 368/2022-P:2022-NGKM5, 1022/2022, 993/2023 P: 2023-N3HJD), and the DSYNE INTPART network (Research Council of Norway project number 309404).

References

1. Ackoff, R.L.: Towards a system of systems concepts. Manage. Sci. **17**(11), 661–671 (1971)
2. de Almeida Falbo, R.: SABiO: systematic approach for building ontologies. In: Guizzardi, G., et al. (eds.) Proceedings of the 1st Joint Workshop ONTO.COM/ODISE on Ontologies in Conceptual Modeling and Information Systems Engineering Co-located with 8th International Conference on Formal Ontology in Information Systems, ONTO.COM/ODISE@FOIS 2014, Rio de Janeiro, Brazil, 21 September 2014. CEUR Workshop Proceedings, vol. 1301. CEUR-WS.org (2014). http://ceur-ws.org/Vol-1301/ontocomodise2014_2.pdf
3. Antunes, G., Borbinha, J.: Capabilities in systems engineering: an overview. In: Falcão e Cunha, J., Snene, M., Nóvoa, H. (eds.) IESS 2013. LNBIP, vol. 143, pp. 29–42. Springer, Heidelberg (2013). https://doi.org/10.1007/978-3-642-36356-6_3
4. Aquino, N.M.R.: A smart assessment of business processes for enterprises decision support. Ph.D. thesis, Université de Lorraine (2021)
5. Azevedo, C.L.B., et al.: An ontology-based well-founded proposal for modeling resources and capabilities in Archimate. In: 17th IEEE International EDOC Conference (EDOC 2013), pp. 39–48. IEEE Computer Society Press (2013)
6. Azevedo, C.L.B., Iacob, M., Almeida, J.P.A., Sinderen, M., Pires, L.F., Guizzardi, G.: Modeling resources and capabilities in enterprise architecture: a well-founded ontology-based proposal for ArchiMate. Inf. Syst. **54**, 235–262 (2015). https://doi.org/10.1016/j.is.2015.04.008
7. Barton, A., et al.: A taxonomy of disposition-parthood. In: Workshop on Foundational Ontology in Joint Ontology Workshops: JOWO 2017, vol. 2050, pp. 1–10. CEUR-WS: Workshop Proceedings (2017)
8. Bertalanffy, L.: General System Theory. George Braziller, New York (1968)
9. Bunge, M.: Treatise on Basic Philosophy: The Furniture of the World. Ontology I. Reidel Publisher (1977)
10. Bunge, M.: Treatise on Basic Philosophy. Ontology II: AWorld of Systems. Springer, Dordrecht (1979)
11. Bunge, M.: Emergence and Convergence: Qualitative Novelty and the Unity of Knowledge. University of Toronto Press (2003)
12. Calhau, R.F., Almeida, J.P.A., Kokkula, S., Guizzardi, G.: Modeling competences in enterprise architecture: from knowledge, skills, and attitudes to organizational capabilities. Softw. Syst. Model., 1–40 (2024)

13. Calhau, R.F., et al.: A system core ontology for capability emergence modeling. In: Proper, H.A., et al. (eds.) EDOC 2023, LNCS 14367, pp. 3–20. Springer, Cham (2023). https://doi.org/10.1007/978-3-031-46587-1_1
14. Calhau, R.F., et al.: Towards ontology-based competence modeling in enterprise architecture. In: 2021 IEEE 25th International Enterprise Distributed Object Computing Conference (EDOC). IEEE, October 2021
15. Compagno, F., et al.: Towards a formal ontology of engineering functions, behaviours, and capabilities. Semantic Web J., 285–318 (2024)
16. Dogan, M.H., Henshaw, M., Johnson, J., Harding, A., INCOSE UK CWG: Capability engineering ontology. INCOSE UK report (2012)
17. Dori, D., Sillitto, H.: What is a system? An ontological framework. Syst. Eng. **20**(3), 207–219 (2017). https://doi.org/10.1002/sys.21383
18. Feng, Y., Zou, Q., Zhou, C., Liu, Y., Peng, Q.: Ontology-based architecture process of system-of-systems: from capability development to operational modeling. Appl. Sci. **13**(9), 5419 (2023)
19. Galton, A., et al.: Dispositions and the infectious disease ontology. In: Formal Ontology in Information Systems: Proceedings of the Sixth International Conference (FOIS 2010), vol. 209, p. 400. IOS Press (2010)
20. Guizzardi, G., Wagner, G., Almeida, J.P.A., Guizzardi, R.S.S.: Towards ontological foundations for conceptual modeling: the unified foundational ontology (UFO) story. Appl. Ontol. (Online) **10**, 259–271 (2015). https://doi.org/10.3233/AO-150157
21. Guizzardi, G.: Ontological Foundations for Structural Conceptual Models. No. 15 in Telematica Institute Fundamental Research Series, Telematica Instituut, Enschede, The Netherlands (2005)
22. Guizzardi, G., et al.: Towards ontological foundations for the conceptual modeling of events. In: Conceptual Modeling, pp. 327–341. Springer, Heidelberg (2013)
23. Guizzardi, R.S., Li, F.L., Borgida, A., Guizzardi, G., Horkoff, J., Mylopoulos, J.: An ontological interpretation of non-functional requirements. In: FOIS, vol. 14, pp. 344–357 (2014)
24. Henshaw, M.J.D.C., et al.: 6.3. 2 capability engineering–an analysis of perspectives. In: INCOSE International Symposium, vol. 21, pp. 712–727. Wiley Online Library (2011)
25. Järvenpää, E., Siltala, N., Hylli, O., Lanz, M.: The development of an ontology for describing the capabilities of manufacturing resources. J. Intell. Manuf. **30**(2), 959–978 (2019)
26. Josey, A.: TOGAF® version 9.1-A pocket guide. Van Haren (2016)
27. Juarrero, A.: Dynamics in action: intentional behavior as a complex system. Emergence **2**(2), 24–57 (2000)
28. Köcher, A., et al.: A reference model for common understanding of capabilities and skills in manufacturing. at-Automatisierungstechnik **71**(2), 94–104 (2023)
29. Koutsopoulos, G., Andersson, A., Stirna, J., Henkel, M.: Application and evaluation of interlinked approaches for modeling changing capabilities. Softw. Syst. Model., 1–30 (2024)
30. Kudryavtsev, D., Grigoriev, L., Bobrikov, S.: Strategy-focused and value-oriented capabilities: methodology for linking capabilities with goals and measures. In: CEUR Workshop Proceedings, vol. 1182, pp. 15–26 (2014)
31. Loucopoulos, P., Kavakli, E.: Capability modeling with application on large-scale sports events. In: AMCIS, vol. 2016, pp. 11–13 (2016)

32. Maier, J.: Abilities. In: Zalta, E.N., Nodelman, U. (eds.) The Stanford Encyclopedia of Philosophy. Metaphysics Research Lab, Stanford University, Fall 2022 edn. (2022)
33. Martin, J.: Enterprise Capability Management (2021)
34. Martin, J., Faisandier, A.: Enterprise systems engineering background (2021)
35. Martin, J.N., O'Neil, D.P.: Enterprise architecture guide for the unified architecture framework (UAF). In: INCOSE International Symposium, vol. 31, pp. 242–263. Wiley Online Library (2021)
36. Martin, J., Axelsson, J., Carlson, J., Suryavedara, J.: The capability concept in the context of systems of systems: a systematic literature review. In: 2022 IEEE International Symposium on Systems Engineering (ISSE), pp. 1–8. IEEE (2022)
37. Merrell, E., et al.: Capabilities (2022)
38. Molnar, G., Bradley, N.: Powers: A Study in Metaphysics. Clarendon Press (2003)
39. Morgan, P.: The Concept of Capacity (Draft Version). Study on Capacity, Change and Performance, pp. 1–19 (2006)
40. Mossio, M., et al.: Emergence, closure and inter-level causation in biological systems. Erkenntnis **78**(S2), 153–178 (2013)
41. Mumford, S., Anjum, R.: Getting Causes from Powers. Oxford University Press (2011)
42. Mumford, S., Anjum, R.L.: Powers of wholes and parts. In: FOIS, p. 4 (2016)
43. Nardi, J.C., et al.: A commitment-based reference ontology for services. Inf. Syst. **54**, 263–288 (2015). https://doi.org/10.1016/j.is.2015.01.012
44. Naudet, Y., et al.: Towards a systemic formalisation of interoperability. Comput. Ind. **61**(2), 176–185 (2010)
45. O'Connor, T.: Emergent properties. Am. Philos. Q. **31**(2), 91–104 (1994)
46. Oliveira, Í., Sales, T.P., Baratella, R., Fumagalli, M., Guizzardi, G.: An ontology of security from a risk treatment perspective. In: Ralyté, J., Chakravarthy, S., Mohania, M., Jeusfeld, M.A., Karlapalem, K. (eds.) ER 2022. LNCS, vol. 13607, pp. 365–379. Springer, Cham (2022). https://doi.org/10.1007/978-3-031-17995-2_26
47. OMG: Unified Modeling Language (OMG UML) version 2.5.1. techreport, Object Management Group (OMG), December 2017. http://www.omg.org/spec/UML/2.5.1
48. Pyster, A., et al.: Guide to the Systems Engineering Body of Knowledge (SEBoK) V. 1.0.1 (2012)
49. Sales, T.P., Almeida, J.P.A., Santini, S., Baião, F., Guizzardi, G.: Ontological analysis and redesign of risk modeling in ArchiMate. In: 22nd IEEE International EDOC Conference (EDOC 2018), pp. 154–163 (2018)
50. Sales, T.P., Baião, F., Guizzardi, G., Almeida, J.P.A., Guarino, N., Mylopoulos, J.: The common ontology of value and risk. In: Trujillo, J.C., et al. (eds.) ER 2018. LNCS, vol. 11157, pp. 121–135. Springer, Cham (2018). https://doi.org/10.1007/978-3-030-00847-5_11
51. Sarkar, A., Šormaz, D.: Ontology model for process level capabilities of manufacturing resources. Procedia Manuf. **39**, 1889–1898 (2019)
52. Saxena, M.: Capability Management. Global India Publications (2009)
53. Sillitto, H.G.: 10.2.1 "Composable Capability" - Principles, strategies and methods for capability systems engineering. In: INCOSE International Symposium, vol. 23, no. 1, pp. 723–738 (2013). https://doi.org/10.1002/j.2334-5837.2013.tb03050.x
54. Specification, OMG: System modeling language (SysML) specification (2006)
55. Spencer-Smith, R.: Reductionism and emergent properties. In: Proceedings of the Aristotelian Society, pp. 113–129. JSTOR (1995)

56. Tell, A.W.: What capability is not. In: Johansson, B., Andersson, B., Holmberg, N. (eds.) BIR 2014. LNBIP, vol. 194, pp. 128–142. Springer, Cham (2014). https://doi.org/10.1007/978-3-319-11370-8_10
57. The Open Group: TOGAF Business Capabilities Guide V2 (2022). https://pubs.opengroup.org/togaf-standard/business-architecture/business-capabilities.html. Accessed 07 Dec 2024
58. The Open Group: Archimate 3.2 specification (2023). https://pubs.opengroup.org/architecture/archimate3-doc/
59. Wilkinson, M.D., et al.: The fair guiding principles for scientific data management and stewardship. Sci. Data **3**(1), 1–9 (2016)
60. Yilma, B.A., et al.: Systemic formalisation of cyber-physical-social system (CPSS): a systematic literature review. Comput. Ind. **129**, 103458 (2021)

Enriching Ontology-Based Data Management with Multidimensional Modeling

Domenico Lembo, Maurizio Lenzerini, Antonella Poggi, and Federico Maria Scafoglieri(✉)

Sapienza Università di Roma, Rome, Italy
{lembo,lenzerini,poggi,scafoglieri}@diag.uniroma1.it

Abstract. We propose a novel framework, *Multi-OBDM*, that extends ontology-based data management (OBDM) by treating multidimensional data cubes and hierarchies as first-class constructs. In our framework, these components are intentionally defined over a domain ontology, which is connected to operational data sources through mappings, in accordance with the OBDM paradigm. This design explicitly and formally clarifies the relationship between aggregated data and the underlying individual-level data, while preserving a declarative specification of data lineage. Furthermore, we introduce essential reasoning services tailored to multidimensional entities, including various types of analysis and quality assessment tasks, as well as query answering.

Keywords: Multi-dimensional modeling · Ontologies · Data warehouse

1 Introduction

Ontologies have long been recognized as powerful tools for data integration and reconciliation. By offering a formal, conceptual, and shared representation of a domain, they enable the specification of a unified schema and can incorporate mappings that declaratively define data flows from operational sources, as in ontology-based data management (OBDM) [8,24,29,33].

While ontology-based integration is well established [10,21,34], their use for modeling and reasoning over aggregate data remains less explored. Aggregate (or macro) data represent summaries derived from individual-level (or micro) data, often sourced from operational systems and integrated across platforms. Commonly managed through Business Intelligence and Data Warehousing tools [14,18–20,22], these data support organizational decision-making via dashboards and reports, enabling trend analysis, comparisons, and the discovery of otherwise hidden insights. Aggregation is typically modeled using the multidimensional paradigm, where data is organized as *cubes* characterized by: *dimensions* (e.g. time, location) along which data is grouped, *hierarchies* defining levels of aggregation, and *measures*, which are numerical values subject to operations like sums or averages (e.g., income, enrollments). These structures support OLAP operations such as roll-up, drill-down, and slice-and-dice.

D. Bork et al. (Eds.): ER 2025, LNCS 16189, pp. 106–124, 2026.
https://doi.org/10.1007/978-3-032-08623-5_6

In this context, ontologies have primarily been used as metadata formalisms. Proposed metamodels serve mainly as vocabularies to standardize terminology, rather than as formal theories supporting reasoning over summarized data (e.g., [1,12]). Moreover, this usage is often disconnected from how data is actually stored or integrated, and mechanisms for explicitly specifying the relationship between aggregate-level and individual-level data are often overlooked in the specialized literature. Similarly, most traditional data warehouse design methodologies lack declarative constructs for specifying the relationship between micro- and macro-data, as such connections are typically hardcoded into ETL processes. This hinders traceability, particularly in contexts such as data provenance or lineage analysis. This paper aims to address these gaps within the context of Ontology-based Data Management (OBDM).

Objectives. Our main goal is to devise a comprehensive formal framework that integrates both analytical and operational data, and to define advanced reasoning services for multidimensional analysis. At the heart of our approach are Description Logic (DL) ontologies, which allow for rigorous modeling of both the application domain concepts [13] and rules [4] and the multidimensional data cubes defined over it. We build on the traditional OBDM framework, which consists of a Description Logic (DL) domain ontology and a set of mappings. These mappings relate operational data sources to ontology predicates, thereby virtually describing how micro-data are loaded into the ontology from the sources. We extend this framework by introducing views over the domain ontology [11], and by defining multidimensional cubes and hierarchies in terms of these views. This explicitly captures how macro-data is derived from micro-data. Our approach considers both cubes and hierarchies as essential constructs. In particular, hierarchies are autonomous entities, defined independently from the cube dimensions they may be associated with. This permits to specify in isolation how hierarchies are populated with data coming from the data sources and favors their reuse across various multidimensional cubes. Data cubes can be defined directly from a view, in which case they are called base (or primary) cubes; alternatively, they can be specified on top of another cube, in which case they are called derived (or secondary) cubes. To define a derived cube we use filters and aggregations, thus capturing classical OLAP operators such as roll-up, drill-down, selection, and slice-and-dice. We equip the framework with a formal epistemic semantics, which allows reasoning over both multidimensional and domain objects in a unified way. We propose some basic reasoning services for both design-time and run-time tasks.

Contribution Overview. Our contributions can be outlined as follows:

- We introduce a comprehensive framework, called *Multi-OBDM*, that extends OBDM by treating multidimensional entities—such as data cubes and hierarchies—as first-class citizens integrated into the ontology. This allows for a unified representation of both micro and macro data.
- We provide a formal and declarative approach to model the derivation of aggregated data from underlying operational sources. This enables transparent specification of data lineage, supporting both data integration and traceability in analytical scenarios.

- We define reasoning services tailored for multidimensional data in OBDM systems. These include hierarchy coherence, cube coherence, cube containment, cube equivalence, and holistic query answering, in which queries span both multidimensional and domain-level predicates. This enables advanced validation and querying capabilities over both domain and aggregate data.
- We show that, for Multi-OBDM systems based on *DL-Lite* [29] ontologies, some reasoning tasks can be solved in polynomial time. As such, our framework is not only grounded in solid theoretical foundations but also practically applicable to data-intensive scenarios, and we are developing an early implementation while testing our approach in real-world statistical settings.

Related Work. Our work is part of a broader effort to conceptualize and formalize multidimensional objects [2,7,18,31,32]. Here, we discuss in more details the approaches that are specifically relevant with respect to the work presented in this paper. [18] is a comprehensive description of a pioneer methodology for formally specifying multidimensional objects at the conceptual level. In [12], a standard vocabulary, called RDF Data Cube [12], for publishing statistical data on the Web is proposed, emphasizing a clear separation between conceptual modeling and physical implementation. Like our work, they aim to provide high-level abstractions for aggregated data, but usually operate at the schema level and place less emphasis on integrating individual-level source data or enabling formal reasoning. Complementary to these, the Cube Algebra framework [15,30] offers an algebraic perspective on multidimensional queries over hierarchical spaces, focusing on structural properties of cube expressions without linking them to data sources or ontological representations. Among works incorporating logical reasoning into multidimensional modeling, two are especially relevant: the Ontological Multidimensional Data (OMD) model [6,25] and the ontology-based OLAP framework by Neumayr et al. [26,27]. OMD uses Datalog$^{\pm}$ rules to encode domain constraints for high-quality data, propagating them along dimensional hierarchies to identify aggregates that meet quality requirements. Neumayr et al. propose a Datalog-based formalism for modeling dimensions, hierarchies, and facts, supporting reasoning tasks such as determining whether one analytical concept is more general than another. While both frameworks add reasoning capabilities, they focus on data quality/validation (OMD) or structural encoding (Neumayr et al.), whereas our approach models cubes, hierarchies, and views as objects over a domain ontology, linked to data sources, and supports both intensional and extensional reasoning. A summary of the comparison discussed above is reported in Table 1.

2 Preliminaries

We employ standard notions of first-order logic (FOL), and assume familiarity with databases [3], Description Logics (DL) [4] and computational complexity [28]. We assume to have the following countably infinite pairwise disjoint alphabets: Const for constants, i.e. identifiers for objects, Val for values,

Table 1. Comparison between different approaches

Approach	Formalism	Micro–Macro Data Linkage	Reasoning	Lineage
Multi-OBDM	extension of OBDM	declarative, based on ontology views	MD specialized reasoning (coherence, containment, queries)	based on mappings and views
[16] Golfarelli & Rizzi 2009	graphical (DFM)	implicit	informal	–
[30] Vassiliadis 2022	cube algebra	–	implicit, based on cube algebra	–
[25] Milani & Bertossi 2015	based on Datalog$^{\pm}$	rule-based, for data assessment or cleaning	based on Datalog$^{\pm}$	based on mappings
[26] Neumayr et al. 2012	based on Datalog	–	consistency and subsumption for MD concepts	–
[12] RDF Data Cube	RDF	–	based on RDF	–

Var for variables, Pred for predicates and Funct for functions. We also use $\mathsf{GT} = \mathsf{Const} \cup \mathsf{Val}$. A *term* is a symbol in $\mathsf{Var} \cup \mathsf{GT}$. A tuple of terms is a sequence $\boldsymbol{t} = \langle t_1, \ldots, t_n \rangle$, where each t_i is a term, called the (i-th) component of $\boldsymbol{t}$, and n is the arity of $\boldsymbol{t}$. If each t_i belongs to GT, $\boldsymbol{t}$ is said *ground*. A tuple of terms $\boldsymbol{t'} = \langle t'_1, \ldots, t'_m \rangle$ is *subtuple* of a tuple $\boldsymbol{t}$ if each t'_i occurs in $\boldsymbol{t}$. Let $\boldsymbol{j} = \langle j_1, \ldots, j_m \rangle$ be a tuple of integers such that $j_i \in \{1, \ldots, n\}$ for every $i \in \{1, \ldots, m\}$, and $j_i \neq j_k$ for every pair of distinct indices $i, k \in \{1, \ldots, m\}$. The *projection of* $\boldsymbol{t}$ *over* $\boldsymbol{j}$, denoted by $\boldsymbol{t}[\boldsymbol{j}]$, is the tuple $\langle t_{j_1}, \ldots, t_{j_m} \rangle$. Let T be a set of ground tuples of arity n, we say that $u = \{\boldsymbol{t}_1, \ldots, \boldsymbol{t}_h\} \subseteq T$ forms a $\boldsymbol{j}$*-cluster* of T if all tuples in u agree on the components at the positions specified by $\boldsymbol{j}$, that is, $\boldsymbol{t}_i[\boldsymbol{j}] = \boldsymbol{t}_k[\boldsymbol{j}]$, for every $i, k \in \{1, \ldots, h\}$. Obviously, there exists one $\boldsymbol{j}$-cluster in T for each distinct combination of ground terms occurring in the positions in $\boldsymbol{j}$. With slight abuse of notation, we sometime treat tuples as sets.

Every symbol P in Pred has an associated *arity*, denoted with $\mathsf{arity}(P)$, which we assume always greater than 0. An *atom* over Pred is an expression $P(t_1, \ldots, t_n)$, where $P \in \mathsf{Pred}$, $n = \mathsf{arity}(P)$, and each t_i is a *term*. An atom with only constants as terms is called *ground*.

Let $\Sigma_{\mathsf{R}} \subseteq \mathsf{Pred}$ denote a countably infinite set of relational predicates. A *database schema* $\mathcal{S}$ is a finite set $\{R_1, \ldots, R_n\}$ of predicates from Σ_{R}, and an $\mathcal{S}$*-database* DB is a set $\{R_1^{DB}, \ldots, R_n^{DB}\}$ where, for $i \in \{1, \ldots, n\}$, R_i^{DB} is a set of ground tuples of arity $\mathsf{arity}(R_i)$, called the *extension of* R_i *in* DB.

A *first-order logic (FOL) query* q over Pred is an expression of the form $\{\boldsymbol{x} \mid \phi(\boldsymbol{x}, \boldsymbol{y})\}$, also denoted $q(\boldsymbol{x})$, where $\boldsymbol{x}$ and $\boldsymbol{y}$ are disjoint tuples of variables in Var. The formula $\phi(\boldsymbol{x}, \boldsymbol{y})$, called the body of q, is a FOL formula in which $\boldsymbol{x}$ are the free variables, $\boldsymbol{y}$ are existential variables and atoms are over Pred. For an atom $P(t_1, \ldots, t_n)$, each t_i is either from GT or from $\boldsymbol{x} \cup \boldsymbol{y}$. For the sake of presentation, we may omit existential quantifiers in $\phi(\boldsymbol{x}, \boldsymbol{y})$. We call $\boldsymbol{x}$ the *target list* of q and also say that the arity of q, denoted $\mathsf{arity}(q)$, coincides with the arity of $\boldsymbol{x}$. *Conjunctive queries (CQs)* are a special case of FOL queries in which the body ϕ is a conjunction of atoms. A *union of conjunctive queries (UCQ)* is a finite disjunction of CQs with the same target list. As customary, a *query* $q_{\mathcal{S}}$ over a database schema $\mathcal{S}$ is a query over the relational alphabet Σ_{R}, which can be evaluated over an $\mathcal{S}$-database DB to return a set of *answers* q^{DB}, each being a tuple of constants.

An $\mathcal{L}$-ontology $\mathcal{O}$ is a finite set of axioms expressed in a DL language $\mathcal{L}$, over a countably infinite alphabet $\Sigma_{\mathsf{O}} \subseteq \mathsf{Pred}$ of unary and binary predicates, disjoint from Σ_{R}. Unary predicates are *concepts*, like `Student` or `School`, binary predicates are *roles*, like `enrolled`, which may associate students schools, or *attributes*, like `gender`, which associates an individual to her/his gender, expressed as a string. A query $q_{\mathcal{O}}$ over an ontology $\mathcal{O}$ is a query over the set of predicates from Σ_{O} occurring in $\mathcal{O}$. The semantics of $\mathcal{O}$ is given in terms of first-order interpretations. The models of $\mathcal{O}$, denoted $\mathsf{Mod}(\mathcal{O})$, are the interpretations satisfying all axioms of $\mathcal{O}$, where the notion of satisfaction depends on $\mathcal{L}$ [5].

An *OBDM specification* Ψ is a triple $\langle \mathcal{O}, \mathcal{M}, \mathcal{S} \rangle$, where $\mathcal{O}$ is an $\mathcal{L}$-ontology, $\mathcal{S}$ is a database schema (called source schema), and $\mathcal{M}$ is a set of *mapping assertions* (or simply mappings) that relate $\mathcal{S}$ to $\mathcal{O}$ [29]. Each mapping in $\mathcal{M}$ is of the form $q_{\mathcal{S}} \rightarrow q_{\mathcal{O}}$, where $q_{\mathcal{S}}$ and $q_{\mathcal{O}}$, called the source and target queries, respectively, are FOL queries of the same arity over $\mathcal{S}$ and $\mathcal{O}$, respectively.

An *OBDM system* is a pair $\Phi = \langle \Psi, DB \rangle$, where $\Psi = \langle \mathcal{O}, \mathcal{M}, \mathcal{S} \rangle$ is an OBDM specification and DB is an $\mathcal{S}$-database, called source database for Ψ. Note that, by definition, DB contains also constants from Const. An interpretation $\mathcal{I}$ for $\mathcal{O}$ is a *model of an OBDM system* Φ if (*i*) it is a model of $\mathcal{O}$, and (*ii*) for every mapping $q_{\mathcal{S}} \rightarrow q_{\mathcal{O}}$ in $\mathcal{M}$, we have $q_{\mathcal{S}}^{DB} \subseteq q_{\mathcal{O}}^{\mathcal{I}}$, where $q_{\mathcal{O}}^{\mathcal{I}}$ denotes the answers of $q_{\mathcal{O}}$ over the interpretation $\mathcal{I}$ (seen as a database). The set of models for Φ is denoted by $\mathsf{Mod}(\Phi)$, and Φ is *consistent* if $\mathsf{Mod}(\Phi) \neq \emptyset$.

Finally, a query over an OBDM system $\Phi = \langle \Psi, DB \rangle$, with $\Psi = \langle \mathcal{O}, \mathcal{S}, \mathcal{M} \rangle$, is a FOL formula over Σ_{O}. The *certain answers* to a query q over Φ are defined as $\mathsf{cert}(q, \Phi) = \{\boldsymbol{t} \mid \boldsymbol{t} \in q^{\mathcal{I}}, \forall \mathcal{I} \in \mathsf{Mod}(\Phi)\}$.

In this paper, we consider one of the most popular settings in OBDM, which we call the *DL-Lite setting*, where the ontology is expressed in *DL-Lite*$_{\mathcal{A}}$ [29] and queries $q_{\mathcal{S}}$ and $q_{\mathcal{O}}$ in mappings are CQs, with $q_{\mathcal{O}}$ containing no existential variables. Below, we provide an example in this setting.

Example 1. Let $\Psi = \langle \mathcal{O}, \mathcal{M}, \mathcal{S} \rangle$ be an OBDM specification. The ontology $\mathcal{O}$ is composed by the following axioms:

(t_1) Student $\sqsubseteq$ Person	(t_2) Person $\sqsubseteq \exists$hasGender	(t_3) Student $\sqsubseteq \exists$enrolled
(t_4) $\exists$enrolled$^-$ $\sqsubseteq$ School	(t_5) School $\sqsubseteq \exists$locatedInDistrict	(t_6) District $\sqsubseteq \exists$locatedInState
(t_7) $\exists$locatedInDistrict$^-$ $\sqsubseteq$ District	(t_8) $\exists$locatedInState$^-$ $\sqsubseteq$ State	(t_9) `funct` enrolled
(t_{10}) `funct` locatedInDistrict	(t_{11}) `funct` locatedInState	(t_{12}) `funct` hasGender

The ontology $\mathcal{O}$ asserts that: students are persons (t_1); every person has exactly one gender (t_2 and t_{12}); a student must be enrolled in exactly one school

(t_3, t_4 and t_9); each school must be located in exactly one district (t_5, t_7 and t_{10}); each district must be located in exactly one state (t_6, t_8 and t_{11}).

The source schema is $\mathcal{S} = \{\mathsf{SI}, \mathsf{OD}, \mathsf{DS}\}$, where SI is intended to store student ID, gender, school and phone number, whereas OD and DS represent associations between organizational units (including schools) and districts, and between districts and states, respectively.

The set $\mathcal{M}$ consists of the following mappings:

$$(m_1)\{id, g, sch \mid \mathsf{SI}(id, g, sch, phn)\} \rightarrow \{id, g, sch \mid \mathsf{Student}(id) \wedge \mathsf{hasGender}(id, g) \wedge \mathsf{enrolled}(id, sch)\}$$
$$(m_2) \quad \{o, dstr \mid \mathsf{OD}(o, dstr)\} \rightarrow \{o, dstr \mid \mathsf{locatedInDistrict}(o, dstr)\}$$
$$(m_3) \quad \{dstr, st \mid \mathsf{DS}(dstr, st)\} \rightarrow \{dstr, st \mid \mathsf{locatedInState}(dstr, st)\}$$

Mapping (m_1) specifies how to populate the ontology—namely, the predicates Student, hasGender, and enrolled—using data extracted from SI. Mapping (m_2) expresses a one-to-one correspondence between OD and locatedInDistrict, and (m_3) does the same for DS and locatedInState.

Let now DB be the following $\mathcal{S}$-database:

$$\mathsf{SI}^{DB} = \{\langle \texttt{st1}, \texttt{'M'}, \texttt{sch1}, \texttt{ph1}\rangle, \langle \texttt{st2}, \texttt{'M'}, \texttt{sch1}, \texttt{ph2}\rangle, \langle \texttt{st3}, \texttt{'F'}, \texttt{sch2}, \texttt{ph3}\rangle\}$$
$$\mathsf{OD}^{DB} = \{\langle \texttt{sch1}, \texttt{dist1}\rangle, \langle \texttt{sch2}, \texttt{dist2}\rangle, \langle \texttt{uni1}, \texttt{dist2}\rangle\}$$
$$\mathsf{DS}^{DB} = \{\langle \texttt{dist1}, \texttt{state1}\rangle, \langle \texttt{dist2}, \texttt{state2}\rangle\}$$

Then, in every model of the OBDM system $\Phi = \langle \Psi, DB\rangle$ the following facts must hold (among others): `st1`, `st2`, and `st3` are students; `st1`, `st2` are both male and enrolled in `sch1`, while `st3` is female and enrolled in `sch2`. Moreover, `sch1` is located in `dist1` and both `sch2` and `uni1` are located in `dist2`, which in turn are located in `state1` and `state2`, respectively.

Consider now the CQ $q = \{st, sch, g \mid \mathsf{Person}(st) \wedge \mathsf{enrolled}(st, sch) \wedge \mathsf{hasGender}(st, g)\}$. It is easy to see that the certain answers to this query are $\{\langle \texttt{st1}, \texttt{sch1}, \texttt{'M'}\rangle, \langle \texttt{st2}, \texttt{sch1}, \texttt{'M'}\rangle, \langle \texttt{st3}, \texttt{sch2}, \texttt{'F'}\rangle\}$. □

3 Multidimensional OBDM: Syntax

To model aggregates, we introduce views, hierarchies, base and derived data cubes, which are instrumental in defining the notion of a Multi-OBDM system. We assume to have the pairwise disjoint countable infinite alphabets Σ_V, Σ_H, Σ_N, Σ_C, Σ_D and Σ_M for the names of views, hierarchies, hierarchy nodes, cubes, cube dimensions and cube measures, respectively. The sets Σ_V and Σ_C are contained in Pred, and Σ_H, Σ_N, Σ_D, Σ_M are disjoint from GT, Pred and Var. We start by adapting the notion of views over DL ontologies [11] to the OBDM setting.

Definition 1 (View). *A* view definition *over an OBDM specification Ψ is an expression of the form $\mathsf{v} \doteq q(\boldsymbol{x})$, where $\mathsf{v} \in \Sigma_\mathsf{V}$ is called view predicate, or simply view, and $q(\boldsymbol{x})$ is a query over Ψ. We say that $\boldsymbol{x}$ is the* signature *of* v*, denoted sig*(v)*; the arity and the components of* v *are the arity and the components of $\boldsymbol{x}$.*

Example 2. The expression $\mathsf{studentView} \doteq q(st, sch, g)$ is a view definition over Ψ, where q and Ψ are the OBDM specification and the query of Example 1. □

Definition 2 (Hierarchy). *Given a set $\mathcal{V}$ of views over an OBDM specification Ψ, a* hierarchy definition *over $\mathcal{V}$ is an expression of the form $\mathsf{h} \doteq G$, where $\mathsf{h} \in \Sigma_{\mathsf{H}}$ is a hierarchy predicate, or simply hierarchy, and $G = \langle N_{\mathsf{h}}, E_{\mathsf{h}}, \gamma_{\mathsf{h}} \rangle$ is an edge-labeled Directed Acyclic Graph (DAG). Here, $N_{\mathsf{h}} \subseteq \Sigma_{\mathsf{N}}$ is the set of* nodes *of h, E_{h} is the set of* edges *of h (i.e. a set of pairs $\langle n^s, n^t \rangle$ with $n^s, n^t \in N_{\mathsf{h}}$, called the* source *and* target *of the edge, respectively), and γ_{h} is a function that labels each edge in E_{h} with a view in $\mathcal{V}$, with the proviso that:*

1. *$\gamma_{\mathsf{h}}(e)$ is a view of arity 2, for every $e \in E_{\mathsf{h}}$;*
2. *there is exactly one node $n \in N_{\mathsf{h}}$ such that $\langle n', n \rangle \notin E_{\mathsf{h}}$, for every $n' \in N_{\mathsf{h}}$; intuitively, such node is the most fine-grained level of the hierarchy and is called the* root *of h, denoted with $root(\mathsf{h})$.*

Example 3. Consider Example 1 and assume that the following views of arity 2 are available:

$$\mathsf{schoolDistrView} \doteq \{x, y \mid \mathsf{locatedInDistrict}(x, y) \wedge \mathsf{School}(x)\}$$
$$\mathsf{distrStateView} \doteq \{x, y \mid \mathsf{locatedInState}(x, y) \wedge \mathsf{District}(x)\}$$

$\mathsf{schoolLocationH} \doteq G$ is a hierarchy, with $G = \langle N, E, \gamma \rangle$ defined as:

$$N = \{\mathsf{school}, \mathsf{district}, \mathsf{state}\} \qquad E = \{\langle \mathsf{school}, \mathsf{district} \rangle, \langle \mathsf{district}, \mathsf{state} \rangle\}$$
$$\gamma(\langle \mathsf{school}, \mathsf{district} \rangle) = \mathsf{schoolDistrView} \quad \gamma(\langle \mathsf{district}, \mathsf{state} \rangle) = \mathsf{distrStateView}$$

Here, school is the root of the hierarchy. □

A *path* π *in* h *from* n_0 *to* n_k is a finite sequence of nodes $\langle n_0, \ldots, n_k \rangle$, with $k \geq 1$, such that $\langle n_i, n_{i+1} \rangle \in E_{\mathsf{h}}$, for each $i \in \{0, \ldots, k-1\}$. A path π is said *complete* if $n_0 = root(\mathsf{h})$ and n_k is a *leaf* node of h, i.e. a node not being the source of any edge of E_{h}. We define the *conjunction of atoms associated with* π, denoted ϕ_π, as the expression $\exists z_1, \ldots, z_{k-1} \bigwedge_{i=0}^{k-1} \Gamma_i(z_i, z_{i+1})$, where $\Gamma_i = \gamma_{\mathsf{h}}(\langle n_i, n_{i+1} \rangle)$ is the view name labeling the edge from n_i to n_{i+1}, and z_i and z_{i+1} are variables from Var. In the next sections, it will be useful to set $z_0 = u$ and $z_k = x$, where $x, u \in \mathsf{Var}$ and x, u are distinct from $z_1, \ldots, z_{k-1}$. We use $\phi_\pi(u, x)$ to denote this variant of ϕ_π, that is:

$$\phi_\pi(u, x) = \exists z_1, \ldots, z_{k-1} \left(\bigwedge_{i=0}^{k-1} \Gamma_i(z_i, z_{i+1}) \wedge z_0 = u \wedge z_k = x \right) \qquad (1)$$

We now define multidimensional cubes, by starting from the so-called base data cube. For ease of exposition we consider cubes having exactly one measure. The generalization to an arbitrary number of measures is straightforward.

Definition 3 (Base Data Cube). *Given a set $\mathcal{V}$ of views over an OBDM specification Ψ and set $\mathcal{H}$ of hierarchies over $\mathcal{V}$, a* base data cube definition *over $\mathcal{V}$ and $\mathcal{H}$ is an expression of the form $\mathsf{c} \doteq \langle \mathsf{v}, \delta, \eta, \mathsf{m} \rangle$, where $\mathsf{c} \in \Sigma_{\mathsf{C}}$ is a base data cube predicate, or simply base data cube, and*

- $\mathsf{v} \in \mathcal{V}$ *is the view that* underlies c, *denoted by* view(c);
- δ *is a total function from a tuple* $\boldsymbol{d} = \langle d_1, \ldots, d_n \rangle$ *to a tuple* $\boldsymbol{x} = \langle x_1, \ldots, x_n \rangle$*, such that each* $d_i \in \Sigma_\mathsf{D}$ *for* $i \in 1, \ldots, n$*, and* $\boldsymbol{x}$ *is a subtuple of* $sig(\mathsf{v})$*; the tuple* $\boldsymbol{d}$ *is called the* signature of c, *denoted by* $sig(\mathsf{c})$*, and each* d_i *in* $\boldsymbol{d}$ *is called the* i-th dimension *of* c, *for* $i \in \{1, \ldots, n\}$*;*
- η *is a partial function from the elements of* $sig(\mathsf{c})$ *to the set* $\mathcal{H}$*;*
- $\mathsf{m} \in \Sigma_\mathsf{M}$ *is the* measure *of* c, *defined by an expression of the form* $\mathsf{m} \doteq \mathsf{op}$, *where* $\mathsf{op} \in \mathsf{Funct}$ *is an aggregation function; we denote* m *as* meas(c).

We say that $n+1$*, where* n *is the arity of* $\boldsymbol{d}$*, is the arity of* c.

As specified above, the data cube is defined on top of the view v, with the function δ associating each cube dimension to a specific component of $sig(\mathsf{v})$. As formally established in the next section, this association enables to populate the cube from the micro-data extracted from the underlying OBDM system. A cube dimension may be in turn associated with a hierarchy by the partial function η. Intuitively, this association enables aggregation of cube facts along dimensions. The measure m is defined by the aggregation function op, which performs computations such as `count`, `sum`, `avg`, `min`, etc., over the answers to the view v. We consider operators tailored to specific aggregation contexts. That is, operators in Funct differ not only in the type of aggregation (e.g., `sum`, `max`, etc.), but also in the components of $sig(\mathsf{v})$ used as grouping keys. For example, to count students in the view studentView (see Example 2) by sch, and to count them by both sch and g, we use different operators.

Example 4. We define a base data cube that aggregates the number of students by school and gender. Let studentView be the view defined in Example 2, with signature $\langle st, sch, g \rangle$. We introduce two cube dimensions: schoolDim and genderDim. The mapping δ assigns these dimensions with components of the view as follows: $\delta(\mathsf{schoolDim}) = sch$ and $\delta(\mathsf{genderDim}) = g$. We associate the dimension schoolDim with the hierarchy schoolLocationH, defined in Example 3, i.e. $\eta(\mathsf{schoolDim}) = \mathsf{schoolLocationH}$. The measure of the cube is defined as $\#\mathsf{enrolled} \doteq \mathsf{count}_{\mathsf{sch,g}}$, where the aggregation function $\mathsf{count}_{\mathsf{sch,g}}$ is intended to count tuples in the answers to $q(st, sch, g)$ grouped by the view components assigned to schoolDim and genderDim. Putting all together, the base data cube is $\mathsf{EnrolCube} \doteq \langle \mathsf{studentView}, \delta, \eta, \#\mathsf{enrolled} \rangle$ and $sig(\mathsf{EnrolCube}) = \langle \mathsf{schoolDim}, \mathsf{genderDim} \rangle$. □

To complete our framework, we next introduce *derived data cubes.* Each derived cube is defined on top of another cube—either base or, in turn, derived—by changing the level of granularity of the aggregation, e.g., through standard OLAP operations such as *roll-up* (also known as *drill-up*) and *drill-down,* or by making selections on the measure, the dimensions, or the hierarchy nodes (if any), thereby capturing, e.g., classical slicing and dicing in data warehousing. To formally define a derived data cube, we make use of a *filter condition* over $\Sigma_\mathsf{D} \cup \Sigma_\mathsf{N} \cup \Sigma_\mathsf{M}$, which is a conjunction of atoms of the form $a_1 \, \beta \, a_2$, where $\beta \in \{=, \neq, <, \leq, >, \geq\}$ and $a_1, a_2 \in \Sigma_\mathsf{D} \cup \Sigma_\mathsf{N} \cup \Sigma_\mathsf{M} \cup \mathsf{Const} \cup \mathsf{Val}$. For instance, $\#\mathsf{enrolled} > 100 \wedge \mathsf{genderDim} = \texttt{'F'} \wedge \mathsf{state} = \texttt{state1}$ is a filter condition.

Definition 4 (Derived Data Cube). *Given a data cube* c_1 *(derived or base), a* derived data cube *definition is an expression of the form tuple* $\mathsf{c}_2 \doteq \langle \mathsf{c}_1, \varphi_2, \theta_2, \mathsf{m}_2 \rangle$*, where* $\mathsf{c}_2 \in \Sigma_\mathsf{C}$ *is a derived data cube predicate, or simply derived data cube, and*

- φ_2 *is a filter condition;*
- θ_2 *is a partial function from* Σ_D *to* $\Sigma_\mathsf{N} \cup \{\mathtt{ALL}\}$*, where* $\mathtt{ALL}$ *is a special symbol not belonging to any alphabet;*
- $\mathsf{m}_2 \in \Sigma_\mathsf{M}$ *is the* measure *of* c_2*, defined by an expression of the form* $\mathsf{m}_2 \doteq \mathsf{op}$*, where* $\mathsf{op} \in \mathsf{Funct}$ *is an aggregation function.*

We say that c_2 is derived from c_1, sometimes expressed as $\mathsf{DerFrom}(\mathsf{c}_2, \mathsf{c}_1)$. As done for base cubes, we denote m_2 as $\mathsf{meas}(\mathsf{c}_2)$. Given a derived data cube c, a *derivation for* c is a sequence of cubes $\mathsf{c}_0, \dots, \mathsf{c}_k$, with $k \geq 1$, such that $\mathsf{c}_k = \mathsf{c}$, $\mathsf{DerFrom}(\mathsf{c}_{i+1}, \mathsf{c}_i)$ for every $i \in \{0, \dots k-1\}$, and derivations (direct or indirect) are non-recursive, i.e. $\mathsf{c}_i \neq \mathsf{c}_j$, for every $i, j \in \{0, \dots k\}$.

We assume that both the filtering condition φ and the function θ only involve symbols from $\Sigma_\mathsf{D} \cup \Sigma_\mathsf{N} \cup \Sigma_\mathsf{M}$ that are relevant for c. Formally, we define the alphabet of c as $\Sigma_\mathsf{c} = \{d \mid d \text{ occurs in } sig(\mathsf{c})\} \cup \{n \mid \text{there is } \mathsf{h} = \langle N_\mathsf{h}, E_\mathsf{h} \rangle \text{ such that } n \in N_\mathsf{h} \text{ and } \eta(d) = \mathsf{h}, \text{ with } d \text{ occurring in } sig(\mathsf{c})\} \cup \{\mathsf{meas}(\mathsf{c}), \mathtt{ALL}\}$, and impose that φ is a filter condition over $\Sigma_\mathsf{c} \cup \mathsf{Const} \cup \mathsf{Var}$, and that θ is a function from $\Sigma_\mathsf{c} \cap \Sigma_D$ to $(\Sigma_\mathsf{c} \cap \Sigma_N) \cup \{\mathtt{ALL}\}$.

Example 5. Consider the following derived data cube definition $\mathsf{EnrolDistrCube} \doteq \langle \mathsf{EnrolCube}, \varphi, \theta, \mathsf{\#enrollDistr} \rangle$, where:

- EnrolCube is the (base) cube of Example 4;
- φ is the filter condition $\mathsf{state} = \mathtt{state1}$;
- θ is such that $\theta(\mathsf{schoolDim}) = \mathsf{district}$;
- $\mathsf{\#enrollDistr} \doteq \mathsf{countDis}_{\mathsf{distr,g}}$, with $\mathsf{countDis}_{\mathsf{distr,g}}$ an operator in Funct.

In words, EnrolDistrCube is defined over EnrolCube via a roll-up on schoolDim to the district level, a selection of facts related to schools in `state1`, and by maintaining genderDim as is. □

We finally give the definitions of Multi-OBDM specification and system.

Definition 5 (Multi-OBDM Specification and System). *A* Multi-OBDM *specification is a tuple* $\Omega = \langle \mathcal{C}, \mathcal{H}, \mathcal{V}, \Psi \rangle$*, where* $\Psi = \langle \mathcal{O}, \mathcal{M}, \mathcal{S} \rangle$ *is an OBDM specification,* $\mathcal{V}$ *is a finite set of views over* Ψ*,* $\mathcal{H}$ *is a finite set of hierarchies over* $\mathcal{V}$*, and* $\mathcal{C} = \mathcal{C}_B \cup \mathcal{C}_D$*, where* $\mathcal{C}_B$ *is a finite set of base data cubes over* $\mathcal{V}$ *and* $\mathcal{H}$ *and* $\mathcal{C}_D = \{\mathsf{c} \mid \mathsf{Base}(\mathsf{c}) \in \mathcal{C}_B\}$*.*
A Multi-OBDM *system is a pair* $\Lambda = \langle \Omega, DB \rangle$*, where* DB *is a source database for* Ψ*. We refer to* Ψ *and* $\langle \Psi, DB \rangle$ *as the* underlying OBDM specification *and the* underlying OBDM system *of* Λ*, respectively.*

4 Multidimensional OBDM: Semantics

The semantics of a Multi-OBDM system is given in terms of an extension of the notion of epistemic interpretation, as originally defined for DL ontologies in [9]. We first introduce the notion of multidimensional interpretations. A *multidimensional interpretation* w over the alphabet $\Sigma = \Sigma_{\mathsf{O}} \cup \Sigma_{\mathsf{V}} \cup \Sigma_{\mathsf{H}} \cup \Sigma_{\mathsf{N}} \cup \Sigma_{\mathsf{C}} \cup \mathsf{Funct}$ is a pair $\langle \Delta, \cdot^w \rangle$, where Δ is the interpretation domain and $\cdot^w$ is an interpretation function that assigns each element of the alphabet with a structure over Δ, which may be a set, an n-ary relation, a graph, or a function, as detailed below. Without loss of generality, we assume $\Delta = \mathsf{Const} \cup \mathsf{Val}$ in each multidimensional interpretation. In other terms, we use *standard names*, as is customary in epistemic semantics [9]. Moreover, we denote with $\mathcal{G}$ the set of all directed graphs over constants and values, that is, $\mathcal{G} = \{\langle \hat{N}, \hat{E} \rangle \mid \hat{N} \subseteq \Delta,\ \hat{E} \subseteq \Delta \times \Delta\}$. The function $\cdot^w$ is defined as follows:

- if $\mathsf{p} \in \Sigma_{\mathsf{O}}$, then $\cdot^w$ behaves as a standard DL interpretation function, by assigning sets of objects in Const to concepts, subsets of $\mathsf{Const} \times \mathsf{Const}$ to roles, and subsets of $\mathsf{Const} \times \mathsf{Val}$ to attributes;
- if $\mathsf{v} \in \Sigma_{\mathsf{V}}$, then $\mathsf{v}^w \subseteq \Delta^n$, where $n = \mathit{arity}(\mathsf{v})$;
- if $\mathsf{n} \in \Sigma_{\mathsf{N}}$ then $\mathsf{n}^w \subseteq \mathsf{Const} \cup \mathsf{Val}$;
- it $\mathsf{h} \in \Sigma_{\mathsf{H}}$ then $\mathsf{h}^w \in \mathcal{G}$;
- if $\mathsf{c} \in \Sigma_{\mathsf{C}}$, then $\mathsf{c}^w \subseteq \Delta^n \times \mathsf{Val}$, where $n = \mathrm{arity}(\mathsf{c}) - 1$.
- if $\mathsf{op} \in \mathsf{Funct}$, then $\mathsf{op}^w : \bigcup_{n \in \mathbb{N}} 2^{\Delta^n} \rightarrow \mathsf{Val}$ (2^{Δ^n} is the powerset of Δ^n).

Note that each tuple in c^w contains an additional component with respect to the arity of c. Intuitively, such component is used for the value that the interpretation w associates to the measure in c. Moreover, the last point says that op^w is a function that computes a value corresponding to applying the aggregation operator op over a set of n-tuples, where n depends on the specific operator op. We assume the semantics of an operator $\mathsf{op} \in \mathsf{Funct}$ to be fixed and predetermined, that is, op^w is the same in each epistemic interpretation w.

With the above notion in place, we define an *epistemic multidimensional interpretation* (or, simply, epistemic interpretation) as a pair $\mathcal{W} = \langle w, W \rangle$, where W is a set of multidimensional interpretations over Σ and $w \in W$.

We are now able to define the semantics of a multi-OBDM System $\Lambda = \langle \Omega, DB \rangle$, where $\Omega = \langle \mathcal{C}, \mathcal{H}, \mathcal{V}, \Psi \rangle$. To this aim, we consider only specific epistemic interpretations $\mathcal{W} = \langle w, W \rangle$, which we call Φ-epistemic-interpretations, where W contains all and only the models of the OBDM system $\Phi = \langle \Psi, DB \rangle$ (note that a multidimensional interpretation is a model of an OBDM system if it meets the standard satisfaction conditions for OBDM systems, recalled in Sect. 2).

A Φ-epistemic-interpretation $\mathcal{W}$ is a model of Φ. For $\mathcal{W}$ to be also a model of Λ, it must satisfy (each element in) $\mathcal{V}$, $\mathcal{H}$ and $\mathcal{C}$. Below, we provide these satisfaction notions. From now on, when we say epistemic interpretation, we always mean Φ-epistemic-interpretation.

View Satisfaction. Given a view $\mathsf{v} \doteq q(\boldsymbol{x})$ in $\mathcal{V}$, we say that $\mathcal{W} = \langle w, W \rangle$ *satisfies* v in Λ if $\mathsf{v}^w = \{\boldsymbol{t} \in \Delta^n \mid \hat{w} \models q(\boldsymbol{t})\ \forall \hat{w} \in W\}$, where n is the arity of v.

In other words, a view is satisfied by $\mathcal{W}$ if the view interpretation coincides with the set of certain answers of the query $q(\boldsymbol{x})$ over the OBDM system Φ.

Example 6. Let $\mathsf{studentView}$ be the view given in Example 2 and $\mathcal{W} = \langle w, W \rangle$ be an epistemic interpretation for a Multi-OBDM system Λ having Φ of Example 1 as underlying OBDM system. Then, $\mathcal{W}$ satisfies $\mathsf{studentView}$ if $\mathsf{studentView}^w = \{(\mathtt{st1}, \mathtt{sch1}, \text{`}\mathtt{M}\text{'}), (\mathtt{st2}, \mathtt{sch1}, \text{`}\mathtt{M}\text{'}), (\mathtt{st3}, \mathtt{sch2}, \text{`}\mathtt{F}\text{'})\}$. □

Hierarchy Satisfaction. Given a hierarchy $\mathsf{h} \doteq \langle N, E, \gamma \rangle$ in $\mathcal{H}$, we say that $\mathcal{W} = \langle w, W \rangle$ *satisfies* h in Λ if $\mathsf{h}^w = \langle \hat{N}, \hat{E} \rangle$ is a graph in $\mathcal{G}$ such that:

- $\hat{N} = \bigcup_{n \in N} n^w$, where $n^w = \{t \mid \exists t', n' \text{ such that } \langle t, t' \rangle \in \gamma(\langle n, n' \rangle)^w\}$;
- $n_1^w \cap n_2^w = \emptyset$, for each $n_1, n_2 \in N$;
- $\hat{E} = \bigcup_{e \in E} e^w$, where $e^w = \{\langle t_1, t_2 \rangle \mid \langle t_1, t_2 \rangle \in \gamma(e)^w\}$.

We set $\mathsf{root}(\mathsf{h}^w) = n_0^w$ where $n_0 = \mathsf{root}(\mathsf{h})$. We remark that both the definition h and the interpretation h^w of a hierarchy are graphs. However, while the edges of a hierarchy definition are pairs of node names labeled with the name of a view, the graph in the hierarchy interpretation is defined over $\mathsf{Const} \cup \mathsf{Val}$. Indeed, each instance of a view labeling an edge of the hierarchy definition, i.e. a pair of constants or values, is an edge of the interpretation graph. Moreover, whereas h is a DAG, h^w is a collection of DAGs, i.e. each connected component of h^w is a DAG. We note also that the above definition of semantics for h is actually saying that a h is satisfied by $\mathcal{W}$ if h^w is a graph whose set of edges coincides with the union of the certain answers over the OBDM system Φ of all the queries defining the views associated to the edges in h.

We now assume on h^w two restrictions typically adopted in Data Warehouses. Firstly, given $n_1 \in N$ and $t_1 \in n_1^w$, we impose that for each edge $e = \langle n_1, n_2 \rangle \in E$ there is at most a $t_2 \in n_2^w$ such that $\langle t_1, t_2 \rangle \in e^w$. By virtue of this restriction, each edge in h actually models a functional dependency between two adjacent nodes of the hierarchy [18]. The second restriction concerns possible convergences in h. A convergence occurs when a node n in h has more than one incoming edge. This implies that in h there are multiple paths ending in n and starting from another node $\tilde{n}$. As a consequence, there might exist $\tilde{t} \in \tilde{n}^w$ and $t, t' \in n^w$ such that in h^w there are paths from $\tilde{t}$ to both t and t' (paths in h^w are defined as in h; see Sect. 3). In such cases, we impose that $t = t'$.

Example 7. Consider the hierarchy $\mathsf{schoolLocationH} = \langle N, E, \gamma \rangle$ introduced in Example 3. Let $\mathcal{W} = \langle w, W \rangle$ be an epistemic interpretation such that:

$$\mathsf{schoolDistrict}^w = \{(\mathtt{sch1}, \mathtt{dist1}), (\mathtt{sch2}, \mathtt{dist2})\},$$
$$\mathsf{districtState}^w = \{(\mathtt{dist1}, \mathtt{state1}), (\mathtt{dist2}, \mathtt{state2})\}.$$

Then, $\mathcal{W}$ satisfies $\mathsf{schoolLocationH}$ in Λ (see Example 6) if $\mathsf{school}^w = \{\mathtt{sch1}, \mathtt{sch2}\}$, $\mathsf{district}^w = \{\mathtt{dist1}, \mathtt{dist2}\}$, $\mathsf{state}^w = \{\mathtt{state1}, \mathtt{state2}\}$, and $\mathsf{schoolLocationH}^w = \langle \hat{N}, \hat{E} \rangle$ is the graph with
$\hat{N} = \{\mathtt{sch1}, \mathtt{sch2}, \mathtt{dist1}, \mathtt{dist2}, \mathtt{state1}, \mathtt{state2}\}$
$\hat{E} = \{\langle \mathtt{sch1}, \mathtt{dist1} \rangle, \langle \mathtt{sch2}, \mathtt{dist2} \rangle, \langle \mathtt{dist1}, \mathtt{state1} \rangle, \langle \mathtt{dist2}, \mathtt{state2} \rangle\}$. □

Base Data Cube Satisfaction. Let c be a base data cube in $\mathcal{C}$ such that $\mathsf{c} \doteq \langle \mathsf{v}, \delta, \eta, \mathsf{m} \rangle$, $sig(\mathsf{c}) = \langle d_1, \ldots, d_n \rangle$, $\mathsf{m} \doteq op$, and $sig(\mathsf{v}) = \langle z_1, \ldots, z_p \rangle$. Let $\boldsymbol{j} = \langle j_1, \ldots, j_n \rangle$ be the tuple of integers such that $\delta(d_i) = z_{j_i}$, for each $1 \leq i \leq n$. We say that $\mathcal{W} = \langle w, W \rangle$ *satisfies* c in Λ if the following conditions hold:

- a tuple $\langle t_1, \ldots, t_{n+1} \rangle$ belongs to c^w if and only if there exists a $\boldsymbol{j}$-cluster u of v^w such that $\langle t_1, \ldots, t_n \rangle = \boldsymbol{t}_u[\boldsymbol{j}]$, where $\boldsymbol{t}_u$ is any tuple in u (note that $\boldsymbol{t}_u[\boldsymbol{j}]$ returns the same tuple for each $\boldsymbol{t}_u \in u$);
- for each $\langle t_1, \ldots, t_{n+1} \rangle \in \mathsf{c}^w$, let u be the $\boldsymbol{j}$-cluster of v^w such that $\langle t_1, \ldots, t_n \rangle = \boldsymbol{t}_u[\boldsymbol{j}]$, for any $\boldsymbol{t}_u \in u$, it holds that $t_{n+1} = \mathsf{op}^w(u)$.

Intuitively, the above definition is saying that the epistemic interpretation $\mathcal{W}$ satisfies a base data cube c if c^w contains exactly a tuple for each cluster "induced" on v by the dimensions of c. Each such tuple contains an additional argument that is the value computed for the cluster by the aggregate operator op. No other tuples occur in c^w.

Example 8. Consider the base cube $\mathsf{EnrolCube} = \langle \mathsf{studentView}, \delta, \eta, \mathsf{\#enrolled} \rangle$ of Example 4. Let $\mathcal{W} = \langle w, W \rangle$ be an epistemic interpretation that satisfies $\mathsf{studentView}$ in Λ (see Example 6). Then, $\mathcal{W}$ satisfies $\mathsf{EnrolCube}$ if $\mathsf{EnrolCube}^w = \{(\mathtt{sch1}, \mathtt{'M'}, 2), (\mathtt{sch2}, \mathtt{'F'}, 1)\}$. □

Derived Data Cube Satisfaction. Let $\mathsf{c}_2 \doteq \langle \mathsf{c}_1, \varphi_2, \theta_2, \mathsf{m}_2 \rangle$ be a derived data cube in $\mathcal{C}$, where $\mathsf{m}_2 \doteq \mathsf{op}_2$ and c_1 is a (arbitrary) data cube such that $sig(\mathsf{c}_1) = \langle d_1, \ldots, d_n \rangle$. By definition, $sig(\mathsf{c}_2) = sig(\mathsf{c}_1)$. To formalize when an epistemic interpretation satisfies c_2, we need to define the query q_{c_2} associated with c_2. Intuitively, q_{c_2} is specified in terms of the base data cube $\mathsf{Base}(\mathsf{c}_2)$ and the views associated with the hierarchy edges that must be traversed to either change the level of data aggregation when moving from c_1 to c_2, as specified by the function θ_2, or to express the selections in φ_2. The semantics of c_2 is then defined in terms of aggregations of the answers to q_{c_2}, obtained by evaluating it over the interpretations in $\mathcal{W}$ of $\mathsf{Base}(\mathsf{c}_2)$ and the aforementioned views. To express the query associated to c_2, we use the function $\mathsf{Cond}(\mathsf{c}_2)$, defined inductively as follows:

1. $\mathsf{Cond}(\mathsf{c}_2) = \varphi_2$ if c_1 is a base data cube;
2. $\mathsf{Cond}(\mathsf{c}_2) = \varphi_2 \wedge \mathsf{Cond}(\mathsf{c}_1)$, otherwise.

Let $\mathsf{c}_0 = \mathsf{Base}(\mathsf{c}_2)$, the query associated with c_2 is defined as follows:

$$q_{\mathsf{c}_2} = \{x_1, \ldots x_n, u_{n+1} \mid \mathsf{c}_0(u_1, \ldots u_n, u_{n+1}) \bigwedge_{i=1}^{n} p(u_i, x_i) \wedge \mu(\mathsf{Cond}(\mathsf{c}_2))\} \tag{2}$$

where each $p(u_i, x_i)$ is a formula that depends on whether the dimension d_i is associated with a hierarchy, and whether $\theta_2(d_i)$ is equal to or different from $\mathtt{ALL}$, whereas $\mu(\mathsf{Cond}(\mathsf{c}_2))$ is a subformula encoding the filter conditions. More precisely, for $i \in \{1, \ldots, n\}$, $p(u_i, x_i)$ is equal to (*i*) a conjunction of atoms of the form (1) associated with a path $\pi = n_0, \ldots, n_\ell$ in $\mathsf{h}_i = \eta(d_i)$, where η is the function in $\mathsf{Base}(\mathsf{c}_2)$ associating dimensions with hierarchies, $n_0 = root(\mathsf{h}_i)$ and $n_\ell = \theta(d_i)$, if both $\eta(d_i)$ and $\theta(d_i)$ are defined and $\theta(d_i) \neq \mathtt{ALL}$;

(*ii*) the atom $x_i = u_i$, if $\theta(d_i)$ is not defined (no matter if $\eta(d_i)$ is defined or not);

(*iii*) the atom $x_i = \mathtt{ALL}$, if $\theta(d_i) = \mathtt{ALL}$ (no matter if $\eta(d_i)$ is defined or not).

Finally, the function $\mu(\varphi)$ is defined as follows: (*a*) it substitutes each occurrence of a dimension $d_i \in \Sigma_{\mathsf{D}}$ in φ with u_i; (*b*) it substitutes each occurrence of a measure $\mathsf{m} \in \Sigma_{\mathsf{M}}$ in φ with u_{n+1}; (*c*) let $\mathsf{h}_i = \langle \mathsf{N}_{\mathsf{h}_i}, \mathsf{E}_{\mathsf{h}_i} \rangle$ be the hierarchy associated with a dimension d_i and let $n_i \in \mathsf{N}_{\mathsf{h}_i}$ occur in φ, $\mu(\varphi)$ substitute n_i with a fresh variable z and extends φ by conjoining it with $\phi_\pi(u_i, z)$, where ϕ_π is a conjunction of atoms of the form (1) associated with a path $\pi = n_0, \ldots, n_i$ in h_i, where $n_0 = root(\mathsf{h}_i)$

Let $\mathcal{W} = \langle w, W \rangle$ be an epistemic interpretation and $q^w_{\mathsf{c}_2}$ denote the evaluation of q_{c_2} over $\mathsf{c}_1{}^w \cup \{\mathsf{v}^w \mid \mathsf{v} \text{ occurs in } q_{\mathsf{c}_2}\}$. Also, let $\boldsymbol{j} = \langle 1, \ldots, n \rangle$ be a tuple of integers. We say that $\mathcal{W}$ *satisfies* c_2 in Λ if the following conditions hold:

- a tuple $\langle t_1, \ldots, t_{n+1} \rangle$ belongs to $\mathsf{c}_2{}^w$ if and only if there exists a $\boldsymbol{j}$-cluster u of $q^w_{\mathsf{c}_2}$ such that $\langle t_1, \ldots, t_n \rangle = \boldsymbol{t}_u[\boldsymbol{j}]$, where $\boldsymbol{t}_u$ is any tuple in u ;
- for each $\langle t_1, \ldots, t_{n+1} \rangle \in \mathsf{c}_2{}^w$, let u be the $\boldsymbol{j}$-cluster of $q^w_{\mathsf{c}_2}$ such that $\langle t_1, \ldots, t_n \rangle = \boldsymbol{t}_u[\boldsymbol{j}]$, for any $\boldsymbol{t}_u \in u$, it holds that $t_{n+1} = \mathsf{op}_2{}^w(u)$.

Note that the last two conditions mirror those for satisfying a base cube, with the only difference being that c_1 is replaced by q_{c_2}.

Example 9. Consider the derived data cube $\mathsf{EnrolDistrCube} \doteq \langle \mathsf{EnrolCube}, \varphi, \theta, \mathsf{\#enrollDistr} \rangle$ introduced in Example 5. Let $\mathcal{W} = \langle w, W \rangle$ be an epistemic interpretation satisfying the base cube EnrolCube in Λ (see Example 8) and the hierarchy schoolLocationH (see Example 7).

The query q associated with EnrolDistrCube is:

$$\{x_1, x_2, u_3 \mid \mathsf{EnrolCube}(u_1, u_2, u_3) \wedge p(u_1, x_1) \wedge x_2 = u_2 \wedge \mu(\varphi)\}$$

where $p(u_1, x_1) = \mathsf{schoolDistrView}(u_1, x_1)$ and, since $\varphi = \mathtt{state} = \mathtt{state1}$ $\mu(\varphi) = \exists y_1, z\, (\mathsf{schoolDistrView}(u_1, y_1) \wedge (\mathsf{distrStateView}(y_1, z) \wedge z = \mathtt{state1}))$.

Then, we have that $q^w = \{(\mathtt{dist1}, \text{'}\mathtt{M}\text{'}, 2)\}$ (remember that q selects only facts concerning $\mathtt{state1}$). For $\mathcal{W}$ to satisfy EnrolDistrCube, it has to be $\mathsf{EnrolDistrCube}^w = q^w$ (in this simple example there is actually only one cluster with one tuple in q^w, thus the two interpretations coincide). □

Model of a Multi-OBDM System. We are now ready to define the semantics of Multi-OBDM systems, which naturally extends those of standard OBDM systems. Specifically, a *model of a Multi-OBDM system* $\Lambda = \langle \Omega, DB \rangle$, where $\Omega = \langle \mathcal{C}, \mathcal{H}, \mathcal{V}, \Psi \rangle$, is a Φ-epistemic interpretation $\mathcal{W}$, with $\Phi = \langle \Psi, DB \rangle$, that satisfies all the views in $\mathcal{V}$, all the hierarchies in $\mathcal{H}$, and all the data cubes (base or derived) in $\mathcal{C}$ (note that each $\mathcal{W}$ is by definition a model of Φ). The set of models of $\Lambda = \langle \Omega, DB \rangle$ is denoted by $\mathsf{Mod}(\Lambda)$.

5 Reasoning Within Multi-OBDM

We now investigate reasoning in our framework, first over Multi-OBDM specifications, then over Multi-OBDM systems. Finally we study the computational complexity of selected tasks in the *DL-Lite* setting. Following the same notational conventions adopted so far, we use $\mathcal{S}$ to denote a relational schema, DB to denote an $\mathcal{S}$-database, Ψ for an OBDM specification $\langle \mathcal{T}, \mathcal{M}, \mathcal{S} \rangle$, Ω for a multi-OBDM specification $\langle \mathcal{C}, \mathcal{H}, \mathcal{V}, \Psi \rangle$, and Λ for a multi-OBDM system $\langle \Omega, DB \rangle$.

Reasoning over the Multi-OBDM Specification. To support the designer of a Multi-OBDM specification, we consider the following tasks:

Hierarchy Coherence: given Ω and $\mathsf{h} \in \mathcal{H}$, verify whether for every complete path $\pi = \langle n_0, \ldots, n_k \rangle$ in h, there exist DB and $\mathcal{W} = \langle w, W \rangle \in \mathsf{Mod}(\Lambda)$ such that h^w contains a path $\langle \ell_0, \ldots \ell_k \rangle$ where $\ell_0 \in \mathsf{root}(\mathsf{h}^w)$ and for every $i \in \{0, \ldots, k-1\}$, $(\ell_i, \ell_{i+1}) \in \gamma(e_i)^w$, with $e_i = \langle n_i, n_{i+1} \rangle$.

Cube Coherence: given Ω and $\mathsf{c} \in \mathcal{C}$, verify whether there exist DB and $\mathcal{W} = \langle w, W \rangle \in \mathsf{Mod}(\Lambda)$ such that $\mathsf{c}^w \neq \emptyset$.

Cube Containment: given Ω and $\mathsf{c}_1, \mathsf{c}_2 \in \mathcal{C}$, verify whether $\mathsf{c}_1^w \subseteq \mathsf{c}_2^w$ for every DB and every $\mathcal{W} = \langle w, W \rangle \in \mathsf{Mod}(\Lambda)$. If this is the case, we say that c_1 *is contained in* c_2 *w.r.t.* Ω and write $\mathsf{c}_1 \sqsubseteq^{\Omega} \mathsf{c}_2$.

Cube Equivalence: given a Multi-OBDM specification Ω and $\mathsf{c}_1, \mathsf{c}_2 \in \mathcal{C}$, verify whether $\mathsf{c}_1 \sqsubseteq^{\Omega} \mathsf{c}_2$ and $\mathsf{c}_2 \sqsubseteq^{\Omega} \mathsf{c}_1$. If this is the case, we say that c_1 *and* c_2 *are equivalent w.r.t.* Ω and write $\mathsf{c}_1 \equiv^{\Omega} \mathsf{c}_2$.

The above reasoning tasks help designers detect ill-defined hierarchies or cubes: a non-coherent one cannot be instantiated, regardless of source data, and cube containment or equivalence holds for any source database.

Reasoning over Multi-OBDM System. The basic reasoning task over Multi-OBDM systems concerns the computation of cubes:

Cube Computation: given $\Lambda = \langle \Omega, DB \rangle$ and $\mathsf{c} \in \mathcal{C}$, compute the *certain extension* of c w.r.t. Λ, denoted $\mathsf{cert}(\mathsf{c}, \Lambda)$, and defined as: $\mathsf{cert}(\mathsf{c}, \Lambda) = \{\boldsymbol{t} \mid \boldsymbol{t} \in \mathsf{c}^w, \forall \mathcal{W} = \langle w, W \rangle \in \mathsf{Mod}(\Lambda)\}$.

Other useful reasoning tasks over Multi-OBDM systems are the following:
Extensional hierarchy coherence: given Λ and $\mathsf{h} \in \mathcal{H}$, verify whether for every complete path $\pi = \langle n_0, \ldots, n_k \rangle$ in h, there exists $\mathcal{W} = \langle w, W \rangle \in \mathsf{Mod}(\Lambda)$ such that h^w contains a path $\langle \ell_0, \ldots \ell_k \rangle$ where $\ell_0 \in \mathsf{root}(\mathsf{h}^w)$ and for every $i \in \{0, \ldots, k-1\}$, $(\ell_i, \ell_{i+1}) \in \gamma(e_i)^w$, with $e_i = \langle n_i, n_{i+1} \rangle$. This reasoning task can be seen as the *extensional* version of **Hierarchy coherence**. We can define in the same way extensional versions of the remaining tasks over Multi-OBDM specifications, which we omit for space reasons.

Holistic $\mathcal{L}$-query Answering: A *holistic $\mathcal{L}$-query* is a query expressed in $\mathcal{L}$ over symbols in $\Sigma_O \cup \Sigma_V \cup \Sigma_C$. The set of answers to q over an epistemic multidimensional interpretation $\mathcal{W} = \langle w, W \rangle$ of Λ is defined as $q^w = \{\boldsymbol{t} \mid \hat{w} \models q(\boldsymbol{t}) \forall \hat{w} \in W\}$. Thus, given Λ and a holistic $\mathcal{L}$-query q, holistic $\mathcal{L}$-query answering amounts to compute the *certain answers to* q w.r.t. Λ, denoted $cert(q, \Lambda)$, and defined as $\mathsf{cert}(q, \Lambda) = \{\boldsymbol{t} \mid \boldsymbol{t} \in q^w, \forall \mathcal{W} = \langle w, W \rangle \in \mathsf{Mod}(\Lambda)\}$.

We next illustrate that holistic query answering is a powerful task, as it combines multidimensional elements with domain ontology predicates in a single query, enabling requests that mix micro and macro data.

Example 10. Consider a Multi-OBDM system $\langle \Omega, DB \rangle$ such that $\Omega = \langle \mathcal{C}, \mathcal{H}, \mathcal{V}, \Psi \rangle$, where $\langle \Psi, DB \rangle$ is the OBDM system introduced in Example 1, and $\mathcal{V}$, $\mathcal{H}$, and $\mathcal{C}$ contain respectively the views, the hierarchies, and the cubes introduced in Examples 2, 3, 4, and 5. Moreover, assume that $\langle \Psi, DB \rangle$ provides also information about districts characteristics, such as the kind of geographic area, i.e. urban, suburban or rural, modeled as the attribute kindGeoArea. Suppose we are interested in computing the students enrolled in a school in `state1` together with their gender, the kind of district of the school they are enrolled in and the number of students of their same gender enrolled in their same district. This is captured by the following holistic CQ query:

$$\{st, g, k, n \mid \mathsf{enrolled}(st, sch) \land \mathsf{hasGender}(st, g) \land \mathsf{locatedInDist}(sch, d) \land \\ \mathsf{EnrolDistrCube}(d, g, n) \land \mathsf{kindGeoArea}(d, k)\}$$

Note that this query captures the combined use of SQL [3] `PARTITION BY` and `OVER` clauses, by returning information about individual students, combined with aggregated information about groups students belong to. Moreover, it illustrates how holistic query answering provides an integrated access to aggregated data and individual-level information (kindGeoArea), without the need of importing it into multidimensional cubes (see also *descriptive attributes* in DFM [17]).

In the rest of this section, we refer to the *DL-Lite* setting and further assume that the queries associated to the views in $\mathcal{V}$ are UCQs over Ψ. Concerning reasoning over a Multi-OBDM specification Ω, it can be shown that the problems of checking the coherence of a hierarchy $\mathsf{h} \in \mathcal{H}$ and of a cube $\mathsf{c} \in \mathcal{C}$, can be reduced to the problem of checking whether there exists an $\mathcal{S}$-database DB such that the certain answers to a UCQ q' (depending on h and c respectively) over the OBDM system $\langle \Psi, DB \rangle$ are non-empty. Intuitively, for a hierarchy h, q' is the union of the CQs obtained as follows. For each complete path π, we construct a conjunctive query q_π whose body is the conjunction of atoms ϕ_π associated with π. We then reformulate q_π into a UCQ q'_π by unfolding the views appearing in ϕ_π with their associated queries. On the other hand, as for a cube c, if c is a base data cube, q' is simply the one defining the view underlying c. Otherwise, if c is a derived data cube, q' is the UCQ q_c (see Eq. 2) associated with c. Combining the above observations with the fact that the non-emptiness of a UCQ query over an OBDM system in the *DL-Lite* setting can be decided in PTIME [29], we have the following.

Proposition 1. *In the DL-Lite setting with UCQ views,* ***Hierarchy*** *and* ***Cube coherence*** *are in* PTIME *with respect to the size of the whole input.*

Concerning reasoning over Multi-OBDM systems, we next provide the outline of the algorithms for **Cube computation** and **Holistic UCQ-query answering**. Intuitively, given an $\mathcal{S}$-database DB, they both resort to first extend DB

with relations storing the sets of tuples that belong to each view and to each cube in every model of $\langle \Omega, DB \rangle$. Then, while **Cube computation** can be reduced to the evaluation of an aggregated query over the extended database, **Holistic UCQ-query answering** can be reduced to compute the certain answer to a UCQ over an OBDM system obtained by accordingly extending $\langle \Psi, DB \rangle$.

More formally, let *the certain extension of a view* v *w.r.t.* Λ be the set of tuples $\mathsf{cert}(\mathsf{v}, \Lambda) = \mathsf{cert}(q_{\mathsf{v}}, \langle \Psi, DB \rangle)$, where q_{v} is the query defining v. Also, let R_{v}^{Λ} be the set of ground atoms $\{R_{\mathsf{v}}(\boldsymbol{t}) | \boldsymbol{t} \in \mathsf{cert}(\mathsf{v}, \Lambda)\}$ where R_{v} is a fresh predicate in Pred, and let $R_{\mathsf{v}_{\mathsf{c}}}^{\Lambda}$ be the set $\{R_{\mathsf{c}}(\boldsymbol{t}) | \boldsymbol{t} \in \mathsf{cert}(\mathsf{c}, \Lambda)\}$, where c is a cube predicate and R_{c} is a fresh predicate in Pred. Finally, let DB' be obtained by extending DB with R_{v}^{Λ} and R_{c}^{Λ} for every $\mathsf{v} \in \mathcal{V}$ and $\mathsf{c} \in \mathcal{C}$.

In order to compute a cube c we can proceed as follows. If c is a base cube, $\mathsf{cert}(\mathsf{c}, \Lambda)$ is the set of tuples $Q^{DB'}$, where Q is the query computing the aggregation specified by $\mathsf{meas}(\mathsf{c})$ for each group of tuples in $R_{\mathsf{v}_{\mathsf{c}}}^{\Lambda}$ that coincide on the components associated by δ to the dimensions of c. Otherwise, if c is a derived cube, $\mathsf{cert}(\mathsf{c}, \Lambda)$ is the set of tuples $Q^{DB'}$, where Q is the query obtained from the query q_{c}, by substituting each predicate c with R_{c} and each view predicate v with R_{v}. Finally, given a holistic UCQ-query q, the set $\mathsf{cert}(\mathsf{c}, \Lambda)$ is the set of tuples $\mathsf{cert}(q', \Phi')$, where $\Phi = \langle \Psi, DB' \rangle$ and q' is obtained from q, by substituting every cube predicate c and view predicate v with the predicates R_{c} and R_{v}.

It is easy to see that the correctness of the above algorithms follows directly from the definition of the semantics of base and derived data cubes and from the observation that, given a Multi-OBDM system Λ, each view v is interpreted by every epistemic multidimensional interpretation $\mathcal{W}$ as the same set of tuples, namely $\mathsf{cert}(\mathsf{v}, \Lambda)$. Also, we have the following.

Proposition 2. *In the DL-Lite setting with UCQ views,* ***Cube computation*** *and* ***Holistic UCQ-query answering*** *are NP-complete with respect to the size of the whole input and in* PTIME *with respect to the size of DB only.*

Finally, one can show that analogous results hold for the extensional versions of hierarchy coherence and of cube coherence, containment and equivalence.

6 Conclusion and Future Work

We are currently developing a first prototype implementation of the Multi-OBDM framework; some details can be found at https://shorturl.at/IAZIm. This development builds on services provided by existing OBDM tools, like query answering over domain ontologies, and extends them to support multidimensional modeling and reasoning. In parallel, we are conducting a comprehensive case study in collaboration with ISTAT, the Italian National Institute of Statistics. This collaboration continues a previous pilot initiative, INTERSTAT, which explored interoperability of statistical data from both cross-border and cross-domain perspectives [23]. Within INTERSTAT, we tested the effectiveness of reconciling micro- and macro-data, an idea that is now rigorously formalized in the framework proposed in this paper. Unlike the earlier approach adopted in INTERSTAT, our current framework offers a more complete and principled formalization, enabling richer reasoning and broader applicability in real-world statistical settings. As future work, we also plan to investigate optimization techniques for holistic query answering and more expressive aggregation operators.

We finally remark that the ability of Multi-OBDM to explicitly model the derivation of macro-data from micro-data through views, hierarchies, and cube definitions fosters transparent data lineage and traceability, which are critical for building trust in data analytics. By enabling users to formally trace aggregated indicators back to their source-level origins, the framework supports accountability, reproducibility, and verification. This is especially important in ethically sensitive domains such as government open data, public health reporting, and educational analytics, where trust and inclusivity are paramount. For example, policy-makers can rely on Multi-OBDM to ensure that published statistics are grounded in verifiable data, and stakeholders can validate whether summary indicators reflect diverse populations and data sources fairly.

Acknowledgements. This work was partially supported by: projects FAIR (PE0000013) and SERICS (PE00000014) under the MUR National Recovery and Resilience Plan funded by the European Union - NextGenerationEU; POLAR project funded by MUR - Progetti di Ricerca di Rilevante Interesse Nazionale (PRIN) Bando 2022 (cup G53D23002870006). Scafoglieri's research was entirely and exclusively supported by the PNRR MUR project PE0000013-FAIR.

We would like to thank Roberta Radini and Michele Riccio (ISTAT) and Valerio Santarelli (OBDA Systems s.r.l.) for the insightful discussions and collaboration during the INTERSTAT project, which fostered the development of the framework presented in this paper.

References

1. The official site for the SDMX community (2023). https://sdmx.org/
2. Abelló, A., Samos, J., Saltor, F.: YAM^2: a multidimensional conceptual model extending UML. Inf. Syst. **31**(6), 541–567 (2006)
3. Abiteboul, S., Hull, R., Vianu, V.: Foundations of Databases. Addison Wesley Publ. Co. (1995)
4. Baader, F., Calvanese, D., McGuinness, D., Nardi, D., Patel-Schneider, P.F. (eds.): The Description Logic Handbook: Theory, Implementation and Applications. Cambridge University Press (2003)
5. Baader, F., Calvanese, D., McGuinness, D., Nardi, D., Patel-Schneider, P.F. (eds.): The Description Logic Handbook: Theory, Implementation and Applications, 2nd edn. Cambridge University Press (2007)
6. Bertossi, L., Milani, M.: Ontological multidimensional data models and contextual data quality. J. Data Inf. Qual. **9**(3), 1–36 (2018)
7. Cabibbo, L., Torlone, R.: A logical approach to multidimensional databases. In: Schek, H.-J., Alonso, G., Saltor, F., Ramos, I. (eds.) EDBT 1998. LNCS, vol. 1377, pp. 183–197. Springer, Heidelberg (1998). https://doi.org/10.1007/BFb0100985

8. Calvanese, D., De Giacomo, G., Lembo, D., Lenzerini, M., Poggi, A., Rosati, R.: Linking data to ontologies: the description logic $DL\text{-}Lite_A$. In: Proceedings of the 2nd International Workshop on OWL: Experiences and Directions (OWLED). CEUR Electronic Workshop Proceedings, vol. 216 (2006). http://ceur-ws.org/
9. Calvanese, D., De Giacomo, G., Lembo, D., Lenzerini, M., Rosati, R.: EQL-lite: effective first-order query processing in description logics. In: Proceedings of the 20th International Joint Conference on Artificial Intelligence (IJCAI), pp. 274–279 (2007)
10. Civili, C., et al.: MASTRO STUDIO: managing ontology-based data access applications. Proc. VLDB Endow. **6**(12), 1314–1317 (2013). https://doi.org/10.14778/2536274.2536304
11. Console, M., De Giacomo, G., Lenzerini, M., Namici, M.: Intensional and extensional views in DL-Lite ontologies. In: Zhou, Z. (ed.) Proceedings of the 30th International Joint Conference on Artificial Intelligence (IJCAI), pp. 1822–1828 (2021). http://ijcai.org/
12. Cyganiak, R., Reynolds, D.: The RDF data cube vocabulary. W3C Recommendation, World Wide Web Consortium (2014). https://www.w3.org/TR/vocab-data-cube/
13. Giacomo, G., Lenzerini, M.: A uniform framework for concept definitions in description logics. J. Artif. Intell. Res. **6**, 87–110 (1997)
14. Devlin, B.: Data Warehouse: From Architecture to Implementation. Addison Wesley Publ. Co. (1997)
15. Gkitsakis, D., Kaloudis, S., Mouselli, E., Peralta, V., Marcel, P., Vassiliadis, P.: Cube query interestingness: novelty, relevance, peculiarity and surprise. Inf. Syst. 102381 (2024)
16. Golfarelli, M., Maio, D., Rizzi, S.: Conceptual design of data warehouses from E/R schemes. In: Proceedings of the 31st Hawaii International Conference on System Sciences, vol. 7, pp. 334–343. IEEE (1998)
17. Golfarelli, M., Maio, D., Rizzi, S.: The dimensional fact model: a conceptual model for data warehouses. Int. J. Coop. Inf. Syst. **7**, 215–247 (1998)
18. Golfarelli, M., Rizzi, S.: Data Warehouse Design: Modern Principles and Methodologies. McGraw-Hill (2009)
19. Inmon, W.H.: Building the Data Warehouse, 2nd edn. Wiley (1996)
20. Jarke, M., Lenzerini, M., Vassiliou, Y., Vassiliadis, P. (eds.): Fundamentals of Data Warehouses, 2nd edn. Springer (2003)
21. Kharlamov, E., et al.: Ontology-based integration of streaming and static relational data with Optique. In: Proceedings of the 2016 International Conference on Management of Data (SIGMOD), pp. 2109–2112. ACM (2016)
22. Kimball, R., Ross, M.: The Data Warehouse Toolkit: The Definitive Guide to Dimensional Modeling, 3rd edn. Wiley (2013)
23. Lembo, D., Lenzerini, M., Poggi, A., Radini, R., Riccio, M., Santarelli, V.: Bridging the gap between micro and macro data: ontologies to the rescue. In: Proceedings of the 31st Italian Conference on Database Systems (SEBD). CEUR Workshop Proceedings, vol. 3478, pp. 220–227. CEUR-WS.org (2023). https://ceur-ws.org/Vol-3478/paper66.pdf
24. Lenzerini, M.: Managing data through the lens of an ontology. AI Mag. **39**(2), 65–74 (2018)
25. Milani, M., Bertossi, L.: Ontology-based multidimensional contexts with applications to quality data specification and extraction. In: Bassiliades, N., Gottlob, G., Sadri, F., Paschke, A., Roman, D. (eds.) RuleML 2015. LNCS, vol. 9202, pp. 277–293. Springer, Cham (2015). https://doi.org/10.1007/978-3-319-21542-6_18

26. Neumayr, B., Anderlik, S., Schrefl, M.: Towards ontology-based olap: datalog-based reasoning over multidimensional ontologies. In: Proceedings of the 15th International Workshop on Data warehousing and OLAP, pp. 41–48 (2012)
27. Neumayr, B., Schütz, C., Schrefl, M.: Semantic enrichment of OLAP cubes: multidimensional ontologies and their representation in SQL and OWL. In: Meersman, R., et al. (eds.) OTM 2013. LNCS, vol. 8185, pp. 624–641. Springer, Heidelberg (2013). https://doi.org/10.1007/978-3-642-41030-7_46
28. Papadimitriou, C.H.: Computational Complexity. Addison Wesley Publ. Co. (1994)
29. Poggi, A., Lembo, D., Calvanese, D., De Giacomo, G., Lenzerini, M., Rosati, R.: Linking data to ontologies. J. Data Semantics **X**, 133–173 (2008)
30. Vassiliadis, P.: A cube algebra with comparative operations: containment, overlap, distance and usability. Computing Research Repository (CoRR) abs/2203.09390 (2022). https://doi.org/10.48550/arXiv.2203.09390
31. Vassiliadis, P., Marcel, P., Rizzi, S.: Beyond roll-up's and drill-down's: an intentional analytics model to reinvent OLAP. Inf. Syst. **85**, 68–91 (2019)
32. Vassiliadis, P., Simitsis, A., Skiadopoulos, S.: Conceptual modeling for ETL processes. In: Proceedings of the 5th ACM International Workshop on Data Warehousing and OLAP, pp. 14–21 (2002)
33. Xiao, G., et al.: Ontology-based data access: a survey. In: Lang, J. (ed.) Proceedings of the 27th International Joint Conference on Artificial Intelligence (IJCAI), pp. 5511–5519. ijcai.org (2018)
34. Xiao, G., et al.: The virtual knowledge graph system ontop. In: Pan, J.Z., et al. (eds.) ISWC 2020. LNCS, vol. 12507, pp. 259–277. Springer, Cham (2020). https://doi.org/10.1007/978-3-030-62466-8_17

LLM-Enabled Modeling

Towards Human-in-the-Loop LLM-Enabled Domain Modeling

Jonathan Silva[1(✉)], Qin Ma[1], Jordi Cabot[1,2], Pierre Kelsen[1], and Henderik A. Proper[3]

[1] University of Luxembourg, Esch-sur-Alzette, Luxembourg
{jonathan.silva,qin.ma,jordi.cabot,pierre.kelsen}@uni.lu
[2] Luxembourg Institute of Science and Technology, Esch-sur-Alzette, Luxembourg
jordi.cabot@list.lu
[3] TU Wien, Vienna, Austria
henderik.proper@tuwien.ac.at

Abstract. The use of Large Language Models (LLMs), combined with advanced prompting strategies, automates the creation of domain models from textual domain descriptions. However, the output is often influenced by mistakes and limitations that arise from the inherent characteristics of LLMs, including hallucinations and inconsistencies. Additionally, ambiguities and incompleteness in the input text further affect the quality of the results.

We propose a new LLM-based modeling method with human in the loop that aims to combine the strengths of automatic model creation with human supervision and interaction to refine and validate the model.

In our approach, the LLM generates an initial draft model from textual descriptions. This draft is then subjected to a feedback loop moderated by a rule-based agent, which engages the user through a Q&A dialogue. The rule-based agent selects the questions based on their potential to clarify the most uncertain aspects of the model up to that point.

Keywords: Domain Modeling · Domain Model Validation · AI-assisted Domain Modeling · Large Language Models

1 Introduction

With the growing interest and adoption of Large Language Models (LLMs) and their rapid update and iteration, the application of LLMs to solve domain modeling problems has also advanced significantly. What began with straightforward single-shot prompting has now evolved into the exploitation of more sophisticated prompting techniques, such as decomposing the modeling process into smaller tasks [4,7,11,30,32,35], assigning specialized roles to LLMs to allow collaborative co-creation [20,22,32], and incorporating self-reflections [17,27,32].

Despite advances, LLM-based domain modeling solutions still face noticeable limitations. For example, in UML class diagram modeling, accurately identifying

D. Bork et al. (Eds.): ER 2025, LNCS 16189, pp. 127–145, 2026.
https://doi.org/10.1007/978-3-032-08623-5_7

relationships among classes remains challenging [11,32,33]. This is largely due to the inherent characteristics of LLMs, including hallucinations and inconsistencies, which can compromise the quality of the output. Moreover, ambiguities and incompleteness in the input text may further degrade the quality of the generated models. As a result, the validity and domain relevance of the created models still require careful verification and validation (V&V).

According to the SEQUAL framework from the model quality V&V literature [21,23], syntactic and semantic quality are considered two fundamental dimensions of model quality. Briefly, syntactic quality refers to a model's adherence to the syntax rules of the modeling language and semantic quality ensures that the model correctly represents the domain and captures all relevant aspects. Recent studies [12] show that when LLMs are used to produce models in widely adopted modeling notations such as (Plant)UML, they tend to produce few syntactic errors, but frequently introduce semantic inaccuracies. The SEQUAL framework recommends consistency checking as a means to achieve semantic validity, whose effective execution requires the involvement of domain experts [19,24], since fully automated validation is considered infeasible [8]. In effect, the specialized knowledge of domain experts is essential to disambiguate and complete the domain understanding captured in textual sources and represented in the model [14,16,18,25].

In line with this, research such as [20] proposed a human-in-the-loop (HITL) approach to LLM-based modeling, aiming to exploit user feedback to refine and eventually enhance the quality of domain models created by LLMs. Specifically, next to leveraging advanced prompting techniques such as role prompting and knowledge injection, [20] incorporated an interactive feedback loop that enables users to identify errors in LLM-generated models and provide corrective feedback, which the LLM then uses to refine the models. This approach demonstrated a promising improvement in the quality of the resulting process models. However, the observed improvement is dependent on users, who are often domain experts, also possessing sufficient modeling expertise. This includes both (1) the ability to comprehend domain models expressed in specialized modeling notations, and (2) the skills to identify and articulate the issues within them. The findings of studies with novice modelers e.g., [33] also support this correlation, indicating that the quality of domain models produced with the assistance of LLMs improves proportionally to the modeling skills and experience of the users.

Given that domain experts often lack a technical modeling background, traditional modeling scenarios, where a domain expert collaborates with a human modeler rather than an LLM, place the responsibility on the modeler to bridge the gap between technical modeling and domain understanding. To enhance model comprehension, the modeler can leverage several strategies such as automatically generating instances from the model and visualizing them using domain-specific notations familiar to the expert [31], transforming the model into natural language representations [8], and explaining the model in natural language through dialogues [5]. These are then followed by strategies to guide and facilitate error detection and feedback elicitation, such as posing pertinent questions derived from pattern matches in the model [5]. The identified issues and feedback for improvement are then translated by the modeler into appropriate modeling refinements to improve the model [18].

However, when the role of modeler is assumed by an LLM, as is the case in current LLM-based domain modeling solutions, the criticality of bridging the gap between technical modeling and domain understanding is often overlooked. Inspired by the strategies employed by human modelers, this paper proposes an extension to existing LLM-based domain modeling approaches by integrating an interactive feedback loop with the domain expert, moderated by a rule-based agent. Specifically, we demonstrate the extension using a previous LLM-based domain modeling solution built on the Tree-of-Thoughts (ToT) prompting technique [32], which we refer to as the ToT-Q framework. In ToT-Q, an LLM generates an initial draft of a UML class diagram model from a textual description by executing a ToT-based modeling process. The rule-based agent then engages the domain expert in an interactive dialogue, posing questions generated based on pattern matches in the draft model to solicit feedback for refinement.

To support this process, we collect a set of controversial modeling patterns from both the literature [5] and our own modeling experience with UML class diagrams. We then design natural language question templates using domain-specific vocabulary to be triggered when pattern matches are found in the draft model. To prevent overwhelming users with an excessive number of questions, we also put in place a confidence scoring mechanism that selectively involves the user only when the confidence is low or multiple competing modeling options have comparable confidence levels. We validate the ToT-Q framework by conducting experiments using two LLMs with contrasting capabilities (GPT-4o and GPT-4o-mini), which are also employed to simulate the domain expert. Our open-source implementation is available on GitHub for customization of the format of the question templates and the conditions under which questions are triggered.

The rest of the paper is organized as follows. Section 2 reviews the state of the art in LLM-enabled domain modeling and HITL approaches. Section 3 presents the ToT-Q framework for conceptual modeling and elaborates on the technical details of the framework. Section 4 reports the experiments and analyzes the results to evaluate the effectiveness of ToT-Q in improving the general LLM domain modeling capabilities. Section 5 describes the tool support and customization options. Finally, Sect. 6 concludes and points to future directions.

2 State of the Art in LLM-Enabled Domain Modeling

Recent research on creating domain models with LLMs has evolved from using prompting techniques such as Few-shot [9,10,15] or Chain-of-Thought (CoT) prompting [10,27] to dividing the process into smaller tasks. This newer approach uses specialized prompts to identify different model elements [4,7,11,29,30,32,35], which are then combined to create a complete domain model. Approaches based on task decomposition have shown better results over direct prompt strategies [7,29,35]; however, there are still challenges in improving the recognition of attributes and relationships [11,32]. Furthermore, other approaches assign specialized roles to create process models. For example, one approach uses the role of team leader, process design expert, and process reviewer [22]. Another approach proposes a process owner and a modeling expert to create process models [20]. However, the models still require further refinement to fully align with the process description [20]. While substantial research has focused on improving domain models generated with LLMs, the results show that LLMs have limitations and human feedback is essential to improve the models.

Human in the loop approaches which involve human interaction to guide, supervise, or enhance the learning process [26] play a crucial role to address the limitations. Specifically, Interactive Machine Learning that involves an iterative interaction with human feedback and shared decision-making [13]. Building on these principles, we propose an interactive HITL approach that explicitly structures the collaboration between LLMs and domain experts. Our method extends the ToT framework by iteratively refining the model through a validation loop.

Exploration of HITL approaches has not been widely explored, with only two approaches found in the literature. Norouzifar et al. [28] uses LLMs to generate clarifying questions from process descriptions. The answers serve to create a list of rules that is used to create an initial process model, which is subsequently presented to the domain expert to continue with further refinements of the rules. However, it remains unclear whether LLMs can generate clarifying questions that will resolve the ambiguous parts of the process descriptions. Kourani et al. [20] allowed users to improve the model with rounds of feedback to provide the changes needed to refine the model; then, the LLM refines the model based on this input. Nonetheless, this approach assumes that the user possesses sufficient modeling expertise to understand the process model and continue with the iterative refinement. Moreover, research with novice UML modelers has identified that models created with LLM assistance include errors caused by the known limitations in relationship identification, which are not detected by the users with low modeling expertise [33]. Our approach addresses these limitations through a structured HITL strategy adapted to non-expert users. The rule-based agent generates questions about model elements with low confidence; these questions are created with templates adapted to users with limited UML expertise. This structured interaction ensures that domain experts focus their attention on answering questions about uncertain parts of the model.

3 The TOT-Q Framework

We present an overview of the ToT-Q framework in Fig. 1. ToT-Q structures the modeling process into three main phases, orchestrated by a rule-based agent: 1) the initial phase starts with a domain description that leads to the creation of a draft domain model; 2) the iterative improvement phase refines the domain model through a Q&A loop, and 3) the final phase is reached once all relevant questions are addressed and the improved domain model is proposed to the user. These phases are enabled by four key technical components (cf. Fig. 2).

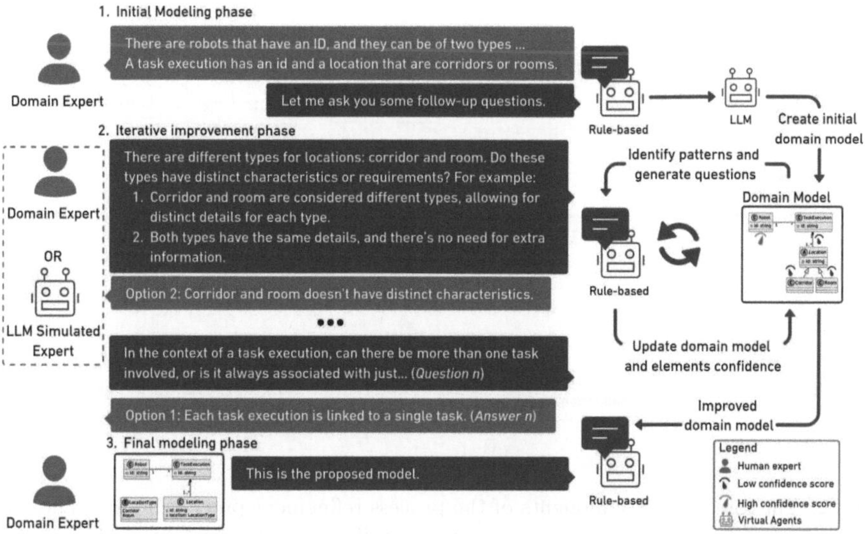

Fig. 1. ToT-Q follows a 3 phases approach moderated by a rule-based agent: 1) Initial modeling phase: delegates the creation of a draft domain model to an LLM, 2) Iterative improvement phase: engages the user in an iterative Q&A loop to refine the domain model, and 3) Final modeling phase: proposes the improved domain model to the user.

1. **ToT and Confidence Quantification:** The initial domain model is created by an LLM using the ToT prompting strategy. During ToT execution, we also let the LLM verbalize its confidence and synthesize it in a hybrid confidence quantification mechanism.
2. **Modeling Pattern Matching:** The rule-based agent identifies matches of modeling patterns in the domain model and prepares data for the generation of questions.
3. **Generation and Selection of Questions:** Questions are generated by instantiating the template linked to the matched modeling pattern. Only those with a confidence score below a defined threshold are presented to the domain expert during the Q&A loop. Moreover, the agent prioritizes these questions by asking those with the lowest confidence scores first.
4. **Model Refinement and Confidence Score Update:** The rule-based agent refines the domain model based on the expert's feedback and updates the corresponding confidence scores, until all questions have been addressed, or a predefined limit on the number of questions has been reached.

We illustrate the ToT-Q framework in the following with an example domain of robots moving in different locations, such as corridors or rooms. Using UML class diagrams, these locations can be either represented as literals of an enumeration type or as subclasses inheriting from a common location class.

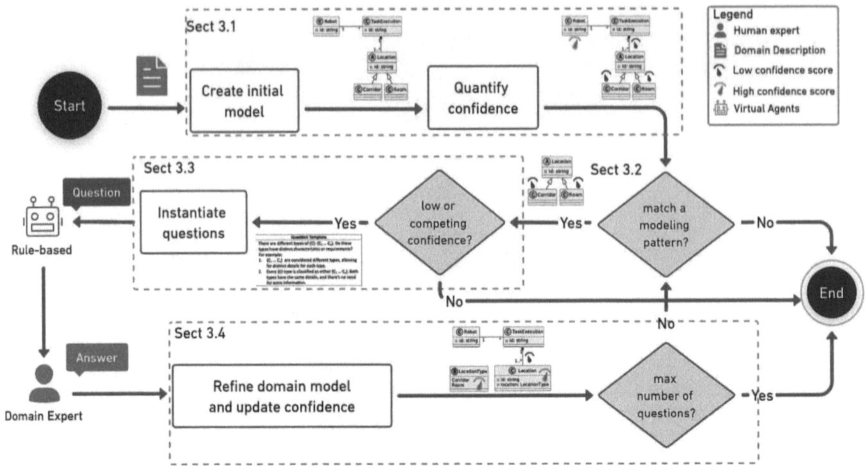

Fig. 2. The four main components of the process refinement process: 1) ToT and confidence quantification, 2) modeling pattern identification, 3) selection and generation of questions, and 4) confidence update based on expert feedback.

3.1 ToT and Confidence Quantification

We use the ToT4DM framework [32] to create the initial domain model. This framework is built upon the ToT prompting strategy [36] designed to enhance the reasoning capabilities of LLMs by decomposing a complex problem into smaller tasks and promoting LLMs to self-assess their responses. In the context of domain modeling, ToT offers the potential to explore and evaluate alternatives of partial models, enabling the creation of domain models with complex abstractions. Specifically, the modeling process is decomposed into a sequence of tasks, referred to as the ToT levels, to build up the classes, attributes, relationships, and association classes of a UML class diagram step by step. For each level, an LLM generates k candidate thoughts, each containing multiple model elements. The LLM then votes for the best thought, and uses the breadth-first search (BFS) to explore the best thought further to complete the draft model. The rest of the thoughts are pruned.

To determine the uncertain parts of the draft model that require domain expert feedback, we quantify it with confidence scores. Our quantification mechanism is inspired by recent advancements in uncertainty quantification for LLMs, particularly methods to estimate confidence in the outputs of closed-source LLMs [37], which do not rely on the logits that are only accessible in open-source LLMs. Specifically, we adopt a hybrid strategy, following the method of Xiong et al. [34], to calculate the confidence scores, combining verbalized confidence scores expressed by LLMs in their responses based on the consistency among the k candidate thoughts of a given level.

To elicit the verbalized confidence scores, we include in the ToT prompts an instruction for the LLM to express a confidence score in $[0, 1]$ alongside each of the following model elements: classes, attributes, enumerations, relationships, their source and target cardinalities, and association classes.

Given a level, let t_i (for $i = 1, \ldots, k$) range over the k thoughts of this level. A thought t_i contains a set of model elements, each paired with a corresponding verbalized confidence score, namely $t_i = \{(e_1, vc_1), (e_2, vc_2), \ldots\}$. Note that different thoughts within the same level may propose model elements that are in a *semantic match*, meaning the name of the elements refer to the same concept but may be expressed differently [6]. We denote the semantic match relation between two elements as $\approx$.

Briefly, the hybrid confidence score of an element e, denoted by $S(e)$, is defined as the average of the verbalized confidence scores of all elements that are in a semantic match with e across the k thoughts at a given level, namely:

$$S(e) = \frac{1}{k} \sum_{i=1}^{k} vc^i_{\approx e} \tag{1}$$

where $vc^i_{\approx e}$, the verbalized confidence score of an element in a semantic match with e in thought t_i, is defined as:

$$vc^i_{\approx e} = \begin{cases} vc' & \text{if } \exists e'.(e', vc') \in t_i \text{ and } e' \approx e \\ 0 & \text{otherwise} \end{cases}$$

Note that if a thought t_i does not contain an element in a semantic match with e, we assume the LLM implicitly verbalizes a confidence score of 0, reflecting the intuition that absence indicates a lack of confidence.

To illustrate the confidence quantification, consider an example where in the level for class modeling, in two out of the $k = 3$ thoughts, the LLM proposes a corridor class to represent the concept of corridor as a location with verbalized confidence scores of 0.70 and 0.80 respectively. In the remaining thought, the LLM proposes to capture corridor as a literal in an enumeration. The confidence score of the corridor class is thus equal to $(0.7 + 0.8 + 0)/3 = 0.5$, according to Eq. 1.

3.2 Modeling Pattern Matching

In this section, we present the modeling patterns used in our proposal, each of which contains two facets. We then explain how a pattern is matched in the model and how the two facets are paired using Algorithm 1.

Figure 3 defines eight modeling patterns, each containing two facets, representing two alternative options to model a concept in UML class diagrams. The list of patterns was created by combining insights from the patterns identified by Bertolino et al. [5] and our modeling experience with UML class diagrams. The goal is to identify scenarios of uncertainty where the domain concept can be represented in the model with two alternative options, which facilitates the generation of contrastive questions. Determining which option is the most appropriate depends on a detailed analysis of the domain being modeled.

Pattern	Facet 1	Facet 2	Question Template
	Decision: Use a class to represent a concept composed by multiple parts, or an attribute for a simple representation.		
1	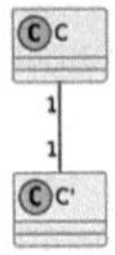		We know that each {C} has an {C'}. When we think about {C'} is it just a simple piece of information, like a line of text? Or is {C'} made up of different parts that might be important? For example: 1. For each { C'}, the information is saved separately, so users can filter {C} based on {C'} details. 2. The {C'} is a single piece of text. This works well when we just need to show the {C'}.
	Decision: Represent concepts with enumeration literals when values are fixed, or use sub classes when concepts involve different details for each one.		
2	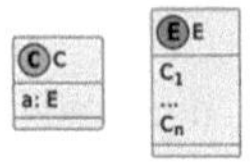	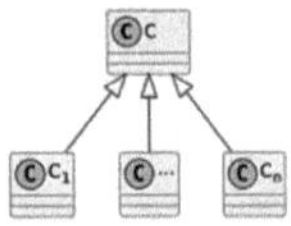	There are different types of {C}: {C_1 ... C_n}. Do these types have distinct characteristics or requirements? For example: 1. {C_1 ... C_n} are considered different types, allowing for distinct details for each type. 2. Every {C} type is classified as either {C_1 ... C_n}. Both types have the same details, and there's no need for extra information.
	Decision: Inheritance with one sub class & Represent a concept as an attribute for a simple representation, or a sub class when the concept requires more details.		
3			When thinking about {C}, what makes a {C_1} different from a regular one? Is there a specific role or responsibility that comes with being a {C_1}? Are there additional factors we need to consider when dealing with {C_1} compared to regular {C}?. For example: 1. A {C_1} is treated as a different kind of {C}. 2. {C} include a status that identifies if it as {C_1} or not.
	Decision: Represent a concept with a concrete class if it can exists independently as instances; otherwise, use an abstract representation.		
4	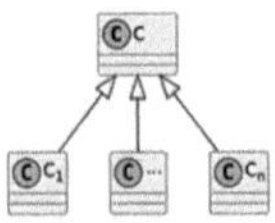	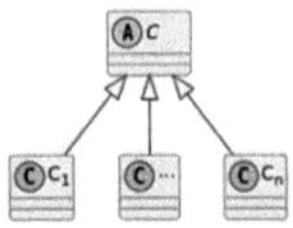	When we talk about {C}, do we always have a clear idea of a specific example, or do we sometimes speak about it in a more general way? Should we think of {C} as a general concept that covers all possible forms, or is it always tied to a particular type or instance?. For example: 1. A general {C} can exists that is not a {C_1 ... C_n}. 2. A {C} is just a concept and cannot exist on its own. We only need specific types like {C_1 ... C_n}.
	Decision: Use composition when the relationship is strong and has lifecycle dependency; otherwise, use association.		
5	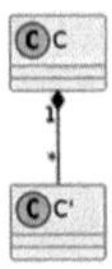	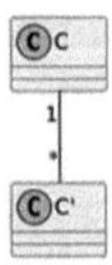	Does a {C'} always require a {C} to exist, or could it exist independently and possibly be linked to multiple {C} instances? If a {C} is removed, would all the associated {C'} also need to be removed, or could a {C'} still make sense on its own?. For example: 1. A {C'} belongs to a {C} and cannot exist without a specific {C}. 2. A {C'} is linked to a {C} but can exist independently of it.
	Decision: The lowerbound cardinality is to zero instance, or one instance.		
6	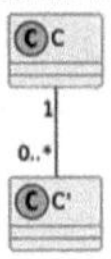	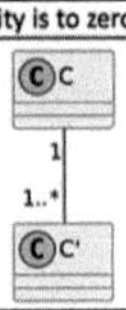	In the context of a {C}, does it always involve at least one {C'} or can it exist without any?. For example: 1. A {C} can exist without any {C'} 2. A {C} must have at least one {C'}
	Decision: The upperbound cardinality is to only one instance, or multiple instances.		
7	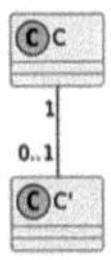	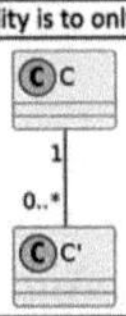	In the context of a {C}, can there be more than one {C'} involved, or is it always associated with just one?. For example: 1. A {C} is linked to a single {C'}. 2. A {C} is linked to multiple {C'}.
	Decision: Represent a concept as an association class when a relationship has attributes; otherwise, use a class.		
8		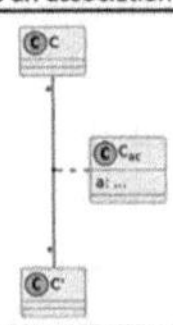	A {C} has multiple {C_{ac}} at different {C'}. Should we think of the link between a {C} and a {C'} as something that only exists when a {C_{ac}} happens? Or would you say a {C} and a {C'} should have a link even outside of specific {C_{ac}}?. For example: 1. A {C} has a direct relationship with a {C'}. {C_{ac}} is a separate event that connects the {C} and {C'} temporarily. 2. The {C_{ac}} is the key event that establishes the link between a {C} and a {C'}. The {C} and {C'} are only linked when a {C_{ac}} occurs.

Fig. 3. Modeling patterns with its corresponding facets, decision, and template question.

Algorithm 1. Find modeling pattern facets

Input: List of facets $F_{\mathcal{DM}}$ with p elements, List of facets $F_{\mathcal{DM}_{alt}}$ with q elements
Output: List containing the alternative pairs: *AlternativePairs*

function FindAlternatives($F_{\mathcal{DM}}$, $F_{\mathcal{DM}_{alt}}$)
  $AlternativePairs \leftarrow \emptyset$
  for $i \leftarrow 1$ to p **do**
    $\mathcal{A}_{\mathcal{DM}} \leftarrow F_{\mathcal{DM}}[i]$
    $Matched \leftarrow$ **false**
    $j \leftarrow 1$
    while $j \leq q$ and not $Matched$ **do**
      $\mathcal{A}_{\mathcal{DM}_{alt}} \leftarrow F_{\mathcal{DM}_{alt}}[j]$
      if Match($\mathcal{A}_{\mathcal{DM}}$, $\mathcal{A}_{\mathcal{DM}_{alt}}$) **then** // True when represent the same concept
        $Matched \leftarrow$ **true**
      end if
      $j \leftarrow j + 1$
    end while
    if not $Matched$ **then**
      $\mathcal{A}_{\mathcal{DM}_{alt}} \leftarrow$ GenerateAlternative($\mathcal{A}_{\mathcal{DM}}$) // Transform $\mathcal{A}_{\mathcal{DM}}$ to $\mathcal{A}_{\mathcal{DM}_{alt}}$
    end if
    $AlternativePairs \leftarrow AlternativePairs \cup \{(\mathcal{A}_{\mathcal{DM}}, \mathcal{A}_{\mathcal{DM}_{alt}})\}$
  end for
  return *AlternativePairs*
end function

The draft domain model consists of a set of model elements, denoted by $\mathcal{DM} = \{e_1, e_2, \ldots, e_n\}$. Let $\mathcal{DM}_{alt} = \{e'_1, e'_2, \ldots, e'_m\}$ be the set of model elements of all the pruned thoughts. To match a pattern, we look for a subset of elements $\mathcal{A}_{\mathcal{DM}} \subseteq \mathcal{DM}$ such that $\mathcal{A}_{\mathcal{DM}}$ constitutes an instance satisfying one facet of the pattern, called a match of the facet. If a match of one facet of a pattern is found in $\mathcal{DM}$, we then look for a match of the other facet of the pattern in $\mathcal{DM}_{alt}$, referred to as $\mathcal{A}_{\mathcal{DM}_{alt}} \subseteq \mathcal{DM}_{alt}$, and pair it with $\mathcal{A}_{\mathcal{DM}}$ to constitute a *configuration*. If no match of the other facet can be found in $\mathcal{DM}_{alt}$, we generate $\mathcal{A}_{\mathcal{DM}_{alt}}$ by transforming the elements from $\mathcal{A}_{\mathcal{DM}}$. Algorithm 1 implements this process to iterate through the patterns and generate the configuration pairs:

$$C = \{(\mathcal{A}_{\mathcal{DM}}{}^1, \mathcal{A}_{\mathcal{DM}_{alt}}{}^1), (\mathcal{A}_{\mathcal{DM}}{}^2, \mathcal{A}_{\mathcal{DM}_{alt}}{}^2), \ldots, (\mathcal{A}_{\mathcal{DM}}{}^n, \mathcal{A}_{\mathcal{DM}_{alt}}{}^n)\}$$

where each configuration $(\mathcal{A}_{\mathcal{DM}}{}^i, \mathcal{A}_{\mathcal{DM}_{alt}}{}^i)$, for $i = 1, \ldots, n$, contains instances of the two alternative facets of a modeling pattern from Fig. 3. These configurations provide input data for instantiating the question templates, as elaborated in Sect. 3.3.

As an example, suppose we identify a subset $\mathcal{A}_{\mathcal{DM}}$ of the draft model satisfying Facet 2 of Pattern 2, consisting of a location class and two subclasses: corridor and room, inheriting it. We then look for a match of the other facet of Pattern 2, namely $\mathcal{A}_{\mathcal{DM}_{alt}}$, in the set of model elements that were once proposed by the LLM during ToT execution, but were not retained. If the match cannot be found, $\mathcal{A}_{\mathcal{DM}_{alt}}$ is created by transforming $\mathcal{A}_{\mathcal{DM}}$: (1) the location class is kept;

(2) the two subclasses and the inheritance relationship to the location class are replaced by an enumeration type with two literals, each of which corresponds to one subclass; and (3) a new attribute of the enumeration type is added to the location class. We pair $\mathcal{A}_{\mathcal{DM}}$ with $\mathcal{A}_{\mathcal{DM}_{alt}}$, include $(\mathcal{A}_{\mathcal{DM}}, \mathcal{A}_{\mathcal{DM}_{alt}})$ in the set of configurations C, and continue to match more patterns.

3.3 Generation and Selection of Questions

To select the configurations that require validation with the domain expert, we filter them based on the confidence scores.

Let $C = \{c_1, c_2, \ldots, c_n\}$ be a set of configurations, where each configuration c_i is a pair of alternatives, corresponding to facets of modeling patterns $c_i = (\mathcal{A}_{\mathcal{DM}}{}^i, \mathcal{A}_{\mathcal{DM}_{alt}}{}^i)$.

For a given alternative $\mathcal{A}_{\mathcal{DM}} = \{e_1, e_2, \ldots, e_m\}$, where e_j are the elements that define the distinctive modeling constructs of the facet (e.g. subclasses or an enumeration), the confidence score is $S(\mathcal{A}_{\mathcal{DM}}{}^i) = min\{S(e_j) | e_j \in \mathcal{A}_{\mathcal{DM}}{}^i\}$. The same applies to $S(\mathcal{A}_{\mathcal{DM}_{alt}}{}^i)$.

For each configuration c_i, we have:

- A confidence score for the alternative in the domain model: $S(\mathcal{A}_{\mathcal{DM}}{}^i) \in [0, 1]$.
- A confidence score for the alternative not selected $S(\mathcal{A}_{\mathcal{DM}_{alt}}{}^i) \in [0, 1]$.

Given a threshold $T \in [0, 1]$, we define the set of configurations selected for question generation as:

$$C_{\text{selected}} = \left\{c_i \in C \mid S(\mathcal{A}_{\mathcal{DM}}{}^i) \leq T \vee \left(S(\mathcal{A}_{\mathcal{DM}}{}^i) \geq T \wedge S(\mathcal{A}_{\mathcal{DM}_{alt}}{}^i) \geq T\right)\right\}$$

This selection ensures that configurations with an alternative confidence below the threshold, or those with both alternatives having the confidence above the threshold, are used to trigger questions for expert validation.

The selected configurations are the input to create questions with a heuristic that indicates which modeling option is more appropriate, based on modeling practices or characteristics of the domain. These heuristics are not strict rules; rather, they provide arguments about the two options, helping domain experts compare and select the best one.

Inspired by Cabot et al. [8], who transform UML/OCL models into natural language to aid non-technical stakeholder understanding, and Bertolino et al. [5], who generate natural language text from UML class diagrams, our implementation employs a template-based question generation mechanism. These templates adapt the content to be accessible to experts, without requiring modeling expertise. In Fig. 3, the templates are populated with the model elements in $\mathcal{A}_{\mathcal{DM}}$, ensuring that the questions are based on the domain context.

The purpose is for the rule-based agent to present the questions with contrastive options, where the domain expert selects one of the alternatives presented. This supports the expert in evaluating both modeling alternatives. Then, the answers will guide the improvement of the model based on the decisions made. By combining the patterns described in Sect. 3.2 with a structured set of template-based questions, we facilitate the participation of domain experts in the modeling process. This enables them to make informed decisions without requiring prior modeling expertise. The complete set of templates and examples is available in GitHub[1].

In the running example, $\mathcal{A}_{\mathcal{DM}}$ contains the subclass representation for corridor and room with a confidence score of 0.50. As this score is below the predefined threshold of 0.80 set in our implementation, the configuration is selected to generate a question for expert validation. Then, the elements class location, and subclasses corridor and room are used to generate the question:

> There are different types of locations: corridors and rooms. Do these types have distinct characteristics or requirements? For example:
> 1. Corridors and rooms are considered different types, allowing for distinct details for each type.
> 2. Every location is classified as either corridor or room. Both types have the same details, and there's no need for extra information.

3.4 Model Refinement and Confidence Score Update

After the domain expert answers the question, one of the alternative pairs $(\mathcal{A}_{\mathcal{DM}}{}^{i}, \mathcal{A}_{\mathcal{DM}_{alt}}{}^{i})$ is selected, where $\mathcal{A}_{sel} \in \{\mathcal{A}_{\mathcal{DM}}{}^{i}, \mathcal{A}_{\mathcal{DM}_{alt}}{}^{i}\}$ is the selected alternative. $\mathcal{A}_{sel}$ may contain elements that are categorized into two types:

- Trusted elements: Elements whose modeling construct are explicitly confirmed by the answer. For example, if a subclass will be replaced by an enumeration literal, we have a high confidence in the enumeration element in the model.
- Uncertain elements: elements whose modeling construct become uncertain as a result of the answer. For example, when enumeration literals are replaced by a subclass, we have a low confidence whether the parent class should be abstract or concrete.

Detailed examples of trusted and uncertain elements for each modeling pattern used in our approach are provided in the GitHub repository (see footnote 1).

For each model element $e \in \mathcal{A}_{sel}$. We define the following confidence update parameters:

- $S_{\text{low}} \in [0, 0.5]$: minimum confidence for uncertain elements.
- $S_{\text{high}} \in (0.5, 1]$: high confidence for trusted elements.

The confidence update is performed as follows:

$$\forall e \in \mathcal{A}_{sel}, \quad S(e) \leftarrow \begin{cases} S_{\text{high}} & \text{if } e \text{ is a trusted element} \\ S_{\text{low}} & \text{if } e \text{ is an uncertain element} \end{cases}$$

[1] https://github.com/BESSER-PEARL/TOT-Q/blob/main/tot_rules_q/modeling_patterns_templates.pdf.

Using this approach, we update the confidence of the elements involved in the question, assigning a high confidence to the trusted elements, while uncertain elements are assigned a low confidence. By increasing the confidence in model elements, we support the creation of a model that is aligned with the domain expert's knowledge.

In the running example, the expert answer indicates that corridor and room have distinct characteristics. Based on this feedback, the most suitable representation is subclasses. Consequently, the confidence score for the subclass elements is set to $S_{\text{high}} = 0.88$, reflecting high confidence after expert validation. Also, the class location confidence is set to $S_{\text{low}} = 0.44$, due to the uncertainty of whether the class should be represented as abstract or concrete.

4 Evaluation

This section evaluates our approach with the following research questions:

RQ1: How does the inclusion of rule-based generated questions (ToT-Q) impact on precision, recall, and F1 score metrics compared to an LLM only approach?

RQ2: How does the number of elements in the domain model affect the number of questions generated by the ToT-Q iterative improvement?

4.1 Experiments Setup

For the experiments, we execute the ToT only approach with $k = 3$ and compare it with ToT-Q. To fully automate the experiment, we use a second LLM to simulate the domain expert. While this introduces a threat to validity in the results, we believe this is a reasonable trade-off to conduct a more controlled experiment, also given that the domain we target in the experiment is well-known and therefore the LLM can do a good job in answering related questions because it has probably seen it during training. Furthermore, we constrain the LLM's behavior with the system prompt, explicitly instructing it to answer the questions based solely on the textual domain description. It is important to emphasize that we do not claim that LLMs can substitute domain experts. Nevertheless, this setup serves as a controlled evaluation to assess how our approach supports the refinement and improvement of a domain model compared to a direct approach where no experts are involved. If there were human experts, the improvement would be even better, especially for complex domains, as the human would perform better than the LLM playing the role of expert in this simulation.

To answer the research questions, we use two OpenAI LLMs: 1) GPT-4o: this model is the most capable outside the o-series models [1], and 2) GPT-4o-mini: the smaller model that provides similar results to GPT-4o on certain tasks [2]. To address RQ1, we compare the improvement on the performance metrics using GPT-4o to GPT-4o-mini. Then, to answer RQ2, we compare the number of questions triggered by ToT-Q using the two LLM models.

Table 1. Performance Comparison of ToT and ToT-Q using GPT-4o and GPT-4o-mini per model elements

Model Element	ToT			ToT-Q			ToT vs ToT-Q	
	Precision	Recall	F1-score	Precision	Recall	F1-score	Δ F1-score	Δ (%)
GPT-4o								
Class	0.800	0.914	0.853	0.943	0.943	0.943	+ 0.090	+ 10%
Attributes	0.586	0.850	0.694	0.773	0.850	0.810	+ 0.116	+ 17%
Relationships	0.400	0.583	0.475	0.692	0.750	0.720	+ 0.245	+ 52%
Assoc. Class	0.600	0.667	0.632	1.000	0.667	0.800	+ 0.168	+ 27%
GPT-4o-mini								
Class	0.775	0.886	0.827	0.914	0.914	0.914	+ 0.088	+ 11%
Attributes	0.452	0.825	0.584	0.593	0.875	0.707	+ 0.123	+ 21%
Relationships	0.353	0.500	0.414	0.452	0.583	0.509	+ 0.095	+ 23%
Assoc. Class	0.500	0.333	0.400	1.000	0.444	0.615	+ 0.215	+ 54%

The dataset includes five domain descriptions with the reference solution from [32], which includes experiments from previous research with LLMs [12], exercises from a university modeling course, and cases proposed by us. The total number of elements includes: 35 classes, 40 attributes, 24 relationships, and 9 association classes.

4.2 Evaluation Criteria

We manually evaluate the models generated by ToT and ToT-Q by doing a comparison against the reference solution in PlantUML. A model element is considered correct if it is in a semantic match with the corresponding element in the reference model, as defined in Sect. 3.1. Furthermore, we are not evaluating the type of the attributes, the relationships should match the lower and upper cardinality, and we consider zero as the default lower cardinality if not specified.

We use precision, recall, and the F1 score to evaluate the experiments. We consider the correct predictions of model elements as true positives, incorrect predictions as false positives, and the elements not predicted as false negatives.

4.3 RQ1: Impact of Using ToT-Q Compared to LLM Only

Our experiment with ToT-Q and GPT-4o in Table 1 shows performance improvements for all the model elements. For classes, both precision and recall increase, resulting in an F1-score of 0.943, an improvement of 10%. Similarly, for relationships, the performance increases for all metrics, with an F1-score of 0.720, an improvement of 52%. Regarding attributes, precision increases while recall remains the same, leading to an F1-score of 0.810, an increase of 17%. Finally, for association classes the recall is the same while precision increases, resulting in an F1-score of 0.800, with an increase in performance of 27%.

In Table 1, the comparison between ToT using GPT-4o and GPT-4o-mini, the smaller LLM model, shows a decrease in performance across all model element types with GPT-4o-mini underperforming relative to GPT-4o. Regarding the experiments using ToT-Q and GPT-4o-mini approach, we observe improvements in the precision, recall, and F1-score for all model elements compared with the ToT. Specifically, the F1-score increases by 11% for classes, 21% for attributes, 23% for relationships, and 54% in association classes. These findings suggest that even smaller models with restricted performance in modeling tasks can benefit from the ToT-Q approach to improve the model recommendations when no human expert is available. The structured Q&A refinement loop can help to compensate for the limitations of smaller LLMs when generating UML models.

These results indicate that ToT-Q achieves improvements ranging from 10% to 54% depending on the element type. Furthermore, using ToT-Q with GPT-4o, we overcome the limitation of relying on LLM only solutions, which are limited by the capabilities of the underlying LLM. The ToT-Q approach shows that incorporating questions discovered with rules and modeling patterns is a viable strategy to initiate a structured refinement loop. These questions emphasize parts of the model that have low confidence and require feedback from domain experts to have a more accurate representation of the domain.

Table 2. Summary of number of elements, number of questions generated, and ratio of questions generated per element (Q/E) across five domains

Domain	Elements	GPT-4o		GPT-4o-mini	
		Questions	Q/E	Questions	Q/E
E-commerce	24	15	0.63	15	0.63
Person & Resources	22	17	0.77	22	1.00
Theaters	25	11	0.44	6	0.24
Courses	20	25	1.25	22	1.10
Robots	17	4	0.24	11	0.65
Total	**108**	**72**	**0.67**	**76**	**0.70**

4.4 RQ2: Impact of Model Elements in Number of Questions

In Table 2, for each domain, we summarize the model size by counting the total number of elements, the number of questions asked by ToT-Q, and the ratio of questions generated by the number of elements. We observe that the smallest model, Robots, with 17 elements, tends to generate fewer questions compared to the larger models, with 4 questions for GPT-4o and 11 for GPT-4o-mini. However, larger models with between 20 and 25 elements show a more complex behavior, as they do not consistently generate more questions. For instance, using ToT-Q with GPT-4o, the Theaters domain with 25 elements requires 11 questions, whereas Courses with 20 elements requires 25 questions. This finding suggests that the number of questions is also influenced by other factors, such as variation in details and ambiguity within the textual descriptions of these domains, which in turn affect the number of questions generated.

Furthermore, we notice that GPT-4o-mini generates more questions overall (76), compared to GPT-4o (72); however, this behavior is not consistent across all the domains. The overall ratio of questions per element is very similar between both LLM models, 0.67 for GPT-4o and 0.7 for GPT-4o-mini, suggesting that on average, about two-thirds of the elements trigger a question in each case.

However, fewer questions do not always result in better models. As shown in Fig. 4, the model generated by ToT-Q with GPT-4o-mini for the Theaters domain differs from the reference solution in three important elements: 1) fails to recognize the association between session and participant, 2) session is not modeled as an association class, and 3) does not reflect in the cardinality that plays have one or more authors.

These results suggest that the size of the model is not the only factor that influences the number of questions. Other factors required may include the ambiguity and completeness of the textual description, as well as the elements that are discovered during ToT execution, influenced by the LLM model. Importantly, despite these variations, our experiments show that the total number of questions remains reasonable. This indicates that the ToT-Q interaction process can guide the model refinement with a manageable number of questions.

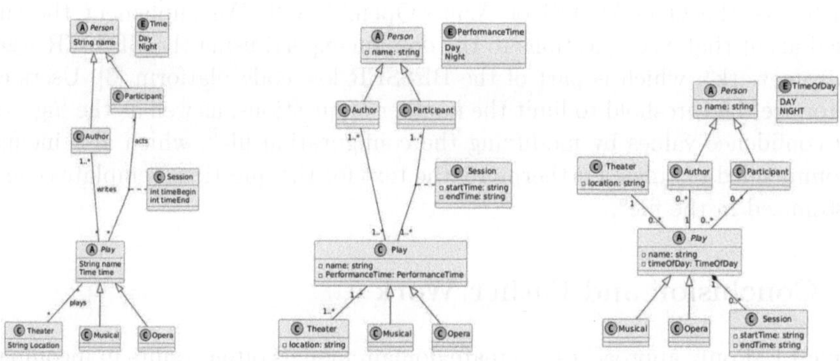

(a) Reference solution (b) ToT-Q (GPT-4o) (c) ToT-Q (GPT-4o-mini)

Fig. 4. Theater domain model used in the experiments

4.5 Threats to Validity

Simulated LLM Domain Expert. LLMs are generative models that produce different responses when given identical prompts. We reduce this variability by using a system prompt to reply using only the domain description, and changing the temperature of the LLM model to zero. While a temperature of zero reduces response variability[2], it does not guarantee complete determinism.

Confidence Variability Using ToT. The ToT approach can lead to variability in confidence levels associated with the model elements. To address this, we employ a hybrid approach that incorporates self-consistent confidence. Using this method, we consider the frequency of the model elements suggested across the ToT multiple paths in the confidence quantification.

Limited Number of Reference Models. Our dataset covers reference models for five domains, which may not represent the complexity and ambiguity that exists in real scenarios. This limitation could affect the generalization of our findings, highlighting the need for evaluation with more diverse and larger models.

5 Tool Support

Our open-source tool is available on GitHub[3]. For the ToT implementation, we use the tool from our previous work [32] to create the initial domain model, which uses the OpenAI API or Azure OpenAI API. We implement the rule-based agent that asks questions to the domain expert; using the BESSER Agentic framework[4], which is part of the BESSER low-code platform [3]. Users can customize the threshold to limit the number of questions, as well as the high and low confidence values by modifying the configuration file[5], which also includes recommended settings. Furthermore, the text for the questions templates can be customized in the file[6].

6 Conclusion and Futher Work

Using LLM only approaches to create domain models often results in incomplete or inaccurate representations. To address this limitation, we propose ToT-Q, a HITL approach that targets uncertain parts of the model that require knowledge from domain experts. Rather than performing an exhaustive revision of all the elements, our method employs a rule-based agent to generate contrastive questions, helping experts to iteratively evaluate and improve the model. Our

[2] https://platform.openai.com/docs/api-reference/chat.
[3] https://github.com/BESSER-PEARL/TOT-Q.
[4] https://github.com/BESSER-PEARL/BESSER-Agentic-Framework/.
[5] https://github.com/BESSER-PEARL/TOT-Q/blob/main/.env_example.
[6] https://github.com/BESSER-PEARL/TOT-Q/blob/main/tot_rules_q/template_questions.py.

open-source tool supports customization of question templates, the number of questions triggered, and the update of confidence score values. Furthermore, we envision extending our proposal by incorporating ontologies and complementary AI techniques to improve element discovery and confidence estimation.

We recognize that human experts have varying expertise levels, which requires adaptability to their diverse profiles. Future work will explore including more modeling patterns and adapting the technical level of the generated questions to different user profiles. Additionally, incorporating a mechanism to capture the degree of certainty in domain expert answers and to aggregate feedback from multiple experts to increase the overall confidence in the model.

While our evaluation relied on simulated expert feedback, it does not fully capture the contextual understanding of human domain experts. Therefore, further work is required to evaluate the effectiveness of the generated questions with domain experts and the quality of models in real scenarios. We expect that involving human experts will lead to even greater improvements.

References

1. GPT-4o (2024). https://platform.openai.com/docs/models/gpt-4o. Accessed 19 May 2025
2. GPT-4o mini (2024). https://platform.openai.com/docs/models/gpt-4o-mini. Accessed 19 May 2025
3. Alfonso, I., et al.: Building BESSER: an open-source low-code platform. In: International Conference on Business Process Modeling, Development and Support, pp. 203–212. Springer (2024)
4. Arulmohan, S., Meurs, M.J., Mosser, S.: Extracting domain models from textual requirements in the era of large language models. In: 2023 ACM/IEEE International Conference on Model Driven Engineering Languages and Systems Companion (MODELS-C), pp. 580–587. IEEE (2023)
5. Bertolino, A., De Angelis, G., Di Sandro, A., Sabetta, A.: Is my model right? Let me ask the expert. J. Syst. Softw. **84**(7), 1089–1099 (2011). https://doi.org/10.1016/j.jss.2011.01.054. https://www.sciencedirect.com/science/article/pii/S0164121211000446
6. Bian, W., Alam, O., Kienzle, J.: Automated grading of class diagrams. In: 2019 ACM/IEEE 22nd International Conference on Model Driven Engineering Languages and Systems Companion (MODELS-C), pp. 700–709. IEEE (2019)
7. Bragilovski, M., Can, A.T., Dalpiaz, F., Sturm, A.: Leveraging machines to derive domain models from user stories. Requirements Eng. (2025). https://doi.org/10.1007/s00766-025-00442-9
8. Cabot, J., Pau, R., Raventós, R.: From UML/OCL to SBVR specifications: a challenging transformation. Inf. Syst. **35**(4), 417–440 (2010). https://doi.org/10.1016/j.is.2008.12.002. https://www.sciencedirect.com/science/article/pii/S030643790800094X
9. Chaaben, M.B., Burgueño, L., Sahraoui, H.: Towards using few-shot prompt learning for automating model completion. In: 2023 IEEE/ACM 45th International Conference on Software Engineering: New Ideas and Emerging Results (ICSE-NIER), Melbourne, Australia, pp. 7–12. IEEE (2023). https://doi.org/10.1109/ICSE-NIER58687.2023.00008. https://ieeexplore.ieee.org/document/10173909/

10. Chen, K., Yang, Y., Chen, B., Hernández López, J.A., Mussbacher, G., Varró, D.: Automated domain modeling with large language models: a comparative study. In: 2023 ACM/IEEE 26th International Conference on Model Driven Engineering Languages and Systems (MODELS), Västerås, Sweden, pp. 162–172. IEEE (2023). https://doi.org/10.1109/MODELS58315.2023.00037. https://ieeexplore.ieee.org/document/10344012/
11. Chen, R., Shen, J., He, X.: A model is not built by a single prompt: LLM-based domain modeling with question decomposition. arXiv preprint arXiv:2410.09854 (2024)
12. Cámara, J., Troya, J., Burgueño, L., Vallecillo, A.: On the assessment of generative AI in modeling tasks: an experience report with ChatGPT and UML. Softw. Syst. Model. **22**(3), 781–793 (2023). https://doi.org/10.1007/s10270-023-01105-5
13. Fails, J.A., Olsen Jr, D.R.: Interactive machine learning. In: Proceedings of the 8th International Conference on Intelligent User Interfaces, pp. 39–45 (2003)
14. Feltus, C., Ma, Q., Proper, H.A., Kelsen, P.: Towards AI assisted domain modeling. In: Reinhartz-Berger, I., Sadiq, S. (eds.) ER 2021. LNCS, vol. 13012, pp. 75–89. Springer, Cham (2021). https://doi.org/10.1007/978-3-030-88358-4_7
15. Fill, H.G., Fettke, P., Köpke, J.: Conceptual modeling and large language models: impressions from first experiments with ChatGPT. Enterprise Modelling and Information Systems Architectures (EMISAJ), pp. 3:1–15 Pages (2023). https://doi.org/10.18417/EMISA.18.3. https://emisa-journal.org/emisa/article/view/318
16. Frederiks, P.J.M., Weide, T.P.: Information modeling: the process and the required competencies of its participants. Data Knowl. Eng. **58**(1), 4–20 (2006). https://doi.org/10.1016/j.datak.2005.05.007
17. Görgen, L., Müller, E., Triller, M., Nast, B., Sandkuhl, K.: Large language models in enterprise modeling: case study and experiences. In: Mayo, F.J.D., Pires, L.F., Seidewitz, E. (eds.) Proceedings of the 12th International Conference on Model-Based Software and Systems Engineering, MODELSWARD 2024, Rome, Italy, 21–23 February 2024, pp. 74–85. SCITEPRESS (2024)
18. Hoppenbrouwers, S.J.B.A., Proper, H.A.E., Weide, T.P.: A fundamental view on the process of conceptual modeling. In: Delcambre, L., Kop, C., Mayr, H.C., Mylopoulos, J., Pastor, O. (eds.) ER 2005. LNCS, vol. 3716, pp. 128–143. Springer, Heidelberg (2005). https://doi.org/10.1007/11568322_9
19. Hoppenbrouwers, S.J., Proper, H., van der Weide, T.P.: Formal modelling as a grounded conversation, pp. 139–155 (2005)
20. Kourani, H., Berti, A., Schuster, D., Aalst, W.M.P.: Process modeling with large language models. In: van der Aa, H., Bork, D., Schmidt, R., Sturm, A. (eds.) Enterprise, Business-Process and Information Systems Modeling, pp. 229–244. Springer, Cham (2024)
21. Krogstie, J., Sindre, G., Lindland, O.I.: 20 Years of Quality of Models, pp. 103–107. Springer, Heidelberg (2013). https://doi.org/10.1007/978-3-642-36926-1_8
22. Lin, L., Jin, Y., Zhou, Y., Chen, W., Qian, C.: Mao: a framework for process model generation with multi-agent orchestration arXiv:2408.01916 (2024). https://doi.org/10.48550/arXiv.2408.01916. arXiv:2408.01916
23. Lindland, O., Sindre, G., Solvberg, A.: Understanding quality in conceptual modeling. IEEE Softw. **11**(2), 42–49 (1994). https://doi.org/10.1109/52.268955
24. Ma, Q., Kaczmarek-Heß, M., Kinderen, S.: Validation and verification in domain-specific modeling method engineering: an integrated life-cycle view. Softw. Syst. Model. **22**(2), 647–666 (2023). https://doi.org/10.1007/s10270-022-01056-3

25. Martini, M., Pinggera, J., Neurauter, M., Sachse, P., Furtner, M.R., Weber, B.: The impact of working memory and the "process of process modelling" on model quality: investigating experienced versus inexperienced modellers. Sci. Rep. **6**(1), 25561 (2016)
26. Mosqueira-Rey, E., Hernández-Pereira, E., Alonso-Ríos, D., Bobes-Bascarán, J., Fernández-Leal, Á.: Human-in-the-loop machine learning: a state of the art. Artif. Intell. Rev. **56**(4), 3005–3054 (2023). https://doi.org/10.1007/s10462-022-10246-w
27. Neuberger, J., Ackermann, L., van der Aa, H., Jablonski, S.: A universal prompting strategy for extracting process model information from natural language text using large language models. In: Maass, W., Han, H., Yasar, H., Multari, N.J. (eds.) Conceptual Modeling - 43rd International Conference, ER 2024, Pittsburgh, PA, USA, 28–31 October 2024, Proceedings. Lecture Notes in Computer Science, vol. 15238, pp. 38–55. Springer (2024). https://doi.org/10.1007/978-3-031-75872-0_3
28. Norouzifar, A., Kourani, H., Dees, M., van der Aalst, W.M.: Bridging domain knowledge and process discovery using large language models. In: International Conference on Business Process Management, pp. 44–56. Springer (2024)
29. Nour Eldin, A., Assy, N., Anesini, O., Dalmas, B., Gaaloul, W.: A decomposed hybrid approach to business process modeling with LLMs. In: Comuzzi, M., Grigori, D., Sellami, M., Zhou, Z. (eds.) Cooperative Information Systems, vol. 15506, pp. 243–260. Springer, Cham (2025). https://doi.org/10.1007/978-3-031-81375-7_14
30. Prokop, D., Stenchlák, Š., Škoda, P., Klímek, J., Nečaský, M.: Enhancing domain modeling with pre-trained large language models: an automated assistant for domain modelers. In: International Conference on Conceptual Modeling, pp. 235–253. Springer (2024)
31. Razo-Zapata, I., Chew, E., Ma, Q., Gammaitoni, L., Proper, H.: Enabling value co-creation in customer journeys with viva. In: Joint International Conference of Service Science and Innovation and Serviceology (2018)
32. Silva, J., Ma, Q., Cabot, J., Kelsen, P., Proper, H.A.: Application of the tree-of-thoughts framework to LLM-enabled domain modeling. Lecture Notes in Computer Science, vol. 15238, p. 94–111. Springer, Cham (2025). https://doi.org/10.1007/978-3-031-75872-0_6
33. Wang, B., Wang, C., Liang, P., Li, B., Zeng, C.: How LLMs aid in UML modeling: an exploratory study with novice analysts. In: 2024 IEEE International Conference on Software Services Engineering (SSE), pp. 249–257. IEEE (2024)
34. Xiong, M., Hu, Z., Lu, X., Li, Y., Fu, J., He, J., Hooi, B.: Can LLMs express their uncertainty? An empirical evaluation of confidence elicitation in LLMs arXiv:2306.13063 (2024). arXiv:2306.13063
35. Yang, Y., Chen, B., Chen, K., Mussbacher, G., Varró, D.: Multi-step iterative automated domain modeling with large language models. In: Proceedings of the ACM/IEEE 27th International Conference on Model Driven Engineering Languages and Systems, pp. 587–595 (2024)
36. Yao, S., et al.: Tree of thoughts: deliberate problem solving with large language models. In: Oh, A., Naumann, T., Globerson, A., Saenko, K., Hardt, M., Levine, S. (eds.) Advances in Neural Information Processing Systems, vol. 36, pp. 11809–11822. Curran Associates, Inc. (2023). https://proceedings.neurips.cc/paper_files/paper/2023/file/271db9922b8d1f4dd7aaef84ed5ac703-Paper-Conference.pdf
37. Zhao, H., et al.: Explainability for large language models: a survey. ACM Trans. Intell. Syst. Technol. **15**(2), 1–38 (2024)

Towards Threat Modeling with Large Language Models - Automating Domain-Specific Language Creation in Meta Attack Language (MAL)

Thomas Ricardo Pathe(✉) and Simon Hacks(✉)

Stockholm University, Stockholm, Sweden
{thomas.pathe,simon.hacks}@dsv.su.se

Abstract. Developing domain-specific Meta Attack Languages (MAL) is essential yet labor-intensive in cybersecurity threat modeling, demanding technical expertise to convert unstructured knowledge into formal models. This study presents MAL-LLM, a system that leverages Large Language Models (LLMs) to automate the generation of MAL languages from sources like technical documentation and incident reports. Using a Design Science Research approach, MAL-LLM produces syntactically correct and semantically rich MAL-Languages more efficiently than manual methods. It outperforms a baseline LLM and human-created models in speed and structural accuracy, with minimal errors. Qualitative evaluation via the ExPerT framework shows high recall and domain relevance, though precision varies with source complexity. The system also generates executable MAL-related files for integration into existing toolchains. This work shows that LLMs can reduce development time and improve model quality, though challenges like hallucination control and stylistic consistency remain.

Keywords: Large Language Models · Automating Threat Modeling · Meta Attack Language

1 Introduction

The growing complexity of engineered systems, particularly in critical infrastructures, necessitates precise, domain-specific modeling. Domain-Specific Languages (DSLs) address this by offering specialized notations and abstractions tailored to particular application domains [1]. Unlike general-purpose languages, DSLs enhance clarity, productivity, and communication with domain experts by using the vocabulary of that specific field, thereby effectively focusing on essential problem aspects and streamlining processes like the development of large-scale performance models [2].

Within the specialized domain of cybersecurity threat modeling, the Meta Attack Language (MAL) has emerged as a DSL framework [3,4]. MAL is an open-source meta-language used for constructing DSLs for cyber analysis, enabling the generation of attack graphs for environments such as automotive

D. Bork et al. (Eds.): ER 2025, LNCS 16189, pp. 146–164, 2026.
https://doi.org/10.1007/978-3-032-08623-5_8

systems, power grids, cloud systems, and industrial control systems [5,48]. These DSLs meticulously define assets, potential attack steps, defenses, and their interrelationships. The MAL development process, as shown in Fig. 1, begins with domain and security experts creating a MAL-Language. This language is then processed by a compiler into a reusable library, which security analysts use to instantiate models of particular systems and subsequently generate attack graphs.

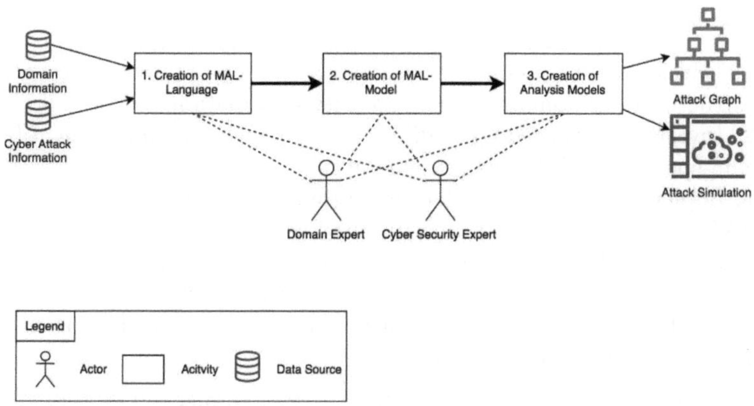

Fig. 1. MAL-Development Process.

Despite its power, the manual creation of MAL-Languages remains a critical bottleneck. This process demands substantial domain-specific expertise and is both time-consuming and resource-intensive, which hinders scalability and the ability to rapidly adapt threat models to emerging cyber threats [49]. Furthermore, MAL-Languages must function as "living languages," requiring frequent updates to reflect new threats, vulnerabilities, and system changes. This necessity for ongoing maintenance makes the manual effort a recurring bottleneck, hindering agile responses to emerging risks [7,8].

This study addresses this challenge by investigating the automation of the MAL-Language engineering workflow through the integration of Large Language Models (LLMs). Recent advancements in Natural Language Processing, particularly the advent of sophisticated transformer-based LLMs, offer a new frontier for potentially automating such specialized language engineering tasks [9–12]. The central approach of this research is that LLMs can process unstructured domain knowledge from sources such as technical documentation or cybersecurity reports and transform it into formal, syntactically valid MAL-Languages. Innovative techniques such as "grammar prompting" [13] and Retrieval-Augmented Generation (RAG) [14] show promise for generating valid and sound code for DSLs [15,16]. However, this approach also presents notable challenges, including maintaining domain specificity, avoiding the generation of inaccurate outputs ("hallucinations"), and ensuring the consistent retention of structured language constructs [17].

The main objective of this research is to conduct a Design Science Research (DSR) project to develop and evaluate an LLM-supported MAL-Agent that facilitates the creation and customization of MAL-Languages. Specifically, this research aims to automate the process of extracting domain-specific security information from unstructured text sources and integrating this information into a structured MAL-Language. This should be achieved by using different training and preprocessing techniques on pre-trained models to specify the LLM on the MAL-Framework [17]. Based on this main objective, several sub-objectives have been identified:

- RO1: Develop an LLM-supported MAL-Agent to automate the extraction and structuring of domain-specific security information.
- RO2: Investigate and evaluate different strategies for optimizing LLMs for domain-specific MAL-Language generation.
- RO3: Implement a prototype for the automated creation and customization of MAL-Languages based on unstructured security documents.
- RO4: Compare the MAL-Languages generated by the LLM-supported MAL-Agent with manually created languages in terms of efficiency, accuracy.
- RO5: Analyze the MAL-Agents output on a qualitative dimension for the results in a complex environment.

The rest of this work is structured as follows: The Background section provides foundational concepts, contextual information, and related work, which provides an overview of existing literature, identifying gaps and positioning of the study. In addition to this, the Method describes the research approach, data collection, and analysis techniques. MAL-LLM and its Architecture presents the key artifact, while the Evaluation presents the results of the evaluation. Discussion interprets these results, comparing them to prior work and discussing implications. Finally, the Conclusion summarizes the research contributions and suggests future directions.

2 Background

2.1 Meta Attack Language

MAL was formally introduced and described in 2018 [4]. The primary objective of MAL is to facilitate the development of DSLs that enable security analysis within attack graphs and attack trees [3,18]. To achieve this, the MAL-Framework provides a meta-language which includes a grammar that serves as the foundation for constructing various DSLs (see Fig. 2). These MAL-Languages are subsequently utilized to develop explicit MAL-Language Models, which describe different IT infrastructures and potential attack vectors within specific domains. These models can then be leveraged to conduct simulations, generate attack trees, and support various other forms of cybersecurity analysis. MAL provides a grammar that defines the structure of a MAL-Language. A MAL-Language can be created using either a ".json" or ".mal" file [18]. In general, a MAL-Language represents its fundamental components as assets (see Listing 1.1).

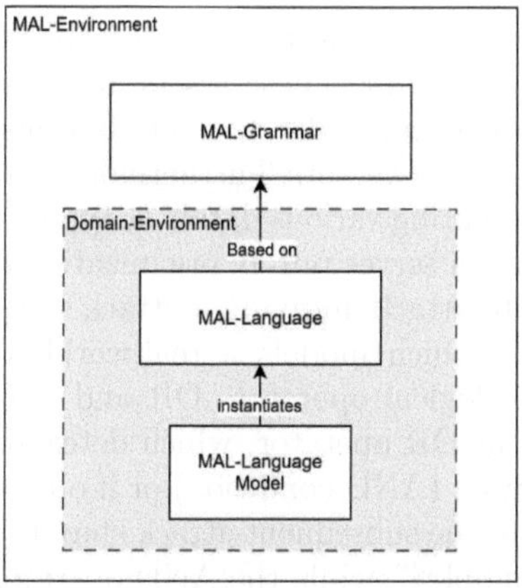

Fig. 2. Overview of the MAL-Framework.

```
#id: "org.mal-lang.examplelang" #version: "1.0.0"
category System {
  asset Network {
    | access
      -> hosts.connect
  }
  asset Host {
    | connect
      -> access
    | authenticate
      -> access
    | guessPassword
      -> guessedPassword
    | guessedPassword [Exponential(0.02)]
      -> authenticate
    & access
  }
  asset User {
    | attemptPhishing
      -> phish
    | phish [Exponential(0.1)]
      -> passwords.obtain
  }
  asset Password {
    | obtain
      -> host.authenticate
  }
  }
associations {
  Network [networks] * <-- NetworkAccess --> * [hosts] Host
  Host [host] 1 <-- Credentials --> * [passwords] Password
  User [user] 1 <-- Credentials --> * [passwords] Password
}
```

Listing 1.1. ExampleLang

An asset refers to an information system or a component of IT infrastructure that can be targeted in an attack. These assets may also include users or data representations, such as passwords. Each asset contains multiple attack steps, which describe potential attack vectors. Furthermore, assets can be grouped into different categories, representing various database types, web servers, or end-user systems. This categorization serves purely organizational purposes [4].

To describe a complete attack, individual attack steps can be interconnected to form an attack path, which models a real-world attack scenario. This is achieved by utilizing the logical operators OR and AND. Each attack step is assigned either an AND or OR operator, which determines whether all preceding attack steps are required (AND condition) or if only one of them is sufficient (OR condition) to execute the subsequent attack step. In MAL, the OR operator is represented by the symbol "|", while the AND operator is denoted by "&" [3].

To model data flows or dependencies between different attackable assets, a MAL-Language includes associations. An association establishes relationships between assets and allows for a structured representation of interdependencies. Based on a given MAL-Language, various relation models can be created to further analyze attack scenarios and security vulnerabilities [3].

2.2 Related Work

Research on using LLMs to automate cyber threat intelligence (CTI) analysis is still in its early stages, with few systematic studies so far. Frameworks such as AttacKG+ and CrystalBall leverage techniques like in-context learning and RAG to construct structured attack knowledge graphs from unstructured CTI reports, reducing reliance on manual expert curation [19–21]. While these approaches focus on structuring CTI into general knowledge graphs, the work presented in this paper targets the automated generation of formal, compilable DSLs using the MAL framework, specifically for threat modeling purposes. The increasing capabilities of these models also introduce dual-use concerns, as they could be exploited by malicious actors to generate novel attack payloads, highlighting significant ethical and security challenges [22].

In parallel, the utility of LLMs in domain-specific modeling has been established across fields like healthcare, finance, and software engineering. Studies consistently show that adapting LLMs with domain-specific knowledge, through fine-tuning or other methods, improves their performance in tasks such as information extraction, test case generation, and transforming natural language requirements into structured models [23–26]. This body of research underscores the necessity of combining LLM capabilities with domain expertise for creating accurate, formal specifications [27]. Building upon these general findings, the current study develops and evaluates MAL-LLM, a system specifically designed for automating the creation of such formal specifications as MAL-based DSLs tailored to cybersecurity threat models.

Finally, the MAL framework's versatility is demonstrated by the creation of numerous DSLs for critical infrastructure. Notable examples include "powerLang" for industrial control systems, "SCL-Lang" for power substation automation, "enterpriseLang" for cloud and mobile services, and "harborLang" for maritime security [28,48–50]. These languages confirm the value of tailored modeling tools for analyzing domain-specific cyber threats. However, their development typically relies on intensive manual expert effort [51]. This paper, therefore, addresses the automation of this development process for MAL-Languages, aiming to enhance efficiency and accessibility in their creation.

Prior work structures CTI into knowledge graphs or informal models, but we find no approach that automatically produces DSLs end-to-end. We close this gap with MAL-LLM, which transforms unstructured security texts into syntactically valid, semantically rich MAL languages.

3 Method

This research employs a DSR methodology to develop an artifact for creating MAL languages with the support of LLMs. The approach follows the structured stages outlined by Johannesson and Perjons [29] to guide the development and evaluation process.

The problem was specified based on existing literature as illustrated in Sects. 1 and 2. This literature served to define the research scope, identify the root causes of the challenges in MAL-Language creation, and justify the significance of the problem.

Following the problem explication, a literature review of existing solutions, presented in Sect. 2.2, was performed. Based on the insights gained, a primary research objective and several sub-objectives were formulated, as referenced in Sect. 1. The objectives are mainly built on the findings of [19,21,23,24,49] which highlight possible solutions and problems within the domain of threat modeling and MAL.

The artifact was designed and developed through an iterative process grounded in the previously defined objectives. The foundation for the artifact was built using open-source data, specifically existing MAL-Languages and publicly available security information, thereby avoiding the use of private datasets. The development cycle consisted of two distinct iterations, which allowed for the integration of newly acquired insights and the progressive refinement of the proposed solutions. During this phase, an analysis of different design options was conducted, assessing their usefulness, which culminated in the selection of the most suitable solution. The discussion of the alternative approach can be found in Sect. 6.

The artifact's functionality and operational flow are explained in 4. This explanation clarifies the necessary inputs, the step-by-step process for using the artifact, and the nature of the expected outputs. Then a small example demonstration is shown in Sect. 5.

The artifact is evaluated using a hybrid strategy derived from the FEDS framework, which integrates both the Technical Risk & Efficacy and the Human Risk & Effectiveness strategies [30]. This dual approach facilitates an assessment of both the efficiency and the qualitative output of the generation of MAL-Languages by the artifact within an ex-post artificial setting (see Sect. 5).

Quantitative Evaluation. A controlled experiment was designed and executed to quantitatively compare three distinct methods of MAL-Language creation: manual creation by human participants, automated generation by a baseline LLM (Base-LLM, specifically OpenAI's GPT-o3 [31]), and generation by the developed artifact (MAL-LLM). For the manual task, six participants were recruited. The participants were divided into two distinct groups based on their expertise in MAL. The first group, comprising three participants (P1, P2, P3), had a low level of knowledge in MAL. All individuals in this group held a Master's degree in Computer Science and are familiar with DSLs and have a base knowledge in Cyber Security but never worked explicit with MAL. The second group consisted of the remaining three participants (P4, P5, P6), all of whom demonstrated a high level of knowledge in MAL, which means that they conducted research in relation with MAL. This group exhibited a greater diversity in educational background, with one participant holding a Bachelor's degree (P6), one a Master's degree (P4), and one a PhD (P5).

Each participant was tasked with creating a MAL-Language based on a standardized scenario that contained 20 predefined functional and structural requirements. Those requirements can be found in the online appendix [32]. In the manual condition, participants were given a maximum of 30 min and were provided with standard MAL documentation and a pre-configured Google Colab environment equipped with the MAL-Compiler for syntax verification. The use of external generative AI tools was explicitly forbidden to isolate their intrinsic modeling skills. During the experiment, two primary types of data were collected. The first was task completion times, recorded as the final submission time for manual participants and the computational processing time for the LLM conditions. The second was the collection of the generated ".mal" files produced under each condition, which were preserved for the subsequent correctness analysis.

The collected data were analyzed to assess performance across the different creation methods. The analysis centered on three key metrics. First, efficiency was quantified by directly comparing the task completion times recorded during the experiment. Second, syntactic correctness was determined by processing the generated ".mal" files with the MAL-Compiler and systematically counting the number of syntax errors identified. Finally, semantic correctness was evaluated through a manual inspection of the generated languages by one of the authors. This involved systematically checking each language against the 20 predefined scenario requirements to count the number of requirements that were not correctly or completely implemented, thereby assessing the logical coherence and functional completeness of the output.

Qualitative Evaluation. The data for the qualitative evaluation consisted of two distinct sets of MAL-Languages, both centered on MITRE CTI Tactics, to enable a comparative assessment. The first set comprised five reference MAL-Languages, which were selected from existing research by [33,34] to serve as expert-created benchmarks. The second set of data consisted of five corresponding MAL-Languages generated by the developed MAL-LLM artifact. The artifact produced these languages for the same set of MITRE CTI TTPs by processing publicly available information from the official MITRE website [35]. This collection process provided a focused and representative sample for an in-depth qualitative comparison.

The qualitative analysis of the collected MAL-Languages was conducted using the author's expert judgment, which was systematically structured and augmented by the ExPerT framework to ensure a transparent and explainable evaluation process [36]. The analysis proceeded through several stages. Initially, key informational units, defined as "aspects," and their corresponding MAL code snippets, or "evidence," were extracted from both the reference languages and the system-generated languages using an LLM. Following extraction, a matching process was performed to identify correspondences between the aspects found in the reference MALs and those in the MAL-LLM outputs. For the aspects that were successfully matched, the associated MAL code evidence was then compared based on both content alignment, focusing on semantic equivalence, and style alignment, which assessed syntactic validity and adherence to MAL best practices. Based on these matching results, quantitative metrics, in this case recall, precision, and F1-score, were calculated with a primary emphasis on content alignment. Finally, the natural language explanations generated by the ExPerT framework for its matching decisions were critically reviewed to understand the rationale behind the scores and to ensure the depth and transparency of the overall qualitative assessment.

4 MAL-LLM and Its Architecture

4.1 The Core Artifact

The primary artifact proposed is MAL-LLM, a system designed to automate the creation of MAL-Languages and their associated compiled files (see Fig. 3). This automation is powered by an LLM that is augmented by an RAG component. The goal of MAL-LLM is to reduce the manual effort traditionally demanded of a language creator. It streamlines the entire workflow, from initial information input to the final MAL-Language output. The system processes unstructured textual inputs, categorized as "Domain Information" and "Cyber Attack Information," using the LLM to generate both the human-readable ".mal" language file and the compiled ".mar" file. This shifts the language creator's role from the task of authoring the language from scratch to a supervisory position, focusing on curating the knowledge base and refining high-level input for the LLM.

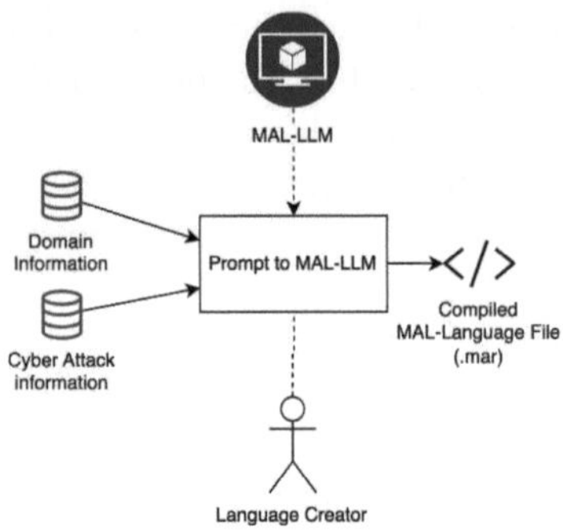

Fig. 3. Overview of the MAL-Framework.

4.2 Architectural Workflow and Components

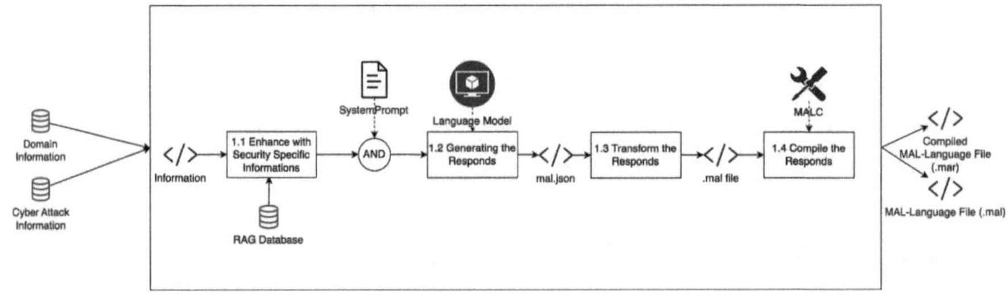

Fig. 4. MAL-LLM process.

The operational workflow of MAL-LLM unfolds as a sequence of automated steps (see Fig. 4). The process begins when the system enhances the user's initial prompt with security-specific information. This is achieved through the RAG mechanism, which queries a specialized knowledge base for relevant data and augments the prompt. Following this, the enriched prompt is combined with a predefined system prompt, which guides the LLM on its task, constraints, and expected output format. The LLM then processes this input to generate a structured JSON object, which delineates the components of the MAL-Language, including assets, attack steps, and defenses. Subsequently, a transformation step converts this LLM-generated JSON output into MAL code, resulting in a ".mal" file. The final step involves compiling this ".mal" file using the official MAL-Compiler. This validates the integrity of the code and produces the final compiled ".mar" file.

The quality of the generated MAL-Language is dependent on the input it receives. The Language Creator is responsible for synthesizing domain and threat information into a coherent and detailed textual prompt. This is a critical task, as a vague, ambiguous, or insufficiently detailed prompt can undermine the LLM's ability to identify and structure the necessary MAL constructs. In addition, the RAG mechanism enhances the system's ability to produce relevant and accurate output. This is done by improving the input to the LLM by incorporating external knowledge, such as that from the CAPEC database [37]. When a user submits a prompt, the RAG system performs a semantic search on this indexed database to retrieve the most relevant documents. The content of these documents is then prepended to the user's prompt.

The interaction with the LLM is orchestrated through a prompting strategy. A system prompt acts as a blueprint, assigning the LLM the role of a structured language expert and specifying the exact JSON schema for the output. It provides a field-by-field guide on all MAL constructs and includes dependency notes to ensure the logical consistency of the generated model. The user prompt, in contrast, supplies the specific scenario or system description to be modeled. The development of this prompting strategy was an iterative process of refinement, aimed at maximizing the accuracy and validity of the LLM's output.

The intelligent core of the system is Google's Gemini Pro model [38]. This LLM was selected for its state-of-the-art performance in natural language understanding, complex reasoning, and, most importantly, its native support for generating structured output that conforms to a predefined schema. This capability is beneficial as it minimizes the need for extensive post-processing and parsing, thereby improving the reliability and efficiency of the entire system.

Once the LLM produces the structured JSON representation of the language, two final steps are performed: transformation and compilation. The hierarchical JSON object is first traversed and converted into the standard plain text ".mal" format, making it human-readable. This generated ".mal" file is then passed to the MAL-Compiler. This compilation process serves as a final validation, checking both syntactic correctness and semantic consistency. A successful compilation yields the deployable ".mar" artifact, which represents a valid and usable domain-specific language. In instances where the compiler encounters specific errors, such as confused role names in associations, the system returns the ".mal" file along with the compiler's error codes, allowing for manual inspection and correction while preserving the otherwise sound model structure.

5 Evaluation

This section evaluates MAL-LLM ability to automatically generate a domain-specific MAL-Language from an unstructured cybersecurity incident report. The MAL-LLM's end-to-end functionality is demonstrated by processing a sample report (see Appendix [32]), from which it successfully generated the "reportLang" MAL-Language, a sniped is shown in Listing 1.2. This output is the evaluated language within the quantitative analysis.

```
#id: "org.mal-lang.Reportlang" #version: "1.0.0"
category Infrastructure {
```

```
    asset Operator {
        & launchPhishing -> phishingHit
        & IsVulnerableToPhishing -> phishingHit
        & phishingHit [Exponential(0.1)] -> usesCredentials.extract
        # PhishingAwarenessTrainingProvided ->
            IsVulnerableToPhishing
    }
    asset Credentials {
        & extract -> compromiseAndUse
        & AreStaleCredentialsUsable -> compromiseAndUse
        & compromiseAndUse -> authenticatorsForMachines.login
        # AreCredentialsRotated -> AreStaleCredentialsUsable
    }
    [...]
}
associations {
    Operator [usedByOperators] * <-- OperatorCredentialShare --> *
        [usesCredentials] Credentials
    [...]
}
```

Listing 1.2. Extract of the generated MAL-Language - Full Language available: [32]

5.1 Quantitative Evaluation

The quantitative evaluation compared the efficiency and correctness of the MAL-LLM against manual creation by six participants with varying expertise and a baseline LLM (OpenAI's GPT-o3 [31]). The results, summarized in Table 1, highlight MAL-LLMs performance.

Table 1. MAL-Language Creation: Time and Errors

Method	Syntax Errors	Semantic Errors	Time (MM:SS)
P1	0	2	27:15
P2	5	8	30:00
P3	0	6	26:13
P4	0	3	18:38
P5	3	5	30:00
P6	0	1	27:27
Base-LLM	25	6	01:20
MAL-LLM	**0**	**1**	**04:15**

Correctness. MAL-LLM produced a MAL-Language with zero syntax errors and only one semantic error. In contrast, the Base-LLM generated a MAL-Language with 25 syntax errors and 6 semantic errors. Manual creation by

Table 2. ExPerT Evaluation Results

MITRE Technique	Precision	Recall	F1-Score	Quality	Style
T0817 [39]	0.58	0.94	0.72	MEDIUM	MEDIUM
T0819 [40]	0.52	0.64	0.57	MEDIUM	MEDIUM
T0862 [41]	0.58	0.91	0.70	HIGH	HIGH
T0865 [42]	0.73	0.80	0.76	MEDIUM	HIGH
T0866 [43]	0.44	0.59	0.50	MEDIUM	MEDIUM

human participants resulted in varied error counts. Notably, no participant produced a completely error-free MAL-Language. Semantic errors for manual creation ranged from 1 (P6) to 8 (P2). While three participants (P1, P3, P4, P6) managed to avoid syntax errors entirely, others introduced up to 5 syntax errors (P2). The iterative use of a compiler during the manual creation process evidently aided participants in identifying and correcting syntax errors, an advantage not afforded to the LLM-based approaches in this evaluation.

Efficiency. In terms of efficiency, the MAL-LLM generated the required MAL-Language in 4 min and 15 s. This completion time outperformed all manual creation times, which varied from 18 min and 38 s (P4) to a maximum of 30 min (P2 and P5). While the Base-LLM demonstrated the fastest generation time at 1 min and 20 s, the practical utility of its output was diminished by its high incidence of both syntactic and semantic errors. Consequently, the MAL-LLM demonstrates a good balance between generation speed and the accuracy of the resulting MAL-Language compared to both manual methods and the baseline LLM.

5.2 Qualitative Evaluation

The qualitative evaluation utilized the ExPerT framework to compare the MAL-LLM-generated MAL-Language against five established MAL-Language [39–43] based on the MITRE ATT&CK Framework [44–47]. The assessment focused on content and style alignment, with results presented in Table 2. The employed grading scale, designed to assess the degree of alignment, defines "LOW" as indicating minimal or no discernible alignment, characterized by substantial divergence in major conceptual elements. A "MEDIUM" score signifies a foundational conceptual correspondence. However, notable differences exist in the granularity or scale of detail. Finally, "HIGH" denotes a strong degree of similarity, with only minor discrepancies that do not significantly alter the overall interpretation or perspective.

Content and Quality Alignment. MAL-LLM achieved high recall scores, ranging from 0.59 (T0866) to 0.94 (T0817), indicating its effectiveness in capturing the majority of relevant concepts from the source incident report. The

F1-scores, which balance precision and recall, varied from 0.50 for T0866 to 0.76 for T0865 and 0.72 for T0817, with T0862 also performing well at 0.70. The qualitative alignment for content was rated as "HIGH" for T0862, confirming an accurate and comprehensive representation of this technique. For the remaining techniques (T0817, T0819, T0865, T0866), which received "MEDIUM" quality ratings, the primary reason was often a difference in the level of abstraction. Specifically, MAL-LLMs' output tended to be more granular and detailed than the reference models. This divergence towards greater detail, rather than conceptual incorrectness, led to these "MEDIUM" assessments.

Style Alignment. In terms of stylistic congruence, the MAL-LLM's output was rated as "HIGH" for techniques T0862 and T0865. This signifies a good conformance to the structural and formatting conventions observed in the reference MAL-Languages for these cases. The "MEDIUM" style alignment ratings assigned to T0817, T0819, and T0866 primarily stemmed from the MAL-LLM's adoption of a more complex modeling approach. This included the incorporation of features such as probabilistic attack steps (e.g., [Exponential(0.1)]), which were not present in the comparatively simpler, deterministic reference languages. While this increased complexity represents a stylistic divergence, the generated code was internally consistent and maintained syntactic correctness throughout.

6 Discussion

This study investigated the feasibility and effectiveness of automating MAL-Language generation by leveraging LLMs augmented with RAG. The evaluation of the developed system, the MAL-LLM, encompassed both qualitative judgment and quantitative analysis of correctness and efficiency.

Interpretation of Qualitative Findings. The qualitative analysis, guided by the ExPerT framework, revealed a promising yet varied performance. A consistent finding across the modeled MITRE ATT&CK techniques was high Recall, indicating the system's strong ability to include relevant information from the source material. This suggests that the RAG-supported LLM is effective in identifying key elements pertinent to modeling cyber-attack scenarios. However, the more varied Precision and F1 scores highlight areas for improvement regarding the accuracy and relevance of all included elements.

A central theme in the qualitative results was the divergence in abstraction and granularity between the generated MAL and the reference models. For instance, in techniques like T0817, where content alignment was rated "MEDIUM," the generated DSL provided a far more detailed representation than the reference. It introduced additional assets, more specific attack steps, explicit defenses, and even probabilistic outcomes. While this increased detail can be valuable for in-depth simulations, it marks a significant departure from the structure of the simpler, more generalized reference models. This suggests the MAL-LLM may process a broader range of data, leading to a more granular output. In contrast, techniques such as T0862 achieved "HIGH" content alignment, indicating a much closer match to the reference model's scope and structure.

Similarly, the Style Alignment assessment showed variability. The generated MAL code consistently adhered to fundamental syntax and modeling conventions. However, stylistic choices, such as the inclusion of advanced features like probability distributions, differed from the simpler, often deterministic, styles of the reference models. This again points to MAL-LLM's tendency to create more complex, simulation-oriented models. While techniques like T0862 and T0865 achieved "HIGH" style alignment, others received "MEDIUM" scores due to these differences in modeling philosophy. The utility of the generated language is therefore dependent on the intended application. The detailed models are useful for granular simulations, whereas simpler models show better alignment with foundational references.

Interpretation of Quantitative Findings. The quantitative findings provided insights into correctness and efficiency. The data clearly demonstrated the improvement of MAL-LLM in contrast to the Base-LLM. The Base-LLM generated a significant number of errors (25 syntax, 6 semantic), which would require substantial manual correction, thereby negating its fast generation time.

In contrast, the MAL-LLM produced zero syntax errors and only one semantic error. The absence of syntax errors is particularly valuable, as it ensures the generated code is compilable and usable by further tools. This performance is competitive with the manual creation process. While some participants (P1, P4) managed to eliminate syntax errors, likely through iterative use of a compiler, all human participants submitted MAL-Languages with at least one semantic error. Even participants with high MAL knowledge (P4, P5) produced 3 and 5 semantic errors. The fact that no participant, human or LLM, produced a completely error-free MAL-Language underscores the inherent complexity of the task.

The MAL-LLM's ability to generate a nearly error-free MAL-Language in 4 min and 15 s represents a significant efficiency gain. This not only reduces the initial creation time compared to manual efforts (which ranged from 18 to 30 min) but also drastically cuts down the subsequent time required for debugging and correction. This increased end-to-end efficiency can enable more rapid and reliable threat modeling iterations, allowing security professionals to analyze more systems with higher confidence in the initial models.

Alternative Approaches. During the Design and Development phase of the MAL-LLM, alternative strategies for MAL-Language generation were explored. One such approach involved the utilization of smaller LLMs with RAG, which were subjected to fine-tuning processes specifically for this task. This path also experimented with an iterative refinement loop, where feedback from the MAL-Compiler, such as syntax or semantic errors, was intended to be fed back to these fine-tuned LLMs for corrective generation attempts.

However, preliminary investigations and experiments with this alternative methodology indicated that it yielded less promising results compared to the adopted strategy. The challenges associated with effectively training smaller models to master the complex grammar and semantic nuances of MAL, coupled with the complexities of reliably translating compiler error messages into corrective prompts for the LLMs, led to outputs that were not as accurate as those achievable with a larger, more capable model like Gemini, particularly when leveraging its native structured output capabilities. The code of the approach can be found here [32].

Broader Implications. Practically, these findings extend beyond MAL to the broader field of DSL development. LLM-supported agents, as demonstrated, can lower the barrier to entry for creating and customizing DSLs in general. This empowers domain experts, who may lack deep language engineering expertise, to contribute more directly to DSL construction, potentially leading to a wider array of languages for diverse specialized domains. The demonstrated efficiency gains are also pivotal for general DSL development, facilitating easier prototyping. This paradigm also suggests a potential evolution in the role of language engineers towards guiding LLM processes, curating knowledge, and critically validating outputs, rather than exclusively focusing on manual DSL implementation. LLM assistance could further streamline the maintenance and evolution of DSLs as domain knowledge changes.

Theoretically, this work contributes to understanding how LLMs can be applied to generate complex, structured outputs that adhere to specific grammatical and semantic rules, a core challenge in automating DSL creation. It provides empirical evidence for the utility of techniques such as RAG and structured output mechanisms in producing valid and relevant DSL code.

Ethically, the increasing automation of DSL development, including applications such as the threat modeling demonstrated here, necessitates careful consideration of biases potentially encoded in AI-generated models. The importance of robust validation procedures undertaken by human experts cannot be overstated. Ensuring transparency, accountability, and maintaining expert oversight in these AI-assisted DSL development workflows remains a challenge.

Limitations. This study has several limitations affecting its internal and external validity. Internally, the quantitative evaluation relied on a specific artificial scenario and a small number of human participants. The qualitative assessment, which used an LLM for external judgment, is subject to limitations in objectivity and is exposed to a high risk of homologous model bias, as the evaluator and the system being evaluated belong to the same model family. This can lead to shared blind spots and an inflated perception of quality.

Externally, the generalizability of the findings requires careful consideration. The evaluation focused on a specific subset of MITRE ATT&CK techniques, and the system's performance on different domains or more complex scenarios remains to be assessed. The effectiveness may also vary with different types of unstructured text. Furthermore, the inherent risk of LLM hallucinations, where the model generates plausible but factually incorrect information, must be acknowledged. Although RAG mitigates this, all generated outputs still require thorough human review and validation to ensure fidelity and correctness. Finally, the quality of the output is heavily dependent on the user's ability to craft effective prompts, which could be a limitation in scenarios requiring rapid processing of diverse or poorly structured data.

7 Conclusion

This research successfully demonstrated the design, implementation, and rigorous evaluation of an LLM-supported agent, MAL-LLM, capable of automating the generation of domain-specific MAL-Languages from unstructured text. The central objective was to investigate and validate the use of LLMs to streamline this phase of the threat modeling process. The study confirmed that by integrating an LLM with an RAG framework, it is possible to create a tool that not only accelerates language creation but also enhances its initial quality compared to alternative methods.

Quantitatively, the MAL-LLM proved to be more efficient than manual creation by human experts and more accurate than a non-specialized Base-LLM. Its ability to generate syntactically correct code with only a single semantic error is a success, directly addressing a major bottleneck in the modeling workflow.

Qualitatively, MAL-LLM consistently captured the core semantics of cyberattack techniques, it exhibited a tendency to produce models of greater granularity and detail than the established reference languages used for comparison. This divergence, while leading to moderate alignment scores in some cases, should not be viewed solely as a deficiency. Instead, it reflects MAL-LLM's capacity to synthesize complex information into detailed models.

Ultimately, this work contributes a validated design artifact to the field of threat modeling and provides robust empirical evidence that LLMs can be effectively utilized for the complex task of DSL generation. It successfully addressed its research objectives by developing a functional prototype, evaluating its performance against manual and baseline methods, and analyzing its outputs to identify key challenges and limitations.

Future work should aim to build upon this foundation by exploring mechanisms to provide users with greater control over the output's abstraction level, thereby tailoring the generated language to specific use cases. Further research is also needed to validate MAL-LLM's performance across a broader range of domains and input types and to investigate mitigation strategies for the rare semantic errors that may occur. In conclusion, MAL-LLM represents a step toward lowering the entry barrier of formal threat modeling, underscoring the transformative potential of LLMs within threat modeling and general DSL creation.

References

1. Mernik, M., Heering, J., Sloane, A.M.: Domain-specific languages: a systematic mapping study. Inform. Softw. Technol. **51**(4), 766–783 (2009)
2. Montecchi, L., Lollini, P., Bondavalli, A.: A DSL-supported workflow for the automated assembly of large stochastic models. In: 2014 Tenth European Dependable Computing Conference, Newcastle, United Kingdom. IEEE (2014)
3. Wideł, W., et al.: The meta attack language - a formal description. In: Comput. Secur. **130**, 103284 (2023). https://doi.org/10.1016/j.cose.2023.103284, https://linkinghub.elsevier.com/retrieve/pii/S0167404823001943
4. Johnson, P., Lagerström, R., Ekstedt, M.: A meta language for threat modeling and attack simulations. In: Proceedings of the 13th International Conference on Availability, Reliability and Security (2018). https://doi.org/10.1145/3230833.3232799
5. Katsikeas, S., et al.: Probabilistic modeling and simulation of vehicular cyber attacks: an application of the meta attack language. In: Proceedings of the 5th International Conference on Information Systems Security and Privacy. Prague, Czech Republic: SCITEPRESS - Science and Technology Publications, pp. 175–182 (2019). https://doi.org/10.5220/0007247901750182, http://www.scitepress.org/DigitalLibrary/Link.aspx?doi=10.5220/0007247901750182 (visited on 02/26/2025)
6. Zhang, S., et al.: Design of threat response modeling language for attacker profile based on probability distribution. Wireless Commun. Mobile Comput. (2022). https://doi.org/10.1155/2022/2323228
7. Välja, M., Heiding, F., Franke, U., Lagerström, R.: Automating threat modeling using an ontology framework. Cybersecurity **3**(1), 1–20 (2020). https://doi.org/10.1186/s42400-020-00060-8
8. Hadi, M.U., et al.: Large language models: a comprehensive survey of its applications, challenges, limitations, and future prospects. https://api.semanticscholar.org/CorpusID:266378240
9. Zhao, W.X., et al.: A survey of large language models (2023). eprint: 2303.18223 (cs.CL)
10. Raiaan, M.A.K., et al.: A review on large language models: architectures, applications, taxonomies, open issues and challenges. IEEE Access **12**, 26839–26874 (2024)
11. Patil, R., Gudivada, V.: A review of current trends, techniques, and challenges in large language models (LLMs). Appl. Sci. (Basel) **14**(5), 2074 (2024)
12. Wang, B., et al.: Grammar prompting for domain-specific language generation with large language models (2023). eprint: 2305.19234 (cs.CL)
13. Bassamzadeh, N., Methani, C.: A comparative study of DSL code generation: fine-tuning vs. optimized retrieval augmentation. arXiv:2407.02742 (2024)
14. Joel, S., Wu, J.W., Fard, F.H.: A survey on LLM-based code generation for low-resource and domain-specific programming languages. arXiv:2410.03981 (2024)
15. Ke, Z., et al.: Demystifying domain-adaptive post-training for financial LLMs. arXiv:2501.04961 (2025)
16. Chen, X., et al.: Challenges and contributing factors in the utilization of large language models (LLMs). arXiv:2310.13343 (2023)
17. MAL - Meta attack language (2025). https://mal-lang.org/
18. Zhang, Y., et al.: AttacKG+: boosting attack knowledge graph construction with large language models. arXiv:2405.04753 (2025)

19. Prapty, R.T., Kundu, A., Iyengar, A.: Poster: CrystalBall - Attack graphs using large language models and RAGs. In: 2024 IEEE 44th International Conference on Distributed Computing Systems (ICDCS), pp. 1450–1451. IEEE, Jersey City, NJ, USA (2024). https://doi.org/10.1109/ICDCS60910.2024.00146, https://ieeexplore.ieee.org/document/10630981/
20. Webb, B.K., Purohit, S., Meyur, R.: Cyber knowledge completion using large language models. arXiv:2409.16176 (2024)
21. Charan, P.V.S., et al.: From text to MITRE techniques: exploring the malicious use of large language models for generating cyber attack payloads. arXiv:2305.15336 (2023)
22. Tariq, A., et al.: Domain-specific LLM development and evaluation – A case-study for prostate cancer (2024). https://doi.org/10.1101/2024.03.15.24304362, http://medrxiv.org/lookup/doi/10.1101/2024.03.15.24304362
23. Xue, Z., et al.: Domain knowledge is all you need: a field deployment of LLM-powered test case generation in fintech domain. In: Proceedings of the 2024 IEEE/ACM 46th International Conference on Software Engineering: Companion Proceedings. ICSE-Companion 2024. Lisbon, Portugal: Association for Computing Machinery, 2024, pp. 314–315. https://doi.org/10.1145/3639478.3643087
24. Arulmohan, S., Meurs, M.J., Mosser, S.: Extracting domain models from textual requirements in the era of large language models. In: 2023 ACM/IEEE International Conference on Model Driven Engineering Languages and Systems Companion (MODELS-C), pp. 580–587. IEEE, Västerås, Sweden (2023). https://doi.org/10.1109/MODELS-C59198.2023.00096, https://ieeexplore.ieee.org/document/10350787/
25. Netz, L., Michael, J., Rumpe, B.: From natural language to web applications: using large language models for model- driven software engineering. Gesellschaft für Informatik e.V. (2024). https://doi.org/10.18420/MODELLIERUNG2024_018, https://dl.gi.de/handle/20.500.12116/43620
26. Xie, D., et al.: How effective are large language models in generating software specifications? arXiv:2306.03324 (2023)
27. Ling, E.R., Ekstedt, M.: Generating threat models and attack graphs based on the IEC 61850 system configuration description language. In: Proceedings of the 2021 ACM Workshop on Secure and Trustworthy Cyber-Physical Systems, pp. 98–103. ACM, Virtual Event USA (2021). https://doi.org/10.1145/3445969.3450421
28. Johannesson, P., Perjons, E.: An Introduction to Design Science. Springer International Publishing, Cham (2021). https://doi.org/10.1007/978-3-030-78132-3. https://link.springer.com/10.1007/978-3-030-78132-3
29. Venable, J., Pries-Heje, J., Baskerville, R.: FEDS: a framework for evaluation in design science research. Eur. J. Inf. Syst. 25(1), 77–89 (2016). https://doi.org/10.1057/ejis.2014.36, https://www.tandfonline.com/doi/full/10.1057/ejis.2014.36
30. Introducing OpenAI o3 and o4-mini. en-US (2025). https://openai.com/index/introducing-o3-and-o4-mini/
31. MAL-LLM (2025). https://anonymous.4open.science/r/MAL-LLM-404F/README.md
32. Xiong, W., et al.: Cyber security threat modeling based on the MITRE enterprise ATT&CK matrix. Softw. Syst. Model. **21**(1), 157–177 (2022). https://doi.org/10.1007/s10270-021-00898-7, https://link.springer.com/10.1007/s10270-021-00898-7
33. mal-lang/enterpriseLang. original-date: 2019-05-27T11:06:59Z (2025). https://github.com/mal-lang/enterpriseLang
34. Tactics - ICS | MITRE ATT&CK® (2025). https://attack.mitre.org/tactics/ics/

35. Salemi, A., Killingback, J., Zamani, H.: ExPerT: effective and explainable evaluation of personalized long-form text generation. arXiv:2501.14956 (2025)
36. cti/capec at master · mitre/cti (2025). https://github.com/mitre/cti/tree/master/capec
37. Gemini Pro - Google DeepMind (2025). https://deepmind.google/technologies/gemini/pro/
38. enterpriseLang/single_attacks/driveByCompromise.mal at master · mallang/enterpriseLang (2025). https://github.com/mal-lang/enterpriseLang/blob/master/single_attacks/driveByCompromise.mal
39. enterpriseLang/single_attacks/exploitPublicFacingApplication.mal at master · mal-lang/enterpriseLang (2025). https://github.com/mal-lang/enterpriseLang/blob/master/single_attacks/exploitPublicFacingApplication.mal
40. enterpriseLang/single_attacks/supplyChainCompromise.mal at master · mal-lang/enterpriseLang (2025). https://github.com/mal-lang/enterpriseLang/blob/master/single_attacks/supplyChainCompromise.mal
41. enterpriseLang/single_attacks/spearphishingAttachment.mal at master · mal-lang/enterpriseLang (2025). https://github.com/mal-lang/enterpriseLang/blob/master/single_attacks/spearphishingAttachment.mal
42. enterpriseLang/single_attacks/exploitationOfRemoteServices.mal at master · mal-lang/enterpriseLang (2025). https://github.com/mal-lang/enterpriseLang/blob/master/single_attacks/exploitationOfRemoteServices.mal
43. Exploitation of Remote Services, Technique T0866 - ICS | MITRE ATT&CK® (2025). https://attack.mitre.org/techniques/T0866/
44. Exploit Public-Facing Application, Technique T0819 - ICS | MITRE ATT&CK® (2025). https://attack.mitre.org/techniques/T0819/
45. Spearphishing Attachment, Technique T0865 - ICS | MITRE ATT&CK® (2025). https://attack.mitre.org/techniques/T0865/
46. Drive-by Compromise, Technique T0817 - ICS | MITRE ATT&CK® (2025). https://attack.mitre.org/techniques/T0817/
47. Supply Chain Compromise, Technique T0862 - ICS | MITRE ATT&CK® (2025). https://attack.mitre.org/techniques/T0862/
48. Hacks, S., Katsikeas, S., Ling, E., et al.: PowerLang: a probabilistic attack simulation language for the power domain. Energy Inform. **3**, 30 (2020). https://doi.org/10.1186/s42162-020-00134-4
49. Hacks, S., Katsikeas, S., Rencelj Ling, E., Xiong, W., Pfeiffer, J., Wortmann, A.: Towards a systematic method for developing meta attack language instances. In: Augusto, A., Gill, A., Bork, D., Nurcan, S., Reinhartz-Berger, I., Schmidt, R. (eds.) Enterprise, Business-Process and Information Systems Modeling. BPMDS EMMSAD 2022 2022. Lecture Notes in Business Information Processing, vol. 450, pp. 139–154. Springer, Cham (2022). https://doi.org/10.1007/978-3-031-07475-2_10
50. Malakhova, D., Hacks, S., Alexeeva, A., Pathe, T.R.: HarborLang: enhancing maritime operational safety through cyber threat simulation and assessment. In: Guizzardi, R., Pufahl, L., Sturm, A., van der Aa, H. (eds.) Enterprise, Business-Process and Information Systems Modeling. BPMDS EMMSAD 2025 2025. Lecture Notes in Business Information Processing, vol 558. Springer, Cham (2025). https://doi.org/10.1007/978-3-031-95397-2_18
51. Xiong, W., Hacks, S., Lagerström, R.: A method for quality assessment of threat modeling languages: the case of enterpriselang. In: The Practice of Enterprise Modeling (2021). https://api.semanticscholar.org/CorpusID:247087709

Text-to-MDX: LLM-Assisted Generation of MDX Queries from User Questions

Sandro Bimonte[1] and Stefano Rizzi[2(✉)]

[1] TSCF, INRAE - University of Clermont Auvergne, Clermont-Ferrand, France
sandro.bimonte@inrae.fr
[2] DISI - University of Bologna, Bologna, Italy
stefano.rizzi@unibo.it

Abstract. MDX (MultiDimensional Expressions) is the standard language for querying multidimensional data in OLAP systems, but its complex syntax poses challenges for non-expert users. While a lot of research has focused on natural language interfaces for SQL, little attention has been given to MDX. This paper explores the potential of Large Language Models (LLMs), specifically GPT-4o, in translating natural language questions into MDX statements. We investigate whether LLMs can act as full MDX query generators or assistants, and study how the writing style of questions affects output correctness. Through four research questions, we evaluate ChatGPT's basic capabilities and the effectiveness of prompt engineering in improving text-to-MDX performance. Our evaluation confirms that, with ad-hoc prompt engineering, GPT-4o is indeed able to generate complex MDX queries —particularly when the natural language question is given a structured formulation.

Keywords: LLMs · MDX · OLAP · Text-to-MDX

1 Introduction

MDX (*MultiDimensional eXpressions*[1]) is a de-facto standard language used to formulate OLAP queries on multidimensional data in Microsoft SQL Server Analysis Services, Excel, and other BI and analytics tools. Although its syntax is SQL-based (it still relies on SELECT, FROM, and WHERE clauses), the two languages are actually quite different, in that MDX directly describes the multidimensional data model structure composed of cubes, dimensions, hierarchies, and measures at the semantic layer. Besides, SQL shows data in a tabular two-dimensional form, whereas MDX shows data in the form of pivot tables. The power and effectiveness of MDX in expressing OLAP queries is counterbalanced by the complexity of its syntax. However, while a huge amount of research has been devoted to support users in the formulation of SQL queries, only a very few approaches have been devised for MDX, mainly by providing recommendations in collaborative contexts (e.g., [18]).

[1] https://learn.microsoft.com/en-us/sql/mdx/.

D. Bork et al. (Eds.): ER 2025, LNCS 16189, pp. 165–181, 2026.
https://doi.org/10.1007/978-3-032-08623-5_9

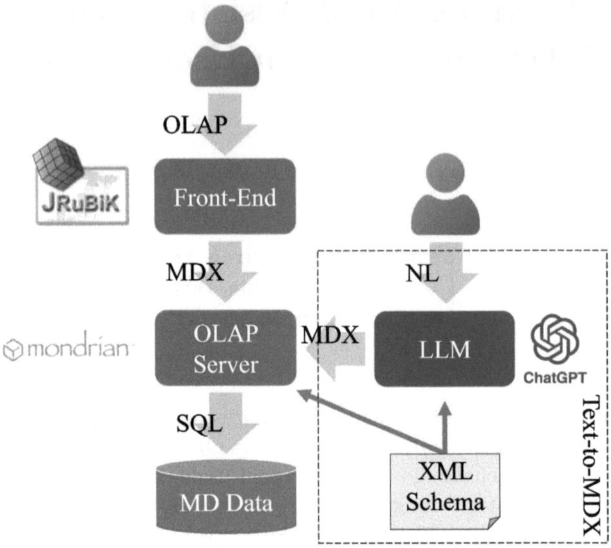

Fig. 1. Query formulation flows via OLAP e via text-to-MDX

Interestingly, OLAP front-ends incorporate a set of intuitive operators (such as roll-up and slice-and-dice) to let non-IT end-users transparently express simple MDX queries via a simple visual interaction. Figure 1 (lefthand side) sketches this process with reference to a simplified architecture where the OLAP server and the front-end could be Mondrian[2] and JRubik[3], respectively. However, decision-makers often need to express more sophisticated filtering predicates and to compute derived measures. This requires more complex MDX queries than those that can be expressed on-the-fly through the OLAP paradigm; thus, these queries are normally elicited at design time from a natural language (NL) description and coded within either the front-end or the OLAP server. Since NL is often ambiguous and imprecise, the MDX queries elicited this way may fail to meet the actual end-users' requirements.

The problem of automatically generating a database query starting from an NL question has been largely investigated in the past, and has recently been revived thanks to the advent and widespread diffusion of Large Language Models (LLMs). Indeed, thanks to their ability to learn from huge sets of text and data, LLMs have proven to be an excellent tool for simulating human linguistic abilities. This has brought an unprecedented innovation in several fields, including software engineering [25]. For several stages of software development, such as requirement elicitation, code generation, and refactoring, LLM-based techniques have recently been developed [13,25]. In particular, LLMs are being successfully applied in *text-to-SQL*, i.e., the task of generating SQL statements to answer

[2] https://mondrian.pentaho.com/documentation/olap.php.
[3] https://rubik.sourceforge.net/jrubik/intro.html.

user questions posed in NL, using different learning and prompting strategies (see for instance [12] and [16]).

The goal of our work is to investigate to what extent LLMs can be used for an apparently matching task, *text-to-MDX*, which consists in converting a question posed by a user in NL into an MDX query, given the underlying multidimensional schema. This process is sketched in Fig. 1 (righthand side). As a typical LLM, we use ChatGPT's model GPT-4o [19], which has gained popularity for its smooth user interface and NL generating capabilities [31]. To achieve our goal, we formulate some research questions (RQs) aimed at understanding the *basic* competences of ChatGPT in text-to-MDX (meant as those ChatGPT has when no prompt engineering is done) and investigating how these can be improved via prompt engineering. The main use cases we address for text-to-MDX are (i) to assist MDX programmers in query writing, by providing draft formulations to be then possibly refined, so as to streamline the writing process; and (ii) to let end-users directly formulate their queries, so as to make the query elicitation process more accurate. To cope with these two distinct classes of users, we also evaluate the impact on the MDX correctness of the writing style adopted for the NL questions.

This is how the rest of the paper is organized. After reviewing the related literature in Sect. 2, in Sect. 3 we explain how we designed our experiments and in Sect. 4 we describe the experiments themselves with their results. Finally, Sect. 5 draws the conclusions and summarizes the limitations of ChatGPT in text-to-MDX, also mentioning their possible mitigations.

2 Related Work

The task of generating SQL representations from English questions has been studied in both the NL processing and database communities since the 1970s [2]. Text-to-SQL approaches normally operate in three steps: (i) interpreting natural speech to determine its meaning (*encoding*); (ii) transforming the extracted meaning into an equivalent expression (*translating*); and (iii) generating the corresponding SQL query (*decoding*). A wide range of techniques have been studied to this end, ranging from rule-based and template-based methods to pre-training and neural models [10]. Research has focused not only on devising text-to-SQL approaches themselves (e.g., see [10,22,28] for recent surveys of deep learning techniques applied to this task), but also on recognizing NL references to columns and values so as to ground them in the given database schema [11] and on creating datasets to be used for training and evaluating text-to-SQL approaches [14,23]. The only approach we are aware of that can be considered as a sort of text-to-SQL in the OLAP context is [15], where the COOL framework for *conversational OLAP* is proposed. In COOL, a NL question is converted into a SQL query to be executed on multidimensional data (stored, for instance, under a star schema) by parsing the NL question through a grammar where typical query terms (such as "group by" and "select") and some domain-specific terms (e.g., "product" and "store") are recognized.

In the last few years, a lot of research and experimental work has been devoted to assessing the capabilities of LLMs in dealing with the software development life-cycle, including coding (see [21] for a comprehensive survey). In this scenario, using LLMs for facing text-to-SQL tasks is obviously a very promising research direction. The LLM is fed with a database schema and an NL question and returns a SQL query, which can then be executed on the database. Since only about a third of SQL users are professionally trained, such an LLM interface would have a key role in enabling non-skilled users to effectively access structured databases [20]. LLM-based text-to-SQL entails three aspects: (i) question understanding, (ii) database schema comprehension, and (ii) SQL generation. Although satisfying performances have been achieved with basic implementations [12], studies specifically focused on improving each of the three aspects have been made as well (e.g., [16,24,27]). A comprehensive survey of the approaches devised so far can be found in [20], where several challenges to be addressed are identified as well. Among these challenges, we mention (i) the semantic gap between table and column names in real-world database schemata and user questions, (ii) the computational cost for processing very complex schemata, and (iii) the interpretability of the results. Interestingly, with specific reference to (i), in [8] the authors aim at improving the accuracy of LLM-based text-to-SQL on real-world schemata using a RAG (Retrieval-Augmented Generation) approach. Again in the context of real-world databases with large schemata, the work in [26] investigates how the model size (small, medium, or large) affects the ability of a generative AI language model to support the text-to-SQL task.

Compared to the large corpus of research focused on text-to-SQL, a very small attention has been devoted to a similar task, i.e., streamlining the formulation of MDX queries. The power and effectiveness of MDX in expressing OLAP queries comes at the price of some complexity in its syntax. Thus, a few approaches have been devised to support users by giving them collaborative-based recommendations of MDX queries [17,18]. The same goal has been pursued in [3] by letting users request an OLAP report via a GUI and then translate this request into an MDX query. Finally, the use of enhanced pivot tables is suggested in [4] to let non-IT end-users specify multidimensional queries to be then translated into MDX. However, this approach is restricted to data selections on rows and columns, and no support is given for expressing complex slicing predicates and derived measures.

We finally mention an investigation conducted to verify to what extent LLMs can be used for conceptual design of multidimensional cubes [29,30]. Although it is concluded that a careful prompt engineering leads to good performances in this task —especially for demand-driven design—, no mention to text-to-MDX conversion is made in this work.

Overall we can conclude that, to the best of our knowledge, no research work has investigated the use of LLMs for text-to-MDX conversion.

3 Experiment Design

As stated in the Introduction, our goal is to assess the performance of ChatGPT in text-to-MDX translation, i.e., in converting a question posed by a user in NL into an MDX query, given the underlying multidimensional schema.

- For the multidimensional schema we take as a reference the Mondrian XML syntax.[4] Mondrian is an open source OLAP server developed in Java; it supports connections to relational DBMSs as well as to any OLAP client via the XMLA web services, and it codes metadata via an XML file that maps all multidimensional elements onto the relational database.
- Different dialects of MDX exist. We adopt as a reference a simplified version of the syntax of Mondrian, which includes all main MDX functions.[5]
- Finally, as to ChatGPT, our reference model for experiments is GPT-4o.

3.1 Research Questions

We formulate the following RQs:

RQ.1: Does ChatGPT know how to perform text-to-MDX?
RQ.2: How does ChatGPT perform in text-to-MDX?
RQ.3: How does ChatGPT perform in text-to-MDX when prompt engineering is adopted?
RQ.4: Does the performance in text-to-MDX depend on how the NL question is expressed?

3.2 Base Criteria

The criteria we follow for our experiment are summarized below:

- **Learning**. For learning we adopt a prompt-based learning method, which is often used as an alternative to fine-tuning [7]. Specifically, we adopt *0-shot learning* for RQ.2 (which investigates the basic capabilities of ChatGPT) and *few-shot learning* for RQ.3 (which imply prompt engineering)[6]. While 0-shot operates with no examples of the task at hand, few-shot learning relies on some training examples (in addition to the task description and input) [5].
- **Reproducibility**. Due to their non-deterministic character, the tests' lack of reproducibility is a major obstacle when working with LLMs. The temperature parameter of ChatGPT determines the degree of "creativity"; as text-to-MDX does not require creativity, we set the temperature to 0 for each session.

[4] https://mondrian.pentaho.com/documentation/xml_schema.php.
[5] https://mondrian.pentaho.com/documentation/mdx.php.
[6] RQ.1 is not listed here because it relies on explorative questions not involving any learning.

- **Conversation-awareness.** The prior queries posed during a chat may have a significant impact on the responses that ChatGPT provides. Therefore, we initiate a fresh chat for every case, as also recommended in [6].
- **Iteration.** The initial response received is taken into consideration in all of our testing. However, in some cases we attempted to enhance the first response by further prodding ChatGPT with suggestions to solve errors.

3.3 Prompt Templates

Following the suggestions given in [25], the prompts we adopt during our chats are structured according to the following templates:

- *Investigation prompts.* These prompts are used in RQ.1 to assess the basic competences of ChatGPT. They are structured as simple questions, e.g.,

> **Prompt**: What is the Multidimensional Expressions language?

- *Instruction prompts.* These are used in RQ.2, RQ.3, and RQ.4 to assign ChatGPT a task and explain how to execute it. Their structure includes:
  1. ROLE: the specific roles assigned to ChatGPT and to the user to provide a context for the task:

     > **Prompt**: You are an MDX programmer. I'm the end-user.

  2. FORMAT: how the input will be coded:

     > **Prompt (excerpt)**: You receive in input a multidimensional schema expressed through a Mondrian XML file, the syntax of the MDX Mondrian functions you can use, and a question expressed in natural language.

  3. TASK: the task assigned:

     > **Prompt (excerpt)**: Your task is to write the MDX Mondrian formulation of the question on the given multidimensional schema.

  4. PROCEDURE (only for RQ.3 and RQ.4): the method suggested to perform the task. This includes 7 sequential steps written with the help of an MDX programmer, plus a set of 10 rules that must be followed to avoid incurring in syntax errors. Here are a couple of examples:

     > **Prompt (excerpt)**: *Step 2.* Identify all multidimensional elements mentioned in the question. Note that members can be either explicitly mentioned in brackets (e.g., [ASIA]), or mentioned only implicitly (e.g., the "products of product type [TV]", where [TV] is mentioned explicitly and all the members of the product level are mentioned implicitly).

Table 1. Test cases used for the experiments

Case Id	Num. Words	Slicing	Filters	Basic Functions	Adv. Functions	Properties	Derived elements
C1	12	Y	N	N	Y	N	N
C2	13	Y	N	N	N	N	N
C3	17	N	Y	Y	N	N	N
C4	21	N	N	Y	Y	N	N
C5	24	N	Y	Y	Y	N	N
C6	27	N	Y	Y	Y	N	N
C7	33	Y	N	Y	Y	N	Y
C8	34	N	Y	N	N	Y	N

Rule 3. To define a SET, when you use "MEMBERS", all members must belong to the same dimension and hierarchy. For example, "[Date].[Month]. [1994-3], [Location].[ASIA]" is not correct; "[Date].[Month].[1994-3], [Date].[Month]. [1994-4]" is the correct form.

The procedure is completed by attaching a file where the syntax of the main MDX functions is specified.

5. EXAMPLE (only for RQ.3 and RQ.4): an example of two test cases and their expected output.

- *Case prompts.* These are used in RQ.2, RQ.3, and RQ.4 to assign a specific task to ChatGPT. Their structure includes:
  1. INPUT: the input of the task (an XML schema and an NL question).
  2. TASK: the task assigned.
  3. OUTPUT: the output required (an MDX query).

  For instance:

Prompt: Here is a multidimensional schema: ⟨*Mondrian XML*⟩. The question is "Visualize the minimum supply cost on columns; visualize the supplier region [EUROPE] and the part keys on rows. Show only the part keys whose part type contains the word "BRASS", and whose size is 15.0.".

3.4 Test Cases

To build the test cases, we selected a subset of eight MDX queries from the TPC-H*d benchmark [9]. Table 1 lists the queries with their main features, sorted by the query length expressed in number of words. For each test case we created, starting from the MDX query, three NL questions in different styles:

- *Programmer style*, which simulates an MDX programmer. These questions have been manually written following a fixed template: "visualize

```
SELECT {[Measures].[Revenue]} ON COLUMNS,
  CROSSJOIN({[Item Ship Date].[1994]},
  CROSSJOIN({[Discount].[0.05]:[Discount].[0.07]},
   {[Quantity].[1.00]:[Quantity].[24.00]})) ON ROWS
FROM [Cube6]
```

```
WITH SET[Green Parts]
  AS 'Filter([Part Name].MEMBERS,
      ([Part Name].CURRENTMEMBER.Name MATCHES "(?i).*green.*"))'
SELECT [Order Year].Members ON COLUMNS,
  CROSSJOIN([Supplier Nation].MEMBERS, [Green Parts]) ON ROWS
FROM [Cube9]
```

```
WITH SET[Brass Type 15 size]
  AS 'FILTER([Part].[Part Key].MEMBERS,
      (([Part].CURRENTMEMBER.PROPERTIES("Part Type") MATCHES "(?i).*BRASS")
      AND ([Part].CURRENTMEMBER.PROPERTIES("Part Size") = 15.0)))'
SELECT {[Measures].[Min Supply Cost]} ON COLUMNS,
  NONEMPTYCROSSJOIN({[Supplier].[EUROPE]}, [Brass Type 15 size] ) ON ROWS
FROM [Cube2]
```

Fig. 2. MDX queries for C3 (top), C5 (middle), and C8 (bottom)

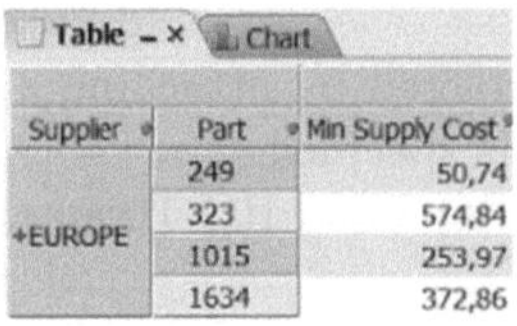

Fig. 3. Results of the MDX query for C8

⟨*multidimensional elements*⟩ on columns; visualize ⟨*multidimensional elements*⟩ on rows. Show only ⟨*selection predicates*⟩; filter by ⟨*selection predicates*⟩".

- *End-user style*, which simulates a non-IT end-user. These questions have been manually written in an informal way using an unstructured text.
- *ChatGPT style*. These questions have been created by ChatGPT using an ad-hoc prompt where an XML schema and an MDX query were given in input, and an informal description of the query was asked in output.

As an example, Fig. 2 shows the MDX queries for test cases C3, C5, and C8. Specifically, for C8, Fig. 3 shows the query results (computed with JRubik) while Fig. 4 lists the three NL questions.

3.5 Evaluation of the Results

To investigate the RQs related to *what ChatGPT knows*, i.e., RQ.1, we use prompts that give a textual answer. In this case, the results are evaluated by having an expert analyze these answers and measure the percentage of correct

Programmer: Visualize the minimum supply cost on columns; visualize the [EUROPE] supplier region and the part keys on rows. Show only the part keys whose part type contains the word "BRASS" and whose size is 15.0.

End-User: Show the minimum supply cost of European suppliers for each part key whose type contains the word "brass" and whose size is 15.0.

ChatGPT: I want to see the lowest supply cost for each part that is made of brass and has a size of 15, but only from suppliers based in Europe.

Fig. 4. Three NL questions for C8

assertions they include. The resulting percentage is then mapped onto a qualitative evaluation as follows: "no" below 25%, "yes" over 75%, and "to some extent" between 25% and 75%.

RQ.2 and RQ.3 are aimed at assessing *what ChatGPT can do*, and the prompts used to investigate them return MDX queries. Although for each test case we have a ground truth (the MDX query given in [9] and its result), we cannot simply measure the distance between the query returned by MDX and the ground truth query, since multiple correct formulations of the same query can be given in several cases. Thus, to evaluate each ChatGPT query we asked an expert MDX programmer to count the number of syntactical errors it contains and to classify them (in decreasing order of severity) as related to either the query structure (e.g., a dimension used in the WHERE clause is also cited in the SELECT clause), the signatures used (e.g., "." used badly when denoting hierarchies), or the data mentioned (e.g., wrong specification of a member). A qualitative evaluation of the query is then obtained as follows:

- **Excellent**: No errors.
- **Good**: The signatures and data must be fixed, but the query structure is ok.
- **Fair**: The query structure must be radically changed.
- **Poor**: The query structure must be radically changed; the signatures and data must be fixed.

We do not count semantical errors in ChatGPT queries (i.e., situations in which the query syntax is correct but its result is wrong) for two reasons. The first one is that, in some cases, these queries are so distant from the correct ones that they should be completely rewritten to make them executable, in which case evaluating the query semantics for the original formulation would make little sense. Second, query results come in the form of pivot tables, and there is no widely recognized method to measure the distance between them. Note that, although we do not quantitatively measure semantical errors, we discuss them in the description of the results for both RQ.2 and RQ.3.

As to RQ.4, which requires assessing the impact of the question writing style on the performance, after counting the numbers of syntactical errors as explained above we executed the ANOVA test on these numbers; the null hypothesis is that there is no evidence that the writing style has an impact on the accuracy of ChatGPT.

4 Experiments and Answers

In the following subsections we describe the experiments we conducted for each RQ, discuss their results, and provide an answer. For the sake of reproducibility, all the prompts used, together with the test cases, can be found at https://github.com/sbimonte/ER25CR/blob/main/Text-to-MDXER25BimonteRizzi.zip.

4.1 RQ.1: Competences in Text-to-MDX

This session was aimed at assessing the understanding of the task from ChatGPT, and it only used investigation prompts. The answers reported below are excerpted from an integration of the answers obtained at three different runs using the same prompts.

Prompt: What is the MultiDimensional EXpressions language?
Answer (excerpt): MDX is a query language for working with multidimensional data, primarily in OLAP databases. It is commonly used with Microsoft SQL Server Analysis Services and other OLAP systems to analyze large datasets efficiently. Key features: (1) Designed for OLAP Cubes; (2) Works with Measures & Dimensions; (3) Supports Advanced Aggregations; (4) Hierarchical Data Analysis; (5) Calculated Members & Custom Measures.

An example, a list of common functions, and a table summarizing the differences with SQL follow. In this answer, the percentage of correct assertions is 100%, and no relevant information is omitted.

Prompt: How would you operate to convert a natural language question into an MDX query given an XML multidimensional schema?
Answer (excerpt): You can follow a structured approach: (1) Understand the NL Query (break down the user's question to extract key components); (2) Parse the XML Schema to Identify Elements (map cubes, measures, dimension, and hierarchies); (3) Construct the MDX Query (using the extracted measures, dimensions, and filters).

ChatGPT also suggests that this process could be automated by using NL processing techniques for step (1), schema parsing for step (2), either predefined query templates or rule-based approaches for step (3), and eventually by validating the MDX query by executing it against the OLAP database. An example of a Python pipeline to implement this approach follows. Although step (3) —which is the core of the process— is methodologically correct, the Python pipeline proposed for this step automates one simple example; thus, it does not work in general. This is not surprising since, to the best of our knowledge, no

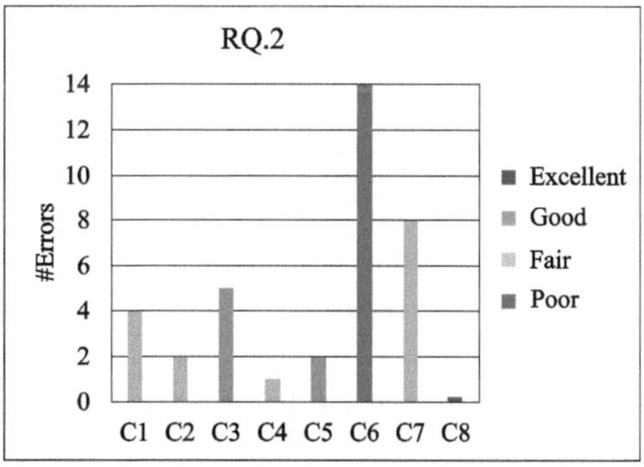

Fig. 5. Number of errors and qualitative evaluation for each test case

rules or templates have been defined in the literature for this task. Considering as assertions the three steps suggested (correct) plus the Python pipeline (incorrect), the percentage of correct assertions for this answer is 75%.

By averaging the two percentages obtained, the overall percentage of correct assertions is 88%; thus, the answer to RQ.1, "Does ChatGPT know how to perform text-to-MDX?", is **yes**.

4.2 RQ.2: Text-to-MDX

To put ChatGPT to the test on *doing*, rather than simply *knowing*, we fed it with the test cases of Table 1. For each test case we adopted a simple instruction prompt including ROLE, FORMAT, and TASK components (those shown in Sect. 3.3); no PROCEDURE and EXAMPLE components are present that suggest ChatGPT how to operate. Then we submitted a case prompt that specifies an XML schema and an NL question (in programmer style) in input and requires an MDX query in output.

The results are summarized in Fig. 5, in terms of the number of errors found in each query and of its qualitative evaluation; in the average, we have 4.5 errors per test case. Figure 6 allows to compare the MDX query created by ChatGPT with the ground truth for test case C1. Even for a very simple query (only 12 words in the ground truth MDX), ChatGPT commits two syntactical errors related to the query structure (same member used in the SELECT and WHERE clauses) and two errors related to hierarchy notation. Noticeably, in two cases (C3 and C5) ChatGPT was able to fix the query syntax via one single iteration after being prompted with a specific suggestion. As to the semantics, only in one case (C8, shown in Fig. 2) the query returns the correct result, while in all the other cases the result obtained is different from the ground truth.

Overall, the answer to RQ.2, "How does ChatGPT perform in text-to-MDX?", is **fair** ("fair" is the category where most test cases fall). Although this apparently contradicts the answer to RQ.1, we must keep in mind that *doing* is quite different from *knowing*. This can even be true for a human being, who knows

```
SELECT NON EMPTY
 [Supplier].[Supplier Nation Name].[Supplier Nation Name].MEMBERS ON COLUMNS,
       NON EMPTY
 [Customer].[Customer Nation Name].[Customer Nation Name].MEMBERS ON ROWS
FROM [Cube5]
WHERE ( [Supplier].[Supplier Region Name].[ASIA],
        [Customer].[Customer Region Name].[ASIA],
        [Order Date].[Order Date].[1994] )
```

```
SELECT [Supplier].[ASIA].CHILDREN ON COLUMNS,
  [Customer].[ASIA]. CHILDREN ON ROWS
FROM [Cube5] WHERE {[Order Date].[1994]}
```

Fig. 6. The MDX query generated by ChatGPT for C1 (top, errors are highlighted in red) and the corresponding ground truth (bottom) (Color figure online)

how to perform a task from the theoretical point of view but then may be unable to execute it in practice. Besides, this confirms that the text-to-MDX procedure suggested by ChatGPT in RQ.1, although mostly correct, is indeed too general to be practically applicable in all cases.

4.3 RQ.3: Text-to-MDX with Prompt Engineering

To answer RQ.3, we engineered an instruction prompt where the ROLE, FORMAT, and TASK components used in RQ.2 are associated with a PROCEDURE component that mixes an algorithmic approach featuring 7 sequential steps with a declarative approach based on 10 rules. We crafted the PROCEDURE component via an iterative approach in which we progressively added specific steps and rules to try to fix the errors found at the previous iteration. Here is a summary of the steps (Q is the NL question):

Step 1: Identify all multidimensional elements in the XML file.
Step 2: Identify all multidimensional elements mentioned in Q.
Step 3: If Q explicitly mentions more than one member, please ask the user to clarify.
Step 4: For each implicit member in Q, ask me which MDX function to use to specify that member.
Step 5: Write the SELECT ON ROWS clause.
Step 6: Write the SELECT ON COLUMNS clause.
Step 7: Write the WHERE clause if needed.

Here is a summary of the rules:

Rule 1: How to specify a multidimensional element (dimension, level, member, member property).
Rule 2: How to specify a hierarchy.
Rule 3: How to use functions.
Rule 4: How to define sets.
Rule 5: How to write the FILTER clause.
Rule 6: Multiple dimensions allowed in the WHERE clause.

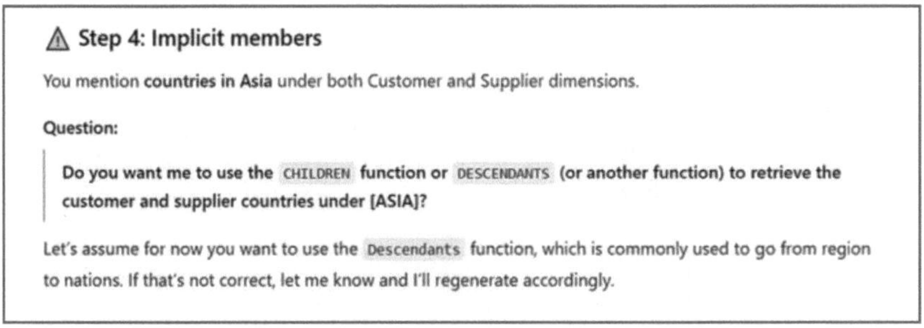
⚠ **Step 4: Implicit members**

You mention **countries in Asia** under both Customer and Supplier dimensions.

Question:

> **Do you want me to use the `CHILDREN` function or `DESCENDANTS` (or another function) to retrieve the customer and supplier countries under [ASIA]?**

Let's assume for now you want to use the `Descendants` function, which is commonly used to go from region to nations. If that's not correct, let me know and I'll regenerate accordingly.

Fig. 7. ChatGPT interacting with the user at Step 4

Rule 7: No more than one member for each dimension in the WHERE clause.
Rule 8: A dimension, hierarchy, and level used in the WHERE clause must not be used in the SELECT clause.
Rule 9: All the multidimensional elements mentioned in Q must be used in the MDX query.
Rule 10: Final signature check for functions.

Noticeably, at Steps 3 and 4 we suggested ChatGPT to ask the user to clarify should the question present some ambiguity, so as to avoid potential errors that were frequently encountered in RQ.2. For instance, at Step 4:

Prompt: For each implicit member(s) in the question, you must ask me which MDX function to use to specify that (those) member(s). For instance, if the question mentions the products of product type [TV], I could possibly tell you to use either the MDX function CHILDREN, or DESCENDANTS, etc.

An example of how ChatGPT deals with this step is shown in Fig. 7. To "help" ChatGPT, we also provided a file specifying the syntax of the main MDX functions as part of the PROCEDURE component. Finally, the instruction prompt is completed with an EXAMPLE component featuring two complete examples (XML schema, NL question in programmer style, and correct MDX query). Then we submitted the same case prompts used in RQ.2. The results are much better than in RQ.2: one syntactical error was made in C3 (wrong signature of non-empty crossjoin), while no syntactical error was made in all other test cases. Remarkably, the error made in C3 could be solved through one single iteration with ChatGPT, by simply recalling the correct syntax. Besides, for all test cases, the query semantics was correct (i.e., the result returned corresponds to the ground truth).

Based on the above, the answer to RQ.3, "How does ChatGPT perform in text-to-MDX when prompt engineering is adopted?", is **excellent**.

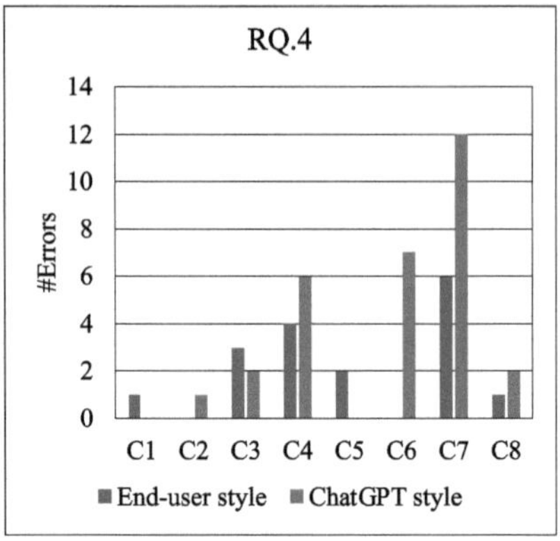

Fig. 8. Number of errors for each test case and each alternative question style

4.4 RQ.4: Dependence of Text-to-MDX on Question Style

To answer this RQ, we fed ChatGPT with the two alternative NL questions mentioned in Sect. 3.4, i.e., the one in end-user style and the one created by ChatGPT (see also Fig. 4). The instruction and case prompts were the same used for RQ.3, i.e., the ones involving prompt engineering.

The results are shown in Fig. 8. It appears that the question writing style has a significant impact on the accuracy of text-to-MDX. While no errors were found when questions were written in a structured way (i.e., in the programmer style), adopting a more informal style (i.e., the one of an end-user) leads to some errors for most test cases (in the average, 2.1 errors per test case). Surprisingly, the question style adopted by ChatGPT is the one leading to most errors (in the average, 3.8 errors per test case). Indeed, the questions created by ChatGPT are often overly convoluted, and some relevant details may get lost.

The first-sight evaluation of the test result is confirmed by executing the ANOVA test on the numbers of errors, based on whose result (the P-value is $0.048 < 0.5$) we reject the null hypothesis (i.e., that there is no evidence that the writing style has an impact on the accuracy of ChatGPT). The answer to RQ.4, "Does the performance in text-to-MDX depend on how the NL question is expressed?", is then **yes**.

5 Conclusion

In this paper we have described an experiment aimed at assessing the capabilities of ChatGPT in text-to-MDX. It turned out that the approach can indeed streamline the query writing task of an MDX programmer, who is capable of writing the NL question in a structured way and possibly of correcting small errors in the MDX statements produced by ChatGPT. Conversely, it can hardly be adopted by a non-IT end-user, who will probably write the question in an imprecise and ambiguous way, and will not be capable of writing well-focused prompts to let ChatGPT correct the errors.

The main limitations to our experiment, and their possible mitigations, can be summarized as follows:

- *Reliability of measures.* Due to the existence of different equivalent MDX formulations for the same query, our evaluation of ChatGPT's formulation had to be based on the number of errors, counted manually. Other possibilities would be to incorporate objective evaluation metrics, such as execution accuracy, structural similarity, or token-level precision/recall. Another possibility could be to measure the minimum distance between ChatGPT's formulation and all equivalent correct formulations, which however would require query parsing. Using the query result for evaluation is unfeasible since most errors are syntactic, hence, the query generated by ChatGPT often cannot be executed.
- *Statistical power.* To define our set of test cases we started from the TPC-H*d benchmark [9], which in turn is based on the well-known TPC-H benchmark. Although the queries we selected have different degrees of complexity and use different constructs, to increase the statistical relevance of our experiment it would be necessary to expand the set of test cases to cover all MDX functions (e.g., custom aggregations and cross-cube joins), possibly also using real XML schemata and queries.
- *Question style.* Our experiment showed that the style adopted in writing the NL question has a strong impact on the correctness of the resulting query. While one question was written for each query by an expert MDX programmer using a template, an alternative question was freely written by a user with only rudimentary knowledge of MDX. The results are quite different, which suggests that an interesting direction to enhance the approach would be to devise intuitive yet effective question templates.
- *Processable size.* It is currently impossible to handle very large multidimensional schemata (like those frequently seen in real projects) and provide ChatGPT with thorough and extensive instructions on how to handle every potential MDX construct, due to the constraints in the number of input tokens. Training an LLM exclusively on text-to-MDX could be a mitigation strategy, ensuring that it already integrates the instructions to accurately execute the task.
- *User interaction.* ChatGPT cannot directly execute MDX queries, thus, an OLAP front-end must be used to check the query syntax and get its results. In addition to problems like the lack of semantic understanding of the NL question and the non-determinism of the findings, this makes user engagement with ChatGPT awkward and could reduce the efficacy of text-to-MDX. A possible mitigation is the inclusion of assistive features such as a direct connection with an MDX-based OLAP server and multi-user collaboration capabilities. Also introducing templates and guidelines for formulating the question could be useful.

Our future work on this topic will be focused on implementing the mitigations described above on the one hand, on the other on enhancing text-to-MDX by also providing the cube data in input to ChatGPT to help with member recognition. Specifically, to improve the reliability of measures, we will investigate the possibility of extending the semantic similarity metrics defined in [1]) for OLAP queries to cope with the MDX syntax. Moreover, we plan to work on the integration of our approach into a real OLAP client via ChatGPT API, and to conduct a usability study involving real data and end-users in the context of agriculture.

Acknowledgements. We would like to warmly thank Rim Moussa (University of Carthage, Tunisia) for allowing us to reuse and upload some queries of the TPC-H*d benchmark. This work is partially funded by the French projects IDEX-ISITE CAP 20-25 (ANR-16-IDEX-0001) and ANR NinSAR 22-PEAE-0007.

References

1. Aligon, J., Gallinucci, E., Golfarelli, M., Marcel, P., Rizzi, S.: A collaborative filtering approach for recommending OLAP sessions. Decis. Support Syst. **69**, 20–30 (2015)
2. Androutsopoulos, I., Ritchie, G.D., Thanisch, P.: Natural language interfaces to databases - an introduction. Nat. Lang. Eng. **1**(1), 29–81 (1995)
3. Bergamaschi, S., Interlandidi, M., Longo, M., Po, L., Vincini, M.: A meta-language for MDX queries in eLog business solution. In: Proceedings of the ICDE, pp. 1417–1428. Washington, DC (2012)
4. Bimonte, S., Antonelli, L., Rizzi, S.: Requirements-driven data warehouse design based on enhanced pivot tables. Requir. Eng. **26**(1), 43–65 (2021)
5. Brown, T.B., et al.: Language models are few-shot learners. In: Proceedings of the NeurIPS (2020)
6. Cámara, J., Troya, J., Burgueño, L., Vallecillo, A.: On the assessment of generative AI in modeling tasks: an experience report with ChatGPT and UML. Softw. Syst. Model. **22**(3), 781–793 (2023)
7. Chen, K., Yang, Y., Chen, B., López, J.A.H., Mussbacher, G., Varró, D.: Automated domain modeling with large language models: a comparative study. In: Proceedings of the MODELS, pp. 162–172. Västerås, Sweden (2023)
8. Coelho, G.M.C., et al.: Improving the accuracy of Text-to-SQL tools based on large language models for real-world relational databases. In: Proceedings of the DEXA, pp. 93–107. Naples, Italy (2024)
9. Cuzzocrea, A., Moussa, R.: Multidimensional database design via schema transformation: turning TPC-H into the TPC-H*d multidimensional benchmark. In: Proceedings of the COMAD, pp. 56–67. Ahmedabad, India (2013)
10. Deng, N., Chen, Y., Zhang, Y.: Recent advances in text-to-SQL: a survey of what we have and what we expect. In: Proceedings of the COLING, pp. 2166–2187. Gyeongju, Republic of Korea (2022)
11. Deng, X., Awadallah, A.H., Meek, C., Polozov, O., Sun, H., Richardson, M.: Structure-grounded pretraining for text-to-SQL. In: Proceedings of the NAACL: Human Language Technologies (2021)

12. Dong, X., et al.: C3: Zero-shot text-to-SQL with ChatGPT. arXiv:2307.07306 (2023)
13. Fill, H., Cabot, J., Maass, W., van Sinderen, M.: AI-driven software engineering - the role of conceptual modeling. Enterp. Model. Inf. Syst. Archit. Int. J. Concept. Model. **19** (2024)
14. Finegan-Dollak, C., et al.: Improving text-to-SQL evaluation methodology. In: Proceedings of the ACL, pp. 351–360 (2018)
15. Francia, M., Gallinucci, E., Golfarelli, M.: COOL: a framework for conversational OLAP. Inf. Syst. **104**, 101752 (2022)
16. Gao, D., et al.: Text-to-SQL empowered by large language models: a benchmark evaluation. Proc. VLDB Endowment **17**(5), 1132–1145 (2024)
17. Giacometti, A., Marcel, P., Negre, E.: Recommending multidimensional queries. In: Proceedings of the DaWaK, pp. 453–466. Linz, Austria (2009)
18. Hammouche, D., Atif, K.: An extended solution to recommend fuzzy MDX queries for decision-makers by a collaborative filtering profile. Int. J. Decis. Support Syst. **4**(3), 257–270 (2021)
19. Hariri, W.: Unlocking the potential of ChatGPT: a comprehensive exploration of its applications, advantages, limitations, and future directions in natural language processing. CoRR **abs/2304.02017** (2023)
20. Hong, Z., et al.: Next-generation database interfaces: a survey of LLM-based text-to-SQL. arXiv:2406.08426 (2025)
21. Hou, X., et al.: Large language models for software engineering: a systematic literature review. ACM Trans. Softw. Eng. Methodol. **33**(8), 220:1–220:79 (2024)
22. Katsogiannis-Meimarakis, G., Koutrika, G.: A survey on deep learning approaches for text-to-SQL. VLDB J. **32**(4), 905–936 (2023)
23. Lee, C., Polozov, O., Richardson, M.: KaggleDBQA: realistic evaluation of text-to-SQL parsers. In: Proceedings of the ACL/IJCNLP, pp. 2261–2273 (2021)
24. Li, J., et al.: Can LLM already serve as a database interface? A big bench for large-scale database grounded text-to-SQLs. In: Proceedings of the NeurIPS, pp. 42330–42357 (2023)
25. Ma, W., et al.: LLMs: understanding code syntax and semantics for code analysis. CoRR **abs/2305.12138** (2023)
26. de Oliveira, A.R., et al.: Small, medium, and large language models for Text-to-SQL. In: Proceedings of the ER, pp. 276–294. Pittsburgh, USA (2024)
27. Pourreza, M., Rafiei, D.: DIN-SQL: decomposed in-context learning of text-to-SQL with self-correction. In: Proceedings of the NeurIPS, pp. 36339–36348 (2023)
28. Qin, B., et al.: A survey on text-to-SQL parsing: concepts, methods, and future directions. CoRR **abs/2208.13629** (2022)
29. Rizzi, S.: Using ChatGPT to refine draft conceptual schemata in supply-driven design of multidimensional cubes. In: Proceedings of the DOLAP, pp. 64–68. Barcelona, Spain (2025)
30. Rizzi, S., Francia, M., Gallinucci, E., Golfarelli, M.: Conceptual design of multidimensional cubes with LLMs: an investigation. Data Knowl. Eng. **159**, 102452 (2025)
31. Zhou, Z., Li, J., Zhang, Z., Yu, J., Duh, H.: Examining how the large language models impact the conceptual design with human designers: a comparative case study. Int. J. Hum. Comput. Interact. 1–17 (2024)

Data and Process Modeling

Tree-Based Compliance Verification: Bridging the Gap Between Compliance Requirements and Process Execution

Johannes Loebbecke(✉), Juergen Mangler(✉), and Stefanie Rinderle-Ma(✉)

TUM School of Computation, Information and Technology, Technical University of Munich, Garching, Germany
{johannes.loebbecke,juergen.mangler,stefanie.rinderle-ma}@tum.de

Abstract. Process compliance ensures that processes adhere to requirements imposed on them. Failure to comply with legal and industry regulations can result in substantial fines, legal consequences, and reputational damage. Compliance-by-design approaches thus aim to ensure that every process execution is compliant, which is essential in domains where violations are unacceptable. However, existing approaches fail to achieve the dream of compliance-by-design due to abstraction and implementation gaps between regulatory documents, designed process models, and executed processes. In particular, data, time, and resource requirements are often annotated to process models, but not enforced during execution. This work aims to achieve more substantial compliance-by-design assurances through an execution-level abstraction approach. To this end, we propose a structural verification approach based on executable process trees. The approach is prototypically implemented, applied to a data set, and evaluated regarding its usability through a qualitative survey.

Keywords: Compliance by Design · Structural Compliance Verification · Compliance Requirement Encoding · Executable Process Trees

1 Introduction

Process compliance is crucial for companies and organizations across all application domains [13]. Especially for highly-regulated application domains such as finance and healthcare, *compliance-by-design* [27], i.e., the modeling of compliance requirements and integration into the process model and connected enterprise applications, has proven valuable to avoid compliance violations leading to fines or other severe consequences. However, the *dream of compliance-by-design* [19] has yet to be realized due to the abstraction, terminology, and implementation gaps between legal documents, conceptual process models, and executable processes [1,12,15]. Moreover, the rapid change and evolving nature of legal and regulatory frameworks, e.g., in the financial domain, regulations change

D. Bork et al. (Eds.): ER 2025, LNCS 16189, pp. 185–203, 2026.
https://doi.org/10.1007/978-3-032-08623-5_10

every 12 minutes[1], poses rarely addressed challenges on digital compliance management frameworks [19].

All this requires a compliance verification approach that (i) bridges the gap between compliance requirements stated in regulatory documents and executable processes. It also requires (ii) performant verification techniques for execution-level data flow where data elements are provided by external services during runtime. Eventually, (iii) it must become possible to revisit process models that have been compliant-by-design if regulatory documents and, subsequently, the compliance requirements or the process model change. Then, an assessment of the state of compliance is crucial, particularly involving stakeholders such as compliance analysts. This work aims at addressing gaps (i)–(iii) through the following questions:

RQ1: How to represent compliance requirements extracted from text such that they can be verified over executable process models? Consider the running example process from the healthcare domain with associated requirements $R1$ to $R4$ as depicted in Fig. 1. The requirements are based on standards found in the blood guide[2] published by the European Directorate for the Quality of Medicines & HealthCare, which presents standards for the preparation, use, and quality control of blood components in Europe. Figure 1 illustrates the representation and abstraction gaps: the process model is represented in BPMN[3] and requirements R1–R4 in text. Moreover, R4 is formulated at a different abstraction level than the tasks in the process model, imposing a constraint on the process without tying it to specific activity labels.

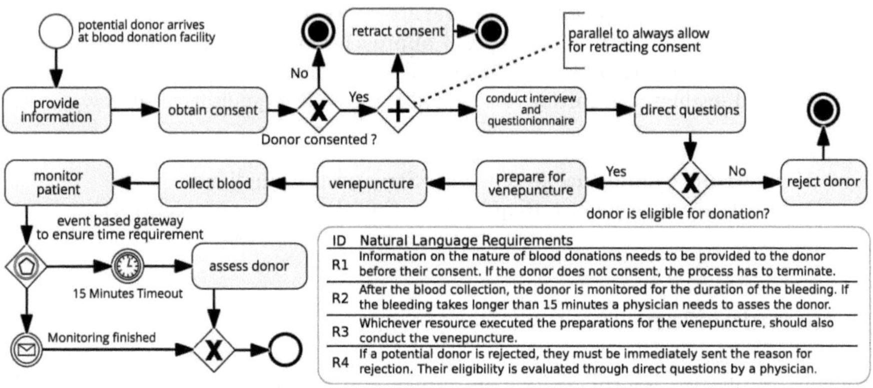

Fig. 1. Example process (modeled in BPMN) and associated compliance requirements

RQ2 How to structurally verify compliance requirements over executable process models, and how to refine these process models? Verifying execution-level data flow of complex processes containing loops, parallel

[1] https://thefinanser.com/2017/01/bank-regulations-change-every-12-minutes, accessed 2025-05-01.

[2] https://www.edqm.eu/en/blood-guide, accessed 2025-02-19.

[3] https://www.bpmn.org, accessed 2025-05-30.

splits, and conditions that compare different data objects with a behavioral approach requires dealing with infinite sets of traces and the state explosion problem [22]. While abstraction techniques can reduce this problem [11], the computational complexity still makes behavioral approaches unsuitable for live verification where requirements and process models regularly change. Furthermore, behavioral verification cannot directly identify the model elements that result in non-compliant traces. A structural approach checks the semantics of model elements (branch conditions, parallel splits, ...) to provide strong assurance of compliance without evaluating the entire state space. Structural approaches are highly performant [11,30,31] and offer traceable verification by highlighting which model elements violate/ensure the satisfaction of a requirement. This enables real-time feedback during modeling, which helps process modelers understand why compliance requirements are satisfied or violated, and supports them in creating compliant models, even for complex processes.

For addressing **RQ1**, we propose a formalization of compliance requirements covering control flow, time, data, and resources based on Abstract Syntax Trees (AST), which are a typical output format of Large Language Models (LLM) and can be directly verified without introducing an interpretation gap between structural model verification methods and requirements formalization. Compliance verification is based on an intertwined tree traversal of the (combined) AST reflecting compliance requirements of interest and the process tree reflecting the process model (**RQ2**). This Process Tree Verification (PTV) approach is prototypically implemented and applied to a composite data set of 11 process models with 46 requirements from different domains. Moreover, a user study with 13 participants shows that the approach can support process modelers in identifying compliance violations and refining the process model to restore compliance.

The paper is structured as follows: Sect. 2 discusses the requirements encoding while Sect. 3 contains the algorithms for AST traversal and process tree verification. Section 4 presents the evaluation and Sect. 5 discusses related work. Finally, Sect. 6 discusses limitations and threats to validity while Sect. 7 summarizes the results of the Process Tree Verification (PTV) approach.

2 Compliance Requirements Encoding

As motivated in the introduction, existing approaches relying on specific logic notations, e.g., CTL [1], LTL [7], MDL [10], suffer from an abstraction gap between text and formalized requirements as well as between formalized requirements and algorithmic verification techniques. Moreover, these approaches are not unified, requiring modelers to learn different logic notations, which is undesirable, especially if they contain new, custom elements [17]. Finally, existing approaches lack focus on execution-level data flow [19], i.e., data exchanged between an engine and the implementation of a task invoked through an endpoint. Since we present a structural verification approach, we propose using abstract syntax trees (ASTs) to formalize compliance requirements (cf. Definition 1).

ASTs are widely used to represent programs or code snippets and benefit from extensive tool support. Furthermore, advances in AI technologies enable the automatic generation of complex ASTs from simple descriptions, which is promising for automatic requirements extraction. While automatic extraction is not the focus of the paper, we conducted some initial experiments with the GPT-4 model and an adapted, existing prompting technique [23] to transform the textual requirements of the example process (cf. Fig. 1) into code form ASTs (cf. Fig. 2a), both from a complete textual process description and natural language requirements[4]. The extracted requirements are preliminary w.r.t. consistency and correctness but always contain required activities, resources, time descriptions, data objects (α), and compliance patterns (CP)(θ).

AST formalization offers three further advantages, i.e., (a) AST tree traversal directly prevents injection attacks, where the requirements contain undesired code pieces since allowed functions and attribute accesses are restricted; (b) it reduces development effort while improving reliability and trustworthiness since sophisticated parsing and performant AST traversal are already developed for compilers and (c) compilers also give extensive feedback in case of syntax errors in the requirements which supports rule modelers. Furthermore, if a temporal logic for requirements representation is still desired (e.g., for formal proofs), a custom parser can be created to translate requirements between a logic system and an AST or vice versa.

Definition 1. (AST-based Compliance Requirements Encoding). *With L = {literals(α), variables(β), operators ($\oplus$), function calls(θ)} an AST is a finite, rooted, ordered tree $T = (V, E, \lambda)$ where:*

- *V is a finite set of nodes*
- *$E \subseteq V \times V$ is the set of ordered edges connecting the nodes*
- *$\lambda : V \rightarrow L$ is a labeling function that assigns each node a label*

To formalize requirements using an AST, literals contain all activity, resource, data object, and time descriptors, while variables can be freely assigned, operators are all standard operators (if, and, or, +, ==, ...), and function calls θ can correspond to any compliance pattern (CP), e.g., existence of activities. Figure 2a) depicts the ASTs of $R1$ to $R4$ of the running example in code form and Fig. 2b) the AST for the *precedence* CP required for $R1$. For simplicity, the *precedence* AST does not contain checks for correct data types and passing identical elements that are included in the implementation.

The literals also define the type of a requirement. Assume an AST T with literals a: if a contains only activity names, then T represents a pure control flow requirement; if a contains activity names and resource descriptors or only resource descriptors, then T represents a resource requirement; if a contains activity names and time descriptors or only time descriptors, then T represents a time requirement; if $a \subseteq \alpha$, then T represents a data flow requirement.

[4] Prompts/Results: https://github.com/JohannesLbck/ProcessTreeVerify.

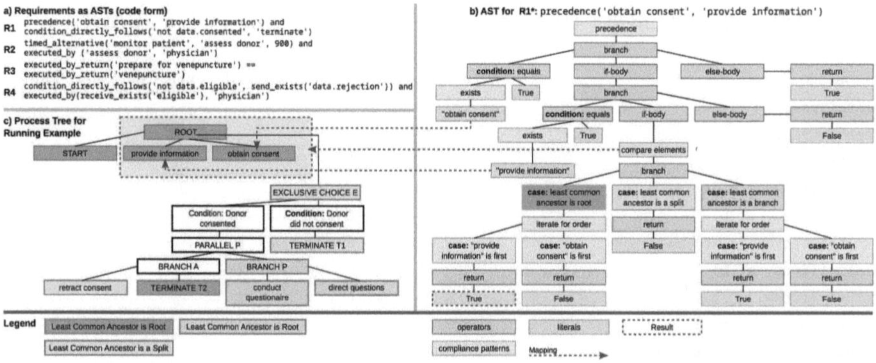

Fig. 2. Requirements as ASTs containing CPs which map to the Process Tree

Since the formalization is directly mapped to the implementation, there is no gap between formalized requirements and verification methods. Furthermore, the expressivity is not limited by the formal language but by the implemented verification methods, which can be freely combined using standard operators to model requirements. In particular, the deontic modalities of obligations, permissions, and prohibitions can be modeled similarly to [14], by defining the prohibition of an AST A, as the obligation of $\neg A$, while if A is a requirement (it is obligatory), then $\neg A$ is prohibited and any AST that is not prohibited is permitted. Based on CPs defined in literature (e.g., [21]), we define two sets of CPs, i.e., Atomic Compliance Patterns (ACP) (Table 1) and extended compliance patterns (ECP)(Table 2). ACP are basic patterns that can be used in combination with literals in the AST, other ACP, and operators to represent any verifiable requirement, which we show by using the ACP to represent the ECP and CP found in related work (See Sect. 4). ACP `C`, for example, compares the positions of activities `a` and `b` in `tree`, representing the process (cf. Sect. 3). The `tree` argument

Table 1. Atomic Compliance Patterns (ACP). *Tree*, *a*, and *b* can all be any node

Atomic Compliance Pattern	Short	Returns	Description
`Existence(tree, a)`	E	Element/None	Node matching to a in tree
`Compare(tree, a, b)`	C	P, X, →, ←	Checks relationship of nodes a and b in tree
`Can directly follow(tree, a, b)`	$\longrightarrow$	True/False	Can directly follow in some traces
`Must directly follow(tree, a, b)`	$\Longrightarrow$	True/False	Must directly follow in every trace
`parallel cancel(tree, a, b)`	PC	Subtree/None	parallels where one branch cancels the other
`executed by(tree, a)`	R	[Resources]	Returns list of resources that execute an activity
`timeouts exists(tree)`	T	[Timeouts].t	List of timeout elements with the times as .t
`due date exists(tree)`	D	[Due Dates].t	List of due date elements with times as .t
`data objects(tree)`	DO	[Data Objects].(s,r)	Data objects, .s for sends and .r for receives
`activity data checks(tree, a)`	DA	[Data Objects].(s,r)	Data objects send(.s)/received(.r) by a activity
`condition finder(tree, condition)`	DC	[Branches]	List of branches with matching condition
`loops(tree)`	L	[Loops]	List of Loop elements

Table 2. Extended Compliance Patterns (ECP) using FOL and ACP

Compliance Patterns for ASTs	Representation using FOL and Atomic Compliance Patterns
`exists(tree, a)`	$E(tree, a)$
`absence(tree, a)`	$\neg E(tree, a)$
`loop(tree, a)`	$\exists x \in loops(tree) : E(x, a)$
`directly_follows(tree, a, b)`	$\Longrightarrow (a, b)$ or $\longrightarrow (a, b)$
`leads_to(tree, a, b)`	$\neg E(tree, a) \vee C(a, b) \equiv a \rightarrow b$
`precedence(tree, a, b)`	$\neg E(tree, a) \vee C(a, b) \equiv a \leftarrow b$
`parallel(tree, a, b)`	$C(a, b) \equiv a\, P\, b$
`exclusive(tree, a, b)`	$C(a, b) \equiv a\, X\, b$
`executed_by(tree, a, r)`	$\exists x \in R(a) : x \equiv r$
`executed_by_return(tree, a)`	$R(a)$
`timed_alternative(tree, a, b, time)`	$\exists x \in T(tree) : PC(x, a) \wedge x.t \equiv time \wedge E(PC(x, a), b)$
`by_due_date(tree, a, time)`	$\exists x \in D(tree) : x \equiv a\ \wedge x.t \equiv time$
`max_time_between(tree, a, b, time)`	$C(a, b) \equiv a \rightarrow b \wedge \exists x \in T(tree) : PC(x, b)$ and $x.t \equiv time)$
`activity_sends(tree, a, data)`	$\exists x \in DA(E(tree, a)) : x.s \equiv data$
`activity_receives(tree, a, data)`	$\exists x \in DA(E(tree, a)) : x.r \equiv data$
`send_exists(tree, data)`	$\exists x \in DO(tree) : x.s \equiv data$
`receive_exists(tree, data)`	$\exists x \in DO(tree) : x.r \equiv data$
`condition_directly_follows(tree, c, a)`	$\exists x \in DC(tree, c) : E(x, a) \wedge \neg \exists y : E(x, y) \wedge C(a, y) \equiv a \leftarrow y$
`condition_branch_eventually_follows(tree, c, a)`	$\exists x \in DC(tree, c) : E(x, a)$
`condition_eventually_follows(tree, c, a)`	$\exists x \in DC(tree, c) : C(x, a) \equiv x \rightarrow a$

is used to indicate the scope of a requirement, and we assume that the CP is obligated for the entire process if the argument is omitted.

The formal base of the ECP is ensured by representing each ECP using the ACP and First Order Logic (FOL). The proposed ACP do not constitute a minimal set, and it would be possible to reduce the set of ACP further by, e.g., replacing the existence patterns with a single $\exists$ at the cost of understandability. Since it is challenging to formalize requirements as ASTs using just the ACP, the ECP improve usability and automatic extraction. AST-based encoding allows combining CPs such as `send/receive exists` and `executed by return`, which return the process element sending/receiving a data object and the resource executing an activity, respectively. Verified independently, they are mapped to satisfied/violated by evaluating `None` as false and any object as true. However, since they return process elements, they can also be combined to model constraints at different abstraction levels. For example, $R3$ compares executing resources, while $R4$ (cf. Fig. 2a) avoids tying the resource and dataflow constraints to activity labels by combining the `condition directly follows`, `executed by`, and `send/receive exists` CP.

In general, condition patterns can be used to model requirements that enforce the existence of an activity in a subset of all traces defined by a condition c that compares one or more data objects to literals or other data objects. We differentiate by whether an activity should a) **directly follow** after c evaluates to true, b) **eventually follow only** when c evaluates to true, or c) **eventually follow** when c evaluates to true. The difference between b) and c) can be regarded as a scoping or *overcompliance* difference, where b) defines that the activity should *only* be executed in the traces defined by the condition, while c) allows the activity to be executed in more traces than defined. As used for $R4$, the activity can also be replaced by any CP that returns a model element.

While we include the `due date` and `max time between` CP that can be identified in literature [6], we also propose the `timed alternative` pattern, which can be found in operationalized requirements such as $R2$ which is based on standard 3.6.2.6 in the Blood Guide. The `timed alternative` CP subsumes the other time CP since it defines an alternative that has to be executed instead of an original activity if a time constraint is not held.

3 AST-Based Process Tree Verification (PTV)

As discussed the formalization of compliance requirements as ASTs bears several advantages. In this section, we focus on how the AST representation can be leveraged for compliance verification of executable processes. To this end, we opt for an executable representation of process models as *process trees* to enable the structural verification of tree-based requirements on a tree-based model.

A process tree is an ordered, tree-based data structure inspired by the Refined Process Structure Tree (RPST) [30], where each node can be either a branch or a leaf. Figure 2c) depicts part of the process tree of the running example. Leaf nodes cannot have children since they represent tasks such as activities, terminates, and events like timeouts or stops. Branches represent control flow splits (exclusive choices, parallels, ...) and exclusive/parallel branches, which require a fitting split as a parent. Notably, tree edges do not represent the edges of the process model, as the execution order is implied by the tree order rather than the edges, which describe a parent-child relationship between two nodes. Activities `provide information` and `obtain consent`, for example, are not connected by an edge since they are both leaf nodes. To enable process execution, a process tree contains implementation details (endpoint addresses, data objects reads/writes, ...), which are added as nodes that do not affect the execution order. Key advantages of the process tree representation are (a) enforced syntactical correctness of the process model, (b) trivial insertion and deletion [26], and (c) performant transformation between workflow graph and process model [30].

3.1 General Verification and Control Flow Patterns

Assuming a set of ASTs representing different requirements and a process tree representing the executable process model, the basic idea of the verification approach is to iterate over the set of ASTs and traverse each AST until we find CPs in each AST that are verified by traversing the process tree. The verification instruction for a CP is encoded in the AST of this CP. Once a complete AST has been traversed, the return value is evaluated towards **satisfied** (true), **violated** (false) or **violable** (true, with reduced assurance) as proposed by [22], since not every requirement can be enforced at design time.

Algorithm 1 shows a generic AST traversal algorithm used for verifying a requirement formalized as an AST by matching the CP contained in the AST to a process tree. Take Fig. 2b) for illustrating the AST representation of requirement $R1^*$: `precedence('obtain consent', 'provide information')` to be verified over the process tree in Fig. 2c). Algorithm 1 traverses the AST and first finds the existence CP for task `obtain consent`. Traversing the process tree, `obtain consent` is matched. Continuing AST traversal, the next CP to be found is the existence of `provide information`, which is again matched in the process tree. Finally, AST traversal checks the precedence relation based on the compare elements CP in the AST by identifying the least common ancestor (LCA) of `obtain consent` and `provide information` in the process tree[5].

Algorithm 1. General AST Traversal Algorithm

Require: Compliance Rule
Ensure: True/False
  Tokenize (extract α, β, $\oplus$ and θ)
  Build AST ($T = (V, E, \lambda)$ where $\lambda : V \rightarrow L = \{\alpha, \beta, \oplus, \theta\}$ and $(n, m) \in E$ is an edge $n \rightarrow m$)
  procedure VISITNODE(Node)
    if λ(Node)$\in \alpha$ **then return** : λ(Node)
    else if λ(Node)$\in \beta$ **then return** : value of λ(Node)
    else if $\lambda(\text{Node}) \in \{\oplus, \theta\}$ **then return** $\lambda(\text{Node})(\{\text{VisitNode}(v) \mid v \in V, (Node, v) \in E\})$
    end if
  end procedure

When traversing the tree upwards from two nodes, the LCA can be used to identify whether two nodes are in a shared parallel/exclusive branch (LCA is the branch, highlighted purple in Fig. 2), in different parallel/exclusive branches (LCA is a split, highlighted blue), or the nodes do not share any splits (LCA is root, highlighted yellow). The compare algorithm (Listing 1) uses the LCA property to first identify whether any two nodes/subtrees are on different branches of the same split (mutually exclusive or in parallel). Otherwise, a node appearing first in the ordered tree will always precede the other in every trace if both appear. Since the LCA of `obtain consent` and `provide information` is the root node, the order of the tree is used to confirm the precedence relationship.

Listing 1. Pseudo code algorithm for comparing tree elements; Top down approach.

```
def compare_ele(tree, node1, node2):
  shared_ancestors = get_shared_ancestors(tree, node1, node2)
  if shared_ancestors[-1].label() == "exclusive split":
    return "node1 and node2 are on different exclusive branches"
  elif shared_ancestors[-1].label() == "parallel split":
    return "node1 and node2 are on different parallel branches"
  ## Otherwise, the nodes are neither in parallel/mutually exclusive, so the tree
      ↪ order decides the control flow
  for node in tree.iter():
    if node in {node1, node2}:
      return node
```

Figure 2b) shows the AST for the `precedence` pattern since more complex CP require large ASTs, and the LCA concept is essential for several CP (see Table 2). The following subsections discuss the CP of the other perspectives.

[5] Simplified; Compilers only visit required children.

3.2 Send/receive and Condition Patterns

In typical process engines [26], data objects can be accessed (1) in preparation before they are sent to an endpoint, (2) when they are sent as arguments towards an endpoint, (3) when results returned from an endpoint are written to data objects, and (4) when an endpoint returns an error message and (partial) results are rescued and written to data objects. Accordingly, for the send CP, the verification has to search for the data objects in the (1) preparation and (2) argument fields, while for the receive CP, it has to check the (3) return and (4) rescue processing fields in the process tree.

For the `condition finder` CP, the condition c_r of a requirement should ideally match to a condition c_t of an exclusive branch in the process tree only if, for every potential data object state where c_r returns TRUE, c_t also returns TRUE. However, evaluating arbitrary condition behavior is infeasible, especially when c_t compares multiple data objects returned by endpoints. Therefore, the `condition finder` distinguishes three cases with different assurances:

(1) $c_r \equiv c_t$: In case of a perfect match, the branch is returned with full assurance
(2) $c_r \in c_t$: If c_r is part of c_t, the branch is returned with reduced assurance since the complete condition might have different behavior.
(3) $c_r \in \neg c_t$: If c_r is part of the negation of c_t, the default branch of the same split is returned with significantly reduced assurance, since, assuming a split with branch conditions $(c_1, c_2, \ldots, c_n)$ then the condition of the default branch is the negation of the disjunction of all c_n, instead of a single $\neg c_n$.

If a c_r is not mapped using any of the cases for all branches in the process, it returns None. Since the condition patterns check the existence of required activities on all branches matched using the `condition finder` in the order of the cases above, the verification will return results with as high assurance as possible while highlighting which conditions have to be re-checked at run time.

3.3 Time Patterns

Since process trees are used to orchestrate distributed systems without globally trusted clocks, enforcing time-related CPs requires comparing the positions and data object read/writes of sync and timeout endpoints. For example, the algorithm for verifying the `timed alternative` CP (Lst. 2) first ensures that both the original activity `a` (that is time-constrained) and the alternative `b` exist, since absence of either violates the requirement. If both are present, the CP checks all timeouts in the process tree to find those in a `parallel cancel` relationship with `a`. For each, it checks if the timeout's parameter matches the required time, and if so, verifies if `b` appears on the alternative branch after the timeout. The `max time between` CP is a relaxed form of `timed alternative` without requiring an alternative, while the `due date` CP checks for a branch condition containing the data object returned by a sync activity before the time-constrained activity.

Listing 2. Simplified pseudo code algorithm for the timed alternative pattern

```
def timed_alternative(tree, a, b, time):
  if not exists(tree, a) then return: false
  if not exists(tree, b) then return: false
  for timeout in timeouts_exists(tree):
    parallel = parallel_cancel(tree, timeout, a)
    if parallel is not None:
      if timeout.t = time:
        return: exists(parallel, b)
  return: false ## No timeout was found to enforce the timed alternative
```

3.4 Resource Patterns

The challenge with resource CP is that the process tree does not enforce how resources are assigned to endpoints. For example, requirement $R4$ mandates that a physician assesses donor eligibility through direct questions. In an executable process, this could be ensured through (1) an endpoint that requires a resource assignment in the REST call header/body, (2) an endpoint implemented to only be executable by a physician, or (3) a resource organization platform such as [16]. For (1), the resource has to be checked in the REST call header/body, while for (2), the resource is assigned in the endpoint implementation, so the requirement cannot be verified in the executable process. Finally, for (3), the compliance rule would be integrated into the allocation algorithms. For a company-specific compliance solution, we can define how resources are assigned to endpoints, reducing flexibility but enabling highly reliable verification. For a generic solution, we can only verify resource CP similar to existing approaches [17] by checking an annotation without assurance that the annotation is followed at run time. For this annotation solution, we do not differentiate between resources and other concepts (roles, departments, teams, ...) since they can be annotated analogously.

4 Evaluation

We provide a prototypical implementation of the approach in Sect. 4.1, apply it to a custom data set in Sect. 4.2, and present the results of a user study regarding its usability in Sect. 4.3.

4.1 Implementation

AST-based requirements are verified on process trees in the Cloud Process Execution Engine (CPEE[6]). The CPEE supports an extensive range of BPMN element types, utilizes a process tree structure called CPEE-trees for representing executable process models, and enables live verification through a subscriber functionality that publishes the updated process tree to a REST-based subscriber whenever the process model is modified. The general structure of the PTV can be seen in Fig. 3 with complete documentation available on GitHub[7].

[6] https://cpee.org/, accessed 2025-03-05.

[7] https://github.com/JohannesLbck/ProcessTreeVerify, accessed 2025-03-05.

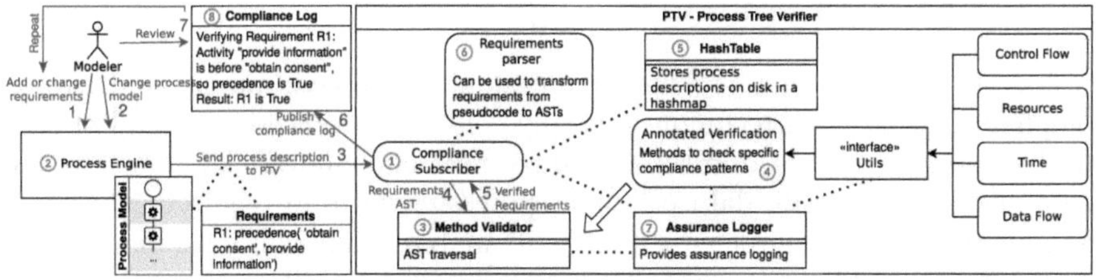

Fig. 3. General structure of the PTV

The main module of the PTV is the compliance subscriber (1), which defines an endpoint towards which the process engine (2) publishes the updated process descriptions containing the process tree, the encoded requirements and additional metadata (instance ID, author, ...) whenever the process modeler changes the process or updates the requirements. The requirement ASTs are traversed by the Method Validator class (3), which inherits the compiler's tree traversal methods to evaluate any ASTs where $\theta \subseteq \text{CP}$ defined in the annotated verification module (4). To improve code clarity and increase extendability, not all CP are part of the annotated verification module. Instead, lower-level abstraction checks (such as the compare ACP from Sect. 3) are organized into different utility modules for control flow, resources, time, and data flow. All utility methods can be accessed through the utils interface for more straightforward access and a better overview. The PTV also contains a Hash Table class (5) for storing previous versions of process descriptions on disk and a requirements parser module (6) to parse simpler pseudo-code requirements into an AST string.

As motivated in the introduction, an additional advantage of structural, AST-based verification is the opportunity to trace all verification steps to highlight which requirements are still violable at design time and support the process modeler with identifying violations and restoring compliance. This functionality is achieved through the Assurance Logger class (7), which inherits from the standard Python logger class. It documents the verification steps, tracks missing activities, and calculates an assurance level by reducing the assurance whenever a CP is verified, which remains violable after verification. For example, the timed alternative CP presented in Sect. 3 reduces the assurance whenever the timeout endpoint identified in a parallel cancel with the other activities is passed a data object instead of a digit since this means that the value of the timeout cannot be predicted at design time, i.e., the timed alternative is still violable even if the alternative activity is found on the alternative branch. A process modeler can acknowledge this warning and either fix a potential syntax error in the timeout or ensure that the value of the data object passed to the timeout will be correct at run time. The compliance logger can automatically generate both simple compliance logs (see (8) or the PTVLogs repository[8]) and complex logs containing information important for debugging and evaluation.

[8] https://power.bpm.cit.tum.de/PTVLogs/, accessed 2025-08-13.

4.2 Application to Custom Data Set

Real-world datasets that are used for evaluating process mining and ex-post compliance verification techniques usually consist of event logs instead of (executable) process models, and associated requirements are rare [3]. Thus, we create a custom composite dataset[9] of 11 processes with 46 requirements out of example processes/requirements used in 20 analyzed contributions, identified by searching digital libraries using the keywords *Business Process* AND *Compliance*. The 46 requirements cover the typical process perspectives of control flow, resources, time, and data flow. Example processes are included in the composite dataset if the process is understandable and at least one of the requirements stated in the paper can be verified through the process ("The information provided to the donor should be understandable" cannot be verified on the process model). For each process, we translate the model into an executable process model close to the original model and the requirements into ASTs. By checking the associated requirements on all processes in the composite dataset and using violations identified by the PTV to adjust the processes until they are compliant, we verify that (a) all the process-related requirements used in related work are verifiable with process tree verification and (b) the verification is reliable and consistent, i.e., the results are deterministic, each check yields the same result for the same input in nearly the same execution time. Table 3 contains an overview of the evaluation results using the composite dataset, including execution times, number of requirements, and whether all the requirements were verifiable and compliance could be restored by checking the generated compliance log.

Table 3. DataSet evaluation results

thline Origin	Exec. Time	# Req.	Verifiable?	Fixable?
[1]	1ms	6	Yes	Yes
[7]	3ms	7	Yes	Yes
[18]	1ms	3	Yes	Yes
[12]	1ms	5	Yes	Yes
[20]	*68*/2ms	2	Yes	Yes
[10]	1ms	3	Yes	Yes
[8]	1ms	4	Yes	Yes
[2]	1ms	2	Yes	Yes
[28]	1ms	4	Yes	Yes
[32]	1ms	3	Yes	Yes
[34]	2ms	7	Yes	Yes

Execution times were logged using the PTV deployed on consumer-grade hardware (Nvidia RTX 4090, AMD Ryzen 9 7950X). As seen in Table 3, the verification finishes in less than four milliseconds as long as the process does not contain any sub-processes (see [20] taking 68 ms). For the PTV to verify a process with sub-processes, the sub-process execution tree is automatically fetched from a URL and merged into the parent tree, introducing unpredictable network delays averaging 68 ms in testing. This can be avoided by checking the parent and sub-processes separately or by storing processes on disk. In general, while sufficient for live verification, the execution times should be regarded as upper bounds.

[9] https://github.com/JohannesLbck/ProcessTreeVerify, `Composite Dataset directory contains data and additional documentation.`

4.3 User Study

The qualitative user study is based on a questionnaire with additional artifacts (available on GitHub) and evaluates whether the PTV can help process modelers identify compliance violations in processes and assist in restoring compliance. The 13 study participants were divided into two groups in order and provided with two process models, i.e., donor registration and blood collection process, containing compliance violations, along with a list of requirements covering all process perspectives for each process. Depending on their group (7 participants in A, 6 in B), participants got access to a generated **compliance log** using the Assurance Logger of the PTV (cf. Fig. 3) for either the donor registration or blood collection process. As discussed, the compliance log directly identifies violations and gives an indication of how compliance could be restored. The participants were then tasked with identifying which requirements are violated in each process and describing how they would restore compliance for all violated requirements. Identification and restoring results were evaluated regarding their correctness by considering an identification incorrect whenever (a) a participant identified an unviolated requirement as violated without giving a valid reason why it could be regarded as violated or (b) a participant did not identify a violated requirement. Meanwhile, restoring was considered incorrect whenever a participant identified a requirement as violated but could not give a valid explanation on how compliance could be restored. After completing the task for each process, the participants answered the survey questions regarding their experience in process modeling, the study execution, how helpful they found the PTV for identifying violations and restoring compliance, and additional features they would be interested in.

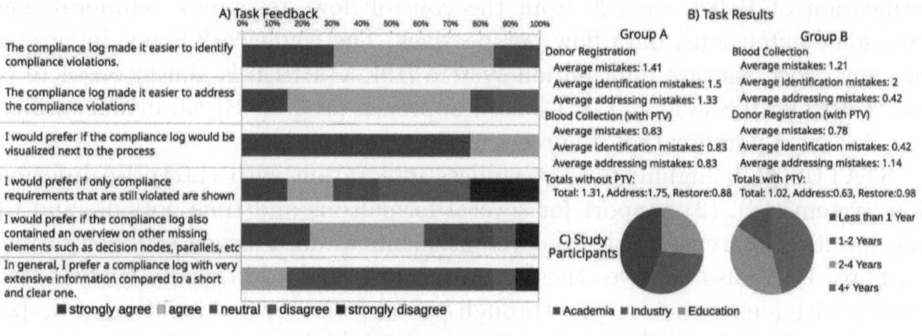

Fig. 4. Overview user study results; Avg. mistakes rounded to the nearest 100th

The study results are promising while highlighting the need for better visualization (Fig. 4a). Out of 13 participants, 11 strongly or weekly agreed that the PTV helped identify the violations. The task results (Fig. 4b) also support this statement since, on average, the PTV reduced the amount of (a) incorrectly or (b) un-identified violations from 1.75 to 0.63 per process. Furthermore, 11 participants agreed that the PTV helped restore compliance. Interestingly, the results show that, on average, the PTV made participants slightly worse at restoring compliance (likely due to an over-reliance on the compliance log). For example, if an activity should directly follow a data condition, the compliance log indicated that the activity was missing, which meant several participants answered that the activity should be added without considering the data condition. However, in practice, the PTV would regenerate the log, informing users of the incorrect position. Regarding information density, participants somewhat preferred extensive compliance logs with additional information, with several participants highlighting the importance of transparency and interpretability. The main criticism was regarding the presentation: all participants agreed that the violations should be visualized next to the actual process instead of in the compliance log. Regarding the study execution, every participant gave a valid explanation of the study's goal, while opinions regarding the complexity of the two processes varied: four found the donor registration more complex, three the blood collection process, and five considered them equally complicated. Most participants were from Academia (Fig. 4c) and had significant experience in process modeling.

5 Related Work

Table 4 compares existing design time process compliance approaches with PTV. In line with compliance surveys such as [13,34] there are no design time compliance verification approaches based on trees. The survey in [19] identifies approaches most similar to PTV as execution-level abstraction approaches and highlights *"an opportunity to integrate compliance-checking frameworks in BPMS to guarantee compliant executions"* as explored by the COMPAS project, which resulted in the Compliance Request Language (CRL) [7]. CRL supports verification of BPEL models from the control flow, resources, temporal, and with some extensions, data flow perspectives. The framework is not integrated into any process-aware information system [19], as BPEL is almost obsolete by now[10]. PROPOLS [33], an OWL-based approach used for BPEL model verification, lacks support for the resource and time perspectives.

STATUS [2,4] highlights (1) seamless integration with enterprise Information Systems(IS), (2) support for several formalisms and time notions, and (3) rule specification reuse by defining requirements as data-driven workflows called mashups. PTV also achieves these requirements, and additionally enables integration with a execution engine through process tree verification. Sun et al. [28] focus on regulatory requirements extraction with high accuracy for certain regulations, e.g., GDPR, but only supports some control flow patterns and annotated resources. Groefsema et al. [11] present an abstraction approach for managing the state space explosion problem using Petri nets and LTL encoding without considering time/resource aspects and the evolution of data objects during process execution. PCL [10] uses Modal Defeasible Logic (MDL) to represent requirements described by the normative requirements typology of obligations, permissions, and compensations [14]. This allows for a more direct mapping

[10] https://ode.apache.org/, accessed 2024-10-30, was retired in 2019.

Table 4. Overview of Compliance Frameworks analyzed regarding Assurance Levels

Approach	LC Phase	Formal	Type	Proofs	Process Perspectives				
					Control	A-DF	EL-DF	Resource	Time
BPMN-Q[1]	DT	CTL	I	yes	yes	yes	no	no	no
CRL[7]	DT	LTL/MTL	I	no	yes	no	no	yes	yes
DECLARE[25]	DT	LTL	D	yes	yes	yes	no	yes	yes
DCR[15]	DT	DL/HL	D	yes	yes	yes	no	yes	yes
eCRG[17]	DT/EP	FOL	I	no	yes	yes	no	yes	yes
PCL[10]	DT	MDL	I	yes	yes	yes	no	yes	yes
PNP[29]	EP	Petri-Net	I	no	yes	no	no	no	yes
PENELOPE[9]	DT	EC	D	yes	yes	yes	no	no	no
PROPOLS[33]	DT	OWL	I	no	yes	no	no	no	yes
PPSL[8]	DT	LTL	I	yes	yes	no	no	no	no
Rule Pattern[5]	EP	FOL/LTL	I	no	yes	yes	no	yes	yes
Status[2]	DT	custom[4]	Mix	no	yes	yes	no	yes	yes
Gro. et al.[11]	DT	CTL	I	yes	yes	yes	no	no	no
Sun et al.[28]	DT	no	I	no	yes	no	no	yes	no
PTV	DT	AST	I	no	yes	yes	yes	yes	yes

LC: Life Cycle; DT: Design Time; EP: Ex-Post; I: Imperative; D: Declarative
A-DF: Annotated Data-flow; EL-DF: Execution Level Data-flow

between formalized requirements and legislation while hindering understandability and automatic extraction due to its highly logical nature. Several approaches attempt to address the understandability problem through visual languages with a mapping towards a logic system [1,17]. BPMN-Q [1] uses model checking for verifying control flow and annotated data flow, similar to [17] who support control flow, time, data, and resource perspectives by verifying annotations. This, however, keeps the implementation gap between models and executed processes. DECLARE [25], DCR [15], and PENELOPE [9] are approaches for declarative process modeling which are suited for compliance since they are more flexible [15,25,34]. A downside of declarative process modeling and verification is that (useful) models can only be generated if there are enough constraints [9]. Finally, several approaches use process mining to conduct ex-post auditing and verification of compliance [5,29], giving an empirical prediction for the subsequent process instance execution, i.e., compliant execution can never be guaranteed.

6 Discussion

We discuss limitations, threats to validity, generalizability, and correctness proofs.

Limitations: As a structural approach, PTV does not create the state space of a process model to produce formal behavioral compliance proofs. Furthermore, verification of annotated resources is prototypical, and real-world adoption would require integration with a resource organization platform [16]. PVT assumes availability of operationalized requirements such that ASTs can be extracted reliably using LLMs. Formalization and interpretation of legal texts, particularly defeasible norms with temporal validity, is a known challenge in research [14,24]. Another limitation is connected with the interpretability of the compliance requirements. Unlike elements of commonly used formalizations, such as LTL, not all compliance patterns proposed in this paper have widely agreed-upon meanings. Another conceptual limitation is the design time focus of PTV. A complete BPC approach must also consider run-time monitoring and ex-post analysis [22]. This necessitates further integration with run-time enforcement and resource organization platforms. Finally, the evaluation dataset is synthetic and relatively small due to a lack of publicly available real-world datasets containing both process models and requirements. A comparative performance evaluation with other BPC approaches was not feasible, as many lack accessible implementations [1,8,10,17,33], have inaccessible interfaces [7], or are limited to predefined models [28]. Moreover, several use fundamentally different paradigms, such as ex-post analysis [5,29], declarative process modeling [9,15,25], or mashup-based modeling [2], making direct performance comparison inappropriate.

Threats to Validity: Regarding evaluation validity, the translation of process models from related work into executable artifacts was conducted manually. Despite independent work and discussion between authors, the resulting models may reflect biases in modeling style. In the user study, we sought to balance confounding variables by randomizing assignment. However, process complexity may have influenced results, even if participants did not agree on a more complex process. Finally, there is a potential bias in interpreting what constitutes a *violation* and what steps suffice to restore compliance. Accordingly, we regarded well-argued violations, such as data quality violations, as correctly identified. Regarding external validity, all 13 user study participants had substantial modeling experience, limiting the generalizability of the user study results.

Generalizability: As an imperative verification approach PTV can not verify declarative models. Considering imperative notations, PTV can be directly applied for control flow verification of block structured workflow graphs, such as executable BPMN models created in Camunda (https://camunda.com/), through a transformation to process trees [30]. The data perspective is more challenging, since BPMN only defines that a activity writes/reads a dataobject without considering execution-level abstraction details. Accordingly, data condition CPs can be verified, while data reads/write CPs depend on the exact notation style. Similarly, for resource and time annotations there is no unified execution-level notation, so the implemented CPs are CPEE-specific. Conceptually, all presented algorithms can be applied to any process tree based representation.

Provability: Formally proving the correctness of PTV requires four artifacts: (1) formal semantics for each CP, verified by legal and domain experts; (2) formal semantics of process trees; (3) a formal specification of the CPEE; and (4) formal specifications of each implemented PTV CP. Since some CPs lack an established formal specification in literature, (1) is necessary to ensure that any proof using the formal specifications is valid; for (2) we can rely on the semantics in [30,31]. A simplified proof can then verify, for each CP, that the structure identified in the process tree according to the CP implies its formal execution semantics. A full proof additionally requires (3) and (4) (e.g., in TLA+) to verify the implementation. Simplified proofs using (1) and (2) can be created for important CP and complete proofs using (3) and (4) in critical environments.

7 Conclusion

The Process Tree Verification (PTV) approach is based on structural compliance verification through intertwined traversal of process models represented as process structure trees and compliance requirements represented as Abstract Syntax Trees. By design, PTV is a structural, deterministic, white-box compliance verification approach designed for use with semi-operationalized requirements and both conceptual and executable process models. Since the verification is highly performant, PTV supports both ex-ante and live verification, making it suitable for environments where process models or requirements frequently change. The use of AST encoding using the presented compliance patterns allows for performant, trustworthy, and traceable compliance verification of control flow, time, annotated resources, and (execution-level) data flow requirements through the creation of a compliance log that explains verification steps to process modelers, while highlighting why requirements are not yet enforced at design time (i.e., violable requirements [22]). Future work will address the discussed limitations and threats to validity through industrial collaborations, the development of PTV towards runtime compliance monitoring, more extensive user studies with different levels of experience and backgrounds, and discussions with legal experts.

Acknowledgment. This work has been funded by the Deutsche Forschungsgemeinschaft (DFG) under project number 514769482.

References

1. Awad, A., Weidlich, M., Weske, M.: Visually specifying compliance rules and explaining their violations for business processes. J. Vis. Lang. Comput. **22**(1), 30–55 (2011). https://doi.org/10.1016/J.JVLC.2010.11.002
2. Bernal, Á., Montero, F., Cabanillas, C., Fernandez, P., Resinas, M.: STATUS: a low-code business process compliance management system. In: BPM Demos, pp. 141–145 (2024). https://ceur-ws.org/Vol-3758/paper-26.pdf

3. Burattin, A., Maggi, F.M., Sperduti, A.: Conformance checking based on multi-perspective declarative process models. Expert Syst. Appl. **65**, 194–211 (2016)
4. Cabanillas, C., Resinas, M., Ruiz-Cortés, A.: A mashup-based framework for business process compliance checking. IEEE Trans. Serv. Comput. **15**(3), 1564–1577 (2022). https://doi.org/10.1109/TSC.2020.3001292
5. Caron, F., Vanthienen, J., Baesens, B.: Comprehensive rule-based compliance checking and risk management with process mining. Decis. Support Syst. **54**(3), 1357–1369 (2013). https://doi.org/10.1016/J.DSS.2012.12.012
6. Chen, Q., Winter, K., Rinderle-Ma, S.: Predicting unseen process behavior based on context information from compliance constraints. In: Di Francescomarino, C., Burattin, A., Janiesch, C., Sadiq, S. (eds.) BPM 2023. LNBIP, vol. 490, pp. 127–144. Springer, Cham (2023). https://doi.org/10.1007/978-3-031-41623-1_8
7. Elgammal, A., Türetken, O., van den Heuvel, W., Papazoglou, M.P.: Formalizing and appling compliance patterns for business process compliance. Softw. Syst. Model. **15**(1), 119–146 (2016). https://doi.org/10.1007/S10270-014-0395-3
8. Förster, A., Engels, G., Schattkowsky, T., Straeten, R.V.D.: Verification of business process quality constraints based on visual process patterns. In: Symposium on Theoretical Aspects of Software Engineering. pp. 197–208 (2007)
9. Goedertier, S., Vanthienen, J.: Designing compliant business processes with obligations and permissions. In: BPM Workshops, pp. 5–14 (2006)
10. Governatori, G., Rotolo, A.: A conceptually rich model of business process compliance. In: Asia-Pacific Conference on Conceptual Modelling, pp. 3–12 (2010)
11. Groefsema, H., van Beest, N.R.T.P., Armas-Cervantes, A.: Efficient conditional compliance checking of business process models. Comput. Ind. (2020). https://doi.org/10.1016/J.COMPIND.2019.103181
12. Haarmann, S., Holfter, A., Pufahl, L., Weske, M.: Formal framework for checking compliance of data-driven case management. J. Data Semant. 143–163 (2021). https://doi.org/10.1007/s13740-021-00120-3
13. Hashmi, M., Governatori, G., Lam, H.-P., Wynn, M.T.: Are we done with business process compliance: state of the art and challenges ahead. Knowl. Inf. Syst. **57**(1), 79–133 (2018). https://doi.org/10.1007/s10115-017-1142-1
14. Hashmi, M., Governatori, G., Wynn, M.T.: Normative requirements for regulatory compliance: an abstract formal framework. Inf. Syst. Front. **18**(3), 429–455 (2016). https://doi.org/10.1007/S10796-015-9558-1
15. Hildebrandt, T.T., Mukkamala, R.R.: Declarative event-based workflow as distributed dynamic condition response graphs. arXiv preprint arXiv:1110.4161 (2011)
16. Ihde, S., Pufahl, L., Völker, M., Goel, A., Weske, M.: A framework for modeling and executing task-specific resource allocations in business processes. Computing (2022). https://doi.org/10.1007/S00607-022-01093-2
17. Knuplesch, D., Reichert, M.: A visual language for modeling multiple perspectives of business process compliance rules. Softw. Syst. Model. **16**(3), 715–736 (2017)
18. Letia, I.A., Goron, A.: Model checking as support for inspecting compliance to rules in flexible processes. J. Vis. Lang. Comput. **28**, 100–121 (2015)
19. López, H.A., Hildebrandt, T.T.: Three decades of formal methods in business process compliance: a systematic literature review. CoRR abs/2410.10906 (2024)
20. Ly, L.T., Indiono, C., Mangler, J., Rinderle-Ma, S.: Data transformation and semantic log purging for process mining. Adv. Inf. Syst. Eng. (2012)
21. Ly, L.T., Maggi, F.M., Montali, M., Rinderle-Ma, S., Aalst, W.M.P.: Compliance monitoring in business processes: functionalities, application, and tool-support. Inf. Syst. **54**, 209–234 (2015). https://doi.org/10.1016/J.IS.2015.02.007

22. Ly, L.T., Rinderle-Ma, S., Göser, K., Dadam, P.: On enabling integrated process compliance with semantic constraints in process management systems - requirements, challenges, solutions. Inf. Syst. Front. 195–219 (2012). https://doi.org/10.1007/S10796-009-9185-9
23. Neuberger, J., Ackermann, L., van der Aa, H., Jablonski, S.: A universal prompting strategy for extracting process model information from natural language text using large language models. In: Maass, W., Han, H., Yasar, H., Multari, N. (eds) ER 2024. LNCS, vol. 15238, pp. 38–55 (2024). https://doi.org/10.1007/978-3-031-75872-0_3
24. Novotna, T., Libal, T.: An evaluation of methodologies for legal formalization. In: Calvaresi, D., Najjar, A., Winikoff, M., Främling, K. (eds.) EXTRAAMAS 2022. LNCS, vol. 13283, pp. 189–203. Springer, Cham (2022). https://doi.org/10.1007/978-3-031-15565-9_12
25. Pesic, M., Schonenberg, H., van der Aalst, W.M.P.: DECLARE: full support for loosely-structured processes. In: Enterprise Distributed Object Computing Conference, pp. 287–300 (2007)
26. Rinderle-Ma, S., Mangler, J., Ritter, D.: Fundamentals of Information Systems Interoperability - Data, Services, and Processes. Springer, Cham (2024)
27. Sadiq, S., Governatori, G., Namiri, K.: Modeling control objectives for business process compliance. In: Alonso, G., Dadam, P., Rosemann, M. (eds.) BPM 2007. LNCS, vol. 4714, pp. 149–164. Springer, Heidelberg (2007). https://doi.org/10.1007/978-3-540-75183-0_12
28. Sun, X., Yang, S., Zhao, C., Yu, D.: Design-time business process compliance assessment based on multi-granularity semantic information. J. Supercomput. **80**(4), 4943–4971 (2024). https://doi.org/10.1007/S11227-023-05626-0
29. Ramezani Taghiabadi, E., Fahland, D., Dongen, B.F., Aalst, W.M.P.: Diagnostic information for compliance checking of temporal compliance requirements. In: Salinesi, C., Norrie, M.C., Pastor, Ó. (eds.) CAiSE 2013. LNCS, vol. 7908, pp. 304–320. Springer, Heidelberg (2013). https://doi.org/10.1007/978-3-642-38709-8_20
30. Vanhatalo, J., Völzer, H., Koehler, J.: The refined process structure tree. In: Dumas, M., Reichert, M., Shan, M.-C. (eds.) BPM 2008. LNCS, vol. 5240, pp. 100–115. Springer, Heidelberg (2008). https://doi.org/10.1007/978-3-540-85758-7_10
31. Vanhatalo, J., Völzer, H., Leymann, F.: Faster and more focused control-flow analysis for business process models through SESE decomposition. In: Krämer, B.J., Lin, K.-J., Narasimhan, P. (eds.) ICSOC 2007. LNCS, vol. 4749, pp. 43–55. Springer, Heidelberg (2007). https://doi.org/10.1007/978-3-540-74974-5_4
32. Winter, K., Aa, H., Rinderle-Ma, S., Weidlich, M.: Assessing the compliance of business process models with regulatory documents. In: Dobbie, G., Frank, U., Kappel, G., Liddle, S.W., Mayr, H.C. (eds.) ER 2020. LNCS, vol. 12400, pp. 189–203. Springer, Cham (2020). https://doi.org/10.1007/978-3-030-62522-1_14
33. Yu, J., Manh, T.P., Han, J., Jin, Y., Han, Y., Wang, J.: Pattern based property specification and verification for service composition. In: Aberer, K., Peng, Z., Rundensteiner, E.A., Zhang, Y., Li, X. (eds.) WISE 2006. LNCS, vol. 4255, pp. 156–168. Springer, Heidelberg (2006). https://doi.org/10.1007/11912873_18
34. Zasada, A., Hashmi, M., Fellmann, M., Knuplesch, D.: Evaluation of compliance rule languages for modelling regulatory compliance requirements. Software **2**(1), 71–120 (2023). https://doi.org/10.3390/software2010004

Detecting Conflicting Object Views in Object-Centric Process Choreographies

Tom Lichtenstein(✉), Anjo Seidel(✉), and Mathias Weske

Hasso Plattner Institute, University of Potsdam, Potsdam, Germany
{Tom.Lichtenstein,Anjo.Seidel,Mathias.Weske}@hpi.de

Abstract. Process choreography models facilitate the coordination of interactions among collaborating organizations. Recent advances integrate data into choreography modeling yet typically confine the scope of shared data to a single instance of a choreography. In practice, however, multiple choreography instances may access the same shared data object concurrently. This can lead to inconsistent views of the object among participants, resulting in conflicts that remain hidden during design. To address this limitation, we propose an object-centric extension of process choreography execution semantics based on typed Petri Nets with Identifiers, enabling the formal detection of conflicting object views during design time. In addition, this paper introduces two coordination patterns—*optimistic conflict handling* and *pessimistic locking*—that can be embedded into BPMN choreography diagrams to proactively prevent these conflicts. These extensions enhance the expressiveness and reliability of choreography models by enabling more robust coordination across concurrent instances with shared data.

Keywords: Process choreographies · Distributed systems · BPMN · Object-centric processes · Object lifecycles · Petri nets with identifiers

1 Introduction

Process choreographies allow the coordination of interactions between the business processes of autonomous participants, facilitating reliable collaboration in distributed settings [33]. While recent advances have integrated data semantics into choreography modeling [24], they typically assume that shared data objects, such as inventory items or appointments, remain confined within a single instance of a choreography. However, in real-world settings, shared data objects are often accessed concurrently by multiple choreography instances, which can lead to unintended behaviors, as discussed in [23].

Traditional choreography models, such as BPMN choreography diagrams [29], focus primarily on coordinating the control flow of collaborators. In contrast, *object-aware choreographies* extend this perspective by explicitly capturing constraints on shared data objects for each participant [24]. In this setting, the views of different participants on a shared data object may diverge during execution due to local updates that must be synchronized via messages. As participants independently update their local data objects, inconsistencies may emerge, particularly when these local updates are synchronized across different choreography instances. If a participant sends a message based on an outdated or inconsistent view, the update to the receiver's local object

D. Bork et al. (Eds.): ER 2025, LNCS 16189, pp. 204–222, 2026.
https://doi.org/10.1007/978-3-032-08623-5_11

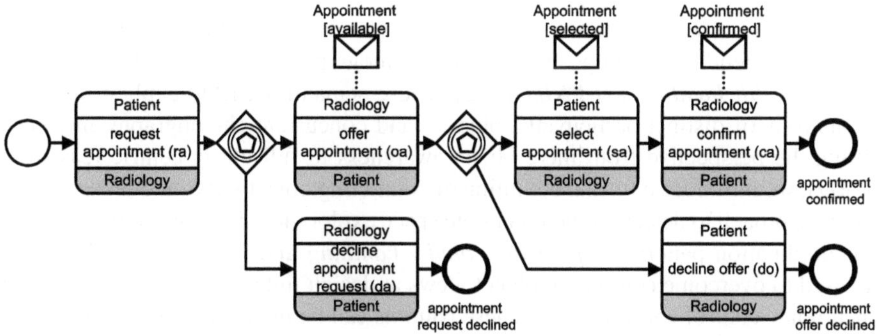

Fig. 1. Radiology appointment scheduling choreography illustrated as a BPMN choreography diagram [29].

view may violate *object lifecycle constraints*, which define an object's valid states and state transitions [24,33]. Such violations can lead to conflicts that disrupt collaboration. Despite this, current choreography semantics typically remain limited to single instance perspectives and do not capture conflicts that emerge across multiple concurrent choreography instances [23].

To illustrate this limitation, we consider an appointment scheduling scenario in the healthcare domain depicted as a BPMN choreography diagram in Fig. 1. This model consists of choreography tasks that refer to data objects in specific states, indicating the transfer of these objects during task execution.

First, a patient sends a message requesting an appointment to the radiology department. If an appointment slot is available, the radiology offers it to the patient, who may either accept or decline. Once the patient selects an appointment, the radiology department confirms it. While this scenario works properly in isolation, sharing the same appointment object across concurrent choreography instances can create conflicts. For example, two patients may receive the same appointment offer at the same time. If one patient's selection is confirmed, then any subsequent selection by another patient would revert the appointment from *confirmed* to *selected*, which could violate the object's lifecycle constraints assuming that a confirmed appointment cannot be selected again. Since choreography models are usually analyzed assuming isolated instances, conflicting object views across instances often go undetected during design and only become apparent during execution, resulting in unexpected behavior and coordination overhead.

To overcome this challenge, this paper investigates how conflicting views on shared data objects can be systematically detected and prevented across concurrent choreography instances. The contributions are organized around the following research questions:

RQ_1. How can participant-specific views of shared data be formally represented in concurrent choreography instances?

RQ_2. How can conflicting object views across instances be detected through formal verification?

RQ_3. How can choreography models be designed to ensure object lifecycle conformance across instances?

To address RQ_1, this paper proposes object-centric semantics for choreography models by extending existing object-aware choreography semantics [24] using *typed Petri Nets with Identifiers (t-PNIDs)* [32]. These semantics enable explicit modeling and analysis of distinct participants, objects, and concurrent choreography instances, shifting the perspective from mere object-awareness to full object-centric reasoning. For RQ_2, we introduce a formal definition of conflicting object views and present a systematic approach to detecting them via state space exploration. Finally, addressing RQ_3, two coordination patterns—*optimistic conflict handling* and *pessimistic locking*—are proposed to overcome conflicting object views at design time, drawing on well-known concurrency control concepts [21]. These patterns can be integrated into choreography models and translated into object-centric formal semantics.

We illustrate the translational semantics, the detection of conflicting object views, and the coordination patterns based on the appointment scheduling scenario depicted in Fig. 1. The results highlight that the extended semantics reveal otherwise hidden conflicts that can be prevented by the proposed coordination patterns. By enabling early detection and resolution of conflicting object views, our approach enhances the robustness of choreography models, contributing directly to trustworthy and efficient collaboration between organizations.

The remainder of this paper is structured as follows: Sect. 2 discusses related work. Section 3 provides background on object-aware choreographies and t-PNIDs. Section 4 introduces our extended semantics and methods for detecting conflicting object views, while Sect. 5 presents the optimistic and pessimistic coordination patterns. Section 6 demonstrates applicability and discusses key findings, and Sect. 7 concludes and outlines future research directions.

2 Related Work

Modeling collaborations between autonomous processes requires capturing data exchanges and dependencies alongside control flow. While standardized choreography languages such as BPMN [29] provide basic support for message-based interactions, their native data-handling capabilities remain limited [12]. To address this, various extensions have been proposed that enrich choreography models with data semantics, capturing concepts such as data awareness, automated data transfer across local schemas, and privacy-aware communication [2,16,18,26,28]. However, these approaches typically assume that data is confined to a single choreography instance and do not consider consistency issues arising from concurrent access to shared data across instances. Related efforts extend choreographies with transactional semantics [19,20]. Still, challenges that arise from diverging views across concurrent choreography instances are not addressed.

The importance of instance-spanning behavior has been recognized in the process modeling literature as well. Foundational classifications and modeling principles for instance-spanning constraints have been proposed [11,22]. Furthermore, cross-case data objects [15] have been introduced to enable the representation and analysis of data shared across process instances, although typically assuming centralized data access.

Artifact-centric approaches model data as first-class entities and track object movement across processes [25]. However, these models assume a uniform view of an object's state across participants. More recently, Haarmann et al. [14] explored the integration of object-centric behavior in service choreographies, but their focus remains on control-flow compatibility with local process behavior rather than consistent data views. Furthermore, Burigana et al. [3] examine the impact of local data views on conformance checking, but do not address model verification.

Several formal models support object-centric process reasoning based on Petri net variants. Typed Petri Nets with Identifiers (t-PNIDs) [32] extend classical Petri nets by associating tokens with typed identifiers. This allows representing and correlating participants and data objects across executions. Gianola et al. [13] further enhance this model with variable arcs to support operations over sets of objects.

Related work on proclets [31] has applied object-centric modeling to both processes involving multiple object types [10] and distributed choreographies [31]. However, they currently cannot simultaneously capture both dimensions—participant and object instances—as required for this paper. For this reason, we rely on the t-PNID formalism.

In summary, prior work has made significant advances in data-aware choreography modeling, instance-level verification, and object-centric semantics. However, the detection and prevention of lifecycle inconsistencies arising from shared data access across choreography instances remains underexplored. This paper addresses this gap by defining object-centric semantics for choreographies and introducing modeling patterns that explicitly coordinate access to shared data across instances.

3 Preliminaries

This section reviews foundational concepts relevant to this paper, focusing first on process choreographies and their extensions to incorporate data semantics. We then introduce typed Petri Nets with Identifiers (t-PNIDs), a formalism well-suited for modeling instance-specific behaviors.

3.1 Process Choreographies with Data Semantics

Process choreographies, particularly BPMN choreography diagrams [29], specify the interaction behavior between processes managed by independent collaborating participants. These models abstract from internal process logic, focusing exclusively on message exchanges. Each interaction is represented as a *choreography task* (hereafter referred to as *task*), denoting both an *initiator* (shown with a white band) and a *receiver* (indicated by a gray band). Following common practice [7], bidirectional tasks are interpreted as pairs of sequential unidirectional interactions. Sequence flows define the execution order between tasks, while gateways express exclusive or parallel branching behavior. An example of a choreography diagram is illustrated in Fig. 1.

Recent advancements integrate data-semantics into choreography modeling [24] by introducing shared data objects which represent a shared understanding of business data objects such as inventory items or appointments among participants. The behavior of shared data objects is defined by supplemental models, specifically a *shared data model*

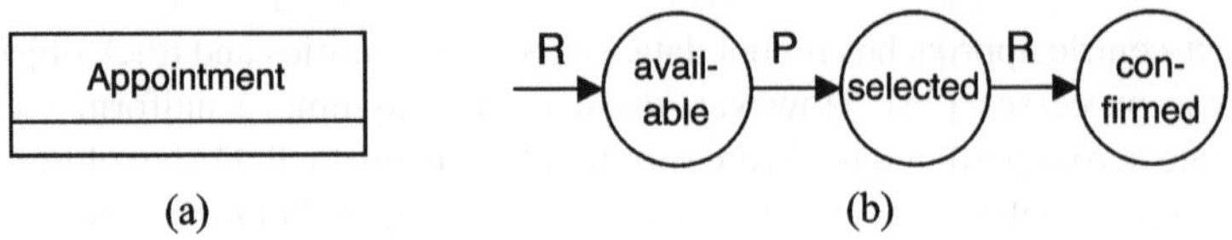

Fig. 2. Supplemental models specifying data semantics for the choreography diagram depicted in Fig. 1 according to [24], including (a) a shared data model consisting of a single class and (b) a shared object lifecycle for appointment objects.

and *shared object lifecycles*. Examples of these supplemental models in the context of the appointment scheduling scenario are depicted in Fig. 2.

The shared data model specifies object classes and their relationships, formally defined as a tuple $D = (C, \mathcal{R}, mul)$, where C is a non-empty, finite set of classes, $\mathcal{R}$ is a symmetric relation over classes representing associations between classes, and *mul* defines cardinality constraints over relations. Each object class in the shared data model is associated with a shared object lifecycle that defines allowed states and transitions. Each state transition (and initialization) is assigned a participant role responsible for its execution:

Definition 1 (Shared Object Lifecycle). *Let $\mathcal{S}$ be the universe of all possible states. A shared object lifecycle for class $c \in C$ is defined by a tuple $\mathcal{L}_c = (S_c, S^i_c, \delta_c, R, act)$, where:*

- *$S_c \subseteq \mathcal{S}$ is a non-empty, finite set of states,*
- *$S^i_c \subseteq S_c$ is a non-empty set of initial states,*
- *$\delta_c \subseteq S_c \times S_c$ is a state transition relation,*
- *R is a non-empty, finite set of participant roles, and*
- *$act : S^i_c \cup \delta_c \rightarrow R$ assigns a role to state transitions and initializations.*

Due to the decentralized nature of choreographies, object state is not globally shared. Instead, each participant maintains a *local view of each data object.* State changes are thus applied locally and must be communicated explicitly via tasks to update the receiver's local object view. To visually represent the exchange of shared data objects, message elements in choreography tasks can be annotated with data object classes and expected states, requiring the initiator to send an object in the respective state, as illustrated in Fig. 1. We formalize these concepts into an object-aware choreography:

Definition 2 (Object-Aware Process Choreography). *An object-aware process choreography is defined as a tuple $C = (\mathcal{N}, SF, R, D, \mathcal{L}, ini, rec, msg)$, where:*

- *$\mathcal{N} \subseteq \mathcal{T} \cup G \cup E$ is a non-empty finite set of nodes (tasks $\mathcal{T}$, gateways G, events E),*
- *$SF \subseteq \mathcal{N} \times \mathcal{N}$ represents sequence flows,*
- *R is a non-empty, finite set of participant roles,*
- *$D = (C, \mathcal{R}, mult)$ is a shared data model,*

- $\mathcal{L} = \{\mathcal{L}_c \mid c \in C\}$ *is the set of object lifecycles,*
- $ini : \mathcal{T} \rightarrow R$ *assigns an initiating role to each task,*
- $rec : \mathcal{T} \rightarrow R$ *assigns a receiving role to each task, and*
- $msg : \mathcal{T} \rightarrow (C \times S_c) \cup \{\emptyset\}$ *associates each task with a class and a state, or indicates that no data object is exchanged.*

The execution semantics of this extension are formally defined in [24] using data-enhanced interaction Petri nets, as illustrated in Fig. 3, which forms the basis for the semantic extension introduced in Sect. 4.

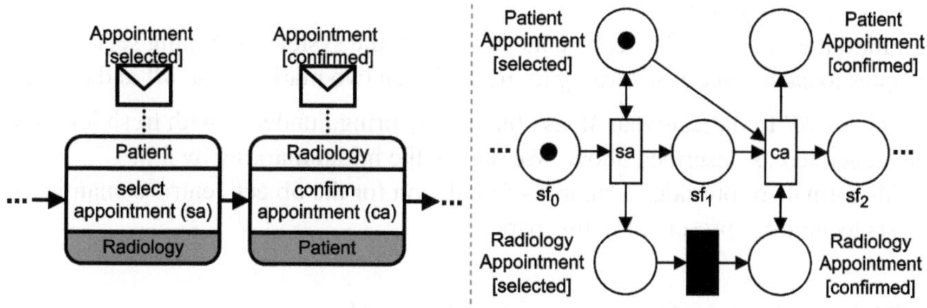

Fig. 3. Excerpt of the appointment scheduling choreography depicted in Fig. 1 (left) and the Petri net (right) representing its object-aware execution semantics based on the supplemental models illustrated in Fig. 2.

3.2 Typed Petri Nets with Identifiers

Petri nets are a well-established formalism for modeling distributed systems and are widely used to define and analyze the semantics of process models [9]. Classical Petri nets consist of places and transitions connected by directed arcs, where transitions fire by consuming tokens from input places and producing tokens in output places.

Typed Petri Nets with Identifiers (t-PNIDs) [32] extend classical Petri nets by associating each token with a typed vector of identifiers, enhancing expressiveness for modeling data-driven and multi-instance behaviors. Each type corresponds to a domain of identifiers, and arc inscriptions specify typed variable tuples that are bound to identifiers of the respective type during transition firing. Formally, we define t-PNIDs following [32]:

Definition 3 (Typed Petri Net with Identifiers). *Let $\mathcal{I}$, Λ, and $\mathcal{V}$ be countable, infinite sets of identifiers, type labels, and variables, respectively, a* typed Petri Net with Identifiers *is a tuple $N = (P, T, F, \alpha, \beta)$, where:*

- (P, T, F) *is a classical Petri net, consisting of places P, transitions T, and a flow relation F,*
- $\alpha : P \rightarrow \Lambda^*$ *assigns a tuple of type labels to each place, defining the type signature of tokens stored there,*

– $\beta : F \rightarrow (\mathcal{V}^*)^\oplus$ *associates arcs with multisets of typed variable tuples, each conforming to the type signature* $\alpha(p)$ *of the connected place* $p \in P$.

A transition may fire if the variables on all connected arcs can be consistently bound to identifiers. A *binding* is a function $\psi : \mathcal{V} \rightarrow \mathcal{I}$ assigning each variable an identifier. Variables on incoming arcs must be bound to identifiers occurring in the current marking. For variables on outgoing arcs that do not appear on any incoming arc of the same transition, ψ must assign *fresh identifiers* from $\mathcal{I}$ not present in the current marking; other outgoing variables reuse the identifiers from their incoming counterparts. A transition t is *enabled* under ψ iff for each input arc $(p, t) \in F$, place p contains tokens matching $\beta((p, t))$ under ψ.

A marking $M : P \rightarrow 2^{\mathcal{I}^*}$ represents the state of the system, assigning sets of identifier tuples to each place p according to $\alpha(p)$[1]. Given two markings M, M' and $t \in T$, we write $M \xrightarrow{t,\psi} M'$ to indicate that M' is obtained by firing t under ψ, with fresh identifiers being generated as described above. We denote the initial marking by M_0.

This formalism provides a rigorous foundation for the object-centric semantics and analysis techniques presented in this paper.

4 Object-Centric Choreography Semantics

As discussed in Sect. 2, current choreography semantics generally assume that data exchanged within choreographies is confined to a single instance of a choreography. In this section, we relax this assumption by allowing the reuse of object views across multiple instances, as depicted in Fig. 4. This enables the detection and analysis of conflicting object views that arise across concurrent choreography instances.

To achieve this, we extend the existing object-aware choreography semantics [24] using *typed Petri Nets with Identifiers (t-PNIDs)* [32], enabling explicit representation of participant, object, and choreography instances. This shift from an *object-aware* to an *object-centric* perspective allows us to analyze how shared objects evolve and diverge across concurrent instances, facilitating early detection of conflicting object views.

4.1 Translational Semantics to Typed Petri Nets with Identifiers

We build upon the translation from object-aware choreography models to Petri nets described in [24]. Our extensions include the introduction of identifiers to distinguish object, participant, and choreography instances and the explicit modeling of receiver-side transitions according to valid lifecycle transitions. Figure 5 illustrates the refined translation for a choreography task and the start event of the running example (see Figs. 1 and 2). Note that t-PNID illustrations usually omit place types labels for readability, as they can be inferred from the variable tuples on their connected arcs, which respect the type signature $\alpha(p)$.

[1] In contrast to the original definition in [32], we restrict ourselves to sets rather than multisets. A transition may still fire even if one of its output tuples already exists in the respective place; in this case, the marking remains unchanged for that place.

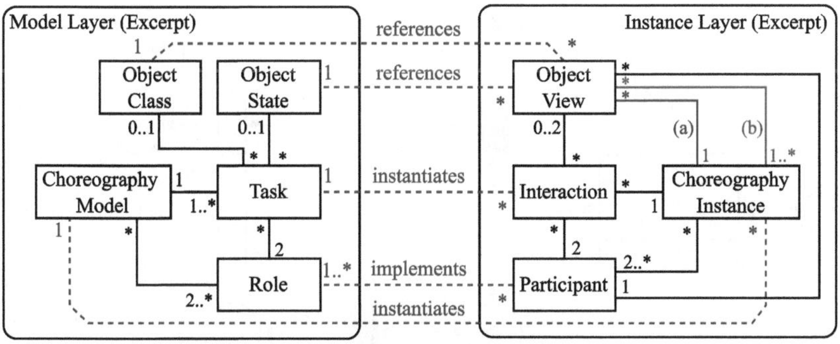

Fig. 4. An excerpt of the relations (blue, dashed lines) between the key constructs of object-centric choreographies on the model layer (left) and the instance layer (right). Data object visibility is represented by *object views* (Color figure online), which relate to an object class and state, and are linked to a single participant. While previous works tie object views to a single choreography instance (a), we remove this assumption to enable their use in multiple instances (b).

Identifier Types. For each *role* $r \in R$ and *object class* $c \in C$, distinct types $\lambda_r, \lambda_c \in \Lambda$ are introduced. A distinct type $\lambda_i \in \Lambda$ represents *choreography instance* identifiers.

Roles and Object Views. Each *role* $r \in R$ is mapped to a place $p_r \in P_R$, storing *participant* identifiers of type λ_r, i.e., $\alpha(p_r) = (\lambda_r)$. Each possible *object view*, i.e., a role-class-state combination (r, c, s), is mapped to a place $p_{rcs} \in P_v$ with $\alpha(p_{rcs}) = (\lambda_r, \lambda_c)$, capturing the association between a participant instance and a shared object instance in a specific state.

Sequence Flows. These are represented as places $p_{sf} \in P_{sf}$, which are typed $\alpha(p_{sf}) = (\lambda_i, \lambda_{r_0}, \ldots, \lambda_{r_m})$ to capture identifiers for the choreography instance and the involved participants $\{r_0, \ldots, r_m\} = R$. This typing enables the correlation of interaction parties for each task execution.

Start and End Events. The *start event* is mapped to a transition t_{start} that initializes a choreography instance by generating a fresh identifier and propagating participant identifiers to the subsequent sequence flow place as illustrated in Fig. 5. To access the participant identifiers, t_{start} consumes and reproduces tokens in all role places P_R. The end event transition t_{end} consumes the final sequence flow token, signaling completion.

Local State Transitions. Each *local transition* $t \in T_s$ moves tokens between object-view places of the same role according to the object lifecycle. Specifically, for $(s, s') \in \delta_c$ and $act(s, s') = r$ given a shared object lifecycle $\mathcal{L}_c$ for a class $c \in C$, the transition consumes a token from p_{rcs} and produces it in $p_{rcs'}$. If a participant creates a new object, i.e., $s'' \in S_c^i$ and $act(s'') = r$, a corresponding local transition generates a fresh object identifier and places it into the appropriate view place $p_{rcs''}$, linking it to the participant identifier read from the respective role place p_r, as depicted in Fig. 5.

Task Execution Semantics. In contrast to the original semantics that represent each task with a single transition (see Fig. 3) [24], we decompose tasks into a *sender transition* t_{ini}^{τ} and a set of *receiver transitions* T_{rec}^{τ}, as depicted in Fig. 5. A sender transition propagates tokens from the sequence flow place and initiator's object view place to a dedicated transmission place p_{τ}, capturing the object identity and choreography context,

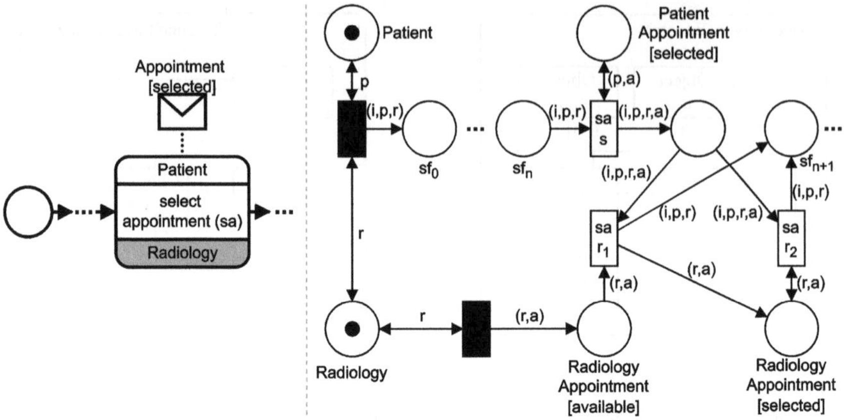

Fig. 5. Excerpt of the appointment scheduling choreography depicted in Fig. 1 (left) and its object-centric semantics based on typed Petri Nets with Identifiers (right), illustrating the translation of a start event and a choreography task. The variables are typed: $i : \lambda_i$ (choreography instance), $p : \lambda_{patient}$, $r : \lambda_{radiology}$, and $a : \lambda_{appointment}$.

i.e., $\alpha(p_\tau) = (\lambda_i, \lambda_{r_0}, \ldots, \lambda_{r_m}, \lambda_c)$. The token consumed from the initiator's object view place is reproduced. We denote the set of all transmission places as $P_{\mathcal{T}}$.

Receiver transitions are generated based on the notion of *valid receiver states*, which ensures lifecycle-conformant message receptions. A receiver state s' is considered valid if the sent state s is reachable from s' through a path of lifecycle transitions *not involving the receiver*. This reflects that the receiver must be able to reach s from their current (or initial) state without being responsible for any intermediate state changes.

Formally, we define a role-excluding transitive closure $\theta_c^r \subseteq S_c \times S_c$ over the lifecycle δ_c to capture all such paths:

$$(s, s') \in \theta_c^r \iff \exists k \geq 1, (s_0, \ldots, s_k) \subseteq S_c^* : \; s_0 = s \wedge s_k = s' \wedge \\ \forall j \in \mathbb{N}_0 : j < k \wedge (s_j, s_{j+1}) \in \delta_c \wedge act(s_j, s_{j+1}) \neq r$$

We then define the set of valid receiver states for a task using the function $vrs : R \times C \times S_c \to 2^{S_c} \cup \bot$. The special symbol $\bot$ denotes that the object can be received in the state $s \in S_c$ if it is unknown to the receiver.

Definition 4 (Valid Receiver States). *Let $\tau \in \mathcal{T}$ be a task with $msg(\tau) = (c, s)$ and $r = rec(\tau)$. The set of valid receiver-side states is given by:*

$$vrs(r, c, s) = \{s' \in S_c \mid (s', s) \in \theta_c^r\} \cup \left\{\bot \mid \exists s_0 \in S_c^i : (s_0 = s \wedge act(s_0) \neq r) \vee (s_0, s) \in \theta_c^r\right\}$$

The intuition behind this definition is twofold. First, a state s' (or an unknown object $\bot$) is only a valid receiver state if there exists a lifecycle path from s' to the received state s. Second, the receiver must not be responsible for any transition along that path; otherwise, it implies that they must have previously observed an intermediate state before receiving s, contradicting their local object view.

For example, suppose that a patient sends an appointment in the state *selected* to the radiology department (see Task 'sa' in Fig. 1). Valid receiver-side states include *available* and *selected* (unchanged), but not *confirmed*, since there is no lifecycle-compliant transition from *confirmed* to *selected* according to Fig. 2. Likewise, when the patient later receives the same appointment in state *confirmed* (Task 'ca'), they must have previously observed it at least in state *selected*. This is due to the fact that the patient is responsible for transitioning from *available* to *selected* before an appointment can be *confirmed*. Consequently, if the appointment is received in state *confirmed*, it cannot be in state *available* from the patient's perspective, resulting in *selected* or *confirmed* (unchanged) as valid states.

Each valid receiver state $s' \in vrs(r, c, s)$ yields a receiver transition $t \in T^{\tau}_{rec}$ consuming a token from p_{τ}, producing a token in a succeeding sequence flow place p_{sf}, and updating the receiver's local object view by transferring a token from $p_{rcs'}$ to p_{rcs}, thus ensuring only lifecycle-conformant state transitions during reception. We formalize the resulting object-centric semantics as follows:

Definition 5 (Object-Centric Choreography Semantics). *An object-centric choreography C is defined by the t-PNID semantics $n_C = (P, T, F, \alpha, \beta)$, where:*

- $P = P_R \cup P_{sf} \cup P_v \cup P_{\mathcal{T}}$,
- $T = \{t_{start}, t_{end}\} \cup T_s \cup \left\{t^{\tau}_{ini} \mid \tau \in \mathcal{T}\right\} \cup \bigcup_{\tau \in \mathcal{T}} T^{\tau}_{rec}$.

For brevity, we omit the explicit reconstruction of F, α, and β, as they are uniquely determined by the typing and flow structure described in this section.

An initial marking M_0 can be defined by distributing participant identifier tokens to each role place $p_r \in P_R$, which enables the creation of a new choreography instance using t_{start}.

4.2 Detecting Conflicting Object Views

Building on the semantics introduced in the previous section, we now formalize how to detect *conflicting object views* across multiple choreography instances. Intuitively, a conflict arises when a message has been sent but cannot be received due to lifecycle constraints on the receiver's side, thus blocking further execution. We define this property formally as follows:

Definition 6 (Conflicting Object View). *A reachable marking M exhibits a conflicting object view if:*

$$\exists e \in \mathcal{I}^*, p_{\tau} \in P_{\mathcal{T}} : e \in M(p^{\tau}) \wedge \nexists t \in T^{\tau}_{rec}, \psi, M' \text{ s.t. } M \xrightarrow{t,\psi} M' : e \notin M'(p^{\tau})$$

That is, a message token exists in a transmission place, but no receiver transition can be fired to consume it in any successor marking, implying that the corresponding message cannot be received. Based on this, we define the notion of conflict-freedom:

Definition 7 (Conflict-free Choreography). *An object-centric choreography C is* conflict-free *if its t-PNID semantics n_C with the initial marking M_0 defines no reachable marking M' that exhibits a conflicting object view according to Definition 6.*

Conflict-freedom ensures that all messages sent within a choreography are eventually received in a lifecycle-conformant manner, thereby preventing execution deadlocks caused by inconsistent object views. This property can be verified using established model checking techniques [1,6]. The semantics defined by the t-PNID n_C induce a reachability graph that captures all markings reachable from an initial marking M_0, also referred to as *state space*. Based on this graph, the first-order condition defined in Definition 6 can be evaluated for each marking. Conflict-freedom then corresponds to a safety property—ensuring that no reachable marking violates the condition—formally expressible and verifiable using temporal logic [5].

In general, the semantics permit unbounded creation of choreography instances and data objects, potentially resulting in an infinite state space. For model checking to remain decidable and tractable, the number of instances must therefore be bounded in practical applications [30].

5 Object Coordination Patterns

The t-PNID semantics introduced in Sect. 4 provide the foundation needed to detect conflicting object views across choreography instances. In practice, however, modelers often require preventive mechanisms to avoid inconsistencies in the first place. Inspired by classical concurrency control approaches [21], this section introduces two *object coordination patterns* to coordinate object access that can be applied selectively to object-centric choreography models. Each pattern defines an extension of the Petri net-based execution semantics presented in Sect. 4.1. The patterns specify coordination at the modeling level; they are not a global runtime enforcement mechanism. Enforcement is realized by the participants' local processes implementing the annotated behavior.

5.1 Optimistic Conflict Handling

The *optimistic pattern* allows the initiator of a task to send an object regardless of the receiver's current view. If the receiver cannot apply the state transition, i.e., the object is received in an incompatible state, an *exceptional sequence flow* is triggered to handle the inconsistency. This pattern trades immediate conformance for flexibility, delegating conflict resolution to custom compensation logic.

To visually indicate this behavior, choreography tasks can be extended with conditional interrupting boundary events on the receiver's band (Fig. 6), in line with BPMN syntax [29]. Since only the receiver can determine whether the message leads to a conflict, they must initiate the tasks following both the normal and exceptional sequence flows to preserve realizability [8].

The execution semantics of such a task $\tau \in \mathcal{T}$ with $msg(\tau) = (c, s)$ and receiver $r = rec(\tau)$ are extended as follows. In addition to the standard sender transition t^{τ}_{ini} and

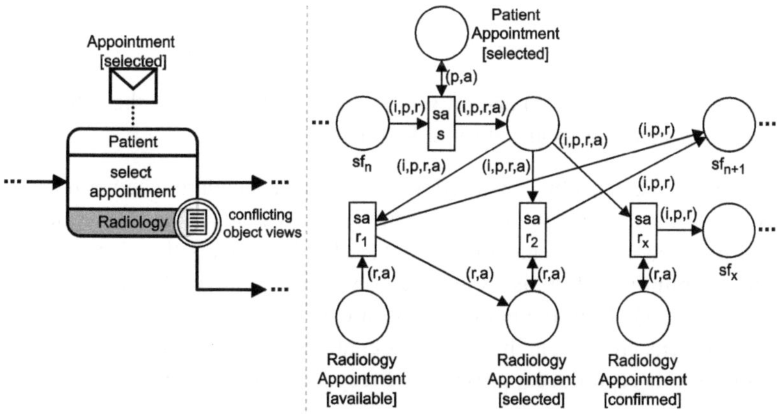

Fig. 6. Optimistic object coordination pattern. A visual extension, illustrated on the left, introduces a conditional interrupting boundary event to indicate the optimistic handling of conflicting object views. The corresponding execution semantics are illustrated on the right. (Variable types as given in Fig. 5.)

conformant receiver transitions T^{τ}_{rec} (Sect. 4.1), we generate a set of *exceptional receiver transitions* T^{τ}_{recx} for each invalid receiver state $s' \in S_c \setminus vrs(r, c, s)$. Each exceptional transition consumes the transmission token from p_{τ}, consumes and reproduces the token in $p_{rcs'}$ (leaving the local view of the receiver unchanged), and produces a token in the exceptional sequence flow place.

The semantic extension is illustrated in Fig. 6, where the transition labeled 'sa r_x' extends the regular translation with a transition to the exceptional sequence flow place sf_x while keeping the local object view unchanged to avoid lifecycle complications.

This pattern guarantees that message receipt always progresses: if the state is valid, the object transitions as defined; if invalid, the receiver's view of the object's state remains unchanged and an exceptional flow is triggered. In both cases, the model remains deadlock-free and lifecycle-conformant, preserving the autonomy of participants with only local state knowledge. By explicitly integrating the optimistic strategy into the choreography, any additional interactions, such as compensation, retries, or escalation, become part of the agreed model and can be verified in the resulting t-PNID.

Theorem 1 (Progress and Lifecycle Conformance with Optimistic Coordination). *Let n_C be a t-PNID representing the semantics of an object-centric choreography C and $\tau \in \mathcal{T}$ a task annotated with the optimistic pattern, with $(c, s) = msg(\tau)$. In any reachable marking M with $M(p_{\tau}) \neq \emptyset$, let $e \in M(p_{\tau})$ be a transmission token. Then, the following properties hold.*

(i) ***Progress.*** *At least one transition in $T^{\tau}_{rec} \cup T^{\tau}_{recx}$ is enabled in M.*
(ii) ***Lifecycle Conformance.*** *Every such enabled transition is lifecycle-conformant, i.e., its firing only yields state transitions that conform with $\mathcal{L}_c$ according to the receiver's object view.*

Hence, in any case, the token e can be consumed immediately from p_τ, and τ can never deadlock due to conflicting object views.

Proof (Sketch). Let $r = rec(\tau)$ and $(c, s) = msg(\tau)$. Exactly one of the following holds for the receiver's current local state $s' \in S_c$ for c:

- $s' \in vrs(r, c, s)$. Then by construction there exists a standard receiver transition $t_{rec}^{\tau,s'}$ consuming tokens from p_τ and $p_{rcs'}$, which already contain the two required tokens (e and the view-token), enabling $t_{rec}^{\tau,s'}$. Once fired, it moves the view token to p_{rcs}, which by definition of vrs is a lifecycle-conformant state transition.
- $s' \notin vrs(r, c, s)$. Then the net contains an exceptional transition $t_{recx}^{\tau,s'}$. Again, both required tokens are present, hence $t_{recx}^{\tau,s'}$ is enabled. Once fired, e is consumed and the token in $p_{rcs'}$ is reproduced, preserving lifecycle conformance.

In both cases (i) and (ii) are satisfied.

Note that this guarantee is strictly local: only tasks employing the optimistic pattern benefit from it. Inconsistencies are not resolved globally but deferred to exception handling logic. Thus, while autonomy and deadlock-freedom are ensured, inconsistencies may still propagate unless explicitly managed.

5.2 Pessimistic Locking

The *pessimistic pattern* enforces exclusive access to a shared object by temporarily restricting its use through explicit locking. A *locking task* prevents the sender from modifying or transmitting the object until a corresponding *unlocking task* is executed. This pattern isolates object access to a single choreography instance, thereby eliminating the risk of conflicting object views across instances at the cost of reduced concurrency and increased modeling responsibility to ensure that locks are eventually released.

Tasks involved in this pattern are visually annotated with closed (locking) and open (unlocking) padlock symbols, as shown in Fig. 7. Although not part of BPMN, this notation provides clear semantic cues to modelers.

Let $\tau \in \mathcal{T}$ be a locking task with $msg(\tau) = (c, s)$ and initiator $r = ini(\tau)$. We adjust its sender transition t_{ini}^{τ} to consume the token from p_{rcs} and place it in a new *locked state place* p_{rcs}^{lock}. This marks the object as locked for r and prevents further use until it is explicitly unlocked while maintaining state information. The receiver transitions T_{rec}^{τ} remain as previously defined.

Let $\tau' \in \mathcal{T}$ be the corresponding unlocking task with $msg(\tau') = (c, s)$ and receiver $r = rec(\tau')$. Each receiver transition $t_{rec}^{\tau',s'} \in T_{rec}^{\tau'}$ now consumes the token from $p_{rcs'}^{lock}$ instead of $p_{rcs'}$ and places it in p_{rcs}, thereby unlocking the object and restoring it for use by r. The sender transition $t_{ini}^{\tau'}$ is unchanged.

Figure 7 illustrates this mechanism: once the radiology department offers an *available* appointment (locking task), it cannot manipulate that appointment again until the patient responds with the *selected* appointment (unlocking task). This ensures that no concurrent instance can change the sender's view during this window, thus preserving consistency. Note that there exists a locked place and receiver transition for the *selected* state as well, since both *available* and *selected* are valid receiver states for a task sending

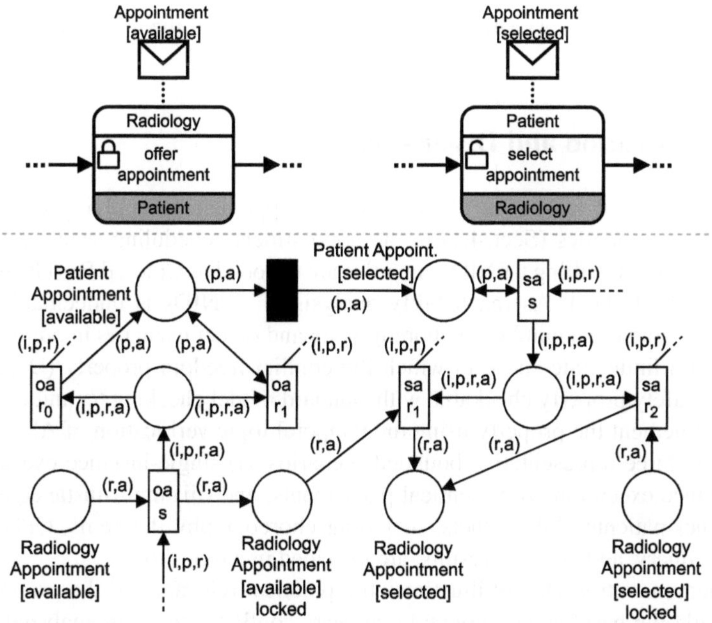

Fig. 7. Pessimistic object coordination pattern with sender-side locking and receiver-side unlocking tasks, indicated by a closed or open padlock icon respectively (top). The extended semantics are depicted at the bottom. This illustration abstracts from sequence flow places to limit complexity. (Variable types as given in Fig. 5.)

an appointment in *selected* according to the lifecycle in Fig. 2. However, since locked objects must not be manipulated until explicitly unlocked, which also includes local state transitions, locked places are not connected to local transitions (T_s).

While the pattern enforces isolation and thus mitigates the risk of conflicting object views across choreography instances, it does not guarantee lock release. It is the modeler's responsibility to ensure that every execution path from a locking task eventually leads to an unlocking task. This limitation highlights a trade-off: higher guarantees of consistency come at the cost of reduced concurrency and added modeling responsibility.

Theorem 2 (Exclusive and Non-Reentrant Locking Under Pessimistic Coordination). *Let n_C be a t-PNID representing the semantics of an object-centric choreography C and $\tau \in \mathcal{T}$ a task annotated with the pessimistic pattern, with $(c, s) = msg(\tau)$. If, in a reachable marking M, a token e is located in p^{lock}_{rcs}, then it holds that no transition which consumes e in an* ordinary *view place p_{rcs} of r is enabled. This also implies that no further locking transition initiated by the same role r on the same object identifier is enabled until e has been unlocked by the designated unlock task.*

Proof (Sketch). When τ fires, it removes the token e from the ordinary view place p_{rcs} and places it *exclusively* in p^{lock}_{rcs}. Since an object view token can only be in one ordinary view place at a time by construction (Sect. 4.1), no other ordinary view place of r contains e. Since all non-unlocking transitions consume tokens from an ordinary view place in their presets, every such transition is disabled until the unlock task moves the token back.

6 Demonstration and Discussion

We demonstrate the feasibility of the proposed approach by applying the proposed object-centric semantics (Sect. 4.1) to the appointment scheduling scenario shown in Figs. 1 and 2. The resulting t-PNID semantics are encoded as Colored Petri Nets (CPNs) using CPN Tools [17]. As reachability analysis of t-PNIDs is undecidable in general [30], we bound the number of choreography and object instances in our evaluation, resulting in a finite state space in which the conflict-freedom property (Definition 7) becomes a safety property checkable with standard model checking techniques. To this end, we implement the property using the temporal logic verification of ASK-CTL [4] and analyze three representative bounded scenarios: (i) single-instance execution, (ii) multi-instance execution with identical participants, and (iii) multi-instance execution with distinct patients. All artifacts, including choreography diagrams, CPN models, ASK-CTL query, and analysis results, are provided in a repository[2].

The demonstration clearly illustrates the practical relevance of the proposed approach. While the baseline choreography appears conflict-free when analyzed in isolation, concurrent executions, both with identical and distinct participants, reveal previously hidden conflicting object views. This underscores the limitation of traditional choreography analysis, which typically assumes isolated execution scenarios. The proposed approach addresses this gap by enabling early detection of potential runtime inconsistencies, which can be costly to resolve when identified late.

Embedding the optimistic and pessimistic coordination patterns in the choreography resolves the conflicts observed in our scenarios while preserving lifecycle conformance. Explicitly modeling the chosen strategy, rather than relying on implicit control, makes coordination and any interactions resulting from a conflict (e.g., compensation, retries, escalation) explicit, so they can be verified globally on the resulting t-PNID before implementation. Using well-known patterns [21] supports adoption in practice.

Reflecting on the research questions, we confirm that the extended object-centric choreography semantics effectively capture multiple concurrent instances while explicitly distinguishing between choreography instances and participants' views of objects (RQ_1). Regarding RQ_2, the formalization of conflicting object views is effective for model analysis, as demonstrated through successful detection via state-space exploration. Addressing RQ_3, the embedded optimistic and pessimistic coordination patterns prove to be capable of preventing conflicting views and preserving lifecycle conformance.

However, some limitations and open questions remain. The current semantics and patterns are evaluated for a single choreography model; handling conflicts over shared objects accessed by multiple, distinct choreography models is left for future work. Moreover, the proposed patterns represent rather simple solutions. Hybrid approaches that combine optimistic and pessimistic mechanisms or more sophisticated concurrency

[2] https://github.com/bptlab/detecting-conflicting-object-views-in-choreographies/.

control strategies could offer better trade-offs between concurrency and safety. While we focused on design-time verification of lifecycle conformance, the runtime impact of these patterns, e.g., on throughput or latency, remains unexplored. Simulation techniques grounded in the proposed formal semantics may help quantify such trade-offs. Furthermore, assessing the usability and understandability of these patterns for business process designers require empirical evaluation. Additionally, the introduced coordination patterns raise new verification challenges, such as ensuring eventual release of locked objects, which is outside the scope of this paper.

Moreover, the demonstration is limited to a bounded number of instances and objects due to rapidly growing state-space complexity caused by concurrency. Consequently, scalability to larger real-world choreographies could benefit significantly from symbolic or modular verification techniques [27]. In addition, object-centric processes typically involve the handling of sets of objects [13], and the extension of choreography semantics to multi-object interactions remains open. Lastly, the relationship between object-centric choreographies and local object-centric processes deserves further investigation, including the impact of coordination patterns on behavior and compliance.

Despite these considerations, the proposed semantics and embedded coordination patterns significantly advance the expressiveness of choreography modeling. By enabling detection and explicit resolution of conflicting object views at design time, we provide a foundation for safer, more robust, and ultimately more trustworthy interorganizational interactions. This represents a meaningful step towards bridging the gap between conceptual choreography models and the complex realities of concurrent, data-driven collaborations.

7 Conclusion

This paper introduces a formal extension of object-aware choreography semantics to detect and prevent *conflicting object views* arising in concurrent choreography instances. By proposing an object-centric translation to typed Petri Nets with Identifiers (t-PNIDs), we enable explicit modeling and analysis of distinct participants, data objects, and choreography instances, enabling the detection of conflicting object views. Additionally, we present two coordination patterns—optimistic conflict handling and pessimistic locking—which can be embedded into choreography models, and demonstrate their effectiveness in resolving conflicts arising from concurrent interactions. The demonstration confirms that the presented approach improves the reliability of choreography models involving shared objects, thus supporting more robust and trustworthy process interactions among collaborating organizations.

Future work will focus on exploring hybrid coordination strategies to better balance concurrency and safety, addressing verification challenges associated with locking patterns, and extending our semantics to support multi-instance handling of object sets.

Disclosure of Interests. The authors have no competing interests to declare that are relevant to the content of this article.

References

1. Baier, C., Katoen, J.: Principles of Model Checking. MIT Press, Cambridge (2008)
2. Belluccini, S., De Nicola, R., Dumas, M., Pullonen-Raudvere, P., Re, B., Tiezzi, F.: Model-based verification of data protection mechanisms in collaborative business processes. Softw. Syst. Model. **24**(2), 489–521 (2025). https://doi.org/10.1007/s10270-024-01217-6
3. Burigana, A., Gianola, A., Montali, M., Winkler, S.: Glocal conformance checking. In: Marrella, A., Resinas, M., Jans, M., Rosemann, M. (eds.) Business Process Management - 22nd International Conference, BPM 2024, Krakow, Poland, September 1-6, 2024, Proceedings. Lecture Notes in Computer Science, vol. 14940, pp. 75–92. Springer (2024). https://doi.org/10.1007/978-3-031-70396-6_5
4. Cheng, A., Christensen, S., Mortensen, K.H.: Model checking coloured petri nets - exploiting strongly connected components. DAIMI Report Series **26**(519) (1997). https://doi.org/10.7146/dpb.v26i519.7048
5. Clarke, E.M., Emerson, E.A.: Design and synthesis of synchronization skeletons using branching-time temporal logic. In: Kozen, D. (ed.) Logics of Programs, Workshop, Yorktown Heights, New York, USA, May 1981. Lecture Notes in Computer Science, vol. 131, pp. 52–71. Springer (1981). https://doi.org/10.1007/BFB0025774
6. Clarke, E.M., Grumberg, O., Peled, D.A.: Model Checking. MIT Press, Cambridge (2001). https://mitpress.mit.edu/books/model-checking
7. Corradini, F., Morichetta, A., Polini, A., Re, B., Tiezzi, F.: Collaboration vs. choreography conformance in BPMN. Log. Methods Comput. Sci. **16**(4) (2020). https://lmcs.episciences.org/6861
8. Decker, G., Weske, M.: Local enforceability in interaction petri nets. In: Alonso, G., Dadam, P., Rosemann, M. (eds.) Business Process Management, vol. 4714, pp. 305–319. Springer Berlin Heidelberg, Berlin, Heidelberg (2007). https://doi.org/10.1007/978-3-540-75183-0_22
9. Dijkman, R.M., Dumas, M., Ouyang, C.: Formal semantics and analysis of BPMN process models using petri nets (2007)
10. Fahland, D.: Describing behavior of processes with many-to-many interactions. In: Donatelli, S., Haar, S. (eds.) Application and Theory of Petri Nets and Concurrency, pp. 3–24. Springer International Publishing, Cham (2019). https://doi.org/10.1007/978-3-030-21571-2_1
11. Fdhila, W., Gall, M., Rinderle-Ma, S., Mangler, J., Indiono, C.: Classification and formalization of instance-spanning constraints in process-driven applications. In: Rosa, M.L., Loos, P., Pastor, O. (eds.) Business Process Management - 14th International Conference, BPM 2016, Rio de Janeiro, Brazil, September 18-22, 2016. Proceedings. Lecture Notes in Computer Science, vol. 9850, pp. 348–364. Springer (2016). https://doi.org/10.1007/978-3-319-45348-4_20
12. Fleischmann, A.: Limitations of choreography specifications with BPMN. In: Freitag, M., Kinra, A., Kotzab, H., Kreowski, H.J., Thoben, K.D. (eds.) Subject-Oriented Business Process Management. The Digital Workplace - Nucleus of Transformation - 12th International Conference, S-BPM ONE 2020, Bremen, Germany, December 2-3, 2020, Proceedings. Communications in Computer and Information Science, vol. 1278, pp. 203–216. Springer (2020). https://doi.org/10.1007/978-3-030-64351-5_14
13. Gianola, A., Montali, M., Winkler, S.: Object-centric conformance alignments with synchronization. In: Guizzardi, G., Santoro, F.M., Mouratidis, H., Soffer, P. (eds.) Advanced Information Systems Engineering - 36th International Conference, CAiSE 2024, Limassol, Cyprus, June 3-7, 2024, Proceedings. Lecture Notes in Computer Science, vol. 14663, pp. 3–19. Springer (2024). https://doi.org/10.1007/978-3-031-61057-8_1

14. Haarmann, S., Lichtenstein, T., Weske, M.: Fragment-based service choreographies. In: Ardagna, C.A., Bian, H., Chang, C.K., Chang, R.N., Damiani, E., Dustdar, S., Marco, J., Singh, M.P., Teniente, E., Ward, R., Wang, Z., Xhafa, F., Zhang, J. (eds.) IEEE International Conference on Services Computing, SCC 2022, Barcelona, Spain, July 10-16, 2022. pp. 164–173. IEEE (2022). https://doi.org/10.1109/SCC55611.2022.00035
15. Haarmann, S., Weske, M.: Cross-case data objects in business processes: semantics and analysis. In: Fahland, D., Ghidini, C., Becker, J., Dumas, M. (eds.) Business Process Management Forum - BPM Forum 2020, Seville, Spain, September 13-18, 2020, Proceedings. Lecture Notes in Business Information Processing, vol. 392, pp. 3–17. Springer (2020). https://doi.org/10.1007/978-3-030-58638-6_1
16. Hahn, M., Breitenbücher, U., Kopp, O., Leymann, F.: Modeling and execution of data-aware choreographies: an overview. Comput. Sci. Res. Dev. **33**(3-4), 329–340 (2018). https://doi.org/10.1007/s00450-017-0387-y
17. Jensen, K., Kristensen, L.M., Wells, L.: Coloured petri nets and CPN tools for modelling and validation of concurrent systems. Int. J. Softw. Tools Technol. Transf. **9**(3–4), 213–254 (2007). https://doi.org/10.1007/S10009-007-0038-X
18. Köpke, J., Franceschetti, M., Eder, J.: Optimizing data-flow implementations for inter-organizational processes. Dist. Parallel Databases **37**(4), 651–695 (2019). https://doi.org/10.1007/S10619-018-7251-3
19. Kopp, O., Görlach, K., Leymann, F.: Extending choreography spheres to improve simulations. In: Kotsis, G., Taniar, D., Pardede, E., Saleh, I., Khalil, I. (eds.) iiWAS'2010 - the 12th International Conference on Information Integration and Web-Based Applications and Services, 8-10 November 2010, Paris, France. pp. 696–699. ACM (2010). https://doi.org/10.1145/1967486.1967598
20. Kopp, O., Wieland, M., Leymann, F.: Towards choreography transactions. In: Kopp, O., Lohmann, N. (eds.) 1st Central-European Workshop on Services and Their Composition, ZEUS 2009, Stuttgart, Germany, March 2-3, 2009. Proceedings. CEUR Workshop Proceedings, vol. 438, pp. 49–54. CEUR-WS.org (2009), https://ceur-ws.org/Vol-438/paper8.pdf
21. Kung, H.T., Robinson, J.T.: On optimistic methods for concurrency control. ACM Trans. Database Syst. **6**(2), 213–226 (1981). https://doi.org/10.1145/319566.319567
22. Leitner, M., Mangler, J., Rinderle-Ma, S.: Definition and enactment of instance-spanning process constraints. In: Wang, X.S., Cruz, I.F., Delis, A., Huang, G. (eds.) Web Information Systems Engineering - WISE 2012 - 13th International Conference, Paphos, Cyprus, November 28-30, 2012. Proceedings. Lecture Notes in Computer Science, vol. 7651, pp. 652–658. Springer (2012). https://doi.org/10.1007/978-3-642-35063-4_49
23. Lichtenstein, T., Weske, M.: Data consistency as a criterion for process choreography design. In: Link, S., Reinhartz-Berger, I., Zdravkovic, J., Bork, D., Srinivasa, S. (eds.) Proceedings of the ER Forum and PhD Symposium 2022 Co-Located with 41st International Conference on Conceptual Modeling (ER 2022), Virtual Event, Hyderabad, India, October 17, 2022. CEUR Workshop Proceedings, vol. 3211. CEUR-WS.org (2022). https://ceur-ws.org/Vol-3211/CR_095.pdf
24. Lichtenstein, T., Weske, M.: Execution semantics for process choreographies with data. In: Francescomarino, C.D., Burattin, A., Janiesch, C., Sadiq, S.W. (eds.) Business Process Management Forum - BPM 2023 Forum, Utrecht, the Netherlands, September 11-15, 2023, Proceedings. Lecture Notes in Business Information Processing, vol. 490, pp. 90–106. Springer (2023). https://doi.org/10.1007/978-3-031-41623-1_6
25. Lohmann, N., Wolf, K.: Artifact-centric choreographies. In: Maglio, P.P., Weske, M., Yang, J., Fantinato, M. (eds.) Service-Oriented Computing - 8th International Conference, ICSOC 2010, San Francisco, CA, USA, December 7-10, 2010. Proceedings. Lecture Notes in Computer Science, vol. 6470, pp. 32–46 (2010). https://doi.org/10.1007/978-3-642-17358-5_3

26. Meyer, A., Pufahl, L., Batoulis, K., Fahland, D., Weske, M.: Automating data exchange in process choreographies **53**, 296–329 (2015). https://doi.org/10.1016/j.is.2015.03.008
27. Nejati, F., Ghani, A.A.A., Ng, K.Y., Jafaar, A.B.: Handling state space explosion in component-based software verification: a review. IEEE Access Pract. Innov. Open Solut. **9**, 77526–77544 (2021). https://doi.org/10.1109/ACCESS.2021.3081742
28. Nikaj, A., Weske, M.: Formal specification of RESTful choreography properties. In: Bozzon, A., Cudré-Mauroux, P., Pautasso, C. (eds.) Web Engineering - 16th International Conference, ICWE 2016, Lugano, Switzerland, June 6-9, 2016. Proceedings. Lecture Notes in Computer Science, vol. 9671, pp. 365–372. Springer (2016), https://doi.org/10.1007/978-3-319-38791-8_21
29. (OMG), O.M.G.: Business Process Model and Notation (BPMN), Version 2.0.2: Standard (2014). https://www.omg.org/spec/BPMN/2.0.2/PDF
30. Rosa-Velardo, F., de Frutos-Escrig, D.: Decidability and complexity of Petri nets with unordered data. Theoret. Comput. Sci. **412**(34), 4439–4451 (2011). https://doi.org/10.1016/J.TCS.2011.05.007
31. Aalst, W.M., Barthelmess, P., Ellis, C.A., Wainer, J.: PROCLETS: a framework for lightweight interacting workflow processes. Int. J. Cooper. Info. Syst. **10**(04), 443–481 (2001)
32. Werf, J.M.E.M., Rivkin, A., Montali, M., Polyvyanyy, A.: Correctness notions for petri nets with identifiers. Fund. Info. **190**(2–4), 159–207 (2024). https://doi.org/10.3233/FI-242169
33. Weske, M.: Business process management - concepts, languages, architectures. Fourth Edition. Springer (2024). https://doi.org/10.1007/978-3-662-69518-0

To Bind or Not to Bind? Discovering Stable Relationships in Object-Centric Processes

Anjo Seidel[1(✉)], Sarah Winkler[2], Alessandro Gianola[3], Marco Montali[2], and Mathias Weske[1]

[1] Hasso Plattner Institute, University of Potsdam, Potsdam, Germany
{anjo.seidel,mathias.weske}@hpi.de

[2] Free University of Bozen-Bolzano, Bolzano, Italy
{winkler,montali}@inf.unibz.it

[3] INESC-ID/Instituto Superior Técnico, Universidade de Lisboa, Lisboa, Portugal
alessandro.gianola@tecnico.ulisboa.pt

Abstract. Object-centric process mining investigates the intertwined behavior of multiple objects in business processes. From object-centric event logs, object-centric Petri nets (OCPN) can be discovered to replay the behavior of processes accessing different object types. Although they indicate how objects flow through the process and co-occur in events, OCPNs remain underspecified about the relationships of objects. Hence, they are not able to represent synchronization, i.e. executing objects only according to their intended relationships, and fail to identify violating executions. Existing formal modeling approaches, such as object-centric Petri nets with identifiers (OPID), represent object identities and relationships to synchronize them correctly. However, OPID discovery has not yet been studied. This paper uses explicit data models to bridge the gap between OCPNs and formal OPIDs. We identify the implicit assumptions of stable many-to-one relationships in object-centric event logs, which implies synchronization of related objects. To formally underpin this observation, we combine OCPNs with explicit stable many-to-one relationships in a rigorous mapping from OCPNs to OPIDs explicitly capturing the intended stable relationships and the synchronization of related objects. We prove that the original OCPNs and the resulting OPIDs coincide for those executions that satisfy the intended relationships. Moreover, we provide an implementation of the mapping from OCPN to OPID under stable relationships.

Keywords: Business Process Management · Data Modeling · Object-centric Petri Nets · Conformance Checking · Synchronization

1 Introduction

Process mining analyzes the behavior of information systems through event logs to gain insight into the behavior of the system [19]. Process mining techniques

D. Bork et al. (Eds.): ER 2025, LNCS 16189, pp. 223–241, 2026.
https://doi.org/10.1007/978-3-032-08623-5_12

strive between two contrasting forces when dealing with process models: capturing complex real-life processes demands *expressiveness*, while performance and memory consumption of the adopted algorithms call for *simplicity*. Balancing these contrasting forces is difficult given that within a process mining pipeline, the same model can be seen as descriptive, like a model discovered from data, or as prescriptive, e.g., when later on used for conformance checking: while a descriptive model can favor simplicity over precision, a prescriptive one should be expressive enough to precisely capture the intended behavior. Achieving a suitable trade-off appears particularly difficult within the novel research area of object-centric process science, where processes co-evolve multiple, interrelated objects at once [17]. Executions of such processes are typically represented in *object-centric event logs* (OCELs) [6], where each recorded event may refer to multiple objects. For example, consider the following OCEL L_1 that records activities in a bicycle manufacturing workshop. For a given order, a frame, a set of wheels, and a handlebar are collected before being assembled:

$$\begin{aligned} L_1 = [&\langle \mathsf{collect}, \{f_1, h_1, w_1, w_2\}\rangle, \langle \mathsf{assemble\_w}, \{f_1, w_1, w_2\}\rangle,\\ &\langle \mathsf{assemble\_h}, \{f_1, h_1\}\rangle, \langle \mathsf{collect}, \{f_2, h_2, w_3, w_4\}\rangle,\\ &\langle \mathsf{assemble\_h}, \{f_2, h_2\}\rangle, \langle \mathsf{assemble\_w}, \{f_2, w_3, w_4\}\rangle] \end{aligned}$$

with f_i of type *frame*, h_i of type *handlebar*, and w_i of type *wheel*. Two bicycles are ordered; the first *collect* event takes the frame, handlebar, and two wheels for the first bike; the `assemble_w` event assembles two wheels to a frame, etc.

To replay the event log and describe the behavior captured in an OCEL, an *object-centric Petri net (OCPN)* can be discovered [20]. For instance, the OCPN in Example 1 allows to replay the behavior of log L_1. In the initial marking (▶), all recorded objects in the log are placed, so that, e.g., all wheel objects $w_1, \ldots w_4$ reside initially in the *wheel* place. The transitions can fire by binding objects and processing them through the net. In OCPNs, a non-variable arc binds a single object, while a variable arc (double line) binds a set of objects. Finally, the net accepts a given execution if all objects are placed in the final marking (■).

Example 1 (OCPN for bicycle manufacturing).

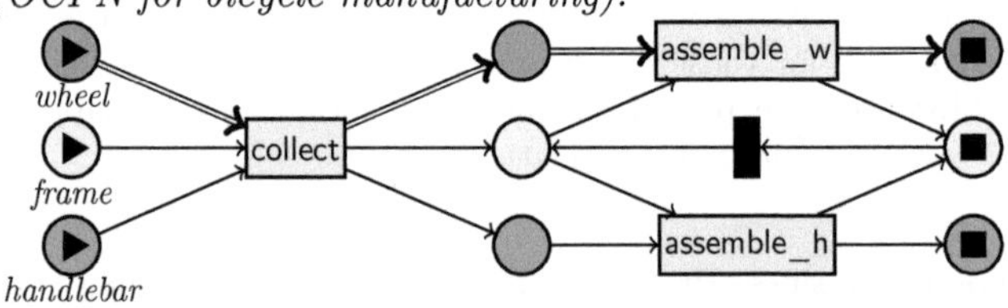

OCPNs favor simplicity over expressiveness: Although discovered OCPNs consider the token flow of multiple object types, OCPNs do not provide mechanisms to track the identity of objects, their relationships, and cardinality constraints. As pointed out in [18], this deliberate underspecification makes discovered OCPNs underfitting, as they allow for too much behavior. This becomes apparent if the expected data model with cardinality constraints for log L_1 is explicitly modeled as a UML class diagram:

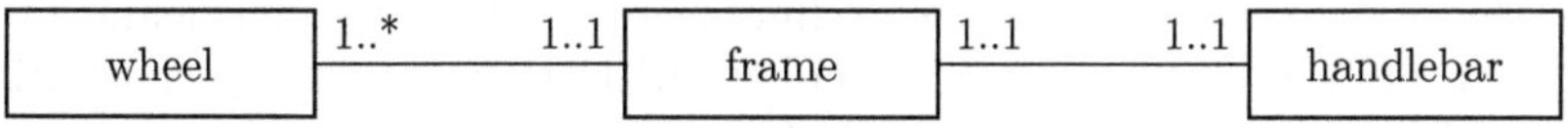

The behavior recorded in L_1 satisfies the cardinality constraints for a many-to-one relationship between the wheels and a frame, and a one-to-one relationship between the frame and handlebar. However, in an OCPN it is impossible to express that a transition should bind objects in accordance with their mutual relationships, and it cannot distinguish transition firings that satisfy this criterion from those that bind unrelated objects, a distinction that is often essential when dealing with synchronization [8]. For example, in the OCPN in Example 1 wheels collected for a given frame may be reshuffled, that is, assembled with a different frame. Hence, it accepts the execution in the following log:

$$L_2 = [\langle \mathsf{collect}, \{f_3, h_3, w_5, w_6\}\rangle, \langle \mathsf{collect}, \{f_4, h_4, w_7\}\rangle, \langle \mathsf{assemble\_w}, \{f_3, w_5\}\rangle, \langle \mathsf{assemble\_h}, \{f_3, h_4\}\rangle, \langle \mathsf{assemble\_w}, \{f_4, w_6, w_7\}\rangle, \langle \mathsf{assemble\_h}, \{f_4, h_3\}\rangle]$$

where wheel w_6 is attached to frame f_4 even though it was collected with frame f_3. This indicates that whenever an OCPN is used in a prescriptive manner for conformance checking or simulation, further so-called "bounding behavior" [18] is needed to ensure the desired synchronization. This bounding behavior can be suitably captured through more sophisticated and expressive object-centric process modeling languages, such as variants of Petri nets with identifiers (PNIDs) [7,21], or synchronous proclets [4]. Recently, object-centric Petri nets with identifiers (OPIDs [8]) have been proposed as a formalism that unifies the features of OCPNs, PNIDs, and synchronous proclets. In contrast to OCPNs, OPIDs are appropriate for prescriptive purposes because of their high expressiveness. However, while conformance for OPIDs is handled in [8], the discovery of OPIDs and related formalisms has not yet been studied. To avoid reshuffling like in the above example, and similar synchronization problems, we start by identifying an important assumption that is implicit in OCELs: executions are supposed to satisfy *stable many-to-one relationship* between two object types which synchronize the corresponding objects throughout the execution. This means that if the relationship between object types σ_m and σ_o is many-to-one, then whenever an object of type σ_m is bound to an object of type σ_o, it is never bound to a different object of type σ_o. This implicit assumption comes from the fact that OCEL assumes global and rigid relationships throughout execution [2,10].

To find a model that satisfies both the simplicity of discovered OCPNs and the expressiveness to enforce the desired bounding behavior, this paper presents a rigorous mapping from an OCPN together with a set of stable many-to-one relationships, to an equivalent *replay OPID* that enforces the intended synchronization. By doing so, we at once provide a fourfold contribution: (1) we provide a first discovery technique for one specific class of OPIDs, (2) we identify the class of relatively simple replay OPIDs that are yet expressive enough to enforce the desired bounding behaviour, (3) we formally prove that a so-obtained replay

OPID is equivalent to the original OCPN for executions that respect the data model (4) we provide a proof-of-concept implementation of our transformation.

To this end, after recapping the preliminaries (Sect. 2), we first define a mapping of an OCPN to an equivalent replay OPID that tracks object identifiers but not object relationships (Sect. 3). In a second step, given a set of stable many-to-one relationships, we define a translation that encodes the synchronization semantics into a more restrictive replay OPID (Sect. 4), which we prove to be equivalent to the original OCPN in replaying OCELs that satisfy the stable many-to-one relationships, while prohibiting violating executions. To illustrate practical relevance, we discuss our contribution in the context of related work, show that stable many-to-one relationships frequently occur in existing OCEL benchmarks, and describe our implementation of the transformations (Sect. 5).

2 Preliminary Definitions

2.1 Object-Centric Event Logs and Object-Centric Petri Nets

To define OCELs and OCPNs, we recall notions by van der Aalst and Berti [20].

Definition 1. *Given a set of object types Σ, a set of activities $\mathcal{A}$, and a set of timestamps $\mathbb{T}$ under a total order $<$, an* object-centric event log *(OCEL) is a tuple $L = (E, \mathcal{O}, \pi_{act}, \pi_{obj}, \pi_{time})$ where:*

- *E is a set of events;*
- *$\mathcal{O}$ is a set of object identifiers, each typed by the function $ot : \mathcal{O} \to \Sigma$;*
- *the functions $\pi_{act} : E \to \mathcal{A}$, $\pi_{obj} : E \to \mathcal{P}(\mathcal{O})$, and $\pi_{time} : E \to \mathbb{T}$, mapping each event to an activity, a set of objects, and a timestamp.*

For example, the event logs L_1 and L_2 in Section 1 are defined for the object types *Wheel*, *Frame*, and *Handlebar*. The event $e = \langle \mathsf{collect}, \{f_1, h_1, w_1, w_2\}\rangle$ in L_1 refers to the activity $\pi_{act}(e) = \texttt{collect}$ and the objects $\pi_{obj}(e) = \{f_1, h_1, w_1, w_2\}$, where $ot(f_1) = \mathit{Frame}$.

Definition 2. *Given a set of object types Σ, and a set of activities $\mathcal{A}$, an* object-centric Petri net *(OCPN) is defined as a tuple $N = (P, T, F, pt, F_{var}, \ell)$, where:*

1. *P and T are finite sets of places and transitions such that $P \cap T = \emptyset$,*
2. *$F \subseteq (P \times T) \cup (T \times P)$ is the flow relation between places and transitions,*
3. *$pt\colon P \to \Sigma$ maps every place to an object type,*
4. *$F_{var} \subseteq F$ is the set of variable flow relations,*
5. *$\ell\colon T \to \mathcal{A} \cup \{\tau\}$ is the transition labelling where τ marks an invisible activity.*

The pre-places of a transition t are all places with ingoing flow relations $\bullet t = \{p \in P \mid (p,t) \in F\}$, while the post-places of t are all those connected with outgoing flow relations $t\bullet = \{p \in P \mid (t,p) \in F\}$. For a transition t, the function $tpl(t)$ returns the types of all its corresponding places $p \in \bullet t \cup t\bullet$. $tpl_{var}(t)$ returns all place types connected via variable flow, and $tpl_{nv}(t)$ all place types connected via non-variable flow. An OCPN is considered well-formed if all flow relations of one transition agree in the variability for the place types, i.e., $\forall t \in T : tpl_{var}(t) \cap tpl_{nv}(t) = \emptyset$.

All possible tokens and their location in a place are defined as $Q = \{(p, o) \in P \times \mathcal{O} \mid pt(p) = type(o)\}$. A marking is generally defined as a multiset of token-object pairs $M: Q \rightarrow \mathbb{N}$ [20]. However, we pose the following specific assumptions about the structure of an OCPN. The contemporary discovery algorithms for OCPN [20,22] utilize the Inductive Miner algorithm [11], which results in sound workflow nets for each object type. As a result, all places are bound to at most one object identity by design. Therefore, we interpret the marking M of an OCPN as a set of objects in a marking such that $M: Q \rightarrow \{0, 1\}$. Furthermore, each object type has one initial place and one final place.

The set of binding executions is $B = \{(t, b) \in T \times (\Sigma \rightarrow \mathcal{P}(\mathcal{O})) \mid dom(b) = tpl(t) \wedge \forall \sigma \in tpl_{nv}(t) : |b(\sigma)| = 1\}$. It contains pairs of transition t and binding b. A binding b is a function that maps an object type $\sigma \in \Sigma$ to a set of objects. We denote by $codom(b)$ the codomain of b, that is, $codom(b) = \bigcup_{\sigma \in \Sigma} b(\sigma)$. This binding execution consumes a set of object tokens from the transition's pre-places $cons(t, b) = \{(p, o) \in Q \mid p \in \bullet t \wedge o \in b(pt(p))\}$. Similarly, it produces object tokens $prod(t, b) = \{(p, o) \in Q \mid p \in t\bullet \wedge o \in b(pt(p))\}$. This binding is enabled in a marking M_i and can be executed if $cons(t, b) \leq M_i$. The resulting marking is $M_j = M_i - cons(t, b) + prod(t, b)$. The firing is denoted as $M_i \xrightarrow{(t,b)} M_j$. Note that by the definition of bindings, if a transition t has two places in $p_1, p_2 \in \bullet t$ of the same object type, then t can only be fired by consuming the same objects from p_1 and p_2. A binding (t, b) for a transition t considers only objects $b \subseteq \mathcal{O}$ that belong to the types of the respective input places and are in line with the variable and non-variable arcs.

An *accepting OCPN* combines an OCPN N with an initial marking $M_{init} \in \mathcal{B}(Q)$ and a final marking $M_{final} \in \mathcal{B}(Q)$. An accepted run is a sequence of binding executions from initial to final marking $M_{init} \xrightarrow{*} M_{final}$. The accepting OCPN can be used to *replay* the behavior of the log. All recorded objects are interpreted as the initial marking M_{init}. An event in the log and its recorded objects are interpreted as a binding execution of the corresponding transition and the involved objects, which results in a new marking. After replaying all events consecutively, the OCPN can accept the log if the run results in the final marking M_{final}. If an event has no corresponding binding execution or M_{final} is not reached, the log is rejected by the OCPN.

2.2 Object-Centric Petri Nets with Identifiers

Example 2. (Simple OPID for bike manufacturing). The OPID combines the object types *Wheel* (red), *Frame* (yellow), and relations for both (orange places).

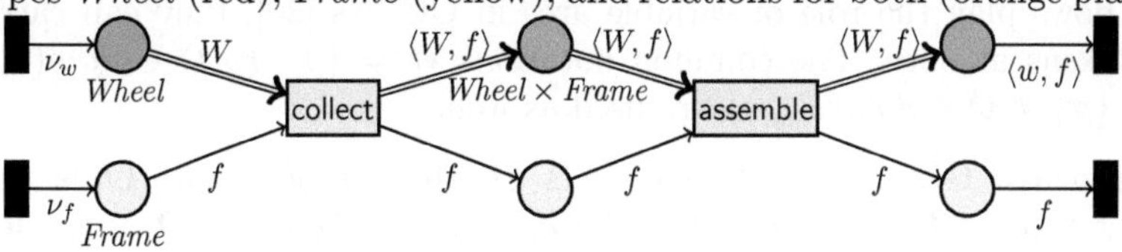

We summarize the definitions from [8]. Every object type $\sigma \in \Sigma$ is assumed to have a domain $dom(\sigma) \subseteq \mathcal{O}$, given by all objects in $\mathcal{O}$ of type σ. List types with a base type in σ are denoted as $[\sigma]$. Each Petri net place has a *color* that is a cartesian product of data types from Σ; precisely, the set of colors $\mathcal{C}$ is the set of all $\sigma_1 \times \cdots \times \sigma_m$ such that $m \geq 1$ and $\sigma_i \in \Sigma$ for all $1 \leq i \leq m$. We fix a set of Σ-typed variables $\mathcal{X} = X \uplus X_{list} \uplus \Upsilon$ as the disjoint union of a set X of "normal" variables that refer to single objects, denoted by lower-case letters like x, with a type $\text{type}(x) \in \Sigma$, a set X_{list} of list variables that refer to a list of objects of the same type, denoted by upper case letters like U, with a type $\text{type}(U) = [\sigma]$ for some $\sigma \in \Sigma$, and a set Υ of variables referring to fresh objects, denoted as ν, with $\text{type}(\nu) \in \Sigma$.

In OPIDs [8], tokens are object tuples associated with a color. To define relationships between objects in consumed and produced tokens when firing a transition, arc *inscriptions* are defined.

Definition 3. *An* inscription *is a tuple* $\boldsymbol{x} = \langle x_1, \ldots, x_m \rangle$ *such that* $m \geq 1$ *and* $x_i \in \mathcal{X}$ *for all* i*, but at most one* $x_i \in X_{list}$*, for* $1 \leq i \leq m$*. We call* $\boldsymbol{x}$ *a* template inscription *if* $x_i \in X_{list}$ *for some* i*, and a* simple inscription *otherwise.*

Template inscriptions capture an arbitrary number of tokens of the same color; they are used to label the correspondent of variable arcs in OCPNs. The color of an inscription $\iota = \langle x_1, \ldots, x_m \rangle$ is given by $\text{color}(\iota) = \langle \sigma_1, \ldots, \sigma_m \rangle$ where $\sigma_i = \text{type}(x_i)$ if $x_i \in X \cup \Upsilon$, and $\sigma_i = \sigma'$ if x_i is a list variable of type $[\sigma']$. We set $\text{vars}(\iota) = \{x_1, \ldots, x_m\}$. The set of all inscriptions is denoted Ω. Based on this, an OPID is formally defined as follows [8].

Definition 4. *An* object-centric Petri net with identifiers *(OPID) is defined as a tuple* $N = (\Sigma, P, T, F_{in}, F_{out}, \text{color}, \ell)$*, where:*

1. *P and T are finite sets of places and transitions such that $P \cap T = \emptyset$,*
2. *$\text{color}\colon P \to \mathcal{C}$ maps every place to a color,*
3. *$\ell\colon T \to \mathcal{A} \cup \{\tau\}$ is the transition labelling where τ marks an invisible activity,*
4. *$F_{in}\colon P \times T \to \Omega$ is a partial function called* input flow*, such that $\text{color}(F_{in}(p,t)) = \text{color}(p)$ for every $(p,t) \in dom(F_{in})$,*
5. *$F_{out}\colon T \times P \to \Omega$ is a partial function called* output flow*, such that $\text{color}(F_{out}(t,p)) = \text{color}(p)$ for every $(t,p) \in dom(F_{out})$.*

We set $\text{vars}_{in}(t) = \bigcup_{p \in P} \text{vars}(F_{in}(p,t))$*, and* $\text{vars}_{out}(t) = \bigcup_{p \in P} \text{vars}(F_{out}(t,p))$*, and require that* $\text{vars}_{in}(t) \cap \Upsilon = \emptyset$ *and* $\text{vars}_{out}(t) \subseteq \text{vars}_{in}(t) \cup \Upsilon$*, for all* $t \in T$*.*

If $F_{in}(p,t)$ is defined, it is called a *variable* flow if $F_{in}(p,t)$ is a template inscription, and *non-variable* flow otherwise; and similar for output flows. Variable flows play the role of variable arcs in OCPNs [20]; they can carry multiple tokens at once. The common notations $\bullet t = \{p \mid (p,t) \in dom(F_{in})\}$ and $t\bullet = \{p \mid (t,p) \in dom(F_{out})\}$ are used as well.

Semantics. Given the set of objects $\mathcal{O}$, the set of *tokens* $\boldsymbol{\mathcal{O}}$ is the set of object tuples $\boldsymbol{\mathcal{O}} = \{\mathcal{O}^m \mid m \geq 1\}$. The *color* of a token $\omega \in \boldsymbol{\mathcal{O}}$ of the form $\omega =$

$\langle o_1, \ldots, o_m \rangle$ is denoted $\text{color}(\omega) = \langle \text{type}(o_1), \ldots, \text{type}(o_m) \rangle$. A *marking* of an OPID $N = \langle \Sigma, P, T, F_{in}, F_{out}, \text{color}, \ell \rangle$ is a function $M \colon P \to 2^{\mathcal{O}}$, such that for all $p \in P$ and $\langle o_1, \ldots o_m \rangle \in M(p)$, it holds that $\text{color}(\langle o_1, \ldots o_m \rangle) = \text{color}(p)$. Let $\mathit{Lists}(\mathcal{O})$ denote the set of objects lists of the form $[o_1, \ldots, o_k]$ with $o_1, \ldots, o_k \in \mathcal{O}$ such that all o_i have the same type; the type of such a list is then $[\text{type}(o_1)]$. Next, *bindings* are defined to fix which objects are involved in a transition firing.

Definition 5. *A* binding *for a transition* t *and a marking* M *is a type-preserving function* $\beta \colon \text{vars}_{in}(t) \cup \text{vars}_{out}(t) \to \mathcal{O} \cup \mathit{Lists}(\mathcal{O})$. *To ensure the freshness of created values,* β *is required to be injective on* $\Upsilon \cap \text{vars}_{out}(t)$, *and* $\beta(\nu)$ *must not occur in* M *for all* $\nu \in \Upsilon \cap \text{vars}_{out}(t)$.

We denote by $\mathit{codom}(\beta) \subseteq \mathcal{O}$ the set of all objects occurring in tuples returned by β. Bindings are extended to inscriptions, denoted $\boldsymbol{\beta}$, to fix which tokens participate in a transition firing. For an inscription $\iota = \langle x_1, \ldots, x_m \rangle$, let $o_i = \beta(x_i)$ for all $1 \le i \le m$. Then $\boldsymbol{\beta}(\iota)$ is the set of object tuples defined as follows: if ι is a simple inscription, then $\boldsymbol{\beta}(\iota) = \{\langle o_1, \ldots, o_m \rangle\}$. Otherwise, there must be one x_i, $1 \le i \le n$, such that $x_i \in X_{list}$, and consequently o_i must be a list, say $o_i = [u_1, \ldots, u_k]$ for some $u_1, \ldots, u_k$. Then $\boldsymbol{\beta}(\iota) = \{\langle o_1, \ldots, o_{i-1}, u_1, o_{i+1}, \ldots, o_m \rangle, \ldots, \langle o_1, \ldots, o_{i-1}, u_k, o_{i+1}, \ldots, o_m \rangle\}$. $\mathcal{B}$ denotes the set of all bindings. Finally, a transition with a binding β is enabled if all object tuples pointed by $\boldsymbol{\beta}$ occur in the current marking:

Definition 6. *A transition* $t \in T$ *and a binding* β *for marking* M *are* enabled *in* M *if* $\boldsymbol{\beta}(F_{in}(p,t)) \subseteq M(p)$ *for all* $p \in \bullet t$.

Definition 7. *Let transition* t *be enabled in marking* M *with binding* β. *The* firing *of* t *yields the new marking* M' *given by* $M'(p) = M(p) \setminus \boldsymbol{\beta}(F_{in}(p,t))$ *for all* $p \in \bullet t \setminus t\bullet$, *and* $M'(p) = M(p) \cup \boldsymbol{\beta}(F_{out}(p,t))$ *for all* $p \in t\bullet \setminus \bullet t$, *and* $M'(p) = M(p) \setminus \boldsymbol{\beta}(F_{in}(p,t)) \cup \boldsymbol{\beta}(F_{out}(p,t))$ *for all* $p \in \bullet t \cap t\bullet$.[1]

We write $M \xrightarrow{t,\beta} M'$ to denote that t is enabled for binding β in M, and its firing yields M'. An *accepting* OPID N is an OPID together with a set of initial markings M_{init} and a set of final markings M_{final}. A run is accepted if it starts in the initial and ends in the final marking $M_{init} \xrightarrow{*} M_{final}$.

3 Equivalent Object-Centric Petri Nets with Identifiers

This section defines the mapping $\mathbb{T}_1$ from an OCPN N to an OPID. We show that the replays of both nets N and $\mathbb{T}_1(N)$ on a given event log are equivalent, that is, they accept and reject the same executions.

In this paper, we assume that for any given OCPN $N = (P, T, F, pt, F_{var}, \ell)$ there are fixed sets of places $P_{\blacktriangleright}, P_{\blacksquare} \subseteq P$ called *play* and *stop places*, respectively, such that for each $\sigma \in \Sigma$ there is exactly one place $p \in P_{\blacktriangleright}$ and $p' \in P_{\blacksquare}$ such that $pt(p) = pt(p') = \sigma$. These are the places that are supposed to be populated by

[1] The case for $p \in \bullet t \cap t\bullet$ was omitted in [8], which is insufficient for cyclic nets.

initial and final markings, respectively. Markings M_{init} and M_{final} are *suitable* initial and final markings for an OCPN with play and stop places $P_{\blacktriangleright}, P_{\blacksquare}$ if they put tokens only in those places, i.e., for all $o \in \mathcal{O}$, $M_{init}(p, o) = 0$ for all $p \notin P_{\blacktriangleright}$ and $M_{init}(p', o) = 0$ for all $p' \notin P_{\blacksquare}$, and similar for M_{final}.

Note that a given set of objects uniquely determines suitable initial and final markings for N: precisely, for a finite set of objects $O \subseteq \mathcal{O}$, let M^O_{init} (resp. M^O_{final}) be the marking such that for each $\sigma \in \Sigma$ and and each $o \in O_\sigma$, $M^O_{init}(p_\sigma, o) = 1$ (resp. $M^O_{final}(p_\sigma, o) = 1$) where p_σ is the unique place in $P_{\blacktriangleright}$ (resp. $P_{\blacksquare}$) of type σ. Our mapping $\mathbb{T}_1$ maps an OCPN N with start and stop places to an OPID $\mathbb{T}_1(N)$ that keeps all the places and transitions of N. The flow relations are adjusted and extended with arc inscriptions. Moreover, $\mathbb{T}_1(N)$ has additional transitions for creating and removing objects. In this way, the OPID can, on demand, populate the places in $P_{\blacktriangleright}$ with objects in an initial marking for N and consume objects from the places in $P_{\blacksquare}$ once a final marking for N is reached. The initial and final markings for $\mathbb{T}_1(N)$ are always empty.

Precisely, the OPID has an emitting transition for every object type, i.e., we set $T_e := \{t_{e,\sigma} \mid \sigma \in \Sigma\}$; and a consuming transition for every object type, i.e., we set $T_c := \{t_{c,\sigma} \mid \sigma \in \Sigma\}$. With its emitting transitions T_e, an OPID allows the creation of arbitrary new objects. However, in the replay of an OCEL L, this set of objects is fixed and denoted as $\mathcal{O}_L$. Hence, when replaying the log L, the inscription variables $\nu_i \in F_{out}(T_e)$ will be bound exclusively to objects in $\mathcal{O}_L$. To be able to define suitable inscriptions, we assume that for every object type $\sigma \in \Sigma$ there is a normal variable $x_\sigma \in X$, a list variable $X_\sigma \in X_{list}$, and a fresh object variable $\nu_\sigma \in \Upsilon$. We then set:

$$F_{out}\colon (T \cup T_e) \times P \to \Omega \qquad F_{out}(t,p) = \begin{cases} \langle x_{pt(p)} \rangle & \text{if } (t,p) \in F \setminus F_{var} \\ \langle X_{pt(p)} \rangle & \text{if } (t,p) \in F_{var} \\ \langle \nu_{pt(p)} \rangle & \text{if } p \in P_{\blacktriangleright} \land t \in T_e \end{cases}$$

$$F_{in}\colon P \times (T \cup T_c) \to \Omega \qquad F_{in}(p,t) = \begin{cases} \langle x_{pt(p)} \rangle & \text{if } (p,t) \in F \setminus F_{var} \\ \langle X_{pt(p)} \rangle & \text{if } (p,t) \in F_{var} \\ \langle x_{pt(p)} \rangle, & \text{if } p \in P_{\blacksquare} \land t \in T_c \end{cases}$$

The equivalent OPID is given by $\mathbb{T}_1(N) = (\Sigma_1, P_1, T_1, F_{in}, F_{out}, color, \ell_1)$ where $\Sigma_1 = \Sigma$, $P_1 = P$, $T_1 = T \cup T_e \cup T_c$, $color(p) = \langle pt(p) \rangle$ for all $p \in P$, and

$$\ell_1\colon T \to \mathcal{A} \qquad \ell_1(t) = \begin{cases} \tau, & \text{if } t \in T_e \cup T_c \\ \ell(t), & \text{otherwise} \end{cases}$$

Example 3 (Equivalent OPID for bike manufacturing). The following OPID is obtained from the OCPN in Example 1 by applying the translation $\mathbb{T}_1$.

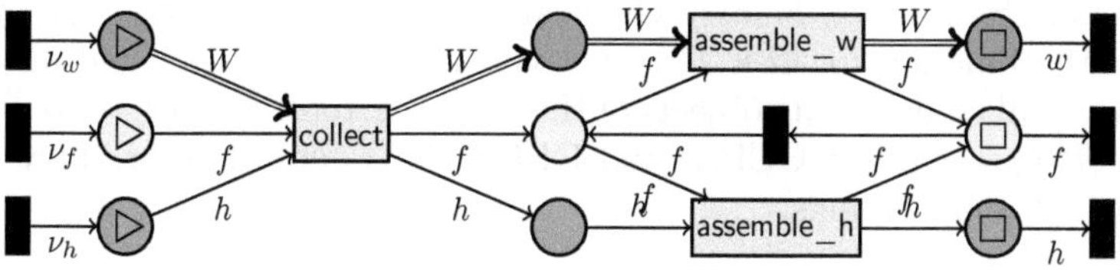

$\mathbb{T}_1(N)$ is interpreted as an accepting OPID where the initial and final markings are defined as the empty marking $M_\emptyset$, which requires that all places be empty. The example OPID can replay the logs L_1 as well as L_2 as it has equivalent semantics to Example 1 in combining objects without additional constraints.

As formalized in Theorem 1, the execution semantics of the OCPN N and the mapped OPID $\mathbb{T}_1(N)$ are equivalent for replaying any OCEL. This theorem can be proven by considering the equivalent definition of binding executions. Considering $M_i' = \mathbb{T}_1(M_i)$ as the mapped markings and $\beta_i = \mathbb{T}_1(b_i)$ as the mapped bindings, $\mathbb{T}_1(N)$ can produce and consume the same set of objects $\mathcal{O}$ as specified in the initial and final marking of the OCPN. For reasons of space, the full proof of Theorem 1 is moved to Appendix A of the extended paper [15].

Theorem 1. *Let $\mathcal{O}$ be a set of objects, N be an accepting OCPN, $N' = \mathbb{T}_1(N)$, and $M_\emptyset$ denote the empty marking of N'. There exists a run of N:*

$$M_0 \xrightarrow{(t_1,b_1)} M_1 \xrightarrow{(t_2,b_2)} \dots \xrightarrow{(t_n,b_n)} M_n$$

with $M_0{=}M_{init}^{\mathcal{O}}$ and $M_n{=}M_{final}^{\mathcal{O}}$ if and only if there is a run of N' over the set of objects $\mathcal{O}$:

$$M_\emptyset \xrightarrow{*} M_0' \xrightarrow{(t_1,\beta_1)} M_1' \xrightarrow{(t_2,\beta_2)} \dots \xrightarrow{(t_n,\beta_n)} M_n' \xrightarrow{*} M_\emptyset$$

such that $M_i' = \mathbb{T}_1(M_i)$ for all $0 \leq i \leq n$ and $\beta_i = \mathbb{T}_1(b_i)$ for all $1 \leq i \leq n$, such that $M_\emptyset \xrightarrow{*} M_0'$ is an emitting sequence, $M_n' \xrightarrow{*} M_\emptyset$ a collapsing sequence, and no emitting or consuming transitions occur in between.

4 Synchronization for Stable Many-to-One Relationships

In this section, we define what constitutes a stable many-to-one relationship for object-centric process executions. Given an OCEL that assumes the stability of relationships, such a stable many-to-one relationship implies that objects on the many-side will always be bound to the same object of the one-side. Hence, the processing of such objects is implicitly synchronized. We then extend the mapping $\mathbb{T}_1$ from Section 3 to implement the expected synchronization for a set of defined stable many-to-one relationships. Finally, we show that any execution replay of the OCPN is accepted by the mapped OPID if and only if it conforms to the stable many-to-one relationships.

In the following, let a pair (σ_m, σ_o) be an *object type relationship* if $\sigma_m \neq \sigma_o$. For example, for the bike manufacturing example, a stable many-to-one relationship may exist for *(Wheel, Frame)*. Given an OCEL $L = (E, \mathcal{O}, \pi_{act}, \pi_{obj}, \pi_{time})$, we define the function $lo\colon \mathcal{O} \times \Sigma \to \mathcal{O}$, which, given an object and an object type, returns all co-occurring objects of this type, i.e. $lo(o, \sigma) = \bigcup_{e \in E}\{o' \mid o, o' \in \pi_{obj}(e) \wedge ot(o') = \sigma\}$. For OCPNs and OPIDs, lo is defined accordingly over a run of the net and bindings.

Definition 8. *An object type relationship* (σ_m, σ_o) *is a* stable many-to-one relationship *in an event log* L *if for all objects* $o_m, o_o \in \mathcal{O}$*, where* $ot(o_m) = \sigma_m$ *and* $ot(o_o) = \sigma_o$ *it holds that* $|lo(o_m, \sigma_o)| = 1$.

Similarly for OCPNs and OPIDs, (σ_m, σ_o) is a *stable many-to-one relationship* if the same holds for a run in the net: The objects o_m of the many-side σ_m in the stable relationship (σ_m, σ_o) are required to be linked to exactly one object o_o of the one-side σ_o. On the other hand, every o_o must have a non-empty set of linked objects o_m. For example, *(Wheel, Frame)* is a stable many-to-one relationship in the log L_1 from Section 1, but not in L_2. Note that the one-to-one relationship between handlebar and frame manifests itself as two stable many-to-one relationships *(Handlebar, Frame)* and *(Handlebar, Frame)*.

4.1 Mapping to Synchronizing OPIDs

The goal of this mapping is to enforce a set of stable many-to-one relationships with synchronization behavior. To this end, for every many-to-one relationship (σ_m, σ_o), the required set of links $(m, o) \in \mathcal{O}^2$ of type (σ_m, σ_o) must be determined *before* the actual execution starts, and must be stable during the whole execution. In general, the idea is to store all links of a relationship in a dedicated place that is accessed by all transitions that operate on both object types. For the Petri net used for the manufacturing of bikes, the translation results in the OPID shown in Example 4. For the log L_1, it determines the links between wheels w_1, w_2 of type W and frame f_1 of type F as $(w_1, f_1), (w_2, f_1)$ before execution starts and they are not changed. The transition's synchronization semantics ensure that only objects in a stable relationship are within one binding.

We assume a given OCPN $N = (P, T, F, pt, F_{var}, \ell)$ and a fixed set of object type relationships R, which are supposed to work as stable many-to-one relationships. The mapping $\mathbb{T}_R$ is defined on top of the mapping $\mathbb{T}_1$ in Section 3. Let $N_1 = \mathbb{T}_1(N) = (\Sigma_1, P_1, T_1, F_{in,1}, F_{out,1}, \text{color}_1, \ell_1)$. In $\mathbb{T}_R(N_1)$, we add the following new places and transitions:

- a set of *link places* $P_L := \{p_{(\sigma_m,\sigma_o)} \mid (\sigma_m, \sigma_o) \in R\}$, storing the links for each relationship $(\sigma_m, \sigma_o) \in R$, such that $\text{color}_2(p_{(\sigma_m,\sigma_o)}) = \langle \sigma_m, \sigma_o \rangle$,
- a set of *link transitions* $T_L := \{t_{\sigma_m,\sigma_o} \mid (\sigma_m, \sigma_o) \in R\}$ that creates links for a set of objects of type σ_m and one object of σ_o to populate P_L,
- new emitting transitions $T_i := \{t_{i,\sigma} \mid \exists \sigma' \in \Sigma : (\sigma, \sigma') \in R \vee (\sigma', \sigma) \in R\}$,
- a set $P_b := \{p_{\sigma,(\sigma_m,\sigma_o)} \mid (\sigma = \sigma_m \vee \sigma = \sigma_o) \wedge (\sigma_m, \sigma_o) \in R\}$ of auxiliary places before the link creation such that $\text{color}_2(p_{\sigma,(\sigma_m,\sigma_o)}) = \langle \sigma \rangle$, and

– a set $P_a := \{p_{(\sigma_m,\sigma_o),\sigma} \mid (\sigma = \sigma_m \vee \sigma = \sigma_o) \wedge (\sigma_m, \sigma_o) \in R\}$ of auxiliary places after link creation such that $\text{color}_2(p_{\sigma,(\sigma_m,\sigma_o)}) = \langle \sigma \rangle$.

The arrangement of the additional places and transitions is schematically shown below for a pair of object types $(\sigma_m, \sigma_o) \in R$. Here, the blue part of the net represents N_1, while the black parts with red labels are extensions by $\mathbb{T}_R$.

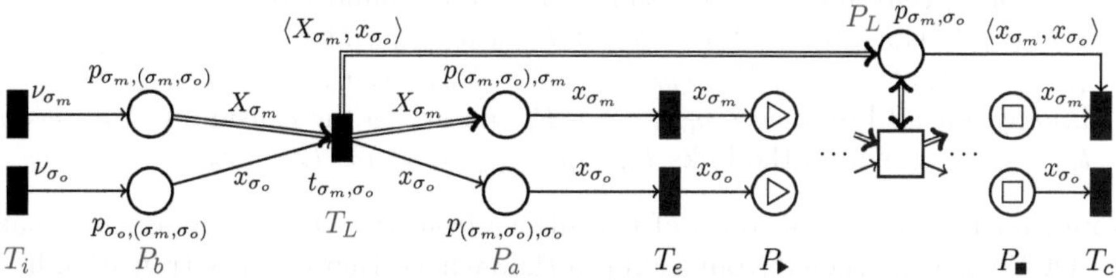

Before defining the new flow relations, we give an intuitive explanation considering the many-to-one relationship between wheels and a frame. The idea is that all links for the later execution are created concurrently before the objects are placed in the initial places $P_\blacktriangleright$ by T_e. To that end, new emitting transitions T_i, instead of T_e, are used to create objects which are placed in P_b. Every link creation transition $t_{\sigma_m,\sigma_o} \in T_L$ is connected with inflow to the according places before link creation P_b, and with outflow to the respective link place $p_{\sigma_m,\sigma_o} \in P_L$ as well as places in P_a after link creation. The places in P_a are connected to the former emitting transitions T_e. When all transitions T_e emitted the objects to the places $P_\blacktriangleright$, the places in P_L are thus populated with a fixed set of links. Instead of emitting the wheels and frames directly to the $P_\blacktriangleright$ places, each frame is considered jointly with a non-empty set of wheels by a transition T_L to create the required links onto a place in P_L. Crucially, to enforce the synchronization for a transition t in N_1, which operates on σ_m and σ_o, that is wheels and a frame, the respective transition in $\mathbb{T}_R(N_1)$ must read and write the required links from the link places P_L. at the end of the execution, any created link on P_L is consumed together with the object of the many-side by the consuming transition in T_c, ensuring that all links are eventually consumed as well.
Precisely, we define the flow relations as follows.

– For a new emitting transition $t_{i,\sigma} \in T_i$, and $p \in P_b$ where $\text{color}_2(p) = \langle \sigma \rangle$, the outflow is set as $F_{out,2}(t_{i,\sigma}, p) = \langle \nu_\sigma \rangle$.
– For a former emitting transition $t_{e,\sigma} \in T_e$ and $p \in P_\blacktriangleright$ with $\text{color}_2(p) = \langle \sigma \rangle$, we set $F_{out,2}(t_{e,\sigma}, p) = \langle x_\sigma \rangle$ if there is a $\sigma' \in \Sigma$ such that (σ, σ') or (σ', σ) in R, otherwise $F_{out,2}(t_{e,\sigma}, p) = \langle \nu_\sigma \rangle$ as before.
– For a place in P_b which is for the one-side of the relationship, the inflow reads a single object $F_{in,2}(p_{\sigma_o,(\sigma_m,\sigma_o)}, t_{\sigma_m,\sigma_o}) = \langle x_{\sigma_o} \rangle$; while for the many-side we have $F_{in,2}(p_{\sigma_m,(\sigma_m,\sigma_o)}, t_{\sigma_m,\sigma_o}) = \langle X_{\sigma_m} \rangle$ reading a list of objects.
– Similarly, for a place in P_a for the one-side of a relationship we have $F_{out,2}(t_{\sigma_m,\sigma_o}, p_{(\sigma_m,\sigma_o),\sigma_o}) = \langle x_{\sigma_o} \rangle$ whereas for a place for the many-side we set $F_{out,2}(t_{\sigma_m,\sigma_o}, p_{(\sigma_m,\sigma_o),\sigma_m}) = \langle X_{\sigma_m} \rangle$.
– Each link creation transition $t_{\sigma_m,\sigma_o} \in T_L$ has an outflow to the respective place $p_{(\sigma_m,\sigma_o)} \in P_L$ with inscription $F_{out,2}(t_{\sigma_m,\sigma_o}, p_{(\sigma_m,\sigma_o)}) = \langle X_{\sigma_m}, x_{\sigma_o} \rangle$.

- Every former emitting transition $t_{e,\sigma} \in T_e$ has an inflow from all related $p \in P_a$ where $\text{color}_2(p) = \langle\sigma\rangle$, so that $F_{in,2}(p, t_{e,\sigma}) = \langle x_\sigma \rangle$.
- For all link places $p_{(\sigma_m,\sigma_o)} \in P_L$ and transitions $t \in T$ such that there exist places $p_1, p_2 \in P$ with $\text{color}_2(p_1) = \langle\sigma_m\rangle$ and $\text{color}_2(p_2) = \langle\sigma_o\rangle$ and both $F_{in,1}(p_1, t)$ and $F_{in,1}(p_2, t)$ are defined, the transition needs to read and write the appropriate links. If t consumes a variable number of σ_m objects, i.e. if $F_{in,1}(p_1, t)$ is a variable flow, we set $F_{in,2}(p_{(\sigma_m,\sigma_o)}, t) = F_{out,2}(t, p_{(\sigma_m,\sigma_o)}) = \langle X_{\sigma_m}, x_{\sigma_o}\rangle$; otherwise, $F_{in,2}(p_{(\sigma_m,\sigma_o)}, t) = F_{out,2}(t, p_{(\sigma_m,\sigma_o)}) = \langle x_{\sigma_m}, x_{\sigma_o}\rangle$.
- Finally, for all link places $p_{(\sigma_m,\sigma_o)} \in P_L$, an arc to the consuming transition $t_{c,\sigma_m} \in T_c$ consumes the links $F_{in,2}(p_{(\sigma_m,\sigma_o)}, t_{c,\sigma_m}) = \langle x_{\sigma_m}, x_{\sigma_o}\rangle$.

Note that for the modification of transitions from the OCPN, we assume that the OCPN is constructed from sound workflow nets. Hence, every transition has an inflow for an object type if and only if it has an outflow for it. For example, if $p_{W,F}$ holds the tokens $(w_1, f_1), (w_2, f_1)$, then the transition `assemble_w` can only bind the frame f_1 to any of the wheels w_1 or w_2 but never to w_3.

For all other $p \in P_1$ and $t \in T_1$ we set $F_{in,2}(p, t) = F_{in,1}(p, t)$, $F_{out,2}(t, p) = F_{out,1}(t, p)$, and $\text{color}_2(p) = \text{color}_1(p)$. The new places are $P_2 = P_1 \cup P_b \cup P_L \cup P_a$, and the new transitions are $T_2 = T_1 \cup T_i \cup T_L$. Then, the result of the mapping $\mathbb{T}_R$ is the OPID $\mathbb{T}_R(\mathbb{T}_1(N)) = (\Sigma_1, P_2, T_2, F_{in,2}, F_{out,2}, \text{color}_2, \ell_2)$ where $\ell_2(t) = \tau$ for all $t \in T_i \cup T_L$ and $\ell_2(t) = \ell_1(t)$ otherwise.

The OPID N_2 is again interpreted as an accepting OPID where the initial marking $M_{init,2}$ and the final marking $M_{final,2}$ require that all places be empty. The OPID in Example 4 accepts L_1 because there exists a run, where the links for wheels and frames can be set as $(w_1, f_1), (w_2, f_1), (w_3, f_2), (w_4, f_2)$ in the orange link place and the tokens for handlebars and frames as $(h_1, f_1), (h_2, f_2)$ in the green link place. The transitions must bind objects correctly according to the links. However, the execution in L_2 is rejected because $\langle \text{collect}, \{f_3, h_3, w_5, w_6\}\rangle$ requires the links (w_5, f_3) and (w_6, f_3) but $\langle \text{assemble\_w}, \{f_4, w_6, w_7\}\rangle$ requires the link (w_6, f_4), which cannot have been created in the same execution.

*Example 4 (Synchronizing OPID for bike manufacturing).*The OPID is obtained from the OCPN in Example 1 by applying $\mathbb{T}_1$ and $\mathbb{T}_R$ for the stable relationships *(Wheel, Frame)* (orange) and *(Handlebar, Frame)* (green).

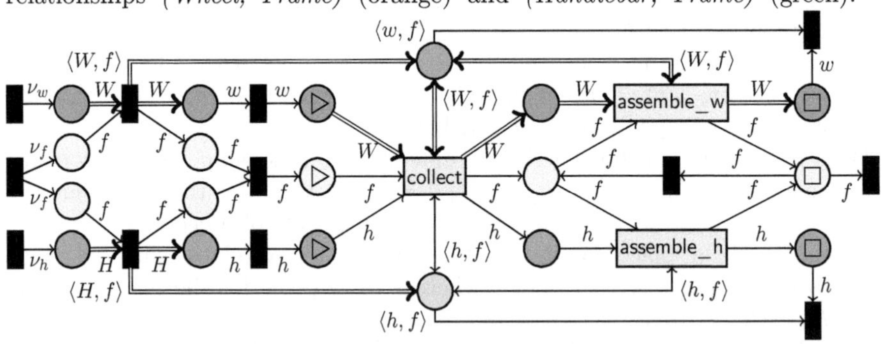

4.2 Equivalence for Executions with Stable Relationships

In Section 3, we show that an OCPN N is equivalent to its OPID representation $N_1 = \mathbb{T}_1(N)$ for event log replay. The mapping $N_2 = \mathbb{T}_R(N_1)$ implements the stable relationships R into N_1. We show that a run in the OCPN N is conform to R if and only if there is an accepted corresponding run in N_2.

Theorem 2. *Let $N_1 = \mathbb{T}_1(N)$ be an equivalent OPID for an OCPN N and $N_2 = \mathbb{T}_R(N_1)$ a synchronizing OPID. There is an accepted run of N_1 of the form*

$$M_\emptyset \xrightarrow{*} M_0 \xrightarrow{(t_1,\beta_1)} M_1 \xrightarrow{(t_2,\beta_2)} \dots \xrightarrow{(t_n,\beta_n)} M_n \xrightarrow{*} M_\emptyset$$

that conforms to the stable relationships R if and only if there is an accepted run of N_2 of the form

$$M_\emptyset \xrightarrow{*} M'_b \xrightarrow{*} M'_a \xrightarrow{*} M'_0 \xrightarrow{(t_1,\beta_1)} M'_1 \xrightarrow{(t_2,\beta_2)} \dots \xrightarrow{(t_n,\beta_n)} M'_n \xrightarrow{*} M_\emptyset$$

such that $\forall p \in P_1 \colon M'_i(p) = M_i(p)$ for all $0 \leq i \leq n$.

While the detailed proof for Theorem 2 is spelled out in Appendix B of the extended paper [15], we outline its three main arguments: (i) Any accepted run in N_2 is accepted in N_1. (ii) Any accepted run in N_1 conforming to R is accepted by N_2. (iii) Any accepted run in N_1 not conforming to R is rejected by N_2.

(i) The emitting and link creating sequence $M_\emptyset \xrightarrow{*} M'_b \xrightarrow{*} M'_a \xrightarrow{*} M'_0$ results in a marking M'_0 that holds only tokens in the places $P_\blacktriangleright \cup P_L$. An equivalent emitting sequence $M_\emptyset \xrightarrow{*} M_0$ exists for N_1 that produces the same objects in the initial places $P_\blacktriangleright$. Any binding execution (t_i, β_i) in the run of N_2 can be replayed in a corresponding marking of N_1 as it is less restrictive. Finally, there exists an appropriate sequence $M_n \xrightarrow{*} M_\emptyset$ of only consuming transitions $t \in T_c$ that removes the same objects as $M'_n \xrightarrow{*} M_\emptyset$.

(ii) For the conforming run $M_\emptyset \xrightarrow{*} M_0$ that places objects to $P_\blacktriangleright$ in N_1, there exists a corresponding run $M_\emptyset \xrightarrow{*} M'_b \xrightarrow{*} M'_a \xrightarrow{*} M'_0$ in N_2, which places the same objects onto the places P_b in M'_b. Then, $M'_b \xrightarrow{*} M'_a$ creates all required links according to the binding executions (t_i, β_i) in the run of N_1, such that for every object o_m of type σ_m in a relationship with an object of type σ_o, the links in P_L are set for all $lo(o_m, \sigma_o)$. Next, $M'_a \xrightarrow{*} M'_0$ places the objects in $P_\blacktriangleright$ such that M'_0 holds tokens only in places $p' \in P_\blacktriangleright \cup P_L$. The created links are not changed and transitions that operate on two object types in a relationship are required to adhere to them. the run in N_1 is conform, it only binds an object o_m to a single object of σ_o, hence, $|lo(o_m, \sigma_o)| = 1$ and there exists a link such that N_2 can accept the run as well. Finally, for $M_n \xrightarrow{*} M_\emptyset$ of only consuming transitions $t \in T_c$, $M'_n \xrightarrow{*} M_\emptyset$ can consume the same objects including their respective links.

(iii) By contradiction, we show that N_2 cannot create links that violate the conformance criteria. No object in a relationship can exist without a link. Any object o_m with $ot(o_m) = \sigma_m$ will receive exactly one link to an object of type σ_o and not more. As the bindings of any run in N_2 are restricted by the links, a non-conforming run of N_1 has no counterpart in N_2.

By expanding the mapping $\mathbb{T}_1$ with stable relationships in $\mathbb{T}_R$ for a given OCPN and its relationships R, we can generate an OPID $\mathbb{T}_R(\mathbb{T}_1(N))$ that accepts an execution in N if and only if it conforms to R.

5 Discussion and Related Work

In the following, we discuss the presence of stable many-to-one relationships in existing benchmark OCELs, and we outline a prototype implementation of our mapping. Both artifacts are available online[2]. Finally, we comment on the implications for the research areas of conformance checking and formal analysis.

5.1 Stable Relationships in OCEL

Stable relationships can be discovered at the type level from OCELs, as described in the TOTeM tool [13]. To substantiate our intuition that, in many contexts, the executions of object-centric processes indeed have stable relationships, we applied an according analysis to existing benchmark logs. The result in 1 shows that all investigated logs contain some stable many-to-one relationships. The full data is available from the repository.

The stability of object relationships is a typical (often implicit) assumption in the literature. In the widely adopted OCEL 2.0 standard [2], links are recorded without a notion of time, assuming global existence and stability. For discovered models, such as OCPNs [20], class diagrams [13], and even simulation models [10], this yields the same notion of stable relationship introduced here.

The intended stable relationships may be violated in OCELs. When investigating noise, that is, infrequent outliers, it can be seen that some logs contain a few violations of the intended stable many-to-one relationships. In 1, we report how the number of stable relationships changes when considering noise. For example, LLM-based simulations for LRMS – O2C contain 20 more stable relationships when only focusing on the 90% most frequent observations. This relates to the approach in [25], where this type of violation is identified in a real-world use case. Our mapping to OPIDs can assist in identifying exact executions that violate stable relationships.

However, our identified notion of stable relationships yield some limitations. Our definition of stable many-to-one relationships only considers existential relations of the type `(1..*,1..1)`. Non-existential relationships (e.g. `(0..*,0..1)`) are not present in the existing OCELs but should be considered in future investigations as well. In general, the need to enrich object-centric event data with data modeling concepts such as non-rigid relationships is being increasingly recognized. Goossens et al. [9] point out that from a database perspective, links between objects might indeed change over time. It is not possible to differentiate between a non-rigid many-to-one relationship and an intended many-to-many relationship without domain knowledge. Therefore, our approach emphasizes

[2] https://github.com/AnjoSs/To-bind-or-not-to-bind.

Table 1. OCELs with their number of object types, all relationships (including one-to-one), stable many-to-one relationships with, and without filtering noise.

OCEL	#obj. types	#relationships	#m2o(noise=0.1)	#m2o(noise=0.0)
Logistics	7	9	6 (4+2*1)	6 (4+2*1)
Order Management	6	13	5 (5+0)	5 (5+0)
Procure to Pay	7	9	10 (6+2*2)	10 (6+2*2)
Hinge Production	12	39	35 (13+2*11)	35 (13+2*11)
Age of Empires	30	135	**87** (77+2*5)	**67** (57+2*5)
LRMS – O2C	9	11	**18** (2+2*8)	**16** (4+2*6)
LRMS – P2P	6	15	**11** (3+2*4)	**0** (0+0)
LRMS – Hiring	6	15	6 (6+0)	6 (6+0)
LRMS – Hospital	8	18	6 (6+0)	6 (6+0)

an explicit declaration of object types and relationships, e.g., as data models. In addition, [16] highlights the need for richer representations of object-centric event data, where the effects of events are explicitly tracked, allowing identification of time intervals within which a relationship exists. An ongoing effort aims to consolidate these different considerations in a single standard for representing object-centric event data [5], motivating further research on the matter.

5.2 Process Discovery and Prototypical Implementation

The original discovery of OCPNs [20] is proposed as a divide-and-conquer approach in which each object type defines an individual workflow net [20]. The proposed mapping from OCPNs to OPIDs is based on this specific characteristic structure of OCPNs. Therefore, our mapping rules and formal proofs are limited to such OCPNs. OCPN discovery [20] has recently been extended in [22], which proposes the discovery of object-centric process trees. From these process trees, identifier-sound [21] OCPNs can be generated, but without synchronization semantics. Analog to [20], the resulting Petri nets are constructed as combinations of workflow nets for each object type. In a second extension, [23] discovers so-called silent objects from an OCEL, which reify and synchronize arbitrary sets of objects. However, the discovered Petri nets are also limited to replaying the behavior of an OCEL. Still, the concept of silent objects may provide insights on how to extend our investigation to many-to-many relationships.

However, the discovery of OPIDs has not yet been tackled. To show how discovered OCPNs can be directly mapped to OPIDs, we provide a prototypical implementation of our proposed mappings. Our prototype implements both transformations $\mathbb{T}_1$ and $\mathbb{T}_R$ in a Python command-line script. The script takes as input an OCPN in json format, and for $\mathbb{T}_R$ the desired stable many-to-one relationships R. The resulting OPID is output in a pnml format, which can be used as input for conformance checking [8], and in the dot format for visualization. The code, as well as the results obtained by applying it to a set of OCPNs collected in earlier work [3], can be obtained from the repository.

5.3 Conformance Checking and Formal Analysis

OCPNs have been studied for conformance checking. Fitness and precision metrics have been introduced to quantify the suitability of an OCPN to replay a log [1], and techniques have been studied to calculate alignments for OCPNs [12]. However, both focus only on individual objects and not on their mutual links. For varying links, these approaches are too liberal in identifying deviations [8], calling for richer formalisms such as PNIDs or OPIDs, which are computationally more demanding [8]. Still, with Theorem 2 we show that conformance checking with OCPNs [1,12] is appropriate if the log satisfies the intended stable relationships. In practice, this check through the discovery of data models [13] can be more performant than the computation of synchronization alignments [8]. If the log violates stable relationships, OPIDs can be used to compute conformance alignments, including specific penalties to quantify the severity of the violations [8]. In the future, the fitness and precision metrics should be extended to respect the object relationships defined in OPIDs. Other process models have also been considered for object-centric conformance checking, that is, object-centric directly follows graphs [14] and object-centric behavioral constraints [24].

Different formal modeling approaches have been proposed for object-centric processes, such as variants of Petri nets with identifiers (PNIDs) [7,21], or synchronous proclets [4]. These two formalisms provide extended orthogonal features when related to OCPNs. On the one hand, PNIDs provide explicit modeling mechanisms for creating, updating, and removing objects and relationships, while lacking variable arcs to evolving multiple objects in a single transition. On the other hand, proclets extend the variable-arc feature of OCPNs, by supporting different forms of synchronization where many objects of a certain type synchronously move together with a single, parent object; however, they lack support for the explicit manipulation of objects and relationships, as supported in PNIDs. In a recent effort, *object-centric PNIDs* (OPIDs [8]) have emerged to provide an integrated formalism that unifies the distinctive features of OCPNs with variable arcs, PNIDs and synchronous proclets. Thus, OPID is the natural candidate for enriching an OCPN with the desired synchronization behavior.

As we show, OPIDs with synchronization can be mapped directly from discovered OCPNs. As OPIDs can emit novel objects, they can serve not only as trace recognizers but also as trace generators. Therefore, our mapping serves as a missing link between object-centric process discovery and their formal analysis and execution. The relationship between the established approaches of Proclets and PNIDs, the novel OPIDs and discovered process models needs to be studied in the future, where our mapping can now also serve as the missing link. For example, van der Werf et al. [21] define correctness notions for PNIDs, which can now be applied to discovered process models through our mapping.

6 Conclusion

This paper shows how discovered object-centric process models can be enhanced with explicit data modeling concepts to ensure precision and trust in object relationships. Our contribution rigorously closes the gap between the two representative formal models for object-centric processes: OCPNs—an underfitting model with efficient discovery and available conformance checking techniques, and OPIDs—a more sophisticated model for which discovery techniques are still missing and conformance checking techniques are computationally more demanding. Our findings indicate that when focusing on executions where many-to-one relationships are stable, that is, once a link is established it is rigidly maintained over time, these two models coincide. These results can serve as a promising link between object-centric process discovery and formal analysis.

Acknowledgements. M. Montali was partially supported by the NextGenerationEU FAIR PE0000013 project MAIPM (CUP C63C22000770006) and the PRIN MIUR project PINPOINT Prot. 2020FNEB27. S. Winkler was partially supported by the UNIBZ project TEKE. A. Gianola was partly supported by Portuguese national funds through Fundação para a Ciência e a Tecnologia, I.P. (FCT), under projects UIDB/50021/2020 (DOI: 10.54499/UIDB/50021/2020). This work was partially supported by the 'OptiGov' project, with ref. n. 2024.07385.IACDC (DOI: 10.54499/2024.07385.IACDC), fully funded by the 'Plano de Recuperação e Resiliência'(PRR) under the investment 'RE-C05-i08 - Ciência Mais Digital', measure 'RE-C05-i08.m04' (in accordance with the FCT Notice No. 04/C05-i08/2024), framed within the financing agreement signed between the 'Estrutura de Missão Recuperar Portugal' (EMRP) and FCT as an intermediary beneficiary.

References

1. Adams, J.N., van der Aalst, W.M.P.: Precision and Fitness in Object-Centric Process Mining. In: Proc. 3rd ICPM. pp. 128–135 (2021)
2. Berti, A., et al.: OCEL (Object-Centric Event Log) 2.0 Specification (2024)
3. Brachmann, T.: Visualizing object-centric Petri nets. Bachelor thesis, RWTH Aachen (2025), https://github.com/rwth-pads/ocpn-visualizer
4. Fahland, D.: Describing Behavior of Processes with Many-to-Many Interactions. In: Donatelli, S., Haar, S. (eds.) PETRI NETS 2019. LNCS, vol. 11522, pp. 3–24. Springer, Cham (2019). https://doi.org/10.1007/978-3-030-21571-2_1
5. Fahland, D., et al.: Towards a simple and extensible standard for object-centric event data (OCED) - core model, design space, and lessons learned. CoRR **abs/2410.14495** (2024)
6. Ghahfarokhi, A.F., et al.: OCEL: A Standard for Object-Centric Event Logs. In: New Trends in Database and Information Systems (Proc. ADBIS 2024). pp. 169–175. Springer (2021)
7. Ghilardi, S., Gianola, A., Montali, M., Rivkin, A.: Petri net-based object-centric processes with read-only data. Inf. Syst. **107**, 102011 (2022)
8. Gianola, A., Montali, M., Winkler, S.: Object-Centric Conformance Alignments with Synchronization. In: Proc. 36th CAiSE. LNCS, vol. 14663, pp. 3–19. Springer (2024)

9. Goossens, A., De Smedt, J., Vanthienen, J.: Object-Centric Event Logs: Characteristics, Comparative Analysis and Road Map. In: Business Process Management Forum. pp. 37–54. Springer (2024)
10. Knopp, B., Pourbafrani, M., van der Aalst, W.M.P.: Discovering Object-Centric Process Simulation Models. In: Proc. 5th ICPM. pp. 81–88 (2023)
11. Leemans, S.J.J., Fahland, D., van der Aalst, W.M.P.: Scalable process discovery and conformance checking. Software & Systems Modeling **17**(2), 599–631 (2018)
12. Liss, L., Adams, J.N., van der Aalst, W.M.P.: Object-centric alignments. In: Proc. 42nd ER. LNCS, vol. 14320, pp. 201–219. Springer (2023)
13. Liss, L., Adams, J.N., van der Aalst, W.M.P.: TOTeM: Temporal Object Type Model for Object-Centric Process Mining. In: Proc. Business Process Management Forum. pp. 107–123. Springer (2024)
14. Park, G., Adams, J.N., van der Aalst, W.M.P.: Conformance Checking and Performance Analysis Using Object-Centric Directly-Follows Graphs. In: Proc. Business Process Management Forum. pp. 179–196. Springer (2024)
15. Seidel, A., Winkler, S., Gianola, A., Montali, M., Weske, M.: To bind or not to bind? Discovering Stable Relationships in Object-centric Processes (Extended Version) (2025)
16. Swevels, A., Fahland, D., Montali, M.: Implementing Object-Centric Event Data Models in Event Knowledge Graphs. In: Process Mining Workshops. pp. 431–443. Springer (2024)
17. van der Aalst, W.M.P.: Object-Centric Process Mining: Dealing with Divergence and Convergence in Event Data. In: Software Engineering and Formal Methods. pp. 3–25. Springer (2019)
18. van der Aalst, W.M.P.: Toward more realistic simulation models using object-centric process mining. In: Proc. 37th ECMS. pp. 5–13 (2023)
19. van der Aalst, W., Adriansyah, A., de Medeiros, A.K.A., Arcieri, F., Baier, T., Blickle, T., Bose, J.C., van den Brand, P., Brandtjen, R., Buijs, J., Burattin, A., Carmona, J., Castellanos, M., Claes, J., Cook, J., Costantini, N., Curbera, F., Damiani, E., de Leoni, M., Delias, P., van Dongen, B.F., Dumas, M., Dustdar, S., Fahland, D., Ferreira, D.R., Gaaloul, W., van Geffen, F., Goel, S., Günther, C., Guzzo, A., Harmon, P., ter Hofstede, A., Hoogland, J., Ingvaldsen, J.E., Kato, K., Kuhn, R., Kumar, A., La Rosa, M., Maggi, F., Malerba, D., Mans, R.S., Manuel, A., McCreesh, M., Mello, P., Mendling, J., Montali, M., Motahari-Nezhad, H.R., zur Muehlen, M., Munoz-Gama, J., Pontieri, L., Ribeiro, J., Rozinat, A., Seguel Pérez, H., Seguel Pérez, R., Sepúlveda, M., Sinur, J., Soffer, P., Song, M., Sperduti, A., Stilo, G., Stoel, C., Swenson, K., Talamo, M., Tan, W., Turner, C., Vanthienen, J., Varvaressos, G., Verbeek, E., Verdonk, M., Vigo, R., Wang, J., Weber, B., Weidlich, M., Weijters, T., Wen, L., Westergaard, M., Wynn, M.: Process Mining Manifesto. In: Daniel, F., Barkaoui, K., Dustdar, S. (eds.) BPM 2011. LNBIP, vol. 99, pp. 169–194. Springer, Heidelberg (2012). https://doi.org/10.1007/978-3-642-28108-2_19
20. van der Aalst, W.M.P., Berti, A.: Discovering Object-centric Petri Nets. Fund. Inform. **175**(1–4), 1–40 (2020)
21. van der Werf, J.M.E.M., Rivkin, A., Montali, M., Polyvyanyy, A.: Correctness Notions for Petri Nets with Identifiers. Fund. Inform. **190**(2–4), 159–207 (2024)
22. van Detten, J.N., Schumacher, P., Leemans, S.J.J.: Discovering Compact, Live and Identifier-Sound Object-Centric Process Models. In: Proc. 6th ICPM. pp. 113–120 (2024)

23. van Detten, J.N., Schumacher, P., Leemans, S.J.J.: Object Synchronizations and Specializations with Silent Objects in Object-Centric Petri Nets. In: Proc. 22nd BPM. LNCS, vol. 14940, pp. 57–74. Springer (2024)
24. Xiu, B., Li, G.: Diagnosing Conformance Between Object-Centric Event Logs and Models. IEEE Access **11**, 110837–110849 (2023)
25. Xiu, B., Li, G.: Quantifying Conformance Between Object-Centric Event Logs and Models. IEEE Access **12**, 91793–91806 (2024)

Discovering Inclusion Dependencies in a Multi-model Scenario

Dominique Hausler[1(✉)], André Conrad[2], Mike Sperling[2], Uta Störl[2], and Meike Klettke[1]

[1] Data Engineering Group, University of Regensburg, Regensburg, Germany
{dominique.hausler,meike.klettke}@ur.de

[2] Chair of Databases and Information Systems, University of Hagen, Hagen, Germany
{andré.conrad,mike.sperling,uta.stoerl}@fernuni-hagen.de

Abstract. Multi-model data stores combine the benefits of different data stores to ensure optimal storage for various datasets. To adequately connect data in a multi-model scenario e.g., to join data in different data models and to consistently evolve multi-model databases, inclusion dependencies (INDs) must be known. INDs are database integrity constraints that define a subset of relationships between attributes or attribute sets. A classic use case for INDs is the definition of foreign keys in relational databases, i.e., single stores. In multi-model systems, we cannot assume the availability of all INDs, especially the intra-model-constraints are often not defined in advance and have to be extracted from the data. In this article, we present a data-driven reverse engineering approach for finding intra- and inter-model-linkages between relational, document, and graph databases and show a proof-of-concept. To do so, we present a flexible framework that is capable of integrating existing as well as one's own algorithm. The meta level at which data dependencies are detected, is represented by a relational database, as most existing IND detection algorithms are based on relational data. Besides integrating the existing algorithms Hopf or Iris-Ds, we additionally implemented a Hybrid approach, combining elements of these existing methods and a classical bottom-up IND search. The evaluation of all four algorithms accessible in our framework, confirmed that a classical bottom-up IND search surpasses all other algorithms, requiring special multi-model algorithms derived from classical IND search methods.

Keywords: Database Integrity Constraints · Inclusion Dependencies · Inter-Model Linkage · Multi-Model Databases · Schema Evolution

1 Introduction

In a multi-model scenario, data from different databases is combined. When we speak of multi-model systems, we include federated database, polyglot, multistore and polystore systems as defined in [40]. Single stores refer to identical database systems. Typically, there exist **In**clusion **D**ependencies (INDs) between

D. Bork et al. (Eds.): ER 2025, LNCS 16189, pp. 242–260, 2026.
https://doi.org/10.1007/978-3-032-08623-5_13

the different data models within multi-model systems. An IND between two attribute sets $X \subseteq Y$ exists if all attribute values of attributes X also occur in Y. The attribute sets X and Y can be in different data models and relations. INDs are often not known in advance and must be derived from the data. This is particularly the case when different data sources are developed independently of each other and then brought together for analysis, querying and updates. We see three main reasons why such INDs exist in multi-model systems but are not known in advance.

1. Natural identifiers (such as IDs, email addresses, product numbers) are used in different data models. They can be utilized to combine data through joins. In most cases these INDs are unary dependencies.
2. Redundancy is an important way of optimizing performance in document-oriented databases to avoid joins. These also occur if multi-model databases have been developed independently. Thus, the INDs are mostly n-ary.
3. The third type of INDs are references between different data models. These occur when data stores are combined in a multi-model scenario.

It cannot be assumed that INDs are known for all data stores of a multi-model system; these must be determined from the data. It is necessary to develop a technique that derives the INDs of different data models (*intra-model linkage constraints*) – here document, relational and graph databases – as well as finds all valid INDs between different data models (*inter-model linkage constraints*).

The concept of our approach tackling the challenge of integrating INDs in a multi-model is shown in Fig. 1. All valid INDs are illustrated by the lines connecting the data models (see local and global schema layer). In order to identify these, the INDs are derived from the local schema and the data level and are then forwarded to a higher level of abstraction, namely the global schema layer. This is due to our approach first comparing entity types and their properties, followed by the data comparison. Compared to known algorithms for INDs in relational data, we must make *two significant extensions*:

1. The *technical heterogeneity* of the different data models must be considered, as the data can be stored in either a relational, document or graph database.
2. The method must efficiently find INDs that have many attributes on the left and right sides i.e., *n-ary INDs*.

Benefit of INDs at the Global Schema Level. In multi-models, INDs are stored on the global schema level (Fig. 1) and are used to:

1. *Handle schema evolution.* Evolution operations executed in a single store [32] can affect INDs, therefore the need to be propagated to the global schema level and the other data stores [15,39] to keep the overall system consistent.
2. *Query execution.* INDs can be used to connect single stores through joins.
3. *Optimization.* To store data in the ideal model, the data needs to be migrated. A complete schema including INDs is necessary to realize the migration of data between different data stores [3,18].

Contribution. We present a framework to extract all INDs in a multi-model system, exemplarily between document, relational and graph databases. The source code of our implementation is available from our GitHub repository[1]. To the best of our knowledge, this is the first approach in which intra-model and inter-model linkages are automatically extracted. The mapping into a flat, relational-like format, enables the usage of existing constraint detection algorithms. A JSON output ensures easy integration in many applications.

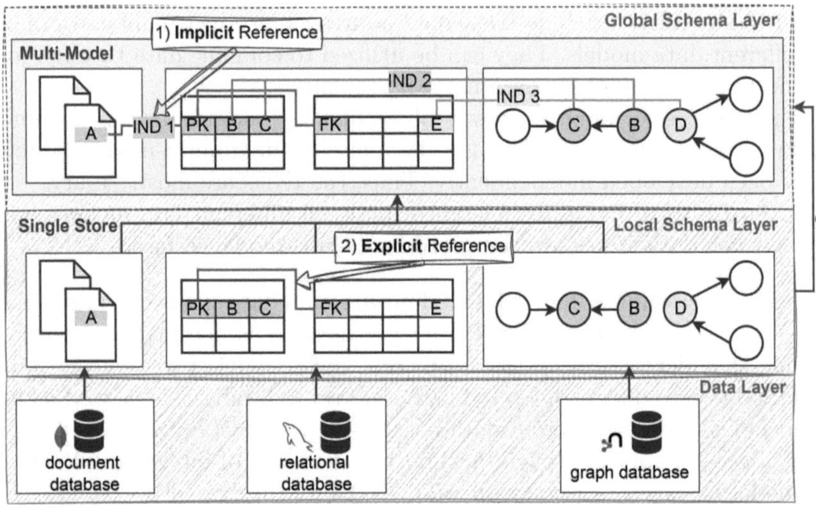

Fig. 1. Approach: The data layer contains the single stores. From each dataset the implicit structure (= schema) is extracted. The local schema layer describes the schema of a single store (= document, relational, graph database), while the global schema layer represents the structure of the multi-model. Here the single stores are connected.

Structure. Section 2 defines important terminology and in Sect. 3 relevant literature for UCCs, INDs and constraint detection is discussed. Subsequently, different search approaches for the lattice of INDs and the resulting optimizations are presented. Afterwards, different concepts to accomplish an integration within a multi-model scenario are illustrated in Sect. 4. Due to the integration of relational and NoSQL stores, relevant challenges for multi-model scenarios are discussed in Sect. 5. In Sect. 6, we present our framework for multi-model systems that allows a flexible integration of either existing or own approaches. Our framework and the different algorithms, momentarily implemented in it, are evaluated in Sect. 7, followed by the conclusion.

[1] The implementation of our framework is available at https://github.com/dbishagen/ref-seeker-extractor.

2 Concepts and Terminology

In this section, reference types and unique column combinations are analyzed. These are highly relevant to reduce the number of false positive INDs in the context of single stores. Afterwards, the formal definition of INDs is given, including the integration of aspects when utilizing them in a multi-model scenario.

Inherent, Explicit and Implicit References. Different types of references have to be considered when searching for INDs. *Inherent references* emerge from the data model e.g., the unique ids of nodes and their usage in relationships to reference the corresponding nodes in graph databases [30]. These are system-specific for each data model. User-defined references such as foreign keys (FKs) are categorized as *explicit* and can be described through a Data Definition Language, e.g., SQL. *Implicit references* are valid in the data itself and are not explicitly defined. Redundant information (1) can be designed on purpose or (2) show that an explicit reference was forgotten or not assigned due to system restrictions. Implicit references can occur between the data models and can also point towards an explicit reference like in the case of IND 1, connecting a document and a relational database (Fig. 1).

Unique Column Combinations. A set of attributes in relational data where no value is contained more than once, are called unique column combinations (UCCs) [29]. Commonly they are unknown and consequently need to be derived from the data which is considered to be a NP-hard problem [13]. Given is the schema S of a relational database with a relation R and its instance r which contains a set of columns C with $C \subseteq R$ under the condition that the projection of r only contains unique, non-null value combinations [2,16].

$$\forall r_i, r_j \in r, i \neq j : r_i[C] \neq r_j[C] \tag{1}$$

Inclusion Dependencies. Figure 2 illustrates examples of INDs (highlighted in green). The two compared instances are called d_i and d_j. NoSQL databases like graph databases can be schemaless; i.e., defining a schema is optional. Nevertheless, data always has an implicit schema which can be extracted in a preprocessing step, to describe these datasets by an explicit schema. D_i and D_j are further specified by the used capital letter (R for relational, J for document-oriented and G for graph databases). Tuples are defined as u and v [9].

$$D_i[A] \subseteq D_j[B] \equiv A \subseteq B \,|\, \forall u \in d_i, \exists v \in d_j : u[A] = v[B] \tag{2}$$

Consequently, the values of all tuples of the attribute(s) A on the left side also exist for the attribute(s) B on the right side. An inclusion dependency represents a subset between two attribute sets. Figure 1 illustrates the unary INDs (IND 1 and IND 3). Higher or n-ary INDs identify proper subsets between $k > 1$ attributes. An example is IND 2, illustrating a binary IND.

Scenario 1 of Fig. 2 illustrates INDs in a **Single Store** i.e., between identical database systems. Scenario 2 shows a multi-model scenario. A n-ary IND (here: binary) is illustrated in Scenario 1, whereas the graph database Scenario 2 shows an unary IND. Different patterns are shown in 1 and 2: In case of Scenario 1 $R_j[DE] \subseteq R_i[AB]$ and of Scenario 2 $J_j[ED] \subseteq R_i[AB]$.

Apriori-Gen. Deriving all valid INDs from the data is a NP-hard problem. In order to be able to solve the problem, heuristics for search space restriction are essential (see Table 1). The most important of these are explained in the following. For Scenario 1 the valid unary INDs $R_j[D] \subseteq R_i[A]$ and $R_j[E] \subseteq R_i[B]$ can be derived from the valid n-ary IND $R_j[DE] \subseteq R_i[AB]$. This validation assumption only works from k to $k-1$ not for k to $k+1$, i.e., $R_j[DE] \subseteq R_i[AB] \rightarrow R_j[D] \subseteq R_i[A] \wedge R_j[E] \subseteq R_i[B]$. Finding unary INDs does not imply that n-ary INDs are automatically valid (Case A). If INDs at k contain not valid INDs (Case B), we can assume that also for a superset $(k+1)$ the IND is not valid. Such derivations are called *apriori-gen* and are used to *decrease the search space* and thus *increase performance*. The gear symbol demonstrates a obligatory search process because an automatic assumption is not possible.

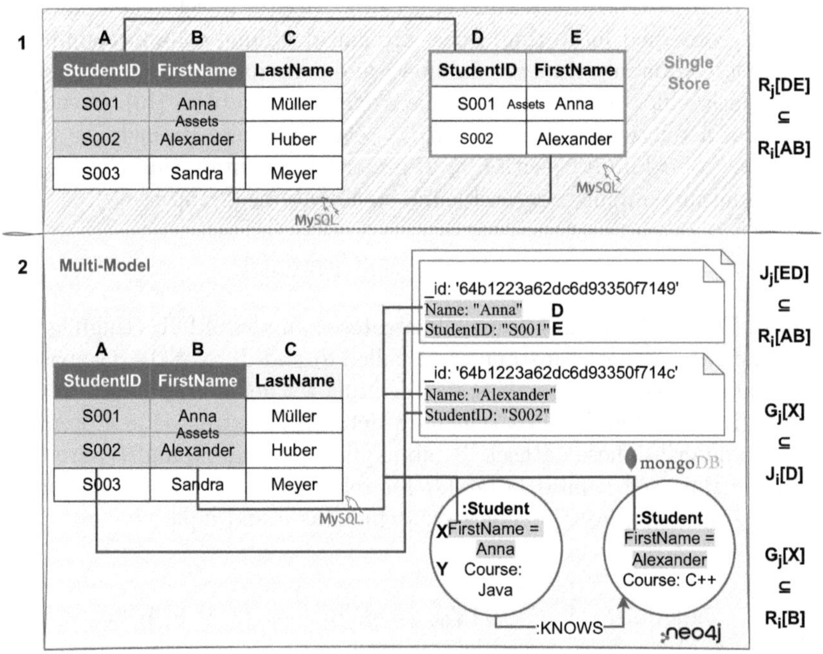

Fig. 2. Visualization of INDs in different scenarios. Scenario 1 illustrates a single store, while Scenario 2 shows a multi-model where INDs are used to connect the single stores.

Table 1. Minimal Example for Search Space Reduction Options with Apriori-gen

Case	Type	INDs	Apriori-gen	
A	unary INDs	$A \subseteq C$ and $B \subseteq D$	↓ k, k+1	↑ k-1, k ✓
	n-ary IND	$AB \subseteq CD$	⚙	
B	unary INDs	$A \not\subseteq C$ or $B \not\subseteq D$	↓ k, k+1	↑ k-1, k ⚙
	n-ary IND	$AB \not\subseteq CD$	✓	

✓ can be assumed automatically

⚙ cannot be assumed automatically → search process mandatory

3 Related Work

There are several methods for deriving semantic constraints from data. Nevertheless, only few thematize graph databases and multi-models. We will concentrate on INDs, as we use these for our own approach. Since some IND extraction methods base on Unique Column Combinations (UCC) detection to identify keys (PK) and foreign keys(FK), we will also present work on UCCs.

(Integrity) Constraints in Multi-Models. So far there are only a few publications on constraints in multi-model scenarios. An approach to handle cross-data-store constraints is presented in [18] and an algorithm which automatically enforces cross-database integrity constraints is presented in [11]. This underlines the importance of handling integrity constraints within multi-models but neither INDs are considered nor graph databases are integrated in these approaches. With our approach, we will fill this gap and extend available IND discovery algorithms for multi-model systems.

(Integrity) Constraints in Graph Databases. In [35,36] graph generating dependencies are thematized. There is also work done on graph functional dependencies in [10,23]. [31] describes a syntax that supports the management of complex integrity constraints for OrientDB. [30] analyzes available options for Titan, OrientDB, and Neo4j. The most relevant for our work is the suggestion of referential integrity constraints and their integration in Neo4j [27]. This article defines how these constraints can be integrated into a graph meta model but does not develop a method to derive them from data. Even though different types of integrity constraints are presented in the work above, to the best of our knowledge, INDs are not yet considered for graph databases or multi-models.

Reference Detection Algorithms. The HOPF algorithm [16] searches for foreign (FKs) and primary keys (PKs) candidates and is based on FastFK [8] and randomness test [45] to determine FKs. For MongoDB, the IRIS-DS was developed in [38]. Both the HOPF and the IRIS-DS rely on UCCs, serving as a precondition to derive key candidates. The HOPF also requires INDs to detect PK candidates. To tackle the shortcoming of multi-model approaches, we combine relational and NoSQL databases. Our implementation includes the HOPF and IRIS-DS, allowing a comparison when used in a multi-model scenario. Moreover, our HYBRID approach combines components of both algorithms.

Unique Column Combinations. UCCs are all attributes or attribute sets where no value occurs more than once. There are many approaches to derive UCCs from datasets available like [2,6,13,14,29,37,41]. Our algorithm is based on the HCA algorithm [1] and uses SQL commands.

IND Search Algorithms. Dürsch et al. presents a detailed analysis and comparison of established IND algorithms [9]. Several algorithms are limited to unary INDs [5,33], while others also consider n-ary INDs [4,20,22,25,26,28,34]. For JSON data, an unary and n-ary IND inference algorithm is suggested in [19]. There are also several variants of IND detection algorithms available, combining data dependencies. To reduce the search space either UCCs can be used as input [16] or statistical methods [42]. Other kinds of INDs are: relaxed INDs in [17] and conditional INDs in [21]. As a precondition of the HOPF INDs are needed. To fulfill this precondition together with the usage of a relational database at the meta level, we use [5] to detect unary INDs, and [24] to find n-ary INDs. This allows us to re-use known algorithms, aiming to use them for multi-models.

4 IND Search Options for Multi-model Scenarios

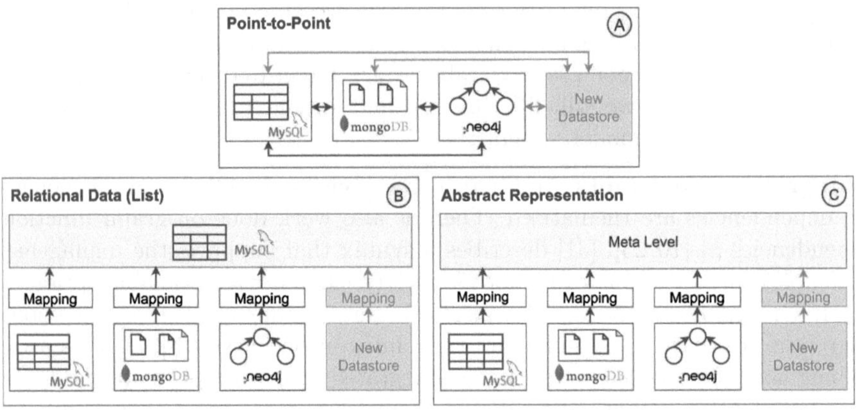

Fig. 3. There are three approaches to extract INDs from multi-model data. Case A represents a point-to-point comparison, while Case B and C include a meta level. B uses a single store to which all data is mapped. C defines an abstracted meta level.

Figure 1 shows different data stores with inclusion dependencies. Imagine, that – in the context of schema evolution – a rename of D to D' in Neo4j takes place with the consequence of losing IND 3 . This must be prevented because

$G_j[D] \subseteq R_i[E]$ is defined (see Sect. 2), but as result of the `rename` evolution operation, this IND would no longer be fulfilled. To tackle such problems, we propose the definition and testing of INDs at the global schema layer. These INDs are stored at the global schema layer for the initial multi-model. In case changes occur, the information about the INDs is used to either decline operations which are violating valid INDs or to realize co-evolution (cascading evolution operations) to adequately handle evolution. In both case, INDs like IND 3 are kept.

Consequently, INDs have to be either *predefined* or *derived from the data* when designing a multi-model. To extract INDs from data, three different approaches are illustrated in Fig. 3. Adding another data model is highlighted green.

(A) shows a point-to-point strategy. This includes mappings between every single data store. Therefore, six mapping algorithms are necessary for the three data stores c_d shown. If another store is added – color coded in green – the obvious disadvantage of this approach is that additional mappings to each data store are required. In (B) the data is mapped into a flat, relational-like format and stored in a relational database. Here SQL commands can be used to find INDs (as proposed by several available approaches, see Sect. 3). Moreover, mapping algorithms into a relational database are at hand for a variety of data models [7,12]. The last approach (C) operates with a meta level consisting of information on kinds (= relations/collections/labels), properties and paths. Similar to (B) only one mapping for each data store is required, significantly decreasing the effort compared to the point-to-point approach in (A).

(B) and (C) are beneficial, as they reduce the number of mappings and thus ensure an easy extensibility together with a higher degree of abstraction. Our framework uses (B), as most existing algorithms are optimized for relational data, while another domain- and system-independent option is shown in (C).

5 Challenges in Multi-model Scenarios

Several challenges and data characteristics need to be considered when integrating NoSQL databases together with relational data stores in a multi-model. Relational databases follow a schema-first approach, meaning the schema is predefined before data can be inserted, allowing reliability on the validity of the structure and constraints. NoSQL databases can follow a schema-second approach where no schema checking component is required. The consequence is a higher degree of heterogeneity in NoSQL data. Especially in real-word data, normalization cannot be assumed for any data store.

Heterogeneous Data. If we want to apply IND search algorithms to NoSQL databases, we have to consider all facets of heterogeneity that may arise due to the schemaless nature of these systems. Heterogeneous data includes optional property keys, unconnected entities (e.g., nodes in a graph database) and enhances the change of semantical overlaps (e.g., synonyms used for labels like customer and buyer, properties or occurring typos). An increasing number of users may lead to greater heterogeneity, posing a key challenge in the integration of NoSQL databases.

Null Value Handling. There are various different *types of null values* that we have to consider. In NoSQL database, *a* `null` *value* is used similar to the `null` value in relational databases. Additionally, the non-existence of information can occur (in schemaless databases as well as in database with optional properties). In graph databases, missing properties and non-available relationships are interpreted as null values, while in JSON databases, non-available properties, fields in arrays and nested objects deliver the same information. The reasons for null values can be manyfold, e.g., non-existence (`Customer` nodes without the property key `bonus_card_number`), unknown (e.g., no `phone_number` of a `Customer`, or not yet existing (e.g., `marriage partner` of a `Person`). Also data protection question (e.g., hide the `salary` value of a `Person`) can cause null values in databases.

Normalized vs. Non-normalized Properties. Another challenge, not limited to NoSQL databases, involves properties in 1.NF vs. composed values (not in 1.NF). For example, the relation `Customer` may use a property key `name` with the value `Anna Müller`, while another relation (not normalized), `Guest`, represents the same information using separate key-value pairs: `firstName: Anna` and `lastName: Müller` (fulfills 1.NF). Even though the structure differs, both relations contain identical data. Detecting such non-normalized properties would be a preprocessing step that we want to add to our framework in the future.

Degree of Difference. Two types of divergence can be identified: at the property name level and at the data level. On the data level, syntactical error like different spelling of values and typos have to be considered when comparing the data to detect INDs. On the property name level, we additionally have to assume synonyms and abbreviations for property name with the same semantic.

Speed Mode with Sampling. Depending on the use case, it may also be of interest to find existing data dependencies that are probably valid. This is especially important in the context of data exploration tasks. In order to handle such cases, we have a so-called *speed_mode* and define the percentage of the dataset to be tested. In this case for each IND candidate only a randomly selected percentage of the data of the left-hand side of a potential dependency is selected and tested. As the test only covers a sample portion of the data sets, these dependencies are associated with uncertainty. If the exact valid inclusion dependencies are required, the complete test must be carried out.

Interim Conclusion. All the challenges discussed in this section intensify the need for an adequate mapping strategy. When NoSQL data (from MongoDB or Neo4j) are translated into relations, the different kinds of null values are ignored. Thus, properties which contain missing values no longer exist. This is necessary as the integrated algorithms use UCCs as a precondition as otherwise addional false positives would emerge during the IND detection. Our framework's speed mode with sampling improves performance for large datasets.

6 Framework for a Multi-model Approach

In this section we present our framework which offers the advantage of integrating existing or an own algorithm for multi-model scenarios. It enables constraint detection with a relational meta level (see Scenario **B** in Fig. 3).

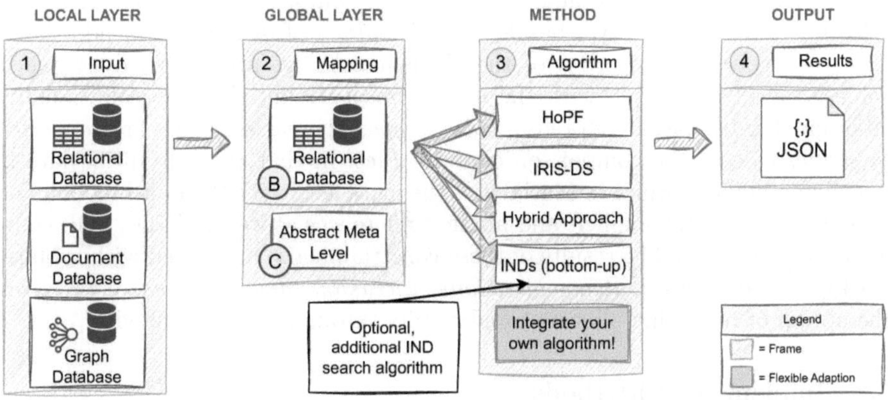

Fig. 4. (1) All input data is (2) mapped to a relational database or an abstract meta level (see Fig. 3). (3) Different existing algorithms or an own algorithm (= green) can be integrated. (4) The INDs are generated and outputted in JSON syntax.

6.1 Approach

First, we present the framework we implemented and discuss conceptual decisions made during the design process. Afterwards, the implementation details of the mapping strategy are presented.

Framework. Figure 4 shows the framework to extract INDs from multi-model data. The method consist of Steps **1**, **2** and **4** which are fixed while the concrete method in **3** is flexible. With this modularity, we achieve an adaptable approach which also allows to *re-use all other available methods* for IND extraction from data in single stores and extend them for multi-model data.

Our framework allows the usage of different databases (relational, document and graph databases), see Step **1**. In Step **2** the data is mapped to a relational database, in our case MariaDB (Sect. 6). The central part of the framework is Step **3**, here the concrete IND inference algorithm (= method) is executed. All available IND extraction algorithms can be used and, of course, also new algorithms can be added here. Step **4** represents the output format. JSON is widely used as exchange format and consequently also used by us to store INDs at the global level. Even though we developed a method for multi-model data, our algorithm is, due to its modularity, applicable for stores of the same data model, e.g., to find INDs between two graph databases.

Mapping. The novelty of our approach lies in our mapping strategy, guaranteeing the integration of various single store. The mapping is analogous to

Scenario Ⓑ in Fig. 3. The mapping unifies the storage in different data models and thus helps handling the heterogeneity of data. In this process the connection data of each data store (= *servers*), and the database names (= *db_name*) are saved in MariaDB. The *datastorage* relation collects information about each kind (= *storage_name*), consisting of each label/type, collection and relation. In case of embedded elements in document-oriented data stores, an additional *parent_id* is stored, to be able to reconstruct complete path information. For a lossless storage of arrays, beside *loaded_values* of *attributes* an additional *entry_no* specifies the order of the elements. Arrays are flattened i.e., each value is saved in a tuple with the *entry_no* of its initial array. Additionally, all original datatypes are stored in *value_type*, whereas all values are *converted to strings* to ease the comparison of the *values*. In that way, all initial data is stored in a unified format in MariaDB – the meta level with the multi-model. For deriving UCCs, PKs, explicit and implicit references as well as INDs, SQL commands can be used. The results of these constraints also are stored within MariaDB (= *unique_attributecombinations*, *inclusion_dependencies*). This gives the option of retrieving all scores and results through SQL commands.

6.2 Implemented Methods

Our implementation offers several algorithms like HoPF, Iris-Ds or Hybrid which are described in detail in this section. Its meta level is relational, as many algorithms thematize relational data. Consequently, optimized algorithms using SQL are utilized. The parameter $maxINDs$ can be used to perform a classical bottom-up approach to extract n-ary INDs.

HoPF [16], **Iris-Ds** [38] and our **Hybrid Approach.** Both the HoPF and Iris-Ds algorithm expect UCCs as input data as restricting precondition. The HoPF, additionally, requires INDs. In contrast to the HoPF, the Iris-Ds is advantageous when handling heterogeneity due to considering a relaxed schema in NoSQL databases.

UCC and Primary Key Detection. Based on the cardinality, value length, position and name suffixes the HoPF algorithm detects primary key (PK) candidates, while the Iris-Ds uses name suffixes, position, datatype as well as value length. The list of name suffixes of the HoPF was extended for the Iris-Ds. Our framework takes a individualized list as input, so that a user can extend or change the suffixes as it seems fit.

Adjustment in the Hybrid approach: Cliff-Method [16,38] **vs. Z-Score.** The PK identification of both algorithms uses the cliff method. To do so, a sorted list with scores $S = \{S_1, S_2, \ldots, S_n\}$ for each kind together with a list of score differences $SD = \{SD_1, SD_2, \ldots, SD_n\}$ are analyzed. The score difference is calculated for all adjusted neighbors as follows: $SD_i = S_i - S_{n-1}$. All values above or identical the highest SD score (= cliff) are considered as PK candidates. We adjusted this method by using the z-score, a well-known statistical method. If the z-score is higher or equal to 1, the z-score is used, otherwise we chose the cliff method.

Foreign Key Detection. Through the usage of join operations, potential FK candidates are identified in the IRIS-DS by calculating the syntactical together with the semantical similarity. The HOPF algorithm uses the data distribution together with the syntactic name similarity.

HYBRID Approach. For the HYBRID approach we adjust the name similarity. Just like in the IRIS-DS, the name of kinds are tokenized and afterwards the syntactic and semantic similarity are calculated; followed by a weighted average value like in the HOPF algorithm. The HYBRID approach can be combined with either the PK algorithm of the HOPF or the IRIS-DS, allowing adjustability depending on the inputted dataset, offering components of both existing and implemented algorithms.

Bottom-Up IND Search. To detect all valid INDs in a multi-model dataset, a bottom-up approach is integrated, too. First, unary INDs are identified based on [5], n-ary INDs are detected with the approach from [24]. Consequently, no preconditions like UCCs in the HOPF algorithm are needed. By adapting the parameter of the algorithm (setting $maxINDs$ to true) all n-ary INDs are searched. The algorithm terminates when no more n+1-ary candidates can be tested. To increase the performance, we apply two strategies: (1) an apriori condition is tested like in [5] and [19]: for all unary INDs the maximum and minimum values are compared before comparing all values. (2) Datasets can be considerably large which is why we implemented a *speed_mode*, that can be individualized. This refers to random samples that are tested for the IND search – a value of 0 indicates that all values are tested.

7 Evaluation of Available Methods in Our Framework

In this section, we evaluate all constraint detection methods, i.e., HOPF, IRIS-DS, the HYBRID approach and the classical bottom-up IND search, within a multi-model scenario. The schema of our dataset is shown in Fig. 5, while all valid data dependencies are visualized in Fig. 6. The evaluation results are presented in Table 2 and Fig. 7 shows the performance results.

Set Up. Our framework is evaluated with a modified version of the UniBench dataset [44]. In the style of [43], the dataset is divided into three parts. Our UniBench version was designed to integrate all possible INDs between normal properties, FKs and PKs. The relational store holds native-relational data, here information about `Customers`, `Invoices` as well as `Vendors`. The property *customer_id* represents a foreign key to connect the `Invoice` relation with `Customer`. MongoDB as the state-of-the-art document store incorporates information about `Orders`. In contrast to other stores, embedding is frequently used in document stores, representing a hierarchical structure. To ensure the integration of this characteristic, `order_item` is embedded into the `Order` document and `vendor` is even further embedded within `order_item`. In accordance with real-world data, the property graph database holds information, representing a social network for the store to tag or post on products. Figure 5 depicts that each

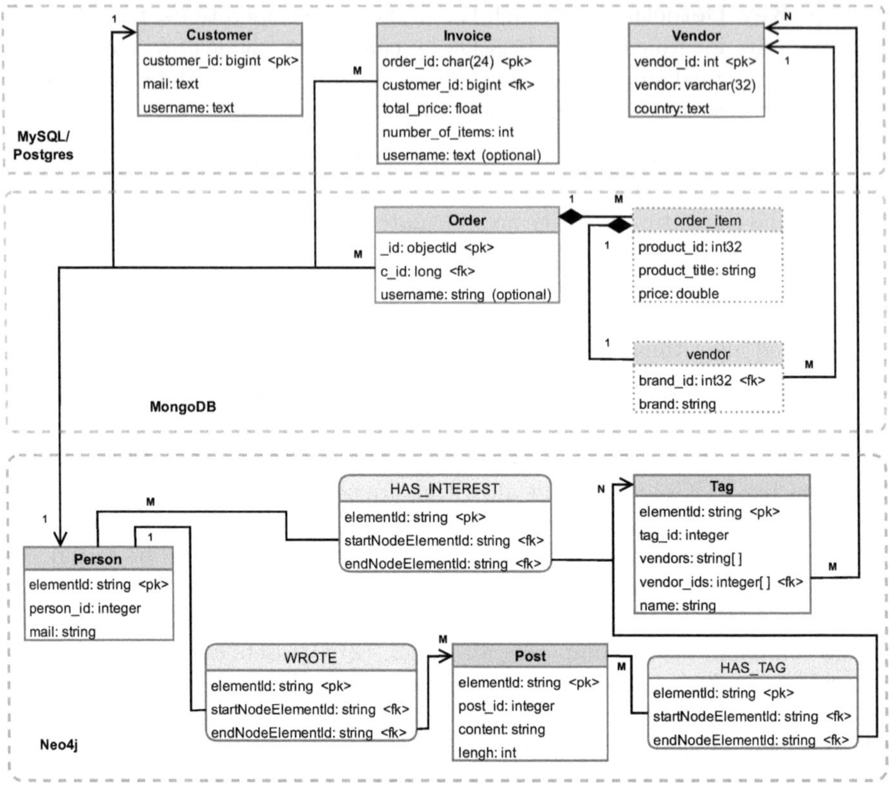

Fig. 5. The schema of the test dataset, based on the UniBench dataset which was divided into three datasets for relational, document oriented and graph stores.

data store contains data dependencies to establish connections to the other two stores. The synthetic datasets are generated by using our own data generator witch's source code is available from our GitHub repository[2].

Data Dependency Graph. The graph in Fig. 6 shows all 24 INDs within the presented dataset. The data stores are color-coded: green represents the document store, violet indicates the graph database, and blue illustrates the relational schema components. Filled nodes indicate properties holding data dependencies, whereas their associated entity types are depicted as white nodes with colored borders. Bold arrows represent valid INDs, while thin arrows indicate potential INDs that could exist, but are not present in the dataset due to the specific data content. Moreover, the dependency graph illustrates that all possible cases are considered and integrated in the multi-model dataset. Namely, these cases are: (1) A foreign key pointing at a primary key and vice versa, (2) foreign keys pointing at each other, (3) properties representing INDs and (4) a foreign key building an IND together with a property.

[2] The code for the data generator is available at: https://github.com/dbishagen/unibench-ind-data-generator.

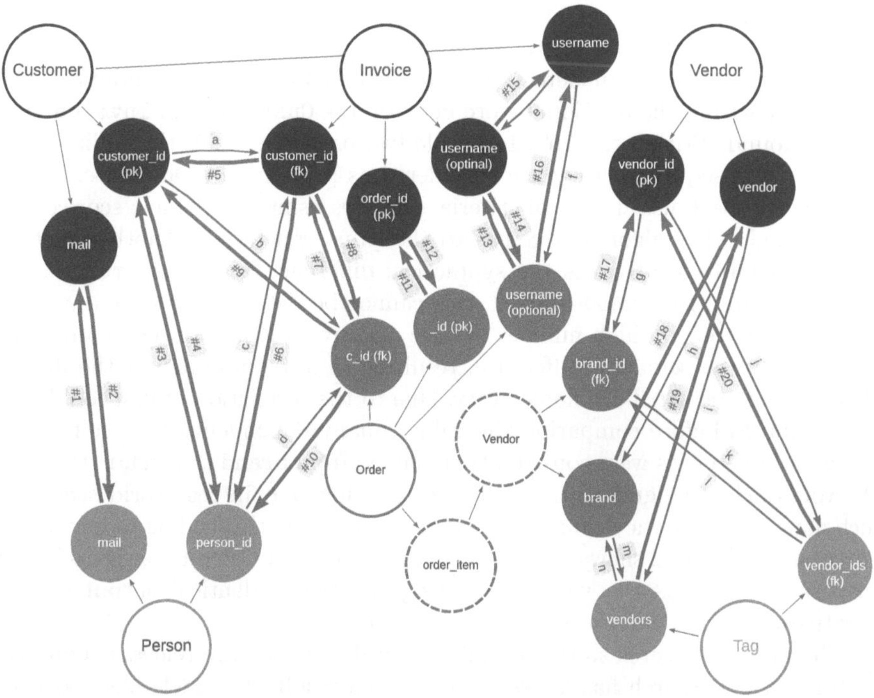

Fig. 6. The data dependency graph shows all 24 INDs present in the schema of our dataset shown in Fig. 5.

Evaluation of Existing Algorithms and Hybrid Approach Fusing Them. First, we evaluate the results for the existing algorithms we integrated in our framework (see Fig. 4), namely Hopf and Iris-Ds together with our Hybrid approach, combining elements of Hopf and Iris-Ds. To enable a comprehensive evaluation and to guarantee the accuracy of each algorithm, we classify the results using the following standard categories: false negatives (missing data dependencies), false positives (falsely determined data dependencies), and true positives (correctly classified data dependency candidates). Table 2 shows the results of our evaluation that illustrate precision, recall, and the F1 score, which are classical static methods to quantify the results.

Table 2. Results of the PK-FK detection and the bottom-up IND search in our multi-model dataset illustrated in Fig. 5.

Algorithm	False negative ✗	False positive ✓✗	True positive ✔	Precision	Recall	F1 score
Ind Search	0	1	24	0.96	1.00	0.98
Hopf	8	0	16	1.00	0.67	0.80
Iris-Ds	16	0	8	1.00	0.33	0.50
Hybrid	8	0	16	1.00	0.67	0.80

Table 2 shows that 16 of 24 inclusion dependencies were accurately identified by the HOPF algorithm, while the eight false negatives are illustrated in Table 3. Although HOPF excels in detecting primary and foreign keys candidates, the foreign key within the relational store between the `Customer` and `Invoice` table was not found. Within the `Invoice` table two properties with the suffix `id` are contained, consequently, they are considered as primary key candidate. As the HYBRID approach uses identical criteria – besides using either the z-score or the cliff method – the algorithm comes to the same conclusion. Another method generating false negatives is the syntactical difference, e.g., `customer_id` and `person_id` are synonymously used, this cannot be detected as too many chars differ. The extremely high number of false negatives of the IRIS-DS, namely 16, is caused by the semantic difference, resulting in a low accuracy if the data is identical but the attribute names vary. Due to the restriction of first looking at the attributes before comparing the values, many dependencies are not found. If, e.g., all references were consistently renamed from `brand` to `vendor`, the IRIS-DS would achieve significantly higher scores. However, in real-world scenarios, such naming consistency cannot be assumed, consequently, leading to low scores. Furthermore, Table 2 shows that the HOPF as well as the HYBRID approach both outperform the IRIS-DS, while outputting an almost identical output of false negatives, differing only in one case (see Table 3).

The precision scores show that all retrieved elements are relevant. Only the bottom-up IND search has a score of 0.96, as a result of a single false positive. The lowest recall with a value of 0.33 was achieved by the IRIS-DS, caused by the naming conventions. Analogously, with a higher consistency in the naming of the properties, the score would increase. Both HYBRID and HOPF show identical values for recall with 0.67 and an F1 score of 0.80. This is a result of both missing the same dependencies with one single difference. The evaluation demonstrated that an IND search is superior for multi-model scenarios.

Performance. Figure 7 illustrates the results of the performance tests with four different scaling factors on the x-axis, analogous to [43,44]. The initial mapping to MariaDB takes the longest with a linear increase in runtime. Consequently, an approach such as Scenario Ⓒ assumes a higher performance (see Fig. 3) if data can be read and processed in the main memory. However, the time taken to process each algorithm is rather low.

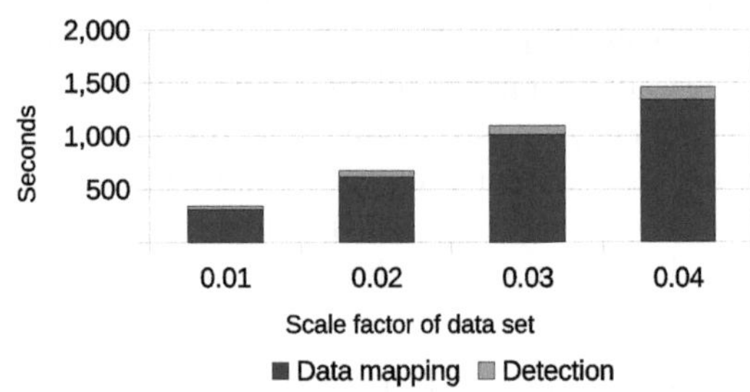

Fig. 7. Performance Results

Table 3. False negatives detected by each of the algorithms available in our framework.

Data Store	*False Negative* Data Dependency	Hopf	Hybrid	Iris-Ds
relational FK	customer.customer_id →invoice.customer_id	✗	✗	✗
relational → document	invoice.customer_id→Order.c_id	✗	✗	✗
	customer.customer_id→Order.c_id	✗	✗	✗
	invoice.username→Order.username	✗	✗	✗
relational → graph	customer.customer_id→Person.person_id			✗
	invoice.customer_id→Person.person_id			✗
document → relational	Order.c_id→invoice.customer_id		✗	✗
	Order.c_id→customer.customer_id	✗		✗
	Order._id→invoice.order_id			✗
	Order.username→invoice.username	✗	✗	✗
	vendor.brand_id→vendor.vendor_id			✗
	vendor.brand→vendor.vendor			✗
document → graph	Order.c_id→Person.person_id			✗
graph → relational	Person.person_id→customer.customer_id			✗
	Person.person_id→invoice.customer_id	✗	✗	✗
graph → document	Person.person_id→.Order.c_id	✗	✗	✗

8 Conclusion and Future Work

In this paper, we present a new approach for detecting INDs in multi-model systems. In contrast to other IND inference algorithms, that only work on a single store, mostly on relational databases, we have developed a method for deriving (1) all intra-model INDs of each data store (relational, JSON and graph) and (2) in parallel within a multi-model. Although the application domain is new and much broader than the available solutions, our framework (see Sect. 6) not only offers a classical IND search but also existing algorithms such as Hopf or Iris-Ds, as well as our own Hybrid approach, which combines the advantages of both existing algorithms. To extend the scope of the established INDs algorithms, we have integrated a mapping strategy (Sect. 6.1) to translate different data sets into relational data, representing our meta level, and thus overcome the technical heterogeneity of the different data models.

With this flexible approach, we achieve a variety of goals: We can build on established algorithms, extend their application domains and thus extract not only INDs for non-relational data but also a completely new class of INDs – representing references between different data models. As a side effect, we can also infer INDs from graph databases for which such algorithms were previously not available. Our framework can be re-used by integrating one's own algorithm.

The evaluation demonstrates that an IND search surpasses a key-foreign key search when working with multi-models. This can be explained, as in NoSQL databases like MongoDB redundancies are designed to improve performance. In our future work, we plan to intensify our work on relaxed inclusion dependencies and their detection in multi-model data including naming inconsistencies. Here, in addition to technical heterogeneity, data errors, and noise will be considered.

Acknowledgements. The work of Dominique Hausler has been funded by Deutsche Forschungsgemeinschaft (German Research Foundation) – 385808805. We thank Stefan Dierks for initial architectural suggestions and fruitful discussions on this topic as well as Marican Seeger for his comments and suggestions.

References

1. Abedjan, Z., Naumann, F.: Advancing the discovery of unique column combinations. In: CIKM, pp. 1565–1570. ACM (2011)
2. Abedjan, Z., Quiané-Ruiz, J., Naumann, F.: Detecting unique column combinations on dynamic data. In: ICDE, pp. 1036–1047. IEEE Computer Society (2014)
3. Bansal, N., Sachdeva, S., Awasthi, L.K.: Database migration tools: from RDB to NoSQL database. In: SoMeT, pp. 563–570. IOS Press (2022)
4. Bauckmann, J., Leser, U., Naumann, F., Tietz, V.: Efficiently detecting inclusion dependencies. In: ICDE, pp. 1448–1450. IEEE (2007)
5. Bell, S., Brockhausen, P.: Discovery of data dependencies in relational databases. Citeseer (1995). https://d-nb.info/1103028413/34
6. Birnick, J., Bläsius, T., Friedrich, T., Naumann, F., Papenbrock, T., Schirneck, M.: Hitting set enumeration with partial information for unique column combination discovery. Proc. VLDB Endow. **13**(11), 2270–2283 (2020)
7. Ceresnák, R., Dudás, A., Matiasko, K., Kvet, M.: Mapping rules for schema transformation : SQL to NoSQL and back. In: IDT, pp. 52–58. IEEE (2021)
8. Chen, Z., Narasayya, V.R., Chaudhuri, S.: Fast foreign-key detection in Microsoft SQL server powerpivot for excel. Proc. VLDB Endow. **7**(13), 1417–1428 (2014)
9. Dürsch, F., et al.: Inclusion dependency discovery: an experimental evaluation of thirteen algorithms. In: CIKM, pp. 219–228. ACM (2019)
10. Fan, W., Hu, C., Liu, X., Lu, P.: Discovering graph functional dependencies. ACM Trans. Database Syst. **45**(3), 15:1–15:42 (2020)
11. Gobert, M., Meurice, L., Cleve, A.: Modeling, manipulating and evolving hybrid polystores with HyDRa. Sci. Comput. Program. **230**, 102972 (2023)
12. Gueidi, A., Gharsellaoui, H., Ahmed, S.B.: Towards unified modeling for NoSQL solution based on mapping approach. In: KES. Procedia Computer Science, vol. 192, pp. 3637–3646. Elsevier (2021)
13. Han, S., Cai, X., Wang, C., Zhang, H., Wen, Y.: Discovery of unique column combinations with Hadoop. In: Chen, L., Jia, Y., Sellis, T., Liu, G. (eds.) APWeb 2014. LNCS, vol. 8709, pp. 533–541. Springer, Cham (2014). https://doi.org/10.1007/978-3-319-11116-2_49
14. Heise, A., Quiané-Ruiz, J., Abedjan, Z., Jentzsch, A., Naumann, F.: Scalable discovery of unique column combinations. Proc. VLDB Endow. **7**(4), 301–312 (2013)

15. Holubová, I., Klettke, M., Störl, U.: Evolution management of multi-model data. In: Gadepally, V., Mattson, T., Stonebraker, M., Wang, F., Luo, G., Laing, Y., Dubovitskaya, A. (eds.) DMAH/Poly -2019. LNCS, vol. 11721, pp. 139–153. Springer, Cham (2019). https://doi.org/10.1007/978-3-030-33752-0_10
16. Jiang, L., Naumann, F.: Holistic primary key and foreign key detection. J. Intell. Inf. Syst. **54**(3), 439–461 (2020)
17. Kaminsky, Y., Pena, E.H.M., Naumann, F.: Discovering similarity inclusion dependencies. Proc. ACM Manag. Data **1**(1), 75:1–75:24 (2023)
18. Kiehn, F., Schmidt, M., Panse, F.: Constraint management and data placement in the context of polyglot persistence. In: GvDB. vol. 3710, pp. 9–15. CEUR-WS.org (2024)
19. Klettke, M., Awolin, H., Störl, U., Müller, D., Scherzinger, S.: Uncovering the evolution history of data lakes. In: IEEE BigData, pp. 2462–2471. IEEE Computer Society (2017)
20. Koeller, A., Rundensteiner, E.A.: Discovery of high-dimensional inclusion dependencies. In: ICDE, pp. 683–685. IEEE (2003)
21. Kruse, S., Jentzsch, A., Papenbrock, T., Kaoudi, Z., Quiané-Ruiz, J., Naumann, F.: RDFind: scalable conditional inclusion dependency discovery in RDF datasets. In: SIGMOD,m pp. 953–967. ACM (2016)
22. Kruse, S., et al.: Fast Approximate discovery of inclusion dependencies. In: BTW. LNI, vol. P-265, pp. 207–226. GI (2017)
23. Langouri, M.A., Mansfield, A., Chiang, F., Wu, Y.: Inconsistency detection with temporal graph functional dependencies. In: ICDE, pp. 464–476. IEEE (2023)
24. Marchi, F., Lopes, S., Petit, J.-M.: Efficient algorithms for mining inclusion dependencies. In: Jensen, C.S., Šaltenis, S., Jeffery, K.G., Pokorny, J., Bertino, E., Böhn, K., Jarke, M. (eds.) EDBT 2002. LNCS, vol. 2287, pp. 464–476. Springer, Heidelberg (2002). https://doi.org/10.1007/3-540-45876-X_30
25. Marchi, F.D., Lopes, S., Petit, J.: Unary and n-ary inclusion dependency discovery in relational databases. J. Intell. Inf. Syst. **32**(1), 53–73 (2009)
26. Marchi, F.D., Petit, J.: Zigzag: A new algorithm for mining large inclusion dependencies in database. In: ICDM, pp. 27–34. IEEE (2003)
27. Masson, T., Ravet, R., Ruiz, F.J.B., Serbout, S., Ruiz, D.S., Cleve, A.: Defining referential integrity constraints in graph-oriented datastores. In: MODELSWARD, pp. 409–416. SCITEPRESS (2020)
28. Papenbrock, T., Kruse, S., Quiané-Ruiz, J., Naumann, F.: Divide and conquer-based inclusion dependency discovery. Proc. VLDB Endow. **8**(7), 774–785 (2015)
29. Papenbrock, T., Naumann, F.: A hybrid approach for efficient unique column combination discovery. In: BTW. LNI, vol. P-265, pp. 195–204. GI (2017)
30. Pokorný, J., Valenta, M., Kovacic, J.: Integrity constraints in graph databases. In: ANT/SEIT. Procedia Computer Science, vol. 109, pp. 975–981. Elsevier (2017)
31. Reina, F., Huf, A., Presser, D., Siqueira, F.: Modeling and enforcing integrity constraints on graph databases. In: Hartmann, S., Küng, J., Kotsis, G., Tjoa, A.M., Khalil, I. (eds.) DEXA 2020. LNCS, vol. 12391, pp. 269–284. Springer, Cham (2020). https://doi.org/10.1007/978-3-030-59003-1_18
32. Scherzinger, S., Klettke, M., Störl, U.: Managing Schema Evolution in NoSQL Data Stores. In: DBPL@VLDB (2013)
33. Shaabani, N., Meinel, C.: Scalable inclusion dependency discovery. In: Renz, M., Shahabi, C., Zhou, X., Cheema, M.A. (eds.) DASFAA 2015. LNCS, vol. 9049, pp. 425–440. Springer, Cham (2015). https://doi.org/10.1007/978-3-319-18120-2_25

34. Shaabani, N., Meinel, C.: Detecting maximum inclusion dependencies without candidate generation. In: Hartmann, S., Ma, H. (eds.) DEXA 2016. LNCS, vol. 9828, pp. 118–133. Springer, Cham (2016). https://doi.org/10.1007/978-3-319-44406-2_10
35. Shimomura, L.C., Fletcher, G.H.L., Yakovets, N.: ProGGD - data profiling on knowledge graphs using graph generating dependencies. In: ISCW 2023, vol. 3632. CEUR-WS.org (2023)
36. Shimomura, L.C., Yakovets, N., Fletcher, G.: GGDMiner - Discovery of Graph Generating Dependencies for Graph Data Profiling. CoRR (2024). https://arxiv.org/pdf/2403.17082
37. Sismanis, Y., Brown, P., Haas, P.J., Reinwald, B.: GORDIAN: efficient and scalable discovery of composite keys. In: VLDB, pp. 691–702. ACM (2006)
38. Souibgui, M., Atigui, F., Yahia, S.B., Cherfi, S.S.: IRIS-DS: A New approach for identifiers and references discovery in document stores. In: HICSS, pp. 1–10. ScholarSpace (2021)
39. Stiemer, A., Vogt, M., Schuldt, H., Störl, U.: PolyMigrate: dynamic schema evolution and data migration in a distributed Polystore. In: Poly/DMAH@VLDB. LNCS, vol. 12633, pp. 42–53. Springer (2020)
40. Tan, R., Chirkova, R., Gadepally, V., Mattson, T.G.: Enabling query processing across heterogeneous data models: a survey. In: IEEE BigData, pp. 3211–3220. IEEE Computer Society (2017)
41. Wang, C., Han, S., Cai, X., Zhang, H., Wen, Y.: Efficient unique column combinations discovery based on data distribution. In: Cui, B., Zhang, N., Xu, J., Lian, X., Liu, D. (eds.) WAIM 2016. LNCS, vol. 9658, pp. 454–466. Springer, Cham (2016). https://doi.org/10.1007/978-3-319-39937-9_35
42. Yamanaka, M.G., de Almeida, D.H., de Almeida, P.R.L., Dominico, S., Peres, L.M., Sunyé, M.S., de Almeida, E.C.: Statistical validation of column matching in the database schema evolution of the brazilian public school census (2024)
43. Zhang, C., Lu, J.: Holistic evaluation in multi-model databases benchmarking. Distributed Parallel Data. **39**(1), 1–33 (2021)
44. Zhang, C., Lu, J., Xu, P., Chen, Y.: UniBench: a benchmark for multi-model database management systems. In: TPCTC. LNCS, vol. 11135, pp. 7–23. Springer (2018)
45. Zhang, M., Hadjieleftheriou, M., Ooi, B.C., Procopiuc, C.M., Srivastava, D.: On multi-column foreign key discovery. Proc. VLDB Endow. **3**(1), 805–814 (2010)

Possibilistic SQL Constraints

Ilya Litvinenko[1], Philipp Skavantzos[1], Henning Koehler[2], and Sebastian Link[1(✉)]

[1] School of Computer Science, University of Auckland, Auckland, New Zealand
{ilit874,philipp.skavantzos,s.link}@auckland.ac.nz
[2] School of Mathematical and Computational Sciences, Massey University, Auckland, New Zealand
h.koehler@massey.ac.nz

Abstract. We equip SQL with reasoning capabilities about the entity integrity of data that may feature volume, variety, and veracity dimensions. We outline applications, and establish axiomatic, algorithmic, and logical characterizations of the PTIME-complete implication problem associated with possibilistic keys, FDs, and NOT NULL constraints. We introduce a tool that creates perfect samples and offers computational support for data stewards in identifying constraints that govern entity integrity in their domain of interest.

Keywords: Functional dependency · Implication · Key · Missing data · Reasoning · SQL · Uncertainty

1 Introduction

Database systems manage data about some domain of the real-world. SQL governs data by the rigid structure of relations [12]. New applications require the handling of large volumes of data from heterogeneous sources (variety) and with different degrees of uncertainty (veracity) [1]. Given the mature and popular technology that SQL provides, many organizations use SQL to manage data that exhibits flexible formats and uncertainty, such as JSON data.

We aim at efficient reasoning about the entity integrity of data that accommodates the volume, variety and veracity dimensions. Codd stipulated entity integrity as one of the three major integrity principles in databases [12]. Entity integrity refers to the principle of representing each entity of the application domain uniquely within the database. Violations of this principle are common in practice, resulting in their own fields of research including entity resolution [11], data de-duplication [37], data cleaning [20], or consistent query answering [6].

While keys and functional dependencies (FDs) have unique and unchallenged definitions in the relational model of data, simple extensions introduce opportunities to define these concepts differently to support different applications [44]. SQL, for example, provides simple means to accommodate missing information. In fact, it permits occurrences of a so-called *null marker*, denoted by $\perp$, to say that there is no information about the value of this record on this column [23,50].

D. Bork et al. (Eds.): ER 2025, LNCS 16189, pp. 261–279, 2026.
https://doi.org/10.1007/978-3-032-08623-5_14

blog	(emp:'Bob', mng: 'Susan', {dpt: 'Biology', dpt: 'Arts'})	*payroll*	(mng:'Simon', {dpt:'Math', dpt:'Stats'})
			(mng:'Shaun', dpt: 'CS', emp: 'Mike', emp: 'Tom')
website	(emp:'John', dpt: 'Music', mng: 'Scott')		(emp: 'Derek', dpt: 'Physics')
	(emp: 'Andy', {mng: 'Sofia', mng: 'Sam'})		(emp: 'John', dpt: 'Music', mng: 'Scott')

Fig. 1. JSON data from different information sources

Moreover, columns can be defined as `NOT NULL` to prevent null marker occurrences. The interpretation of $\perp$ is deliberately kept simple to uniformly accommodate many types of missing information, including values that do not exist or values that exist but are currently unknown [50]. In modern applications, for example data integration, null markers are used frequently by SQL to fit data of heterogeneous structure within a uniform table. SQL also permits the duplication of rows in support of the volume dimension to minimize costs for duplicate elimination. When duplicates are present, FDs can no longer express keys [26]. Hence, for SQL we need to study the combined class of keys and FDs. These considerations also apply in the modern context of graph databases where information is managed on nodes and/or edges, and properties may be missing or duplicated [2,3,40,41]. The veracity dimension abandons the restriction that all data need to be considered equal. Clearly, this provides an opportunity to capture real-world requirements to derive more trust in data-driven decision making. Probabilistic and possibilistic databases offer complementary approaches to uncertain data. Essentially, there is a trade-off as probabilistic databases offer continouous degrees of uncertainty and real probability distributions are hard to come by and maintain, while possibilistic databases offer discrete degrees of uncertainty and are simpler to come by and maintain [15,42].

Contributions and Organization. We introduce our running example in Sect. 2. Section 3 reviews previous work in a framework that can handle all combinations of the volume, variety, and veracity dimension of data within possibilistic SQL. We define our possibilistic SQL model in 4, and the constraints in Sect. 5. The implication problem and its centrality for data management are explained in Sect. 6. In Sects. 7 and 8, respectively, we establish axiomatic and linear-time algorithmic characterizations for the associated implication problem. As a logical characterization, we show in Sect. 9 that the implication problem is equivalent to propositional HornSAT, showing that it is PTIME-complete but also solvable with linear resolution. Hence, we can reason about the entity integrity of possibilistic SQL data efficiently and with familiar tools. Section 10 discusses a prototype system that creates perfect sample data for any given set of keys, FDs, and `NOT NULL` constraints over possibilistic SQL. The tool provides thus computational support for acquiring entity integrity rules for any given application domain. We conclude in Sect. 11. Full proofs and more extensive results are available in the first author's dissertation [35].

Table 1. A University Employment Table

row	*emp*	*dpt*	*mng*	p-degree	interpretation	origin
1	$\perp$	Math	Simon	α_1	fully possible	payroll
2	$\perp$	Stats	Simon	α_1	fully possible	payroll
3	Mike	CS	Shaun	α_1	fully possible	payroll
4	Tom	CS	Shaun	α_1	fully possible	payroll
5	Derek	Physics	$\perp$	α_1	fully possible	payroll
6	John	Music	Scott	α_1	fully possible	payroll
7	John	Music	Scott	α_2	quite possible	website
8	Andy	$\perp$	Sofia	α_2	quite possible	website
9	Andy	$\perp$	Sam	α_2	quite possible	website
10	Bob	Biology	Susan	α_3	somewhat possible	blog
11	Bob	Arts	Susan	α_3	somewhat possible	blog

2 The Running Example

As a simple running example consider Fig. 1 that shows some JSON data. JSON is the de-facto standard for managing and exchanging semi-structured data, due to its capability to accommodate different information structures [36]. In our example, data originates from three sources: payroll data, web data, and blog data. As the data stewards associate different levels of trust with these sources, they would like to attribute these levels of trust to the data from the sources. We are using an SQL-based DBMS, and the data stewards have transformed the JSON data into SQL-compliant format as shown in Table 1.

The null marker $\perp$ indicates that no information is available for a data element for a given attribute, such as information on employees working in Maths or Stats. The column *p-degree* represents the level of trust in the data elements. The highest p-degree α_1 is assigned to payroll data, α_2 to web data, and α_3 to blog data. This application will be used to illustrate concepts and results.

3 Related Work

Figure 2 shows all combinations of the three dimensions, ordered as a lattice. A directed edge represents the addition of another dimension from source to target node. We assign a data structure to each combination of dimensions. At the bottom are relations. The nodes on top of relations are bags, partial relations, and p-relations. Bags model the volume dimension by permitting duplicate rows to avoid costly duplicate removal, partial relations model the variety dimension by permitting null markers, and p-relations model the veracity dimension. Above these single dimensions we then have every combination of two dimensions, and the top node combines all three dimensions.

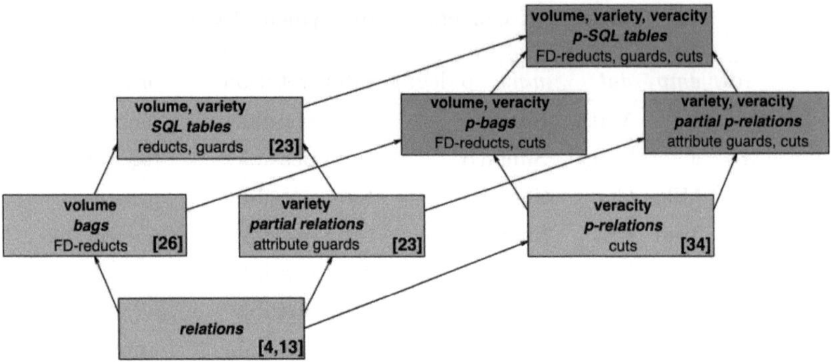

Fig. 2. Framework for data dimensions, related work, and new contributions

Table 2. Table over WORK

emp	dpt	mng
John	Music	Scott
John	Music	Scott
Derek	Physics	$\perp$
Derek	Physics	$\perp$

Previous work on entity integrity rules are marked in the color cyan in Fig. 2. Well-known are Armstrong's axioms for the implication problem of FDs in the relational model [4,13]. For bags, the interaction of keys and FDs was characterized in [26], using *FD-reducts*. Over partial relations, the implication problem for keys and FDs in the presence of `NOT NULL` constraints was solved in [23], using *attribute guards*. The implication problem over SQL tables, which combine bags and partial relations, was solved by [23]. Finally, the implication problem of FDs over p-relations was solved in [34], using *β-cuts*.

We view these isolated results under our possibilistic SQL framework. This view motivates us to extend the previous techniques to new combinations of these dimensions. These include the combination of i) volume and veracity, ii) variety and veracity, and iii) volume, variety, and veracity (marked green in Fig. 2).

4 Possibilistic SQL Tables

This section generalizes SQL schemata and tables from [23] to possibilistic ones.

An *SQL table schema*, denoted by T, is a finite non-empty set of attributes. Each attribute $A \in T$ has a domain $dom(A)$, which is a countably infinite set of values. Each domain contains the null marker as a distinguished element, which we denote by $\perp$. As a running example, we use the table schema WORK=$\{emp, dpt, mng\}$ with the uniform domain `string`.

Table 3. Possible Worlds of p-SQL table from Table 1

t_1

emp	*dpt*	*mng*
⊥	Math	Simon
⊥	Stats	Simon
Mike	CS	Shaun
Tom	CS	Shaun
Derek	Physics	⊥
John	Music	Scott

t_2

emp	*dpt*	*mng*
⊥	Math	Simon
⊥	Stats	Simon
Mike	CS	Shaun
Tom	CS	Shaun
Derek	Physics	⊥
John	Music	Scott
John	Music	Scott
Andy	⊥	Sofia
Andy	⊥	Sam

t_3

emp	*dpt*	*mng*
⊥	Math	Simon
⊥	Stats	Simon
Mike	CS	Shaun
Tom	CS	Shaun
Derek	Physics	⊥
John	Music	Scott
John	Music	Scott
Andy	⊥	Sofia
Andy	⊥	Sam
Bob	Biology	Susan
Bob	Arts	Susan

A *row* (or *tuple*) over table schema T is a function $r : T \to \cup_{A \in T} dom(A)$ assigning to every attribute a value from the attribute's domain. The image $r(A)$ of a row r on attribute A is the *value* of r on A. For $X \subseteq T$, a row r over T is X-*total*, if $r(A) \neq \perp$ for all $A \in X$. A row r is *total*, if it is T-total.

We adopt Zaniolo's interpretation of $\perp$ as "no information" [23,31,50]. That is, $r(A) = \perp$ means no information about the value of row r on attribute A is available. It may mean there is no value at all, or that there is a value which is currently unknown. We do not know which interpretation holds.

Our data model handles duplicates as tables are multisets of rows. An *SQL table* over table schema T is a finite multiset t of rows over T. For $X \subseteq T$, the table t is X-total, if every row $r \in t$ is X-total. Table t is total, if t is T-total. A total table is also called a bag. Table 2 shows an example of a table over table schema WORK. The first and second row are total, and the table itself is $\{emp, dpt\}$-total. The first and second row, as well as the third and fourth row, respectively, are duplicate tuples, since they match on all attributes.

SQL does not accommodate (degrees of) uncertainty. For example, one cannot say tuple (Derek, Physics, $\perp$) is less likely to occur than tuple (John, Music, Scott). We extend our data model by assigning degrees of possibilities (p-degrees) to tuples. This extends the model of [34] where no duplicate nor partial information was used. In our example, p-degrees result from the source tuples originate from. Rows in Table 1 come from payroll, website or blog data, respectively. Payroll data is 'fully possible', website data 'quite possible', and blog data 'somewhat possible'. Other tuples are 'impossible' to occur in the current table. Since p-degrees can have different meanings, we use abstract symbols $\alpha_1, \ldots, \alpha_k, \alpha_{k+1}$. Table 1 shows an instance with p-degrees assigned to tuples. The table has meta-data: 'row' assigns an identifier to each tuple, while 'interpretation' and 'origin' show the interpretation of p-degrees and the source of tuples, respectively.

A *possibility scale* is a strict finite linear order $\mathcal{S}_p = (S_p, >_p)$, denoted by $\alpha_1 >_p \cdots > \alpha_k >_p \alpha_{k+1}$, where k is at least one. The elements α_i are *possibility degrees* (p-degrees). In Table 1, $k = 3$ where fully possible rows have p-degree α_1, while the least possible rows have p-degree α_3. The bottom p-degree $\alpha_{k+1} = \alpha_4$ captures rows 'impossible' for the current table. Non-possibilistic tables are a special case of possibilistic ones where $k = 1$.

A *possibilistic SQL table schema* (or p-SQL table schema) is a pair $(T, \mathcal{S}_p)$, where T is a table schema and $\mathcal{S}_p$ is a possibility scale. A *possibilistic SQL table* (or p-SQL table) over $(T, \mathcal{S}_p)$ consists of a table t over T, and a function $Poss_t$ that maps each row $r \in t$ to a p-degree $Poss_t(r) \neq \alpha_{k+1}$ in the p-scale $\mathcal{S}_p$. The p-SQL table of our example is shown in Table 1. It consists of an SQL table over WORK in which rows are assigned p-degree α_1, α_2 or α_3. P-SQL tables enjoy a possible world semantics. The possible worlds form a linear chain of k SQL tables in which the i-th possible world contains tuples with p-degree α_i or higher. Given a p-SQL table t over $(T, \mathcal{S}_p)$, the possible world t_i associated with t is defined by $t_i = \{r \in t \mid Poss_t(r) \geq \alpha_i\}$, that is, t_i is an SQL table of those rows in t that have p-degree α_i or higher. Since t_{k+1} would contain impossible tuples it is not considered a possible world. Table 3 shows the possible worlds of the p-SQL table from Table 1. The possible worlds of t form a linear chain $t_1 \subseteq t_2 \subseteq t_3$.

The linear order of the p-degrees $\alpha_1 > \cdots > \alpha_k$ results in a reversed linear order of possible worlds associated with a p-SQL table t: $t_1 \subseteq \cdots \subseteq t_k$. We point out the distinguished role of the top p-degree α_1. Every row that is fully possible belongs to every possible world. Therefore, every fully possible row is also fully certain. This explains why p-SQL tables subsume SQL tables as a special case.

5 Possibilistic SQL Constraints

We introduce possibilistic constraints to restrict SQL tables to those that actually occur in an application domain.

5.1 SQL Constraints

We recall the definitions of SQL FDs and `NOT NULL` constraints [23]. Keys have not been studied in this context, but are essential to entity integrity and cannot be expressed by FDs, in contrast to the special case where multisets of partial rows reduce to sets of complete rows.

Intuitively, a key is an attribute collection that can separate different rows by their values on the key attributes. We adopt the semantics for the SQL constraint `UNIQUE` by separating different rows whenever they are total on the key attributes. A *key* over an SQL table schema T is an expression $u(X)$ where $X \subseteq T$. An SQL table t over T *satisfies* $u(X)$ over T, denoted by $\models_t u(X)$, if for all $r_1, r_2 \in t$ we have: if $r_1(X) = r_2(X)$ and r_1, r_2 are X-total, then $r_1 = r_2$. The possible world t_1 of Table 3 satisfies $u(emp)$, while t_2 and t_3 violate this key.

The following semantics of FDs goes back to Lien [31]. A *functional dependency* (FD) over an SQL table schema T is an expression $X \to Y$ where $XY \subseteq T$. An SQL table t over T *satisfies* $X \to Y$ over T, denoted by $\models_t X \to Y$, if for all $r_1, r_2 \in t$ we have: if $r_1(X) = r_2(X)$ and r_1, r_2 are X-total, then $r_1(Y) = r_2(Y)$. The possible world t_2 of Table 3 satisfies *emp* $\to$ *dpt* and *dpt* $\to$ *mng*, while t_3 satisfies *dpt* $\to$ *mng*, but not *emp* $\to$ *dpt*.

SQL `NOT NULL` constraints control occurrences of the null marker. They have been studied in combination with FDs and multivalued dependencies [23]. A `NOT NULL` constraint over an SQL table schema T is an expression $n(X)$ where $X \subseteq T$. An SQL table t over T *satisfies* the `NOT NULL` constraint $n(X)$ over T, denoted by $\models_t n(X)$, if t is X-total. For a given set Σ of constraints over T we call $T_s = \{A \in T \mid \exists n(X) \in \Sigma \wedge A \in X\}$ the *null-free subschema* (NFS) over T. If $T_s = T$, we call T a *bag schema*, as instances over T are bags. For example, *n(dpt)* is satisfied by the possible world t_1 in Table 3, but not by t_2 or t_3.

5.2 Possibilistic SQL Constraints

We extend our semantics of SQL constraints to possibilistic SQL tables. Following [34], we use the p-degrees of rows to specify with which certainty an SQL constraint holds. Similar to how α_i denotes p-degrees of rows, β_i denotes c-degrees by which constraints hold. Let us inspect some SQL constraints on the possible worlds t_1, t_2, t_3 in Table 3. The constraint *dpt* $\to$ *mng* is satisfied by t_3, and therefore by t_2 and t_1. Since the constraint is satisfied by every possible world, it is 'fully certain' to hold, denoted by β_1. The constraint *emp* $\to$ *dpt* is satisfied by t_2 and therefore by t_1, but it is not satisfied by t_3. Since the constraint is only violated by the 'somewhat possible' world t_3, it is 'quite certain' to hold, denoted by β_2. The constraint *u(emp)* is satisfied by t_1, but it is not satisfied by t_2 and therefore not by t_3. Since the smallest possible world that violates the constraint is 'quite possible', it is 'somewhat certain' to hold, denoted by β_3. The constraint *n(emp)* is not even satisfied in the 'fully possible' world t_1. It is 'not certain at all' to hold, denoted by β_4.

The examples illustrate how the p-degrees of rows motivate degrees of certainty (c-degrees) with which constraints hold on p-SQL tables. If the smallest world that violates a constraint has p-degree α_i (this world is impossible only when all possible worlds satisfy the constraint), then the constraint holds with c-degree β_{k+2-i}. For example, the p-key *u(emp)* holds with c-degree β_3 in the p-SQL table t of Table 1, meaning the smallest possible world that violates *u(emp)* is t_2, which is 'quite possible', that is *u(emp)* is 'somewhat certain' to hold in t. We introduce the certainty scale derived from a given possibility scale.

Let $(T, \mathcal{S}_p)$ denote a p-SQL table schema where the bottom p-degree of $\mathcal{S}_p$ is $k+1$. The certainty scale $\mathcal{S}_p^T$ for $(T, \mathcal{S}_p)$ is the strict finite linear order $\beta_1 >_p \cdots >_p \beta_k >_p \beta_{k+1}$. The top c-degree β_1 is for constraints that are 'fully certain', while the bottom c-degree β_{k+1} is for constraints that are 'not certain at all'. Indeed, p- and c-degrees exhibit an inherent duality: a constraint is more certain to hold when it applies to less possible data.

Table 4. SQL Queries Q_1, Q_2, and Q'_2

SELECT DISTINCT *emp*	SELECT DISTINCT *emp*	SELECT *emp*
FROM WORK	FROM WORK	FROM WORK
WHERE *p-degree*=‘α_2’;	WHERE *p-degree*=‘α_1’;	WHERE *p-degree*=‘α_1’;

We define by which c-degree an SQL constraint holds on a p-SQL table. Similar to marginal probabilities in probability theory, we call this c-degree the *marginal certainty*. In SQL tables an SQL constraint either holds or does not hold. In a p-SQL table, an SQL constraint always holds with some c-degree.

Definition 1. (Marginal Certainty). *Let σ denote an SQL key, FD or* NOT NULL *constraint over table schema T. The* marginal certainty $c_t(\sigma)$ *by which σ holds in the p-SQL table t over $(T, \mathcal{S}_p)$ is the c-degree β_{k+2-i} that corresponds to the p-degree α_i of the smallest possible world t_i of t in which σ is violated, that is, $c_t(\sigma) = \beta_1$ if $\models_{t_k} \sigma$, and $c_t(\sigma) = \min\{\beta_{k+2-i} | \not\models_{t_i} \sigma\}$ otherwise.*

For example, when t denotes the p-SQL table of Table 1, then $c_t(dpt \rightarrow mng) = \beta_1$, $c_t(emp \rightarrow dpt) = \beta_2$, $c_t(u(emp)) = \beta_3$, and $c_t(n(emp)) = \beta_4$.

Constraints specify the semantics of an application domain. They govern which databases are regarded as meaningful for the application. We classify a p-SQL table as meaningful whenever it satisfies a given set of possibilistic constraints (σ, β) (key, FD, NOT NULL constraint), which allow us to stipulate the minimum marginal c-degree β by which the constraint σ must hold in every p-SQL table that is considered to be meaningful in the application domain.

Definition 2. (Possibilistic Constraints). *Let $(T, \mathcal{S}_P)$ denote a p-SQL table schema. A* possibilistic SQL key, possibilistic SQL FD, *or* possibilistic NOT NULL constraint *is a pair (σ, β) where σ denotes an SQL key, FD or* NOT NULL *constraint over T, respectively, and β denotes a c-degree from $\mathcal{S}_P^T$. The p-constraint (σ, β_i) is* satisfied *by a p-SQL table t over $(T, \mathcal{S}_P)$ iff $c_t(\sigma) \geq \beta_i$.*

For example, when t denotes the p-SQL table of Table 1, then the following examples of p-constraints are satisfied by t: $(dpt \rightarrow mng, \beta_3)$ since $c_t(dpt \rightarrow mng) = \beta_1 \geq \beta_3$, $(emp \rightarrow dpt, \beta_2)$ since $c_t(emp \rightarrow dpt) = \beta_2 \geq \beta_2$, and $(u(emp), \beta_4)$ since $c_t(u(emp)) = \beta_3 \geq \beta_4$. However, t violates the following p-constraints: $(emp \rightarrow dpt, \beta_1)$ since $c_t(emp \rightarrow dpt) = \beta_2 < \beta_1$, $(u(emp), \beta_2)$ as $c_t(u(emp)) = \beta_3 < \beta_2$, and $(n(emp), \beta_3)$ as $c_t(n(emp)) = \beta_4 < \beta_3$.

6 Motivating the Core Reasoning Problem

We illustrate the centrality of the implication problem on the two most common database tasks: updates and queries, and its application to normalization.

6.1 Efficient Updates

Suppose a design team has specified the set Σ_1 of the following p-constraints on our p-table schema ($\text{WORK}, \alpha_1 > \alpha_2 > \alpha_3 > \alpha_4$): $(emp \rightarrow dpt, \beta_2)$, $(dpt \rightarrow mng, \beta_1)$, $(u(emp), \beta_3)$, $(n(dpt,mng), \beta_1)$, and $(u(mng), \beta_2)$. Since p-tables are typically large, we must not delay insertions into the table. Since the DBMS must validate that the updated table does not violate any p-constraint in Σ_1, we ensure that none of these checks is redundant. For example, validating that $(u(emp), \beta_3)$ is redundant if we already know that the updated table satisfies all the other constraints in Σ_1. Here, redundancy means that $\sigma = (u(emp), \beta_3)$ is implied by $\Sigma_1 - \{\sigma\}$: every p-table that satisfies $\Sigma_1 - \{\sigma\}$ also satisfies σ. Hence, if we can decide at design time whether a set of p-constraints implies another p-constraint, then we can avoid any redundant validation checks at run time of the database. This saves more time the more rows our table contains.

6.2 Query Optimization

Consider the same p-table schema ($\text{WORK}, \alpha_1 > \alpha_2 > \alpha_3 > \alpha_4$) and our set Σ of p-constraints: $(emp \rightarrow dpt, \beta_2)$, $(dpt \rightarrow mng, \beta_1)$, $(u(emp), \beta_3)$. The SQL query Q_1 on the left of Table 4 selects all distinct employees from rows with p-degree α_2. When evaluated on the p-table t in Table 1, the answers 'John' and 'Andy' are returned. Removing the keyword `DISTINCT` from Q_1 results in: 'John', 'Andy', and 'Andy', in which duplicate answers are not removed. Duplicate removal must be explicitly specified by users of SQL as the default is not to remove duplicates. The reason is that duplicates are important for aggregation queries, and duplicate removal is an expensive operation. The SQL query Q_2 in the middle of Table 4 selects all distinct employees from rows with p-degree α_1. Here, the clause `DISTINCT` is redundant. That is, the query Q_2' on the right of Table 4 returns the same answers as Q_2 over every legal table. Here, legal means that the table satisfies the given constraints in Σ. However, Q_2' is more efficient to run than Q_2. The latter will (unsuccessfully) look for duplicates. The reason is the p-key $(u(emp), \beta_3)$, which says that there are no two different rows with p-degree α_1 that have matching non-null values on *emp*. Hence, a query optimizer that can infer the maximum c-degree by which a given p-constraint is implied by a given set of p-constraints is able to optimize SQL queries. In our example, the maximum c-degree by which $u(emp)$ is implied by Σ is β_3, meaning that Q_2 can be rewritten into the equivalent query Q_2' but removal of `DISTINCT` from Q_1 will result in a non-equivalent query. Again, this highlights the centrality of the implication problem.

6.3 The Implication Problem

The (finite) implication problem for a class $\mathcal{C}$ of constraints is to decide for any given finite set $\Sigma \cup \{\varphi\}$ in $\mathcal{C}$ whether Σ (finitely) implies φ, that is, whether every (finite) instance that satisfies all constraints in Σ also satisfies φ. For us Σ will always be defined over a single p-SQL table schema, and as the p-scale is finite,

Table 5. Implication Problem

PROBLEM:	IMPLICATION
INPUT:	P-SQL table schema $(T, \alpha_1 > \cdots > \alpha_{k+1})$
	Set $\Sigma \cup \{\varphi\}$ of p-SQL keys, FDs and NOT NULL constraints
OUTPUT:	Yes, if $\Sigma \models \varphi$
	No, otherwise

so is Σ. We are interested in the class $\mathcal{C}$ of p-SQL keys, FDs, and NOT NULL constraints. For this class, the finite implication problem and the implication problem coincide. In particular, if there is an infinite p-SQL table that satisfies all elements of Σ but violates φ, then - by the semantics of our constraints - there must be two rows in that table that violate φ. However, those two rows satisfy all elements of Σ, so there is also a finite p-SQL table showing that Σ does not finitely imply φ. In the remainder we will therefore speak of *the* implication problem. We write $\Sigma \models \varphi$, if Σ implies φ. The problem is defined in Table 5.

Consider the p-SQL table schema $(\text{WORK}, \alpha_1 > \alpha_2 > \alpha_3 > \alpha_4)$ with the following set Σ: $(dpt \rightarrow mng, \beta_1)$, $(emp \rightarrow dpt, \beta_2)$, and $(u(emp), \beta_3)$. Then Σ does not imply $(emp \rightarrow mng, \beta_2)$, as Table 1 shows. If Θ results from Σ by adding the NOT NULL constraint $(n(dpt), \beta_3)$, then Θ still does not imply $(emp \rightarrow mng, \beta_2)$, as rows 8 and 9 of Table 1 show. However, if Ω results from Σ by adding the NOT NULL constraint $(n(dpt), \beta_2)$, then Ω does imply $(emp \rightarrow mng, \beta_2)$.

6.4 Database Normalization

Classical normalization for relational databases transforms database schemata such that non-trival functional dependencies become keys [7]. The reason is that non-trivial FDs cause data redundancy, while keys prevent them. While data redundancy may benefit query evaluation they cause integrity flaws when redundant values are not updated consistently. The ultimate goal in database normalization with the class of functional dependencies is a dependency-preserving decomposition into Boyce-Codd Normal Form, where the left-hand side of every FD forms a key [7,17,38]. Dependency-preservation cannot always be guaranteed, which is why we sometimes have to settle for a dependency-preserving decomposition into Third Normal Form, which minimizes the sources of data redundancy but cannot guarantee their absence [29]. Recent efforts have shown how to achieve decompositions into Boyce-Codd or Third Normal Form that minimize integrity maintenance [51–53]. Several lines of work have generalized classical normalization theory to some dimensions of big data. There are theories that accommodate missing data in the form of null marker occurrences [28,30,48], duplicate [26] and possibilistic information [34]. Without solutions to the underlying implication problem it is impossible to characterize the absence of data redundancy and update inefficiency by syntactic definitions of normal forms. As a consequence, the results in our work are necessary for any normalization theory

Table 6. Axiomatization $\mathfrak{pS}$ of p-SQL keys, FDs, and NOT NULL constraints

$$\frac{}{(XY \to X, \beta_i)} \text{ (FD reflexivity)} \qquad \frac{(X \to YZ, \beta_i)}{(X \to Y, \beta_i)} \text{ (FD decomposition)} \qquad \frac{(X \to Y, \beta_i)\ (Y \to Z, \beta_i)}{(X \to Z, \beta_i)} Y \subseteq XT_s^i \text{ (null FD transitivity)}$$

$$\frac{(X \to Y, \beta_i)\ (X \to Z, \beta_i)}{(X \to YZ, \beta_i)} \text{ (FD union)} \qquad \frac{(uX, \beta_i)}{(X \to Y, \beta_i)} \text{ (key weakening)} \qquad \frac{(X \to Y, \beta_i)\ (uY, \beta_i)}{(uX, \beta_i)} Y \subseteq XT_s^i \text{ (null pullback)}$$

$$\frac{(\sigma, \beta_i)}{(\sigma, \beta_{i+1})} \text{ (submodel)} \qquad \frac{}{(\sigma, \beta_{k+1})} \text{ (triviality)}$$

in the context of missing, duplicate, and possibilistic information. Our results illustrate what impact these dimensions will have on normalization.

As a simple illustration on our running example consider again the p-SQL table schema (WORK, $\alpha_1 > \alpha_2 > \alpha_3 > \alpha_4$) with the set Σ.Classically, we may decompose into $\{dpt, mng\}$ and $\{emp, dpt\}$ but this may not necessarily transform the FDs into keys, depending on how projections and join are defined in the context of duplicate and missing information [28]. Likewise, the presence of NOT NULL constraints has an impact on dependency-preservation. For example, when $(n(dpt), \beta_2)$ is present, then the FD $(emp \to mng, \beta_2)$ will be implied, which is not preserved by the decomposition.

7 Axiomatic Characterization

We will now present an axiomatic, algorithmic, and logical characterization for the implication problem of our p-constraint class, illustrate them by examples, and highlight important consequences. For their detailed proofs we need to establish additional results about the non-possibilistic class.

The set $\Sigma^* = \{\varphi \mid \Sigma \models \varphi\}$ denotes the *semantic closure of* Σ, that is, the set of all (p-)constraints that are implied by Σ. In principle, the definition of the semantic closure does not tell us whether we can compute it, nevermind how. It is a core reasoning task to investigate whether/how a semantic notion can be characterized syntactically. In fact, we determine the semantic closure Σ^* of a set Σ of (p-)constraints by applying *inference rules* or *axioms* of the form $\frac{\text{premise}}{\text{conclusion}}$ condition. For a set $\mathfrak{R}$ of inference rules let $\Sigma \vdash_{\mathfrak{R}} \varphi$ denote the *inference* of φ from Σ by $\mathfrak{R}$. That is, there is some sequence $\sigma_1, \ldots, \sigma_n$ such that $\sigma_n = \varphi$ and every σ_i is an element of Σ or is the conclusion that results from an application of an inference rule in $\mathfrak{R}$ to some premises in $\{\sigma_1, \ldots, \sigma_{i-1}\}$. Let $\Sigma^+_{\mathfrak{R}} = \{\varphi \mid \Sigma \vdash_{\mathfrak{R}} \varphi\}$ be the *syntactic closure* of Σ under inferences by $\mathfrak{R}$. $\mathfrak{R}$ is *sound* (*complete*) if for every (p-)SQL table schema, and for every set Σ of (p-)SQL constraints over this schema we have $\Sigma^+_{\mathfrak{R}} \subseteq \Sigma^*$ ($\Sigma^* \subseteq \Sigma^+_{\mathfrak{R}}$). The (finite) set $\mathfrak{R}$ is a (finite) *axiomatization* if $\mathfrak{R}$ is both sound and complete.

Table 7. Axiomatization $\mathfrak{B}$ of keys and FDs over bag schemata

$\dfrac{}{XY \rightarrow X}$	$\dfrac{X \rightarrow Y}{X \rightarrow XY}$	$\dfrac{X \rightarrow Y \quad Y \rightarrow Z}{X \rightarrow Z}$	$\dfrac{uX}{X \rightarrow Y}$	$\dfrac{X \rightarrow Y \quad uY}{uX}$
(FD reflexivity)	(FD extension)	(FD transitivity)	(key weakening)	(pullback)

Our first main result is that the set $\mathfrak{pS}$ of inference rules from Table 6 forms a finite axiomatization for the implication problem of our combined class of p-SQL keys, FDs, and NOT NULL constraints. For the set of inference rules we assume that X, Y, Z denote attribute subsets of T from the given p-SQL table schema $(T, \alpha_1 > \cdots > \alpha_{k+1})$, and for $i = 1, \ldots, k$, T_s^i denotes the attribute subset of T whose elements belong to some (nX, β_j) where $j \leq i$, that is, the attributes declared NOT NULL with c-degree β_i or higher: $T_s^i = \{A \in T \mid \exists(nX, \beta_j) \in \Sigma \wedge A \in X \wedge j \leq i\}$. Then $\Sigma \models (nX, \beta_i)$ if and only if $X \subseteq T_s^i$. Finally, σ may denote any SQL key or FD over T.

Theorem 1. *The set $\mathfrak{pS}$ forms a finite axiomatization for the implication problem of the combined class of p-SQL keys, FDs, and NOT NULL constraints.*

The main ideas for the proof of Theorem 1 are as follows. Firstly, we establish the first axiomatization $\mathfrak{S}$ for SQL keys, FDs, and NOT NULL constraints in the non-possibilistic case. The rules in $\mathfrak{S}$ results from those in $\mathfrak{pS}$ by removing *submodel* and *triviality*, removing the p-degrees β_i from all remaining rules in $\mathfrak{S}$, and replacing T_s^i by T_s in the conditions of *null FD transitivity* and *null pullback*. The completeness proof for $\mathfrak{S}$ uses the completeness of the existing axiomatization $\mathfrak{B}$ from Table 7 for the class of keys and FDs over bag schemata (table schemata where all columns are NOT NULL) [26]. Indeed, we can show that every SQL key $\varphi = uX$ and every SQL FD $\varphi = X \rightarrow Y$ that is implied by a set Σ of SQL keys and FDs over the table schema T with NFS T_s, φ is also implied by the *XT_s-guarded FD set* $\Sigma[XT_s] = \{V \rightarrow W \in \Sigma \mid V \subseteq XT_s\} \cup \{uV \in \Sigma \mid V \subseteq XT_s\}$ over the bag schema T. The completeness of $\mathfrak{B}$ entails that $\Sigma[XT_s] \vdash_{\mathfrak{B}} \varphi$ holds, and we can show that this implies $\Sigma \vdash_{\mathfrak{S}} \varphi$, establishing completeness of $\mathfrak{S}$.

Secondly, we can establish the completeness of $\mathfrak{pS}$ by the completeness of $\mathfrak{S}$ using the *β_i-cut* $\Sigma_i = \{\sigma \mid \exists(\sigma, \beta) \in \Sigma \wedge \beta \geq \beta_i\}$ for a p-constraint set Σ. Indeed, given a set $\Sigma \cup \{(\varphi, \beta_i)\}$ of p-SQL keys, functional dependencies, and NOT NULL constraints over a p-SQL table schema $(T, \alpha_1 > \cdots > \alpha_{k+1})$ where $1 \leq i \leq k$, we can show that $\Sigma \models (\varphi, \beta_i)$ if and only if $\Sigma_i \models \varphi$. Consequently, given a p-SQL key or p-SQL FD $\varphi = (\sigma, \beta_i)$ that is implied by a set Σ of p-SQL keys, p-SQL FDs, and p-SQL NOT NULL constraints over p-SQL schema T, it follows that the SQL key $\sigma = uX$ or SQL FD $\sigma = X \rightarrow Y$ is implied by the SQL key/FD set Σ_i over SQL table schema T with NFS T_s^i. By the completeness of $\mathfrak{S}$ we obtain $\Sigma_i \vdash_{\mathfrak{S}} \sigma$, and we can then show that also $\Sigma \vdash_{\mathfrak{pS}} (\sigma, \beta_i) = \varphi$. This shows the completeness of $\mathfrak{pS}$.

Consider the p-table schema $(\text{WORK}, \alpha_1 > \alpha_2 > \alpha_3 > \alpha_4)$ with the following set Σ of p-constraints: $(dpt \rightarrow mng, \beta_1)$, $(emp \rightarrow dpt, \beta_2)$, and

$(u(emp), \beta_3)$. Table 1, in particular rows 8 and 9, shows that Σ does not imply $\varphi = (emp \to mng, \beta_2)$. However, if Ω results from Σ by adding the NOT NULL constraint $(n(dpt), \beta_2)$, then Ω does imply $(emp \to mng, \beta_2)$. Using Theorem 1 this is equivalent to showing that $(emp \to mng, \beta_2)$ can be inferred from Ω using $\mathfrak{pS}$. Indeed, we can apply the *submodel* rule to $(dpt \to mng, \beta_1)$ to infer $(dpt \to mng, \beta_2)$. Subsequently, we can apply the *null FD transitivity* rule to $(emp \to dpt, \beta_2)$, $(dpt \to mng, \beta_2)$, and $T_s^2 = \{dpt\}$ to infer $(emp \to mng, \beta_2)$.

8 Algorithmic Characterization

We reduce the possibilistic implication problem to the standard computation of an attribute set closure in the relational model of data. This constitutes a clean solution that makes effective use of already existing research, and, as an outcome, results in an efficient computation in linear time.

As usual, for an attribute subset $X \subseteq T$ and an FD set Σ, let $X_\Sigma^+ = \{A \in T \mid \Sigma \models X \to A\}$ be the attribute set closure of X under Σ [13]. The reduction is achieved by the *FD reduct* $\Sigma[\text{FD}] = \{V \to W \mid V \to W \in \Sigma\} \cup \{V \to T \mid uV \in \Sigma\}$ for a set Σ of keys and FDs over bag schema T. Given these definitions we can now state the following result.

Theorem 2. *Let Σ denote a set of p-SQL keys, FDs, and NOT NULL constraints over p-SQL table schema $(T, \alpha_1 > \cdots > \alpha_{k+1})$. For all $(X \to Y, \beta_i)$, (uX, β_i) and (nX, β_i) over $(T, \alpha_1 > \cdots > \alpha_{k+1})$ the following hold:*

1. *$\Sigma \models (X \to Y, \beta_i)$ if and only if $Y \subseteq X^+_{\Sigma_i[XT_s^i][FD]}$.*
2. *$\Sigma \models (uX, \beta_i)$ if and only if $X^+_{\Sigma_i[XT_s^i][FD]} = T$ and there is some $uZ \in \Sigma_i[XT_s^i]$.*
3. *$\Sigma \models (nX, \beta_i)$ if and only if $X \subseteq T_s^i$.*

Consider the p-SQL table schema $(\text{WORK}, \alpha_1 > \alpha_2 > \alpha_3 > \alpha_4)$ with the previous set Ω of p-constraints. While Ω does imply $(emp \to mng, \beta_2)$, Ω does not imply $(u(emp), \beta_2)$. Indeed, $\Omega_2[emp, dpt] = \{emp \to dpt, dpt \to mng\}$. Hence, $emp^+_{\Omega_2[emp,dpt]} = \text{WORK}$, but there is no $uY \in \Omega_2[emp, dpt]$. Indeed, rows 6 and 7 from Table 1 form a two-row table that satisfies Ω but not $(u(emp), \beta_2)$.

According to Theorem 2 deciding instances of the possibilistic implication problem are effectively reduced to the standard computation of the attribute set closure $X^+_{\Sigma_i[XT_s^i][FD]}$ under the set $\Sigma_i[XT_s^i][FD]$ of FDs. Algorithms that work in linear input time for this computation are well-known [13]. As a summary of our reductions, we present here Algorithm 1 that computes $X^+_{\Sigma_i[XT_s^i][FD]}$ as the attribute set closure $\text{CLOSURE}(T, \Sigma, i, X)$ of X with respect to the set Σ of p-SQL keys, FDs and NOT NULL constraints.

Algorithm 1 shows that each attribute that occurs in the input is visited at most once. We therefore obtain the following linear-time complexity, which follows from results in [13]. Here, we define the size $||\Sigma||$ of a set Σ of p-constraints as the total number of attribute occurrences in Σ.

Algorithm 1. $\text{CLOSURE}(T, \Sigma, i, X)$ - Attribute Set Closure

Require: p-SQL table schema T, set Σ of p-SQL keys, FDs, and NOT NULLs over T, c-degree β_i, set $X \subseteq T$

Ensure: Attribute set closure $X^+_{\Sigma_i[XT^i_s][FD]}$ of X with respect to set $\Sigma_i[XT^i_s][FD]$ of FDs over T

$Closure \leftarrow X$;
$FDList \leftarrow$ List of FDs in $\Sigma_i[XT^i_s][FD]$;
repeat
  $OldClosure \leftarrow Closure$;
  Cut attributes in Closure from LHS of FDs in FDlist;
  for all $\{\emptyset \rightarrow Y\} \in FDList$ **do**
    $Closure \leftarrow Closure \cup Y$;
    $FDList \leftarrow FDList - \{\emptyset \rightarrow Y\}$;
until $Closure = OldClosure$ **or** $FDList = \emptyset$ **or** $Closure = T$
return $Closure$

Theorem 3. *The instance (Σ, φ) of the implication problem for the class of p-SQL keys, FDs, and NOT NULL constraints over p-SQL table schema $(T, \alpha_1 > \cdots > \alpha_{k+1})$ can be decided in time in $\mathcal{O}(\max\{|T|, ||\Sigma \cup \{\varphi\}||\})$.* □

9 Logical Characterization via HornSAT

In this section we use our results to realize that we can reason very efficiently about p-keys and p-FDs over p-SQL tables and with very familiar tools. Hence, our formalizations of keys and FDs as well as those of the variety and veracity dimensions of big data have led us to a framework where we can express integrity constraint for entities in big data sets, and can reason about these entities confidently and efficiently.

Indeed, we have successfully reduced instances $\Sigma \models (\sigma, \beta_i)$ for keys $\sigma = uX$ or FDs $\sigma = X \rightarrow Y$ of the implication problem for our class of p-constraints to instances $\Sigma_i[XT^i_s] \models \sigma$ for the implication problem of keys and FDs over bag schemata. For the latter, keys behave like propositional goal clauses and FDs behave like propositional definite clauses [14,26].

More formally, we map a key $\sigma = u(A_1, \ldots, A_n)$ over T to the goal clause $\sigma' = \neg A'_1 \vee \cdots \neg A'_n$ over the set $T' = \{A' \mid A \in T\}$ of propositional variables that correspond to attributes in T, and we map an FD $\sigma = A_1, \ldots, A_n \rightarrow A$ to a definite clause $\sigma' = \neg A'_1 \vee \cdots \neg A'_n \vee A'$ over the set T'. If $\models_2$ denotes classical propositional entailment, then it is known that $\Sigma \models \varphi$ if and only if $\Sigma' = \{\sigma' \mid \sigma \in \Sigma\} \models_2 \varphi'$.

We therefore obtain the following logical characterization of the implication problem for our class of entity integrity constraints on possibilistic SQL tables. The main insight is that reasoning about entity integrity for semi-structured big data can be done efficiently by using linear resolution, based on our framework.

Theorem 4. *The implication problem of p-SQL keys, FDs, and NOT NULL constraints is* PTIME*-complete and equivalent to* HORNSAT. □

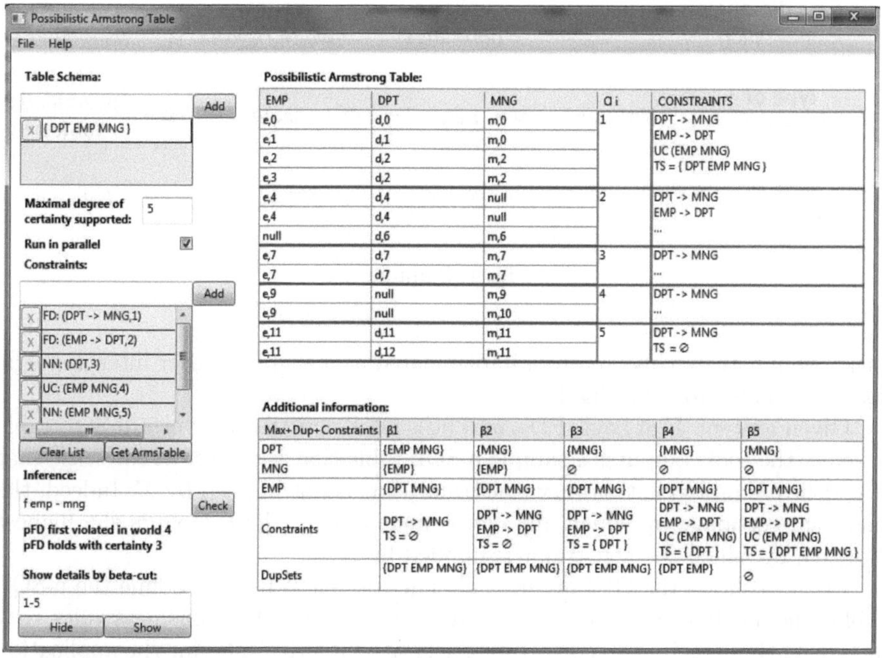

Fig. 3. GUI for Computational Tool that Creates Perfect Data Samples

Concluding our illustrations on our running example, reconsider the instances $\Omega \models (emp \to mng, \beta_2)$ and $\Omega \models (u(emp), \beta_2)$ of the implication problem over p-SQL table schema WORK. Recall that $\Omega_2[emp, dpt] = \{emp \to dpt, dpt \to mng\}$. Consequently, $(\Omega_2[emp, dpt])' = \{\neg emp' \vee dpt', \neg dpt' \vee mng'\}$. Applying linear resolution, for example, it is easy to see that the Horn formulae set $(\Omega_2[emp, dpt])' \cup \{emp', \neg mng'\}$ is unsatisfiable, while the Horn formulae set $(\Omega_2[emp, dpt])' \cup \{emp'\}$ is satisfiable by interpreting all atoms as `true`. Indeed, the latter model corresponds to the two-row table with row 6 and 7 from Table 1, which shows that Ω does not imply $(u(emp), \beta_2)$. This illustrates the fact that our correspondence does not just hold between the implication problems of constraints and Horn clauses, but extends to counter-example two-row tables and truth assignments.

10 Acquisition Tool

Constraints that encode application semantics are known as *business rules*, or entity integrity rules in our context. These are different from constraints that may hold accidentally on some instances, but do not encode application semantics. Data stewards must identify the entity integrity rules for the underlying application domain. Our techniques can offer computational support for this

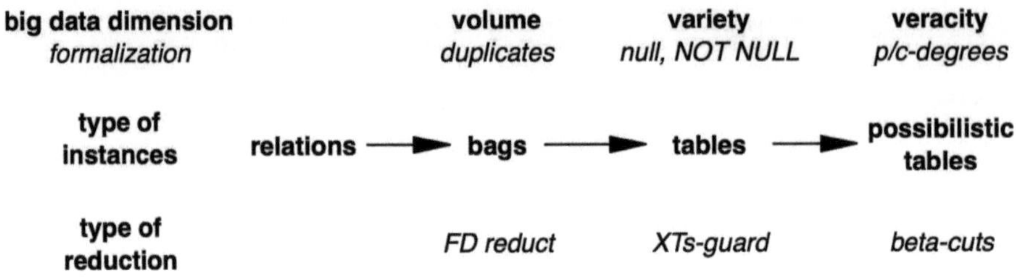

Fig. 4. Summary

task. We illustrate this on a tool implemented as a graphical user interface. The tool is available for download[1].

Given any set Σ of keys, FDs, and `NOT NULL` constraints over a p-SQL table schema, the tool computes a sample p-SQL table that is perfect in the sense that it satisfies Σ and violates every constraint that is not implied by Σ. Indeed, the marginal certainty by which any constraint holds in the sample is the highest c-degree by which the constraint is implied by Σ.

Figure 3 shows the GUI of our tool. The top left is used to define the p-SQL table schema. Below is the interface to define the set Σ of business rules that are currently perceived to constitute the entity integrity rules for the application domain. The tool then creates the perfect sample for Σ on the top right. On the left, users can enter some constraint, such as $emp \rightarrow mng$, and check its marginal certainty in the sample. In the example it is β_3 since the FD is only violated by the two tuples with p-degree α_4. If the constraint should hold with a higher c-degree, then it needs to be added to Σ. Alternatively, some other constraint needs changing. For instance, if Σ' results from changing $(n(dpt), \beta_3)$ to $(n(dpt), \beta_2)$, then Σ' implies $(emp \rightarrow mng, \beta_2)$. The example illustrates how our tool assists data stewards in identifying entity integrity rules of an application domain.

11 Conclusion and Future Work

We have established a comprehensive toolbox for automated reasoning about the integrity of real-world entities in semi-structured big data, including axiomatic, algorithmic and logical characterizations. As an underlying data model we chose a possibilistic extension of SQL. With adequate definitions, automated reasoning can be done by applying off-the-shelf tools, such as linear resolution for propositional HornSAT. Our tool for computing perfect samples helps data stewards identify entity integrity rules for their application domain.

Our approach suggests various future work. Here, different approaches should be applied to the big data dimensions, see Fig. 4, such as probabilistic approaches to the veracity dimension [9], different approaches of handling missing information to the variety dimension such as different null marker interpretations [19,46], embedded keys and FDs [48], genuine FDs [5], and different approaches to entity

[1] https://www.dropbox.com/sh/apdu872jurr1ega/AADIUar7Zr-gwG12ur4ihnVga?dl=0.

integrity such as key sets [22,43] or soft keys [25]. Likewise, we may extend the approach to more expressive classes of constraints such as cardinality constraints [18,21,33,39,45,49], multivalued dependencies [8,16,32,47], or inclusion dependencies to capture referential integrity [10,27]. Finally, we can add further big data dimensions. For example, temporal extensions [24] support the velocity dimension.

References

1. Amalina, F., et al.: Blending big data analytics: review on challenges and a recent study. IEEE Access **8**, 3629–3645 (2020)
2. Angles, R., et al.: PG-schema: schemas for property graphs. Proc. ACM Manag. Data **1**(2), 198:1–198:25 (2023)
3. Angles, R., et al.: PG-keys: keys for property graphs. In: Li, G., Li, Z., Idreos, S., Srivastava, D. (eds.) SIGMOD '21: International Conference on Management of Data, Virtual Event, China, June 20-25, 2021, pp. 2423–2436. ACM (2021). https://doi.org/10.1145/3448016
4. Armstrong, W.W.: Dependency structures of data base relationships. In: Rosenfeld, J.L. (ed.) Information Processing, Proceedings of the 6th IFIP Congress 1974, Stockholm, Sweden, August 5-10, 1974, pp. 580–583. North-Holland (1974)
5. Berti-Équille, L., Harmouch, H., Naumann, F., Novelli, N., Thirumuruganathan, S.: Discovery of genuine functional dependencies from relational data with missing values. Proc. VLDB Endow. **11**(8), 880–892 (2018)
6. Bertossi, L.E.: Database Repairing and Consistent Query Answering. Morgan & Claypool Publishers, Synthesis Lectures on Data Management (2011)
7. Biskup, J.: Achievements of relational database schema design theory revisited. In: Libkin, L., Thalheim, B. (eds.) Semantics in Databases, Selected Papers from a Workshop, Prague, Czech Republic, 1995. Lecture Notes in Computer Science, vol. 1358, pp. 29–54. Springer (1995). https://doi.org/10.1007/BFB0035004
8. Biskup, J., Link, S.: Appropriate inferences of data dependencies in relational databases. Ann. Math. Artif. Intell. **63**(3–4), 213–255 (2011)
9. Brown, P., Link, S.: Probabilistic keys. IEEE Trans. Knowl. Data Eng. **29**(3), 670–682 (2017)
10. Casanova, M.A., Fagin, R., Papadimitriou, C.H.: Inclusion dependencies and their interaction with functional dependencies. J. Comput. Syst. Sci. **28**(1), 29–59 (1984)
11. Christophides, V., Efthymiou, V., Stefanidis, K.: Entity Resolution in the Web of Data. Theory and Technology, Morgan & Claypool Publishers, Synthesis Lectures on the Semantic Web (2015)
12. Codd, E.F.: A relational model of data for large shared data banks. Commun. ACM **13**(6), 377–387 (1970)
13. Diederich, J., Milton, J.: New methods and fast algorithms for database normalization. ACM Trans. Database Syst. **13**(3), 339–365 (1988)
14. Dowling, W.F., Gallier, J.H.: Linear-time algorithms for testing the satisfiability of propositional horn formulae. J. Log. Program. **1**(3), 267–284 (1984)
15. Dubois, D., Prade, H., Schockaert, S.: Generalized possibilistic logic. Artif. Intell. **252**, 139–174 (2017)
16. Fagin, R.: Multivalued dependencies and a new normal form for relational databases. ACM Trans. Database Syst. **2**(3), 262–278 (1977)

17. Fagin, R.: A normal form for relational databases that is based on domains and keys. ACM Trans. Database Syst. **6**(3), 387–415 (1981)
18. Ferrarotti, F., Hartmann, S., Link, S.: Efficiency frontiers of XML cardinality constraints. Data Knowl. Eng. **87**, 297–319 (2013)
19. Franconi, E., Tessaris, S.: On the logic of SQL nulls. In: Freire, J., Suciu, D. (eds.) Proceedings of the 6th Alberto Mendelzon International Workshop on Foundations of Data Management, Ouro Preto, Brazil, June 27-30, 2012. CEUR Workshop Proceedings, vol. 866, pp. 114–128. CEUR-WS.org (2012)
20. Ganti, V., Sarma, A.D.: Data Cleaning: A Practical Perspective. Morgan & Claypool Publishers, Synthesis Lectures on Data Management (2013)
21. Hall, N., Köhler, H., Link, S., Prade, H., Zhou, X.: Cardinality constraints on qualitatively uncertain data. Data Knowl. Eng. **99**, 126–150 (2015)
22. Hannula, M., Li, X., Link, S.: Controlling entity integrity with key sets. J. Comput. Syst. Sci. **136**, 195–219 (2023)
23. Hartmann, S., Link, S.: The implication problem of data dependencies over SQL table definitions. ACM Trans. Database Syst. **37**(2), 13:1–13:40 (2012)
24. Jensen, C.S., Snodgrass, R.T., Soo, M.D.: Extending existing dependency theory to temporal databases. IEEE Trans. Knowl. Data Eng. **8**(4), 563–582 (1996)
25. Jha, A.K., Rastogi, V., Suciu, D.: Query evaluation with soft-key constraints. In: Proceedings of the Twenty-Seventh ACM SIGMOD-SIGACT-SIGART Symposium on Principles of Database Systems, PODS 2008, June 9-11, 2008, Vancouver, BC, Canada, pp. 119–128 (2008)
26. Koehler, H., Link, S.: Armstrong axioms and Boyce-Codd-Heath normal form under bag semantics. Inf. Process. Lett. **110**(16), 717–724 (2010)
27. Koehler, H., Link, S.: Inclusion dependencies and their interaction with functional dependencies in SQL. J. Comput. Syst. Sci. **85**, 104–131 (2017)
28. Koehler, H., Link, S.: SQL schema design: foundations, normal forms, and normalization. Inf. Syst. **76**, 88–113 (2018)
29. Kolahi, S.: Dependency-preserving normalization of relational and XML data. J. Comput. Syst. Sci. **73**(4), 636–647 (2007)
30. Levene, M., Loizou, G.: Database design for incomplete relations. ACM Trans. Database Syst. **24**(1), 80–125 (1999)
31. Lien, Y.E.: On the equivalence of database models. J. ACM **29**(2), 333–362 (1982)
32. Link, S.: Characterisations of multivalued dependency implication over undetermined universes. J. Comput. Syst. Sci. **78**(4), 1026–1044 (2012)
33. Link, S., Koehler, H., Gandhi, A., Hartmann, S., Thalheim, B.: Cardinality constraints and functional dependencies in SQL: taming data redundancy in logical database design. Inf. Syst. **115**, 102208 (2023)
34. Link, S., Prade, H.: Relational database schema design for uncertain data. Inf. Syst. **84**, 88–110 (2019)
35. Litvinenko, I.: On the semantics of uncertain data in possibilistic SQL tables: reasoning and armstrong samples. Master of Science thesis, University of Auckland (2015). https://hdl.handle.net/2292/27325
36. Liu, Z.H., Hammerschmidt, B.C., Mcmahon, D.: JSON data management: supporting schema-less development in RDBMS. In: Dyreson, C.E., Li, F., Özsu, M.T. (eds.) International Conference on Management of Data, SIGMOD 2014, Snowbird, UT, USA, June 22-27, 2014, pp. 1247–1258. ACM (2014). https://doi.org/10.1145/2588555.2595628
37. Naumann, F., Herschel, M.: An Introduction to Duplicate Detection. Morgan & Claypool Publishers, Synthesis Lectures on Data Management (2010)

38. Ndefo, N., Franconi, E.: A study on information-preserving schema transformations. Int. J. Semantic Comput. **14**(1), 27–53 (2020)
39. Roblot, T., Hannula, M., Link, S.: Probabilistic cardinality constraints - validation, reasoning, and semantic summaries. VLDB J. **27**(6), 771–795 (2018)
40. Skavantzos, P., Link, S.: Entity/relationship graphs: Principled design, modeling, and data integrity management of graph databases. Proc. ACM Manag. Data **3**(1), 40:1–40:26 (2025)
41. Skavantzos, P., Link, S.: Third and Boyce-CODD normal form for property graphs. VLDB J. **34**(2), 23 (2025)
42. Suciu, D., Olteanu, D., Ré, C., Koch, C.: Probabilistic Databases. Morgan & Claypool Publishers, Synthesis Lectures on Data Management (2011)
43. Thalheim, B.: On semantic issues connected with keys in relational databases permitting null values. Elektronische Informationsverarbeitung und Kybernetik **25**(1/2), 11–20 (1989)
44. Thalheim, B.: Dependencies in relational databases, Teubner-Texte zur Mathematik, vol. 126. Teubner (1991)
45. Thalheim, B.: Fundamentals of cardinality constraints. In: Pernul, G., Tjoa, A.M. (eds.) Entity-Relationship Approach - ER'92, 11th International Conference on the Entity-Relationship Approach, Karlsruhe, Germany, October 7-9, 1992, Proceedings. Lecture Notes in Computer Science, vol. 645, pp. 7–23. Springer (1992)
46. Thalheim, B., Schewe, K.: NULL 'value' algebras and logics. In: Heimbürger, A., Kiyoki, Y., Tokuda, T., Jaakkola, H., Yoshida, N. (eds.) Information Modelling and Knowledge Bases XXII, 20th European-Japanese Conference on Information Modelling and Knowledge Bases (EJC 2010), Jyväskylä, Finland, 31 May - 4 June 2010. Frontiers in Artificial Intelligence and Applications, vol. 225, pp. 354–367. IOS Press (2010). https://doi.org/10.3233/978-1-60750-690-4-354
47. Wei, Z., Link, S.: A Fourth normal form for uncertain data. In: Giorgini, P., Weber, B. (eds.) Advanced Information Systems Engineering - 31st International Conference, CAiSE 2019, Rome, Italy, June 3-7, 2019, Proceedings. Lecture Notes in Computer Science, vol. 11483, pp. 295–311. Springer (2019)
48. Wei, Z., Link, S.: Embedded functional dependencies and data-completeness tailored database design. ACM Trans. Database Syst. **46**(2), 7:1–7:46 (2021)
49. Wei, Z., Link, S.: The Bounded Cardinality Normal Form for the logical design of relational database schemata. ACM Trans. Database Syst. **50**(4) (Jul 2025). https://doi.org/10.1145/3744897
50. Zaniolo, C.: Database relations with null values. J. Comput. Syst. Sci. **28**(1), 142–166 (1984)
51. Zhang, Z., Chen, W., Link, S.: Composite object normal forms: parameterizing Boyce-Codd normal form by the number of minimal keys. Proc. ACM Manag. Data **1**(1), 13:1–13:25 (2023)
52. Zhang, Z., Link, S.: Mixed covers: optimizing updates and queries using minimal keys and functional dependencies. VLDB J. **34**(3), 29 (2025)
53. Zhang, Z., Link, S.: Synthesizing third normal form schemata that minimize integrity maintenance and update overheads: parameterizing 3nf by the numbers of minimal keys and functional dependencies. Proc. ACM Manag. Data **3**(3), 225:1–225:25 (2025)

Knowledge Graphs and Graph Databases

Shaping Your World – Conceptualizing Viewpoint Dynamics in Event-Centric Knowledge Graphs

Till Affeldt, Florian Plötzky(✉), and Wolf-Tilo Balke(✉)

Institute for Information Systems, TU Braunschweig, Braunschweig, Germany
{ploetzky,balke}@ifis.cs.tu-bs.de

Abstract. In recent years, major *events*, such as wars and political tensions, have occurred in rapid succession. Naturally, most events are complex and can be interpreted in different ways, which spawns the question of how to actually integrate different *viewpoints* in event-centric knowledge graphs (ECKGs). One way is to limit the validity of statements to respective viewpoints, which allows for the representation of conflicting information in ECKGs without causing ontological *inconsistencies*. To consistently fuse such statements in queries or reasoning processes, a *viewpoint model* deciding whether two given viewpoints are compatible has to exist. Prior work utilized *viewpoint hierarchies* to describe aggregations of stances between different groups; yet, in the real world, viewpoints of individuals and groups are usually formed by complex mutual influences that cannot be captured by simple hierarchical models. To cater for such influences, in this paper we propose *influence networks* as a novel viewpoint model based on *opinion dynamics* for ECKGs. In contrast to simple hierarchical aggregations, our model captures fine-grained social interactions between different agents enabling the inference of stances towards claims. To illustrate the effectiveness of our model in practical applications, we conduct extensive simulation studies to compare the model with established results in social physics and provide a case study to contrast our model to viewpoint hierarchies for ECKGs.

Keywords: Knowledge Graphs · Viewpoints · Opinion Dynamics

1 Introduction

Over the past decade, there has been growing interest in real-world *events* both in terms of data collection [13,14,30] and event representation [8,28]. In this regard, event-centric knowledge graphs (ECKGs) as a structured way to provide event data have gained traction [7,23]. Besides storing event information on a large scale, such ECKGs allow for reasoning about real-world events and therefore offer a means of understanding the world through events. However, especially for large-scale and complex events such as wars and political conflicts,

D. Bork et al. (Eds.): ER 2025, LNCS 16189, pp. 283–301, 2026.
https://doi.org/10.1007/978-3-032-08623-5_15

managing ontological *consistency*, i.e., ensuring the absence of conflicting statements in an ECKG, can become difficult if there are multiple perspectives on some event. For instance, there might be a dispute concerning the role or certain properties of some participant in a specific event or events may even be narrated in a completely different way depending on the perspective taken. This can especially be observed in conflicts like the ongoing wars in Ukraine and Gaza, or in diplomatic affairs such as tariff negotiations. To represent those potentially conflicting event information, we recently proposed the idea of *viewpoints* in ECKGs [20,21]. A viewpoint encapsulates the stance of a specific group towards a particular statement, i.e., viewpoints determine the validity of some statement for each group. Such viewpoints are linked to ECKGs by annotating all predicates allowing for subjective stances (called *attributions*) with respective viewpoints. Triples from some ECKG containing an attribution (called *claims*) are thus only valid in the context of that respective viewpoint. Attributions can be subject to further constraints to achieve consistency on the viewpoint level. Thus, while the ECKG as a whole is not consistent, reasoning about a single viewpoint is locally consistent. To safely fuse different viewpoints, they are subject to *viewpoint hierarchies* that describe how claims from different viewpoints can be consistently combined.

By using our previous model, ECKGs are enabled to represent potentially contradicting claims while still allowing for consistent reasoning from different perspectives. However, the practical applicability of this approach is severely limited by the assumption that all viewpoints are formed by consensus within a hierarchically organized group structure. This simplification does not cater for real-world mutual influences between groups that are typically formed by social dynamics (e.g., by social pressure [18]). Furthermore, the model assumes that explicit positive or negative stances towards a specific claim exist in order to perform aggregations in the viewpoint hierarchy. In reality, we might not have explicit stances from all viewpoints and thus, need a way to infer unknown stances for a given claim. This was already discussed as a limitation in [21].

In this paper, we enhance the viewpoint model portion from our prior work [20] to better match real-world opinion influences. We analyze the limitations of viewpoint hierarchies and introduce *influence networks*, inspired by the fields of social physics and opinion dynamics, as a more expressive alternative. Additionally, we operationalize our model in terms of opinion dynamics to infer attributions by network dynamics in contrast to the static aggregation of viewpoints in a hierarchy, without the need for explicit stances for all groups. We show that our model is more expressive than viewpoint hierarchies, while still maintaining its utility in ECKGs in two ways: (i) by conducting an extensive simulation study to compare our model's results with known results from opinion dynamics, and (ii), by comparing it to a viewpoint hierarchy in a case study concerning a recent event.

2 On Viewpoint Hierarchies and Opinion Dynamics

In this section, we briefly introduce viewpoint hierarchies, analyze their limitations, and discuss opinion dynamics as a remedy.

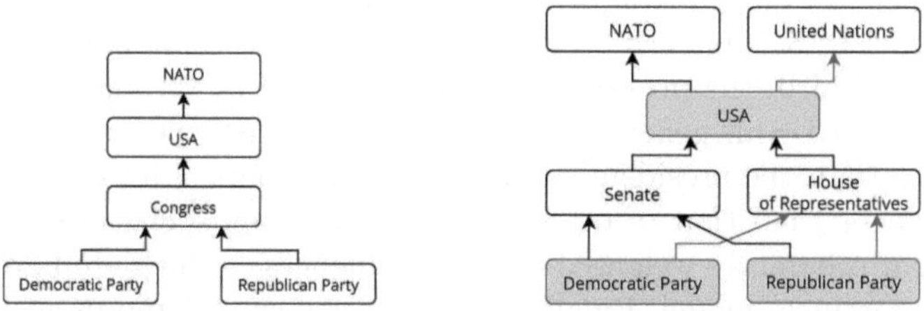

(a) Valid Hierarchy (b) Invalid Hierarchy

Fig. 1. A viewpoint hierarchy according to [20] and an invalid one.

Viewpoint Hierarchies. A viewpoint is a consensual stance towards a given statement of a particular group. A *group* is defined as a set of entities where each entity must be capable of expressing a stance towards a statement, i.e., state whether the statement is valid or invalid. Those stances can be determined by using stance detection [1] on a multitude of sources. The viewpoint is then formed by a consensus of all group members. On top of that, *viewpoint hierarchies* have been introduced to describe the aggregation of stances between different groups. A viewpoint hierarchy is a tree-shaped directed acyclic graph where the nodes are viewpoints and the edges describe (potentially weighted) aggregation relationships [21]. As an example, Fig. 1a depicts a viewpoint hierarchy for political entities. Here, any statement that is valid for the Democratic Party and the Republican Party is also valid in Congress, i.e., it is valid for a broader group. Thus, even if we do not have an explicit stance of Congress, we can infer its stance by aggregation. The "downward direction" for inference, however, is not trivial. In reality, a statement valid in Congress need not be valid for the Democratic Party. This is the case, for instance, if it is only valid in Congress because of a Republican majority. To tackle this problem, we introduced two hierarchy variants: winner takes all hierarchies (WTAH) and view-preserving hierarchies (VPH). In a VPH each minority preserves its stance towards a particular statement, while in WTAH, any statement valid in a node of the hierarchy is also valid in all of its subtrees. In our example, in the WTAH variant, a statement valid in Congress is also valid for both the Democratic and Republican party, whereas in VPH, the parties may preserve a different stance on the statement. With a hierarchy and variant in place, one can then determine the set of statements that is valid for a specific viewpoint.

Limitations of Viewpoint Hierarchies. Naturally, the model is not fit to represent non-hierarchical viewpoint dynamics. First, most members of both the Republican Party and Democratic Party are not members of Congress and should therefore not contribute to its opinion, but they may still contribute to the US viewpoint. Second, if one wants to model the Congress in its two chambers (Senate and House of Representatives) both parties would contribute to them (depicted in Fig. 1b). However, in this case, a paradox can arise if the same statement is valid in the Senate and invalid in the House of Representatives. In this case, it is unclear whether this statement is valid or invalid for one of the parties. Third, the president is in a position of power and can contribute to Congress, the US in general, and the political party he or she is affiliated with. Besides that, the president's influence on members of his or her own party may be stronger than that of other party members by social pressure, leading to mutual but differently weighted opinion influences – which are hard to represent in a hierarchical model. Finally, the hierarchy cannot represent viewpoints with multiple parent nodes, which weakens the constitution of a viewpoint. For instance, the Republican Party can be characterized from multiple perspectives, e.g., nationally, ideologically, and economically. Viewpoint hierarchies limit this spectrum to only one aspect (the affiliation with Congress). As a effect, the influence on the Republican Party by, e.g., political organizations such as the Heritage Foundation are neglected, which leads to a less realistic depiction of real-world influences.

Opinion Dynamics in Social Physics. We introduce a more realistic model on viewpoint interaction, while maintaining compatibility with our prior work, by transferring ideas from social physics (also known as *sociophysics*). In general, social physics applies methods from physics to model topics from the social sciences and is applied in different areas such as social networks, population dynamics analysis, and the analysis of epidemic spreading [6]. Opinion Dynamics is a subfield of social physics used to model how opinions of individuals are shaped in a social context, oftentimes by using statistical or network models [3]. Most recent research in this direction is typically conducted in the area of social media research on how opinion formation on social platforms can be modeled and inferred [15,18]. Such works are more realistic depictions of opinion formation by mutual influences than viewpoint hierarchies; thus this paper borrows ideas from the aforementioned literature and transfers them to viewpoint models for ECKGs. Specifically, we rely on the standard notion of *agent-based models*, i.e., we consider different agents, their opinions, and influences on their opinions on each other. While there are a myriad of potential social interaction models in the literature, we focus on two common types of interactions, namely polarizing and converging opinion dynamics. Hence, our model should be able to reproduce some basic results of opinion dynamics. On a conceptual level, we rely on our previous work in terms of the overarching model and specifically focus on the viewpoint portion.

3 A Viewpoint Inference Model

As mentioned before, in social physics, the dynamics of opinions are commonly implemented with agent-based models. In order to comply with the nomenclature of social physics, we refer to an entity that can express a stance towards a statement as *agent*. Furthermore, we call such statements *claims*. The objectives of our model are twofold: First, our model should describe interactions between different agents and groups more faithfully to real-world social interactions and influence (opinion dynamics) as outlined in the previously discussed limitations (specifically in terms of a clear semantics of agents and groups). Second, while a viewpoint hierarchy can be used to infer missing attributions either by aggregation towards the root, or via either WTAH or VPH towards the leaves, they heavily rely on the availability of explicit positive or negative stances (neutral stances or degrees of agreement or disagreement are excluded in [20]). Our model should be able to infer attributions even if we do not have clear-cut stances of all agents. This is performed by simulating the social pressure on agents with missing stances. We outline the prerequisites and opinion dynamic models in Sect. 3.1 and develop our inference and attribution derivation model in Sect. 3.2.

3.1 Influence Networks and Opinion Dynamics

Stances and Opinions. In order to model opinion dynamics, we need to determine the respective stances and opinions of agents we want to consider. For that, each agent's statements towards each relevant claim are assessed via stance detection over multiple sources, e.g., textual documents or multimedia content. Here, a stance is a numeric representation of an expressed position $p \in [-1, 1]$ towards a statement by an agent, where -1 means total rejection, 1 total affirmation, and 0 neutrality. All other values indicate tendencies towards one of the aforementioned extremes. In this paper, we rely on well-known techniques in the area of stance detection and focus on opinion dynamics based on those results, i.e., we do not contribute a new way of stance detection but assume that such results can be obtained (cf. [1] for a survey).

The resulting stances are aggregated and scaled by the source's reliability to create *opinion values*. Measuring and determining such reliability is out of scope for this paper; we assume a reliability function $rel : S \rightarrow [0, 1]$ for all sources $s \in S$. Each opinion value $o_i^c(t_0)$ represents the opinion of agent i towards statement c over all sources at a point in time $t_0 \in \mathbb{Z}$ and can be computed as

$$o_i^c(t_0) := \begin{cases} 0 & \text{if } \sum_{s \in S_i^c} rel(s) = 0, \\ \dfrac{\sum_{s \in S_i^c} stance(s) \cdot rel(s)}{\sum_{s \in S_i^c} rel(s)} & \text{otherwise.} \end{cases} \quad (1)$$

where $S_i^c \subseteq S$ denotes the set of sources that contain claim c and a stance of agent i, and $stance : S_i^c \rightarrow [-1, 1]$ returns the position that agent i took towards claim c according to the source. Therefore, $o_i^c(t_0)$ is an estimate for the opinion of agent i based on all sources in S_i^c. Naturally, such an estimation does not always reflect the true state of affairs, e.g., in cases of a neutral stance (i.e., a score of 0) it is not clear whether this means neutrality of the agent towards the claim or a lack of sources. We therefore also introduce a measure of confidence $conf_i^c(t_0) \in [0,1]$, i.e., the information quality regarding whether the opinion score $o_i^c(t_0)$ accurately reflects the opinion of the agent. A high confidence would then, for instance, resolve the question whether a neutral score actually expresses neutrality or just a lack of sources. Such a confidence measure can be defined in various ways, e.g., on linear scale with a reference point ref:

$$conf_i^c(t_0) := \min\left\{\frac{\sum_{s \in S_i^c} rel(s)}{ref}, 1\right\} \tag{2}$$

Other features like the consistency of stances can be taken into account for $conf$ but are out of scope for this paper. With the notion of stances and opinions in place, we can proceed with the objective of this paper, i.e., to provide a viewpoint model based on social interactions on the opinion values. For that, we introduce influence networks in the following.

Influence Networks. The desiderata of this model are to clearly distinguish agents and groups and to generalize group similarity. An agent in this model is a person, role, legal entity, or any other constellation that can express an opinion. We extend the definition of agents to also allow the modeling of larger *groups* and organizations that are able to express a collective opinion. Whether a group possesses that ability depends not only on the group but also on the context, e.g., whether the internal group dynamics are known or not. We therefore define groups and *group agents*. A group is an aggregated view of a set of agents represented by the average opinion value of all agents in the group, similar to [20]. A group agent is then a type of agent that is not a person or role but a constellation of multiple people that is used as a stand-in for a group and the agents within. With agents, groups, and group agents, we can model their respective influence on themselves and each other in varying granularity.

We utilize an influence network to define the frequency and intensity of interaction between these agents and groups. This approach enables a very flexible way of modeling social dynamics by applying interactions pair-wise and with asymmetric effects. The network can be expressed via a weighted, directed simple graph with loops $G := (N, E, W)$ that spans over agents N as nodes, edges E, and edge weights W where each $w \in W$ describes the influence of one agent on another. We assume that an edge only exists if its weight is not 0. By allowing agents to influence themselves, we are able to simulate the internal dynamics of homogeneous groups without using additional nodes. The modeled influence affects the properties of the social model. The distance between agents determines how quickly information can travel, the weight of influence an agent receives determines its susceptibility to opinion changes, and the quantity of connections impacts the general trend toward polarization or consensus. Figure 2 depicts an influence network on different levels of granularity. POTUS,

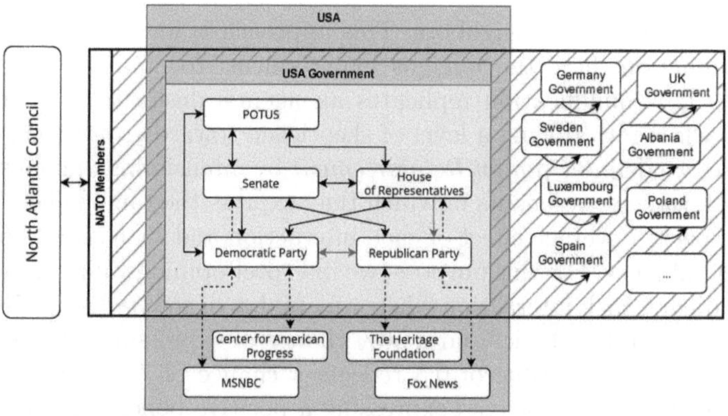

Fig. 2. An example influence network with different agents, groups, and group agents. Arrows depict influences, circles self influence, dashed arrows weak influence, solid arrows strong influence, and red arrows negative influence. (Color figure online)

Senate, House, the North Atlantic Council, and the two parties are agents in this model, whereas the USA government, USA, and all NATO members are groups comprised of the agents. Except for the USA all other governments are modeled as group agents since we might know that they exist but do not know or do not want to model their internal structure.

Operationalization in Opinion Dynamics. Having now defined the different agents and influences, we can now define opinion dynamics in influence networks to derive stances from agents and groups. We utilize the currently predominant social pressure to infer additional information about the status quo. Therefore, we refrain from using any type of social dynamic that introduces randomness or sudden shifts in group opinions and instead rely on small, gradual shifts. We use two opposing dynamics that drive the network towards either convergence or polarity, respectively, namely *Opinion Alignment* and *Opinion Reinforcement*. Opinion Alignment (based on [24]) promotes the formation of clusters and drives network convergence by simulating how people change or misrepresent their opinions under social pressure. Opinion Reinforcement uses positive reinforcement to strengthen an agent's beliefs when interacting with another agent who expresses the same opinion, ultimately creating a drift toward the extremes.

We define *Opinion Alignment* using the function depicted in Eq. 3 where $w_{j,i}$ represents the influence of agent n_j on agent n_i with $n_j, n_i \in N$; t represents the current prediction iteration; and $o_i^c(t) \in [-1, 1]$ represents the opinion of agent $n_i \in N$ on claim c at iteration step t.

$$A_i^c(t+1) := \sum_{j \mid n_j \in N_i} \left[w_{j,i} \cdot \tanh\left(o_j^c(t) - o_i^c(t)\right)\right] \tag{3}$$

The expected or average effect on the opinion of an agent n_i throughout all interactions during iteration t is modeled as a pull effect on $o_i^c(t+1)$ towards the weighted average of its in-neighbors. This approach is improved upon by using a sigmoid function, here the tangens hyperbolicus, to qualify each individual interaction. This qualification replicates an agent's desire to fit in with their peer-group while introducing a level of skepticism towards contrarian views.

Likewise, we define *Opinion Reinforcement* by intensifying opinions for every interaction between two agents in which they express the same belief. We determine the expected average effect of each interaction and then scale the result by the exerted influence. For this purpose, we interpret opinion values as a chance of expression during each interaction where an opinion of zero reflects a 50% chance of expressing a positive belief and a 50% chance of expressing a negative belief. Meanwhile, an opinion value of 0.5 reflects a chance of 75% and 25% respectively. The chance of two agents expressing a positive belief is given by xy and the chance of both agents expressing a negative belief is given by $(1-x)(1-y)$ where $x = [o_i^c(t)+1]/2$, $y = [o_j^c(t)+1]/2$. The average effect of reinforcement on an agent's opinion is then described by the difference in positive and negative reinforcement chance $xy - (1-x)(1-y) = x + y - 1$, scaled by the intensity of the interaction w.

$$\left[\frac{o_i^c(t)+1}{2} + \frac{o_j^c(t)+1}{2} - 1\right] w = \frac{o_i^c(t) + o_j^c(t)}{2} w \tag{4}$$

This approach leads to the following definition where we aggregate the effects of interacting with all agents and also disallow negative influence to cause reinforcement.

$$R_i^c(t+1) := \sum_{j \mid n_j \in N_i} \left[\max\{w_{j,i}, 0\} \cdot \frac{o_i^c(t) + o_j^c(t)}{2} \right] \tag{5}$$

By applying both social dynamics, we can model the change of opinion over time. In order to restrict values to the allowed range, we have to apply a limiter $L(x) := \max\{\min\{x, 1\}, -1\}$. We also introduce two scaling parameters α, ϱ that can be used to fine-tune the model.

$$o_i^c(t+1) := L(\; o_i^c(t) \quad + \quad \alpha A_i^c(t+1) \quad + \quad \varrho R_i^c(t+1)\;) \tag{6}$$

A high α means that the agent is more likely to align its opinion to the group's average (e.g., in areas with high group pressure), whereas a high ϱ means that the positive reinforcement leads to more extreme positions. This function can be utilized to iteratively predict changes in opinion over time, in a similar way as other works of social physics.

3.2 Deriving Attributions Through Opinion Inference

In the last section, we modeled agent-based influence graphs and defined how opinion dynamics is represented in such graphs. Given such networks, we will now illustrate how opinions of agents are mutually influenced and how we can derive attributions based on this inference. With that, we can construct the set of claims that is valid for a specific agent, analogous to viewpoints in [20].

Inference of opinions. An initial opinion of an agent can be formed from different sources based on our elaborations in Sect 3.1. However, the information quality of such an initial opinion can be impeded when a lack of source material prevents the use of stance detection or when inconsistent statements are derived from multiple sources. To cater for that, our model applies ongoing trends in the social dynamic retrospectively, in order to predict the most likely information gained if those sources were to exist. To keep already verified information intact, we specifically target information gaps, defined by low confidence in an agent's opinion. We can scale the effect of opinion dynamics so that fully known opinions remain unchanged while fully unknown opinions behave like before. By extending Eq. 6 we arrive at the following opinion function:

$$o_i^c(t+1) := L\big(\, o_i^c(t) + (1 - conf_i^c(t)) \cdot [\alpha A_i^c(t+1) + \varrho R_i^c(t+1)] \,\big) \tag{7}$$

Here, $(1 - conf_i^c(t))$ describes the information gap of an opinion at time t by using the confidence value as depicted in Eq. 2. Additionally, we adjust the model so that information of higher quality gets passed through the network faster than low-quality information. For each $n_i \in N$, let $N_i \subseteq N$ be the set of all in-neighbors of n_i. Then the function $nconf_i^c : T \to [0,1]$ describes the average confidence of an agent's in-neighbors.

$$nconf_i^c(t) := \begin{cases} 0 & \text{if } |N_i| = 0, \\ \dfrac{\sum_{n_j \in N_i} |w_{j,i}| \cdot conf_j^c(t)}{\sum_{n_j \in N_i} |w_{j,i}|} & \text{otherwise.} \end{cases} \tag{8}$$

Given this point of reference, we dynamically weigh the influence between agents based on their relative information quality.

$$\widehat{w_{i,j}}(t+1) = \frac{w_{i,j} \cdot conf_i^c(t)}{nconf_j^c(t)} \tag{9}$$

This weight function can now be applied by replacing $w_{j,i}$ with $\widehat{w_{i,j}}(t+1)$ in the definition of $A_i^c(t+1)$ and $R_i^c(t+1)$ respectively.

Finally, the confidence of an agent's opinion can be improved by including additional information from in-neighbors. That is, during each iteration, new information is inferred by the agent. The potential improvement depends on multiple factors: (i) the information quality of immediate in-neighbors (approximated by $nconf_i^c(t)$), (ii) the unresolved information gap of the agent (i.e., $1 - conf_i^c(t)$), and (iii), the intensity of each interaction (given by the model parameters α, ϱ). We model the improvement as an additive term to the current confidence:

$$conf_i^c(t+1) := conf_i^c(t) + (1 - conf_i^c(t)) \cdot nconf_i^c(t) \cdot \frac{\alpha + \varrho}{2} \tag{10}$$

By amplifying short-term effects in a regressive manner, opinions are shifted towards their immediate environment until they stabilize or have lost momentum. The resulting new opinion indicates the expected behavior of the social environment at the current phase of opinion formation.

Deriving Attributions. Finally, our objective is to predict attributions. An attribution links a claim in a ECKG to the respective group by annotating the former's predicate. For that, we assume a set of claims and use our model to predict the respective opinion values by simulating opinion dynamics over a period $1 \dots \tau$. From those values in $t = \tau$ we construct the set of attributions which can then be materialized in an ECKG. In the most simple case, the validity of each claim is independent of all other claims. For each agent n_i, the set C_i describes the suspected attributions.

$$C_i = \{c \in C \mid o_i^c(\tau) \geq 1 - \varepsilon\} \cup \{\neg c \in \neg C \mid o_i^c(\tau) \geq -1 + \varepsilon\} \tag{11}$$

The final confidence ratings indicate how much information the prediction model was able to utilize. The likelihood that an attribution is suspected accurately can be estimated by a linear function ϕ over the respective confidence value, where $\varepsilon \in [0, 1]$ can be freely chosen as a model parameter.

$$\phi_i(c) = \left(1 - \frac{\varepsilon}{2}\right) \cdot conf_i^c(\tau) + \frac{\varepsilon}{2} \tag{12}$$

The most likely set of attributions for an agent n_i is given by the suspected attributions C_i that are more likely to be accurate than not.

$$Attr_i = \{c \in C_i \mid \phi_i(c) > 0.5\} \tag{13}$$

In the more general case that claims (or their negations) may be interdependent, it is not sufficient to evaluate each attribution. Instead, each possible combination of interdependent attributions must be evaluated and compared. This also includes claims not previously considered as suspected attributions. The best attribution set $Attr_i$ for an agent n_i is given by the claim set that maximizes the combined likelihood of choosing or discarding each attribution accurately. However, this approach is only feasible for small sets of interdependent claims, as each set requires exponential time for evaluation. We therefore leave this as an open research question and focus on the opinion dynamic model in the remainder of this paper.

4 Evaluation

In this section, we evaluate our model based on a simulation study and a case study that compares it to viewpoint hierarchies. Our objectives are to demonstrate that (i) the model converges and can therefore be used to infer attributions, (ii) our model can replicate a well-known social phenomenon (vocal minorities) that can be observed in the real world but not replicated with viewpoint hierarchies, and (iii), our model achieves a more realistic result when inferring attributions than viewpoint hierarchies.[1]

[1] All evaluation artifacts are available at: https://github.com/fploetzky/ER2025.

4.1 Model Properties

We first evaluate two aspects concerning our model's properties. The first aspect concerns whether group agents behave as expected, i.e., whether their opinion over time converges similarly to the average opinion of the group they proxy. The second aspect concerns the aspect of vocal minorities and how it can shape public discourse. According to [5], this is especially the case for well-organized minority groups with strong levels of reaffirmation in the group. Therefore, if our model can replicate such movements, it is fit to model opinion shifts that cannot be replicated by viewpoint hierarchies since minorities are either merely able to preserve their stance (in a view-preserving hierarchy) or are overruled by the majority (in a winner takes all setting). Finally, we evaluate the performance of attribution prediction in terms of complexity and runtime.

Group Agent Behavior. Agent-based social physics models usually describe networks of individuals. In order to also allow for groups such as political parties, we allow them to be modeled as agents by approximating their internal dynamics using self-influence (i.e., self-loops in the influence graphs). Agents with identical opinions and influences behave in the same way and can be accurately aggregated into a single node. The influence between these nodes can then be supplemented by an influence vector from the new node to itself. In this part of the evaluation, we demonstrate that this principle is also applicable to groups with heterogeneous opinions. All model parameters are depicted along with the respective simulation figures.

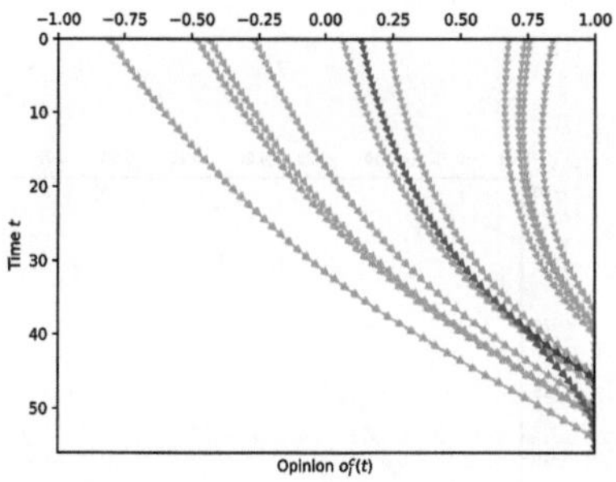

(a) Explicit vs implicit agents; $\tau = 55$, $\alpha = 0.1$, and $\varrho = 0.1$.

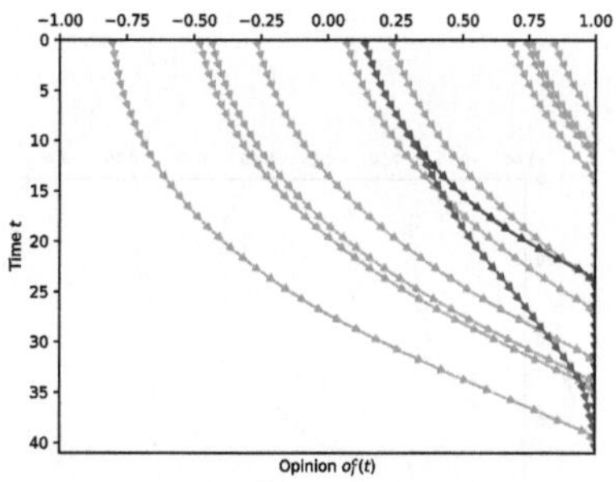

(b) Increased model discrepancy; $\tau = 40$, $\alpha = 0.1$, and $\varrho = 0.2$.

Fig. 3. Group agent behavior tests. Grey lines are simulations of random agents, the red line depicts their average opinion shift, and the blue line a group agent as approximation for the total group's opinion. (Color figure online)

As a first experiment, we create a group consisting of ten members with randomized initial opinions (based on a Gaussian distribution with $\sigma = 0.5$) and homogeneous influence between them and run the model until it stabilizes.

The result is depicted in Fig. 3a. Individual opinion values are shown in gray, and their average is in red. We then use a single agent to approximate the group's behavior (shown in blue) by setting its opinion to the average group opinion and substituting the influence vectors with self-influence. We see that this single group agent's opinions are identical to the group's average for most of the time, as expected. However, groups with higher self-reinforcement can lead to a faster opinion divergence between the group agent and the group. This is because the self-influence vector overshoots since it follows the current trend rather than the actual opinion changes. We show this in a second test, depicted in Fig. 3b, with doubled reinforcement intensity. One can observe that indeed a discrepancy arises at the edges of the opinion scale due to the faster convergence of the group agent. However, we argue that this error can be neglected if the groups have reasonably similar members, since it is mostly caused by the first group members reaching their opinion limit. Therefore, approximating group behavior with a single agent can be deemed suitable and leads to drastically lower modeling efforts, since the underlying influence network need not be modeled.

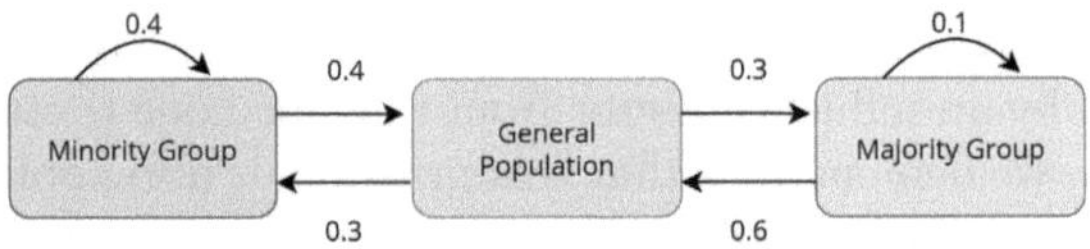

Fig. 4. Influence Network with Vocal Minority

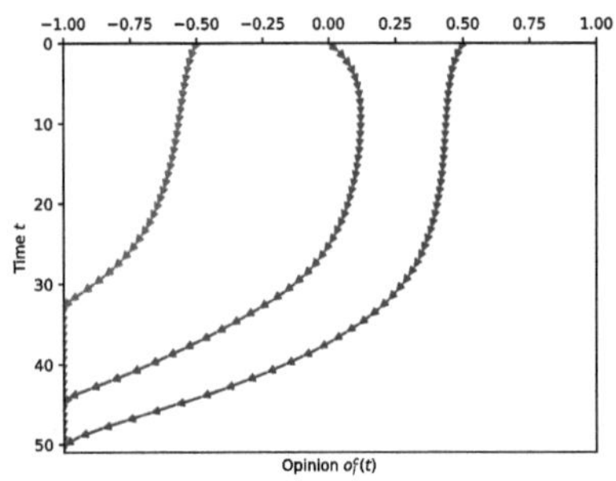

(a) Unaltered model; $\tau = 50$, $\alpha = 0.3$, and $\varrho = 0.2$.

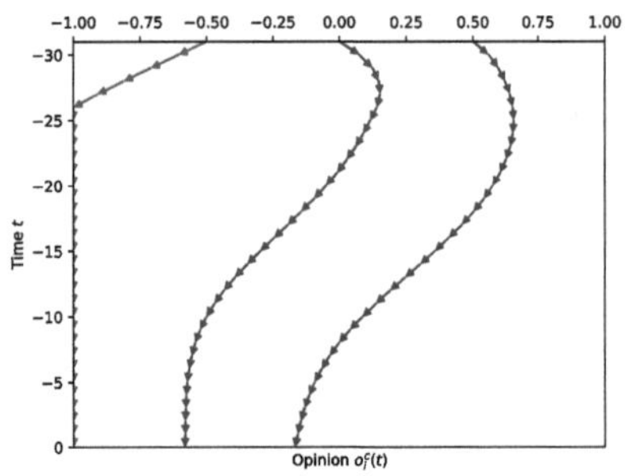

(b) Inference model; $\tau = 30$, $\alpha = 0.3$, and $\varrho = 0.2$.

Fig. 5. Public discourse dominated by a minority (based on Fig. 4). In both figures, the red curve (left-hand side) depicts the minority group, the green one (middle) the general population, and the blue one the majority.

Minority Domination. Besides the behavior of group agents, the last experiments also showed that the opinions in the underlying influence network stabilize over time. In this part, we show that a network can also stabilize in favor of a minority group's opinion if that group is very consistent and vocal about the issue, e.g., in terms of advocacy groups or think tanks. If such a group has a lot of internal interaction, then its members are less likely to adopt external feedback, and it can ultimately dominate public discourse [5]. Such a scenario is not possible in an aggregation hierarchy but can be modeled in an influence network (see Fig. 4). The larger majority group has more interactions with the general population and thus, more influence on it. On the other hand, the minority group is said to have stronger internal communication and thus, more self-influence. With these influence values, we can predict future opinion shifts using our unaltered model of opinion dynamics. The output is shown in Fig. 5a and matches the expected results. While the initial trend suggests the majority dominates based on its greater influence, the minority opinion eventually dominates.

In a second experiment, we focus on the effects of vocal minorities in cases of insufficient sources, i.e., sources with low confidence. In general, to infer an attribution, we are generally more interested in an agent's current opinions as opposed to their predicted future ones. Therefore, we need to adjust the model in order to apply current trends towards information gaps. We can expand on the previous example by assuming that information on both groups is limited (with a confidence of .25) and nothing is known about the general population. We can then improve our confidence by incrementally applying information from the network (cf. Fig. 5b). The example illustrates how the inference model emphasizes initial trends much more strongly (especially on low confidence ratings) and then slowly stabilizes without necessarily reaching consensus or polarization. This behavior allows the model to keep known information intact and to represent heterogeneous groups by maintaining nuanced opinion values.

Performance. Usage of the prediction framework is only viable if it is computationally feasible for moderately sized networks. Opinions are inferred in a predefined number of prediction steps τ. Each step requires every opinion to be updated based on all applied influences. This means that computation time depends on the defined time frame and the number of edges in the network, thus all inferences for a single claim can be made in $\mathcal{O}(\tau \times |E|) \subseteq \mathcal{O}(\tau \times |N|^2)$. Even a small τ is sufficient for the model to reach a stable state, as speed can be controlled with the other model parameters. The worst case of quadratic complexity is only reached in models where each agent influences all other agents. Additionally, for a runtime test, we generate 2,000 entities with random initial opinions and a matrix of 400,000 influence values for a fully connected network. Using a rudimentary model implementation in Python and a commodity PC (CPU: Intel Core i5-12400F and 32GB of DDR5 RAM), the program finishes after *193.44 s*. This test shows that it is generally viable to use agent-based opinion prediction on moderately sized networks.

4.2 Case Study

In this section, we conduct a case study for a specific event to show the differences between our model and viewpoint hierarchies. For that, we focus on a particular claim concerning a recent event, model the respective viewpoints and agents, and show what particular attributions are inferred in the models.

Background and Objective. In October 2024, nearly 50,000 union members of the International Longshoremen's Association initiated a three-day strike against the US East and Golf Coast ports as part of their contract negotiations with the United States Maritime Alliance for new contracts [11]. Based on this event, we focus on the claim: **"The port strikes of October 2024 caused major disruptions"**. As sources, we include positions of a labor union [10], two business groups [2,19], and the Federal Reserve [25] that we manually extracted from the documents. In short, the Federal Reserve and International Longshoremen's Association disagreed with the claim, and both the National Association of Manufacturers and the Chamber of Commerce agreed with it. The objective is now to infer different viewpoints using a viewpoint hierarchy and our model and to compare the results. In particular, we focus on the inferred viewpoints of the Democratic and Republican parties, along with the viewpoint of the US as a whole. As a ground truth, we refer to the real-world stances of both parties towards the claim, i.e., Republicans rather agreed to the claim [4] and Democrats remained neutral [26].

Fig. 6. Relevant institutions in a viewpoint hierarchy for the case study. Green nodes indicate groups with a positive stance towards the claim, red nodes are groups with a negative stance, and for white nodes we assume neutrality. (Color figure online)

Viewpoint Hierarchies. Figure 6 shows these institutions in a viewpoint hierarchy with green nodes indicating entities with positive positions and red nodes indicating entities with negative positions (as discussed before). Information needs to be aggregated to derive positions at more abstract levels, e.g., the Government position is derived by aggregating Congress and the Federal Reserve. Our prior [20] did not focus on neutral stances and thus, for this case study, missing positions can either be ignored or treated as disagreement during aggregation. In both cases, the government and US positions are derived as a disagreement

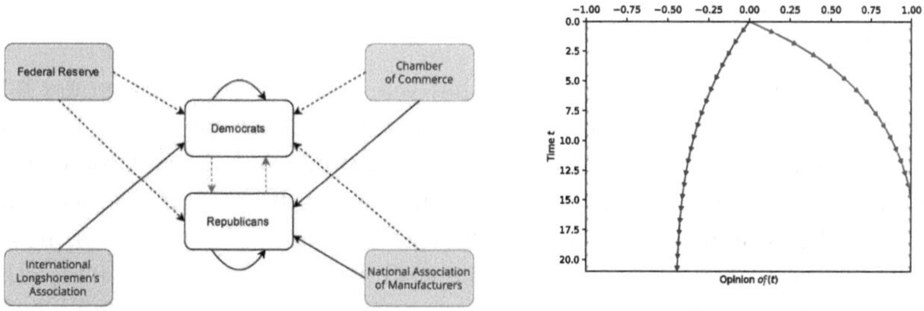

(a) Influence Graph. (b) Opinion Dynamic

Fig. 7. Relevant Institutions in an Influence Graph and the resulting opinions of Democrats (blue) and Republicans (red) respectively. (Color figure online)

and then used to substitute both parties' positions accordingly in a winner takes all hierarchy (since the topmost viewpoint is pushed downwards to all leaves). While this result matches the actual Democrats' viewpoint (assuming that neutrality is considered as disagreement as done in [20]), it does not match the Republican viewpoint (in reality, they agreed to the claim). The US viewpoint also disagrees with the claim. The major concern with the US viewpoint (and large viewpoints in general) is that the opposing positions of business groups and labor unions cancel each other out so that the result mirrors the government's position as the remaining third party. This is a side effect that a modeler must consider and that can lead to unexpected results.

Influence Graph and Opinion Dynamics. In our new model, we consider the relationships between institutions rather than their ontological classification. We use political alignment to estimate influence. In this example, we consider both parties to be somewhat influenced by business interest groups and the Federal Reserve. We also consider the Democratic Party to be strongly influenced by the union and the Republican Party to be more strongly influenced by business interest groups. Lastly, we consider the two parties to have a negative influence on each other to reflect their antagonistic behavior [27]. The resulting influence network is depicted in Fig. 7a. We use this model to predict the missing opinions of the Democratic party (blue) and the Republican party, as shown in Fig. 7b. The resulting slight disagreement and strong agreement match the parties' real statements towards the claim [4,26].

Comparison. The difference in results is achieved by our model's increased flexibility. A hierarchy enforces a strict tree shape based on ontological similarity, leading to a misrepresentation of group opinions by omitting minority positions. Having to rely on a single similarity metric leads to groups of dissimilar members with vastly different political agendas. In contrast, our proposed influence model offers an extremely flexible way of modeling. It is able to apply a given social structure and create predictions based on implicit short-term trends. This advantage can drastically improve the accuracy of attributions.

4.3 Discussion and Limitations

In this section, we have demonstrated that our opinion dynamics model follows established results in social physics and compared it with viewpoint hierarchies in a case study. The model can be seen as a "drop-in" replacement for viewpoint hierarchies when constructing viewpoint-enabled ECKGs as introduced in our prior work. In contrast to viewpoint hierarchies, our new model is also able to predict attributions in cases where neutral stances are dominant or stances are not available at all. This fixes two major limitations of our prior model as discussed in [21]. With that, the expressiveness of representing viewpoints in ECKGs is further enhanced while the semantics of attributions, as introduced in [20], is preserved. Of course, our viewpoint inference model has limitations. For one, we still need to know all actors and their interactions beforehand, i.e., the model needs domain knowledge to be constructed. Furthermore, we need to know the reliabilities for all sources considered. In practical applications, they might be proxied, e.g., by trustworthiness scores. In addition, we did not evaluate how realistic it is to automatically extract stances from sources as setup for the simulation, although recent advances in stance detection for both texts (e.g., [29]) and multi-modal content (e.g., [16]) are positive hints that this task is solvable in real-world applications of the model. The biggest limitation currently is the choice of initial weights for the influence networks and potentially automatic adjustments over time, which requires future work to enhance the result quality.

5 Related Work

Viewpoints in Knowledge Graphs. Introducing multiple perspectives or viewpoints to knowledge graphs and ECKGs has been studied in multiple ways, e.g., modeling different viewpoints explicitly for participants [28] or based on parameterized predicates [20,21] or implicitly by linking the respective document sources from which the graph was constructed [23]. This paper focuses on the prior and introduces an agent-based viewpoint model.

Opinion Dynamics in Social Physics. Modeling opinions is a vast field. Most relevant to this paper are dynamic models that focus on the expression of opinions by agents and social interactions. In this regard, [5] propose a model focused on how the expression of public opinion evolves over time based on the willingness of each actor to express themselves in social interaction. Similarly, [6] focuses on how opinions change over time based on social influence and interaction between agents. In this paper, we focus on a model that obeys the findings of the previous papers but also allows for inferring opinions.

Predictive Modeling and Inference. Concerning predictive modeling, [24] propose an agent-based model to investigate how opinions are propagated through a network over time. [12] analyze the effects of modeling private and public opinion separately. [18] combine the usual agent-based model with a generative machine learning model. [22] propose a framework with the goal of predicting social influence in a network. [17] introduce a framework using a deep neural network to model social influence and predict human behavior. Finally, [9] creates a prediction model for missing or future links in social networks.

6 Conclusion

In this paper, we proposed a viewpoint model that advances the representation of contested claims in ECKGs. We showed that our model is more fit to describe complex relationships and infer attributions from them than prior works in this area. We argue that such representations are increasingly important, especially in times of worldwide tension and, therefore, an increasing amount of contested information. Future work in this direction can show the application of such a model for downstream tasks like automatic reasoning about different viewpoints.

Acknowledgements. Supported by the Leibniz-ScienceCampus Postdigital Participation funded by the Leibniz Association (Leibniz-Gemeinschaft).

References

1. AlDayel, A., Magdy, W.: Stance detection on social media: state of the art and trends. Inf. Process. Manage. **58**(4), 102597 (2021)
2. Bradley, N.: U.S. ports reopen as talks continue: what it means. https://www.uschamber.com/economy/looming-port-strike-what-it-means-for-you, statement by the US Chamber of Commerce regarding the port strikes
3. Castellano, C., Fortunato, S., Loreto, V.: Statistical physics of social dynamics. Rev. Mod. Phys. **81**(2), 591–646 (2009)
4. Committee on transportation and infrastructure: republicans urge biden-harris administration action to prevent strike at east and gulf coast ports (2024). https://transportation.house.gov/news/documentsingle.aspx?DocumentID=407803, call to action by Republicans on the Committee of Transportation regarding the port strikes
5. Gaisbauer, F., Olbrich, E., Banisch, S.: Dynamics of opinion expression. Phys. Rev. E **102**(4), 042303 (2020)
6. Galam, S.: Sociophysics and the forming of public opinion: threshold versus non threshold dynamics. arXiv preprint arXiv:0803.2453 (2008)
7. Gottschalk, S., Demidova, E.: EventKG: A Multilingual Event-Centric Temporal Knowledge Graph. In: Gangemi, A., Navigli, R., Vidal, M.-E., Hitzler, P., Troncy, R., Hollink, L., Tordai, A., Alam, M. (eds.) ESWC 2018. LNCS, vol. 10843, pp. 272–287. Springer, Cham (2018). https://doi.org/10.1007/978-3-319-93417-4_18
8. Guizzardi, G., Wagner, G., Almeida Falbo, R., Guizzardi, R.S.S., Almeida, J.P.A.: Towards ontological foundations for the conceptual modeling of events. In: Ng, W., Storey, V.C., Trujillo, J.C. (eds.) ER 2013. LNCS, vol. 8217, pp. 327–341. Springer, Heidelberg (2013). https://doi.org/10.1007/978-3-642-41924-9_27
9. Huo, Z., Huang, X., Hu, X.: Link prediction with personalized social influence. In: AAAI Conference on Artificial Intelligence (AAAI) vol. 32, no. 1 (2018). https://doi.org/10.1609/aaai.v32i1.11892

10. International Longshoremen's Association: ILA Rank and File Members Ready to Take Ultimate Stand to Win Fair Contract (2024). https://ilaunion.org/ila-rank-and-file-members-ready-to-take-ultimate-stand-to-win-fair-contract-they-will-strike-on-october-1-for-wages-and-benefits-they-believe-they-deserve/, statement by the International Longshoremen's Association regarding the port strikes
11. Isidore, C., Yurkevich, V.: Massive port strike begins across America's East Coast, threatening shortages and rising prices (2024). https://edition.cnn.com/2024/10/01/business/us-port-workers-strike-tuesday/index.html
12. Jadbabaie, A., Makur, A., Mossel, E., Salhab, R.: Inference in opinion dynamics under social pressure. IEEE Trans. on Automatic Control **68**(6), 3377–3392 (2022)
13. Leban, G., Fortuna, B., Brank, J., Grobelnik, M.: Event registry: learning about world events from news. In: Int. World Wide Web Conf. (WWW), pp. 107–110 (2014). https://doi.org/10.1145/2567948.2577024
14. Leetaru, K., Schrodt, P.: GDELT: global data on events, location, and tone, 1979–2012. Pennsylvania State University, Tech. rep. (2013)
15. Lenti, J., Silvestri, F., Morales, G.D.F.: Variational inference of parameters in opinion dynamics models. In: Proceedings of the AAAI Conference on Web and Social Media (ICWSM), pp. 2622–2627. AAAI Press (2025). https://doi.org/10.1609/ICWSM.V19I1.35963
16. Liang, B., et al.: Multi-modal stance detection: new datasets and model. In: Findings of the Association for Computational Linguistics (ACL-Findings), pp. 12373–12387. Association for Computational Linguistics (2024). https://doi.org/10.18653/V1/2024.FINDINGS-ACL.736
17. Luceri, L., Braun, T., Giordano, S.: Social influence (deep) learning for human behavior prediction (2018). https://arxiv.org/abs/1801.09471
18. Monti, C., De Francisci Morales, G., Bonchi, F.: Learning opinion dynamics from social traces. In: Int. Conf. on Knowledge Discovery & Data Mining (KDD), pp. 764–773 (2020)
19. National Association of Manufacturers : Nam, allies: Port talks need intervention (2024). https://nam.org/nam-allies-port-talks-need-intervention-32113/, statement by the National Association of Manufacturers regarding the port strikes
20. Plötzky, F., Britz, K., Balke, W.T.: Shards of knowledge–modeling attributions for event-centric knowledge graphs. In: Int. Conf. on Conceptual Modeling (ER), pp. 259–276. Springer (2023)
21. Plötzky, F., Britz, K., Balke, W.T.: A conceptual model for attributions in event-centric knowledge graphs. Data Knowl. Eng. **159**, 102449 (2025). https://doi.org/10.1016/j.datak.2025.102449
22. Qiu, J., Tang, J., Ma, H., Dong, Y., Wang, K., Tang, J.: Deepinf: social influence prediction with deep learning. In: Int. Conf. on Knowledge Discovery & Data Mining (SIGKDD), pp. 2110–2119 (2018)
23. Rospocher, M., et al.: Building event-centric knowledge graphs from news. J. Web Semantics **37–38**, 132–151 (2016). https://doi.org/10.1016/j.websem.2015.12.004
24. Saini, A., Markuzon, N.: Predictive modeling of opinion and connectivity dynamics in social networks. arXiv preprint arXiv:1603.08252 (2016)
25. Saphir, A., Simao, P.: Fed's goolsbee says dockworkers' strike could lead to higher prices (2024). https://www.reuters.com/markets/us/feds-goolsbee-says-dockworkers-strike-could-lead-higher-prices-2024-10-03/, Reuters News Report regarding the port strikes
26. The White House: Statement from President Joe Biden on the Negotiations Between USMX and the International Longshoremen's Association (2024).

https://www.whitehouse.gov/briefing-room/statements-releases/2024/10/01/statement-from-president-joe-biden-on-the-negotiations-between-usmx-and-the-international-longshoremens-association/
27. Tuttnauer, O., Wegmann, S.: Voting for votes: opposition parties' legislative activity and electoral outcomes. Am. Political Sci. Rev. **116**(4), 1357–1374 (2022)
28. Hage, W.R., Malaisé, V., Segers, R., Hollink, L., Schreiber, G.: Design and use of the simple event model (SEM). J. Web Semantics **9**(2), 128–136 (2011)
29. Zhao, C., Caragea, C.: Bilingual zero-shot stance detection. In: Proc. of the Annual Meeting of the Association for Computational Linguistics (ACL), pp. 29900–29919. ACL (2025). https://aclanthology.org/2025.acl-long.1446/
30. Zhu, M., et al.: EventSum: a large-scale event-centric summarization dataset for chinese multi-news documents. In: AAAI Conference on Artificial Intelligence (AAAI), pp. 26138–26147. AAAI Press (2025). https://doi.org/10.1609/AAAI.V39I24.34810

Comparative Experiments on Natural Language Querying of Knowledge Graphs Using a Graph RAG Approach

Teodora Cristiana Nemțoc(✉), Robert Andrei Buchmann(✉), and Gheorghe Cosmin Silaghi(✉)

Business Informatics Research Center, Babeș-Bolyai University, Cluj-Napoca, Romania
{teodora.nemtoc,robert.buchmann,gheorghe.silaghi}@ubbcluj.ro

Abstract. Recent developments in the synergy between Large Language Models (LLMs) and Knowledge Graphs have introduced Graph Retrieval-Augmented Generation (Graph RAG) as an extension to traditional RAG. Graph RAG replaces the unstructured textual 'knowledge base' obtained in the retrieval phase of the RAG with Knowledge Graphs to improve entity identification and traceability. In this paper we present a customized Graph RAG framework for handling natural language queries over a knowledge graph with the help of Large Language Models. We conduct a comparative evaluation of several LLMs in responding to different query patterns on a domain-specific knowledge graph, employing four prompting levels defined by the TELeR taxonomy. The outputs are evaluated against ground truth results obtained by executing the corresponding SPARQL queries within a GraphDB triplestore. The content on which the experiments are performed is the Unified Medical Language System (UMLS) semantic network. The results summarize several strengths and weaknesses of the different LLMs relative to the complexity of selected query types, triple patterns, and prompting techniques involved in our Graph RAG setup.

Keywords: Graph RAG · Knowledge Graphs · Large Language Models · UMLS · SPARQL Queries · Prompt Engineering

1 Introduction

The synergy of Knowledge Graphs (KGs) with Large Language Models (LLMs) has become an increasingly discussed topic in recent research. As outlined in [9] this confluence can take multiple forms: (1) *KG-enhanced LLMs*, where the structured knowledge from a KG is incorporated into a LLM setup; (2) *LLM-assisted KGs* where LLMs assist KG-related processes such as graph construction, graph completion, embedding generation, and query resolution; and (3) *hybrid models where both parts co-evolve* as LLMs add refinements for KGs while KGs adjust

D. Bork et al. (Eds.): ER 2025, LNCS 16189, pp. 302–319, 2026.
https://doi.org/10.1007/978-3-032-08623-5_16

LLM settings in return. Graph RAG (Graph Retrieval-Augmented Generation) proposes a hybrid strategy regarding the coordination between LLMs and KGs. This technique replaces the unstructured textual 'knowledge base' obtained in the retrieval phase of a traditional RAG with graph-based representations that may be lifted from legacy data sources and/or constructed from raw textual inputs [10]. The graph content exposed to an LLM allows it to achieve traceability of entity connections and to provide more relevant answers to natural language queries.

Graph RAG has garnered significant attention and triggered the development of numerous adaptations within the industry [10]. Microsoft Graph RAG[1] [3] represents one such development, which relies on node community summaries to improve query answers. Graph RAG is expected to improve LLM responses, especially in cases where private data or deep domain specificity is required. However, nuances and suitability may vary between competing LLMs.

In terms of domain-specificity, in our paper we tackle the biomedical domain - for which a well established conceptualization is available in the form of UMLS (Unified Medical Language System)[2]. UMLS [7] provides a "semantic network" comprising an upper conceptual layer (event, activity, physical object etc.) specialized for the biomedical domain (into injury, organ etc.) with a hierarchy of relationships defining relational mappings between concepts from various taxonomical levels. Considering this domain-specificity, our objective is to evaluate and compare the effectiveness of various general-purpose LLMs in answering natural language questions within a Graph RAG framework that we adapted from the Microsoft Graph RAG flavor. The answers are compared against deterministic SPARQL responses over the KG hosted in a triplestore. The KG was built as an RDF rendering of the original UMLS "semantic network" – which is extractable as an "array of triples" dataset in the PyKEEN[3] package.

The tested queries probe structural aspects of the chosen knowledge structure based on triple elements and relationship direction, establishing a basis that can be further expanded towards deeper semantic features. They are not strictly tied to the domain of choice and are suitable for application across diverse datasets.

With this work, we seek to investigate the trade-off between the ease of formulating natural language questions which do not depend on a formal querying language and the accuracy of the returned answers. To this aim, Graph RAG enables a bridge for non-technical users interacting with formal domain-specific knowledge representation. The study examines the strengths and weaknesses of the Graph RAG approach, scrutinizing how the performance varies across different LLMs and depending on the complexity of queries. The LLMs evaluated in our experiments are Mixtral-8x7B-Instruct-v0.1, GPT-3.5 Turbo and GPT-4o. Each LLM was tested with several query types derived from SPARQL patterns of varying complexity, with the deterministic results serving as ground truth for evaluating answer quality.

---

1 https://github.com/microsoft/graphrag.
2 https://uts.nlm.nih.gov/uts/umls/semantic-network/root.
3 https://pykeen.readthedocs.io/en/stable/api/pykeen.datasets.UMLS.html.

Given the critical role of prompt complexity, we follow TELeR taxonomy [12] and conduct experiments with progressively more detailed prompting levels. These prompting levels are systematically combined with RDF triple query patterns across the compared LLMs. Thus, this study aims to identify the query types that LLMs can effectively answer, to highlight existing limitations, as well as to explore strategies for mitigating them through optimized prompting. The UMLS conceptual model was employed as a reference domain knowledge base due to its popularity as a benchmarking and KG embeddings resource available in the PyKEEN (see footnote 3) package.

The paper evolves as follows: Sect. 2 reviews related work. In Sect. 3 we describe our methodology including our Graph RAG approach. Section 4 presents the results and discusses them, and Sect. 5 concludes the paper.

2 Related Work

The interplay between Knowledge Graphs (KG) and Large Language Models (LLM) has gained significant prevalence over the past few years. Fatemi et al. [4] conducted a comprehensive analysis around the capabilities of LLMs of processing graph-structured data, as well as reasoning prospects and associated limitations. The findings suggest that effective reasoning within graph-encoded knowledge depends on several factors including the encoding model used to represent the graph, prompt optimization techniques and the reasoning objective âĂŞ e.g. link prediction, node classification, pathfinding. He et al. [5] introduced the first RAG approach using a KG-based question-answering architecture. The role of graphs in preserving explicit connections between pieces of information within a text emphasized the KG potential to enhance the understanding of connected entities, ultimately achieving KG reasoning. The same conversational approach with a graph is adopted by Sun et al. [14] where LLMs and KGs work in tandem for improved deep reasoning and knowledge traceability. Their interaction with suitable techniques such as beam search mitigates the risk of potential hallucinations.

The very first integration of a Graph RAG setup in a graph database is attributed to NebulaGraph[4], which proposes a lightweight interface for KG-driven applications. Other recent implementations include OntoText GraphDB[5] which supports customizable indexing and retrieval procedures. It also introduces an intuitive and accessible interface for non-technical users for communicating directly with the graph using a ChatGPT Retrieval Plugin Connector or SPARQL extensions. The latter has been probed in [2] where an LLM interacts with serialized BPMN (Business Process Model and Notation) diagrams, in two distinct formats: RDF graph and XML serialization. By adopting the RDF standard to represent domain-specific diagrammatic knowledge the authors explored, through various prompt engineering techniques, the capability of LLMs to understand and analyze open-world process-centric semantic networks.

[4] https://www.nebula-graph.io/posts/graph-RAG.
[5] https://www.ontotext.com/products/graphdb.

Other studies explore the ability of LLMs to generate SPARQL queries, aiming to circumvent technical expertise on the standardized RDF retrieval language. Sima et al. [13] introduced a natural language processing engine for generating SPARQL queries based on a generic graph-based approach, while Rangel et al. [11] outlined a methodology for fine-tuning LLMs in the direction of generating ready-to-use SPARQL queries for tasks formulated in natural language.

While most studies [11,13] evaluated exclusively the ability of an LLM to generate correct SPARQL queries starting from natural language input, in our setup the goal shifts towards obtaining a direct response from natural language, mimicking a response generated by the SPARQL query execution engine. In this way, the response can be readily streamlined with SPARQL client apps. Although various types of questions differing in complexity and diverse associated graph paths have been verified, there are still literature gaps in setting up a catalog of query patterns that clearly pinpoint areas where an LLM excels and where it faces challenges in generating the responses. For this reason, our study incorporates a simple classification of SPARQL queries, based on their applicability to triplestore datasets, therefore allowing 1:1 triple comparison as a strict evaluation method. For prompting patterns, we adopt the TELeR taxonomy [12], including Zero-Shot and One-Shot techniques, the latter branching into ICL (In-Context Learning) and COT (Chain-of-Thought).

Existing studies [6,9,14] on the interaction between knowledge graphs (KGs) and large language models (LLMs) highlight the potential of LLMs in supporting KG-related tasks, while also identifying their limitations and conditions of applicability. In this sense, we adopted key features related to model selection, advanced prompting techniques, the KG construction step, followed by its integration in a RAG pipeline. This paper builds upon these areas and explores the capacity of selected LLMs to respond to a series of queries according to a taxonomy of query patterns. Our approach combines multiple prompt engineering strategies with a context generated through an adapted Microsoft Graph RAG setup and leverages a benchmark knowledge graph based on the UMLS conceptual model. Generated responses are evaluated against ground-truth triples from equivalent SPARQL queries on the knowledge graph, allowing us to determine which combinations of parameters yield the most accurate alignment with deterministic query outputs.

3 Methodology and Experimentation Setup

In this section we present our Graph RAG framework for leveraging LLMs in responding natural languages queries over knowledge graphs. We also introduce our experimentation setup, including the query types, the dataset, the metrics, and the prompt templates.

3.1 Retrieval Augmented Generation and Graph RAG

Retrieval-Augmented Generation (RAG) [6] is a technique that retrieves relevant context from a knowledge base and provides it to a large language model, enabling the model to generate answers to queries by leveraging this external information. For Graph RAG the knowledge base is not a repository of unstructured documents, but instead graph-structured content such as the content of a KG. In the retrieval phase, a Graph RAG approach returns a relevant subgraph from the initial KG, containing nodes and edges considered fit for the input query according to some chosen relevance criteria. Our work employs an already existing benchmark KG, therefore, we ensure that potential errors with the KG construction phase do not propagate through our Graph RAG pipeline, while also leveraging the reliability of a well-formed domain-specific graph.

The default prompt integrated into the Microsoft's (see footnote 1) Graph RAG implementation is not designed to generate answers in a structured format that we need for our direct 1:1 comparison against reference SPARQL results. For this reason, our approach preserves the context generated by the preliminary Graph RAG steps, but defines custom prompting texts to integrate the retrieved context with the user query.

3.2 The Adapted Graph RAG Pipeline

Since our task involves responding natural language queries over a benchmark KG, we adapt the Microsoft Graph RAG [3] implementation to suit our specific objectives.

While retrieving the most relevant entities and relationships for the input query, Microsoft Graph RAG performs community detection where a community represents a group of similar entities based on certain criteria. For each community, a textual summary is returned to support the query answer not only with the most relevant entities, but also with those in the same similarity-based community. Our experiments still employ the Microsoft's community detection approach, but with a restructured pipeline at the indexing time, as represented in Fig. 1.

In the indexing phase, the original Microsoft approach involves processing unstructured text, chunking, and identifying entities and relationships. In our setup, we modify these steps by omitting the KG construction phase, instead operating directly on PyKEEN-derived nodes and relations to build a well-formed in-memory graph structure. However, some preprocessing methods from the Microsoft Graph RAG package are retained to prepare the nodes for community generation based on their associated descriptions.

The original pipeline relies on LLMs to extract entity-relation tables for community generation and summarization and creates entity descriptions from surrounding raw text. Since our setup operates directly on structured triples, an alternative method for attaching textual descriptions is required in order to retain the input expected by the Microsoft Graph RAG package during indexing and retrieval subsequent phases. Our adaptation generates textual descriptions based on the roles each entity plays in the triple dataset, by generating predicate-object and subject-predicate pairs that summarize everything connected to that specific node. For example, the entity `Vitamin` would be

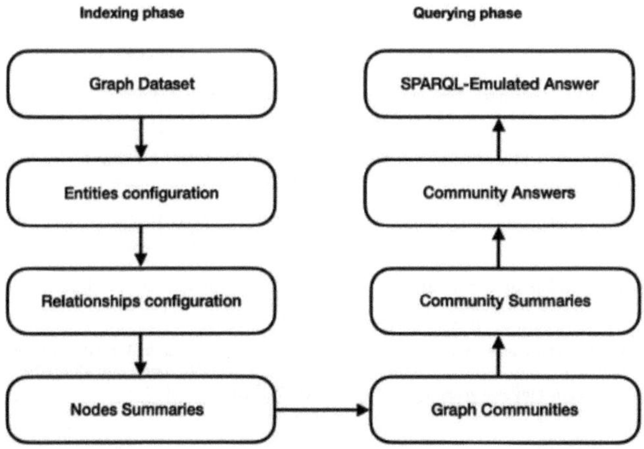

Fig. 1. The adapted Graph RAG pipeline

described as: "affects cell_function, affects disease_or_syndrome, affects experimental_model_of_disease." Similarly, relationship entries are structured to clearly define source and target entities to maintain the connections that would determine the graph.

Microsoft Graph RAG groups elements based on similarity and connectivity, weighting the entities and relationships according to their frequency of occurrence and relevance, detecting potential communities using Leiden algorithm [15]. The system constructs a hierarchical structure and performs community clustering, enabling graph traversals at specific levels. Each cluster produces a summarized textual report based on node descriptions, which facilitates the extraction of relevant answers during the query phase. When a user submits a question, the system identifies the relevant entities and relationships, which are then searched within the appropriate communities. Each relevant community generates a response, and these responses are subsequently combined to form a global answer that is presented to the user. This approach, known as *Query-Focused Summarization*, enables the identification of both broad, general responses within the dataset, and specific answers for the identified nodes. These particularities enable richer contextual grounding for LLM responses, making the Microsoft Graph RAG approach a suitable retrieval framework for our current use case. The well-documented architecture allows for the customization of the processing steps to operate with a custom benchmark dataset instead of an automatically generated KG derived from a textual dataset. These adjustments facilitate dynamic and straightforward evaluation of multiple variations in query types, prompt design, and LLMs without affecting the retrieval mechanisms.

Thus, we kept the original Microsoft Graph RAG logic for the retrieval step in which the input query is matched to the most relevant nodes and relationships via similarity scoring against the initial data structures that conceptually form a graph. The most relevant nodes are selected using the default Graph RAG

	Query Type	Generic Pattern
1	Reading the object for a known relationship with a known subject	SELECT ? object WHERE {@node @predicate ?object.}
2	Reading the subject for a known relationship with a known object	SELECT ?subject WHERE {?subject @predicate @node.}
3	Reading the entity(ies) related to a known node through a known relationship	SELECT ?ent WHERE {{@node @relationship ?ent.} UNION {?ent @relationship @node.}}
4	Reading the relationship(s) that directly connect two known entities	SELECT ?predicate WHERE{{@node1 ?predicate @node2.}UNION {@node2 ?predicate @node1.}}
5	Discovering all relationships of an entity and their targets	SELECT ?predicate ?target WHERE {@node ?predicate ?target.}
6	Return pairs of nodes connected by a relationship	SELECT ?source ?target WHERE {{?source @predicate ?target.} UNION {?target @predicate ?source.}}
7	Discovering all triples that involve an entity	DESCRIBE @x

Fig. 2. Query patterns involved in the experiments

ranking mechanism and are returned along with a structured textual summary of the communities to which they belong. The final report, which serves as context for LLMs, includes these community summaries as well as the list of entities and relationships relevant for the query. In this way, the LLMs receive semantic distinctions and contextual grounding for the input query. At this point, a key task is the extraction of information that directly answers the query based on the instructions provided in the prompt and structuring the response as a list of triples to be directly compared to those obtained with straightforward SPARQL over an RDF Schema representation of the KG.

3.3 Query Types and Their SPARQL Corresponding Pattern

Standard SPARQL queries return SPARQL Results Format[6] or standard triples as responses. Since the goal is to assess the retrieval capability of an LLM against SPARQL resulting triples, all results are transformed at execution time to take the form of an array of triples. This adjustment enforces the uniformity and comparability of the responses between the LLM and the SPARQL deterministic query.

For the experimentation pursued in this paper we limited the study to several query patterns based on the triple structure and direction, as shown in Fig. 2, where each query type is presented both as natural language description and a corresponding parameterized SPARQL pattern. In the currently reported stage of our work, we have selected only simple queries where the objective is to identify missing triple elements when the others are known, and by varying the triple navigation direction (spo, ops, pso etc.). A concrete example of a query in both natural language and SPARQL format is presented in Table 1, alongside the returned triples.

[6] https://www.w3.org/TR/sparql11-results-json/.

Table 1. Query Input and Output Examples for LLM and SPARQL

	LLM	**SPARQL**
Query	Retrieve all triples where the predicate is 'uses' and the subject is 'age_group'.	PREFIX rag: SELECT ?subject ?predicate ?object WHERE {{ rag:age_group rag:uses ?object. }}
Results	'age_group uses manufactured_object' 'age_group uses medical_device' 'age_group uses regulation_or_law' 'age_group uses classification' 'age_group uses clinical_drug' 'age_group uses intellectual_product' 'age_group uses drug_delivery_device' 'age_group uses research_device'	'age_group uses medical_device' 'age_group uses manufactured_object' 'age_group uses regulation_or_law' 'age_group uses drug_delivery_device' 'age_group uses clinical_drug' 'age_group uses intellectual_product' 'age_group uses research_device'
Common Triples	'age_group uses medical_device' 'age_group uses regulation_or_law' 'age_group uses manufactured_object' 'age_group uses clinical_drug' 'age_group uses intellectual_product' 'age_group uses drug_delivery_device' 'age_group uses research_device'	

3.4 Metrics

The evaluation of results consists in examining the triples generated by LLMs and those returned by SPARQL - executed in Ontotext GraphDB hosting an RDF Schema representation of the KG. Evaluation is performed by strictly comparing the two sets element by element. We report the following metrics, described by the equations below:

Precision, which computes the correctly identified triples based on the golden truth out of the total triples returned, focusing on the quality of predictions;

Recall emphasizes the completeness of the predictions, measuring how many triples from the entire benchmark set are successfully discovered by the LLM;

F1-score, which combines Precision and Recall metrics, reflecting both the quality of the prediction and completeness of the model.

$$P = \frac{|\text{LLM Triples} \cap \text{SPARQL Triples}|}{|\text{LLM Triples}|} \tag{1}$$

$$R = \frac{|\text{LLM Triples} \cap \text{SPARQL Triples}|}{|\text{SPARQL Triples}|} \tag{2}$$

$$F1 = \frac{2 \times P \times R}{P + R} \tag{3}$$

3.5 Dataset

To ensure the correctness and reliability of the input KG, we picked UMLS (see footnote 2) [1], a conceptual model extracted from PyKEEN (see footnote

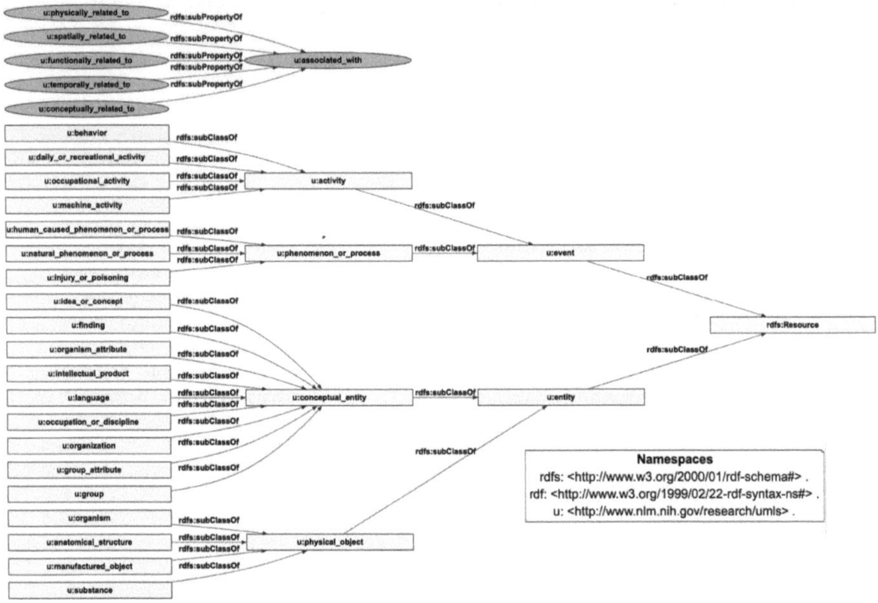

Fig. 3. Upper layers of the UMLS vocabulary

3) - a Python library designed for KG integrations and embeddings that provides access to several established domain-specific graph datasets or tailored to specific tasks. The dataset selection was guided by its alignment with the input requirements for Graph RAG, wide adoption and its apparent focus on a specific domain. UMLS [7,8] offers a semantic network for biomedical information systems, by incorporating 5216 entries with triples containing biomedical vocabulary terms. It provides a standardized semantic network for the biomedical domain and ensures adherence to the principles of KG construction. The PyKEEN-derived triples preserve this UMLS ontology and its semantic consistency, as we ensure that equivalent graph content is made available to both the community building Graph RAG step and to the SPARQL ground truths retrieval.

4 Figure 3 illustrates the upper layers of the UMLS vocabulary, from the superior generic concepts (event, physical object) down to more specialized ones (injury, anatomical structure etc.). Further details on the complete vocabulary can be consulted at the National Health Institute page on the UMLS Semantic Network (see footnote 2). Since this conceptual model is offered through PyKEEN (see footnote 3) we derived from that an array of entity-relation-entity mappings also covering subclass/subproperty specializations (distinguishable as "isA" triples); moreover, a pre-processing phase of turning it into an RDF schema was necessary to apply the SPARQL retrieval treatment. This mapping allows the full execution of the query catalog while simultaneously maintaining compatibility with the Graph RAG pipeline, both using the same set of triples.

You are a Knowledge Graph Expert. You will be provided with a community summary report and a query, both written in natural language. Your task is to extract relevant knowledge in the form of RDF triples to accurately answer the query based on the information contained in the community reports. Provide the extracted RDF triples in the format: subject predicate object as a structured list without additional explanatory descriptions, avoid numbering the elements and do not include additional special characters or additional text. If no matching triples are found, return 'No matching triples found'.

Fig. 4. Level 1 Prompting

3.6 Prompt Engineering

The prompting technique impacts the responses it returns. Each prompting style requires the textual input as context in conjunction with the query. In its simplest form, known as Zero-Shot, LLM receives only the task description. More complex approaches such as One-Shot and Few-Shot involve sending one or more examples to further support the task, the number of examples determining the prompting type: 1) One-Shot if it involves a single example, 2) Few-Shot if multiple examples are provided.

Santu & Feng [12] introduce the TELeR taxonomy for prompt design, supplying guidelines for constructing prompts in a stepwise manner, depending on the complexity and desired technique. Based on the prompt levels defined in the paper, we selected the first four, varying the prompting technique from solely the task definition to the provision of concrete examples that guide the returned responses. Given that the experiments involve multiple query types requiring complete triple reconstruction, regardless of the elements defined as input and output, the degree of prompt detail may influence the final assembly. TELeR taxonomy allows us to examine whether less detailed prompt levels suffice for queries involving simple searches, and whether a more detailed task specification contributes to improved performance for more complex queries. For Level 1, shown in Fig. 4, the LLM is positioned as a KG expert. The input consists of a community summary report and a query, with the objective of returning an answer in triple format derived from the relevant contextual information.

All prompts share the same core content as the initial level with the task definition, additional details being added progressively at each subsequent level. At Level 2, an additional subtask is introduced to filter results by the exact predicate corresponding to the query. This reduces the number of LLM answers with partially correct triples. The subtasks are further expanded at Level 3, where the LLM is fed with a detailed list of steps that guide the model on where to search for relevant information within the community report generated by Microsoft RAG. The LLMs are instructed to focus on dedicated Entities and Relationships sections which contain entity descriptions, sources and targets for each node matching the query. A concrete example with a part of a community report, together with the dedicated Entities and Relationships section is

```
# Role of Professional or Occupational Groups
Professional or occupational groups play a crucial role in diagnosing cell or molecular dysfunction, diseases, mental or behavioral dysfunctions, neoplastic processes, and pathologic functions. They also exhibit various behaviors, interact with different groups, and manage health care-related organizations, among other activities. The expertise and activities of these groups are essential in the biomedical field, contributing significantly to the community's impact.
Relationships:
professional_or_occupational_group|neoplastic_process|diagnoses|
professional_or_occupational_group|biomedical_occupation_or_discipline|issue_in|
professional_or_occupational_group biomedical_occupation_or_discipline|practices|
Entities:
professional_or_occupational_group -> diagnoses cell_or_molecular_dysfunction; diagnoses disease_or_syndrome; diagnoses mental_or_behavioral_dysfunction; diagnoses neoplastic_process; diagnoses pathologic_function; biomedical_occupation_or_discipline; issue_in occupation_or_discipline; manages health_care_related_organization; manages organization; manages professional_society; manages self_help_or_relief_organization; performs individual_behavior; performs social_behavior; practices occupation_or_discipline.
```

Fig. 5. Community summary with detected *Relationships* and *Entities*

presented in Fig. 5. The last level follows the ICL pattern, providing concrete examples for each query type along the expected responses.

4 Results and Discussions

This section presents the results of our experiments. For reproducibility purposes, the source code and results are available via GitHub[7]. Results highlight key observations in relation to the involved parameters.

The analysis kicked off with the dedicated Graph RAG package provided by Microsoft, with its results interacting with three LLMs: Mixtral-8x7B-Instruct-v0[8], accessed via Hugging Face Serverless API, and the two GPT models, GPT-3.5 Turbo[9] and GPT-4o[10], queried through Open AI API. The evaluation covers the four distinct prompt levels, the seven types of queries with 25 examples per each category, all the combinations being tested across the three LLMs, resulting in a total of 2100 trials. The results for each possible combination of parameters: model type, prompting level, and query type are presented in Table 2 along with the three performance evaluation metrics: Precision, Recall, and F1-score. This section presents and analyzes various noteworthy conclusions.

LLMs yield strong results when the query involves s-p-o searching, i.e. when the subject and predicate in the triples are explicitly defined. The simplest type of query (Q1) consists of specifying the first two elements of a triple, requiring the last one to be discovered. In this case, the Graph RAG pipeline manages to determine the most relevant entities and relationships that correspond to those mentioned in the query, effectively preparing the context

[7] https://github.com/teodoracristiananemtoc/Graph-RAG-for-Querying-Knowledge-Graphs.

[8] https://huggingface.co/mistralai/Mixtral-8x7b-Instruct-v0.1.

[9] https://platform.openai.com/docs/models/gpt-3-5-turbo.

[10] https://platform.openai.com/docs/models/gpt-4o.

Table 2. Performance Metrics for LLMs Across Prompting Levels for Query Taxonomy Types

Query	Metric	Mixtral				GPT-3.5 Turbo				GPT-4o			
		L1	L2	L3	L4	L1	L2	L3	L4	L1	L2	L3	L4
Q1	Precision	0.47	0.51	0.20	0.34	0.60	0.69	0.52	0.22	1	1	1	0.86
	Recall	0.53	0.58	0.33	0.39	0.60	0.59	0.69	0.58	0.93	0.93	0.99	0.99
	F1	0.45	**0.49**	0.20	0.34	0.50	**0.57**	0.47	0.25	0.95	0.94	**0.99**	0.87
Q2	Precision	0.37	0.57	0.42	0.36	0.49	0.47	0.36	0.10	0.92	0.90	1.00	0.79
	Recall	0.27	0.32	0.32	0.29	0.28	0.22	0.35	0.30	0.44	0.45	0.48	0.43
	F1	0.25	**0.35**	0.30	0.27	0.28	0.23	**0.29**	0.12	0.52	0.55	**0.60**	0.48
Q3	Precision	0.20	0.20	0.20	0.14	0.14	0.27	0.07	0.03	0.79	0.81	0.74	0.62
	Recall	0.35	0.22	0.36	0.48	0.42	0.43	0.54	0.25	0.78	0.77	0.75	0.78
	F1	**0.22**	0.15	0.18	0.19	0.18	**0.29**	0.09	0.05	**0.77**	0.76	0.73	0.65
Q4	Precision	0.00	0.00	0.06	0.02	0.03	0.09	0.02	0.01	0.28	0.24	0.24	0.16
	Recall	0.00	0.00	0.05	0.01	0.00	0.01	0.01	0.04	0.05	0.03	0.03	0.03
	F1	0.00	0.00	**0.05**	0.01	0.01	0.01	0.01	**0.02**	**0.08**	0.06	0.05	0.05
Q5	Precision	0.61	0.66	0.67	0.71	0.76	0.81	0.71	0.51	0.96	0.91	0.91	0.89
	Recall	0.38	0.31	0.40	0.58	0.66	0.62	0.74	0.70	0.91	0.83	0.95	0.93
	F1	0.41	0.38	0.42	**0.57**	0.65	0.64	**0.70**	0.49	**0.92**	0.83	0.91	0.90
Q6	Precision	0.08	0.11	0.08	0.15	0.12	0.05	0.32	0.06	0.27	0.52	0.04	0.25
	Recall	0.00	0.01	0.02	0.02	0.02	0.01	0.02	0.02	0.01	0.04	0.00	0.02
	F1	0.00	0.02	0.02	**0.03**	0.02	0.01	**0.03**	0.02	0.02	**0.07**	0.01	0.03
Q7	Precision	0.59	0.66	0.78	0.64	0.82	0.84	0.74	0.61	0.84	0.72	0.93	0.97
	Recall	0.12	0.12	0.15	0.16	0.32	0.38	0.44	0.34	0.38	0.43	0.51	0.52
	F1	0.18	0.19	0.23	**0.23**	0.40	0.47	**0.51**	0.40	0.47	0.51	0.62	**0.65**

for subsequent response generation processes. This scenario does not entail any reasoning steps, relying solely on textual matching within the specified triples. For this reason, the model includes a single subtask for identifying the triples in which the exact entity from the query appears as a subject. The results show similar performance regardless of the complexity of the prompt implied when using cost-effective models such as GPT-3.5 Turbo and Mixtral which return quite satisfactory F1-Scores and high values for Precision. Meanwhile, GPT-4o consistently delivers strong results, by correctly identifying almost all triples from the total benchmark set, achieving Precision close to 1. A few triples from the total set are still omitted, slightly affecting Recall, but the final scores reach optimal thresholds in all cases.

LLMs provide the best results when starting from a single entity for which all information is requested, whether the question is formulated in a general manner or specifies the return for predicate-object pairs.

When the starting element is maintained but the search scope and flexibility are expanded, queries requesting pairs of predicates and objects/attributes derived from a subject (Q5) yield strong results across all evaluated models. This demonstrates the effectiveness of LLMs for straightforward queries, with performance largely dependent on the context preparation within the Graph RAG pipeline, which efficiently handles such queries through its robust entity and relationship selection mechanisms. As a result, LLMs receive a semantically valid context, with a task composed by easy-to-follow logical steps, involving returning the triples as they are, without additional filtering or pattern matching requirements. As foreseen, when the queries are formulated in a discovery-based manner, such as "return everything you know about Entity (E)" (Q7), the results are satisfactory given the clear definition of the entity, as well as the flexibility involved. However, the accuracy is restricted, since Graph RAG sets limits for the entities and relationships returned, detecting only the first k objects that match the query in the retrieval step. This may lead to the omission of potential triples, especially when dealing with SPARQL `DESCRIBE` statements, where the total number of results is significantly large. Therefore, Precision remains strong, as the returned triples are mostly correct, though there are still undiscovered triples, as reflected by Recall results.

Graph RAG encounters difficulties in returning triples when the search is based on the object rather than the subject (o-p-s). Contrary to the favorable results obtained with s-p-o searching, when the direction changes (Q4 queries), the results drop drastically in their precision. The root cause may be the Graph RAG algorithm which is designed to specific query patterns and returns the entities and relationships present in the query, around which the community report is subsequently built. The retrieval mechanism ensures that the returned entities are those present in the query, but it fails in understanding their role, leading to erroneous triples where the searched entity represents a subject and not an object. This means that the context reaching the LLM for composing triples is already incomplete. Therefore, the Graph RAG pipeline is less suitable for such a scenario. However, from the limited constructed context, GPT-4o manages to capture quite good precision results compared to the other two LLMs. In this scenario, Mixtral fails to correctly identify any triples, resulting in a performance score of zero across the first two levels, even if it manages to detect the corresponding predicate. In addition, the results slightly improve when the query is less restrictive, eliminating the role constraint and permitting the detection of a term that can have different positions in the triple (Q2 queries). GPT-4o manages to return high values for precision, approaching 1 for all levels, while showing acceptable values for recall and F1-score. GPT-3.5 and Mixtral return similar moderate results, with scores revolving around 30%, performing about halfway to the top model.

Graph RAG fails to return enough triples when the search is based solely on the predicate or involves finding the predicate. The outcomes are subpar for the scenario in which the query includes only the predicate (Q6), even if the searched spectrum becomes broader: identifying the set of entities linked to the specified relationship. Graph RAG results provide low-quality outcomes, as no entity names are provided to help the subsequent step of relationships matching, as its algorithm is suitable for a combination of the relationship and the entity to be searched in the dataset. As a result, the first k entities that seem pertinent to the query are captured, which proves ineffective since these entities are absent. However, a few arbitrary entities are still returned, with their relationships filtered based on the specified predicate. This use case may fail to discover any relevant triples if the selected entities do not appear in a relationship with the key predicate. Even in the best-case scenario where some elements fulfill this criterion, the number of relationships detected is significantly lower compared to all possible triples from the dataset in which several entities are connected through that predicate. This is the reason why even with GPT-4o, the results remain weak, highlighting the dependence of LLMs on the complexity of query formulation in the context of Graph RAG. Similar limitations are encountered when the source and the target are specified, and the relationship that connects them needs to be retrieved (Q3). Even though the Graph RAG algorithm correctly determines the entities in this scenario, it returns the relationship for each entity separately and does not treat them as neighbors.

Furthermore, the algorithm is restricted to return only a limited number of relationships, so it may skip the relationships that share the two entities in the query. GPT-3.5 and Mixtral struggle to reconstruct triples pieces based on head and tail elements, resulting in relatively poor performance, characterized by low Precision scores, although they exhibit moderate Recall values. These additional steps do not pose an issue for models like GPT-4o which manages to capture optimal values for the metrics, typically in range of $70 - 80\%$.

The choice of model significantly influences the results, with more expensive models typically yielding better performance. In Fig. 6, the F1-scores for each type of query are presented at each level of prompting, grouped by LLM. The cost of the model has implications for the final results as Mixtral returned weaker results compared to the other LLMs for the majority of cases, with the surprising note that its performance was not significantly different from that of GPT-3.5-Turbo. Although GPT-4o involves high costs, it significantly surpasses the performance of the other two LLMs and demonstrates exceptional capabilities in responding to complex queries.

Prompt engineering plays an important role in understanding the task of returning the triples that answer the inputted query. In general, Level 3 prompts which involves Zero-Shot prompting paradigm with detailed series of instructions, achieved the best results across the majority of query type and LLM pairings. The more detailed prompt level, i.e. the ICL One-Shot prompting (Level 4), did not deliver the expected performance, likely due to the variety of query types and associated examples, which led to cognitive overload that implicitly affected the model's ability to generalize. For certain query types, particularly the simpler ones, even Level 2—which only imposes a filtering restriction on the predicate—produced promising results. As expected, Level 1, which includes only a general description of the task, yielded the weakest outputs. Nevertheless,

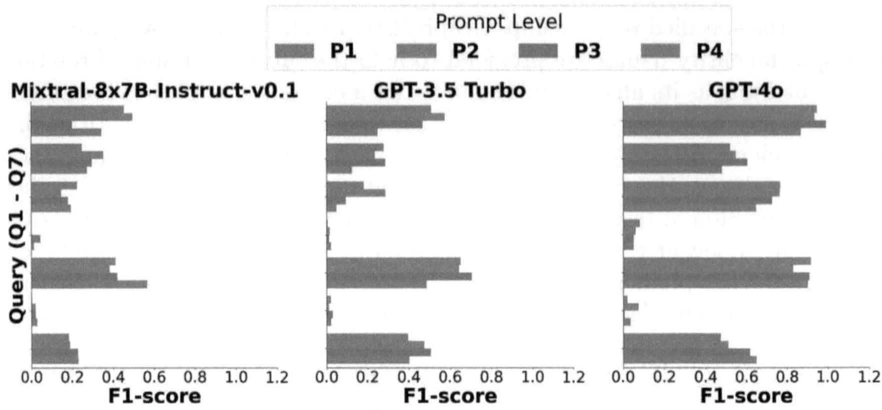

Fig. 6. F1-Scores across prompt levels for each query and LLM

depending on the query type and the LLM used, Level 1 was still able to produce reasonably valid results.

Graph RAG influences the completeness of the extracted triples. With respect to the precision metric, LLMs demonstrated robustness by correctly identifying triples from the benchmark SPARQL set, with challenges arising for omitted triples, which may be related to the prior Graph RAG step in which triples are prepared. Microsoft Graph RAG returns community summaries and the list of entities and relationships, with the completeness directly affected by the type of query addressed. This impacts the recall metric, given that the golden label set is not always entirely captured. However, the F1-scores are adjusted by precision, which yielded strong results for all models, with GPT-4o correctly identifying the majority of triples as they appear in the benchmark across nearly all scenarios. Figure 7 shows the precision differences between the three LLMs, highlighting a clear hierarchy of results.

5 Conclusion

This study evaluates the ability of a selection of open-source and commercial LLMs for responding natural language questions over a domain-specific knowledge graph, through a customized Graph RAG pipeline. LLM results were compared with the deterministic ones supplied by SPARQL queries, across a variation of query patterns and their equivalent natural language questions. Prompts supplied to the LLMs were formulated according with the prompting levels provided by the TELeR taxonomy [12]. Findings highlight differences in performance between the open source and commercial models, as well as shortcomings pertaining to triple navigation direction and the requirement to isolate certain entities and relationships.

By selecting three different LLMs, ranked by cost implications, and refining their prompts using Zero-Shot and One-Shot ICL paradigms, the findings suggest

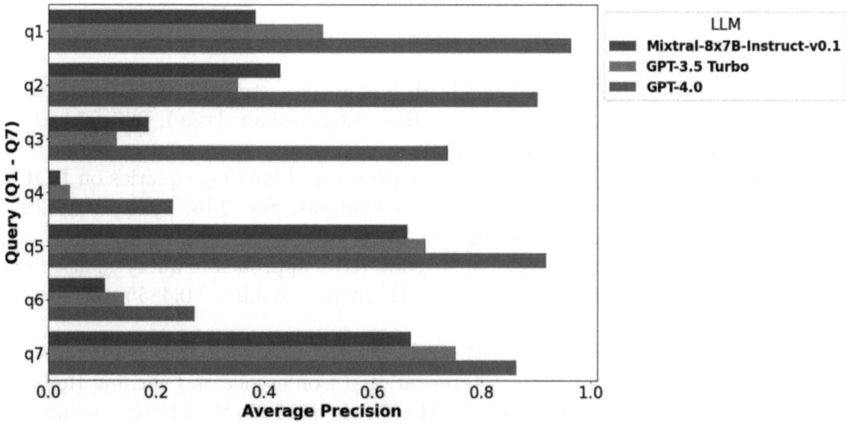

Fig. 7. Query precision comparison across LLMs for each query

that, with appropriate combinations of parameters, it is possible to interact with a knowledge graph using natural language and receive answers nearly as if operating in a programmatic environment where SPARQL queries are executed. The query type and complexity has a significant impact on performance, as when additional reasoning and triple-building steps are required, not all LLMs are able to respond with adequate results. Another limitation lies in constructing the LLM context for query answering, as this process depends directly on the Graph RAG retrieval steps, which proved effective only for certain query types.

The paper has a limited scope in terms of query pattern variety. Instead, it focuses on the experimentation protocol and the Graph RAG pipeline, with the employed query patterns varied by structural considerations. Future work will extend this study to semantically richer patterns, including ABOX/TBOX combinations and domain-specific reasoning. In addition to expanding the query catalog, future experiments will extend the evaluation beyond UMLS by incorporating other datasets relevant for Knowledge Graph Query-Answering. We also plan to investigate alternative Graph RAG algorithms to better handle queries where the current framework showed limitations, with the goal of identifying mechanisms that improve recall, particularly by reducing omitted triples.

This study reports on a Graph RAG pipeline and involves it in probing the answer quality for natural language questions prompted to a selection of open-source and commercial LLMs. The pipeline customizes Microsoft's Graph RAG approach and the experiments employed as graph content the UMLS reference conceptual model. Results have been compared with the deterministic SPARQL queries across a variation of triple query patterns and their equivalent natural language questions formulated over different TELeR [12] prompting levels. Findings highlight differences in performance between the open source and commercial models as well as shortcomings pertaining to triple navigation direction and the requirement to isolate certain entities and relationships.

References

1. Bodenreider, O.: The unified medical language system (UMLS): integrating biomedical terminology. Nucleic Acids Res. **32**(Database-Issue), 267–270 (2004). https://doi.org/10.1093/NAR/GKH061
2. Dolha, D., Buchmann, R.: Experiments with natural language queries on RDF vs. xml-serialized BPMN diagrams. Procedia Comput. Sci. **246**, 3246–3255 (2024). https://doi.org/10.1016/j.procs.2024.09.315
3. Edge, D., et al.: From local to global: a graph RAG approach to query-focused summarization. CoRR abs/2404.16130 (2024). https://doi.org/10.48550/arXiv.2404.16130
4. Fatemi, B., Halcrow, J., Perozzi, B.: Talk like a graph: encoding graphs for large language models. In: The Twelfth International Conference on Learning Representations, ICLR 2024, Vienna, Austria, May 7–11, 2024 (2024). https://openreview.net/forum?id=IuXR1CCrSi
5. He, X., et al.: G-retriever: retrieval-augmented generation for textual graph understanding and question answering. In: Advances in Neural Information Processing Systems 38: Annual Conference on Neural Information Processing Systems 2024, NeurIPS 2024, Vancouver, BC, Canada, December 10–15, 2024 (2024). http://papers.nips.cc/paper_files/paper/2024/hash/efaf1c9726648c8ba363a5c927440529-Abstract-Conference.html
6. Lewis, P., et al.: Retrieval-augmented generation for knowledge-intensive NLP tasks. In: Advances in Neural Information Processing Systems 33: Annual Conference on Neural Information Processing Systems 2020, NeurIPS 2020, December 6–12, 2020, virtual (2020). https://proceedings.neurips.cc/paper/2020/hash/6b493230205f780e1bc26945df7481e5-Abstract.html
7. McCray, A.T.: An upper-level ontology for the biomedical domain. Comp. Funct. Genomics **4**(1), 80–84 (2003). https://doi.org/10.1002/cfg.255
8. McInnes, B., Pedersen, T., Pakhomov, S., Liu, Y., Melton-Meaux, G.: UMLS::similarity: measuring the relatedness and similarity of biomedical concepts. In: Proceedings of the 2013 NAACL HLT Demonstration Session, pp. 28–31. Association for Computational Linguistics, Atlanta, Georgia (2013). https://aclanthology.org/N13-3007/
9. Pan, S., Luo, L., Wang, Y., Chen, C., Wang, J., Wu, X.: Unifying large language models and knowledge graphs: a roadmap. IEEE Trans. Knowl. Data Eng. **36**(7), 3580–3599 (2024). https://doi.org/10.1109/TKDE.2024.3352100
10. Peng, B., et al.: Graph retrieval-augmented generation: A survey. CoRR abs/2408.08921 (2024). https://doi.org/10.48550/arXiv.2408.08921
11. Reyes, J.C.R., de Farias, T.M., Sima, A.C., Kobayashi, N.: SPARQL generation: an analysis on fine-tuning openllama for question answering over a life science knowledge graph. In: 15th International Conference on Semantic Web Applications and Tools for Health Care and Life Sciences, SWAT4HCLS 2024, Leiden, The Netherlands, February 20–26, 2024, pp. 36–45. CEUR Workshop Proceedings, CEUR-WS.org (2024). https://ceur-ws.org/Vol-3890/paper-4.pdf
12. Santu, S.K.K., Feng, D.: Teler: a general taxonomy of LLM prompts for benchmarking complex tasks. In: Bouamor, H., Pino, J., Bali, K. (eds.) Findings of the Association for Computational Linguistics: EMNLP 2023, Singapore, December 6–10, 2023, pp. 14197–14203. Association for Computational Linguistics (2023). https://doi.org/10.18653/V1/2023.FINDINGS-EMNLP.946

13. Sima, A.C., et al.: Bio-soda UX: enabling natural language question answering over knowledge graphs with user disambiguation. Distrib. Parallel Databases **40**(2–3), 409–440 (2022). https://doi.org/10.1007/S10619-022-07414-W
14. Sun, J., et al.: Think-on-graph: deep and responsible reasoning of large language model on knowledge graph. In: The Twelfth International Conference on Learning Representations, ICLR 2024, Vienna, Austria, May 7–11, 2024. OpenReview.net (2024). https://openreview.net/forum?id=nnVO1PvbTv
15. Traag, V., Waltman, L., van Eck, N.J.: From Louvain to Leiden: guaranteeing well-connected communities. Sci. Rep. **9**, 5233 (2019). https://doi.org/10.1038/s41598-019-41695-z

Model-Driven Schema Transformation for Graph Databases

Dominique Hausler[1(✉)], Torben Eckwert[2(✉)], Meike Klettke[1], Michael Guckert[2], and Gabriele Taentzer[3]

[1] University of Regensburg, Data Engineering Group, Bajuwarenstrasse 4, 93053 Regensburg, Germany
{dominique.hausler,meike.klettke}@ur.de

[2] KITE - University of Applied Sciences Mittelhessen, Wiesenstraße 7, 35390 Gießen, Germany
{torben.eckwert,michael.guckert}@kite.thm.de

[3] Philipps-University Marburg, Biegenstraße 10, 35037 Marburg, Germany
taentzer@mathematik.uni-marburg.de

Abstract. In modern, agile software development continuous software evolution is the standard. Software changes can also affect the underlying database and its schema, resulting in schema evolution. Although schema evolution has traditionally been associated with relational databases, similar challenges arise in NoSQL databases, including graph databases. Graph databases are often described as schemaless because they do not enforce a predefined schema at the database level. However, they still have an implicit schema. When a graph database changes, the schema changes are typically implicit and often unknown, which can cause data quality problems. Making the evolutionary process between two schema versions explicit can help migrating the data to conform to the changed schema. In this paper, we present a model-driven approach that uses schema transformation techniques to reconstruct the evolutionary process between two schema versions. Our work is based on Graph Query Language, an ISO standard for graph databases, which makes our approach technology-independent. We present a semi-automated approach that first extracts the implicit schemas as graph models that ensure an abstract representation of the graph schemas. Next, we compare the graph models to identify possible transformations executed from the source and to the target model. An initial evaluation shows that schema extraction and schema transformation are both accurate and require only minimal manual user input.

Keywords: Model-driven engineering · Schema transformation · Schema evolution · Schema extraction · Graph database

1 Introduction

In modern, agile software development continuous software evolution is the standard. Changes to the software can also affect the domain model, which

D. Hausler and T. Eckwert—Joined first authorship.

D. Bork et al. (Eds.): ER 2025, LNCS 16189, pp. 320–338, 2026.
https://doi.org/10.1007/978-3-032-08623-5_17

may require changes to the underlying database and its schema, resulting in schema evolution. Although schema evolution is traditionally associated with relational databases, similar challenges arise in NoSQL databases, including graph databases. Graph databases are known as schemaless, since they do not enforce a predefined schema at the database level. Nevertheless, graph databases still hold an implicit schema.

Graph schema transformation is realized through schema transformation techniques. These techniques refer to the process of converting a source schema into a target schema (see Fig. 1). In contrast, schema evolution starts from a source schema and applies evolution operations. For example, [25] describes specific evolution operations for graph schemas, namely `add`, `rename`, `delete`, `copy`, `move`, `split`, `merge` and `transform`.

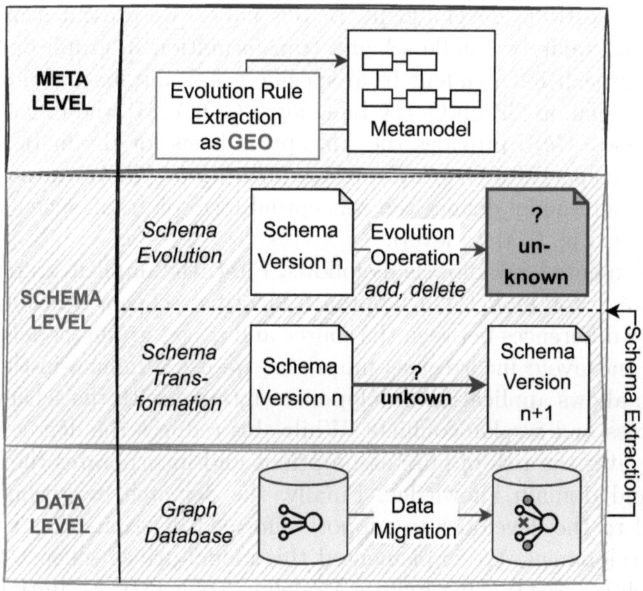

Fig. 1. Intertwine of schema evolution and schema transformation.

Problem Statement. Changes to a graph database often occur during the development process, such as when adapting the data model to evolving requirements or introducing new features. These modifications can affect the implicit schema of the graph database. Making the evolutionary process between two schema versions explicit can support developers in understanding, documenting, and controlling the effects of such changes. By extracting their implicit schemas, an evolution can be visualized and analyzed in terms of the transformation steps required to convert the source schema into the target schema.

Schema transformation, as illustrated in Fig. 1 presents a particularly challenging problem in the context of graph databases. These systems often contain heterogeneous data structures, such as optional properties, which increases the complexity of transformation tasks. The varying degree of disparity between the source and the target schema affects both the number and complexity of the evolution operations required to align them. It also affects the data level at which data migration occurs. Research on schema transformation for graph databases is still limited (see, e.g., [8,17,32]) and it is further complicated by the absence of standardized languages for describing schema transformations.

Contribution. Model-driven engineering [10,19] (MDE) raises the level of abstraction by treating models as primary artifacts. In particular, modeling languages tailored to specific application domains can enhance the productivity and quality of software development. In this paper, we present a model-driven approach to adequately handle schema transformation in graph databases. To make our approach independent from specific graph database technologies, we base our approach on Graph Query Language (GQL) [27], the ISO standard for graph databases. GQL provides the conceptual basis for the meta level of our approach, which specifies Graph Evolution Operations (GEO) based on a metamodel. This metamodel defines the conceptual form of graph schemas based on GQL concepts (Fig. 1: Meta level).

The implemented workflow is as follows: First, the implicit graph schema is extracted as a graph model. Our approach identifies schema transformations by analyzing the differences between the source and target graph models. To reduce uncertainty and avoid incorrect assumptions, we use a human-in-the-loop approach, which allows application developers to interact with the schema transformation process and resolve conflicts. While this reduces the degree of automation, it mitigates the risk of false assumptions and incorporates the developer's intentions and domain knowledge. Finally, the detected evolution operations are returned to the developer to support informed decisions about the further database development. We implemented this model-driven schema transformation approach for Neo4j using Eclipse Modeling Tools [37]. An initial evaluation using three selected Neo4j example datasets shows that schema extraction and transformation are both accurate and require only minimal manual user input.

Outline. The structure of this paper is as follows: Sect. 2 introduces an illustrative example. Section 3 discusses the differences between bottom-up and top-down approaches to schema transformation and presents key concepts of graph databases. Our proposed solution, based on the illustrative example, is presented in Sect. 4. Section 5 describes the implementation of our prototype, which is evaluated in Sect. 6. Section 7 gives a brief overview of the related work. Finally, Sect. 8 concludes the paper and outlines future work.

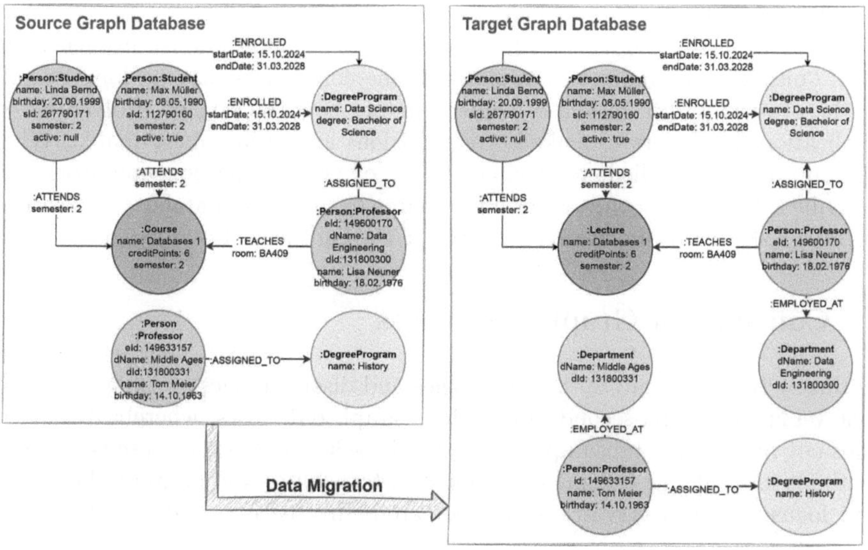

Fig. 2. Source and target database of our illustrative example.

2 Illustrative Example

To illustrate the model-driven schema transformation, we use an example graph database involving two versions of an academic domain that store course data. The source and target schema are shown in Fig. 2. Our goal is to determine the schema transformation and the associated data migration operations.

The source graph database has five distinct node labels. The `Professor` and `Student` nodes exhibit multi-labeling, meaning they are associated with more than one label. Multi-labeling is considered one of the challenges of schema transformation, so proper processing is essential. Furthermore, the example illustrates two kinds of null values: The `degree` property in `DegreeProgram` is optional, while the `active` property in `Student` labeled nodes refers to unknown information. All edges, except `ASSIGNED_TO`, contain properties. In addition, the data set contains different types of constraints. (1) *Type constraints* are defined for the following properties: `startDate` and `endDate` of `ENROLLED` edges and `birthday` of `Person` nodes must be dates. (2) Each `Person` node must have a `name` property. (3) The `sId` and `eId` properties must be keys.

```
GEO1: 'rename' label Course 'of' node 'with' label Course 'to'
    Lecture.
GEO2: 'move' properties dName, dID 'from' node 'with' label
    Professor 'to' node 'with' label Department.
```

Listing 1.1. Two of the Graph evolution operations describing the schema evolution with the evolution language GEO

The target dataset now includes `Department` nodes, and all `Professor` nodes no longer have the properties `dName` and `dId` of departments. Additionally, the label `Course` was renamed to `Lecture`. Some constraints may no longer apply to the evolved graph database. Understanding how the schema evolved allows application developers to make better decisions and ensure data quality. When our approach is applied, it produces a set of graph evolution operators that describe the schema evolution from the source to the target database. A selection of these operators is illustrated in Listing 1.1 using the evolution language GEO.

3 Concepts of Graph Databases

In this section, we analyze the advantages and disadvantages of using a schema-first versus a schema-second approach to graph databases, whereby the latter does not require any presumptions about the schema. Next, we discuss existing methods for realizing schema evolution and transformation in graph databases. Our focus is on property graphs as they are addressed by the ISO GQL.

3.1 Schema-First vs. Schema-Second Approach

NoSQL database systems, such as JSON and graph databases, provide the ability to manage schemas and semantic constraints. These extensions allow the usage of NoSQL databases with a schema-first approach, which involves defining the structure of entities, data types, and constraints. Since the schema management component checks all added data, a homogeneous dataset is created, which reduces the number of errors resulting from reorganization tasks. In case of a schema-second approach users can directly start inserting data without predefining a schema, causing an increased degree of heterogeneity, such as optional properties, or typos, since no schema management mechanism is utilized. In addition, a growing demand to reorganize and restructure the dataset emerges. Thus, an explicit schema must be derived from the data to ensure the quality of the graph data and to make constraints explicit.

We consider the latter for our approach, as it is consider to be the sate-of-the-art usage of schemaless databases. With such a bottom-up usage, the complexity of the transformation task increases because no preliminary considerations about the schema were made.

3.2 Schema Evolution and Schema Transformation

Evolution operations for graph databases such as moving a property, directly cause data migration. Data migration and schema evolution tasks may include optimization, reorganization of the data, or adjustments due to changes in requirements. When comparing the source and target graph databases at the data level (green box in Fig. 1), the following evolution operations can be identified: (1) adding nodes with its edges, colored blue, and (2) deleting a node and its edge, shown by the red cross.

The schema level (i.e. the blue box in Fig. 1) illustrates that both schema evolution and transformation return the same outcome, but differ in the known components. Schema evolution has the goal to obtain the target schema by a known source schema and specific evolution operations. In contrast, for schema transformation, both the source and target schemas are given and the executed evolution operations are sought. Our approach focuses on transformation tasks by extracting the evolution operations conducted between schemas to introduce transparency on the conducted changes between schema versions.

4 Model-Driven Schema Transformation

In this section, we present our approach to model-driven schema transformation in graph databases. This presentation is based on the example in Sect. 2.

The key idea of model-driven schema transformation is the introduction of a meta level, as shown in Fig. 1, which guarantees a generalizable approach. Schema transformation and evolution are handled directly based on technology-independent schema models. The meta level contains our metamodel, which controls schema transformation; it is shown in gray in Fig. 1. Based on the metamodel, rules can be defined to specify valid changes of schema models. First, the source and target models are compared with each other to identify all changes. Then, model-based rule extraction is used to detect all executed evolution operations. The meta level enables the schema transformation process to be formulated in a reusable, technology-independent way.

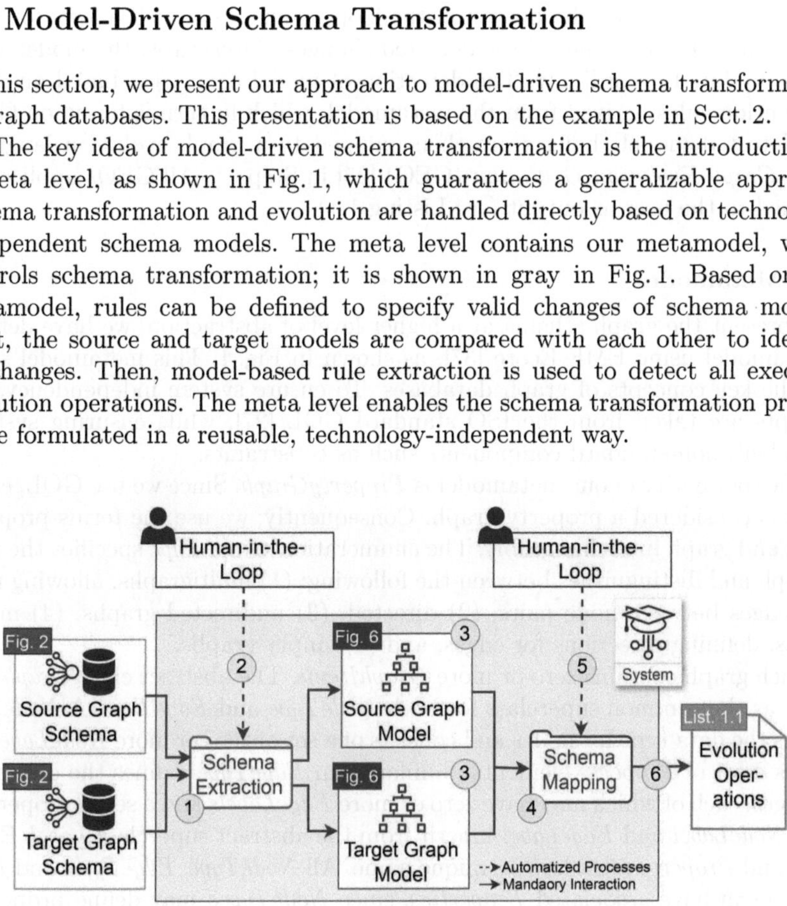

Fig. 3. Workflow, showing all components of the model-driven schema transformation.

Workflow. An overview of the implemented workflow for model-driven schema transformation is shown in Fig. 3. Two versions of a graph database are provided as input at the data level (green boxes). Since graph databases are typically schemaless, schema extraction is required for Step ①. The implicit schema is extracted and transformed into graph models (see Step ③) that conform to our metamodel (the gray box in Fig. 1). The schema extraction result for our example is shown in Fig. 6. Schema extraction is actually performed twice, once on the source database and once on the target database. If multi-labeling is detected, any resulting ambiguities are resolved by the human-in-the-loop (the red box in Fig. 3) in Step ②, which allows for manual adjustments. These adjustments include assigning properties to an appropriate label (see Subsect. 4.2). In Step ④, the differences between the two graph models are analyzed. The detected changes are then forwarded to the human-in-the-loop (Step ⑤), which allows for user validation and adjustment of the detected changes. Afterwards, the model mapping is updated accordingly. The detection of model changes is based on a set of evolution rules derived from the metamodel, which in turn is based on GQL. The detected model changes are then mapped to a graph evolution language called *Graph Evolution Operation* (GEO) [25] in Step ⑥. All GEOs applied are returned to the user as output (see Listing 1.1).

4.1 Metamodel

To represent the graph schema at a higher level of abstraction, we have defined a metamodel using EMF Ecore [37], as shown in Fig. 4. This metamodel specifies the key concepts of graph databases. To ensure system independency, the concepts are taken from the ISO standard GQL [27], while ensuring system-dependent, non-standard components such as constraints.

The root entity of our metamodel is *PropertyGraph*. Since we use GQL, every graph is considered a property graph. Consequently, we use the terms property graph and graph interchangeably. The enumeration *GraphType* specifies the type of graph and distinguishes between the following: (1) multigraphs, allowing multiple edges between node pairs, (2) directed, (3) undirected graphs, (4) mixed graphs, defining directions for edges, and (5) empty graphs.

Each graph contains zero or more *GraphItems*. The abstract class *GraphItem* serves as the common superclass for both *NodeType* and *EdgeType*. A *NodeType* defines the data type for nodes and consists of a set of zero or more *NodeLabels* as well as a set of *Property* elements. Similarly, an *EdgeType* defines the data type for edges, each of which may have zero or more *EdgeLabels* and a set of properties. Both *NodeLabel* and *EdgeLabel* inherit from the abstract superclass *Label*. Every *Label* and *Property* must have a unique name. All *NodeType*, *EdgeType*, and *Label* entities can have associated *Properties*, since *NodeTypes* may define properties that are not explicitly specified by any associated label. Each *Property* has a value type, represented by the abstract class *PropertyValueType* and its concrete subclasses. The value type can be any supported property value type. If the type cannot be determined, a *UnionType* is used to allow values of arbitrary types. Each *PropertyValueType* may have additional attributes specific to the type. For example, a *string type* has a *minlength* and a *maxlength*.

Although graph databases are schemaless, they often provide mechanisms to define constraints, which are not included in the standard, particularly when a

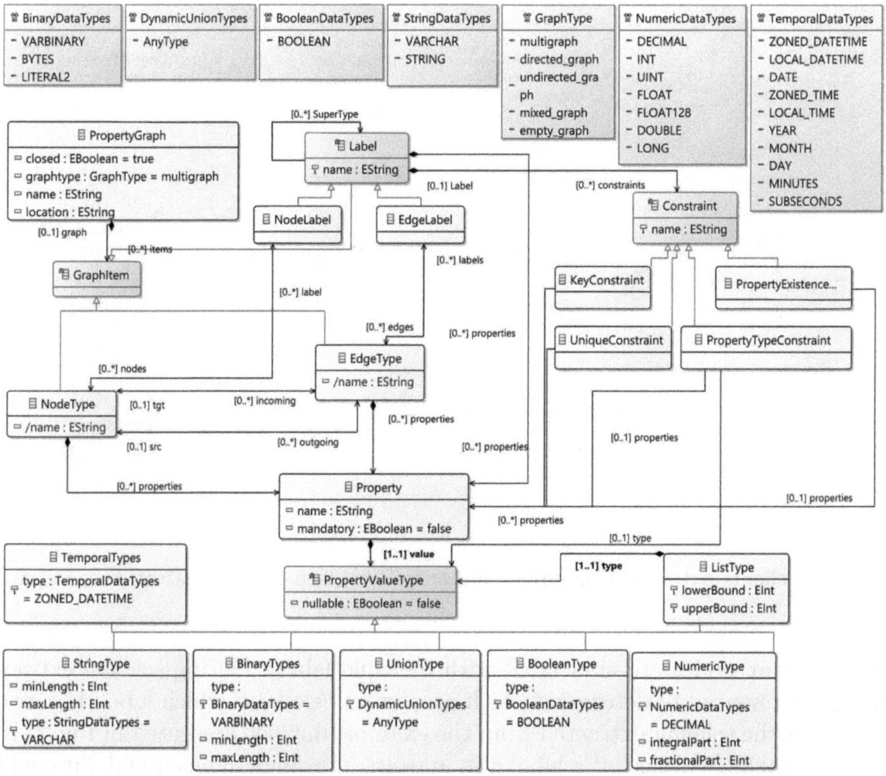

Fig. 4. Graph database metamodel.

certain degree of structure is required. Our metamodel supports different types of constraints, which are represented by the abstract class *Constraint* and its concrete subclasses. Each *Constraint* has a *name*, which serves as a unique identifier. The four subclasses represent the different kind of constraints:

- *UniqueConstraint*: Unique property values across all specified entity types.
- *PropertyExistenceConstraint*: Requires existence of a given property within the stated entity type.
- *PropertyTypeConstraint*: Enforces that a property has a specific data type for all outlined entity types.
- *KeyConstraint*: Combines existence and uniqueness requirements.

4.2 Schema Extraction

The implicit schemas of both database versions (see Fig. 2) are extracted and transformed into instances of our metamodel (see Fig. 3 Step ①). This process presents several challenges. For example, in the example dataset, two `Professor`

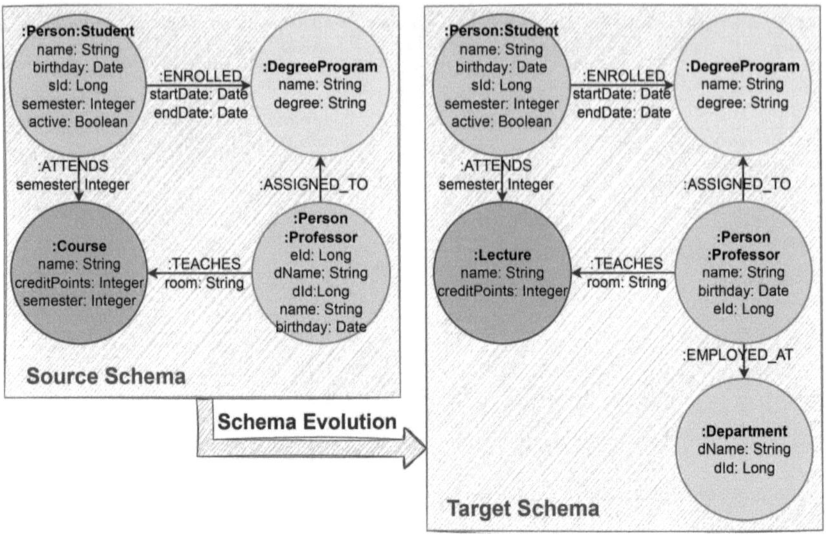

Fig. 5. Schema extraction, mapping and transformation of the illustrative example.

and `Student` nodes are associated with multiple labels. During schema extraction, it is essential to determine which properties belong to which label. Figure 5 visualizes the schema extracted from the example dataset presented in Fig. 2. In a multi-labeling context, if a label also appears in a single-labeled node, it could serve as a point of reference. However, such a node may not be present in the dataset. In our dataset, nodes labeled `Person` never occur without edges. However, all nodes that include this label, share the properties `name` and `birthday`. The constraints on these properties offer valuable insights, since they are associated with the `Person` label (see Paragraph Constraints in Sect. 2). Although this information could support a partially automated solution, such as a best-guess algorithm, we prefer a human-in-the-loop approach (see Fig. 3 Step ②). This approach provides greater control to the user, eliminating the need for further system-sided validation. Moreover, the challenge of possibly optional properties for the `Person` label can only be solved by a human-in-the-loop approach, since there are no single-labeled `Person` nodes in the dataset.

After the user has solved ambiguous cases, the graph models are created automatically. Figure 6 shows an excerpt of the graph model extracted from the source database on the left, and the model of the evolved graph database on the right. The evolved version reflects the conducted changes. In particular, a new node label `Department` was introduced, and both the department id `dId` and its name `dname` were moved to this new label. Additionally, the label `Course` was renamed `Lecture`.

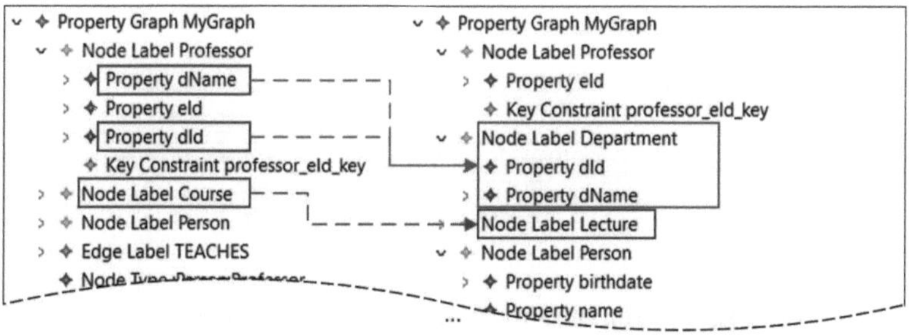

Fig. 6. Graph database model: The original model is displayed on the left, while the edited model version is displayed on the right.

4.3 Schema Comparison

The next step is to analyze the differences between the two model versions (Fig. 3 Step ③). We use SiLift [28] for model comparison since it does not only compare models but also computes high-level change sets. The comparison process consists of three successive steps.

First, a matcher identifies pairs of corresponding elements that are considered to represent the *same* entity. Matching can be challenging. For example, in Fig. 5, the department name `dName` was moved to the `Department` node, allowing for different interpretations. If it is seen as a `move` operation, matching both elements would be correct. Conversely, if it is treated as an `add` operation, matching would be incorrect. Therefore, as with schema extraction, the user is prompted to review the results of the matching and, if necessary, modify them by adding correspondences for unrecognized elements (Fig. 3 Step ⑤). The outcome is a list of correspondences between the two models.

Second, a difference derivator identifies single-type changes based on established correspondences. These changes are atomic modifications that cannot be decomposed into smaller editing steps, such as `create` or `delete`. In practice, user editing operations often consist of multiple single-type changes, because even seemingly simple edits can result in numerous underlying modifications.

Therefore, in the third step, we use SiLift's Semantic Lifting Engine to group changes into *semantic change sets*. Each set represents the effect of a user-level editing operation. In order to adapt SiLift to our modeling language, we need a set of edit rules that define the available editing operations and specify how the structure or content of a model can be modified or updated. These rules describe the permitted or intended changes when evolving a model. The rule set, which is specific to the metamodel used (Sect. 4.1) and was created once for our setup; it does not need to be redefined for each use.

Figure 7 shows two exemplary edit rules specified with Henshin (introduced in 5), a model transformation engine for EMF models. The simple edit rule `create Node Label` (top) identifies the creation of a new `NodeLabel` element. The lower rule illustrates how the `delete` and `add` operations are combined to represent a `moveProperty` operation. Each object is annotated as `preserve`,

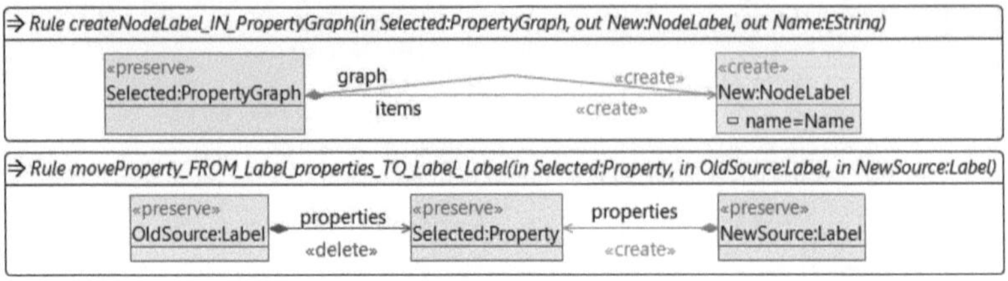

Fig. 7. Edit rules for graph database schemata.

delete, or create. When a Property is moved, the reference to the original label is deleted, and a new reference to the target label is created. SiLift uses these rules to search the list of correspondences for patterns that match the criteria and conditions defined by the respective edit rule. If a pattern matches, the corresponding single-type changes are combined into one edit operation.

4.4 Evolution Language

SiLift compares models to produce a symmetric-difference model containing all correspondences, differences, and grouped single-type changes, called *semantic change sets*. These changes represent the edits between the two models.

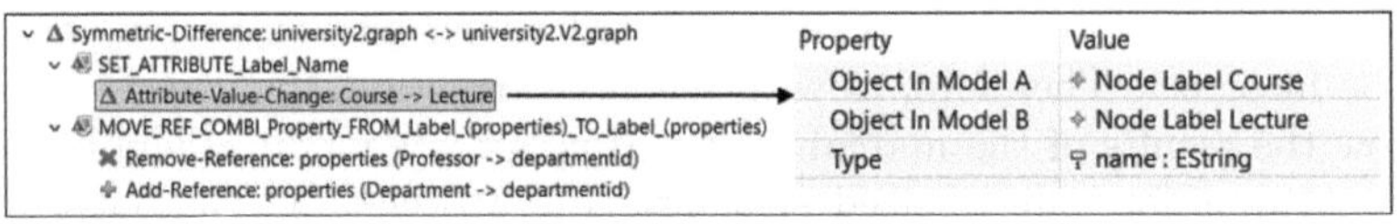

Fig. 8. Symmetric difference model.

Figure 8 shows part of the symmetric difference model for our illustrative example (Fig. 2). The set *SET_ATTRIBUTE_Label_name* represents the renaming of Course to Lecture. The property "Object in Model A" refers to the modified element in the original version, and "Object in Model B" refers to the corresponding element in the evolved version. The *Type* property indicates which aspect of the element was changed. In our case, the value of name. The second set shown, describes the relocation of the property dId from Professor to Department. Accordingly, the reference of this property is moved as well.

In the next step, these sets are mapped to their corresponding GEOs (see Fig. 3, Step ⑥). This approach is beneficial over using commands, as GQL lacks a dedicated evolution language. Without GEO, expertise in GQL is required to understand complex operations. GEO is designed to describe evolution operations in a clear and intuitive manner. A full list of all supported GEOs can be found in[1]. The simple edit rule shown at the top of Fig. 8 is translated

[1] GEO file: https://zenodo.org/records/15958412.

into a `rename label` operation. The second edit rule represents a `move` operation, which is considered a complex evolution operation. Such operations can be decomposed into a combination of single-type operations, namely `add`, `rename` and `delete`. The mapping results in the two GEOs shown in Listing 1.1. The first GEO corresponds to the `rename` operation, while the second represents the `move` operation. Finally, these GEOs are visualized as output for the application user.

5 Implementation

We implemented our approach for Neo4j[2] because of its widespread use in industry and research. Moreover, GQL is based on the Neo4j's query language, Cypher, making it an ideal candidate. Additionally, we used the APOC[3] (Awesome Procedures on Cypher) library as the basis for our schema extraction algorithm. APOC provides access to useful procedures and functions that extend the use of the Cypher query language into areas such as data integration, graph algorithms, and data conversion. Our prototype is implemented as a feature for the Eclipse platform. We did so, because the Eclipse Modeling Tools and the Eclipse Modeling Framework [37] provide a powerful platform for creating, editing, and managing structured data models. EMF provides a comprehensive framework for code generation and model handling, making it highly efficient for model-driven development. For model comparison, we used Henshin[4] and the Silift [28] framework. Henshin supports in-place model transformations, enabling changes directly within the existing model structure. We chose the SiLift framework for model comparison, since SiLift can group low-level changes into *semantic change sets*, each of which represents the impact of a user-level editing operation. The source code of our implementation is available in our GitHub repository[5].

Our current implementation supports the key functionalities of model-driven graph transformation. However, some features and system-specific refinements have yet to be implemented. As described in Sect. 4.1, the metamodel design aligns with the GQL standard. Using this standard ensures that our model-driven approach is domain-independent and allows for the integration of various graph database systems. However, several aspects of the ISO standard are not directly applicable when working with a specific graph database. For example, Neo4j enforces exactly one label per relationship, whereas GQL allows zero to many. Such system-specific constraints must be considered in future refinements. In addition, some complex schema transformation operations, such as copying or splitting of nodes, are not currently accurately detected.

---

2 https://neo4j.com/.
3 https://neo4j.com/docs/apoc/5/introduction/.
4 https://projects.eclipse.org/projects/modeling.emft.henshin.
5 https://github.com/tekw24/evolveDB.

6 Initial Evaluation

We evaluated the effectiveness of our approach in handling schema extraction and transformation using three Neo4j example graph databases[6].

Set Up. To ensure diversity, we selected three sample databases from the Neo4j example collection that differ in both schema size and number of values. Table 1 provides an overview. We applied realistic operations to each dataset to simulate typical schema changes and obtain the evolved version. Specifically, six evolution operations were executed on the *Twitch* dataset, while the *Pole* dataset was evolved with five operations. Eight operations were carried out on the *Bloom* dataset. Taking advantage of real-world user behavior, the `add` operation was executed with the highest frequency across all datasets, followed by `rename` and `delete` (for single-type), `copy`, `move` and `split` (for multi-type operations).

Table 1. Data and schema statistics for each dataset used in the evaluation

	Data Statistics			**Schema Statistics**			
	Total Nodes	**Total Edges**	**Total Properties**	**Node Labels**	**Edge Labels**	**Property keys**	$\sum$
Twitch	4.680.870	10.076.938	4.710.878	10	15	13	38
Pole	61.521	105.840	200.364	22	35	34	91
Bloom	30.960	29.731	101.353	36	38	60	134

RQ1: How Accurate is the Schema Extraction from a Given Graph Database? Accurate results require that the user correctly assigns properties to the appropriate labels in cases of multi-labeling. This is a prerequisite for the subsequent automatic schema extraction. After the assignment, the duration of automatic schema extraction increases with the size of the database. The largest dataset was extracted in under 20 s. *With the human-in-the-loop support, the system can achieve 100% accuracy in schema extraction.*

RQ2: How Accurate is the Schema Transformation? A detailed quantification of the evaluation results is given in Table 2. In addition to the total number of executed operations ($\sum$), the number of evolution operations that were automatically identified is shown by ⚙. The ✗ symbol indicates that no evolution operator of this type was applied to the source version. 👤 represents operations requiring additional manual assignments from the user. The `split` and `copy` operations are not reliably detected by the system. This outcome was expected, as the system currently lacks full support for these complex evolution operators. In such cases, user input is necessary to resolve ambiguities and ensure the transformation is interpreted correctly. *With the human-in-the-loop support, the system can achieve 100% accuracy in schema transformation.*

[6] https://github.com/neo4j-graph-examples.

Table 2. Number and kind of executed evolution operations together with the results of the schema extraction and schema mapping

	Executed Evolution Operations																		Results				
	Single-type									Multi-type									Extr.		Mapping		
	add			rename			delete			copy			move			split			S	T			
	Σ	⚙	👤	Σ	⚙	👤	Σ	⚙	👤	Σ	⚙	👤	Σ	⚙	👤	Σ	⚙	👤	👤	👤	Σ	⚙	👤
Twitch	3	3	0	1	1	0	✗	✗	✗	✗	✗	✗	1	1	0	✗	✗	✗	1	1	38	37	1
Pole	2	2	0	1	1	0	2	2	0	1	0	1	✗	✗	✗	✗	✗	✗	0	0	88	82	6
Bloom	5	5	0	2	2	0	✗	✗	✗	✗	✗	✗	1	1	0	1	0	1	1	2	134	131	3

RQ3: What Proportion of Manual User Input is Required for Schema Extraction and Transformation? More multi-labeled nodes require more user input for property assignment. Based on real-world data, our datasets show that multi-labeling rarely occurs. Specifically, the source graphs contain only two cases of multi-labeling, while the target graphs contain an additional instance, resulting in three cases of multi-labeling in the target graph and five cases in total. During schema comparison, the user is prompted to review and modify the matching results by adding correspondences for unrecognized elements, if necessary. Consequently, the interaction rate indicates the proportion of unmatched or incorrectly matched elements. Table 1 summarizes the number of element pairs that could potentially form correspondences between the source and target models in the rightmost column. Table 2 shows information about schema extraction and transformation results in the five rightmost columns. The *Twitch* example includes 38 correspondences, 37 were automatically identified correctly, and one element pair was missing, resulting in an interaction rate of 2.63%. The source model of the *Pole* example contains 91 elements. Due to deleted elements in the target model, only 88 potential correspondences remained. Of these, 82 were automatically identified correctly, five were not detected, and one pair was incorrectly matched. This results in an interaction rate of 6.81%. The *Bloom* example contains 134 expected correspondences. Of these, 131 were identified automatically. Three element pairs were not recognized, resulting in an interaction rate of 2.23%. The evaluation also revealed that applying an increasing number of changes to a single element in the *Pole* example leads to a higher likelihood of unrecognized or incorrect correspondences. Of the three examples, five cases of multi-labeling required user interaction during the schema extraction. Ten out of 260 correspondences required user intervention during schema mapping, corresponding to an overall interaction rate of 3.84%. *These findings show that although most of the work can be automated, carefully reviewing the extraction and mapping results is crucial, as undetected or incorrect correspondences can compromise the accuracy of the schema transformation.*

Threats to Validity. One potential threat is that our evaluation was limited to three example databases, which constrains the generalizability of the results.

Additionally, the evolution operations applied to the graph databases were defined by the authors and may not accurately reflect the full range of changes encountered in other systems or contexts. Consequently, the findings may not be directly transferable to different settings. Moreover, the authors performed the required user interaction for schema extraction and mapping, as well as the validation of the resulting correspondences. To address this issue, we deliberately applied a diverse set of evolution operators and had two authors validate the results independently. Future studies should incorporate graph databases with real-world data to ensure broader coverage of schema transformation scenarios and to validate the generalizability of the results.

7 Related Work

This section discusses related work on *graph schemas*, *schema extraction*, *schema evolution*, *schema transformation*, and *model-driven engineering*.

Graph Schema. The most renowned paper on graph schemas is [3], which emphasizes the necessity of formalized schema descriptions and proposes *PG-Schema*. The importance of schema constraints for query optimization is discussed in [35]. [23] uses a formalization of the schema through description logic. In addition, ensuring data quality through constraints is done in [33], with [31] focusing on integrity constraints. Regular path constraints to measure inconsistency are presented in [22]. Work has been done on keys [4] and triggers for property graphs [14]. An extendable schema language is presented in [6]. *All these works highlight the necessity of deriving schemas with constraints for semi-structured data in schema-less graph databases.* To this end, we present a metamodel derived from the GQL standard, and use it for model-based schema extraction.

Schema Extraction. Several papers focus on graph schema extraction with a schema-second method, e.g., [9,16,20]. The relevance of schema extraction for NoSQL databases, here document stores, is emphasized in [30]. *Extracting the schemas of given source and target graph data is a prerequisite for schema transformation.* In contrast to other approaches, we use a conceptual model – our metamodel – to transform the graph schema into a schema model of the graph. Consequently, (1) raising the abstraction, (2) ensuring technology-independence by integrating GQL and (3) integrating a human-in-the-loop.

Schema Transformation. Schema mapping is often discussed when migrating data between a NoSQL and a relational database, as described in [2,5,13]. [34] shows how to transform data warehouses which are based on multidimensional conceptual models into graph models. To overcome the absence of a schema description standard, `FLASc` is presented in [36], which defines a schema through formal algebra. We also use a model independent of graph database technology to represent a graph schema, but our approach is closer to implementation. [32] focuses on schema transformation between RDF and property graphs. [1] illustrates a transformation approach by using a meta level. *However, a domain-independent language for implementing schema transformations is still missing.* Our metamodel, which performs model-driven schema transformation, is technology-independent and guarantees standard conformity. GEO [25], the language of graph evolution operations, is based on this metamodel and is also technology-independent.

Schema Evolution. Work on RDF-Graph is shown in [7,15], nevertheless, we focus on property graphs for which GQL was designed. The importance of adequately handling schema evolution is evident from the variety of database systems for which evolution has been considered. [18,21,40] focus on relational, and [38] on document stores. `MigCast` [26] can handle data migration tasks for evolving NoSQL databases. [39] presents an approach for adapting wide-column stores when an underlying conceptual model evolves. `Nautilus`, a tool for evolving graph databases is presented in [24]. The preservation of constraints during evolutionary tasks is presented in [12]. [11] proposes using a graph schema to properly model heterogeneous web data and manage evolution through version control. *These approaches to schema evolution are all technology-dependent, so they cannot be directly reused for other graph database technologies.* In contrast, our approach to schema transformation is applicable to all graph databases because it is based on GQL. It also forms the basis for technology-independent schema evolution.

Model-Driven Engineering. Since we use a model-driven approach, we also analyze approaches that use model-driven techniques for schema evolution, transformation, and data migration. [41] extracts schemas to JSON files, which are then mapped to Ecore. This approach aims to transform schemas to improve the data quality of an extracted schema. The relevance of a model-driven approach for handling transformation tasks, especially in at the meta level, is demonstrated in [29], whereas our approach specializes on graph databases by using an abstract meta level containing a domain-independent meta model to perform schema transformation. *Both approaches are model-driven but not GQL compatible.* This is in contrast to our approach.

8 Conclusion

Changes to a graph database can affect the implicitly given schema, which may lead to data quality issues. Explicitly documenting the evolution between two schema versions can help developers understand, document, and control the effects of such changes, as well as migrate the graph data to conform to the updated schema. In this paper, we present a model-driven approach and tool to reconstruct the evolution between two implicitly given schema versions of a graph database. With this tool, developers do not need to manually construct schema transformations. To ensure independence from specific graph database technologies, our metamodel is based on the recent GQL standard.

The initial evaluation of our model-driven approach revealed that schema extraction and transformation are both accurate and require only minimal user intervention. However, the results also underscore the importance of carefully reviewing the matching results, as undetected or incorrect correspondences can compromise the accuracy. Consequently, we integrated a human-in-the-loop approach, allowing users to validate the results and make manual adjustments.

In the future, we plan to improve the proposed solution by addressing its current limitations. Currently, during schema extraction, users need to decide which properties belong to which label in cases of multi-labeling. To reduce manual input further, we plan to integrate an algorithm that provides suggestions to support this decision. Based on our initial evaluation, we are confident that our approach has great potential for practical application. We plan to demonstrate this by applying it to various real-world graph databases in the future.

Acknowledgments. The work of Dominique Hausler has been funded by Deutsche Forschungsgemeinschaft (German Research Foundation) – 552691270.

References

1. Abdelhédi, F., Brahim, A.A., Atigui, F., Zurfluh, G.: UMLtoNoSQL: automatic transformation of conceptual schema to NoSQL databases. In: AICCSA, pp. 272–279. IEEE Computer Society (2017)
2. Aftab, Z., Iqbal, W., Almustafa, K.M., Bukhari, F., Abdullah, M.: Automatic NoSQL to relational database transformation with dynamic schema mapping. Sci. Program. **2020**, 8813350:1–8813350:13 (2020)
3. Angles, R., et al.: PG-schema: schemas for property graphs. Proc. ACM Manag. Data **1**(2), 198:1–198:25 (2023)
4. Angles, R., et al.: PG-keys: keys for property graphs. In: SIGMOD Conference, pp. 2423–2436. ACM (2021)
5. Bansal, N., Sachdeva, S., Awasthi, L.K.: Query-based denormalization using hypergraph (QBDNH): a schema transformation model for migrating relational to NoSQL databases. Knowl. Inf. Syst. **66**(1), 681–722 (2024)
6. Beeren, N., Fletcher, G.: A formal design framework for practical property graph schema languages. In: EDBT, pp. 478–484. OpenProceedings.org (2023)
7. Bobed, C., Maillot, P., Cellier, P., Ferré, S.: Data-driven assessment of structural evolution of RDF graphs. Semant. Web **11**(5), 831–853 (2020)
8. Boneva, I., Groz, B., Hidders, J., Murlak, F., Staworko, S.: Static analysis of graph database transformations. In: PODS, pp. 251–261. ACM (2023)
9. Bonifati, A., et al.: DiscoPG: property graph schema discovery and exploration. Proc. VLDB Endow. **15**(12), 3654–3657 (2022)
10. Brambilla, M., Cabot, J., Wimmer, M.: Model-Driven Software Engineering in Practice. Morgan & Claypool Publishers, San Rafael (2017)

11. Braunschweig, K., Thiele, M., Lehner, W.: A flexible graph-based data model supporting incremental schema design and evolution. In: Harth, A., Koch, N. (eds.) ICWE 2011. LNCS, vol. 7059, pp. 302–306. Springer, Heidelberg (2012). https://doi.org/10.1007/978-3-642-27997-3_29
12. Calvanese, D., Ortiz, M., Simkus, M.: Evolving graph databases under description logic constraints. In: Description Logics. CEUR Workshop Proceedings, vol. 1014, pp. 120–131. CEUR-WS.org (2013)
13. Ceresnák, R., Dudás, A., Matiasko, K., Kvet, M.: Mapping rules for schema transformation: SQL to NoSQL and back. In: IDT, pp. 52–58. IEEE (2021)
14. Ceri, S., Bernasconi, A., Gagliardi, A., Martinenghi, D., Bellomarini, L., Magnanimi, D.: PG-triggers: triggers for property graphs. In: SIGMOD Conference Companion, pp. 373–385. ACM (2024)
15. Chabin, J., Eichler, C., Ferrari, M.H., Hiot, N.: Graph rewriting rules for RDF database evolution: optimizing side-effect processing. Int. J. Web Inf. Syst. **17**(6), 622–644 (2021)
16. Comyn-Wattiau, I., Akoka, J.: Model driven reverse engineering of NoSQL property graph databases: the case of Neo4j. In: IEEE BigData, pp. 453–458. IEEE Computer Society (2017)
17. Dumbrava, S., Oudemans, M.W.M., Ozkan, B.K.: Fuzzing graph database applications with graph transformations. In: ICGT. Lecture Notes in Computer Science, vol. 15720, pp. 135–156. Springer, Heidelberg (2025). https://doi.org/10.1007/978-3-031-94706-3_7
18. Eckwert, T., Guckert, M., Taentzer, G.: EvolveDB: a tool for model driven schema evolution. In: MoDELS (Companion), pp. 61–65. ACM (2022)
19. Fowler, M.: Domain-Specific Languages. Pearson Education, Boston (2010)
20. Frozza, A.A., Jacinto, S.R., dos Santos Mello, R.: An approach for schema extraction of NoSQL graph databases. In: IRI, pp. 271–278. IEEE (2020)
21. Giachos, F., Pantelidis, N., Batsilas, C., Zarras, A.V., Vassiliadis, P.: Parallel lives diagrams for co-evolving communities and their application to schema evolution. In: ER (Companion). CEUR Workshop Proceedings, vol. 3618. CEUR-WS.org (2023)
22. Grant, J., Parisi, F.: On measuring inconsistency in graph databases with regular path constraints. Artif. Intell. **335**, 104197 (2024)
23. Gutiérrez-Basulto, V., Gutowski, A., Ibáñez-García, Y.A., Murlak, F.: Containment of graph queries modulo schema. Proc. ACM Manag. Data **2**(2), 77 (2024)
24. Hausler, D., Klettke, M.: Nautilus: implementation of an evolution approach for graph databases. In: MoDELS (Companion), pp. 11–15. ACM (2024)
25. Hausler, D., Klettke, M., Störl, U.: A language for graph database evolution and its implementation in Neo4j. In: ER (Companion). CEUR Workshop Proceedings, vol. 3618. CEUR-WS.org (2023)
26. Hillenbrand, A., Levchenko, M., Störl, U., Scherzinger, S., Klettke, M.: MigCast: putting a price tag on data model evolution in NoSQL data stores. In: SIGMOD Conference, pp. 1925–1928. ACM (2019)
27. Information technology—Database languages—GQL. Standard, International Organization for Standardization, Geneva, CH (2024)
28. Kehrer, T., Kelter, U., Ohrndorf, M., Sollbach, T.: Understanding model evolution through semantically lifting model differences with SiLift. In: 2012 28th IEEE International Conference on Software Maintenance (ICSM), pp. 638–641. IEEE (2012)

29. Khelladi, D.E., Kretschmer, R., Egyed, A.: Change propagation-based and composition-based co-evolution of transformations with evolving metamodels. In: MoDELS, pp. 404–414. ACM (2018)
30. Klettke, M., Störl, U., Scherzinger, S.: Schema extraction and structural outlier detection for JSON-based NoSQL data stores. In: BTW. LNI, vol. P-241, pp. 425–444. GI (2015)
31. Pokorný, J., Valenta, M., Kovacic, J.: Integrity constraints in graph databases. Procedia Comput. Sci. **109**, 975–981 (2017)
32. Rabbani, K., Lissandrini, M., Bonifati, A., Hose, K.: Transforming RDF graphs to property graphs using standardized schemas. Proc. ACM Manag. Data **2**(6), 242:1–242:25 (2024)
33. Reina, F., Huf, A., Presser, D., Siqueira, F.: Modeling and enforcing integrity constraints on graph databases. In: Hartmann, S., Küng, J., Kotsis, G., Tjoa, A.M., Khalil, I. (eds.) DEXA 2020. LNCS, vol. 12391, pp. 269–284. Springer, Cham (2020). https://doi.org/10.1007/978-3-030-59003-1_18
34. Sellami, A., Nabli, A., Gargouri, F.: Transformation of data warehouse schema to NoSQL graph data base. In: Abraham, A., Cherukuri, A.K., Melin, P., Gandhi, N. (eds.) ISDA 2018 2018. AISC, vol. 941, pp. 410–420. Springer, Cham (2020). https://doi.org/10.1007/978-3-030-16660-1_41
35. Sharma, C., Genevès, P., Gesbert, N., Layaïda, N.: Schema-based query optimisation for graph databases. Proc. ACM Manag. Data **3**(1), 72:1–72:29 (2025)
36. Sharma, C., Sinha, R.: FLASc: a formal algebra for labeled property graph schema. Autom. Softw. Eng. **29**(1), 37 (2022)
37. Steinberg, D., Budinsky, F., Merks, E., Paternostro, M.: EMF: Eclipse Modeling Framework. Pearson Education, Boston (2008)
38. Störl, U., Klettke, M.: Darwin: a data platform for schema evolution management and data migration. In: EDBT/ICDT Workshops. CEUR Workshop Proceedings, vol. 3135. CEUR-WS.org (2022)
39. Suárez-Otero, P., Mior, M.J., Suárez-Cabal, M.J., Tuya, J.: CoDEvo: column family database evolution using model transformations. J. Syst. Softw. **203**, 111743 (2023)
40. Vassiliadis, P., Karakasidis, A.: Time-related patterns of schema evolution. In: EDBT, pp. 310–323. OpenProceedings.org (2025)
41. Wischenbart, M., et al.: User profile integration made easy: model-driven extraction and transformation of social network schemas. In: WWW (Companion Volume), pp. 939–948. ACM (2012)

Applications of Conceptual Modeling

Ontology-Informed Design of Legal Visualisations

Paul Johannesson(✉) and Jöran Lindeberg

Department of Computer and Systems Sciences (DSV), Stockholm University, Stockholm, Sweden
{pajo, joran}@dsv.su.se

Abstract. Legal regulations governing digital infrastructures and data spaces, such as the European Health Data Space (EHDS), are becoming increasingly complex and difficult to interpret, particularly for non-experts in law, including citizens and small and medium-sized enterprises. To address this challenge, we propose a method for visualising legal regulations that integrates legal ontology with legal design techniques. The method proceeds through three main stages: an ontology-informed reading of regulatory text supported by large language models (LLMs); the pre-processing of ontological constructs into structured tables enriched with explanations and examples; and the rendering of interactive concept maps using visualisation tools such as Kumu. In order to show the feasibility of the approach, we demonstrate the method using the EHDS as a case. The approach not only supports legal understanding but also contributes to the broader goal of trustworthy digital governance.

Keywords: Ontology · Conceptual Model · Legal Ontology · Legal Design

1 Introduction

Digital transformation is increasingly organised around digital infrastructures and the data spaces that run on top of them. A digital infrastructure comprises the technical artifacts (networks, protocols, platforms) and governance mechanisms that allow heterogeneous systems to interoperate at scale. However, digital infrastructures alone mainly provide connectivity and basic services. An additional organisational layer, the data space, is required to turn this connectivity into structured and trustworthy data exchange. A data space offers a governed environment where multiple parties pool and reuse data under common semantic, technical and legal rules, [12]. Its purpose is to enable cross-organisational data use while protecting fundamental rights and commercial interests.

While such shared infrastructures can emerge more or less spontaneously, they often require legislators to intervene to create them through regulations. For example, the EU's Revised Payment Services Directive (PSD2) forces banks to share account data through secure APIs, thereby giving fintechs a standardised entry point to the European payments infrastructure. The newly adopted

D. Bork et al. (Eds.): ER 2025, LNCS 16189, pp. 341–357, 2026.
https://doi.org/10.1007/978-3-032-08623-5_18

European Health Data Space (EHDS) Regulation establishes common rules, bodies, and technical services so that health data can be shared safely for clinical care and research.

These regulations inevitably become highly complex, as they weave together technical standards and sector-specific duties such as data protection and consumer rights, resulting in layered rule-sets that evolve over time. As infrastructures expand, so too does the complexity of the rules that govern them. For example, the PSD2 regulation has additional rules from delegated regulations and country-specific adaptations. Likewise, the EHDS works alongside the GDPR, AI Act, and MDR regulations. Navigating these multi-level, multi-source regulations can overwhelm even specialised lawyers, let alone the citizens, SMEs and public agencies expected to comply.

This growing cognitive load calls for intelligible representations of the regulatory structure. To achieve this, legal ontologies and legal design techniques can provide tools for turning dense legal text into easily digestible representations. Legal ontologies rigorously capture the legal elements and relationships of data spaces in terms of legal entities, legal positions, and legal relators. These legal ontology representations can then be translated into human-centered visualisations, narratives, and interaction patterns using legal design methods and techniques. Together, these approaches promise to reduce the interpretive burden on stakeholders, thereby assisting them in complying with the regulations.

To address the need for clarity and accessibility of complex regulations, we develop an approach based on combining legal ontology with legal design. More specifically, we propose an ontology-informed method for visualising legal regulations through concept maps, tailored to the needs of non-experts-including SMEs, patients, healthcare staff, and citizens—rather than legal professionals. To implement this method in practice, we rely on large language models (LLMs) to analyse legal texts, complemented by tools for visualising network structures.

The research presented in this paper was conducted as part of a European project focusing on supporting innovation through health data spaces. One objective of the project is the development of a "legal toolbox", a structured set of resources designed to assist SMEs, patients, and healthcare professionals in navigating the complexities of the EHDS and related legal frameworks. Consequently, our work explicitly targets this audience of legal non-experts.

The paper is structured as follows. Section 2 provides background on the EHDS, legal design principles, analytical jurisprudence, and core legal ontologies. Section 3 elaborates the UFO-L Legal Core Ontology and its relevance to digital infrastructures. Section 4 introduces the proposed ontology-informed method for visualising legal regulations. Finally, Sect. 5 summarises the paper, discusses the implications of the method, and outlines directions for future research.

2 Background and Ontological Foundations

The method proposed rests primarily on the use of legal ontology, specifically the UFO-L Legal Core Ontology, [15], which is described below and in the next section, together with underlying concepts from analytical jurisprudence. In addition, the field of legal design is outlined. The method is illustrated by applying it to the EHDS, for which a brief overview is also provided.

2.1 The EHDS—The European Health Data Space

The European Health Data Space (EHDS) is an initiative of the European Union designed to improve the use and governance of health data across EU member states, [2]. The EHDS builds on existing EU legislation, such as the GDPR, but also introduces specific rules for health data. It has two main goals: to give individuals better control over their personal health data, and to create a framework that supports the use of health data for research, innovation, policymaking, and public health. By setting out transparent procedures and safeguards, the EHDS seeks to build public trust in how health data is used.

For primary use, the EHDS grants citizens the right to access and share their electronic health records (EHRs) across borders. Citizens can request corrections and add their own health data, and they also have the right to restrict access to certain parts of their data. The system will rely on EU-wide formats and infrastructures to ensure interoperability between national health systems, making cross-border healthcare safer and more efficient. For secondary use, the EHDS introduces a legal and technical framework that allows researchers, public institutions, and innovators to access health data under strict conditions. The goal is to support innovation in areas such as AI, drug development, and public health responses, while respecting patients' rights.

The regulation introduces several new legal actors, including National Contact Points for Digital Health (for primary use coordination), Health Data Access Bodies (for secondary use governance), and the European Health Data Space Board (to ensure consistent implementation across the EU). The EHDS regulation was adopted in January 2025 and entered into force in March 2025, with implementation expected to be phased in over several years.

2.2 Legal Design

Legal design is an interdisciplinary field that integrates methods and techniques from law, design thinking and information technology to improve how legal information is presented. Its main goal is to make the information clearer, easier to understand and more usable by focusing on the needs of people interacting with the law, [9]. For these purposes, legal design applies techniques such as plain language, visual communication, user stories, iconography, and decision trees, [19]. This makes legal materials not only more accessible but also more likely to be trusted and used correctly.

Legal design techniques are helpful for people who often find legal materials difficult to access, such as citizens trying to understand not only laws but also other legal documents, including contracts and court decisions. Small businesses can also benefit, especially when they face complex rules but lack in-house legal teams. For example, under the EHDS regulation, visual maps and user stories can help patients understand the rules governing their access to their own data, as well as their rights to restrict data access for care providers. Analogously, suppliers of EHR systems can benefit from an accessible overview of the EHDS requirements, allowing them to address all of these in an early stage, rather than facing costly redesigns later.

2.3 Analytical Jurisprudence

Analytical jurisprudence, as a tradition within legal theory, has long sought to systematically clarify core legal concepts and their relationships. By analysing these notions with philosophical rigour and bracketing moral or policy considerations, it aims to supply precise conceptual frameworks that can be applied across diverse legal areas. An early work in this tradition was Wesley Newcomb Hohfeld's analysis of legal positions, [22], which distinguished four basic types: claim-rights, privileges, powers, and immunities.

- *Claim-right.* If an actor A has a claim-right against another actor B to do (or not do) some act, then B has a correlative duty toward A to fulfill that claim by doing (or not doing) the act.
- *Privilege.* If an actor A has a privilege to do an act, it means A is under no duty not to do the act. The correlative of A's privilege is that any other actor lacks a claim-right to require A to do otherwise.
- *Power.* A power is the legal ability to alter legal positions, i.e., to create, modify, or extinguish claim-rights, duties, privileges or other powers. Whenever A has a power regarding B, B correspondingly has a liability, meaning B's legal position can be changed by A's exercise of the power.
- *Immunity.* An immunity is the flipside of a power: it is an exemption from having one's legal status altered by another. If A has an immunity against B, it means B lacks the power to change A's legal position in some respect.

This analysis of basic legal positions makes it possible to disaggregate complex legal relations into combinations of legal positions. For instance, ownership of property can be analysed as a bundle of legal positions (claim-rights against others' interference, privileges to use, powers to transfer, etc.).

Herbert L.A. Hart was also a central figure in analytical jurisprudence, but with a broader focus. Rather than analysing individual legal relations in isolation, Hart aimed to explain the nature of a legal system, [20]. One of his major contributions was the concept of secondary rules, i.e., rules that empower actors to create, modify, or extinguish primary rules, i.e., rules that impose or remove duties. Examples include rules that confer legislative power, or the rules for making wills or contracts. There is a correspondence between these notions and Hohfeld's typology: privileges and claim-rights map onto primary rules (governing conduct), while powers and immunities map onto secondary rules (governing legal change). Unlike Hohfeld, who only classified legal relations already assumed to exist, Hart also explained how such relations arise from a structured system of rules. For instance, a contract or statute is valid only if created in accordance with applicable secondary rules.

Legal Institutional Theory, as developed by MacCormick and Weinberger, encompasses the key contributions of both Hohfeld and Hart. However, it differs from them by conceiving of law as an "institutional normative order"—a system of norms founded on, and shaped by, social institutions, [25]. Norms can be understood logically (in terms of their content and relations to other norms) and at the same time as observable social phenomena (in terms of being followed and enforced in institutional settings). Legal Institutional Theory diverges from Hohfeld by being less focused on the pure classification of legal rules and more on explanation: how those rules come about through institutional norms and what role they play in practical reasoning. Practical legal reasoning means that when applying the law, one must often interpret rules or precedents purposively, weigh principles, and ensure coherence in the law as a whole; solely applying legal rules is sometimes insufficient for deciding cases. Thus, judges also utilise principles and reasoned arguments concerning the purpose of legal rules. And these arguments are guided by the traditions and values of specific institutions.

2.4 Core Legal Ontologies

Core legal ontologies are conceptual frameworks that aim to capture the basic conceptual structure of law in a domain-independent way. Their primary purpose is to support the formal representation of legal knowledge in a consistent and uniform manner, thereby enabling interoperability among legal representations and providing a basis for designing legal domain ontologies. A well-established core legal ontology is the Legal Knowledge Interchange Format (LKIF-Core), [21], which was informed by multiple foundational ontologies and provides a comprehensive set of legal notions to support practical legal reasoning. Another example is CLO, [13], based on the DOLCE foundational ontology. Similarly to CLO, UFO-L, [16], builds on a solid foundational ontology: The Unified Foundational Ontology, UFO, [18]. UFO-L takes a relational perspective on core legal concepts based on the work by Hohfeld, [22] and Alexy, [5]. We have chosen UFO-L as the basis of our work, as it offers a relational and event-aware structure that is able to capture the multi-party, evolving legal relationships that are characteristic of digital infrastructures and data spaces.

In preparation for the description of UFO-L in the next section, we here review some key constructs of UFO. UFO makes a key distinction between individuals and universals. *Individuals* in UFO are entities that possess a unique identity, while *universals* are abstract patterns of features that can be realised in one or several individuals. Individuals can be divided into endurants and events, see Fig. 1. An *endurant* is an individual that is wholly present whenever it is present, e.g., a mountain or a car. An *event*, on the other hand, is made up of temporal parts, which are not all present whenever the event is present.

Endurants can be specialised into substantials and moments. *Substantials* are existentially-independent endurants, e.g., a tree or a person. In contrast, *moments* are individuals that inhere in other individuals, meaning that they are existentially-dependent on their bearers, e.g., the smile of a person or the marriage between two spouses. Moments can be either intrinsic moments or relators. *Intrinsic moments* are moments that inhere in a single endurant, e.g., the colour of a car, while *relators* are dependent on two or more endurants, e.g., a marriage.

2.5 Visualisation

Legal conceptual models on the level of granularity of legal positions quickly become very large. The EHDS regulation is around 60,000 words long, including annexes, composed by 105 articles, most of which contain several numbered paragraphs. While a model does not have to cover the complete regulation to be useful, also a limited model will be rather large. How to visually represent the model becomes crucial if lay users are to increase their understanding.

Visualisations can bring new insights to complex information, such as legal texts made more accessible. Legal visualisation has mostly focused on the relations between legal texts, for example, citations, but has also been used to understand the relations between concepts [26]. Legal texts can be analysed with natural language processing (NLP) to create visualisations.

In visualisation of large models, secondary notation becomes increasingly important. As explained by Moody, [27], while the primary notation of a modelling language is defined by its formal rules, the secondary (informal) notation provides other visual clues to how interpret a diagram. The informality of secondary notation does not make it unimportant, however. In fact, Ghiran et al. propose that secondary notation should be understood as an "explicit building block of a modelling method" [14, p. 1], including dynamic rendering through visualisation tools.

As argued by Cerioli et al. [7], for a network visualization to be effective, users must be able to navigate across multiple object types, including actors, rules, contracts, and other legal entities. To support this, the visualization should employ metaphors that resonate with users' mental models. Cerioli et al. propose a map-based approach, which they term *wayfinding*, enabling users to move in and out of the map, discern direct and indirect connections, and explore the broader context. In the legal domain, such a map metaphor is particularly valuable: as Ruhl and Katz [29] note, it provides an intuitive framework for designing *legal maps*, allowing practitioners and scholars to navigate complex legal structures and relationships more effectively.

3 UFO-L and Digital Infrastructure Regulations

This section provides an overview of UFO-L, with particular attention to its relevance for digital infrastructure regulations. The overview integrates elements from the models presented in [16,17], extended by two additional classes. A representation of UFO-L is shown in Fig. 1 as a UML class diagram.

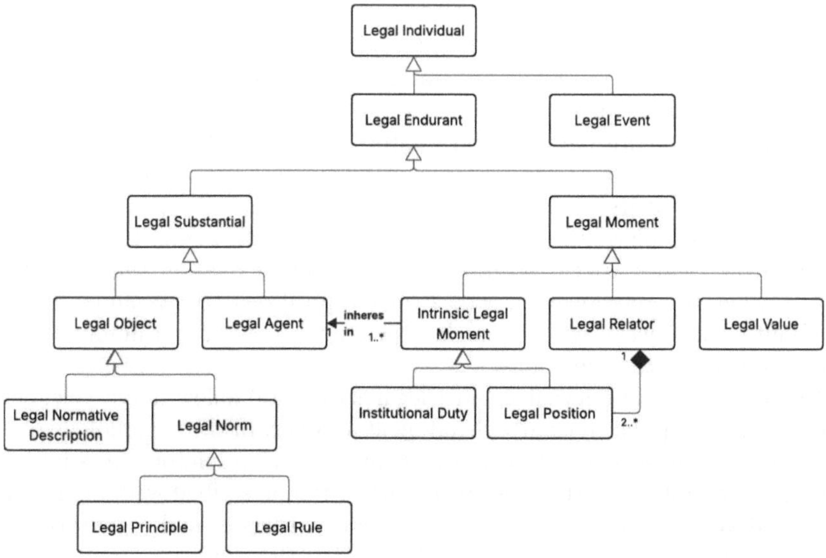

Fig. 1. A Fragment of UFO-L

3.1 Legal Agents and Legal Objects

A *legal individual* is an individual that is recognised and regulated by a legal system. Legal individuals are divided into legal events and legal endurants, which in turn are divided into legal substantials and legal moments. A *legal agent* is a legal substantial recognised by the legal system as capable of having rights, privileges and other legal positions. They can typically own property, enter into legal relations, or be held responsible. Legal agents can be natural persons (corresponding to human beings) or juridical persons, such as companies, associations, and authorities. Some examples of legal agents in the EHDS are patients, health professionals, member states, and national contact points.

A *legal object* is a legal substantial that can be the target of primary legal positions, i.e., claim-rights and privileges. Legal objects are what these legal positions are about, but they cannot themselves hold legal positions. Instead, legal agents hold legal positions concerning legal objects. An example is that a patient (legal agent) has the right to access their health data (legal object), and a hospital (legal agent) has the duty to provide it. Other examples of legal objects from the EHDS are personal e-health data, electronic health record (EHR) systems, metadata, standardised data formats, and datasets.

3.2 Legal Relators and Legal Positions

A *legal moment* is a legal endurant that is dependent on at least one legal agent. A *legal relator* is a legal moment dependent on two or more legal agents, e.g., a marriage that is dependent on two legal agents. In contrast, an *intrinsic legal moment* inheres in only one legal agent. In UFO-L, a *legal position* is modelled as an intrinsic legal moment that is externally dependent on a legal agent. For example, a duty for A to pay an amount of money to B is viewed as an intrinsic legal moment that inheres in A, but it is also externally dependent on B.

Legal positions are part of legal relators. For example, a marriage relator can include a duty of one spouse to financially support the other spouse (a legal position) as one of its parts. It can also be noted that Hohfeld views a legal position as a two-place relation between two agents. However, UFO-L, as well as others, [5], views a legal position as a three-place relation that also makes explicit what the relation concerns. Primary positions (rights and privileges) are about legal objects, while secondary positions (powers and immunities) are about modifying other positions.

Every legal relator (as well as other legal endurants) follows a lifecycle, beginning at a specific point in time and ending at another. In the terminology of [25], an *institutive rule* specifies the conditions under which a relator comes into existence. For example, a marriage is created when the prescribed wedding has been performed and the prerequisites (e.g., consent, witnesses, and registration) are fulfilled. Analogously, a *terminative rule* specifies the conditions under which a given relator ceases to exist. In a law text, these rules are typically not detailed procedural descriptions but instead constraints outlining necessary conditions.

3.3 Institutional Duties

A key feature of Hohfeld's framework is its strict correlativity: every legal position has a correlative. For instance, if one agent has a duty, another agent must hold a claim-right. Yet, in practice, there are situations where the identity of a specific claim-right holder is unclear or indirect. As MacCormick, [24], observes, "not all duties are relevantly 'owed to' determinate other individuals." Public authorities, for example, may bear duties such as safeguarding public safety or protecting the environment, where no clearly identifiable individuals hold the corresponding claim-right. Instead, these duties are generally understood as owed to "the public", "society at large", or even "the environment".

Such institutional duties are ubiquitous in regulations of digital infrastructures and data spaces, as these are designed to ensure the systemic functioning of digital ecosystems. And they do this by imposing duties aimed at securing system properties, such as interoperability, stability, and trust. Thereby, these duties, such as adhering to technical standards or contributing to governance mechanisms, serve the integrity of the system rather than corresponding directly to the claim-rights of specific agents. The EHDS also illustrates how such regulations often pursue public interest goals, such as facilitating cross-border health research, which benefits society as a whole rather than specific individuals. An example of an institutional duty from Article 19 in the EHDS is "Each digital health authority shall be entrusted with the following tasks ... ensuring the implementation at national level of the European electronic health record exchange format". In Fig. 1, we have added a class "Institutional Duty", which is not in UFO-L.

3.4 Legal Norms, Legal Values, and Legal Normative Descriptions

Legal norms are standards that tell agents what behaviours are required, permitted, prohibited, or enabled in a legal system. A *legal rule* is a particular kind of legal norm characterised by a high degree of specificity and an all-or-nothing mode of application. For example, Article 3.2 of the EHDS states, "Natural persons . . . shall have the right to download free of charge an electronic copy of at least the personal electronic health data in the priority categories referred to in Article 14 related to those natural persons". This rule grants people in the EU access to their health data.

Because of their clarity and specificity, legal rules provide certainty and predictability, but can be difficult to apply in hard cases. In contrast, *legal principles* are norms that guide legal interpretation and influence the application of legal rules. Dworkin distinguished principles from rules by noting that principles are not applied in an all-or-nothing fashion; instead, they have a dimension of weight or importance, [11, p. 77–78]. A principle provides a reason that may influence, but not determine, a decision, and it can coexist with competing principles. An example, often referred to in the EHDS, is the principle of data minimisation in the GDPR, which requires that personal data collected and processed must be adequate, relevant, and limited to what is necessary in relation to the purposes for which it is processed.

Legal values are foundational ethical and social ideals within a society that a legal system intends to uphold. They represent the "general, basic and framework norms upon which a legal system is built", [10]. Typical examples of legal values are order, fairness, equality, and freedom. Some legal values relevant for the EHDS are patient autonomy, privacy, trust, accountability, and innovativeness.

Legal values and legal principles differ in their functions for the legal system. The primary function of principles lies within the legal system, as they guide interpretation and ensure consistency of rules—legal principles are tools for legal reasoning and application. In contrast, the primary function of legal values is justificatory, as they provide the underlying rationale for the norms of the legal system, grounding it in the broader ethical and social commitments of a society—legal values answer the 'why'. Legal rules and legal principles are included in UFO-L but not legal values, and we have added a class to Fig. 1.

A legal norm is linguistically represented through a *legal normative description*, which is a linguistic object, such as an article or a paragraph in a legal text. The distinction between norm and description helps differentiate between normative content (the "ought") and legal documentation (the symbolic expression of that ought).

4 A Method for Visualising Legal Regulations

We propose a method for visualising legal regulations using concept maps, where the map components correspond to the ontological constructs defined in UFO-L. The method includes three main activities that are described in the following subsections. We also describe the specific tools we used to implement the method. Doing so demonstrates the feasibility of the method by showing that widely available tools can operationalise each step in the method. It also supports transferability: if future researchers choose to use alternative tools, the pairing of method steps with concrete tools clarifies the functional requirements that any replacements must meet. For an overview of the method, see Fig. 2.

4.1 Ontology-Informed Analysis of Regulations with LLM

The method begins with an ontology-informed analysis of the regulatory text. The goal of this step is to re-express the text in UFO-L terms, with a focus on identifying the relevant universals it contains. The step proceeds through a systematic reading and interpretation of the text. In this work, LLM tools can provide support through suggestions on interpretations of articles and paragraphs, as well as feedback on proposed interpretations. For this purpose, we have developed several prompts. First, a priming instruction was given explaining the terms used in the succeeding prompts. Second, for each paragraph and legal relation contained in it, the type of the legal relation was identified. Third, for each paragraph and legal relation, a specific prompt, based on the type of the relation, was given to extract its contents. Three examples of specific prompts are shown below.

- Read Paragraph X, which concerns a *claim-right.* Describe it in a table format with the following columns: Rights Holder, Duty Bearer, Original Wording, Action, Legal Object, Condition, Purpose.
- Read Paragraph X, which concerns an *institutional duty.* Describe it in a table format with the following columns: Duty Holder, Original Wording, Action, Legal Object, Condition, Purpose.
- Read Paragraph X, which concerns a *power.* Describe it in a table format with the following columns: Power Holder, Subjection Holder, Original Wording, Legal Position Created or Modified by the Power, Action, Legal Object, Condition, Purpose.

For the first prompt, Rights Holder and Duty Bearer are universals whose instances are legal agents; Original Wording is the original text of the paragraph; Action is the act that the claim-right concerns; Legal Object is a universal whose instances are legal objects; Condition describes a prerequisite or a restriction of the application of the claim-right; and Purpose is about the rationale of the claim-right.

Our experience using an LLM tool (ChatGPT 4.5 and o3) as support has been generally promising, with the generated responses being both accurate and practically useful in almost all cases. However, outputs still require manual verification and, occasionally, some rephrasing. Beyond generating responses for our pre-defined prompts, the LLM tool has been valuable as a dialogue partner in more complex analytical tasks, particularly those requiring iterative work on interpretations.

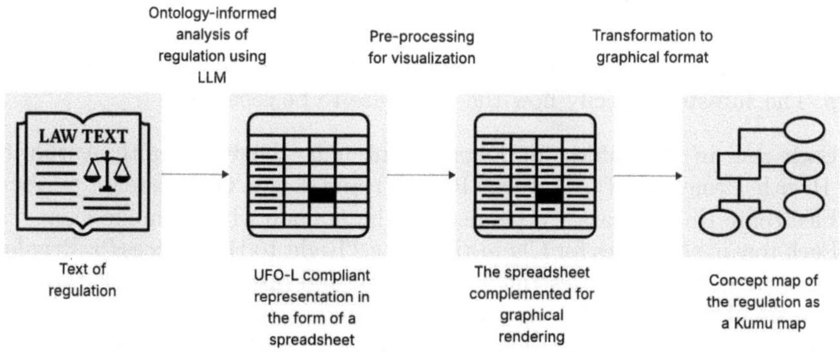

Fig. 2. Overview of the Method for Visualising Legal Regulations

4.2 Pre-processing for Visualisation

The second step involves pre-processing the results from the previous step into a tabular format—specifically, a spreadsheet—that can be used by a tool to render the concept map. Three sub-steps are included:

- A table is created for universals that contain instances of Legal Agent (Legal Object, Role, Claim-right, Privilege, Power, Immunity, Institutional Duty, Legal Relator, and Value). The columns of the tables may vary, as suggested by the above prompts.
- For each table above, two columns Explanation and Example are added. Explanation is a paraphrase of an original text in the regulation in plain language, and Example is a concrete case illustrating an item in easily understandable language. An LLM tool assists in generating these paraphrases.
- A table Connections is created for all relations between universals, in particular, for inheres-in and external-dependency relations.

These steps are informed by the following principles for visual notations by [27]:

Semiotic Clarity. There should be a 1:1 correspondence between ontological constructs and graphical symbols. This principle is the basis of our visualisation approach; the rows of the tables corresponding to universals will become the nodes in the concept map.

Dual Coding. Text annotations should be used to complement graphical symbols to offer additional information. To operationalise this principle, we have prepared clear explanations and illustrative examples using accessible language, guided by the principles of plain legal language [4].

Graphic Economy. The number of different symbols should be kept small so that users will not become overwhelmed and struggle to remember the meanings of the symbols. We have primarily addressed graphic economy through symbol deficit, i.e., by deliberately omitting graphical representations for certain ontological notions. In particular, we have not graphically modelled normative descriptions (articles and paragraphs), but instead included these only in text annotations.

4.3 Transformation to Graphical Form

The third step transforms the tables obtained in the previous step into a concept map. The sub-steps specify how the nodes are to be rendered:

- Each row in the tables for Legal Agent (e.g. "Digital Health Authority", "Health Professional", "Natural Person") and Legal Object (e.g., "Personal Electronic Health Data") gives rise to a large node with a unique icon.
- Each row in the tables for Claim-right (e.g. "Right to Have Access"), Privilege, Power (e.g. "Power to Restrict"), Immunity, and Institutional Duty, gives rise to a small node with the same icon.
- Each row in the table for Legal Relator (e.g. "Restriction of Access") gives rise to a mid-sized node with the same icon.
- Each row in the table for Value (e.g. "Trust") gives rise to a large node with the same icon.
- Each row in the Connections table gives rise to an edge between the related nodes.

For the actual rendering of the map, we have used Kumu, [3], which is a web-based tool designed to support the analysis and visualisation of complex systems through interactive network maps. It enables users to model and explore relationships among diverse elements such as stakeholders, concepts, and policies. Kumu allows for customisation: users can employ visual variables like colour, size, shape, icons, and layout to highlight key elements and distinguish between different types of nodes and edges. The tool also supports filtering and zooming functionality, enabling users to explore a map interactively.

In this step, we also draw on the visualisation principles in [27]:

Semantic Transparency. The appearance of a symbol should suggest its meaning, preferably so that it can be directly perceived. To this end, we have selected icons that are both intuitive and familiar to the intended audience. The icons have been informed by DaPIS: the Data Protection Icon Set, [1].

Perceptual Discriminability. Different symbols should be clearly distinguishable from each other, so that users can easily differentiate between various elements on the map. We have addressed this issue by employing different shapes and colours, as well as drawing icons in a minimalistic style with high internal contrast.

Visual Expressiveness. The full range and capacity of visual variables (such as shape, colour, size, and texture) should be utilised to support both semantic transparency and perceptual discriminability. We have addressed this principle using Kumu's features to render map elements. For example, we use larger sizes and distinct icons for legal agents to highlight their importance and ensure they are clearly distinguishable from other map elements.

Manageable Complexity. The visualisation should include mechanisms for handling complexity, such as modularisation and hierarchical structuring, to ensure that users are not overwhelmed by large and complex maps. For this purpose, we rely on Kumu's functionality, which offers zooming and filtering to focus on specific elements as well as grouping to divide large maps into segments.

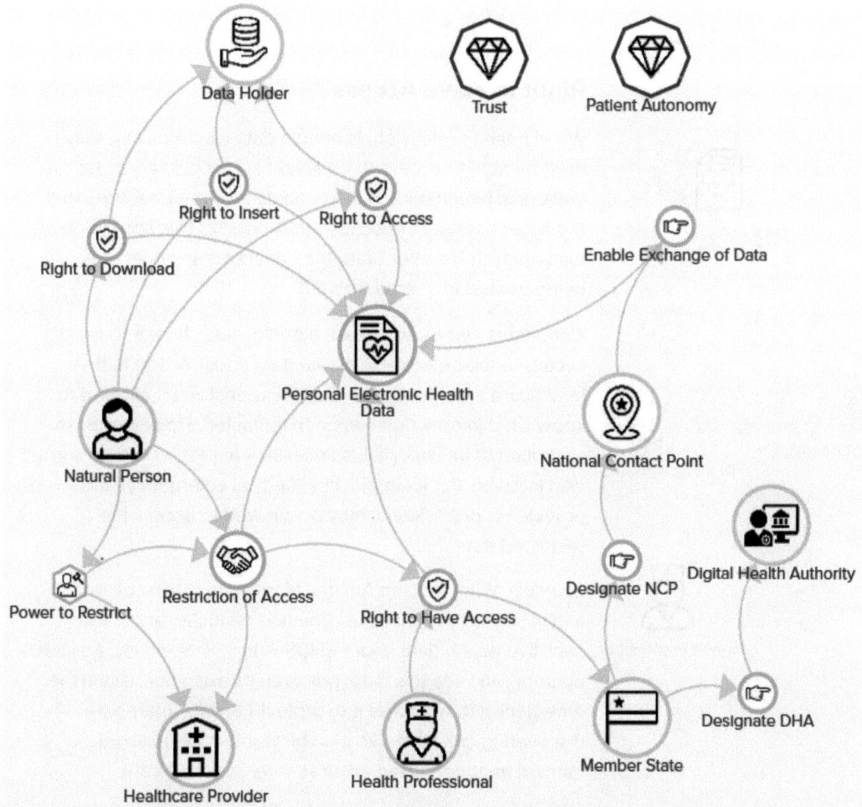

Fig. 3. A Fragment of a Concept Map for EHDS Chapter 2

For example, certain edges in a map can be hidden by default in order to reduce clutter, as shown in Fig. 3, where the edges from the Value nodes are initially suppressed but can be made visible interactively if so desired.

Figure 3 shows a small fragment of a concept map based on Chap. 2 of the EHDS, which addresses the primary use of health data. (Large circles with a blue border represent legal agents; large circles with an orange border represent legal objects; octagons represent values; medium-sized circles with a handshake icon represent legal relators; and all other nodes represent legal positions.) The figure illustrates the output from a method application. As a static image, it cannot display the map's interactive features, but a live, navigable version is available online[1]. Figure 4 displays a pop-up window that contains a text annotation for a node in the map.

[1] https://embed.kumu.io/cf43985dcc788d7b433ec3bd22d0f8fb.

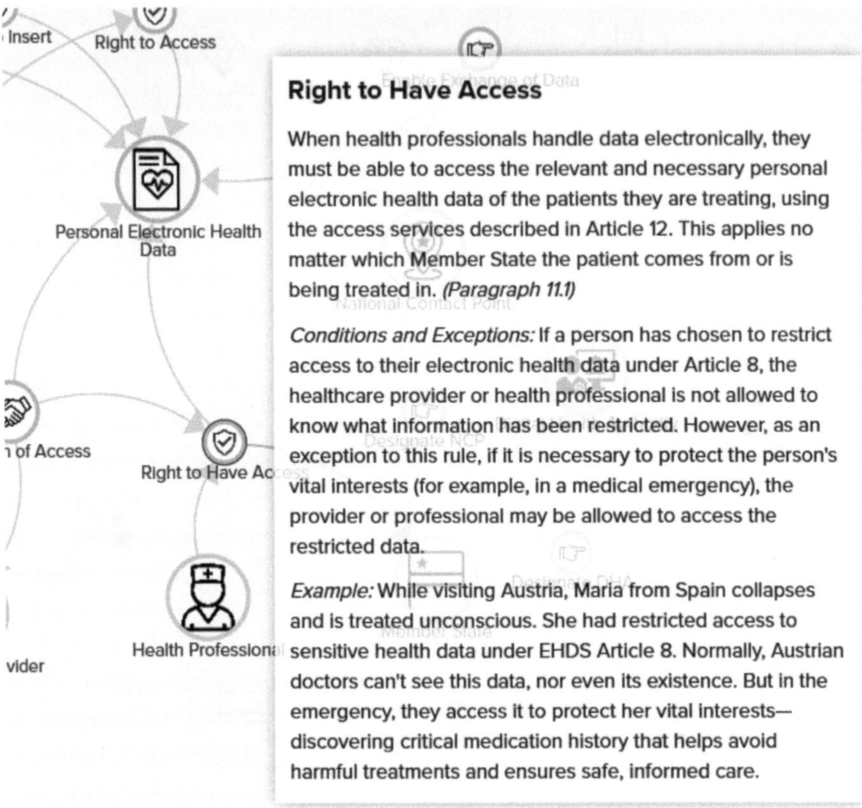

Fig. 4. A popup window containing a textual annotation

5 Discussion

We have proposed an ontology-informed method for visualising complex legal regulations using concept maps, demonstrated through a case study of the EHDS regulation. By applying UFO-L, we showed how to systematically analyse legal texts to identify and represent legal core elements. To support and streamline this analysis, we used LLMs, which helped interpret statutory texts and generate easily understandable paraphrases and illustrative examples. The resulting concept maps facilitate navigation and interpretation of regulatory material, particularly benefiting legal non-experts. While the proposed method has been developed with a primary focus on digital infrastructures and data spaces, it has broader applicability across other legal domains.

Methodologically, our research process can be seen as an instance of design science research, [28]. Using ontology as a knowledge base, we have addressed a persistent and widely recognised problem: making legal material comprehensible for non-experts. We have developed a method for creating concept maps of complex regulations, which we have demonstrated in a case study, applying it to a part of Chapter 2 of the EHDS. A thorough evaluation of the method is a topic for future research.

Scholarship on the visualisation of legal materials has produced a comprehensive body of work, much of it centered on network graphs that depict how statutes or regulations cross-reference and influence one another. For example, Koniaris et al. introduced the Legislation Network and applied it to a corpus of EU law, in which each legislative act appears as a node and citations form the connecting edges [23]. A distinct line of inquiry examines the logical form of norms: Tosatto et al. proposed a graphical representation that encodes premises, deontic operators and conditional clauses, allowing researchers to trace the inferential architecture of articles and paragraphs, [8].

Although these approaches support detailed inferential analysis valuable to legal professionals, their granularity may hinder lay comprehension. Closer to our objectives are studies that visualise networks of agents and their legal positions without delving into the syntactic minutiae of the underlying legal text. The pioneering efforts of Burkhardt and Nazemi, [6], as well as Griffo et al., [15], illustrate this approach; however, their models still presuppose that users are familiar with legal constructs, targeting legal professionals rather than non-expert stakeholders.

Our method for converting natural language legal text to structured legal relations can be considered a form of ontology-guided prompting. A limitation of our proposed approach is that we did not engineer the prompts according to any systematic methods or frameworks. This likely affects the quality of the LLM-generated legal relations. In future studies, a possible approach could be to employ schema-guided prompting, in other words, that both the input is given in a structured form, for example, JavaScript Object Notation (JSON). This would lead to improved predictability.

For future work, we plan to consolidate and extend the use of UFO-L. While UFO-L has proven to be a robust foundation for analysing legal texts and developing concept maps, we have not fully utilised its potential. Specifically, we have not accounted for legal events, and more importantly, we have focused solely on legal universals in our analysis without addressing legal individuals. One of the challenges with modelling legal systems is that they offer an intriguing interaction between universals and individuals. For example, an individual law (EHDS) creating a new universal (National Contact Point), which in turn will be instantiated through a combination of national regulations and tangible information infrastructure design. Another universal created by the EHDS—Personal Electronic Health Data—will have a massive number of instances from the moment it is created, since much data will fit the definition in the EHDS.

Moreover, the concept of legal value merits deeper examination, for which Sales's work offers a promising foundation, [30]. As indicated in Fig. 3, the relationships between Values and other elements remain challenging. One reason is that Values interact with the larger system rather than its individual components. One approach, then, would be to represent the larger system and connect it with its parts. However, a weakness of this solution is that legal systems have fuzzy borders, making it rather arbitrary where to draw the line.

Another topic for further research is to apply ontology-informed analysis to legal design techniques other than concept maps. Process diagrams and scenario narratives, for instance, could give non-expert stakeholders intuitive guidance, and they can be generated methodically from the very analysis used here. Thus, one ontological analysis could underpin several complementary forms of representation.

References

1. DaPIS: the data protection icon set. http://gdprbydesign.cirsfid.unibo.it/dapis-the-data-protection-icon-set/. Accessed 17 May 2025
2. European health data space regulation (EHDS). https://health.ec.europa.eu/ehealth-digital-health-and-care/european-health-data-space-regulation-ehds_en. Accessed 27 May 2025
3. Kumu. https://kumu.io/. Accessed 29 May 2025
4. Plain legal language. https://www.clarity-international.org/plain-legal-language/?utm_source=chatgpt.com. Accessed 7 May 2025
5. Alexy, R., Rivers, J.: A Theory of Constitutional Rights, 2 edn. Oxford University Press (2002)
6. Burkhardt, D., Nazemi, K.: Visualizing law - a norm-graph visualization approach based on semantic legal data. In: Proceedings of the International Conference of the Virtual and Augmented Reality in Education. Zenodo (2018)
7. Cerioli, N., Vyas, R., Reeve, M.P., Masoodian, M.: Designing complex network visualisations using the wayfinding map metaphor. Inf. Visualization **23**(4), 384–403 (2024). https://doi.org/10.1177/14738716241270341
8. Colombo Tosatto, S., Boella, G., Torre, L., Villata, S.: Visualizing normative systems: an abstract approach. In: Ågotnes, T., Broersen, J., Elgesem, D. (eds.) DEON 2012. LNCS (LNAI), vol. 7393, pp. 16–30. Springer, Heidelberg (2012). https://doi.org/10.1007/978-3-642-31570-1_2
9. Compagnucci, M.C., Haapio, H., Hagan, M., Doherty, M.: Legal Design: Integrating Business, Design and Legal Thinking with Technology. Edward Elgar Publishing, Cheltenham, England (2021)
10. Daci, J.: Legal principles, legal values and legal norms: are they the same or different? Academicus Int. Sci. J. **2**(02), 109–115 (2010)
11. Dworkin, R.: Taking Rights Seriously: With a New Appendix, a Response to Critics, 5th edn. Harvard University Press, UK (1978)
12. European Union Official Website: Common European data spaces. https://digital-strategy.ec.europa.eu/en/policies/data-spaces. Accessed 2 May 2025
13. Gangemi, A., Sagri, M.T., Tiscornia, D.: A constructive framework for legal ontologies. In: Benjamins, V.R., Casanovas, P., Breuker, J., Gangemi, A. (eds.) Law and the Semantic Web, 2005 edn. LNCS. Springer, Berlin, Germany (2005)
14. Ghiran, A.M., Buchmann, R.A., Karagiannis, D.: Towards a framework of techniques for enabling semantics-driven secondary notation in conceptual models. In: 2018 12th International Conference on Research Challenges in Information Science (RCIS), pp. 1–6 (2018). https://doi.org/10.1109/RCIS.2018.8406684

15. Griffo, C., Da Silva Teixeira, M.D.G., Almeida, J.P.A., Gailly, F., Guizzardi, G.: LawV: towards an ontology-based visual modeling language in the legal domain. In: XIII Seminar on Ontology Research in Brazil (Ontobras 2020), vol. 2728, pp. 75–88. CEUR-WS (2020)
16. Griffo, C., Almeida, J.P.A., Guizzardi, G.: Legal theories and judicial decision-making: an ontological analysis. In: Frontiers in Artificial Intelligence and Applications, pp. 63–76. Frontiers in Artificial Intelligence and Applications, IOS Press (2020)
17. Griffo, C., Almeida, J.P.A., Lima, J.A.O., Prince Sales, T., Guizzardi, G.: Legal powers, subjections, disabilities, and immunities: ontological analysis and modeling patterns. Data Knowl. Eng. **148**, 102219 (2023)
18. Guizzardi, G., Botti Benevides, A., Fonseca, C.M., Porello, D., Almeida, J.P.A., Prince Sales, T.: UFO: unified foundational ontology. Appl. Ontol. **17**, 1–44 (2022)
19. Hagan, M.: Law by design. https://lawbydesign.co/. Accessed 22 June 2023
20. Hart, H.L.A.: The Concept of Law. Clarendon Law Series, 3rd edn. Oxford University Press, London, England (2012)
21. Hoekstra, R., Breuker, J., Bello, M., Boer, A., et al.: The LKIF core ontology of basic legal concepts. LOAIT **321**, 43–63 (2007)
22. Hohfeld, W.N.: Some fundamental legal conceptions as applied in judicial reasoning. Yale Law J. **23**(1), 16–59 (1913)
23. Koniaris, M., Anagnostopoulos, I., Vassiliou, Y.: Network analysis in the legal domain: a complex model for European union legal sources. J. Complex Netw. **6**(2), 243–268 (2018)
24. MacCormick, N.: H.L.A. Hart. Stanford University Press, Palo Alto, CA (2008)
25. MacCormick, R., MacCormick, N.: Institutions of Law: An Essay in Legal Theory. Oxford University Press, Cary, NC (2007)
26. Mentzingen, H., António, N., Bacao, F.: Unveiling legal complexity: a systematic review on the visual analytics of legal corpora. Int. Rev. Law Comput. Technol., 1–36 (2025). https://doi.org/10.1080/13600869.2025.2497630
27. Moody, D.: The "physics" of notations: toward a scientific basis for constructing visual notations in software engineering. IEEE Trans. Softw. Eng. **35**(6), 756–779 (2009)
28. Peffers, K., Tuunanen, T., Rothenberger, M.A., Chatterjee, S.: A design science research methodology for information systems research. J. Manag. Inf. Syst. **24**(3), 45–77 (2007)
29. Ruhl, J.B., Katz, D.M.: Mapping law's complexity with "Legal Maps". In: Complexity Theory and Law, pp. 23–44. Routledge (2018)
30. Sales, T.P.: ontological foundations for strategic business modeling: the case of value, risk and competition, Ph.D. thesis, University of Trento (2019)

Conceptual Modeling of Disinformation Campaigns

Sidbewendin Angelique Yameogo[1(✉)], Régis Fleurquin[1], Nicolas Belloir[1,2], and Wassila Ouerdane[3]

[1] IRISA, Université de Bretagne Sud, Vannes, France
sidbewendin.yameogo@univ-ubs.fr
[2] CREC St-Cyr, Académie Militaire de St-Cyr Coëtquidan, Guer, France
[3] MICS, Université Paris-Saclay, CentraleSupélec, Gif Sur Yvette, France

Abstract. Online disinformation campaigns represent an increasingly serious threat to democratic societies. Although numerous tools have been developed to assist analysts in detecting and countering such operations, our comprehensive survey of the state of the art reveals persistent shortcomings in terms of coverage, interoperability, and explainability. To address these limitations, we first advocate a unifying conceptual framework that can serve as a semantic backbone. This framework harmonizes the heterogeneous outputs of existing tools and, in the longer term, supports the design of hybrid systems aligned with the principles of Explainable Artificial Intelligence (XAI). We then introduce a domain-specific Conceptual Data Model (CDM) that captures the strategic, structural, and behavioral dimensions of influence operations. Finally, we demonstrate the utility of this model through a real-world case study, illustrating how it enables a deeper and more transparent analyses of disinformation campaigns.

Keywords: Conceptual Modeling · Disinformation Campaign · Explainable Artificial Intelligence

1 Introduction

Democratic societies are increasingly confronted with the rise of online disinformation campaigns. Fueled and amplified by social networks, these malicious operations aim to manipulate public opinion, disrupt electoral processes, and undermine trust in scientific and health institutions [8]. Professionals responsible for countering such dynamics, whether civilian (such as investigative journalists or fact-checkers) or military (such as information warfare units), must continuously process massive volumes of heterogeneous and often volatile data.

To support them, two main categories of tools have emerged. The first includes content analysis systems, which rely primarily on natural language processing (NLP) and deep learning techniques to detect false information [13]. The second consists of social graph monitoring systems, designed to uncover

D. Bork et al. (Eds.): ER 2025, LNCS 16189, pp. 358–375, 2026.
https://doi.org/10.1007/978-3-032-08623-5_19

abnormal or coordinated activity patterns [15]. Recently, hybrid approaches have appeared [6], combining content analysis (text, images, data) with dissemination analysis (who shares what, how quickly, through which subnets and through which types of profiles). However, existing analytical tools still fail to capture the full complexity of disinformation campaigns, as their scope remains narrow and their analyses fragmented. In the absence of a systemic perspective, practitioners must consolidate the results manually and almost always post hoc [26,30]. This situation is aggravated by the widespread reliance on black-box machine learning models (for example, deep neural networks), which are difficult to interpret, prone to bias, and unable to explain why a particular piece of content is classified as deceptive. This lack of transparency reduces trust in the output of these tools among journalists, policymakers, and citizens. Such limitations hinder the detection of weak signals, obstruct the real-time tracking of adversarial maneuvers, and delay the deployment of timely and effective countermeasures.

We introduce a Conceptual Data Model (CDM) designed as the foundation for a unified and interoperable approach to the analysis of disinformation campaigns. We begin by clarifying the core concepts, mapping existing analysis tools, and identifying the recurring limitations in interoperability and explainability in Sect. 2. Based on these observations, we show that a CDM can provide a semantic backbone that coordinates such tools and supports the development of hybrid, CDM-aware machine learning models producing explainable results. The model is represented as a UML class diagram, offering a structured view that captures the strategic, structural, and behavioral dimensions of influence operations, as detailed in Sect. 3. Finally, in Sect. 4, we illustrate the relevance of this CDM through an empirical case study, showing its potential to aggregate weak signals, structure dissemination dynamics, and support the strategic interpretation of disinformation content, before concluding in Sect. 5.

2 Background and Motivation

In this section, we define what constitutes a disinformation campaign. We then examine existing tools and identify their limitations. Finally, we underscore the relevance of a Conceptual Data Model as a means of addressing these limitations.

2.1 Definition and Characterization of Disinformation Campaigns

Disinformation is defined as the intentional dissemination of false information to deceive or manipulate the public [26]. Such definitions rarely account for the organized, large-scale forms that disinformation can take. In contrast, *information warfare* refers to the deliberate use of information to spread confusion, mislead, and influence the actions of an adversary's population [17], thus highlighting the strategic and coordinated nature of such activities. NATO adopts a similar position, referring to "information threats" as intentional, harmful, manipulative, and coordinated activities conducted by state and non-state actors [20].

These perspectives suggest that disinformation goes beyond isolated pieces of content and operates as a strategic instrument within broader influence operations. To account for the organized and sustained nature of these disinformation operations, the concept of *disinformation campaign* has been introduced. Although widely used, this concept remains rarely formalized, and its meaning often varies across disciplines and research contexts. We introduce a definition specifically crafted to serve as the foundation for our analysis. This definition distinguishes campaigns from viral rumors or isolated misinformation and emphasizes their organizational structure, temporal dynamics, and strategic intent.

Definition. *A disinformation campaign is a set of deliberate, coordinated, and structured informational actions carried out by one or more actors, aimed at influencing the opinions, behaviors, or decisions of one or more target audiences through large-scale dissemination of false, misleading, or manipulated content through digital channels, according to strategic logic.*

To operationalize this definition and enable systematic analysis, several conceptual frameworks have been proposed, notably DISARM [28] and MITRE ATT&CK [27]. From the analysis of these frameworks, six main dimensions can be identified to capture the nature of disinformation campaigns:

- **Strategic architecture**: objectives pursued, narratives deployed, and the timing of actions.
- **Actors involved**: states, organized groups, bots, trolls, and other influence agents.
- **Dissemination vectors**: digital platforms used according to the target audience.
- **Manipulation techniques**: content falsification, information overload, fake experts, microtargeting, etc.
- **Target audiences**: vulnerable or strategically significant groups.
- **Impact indicators**: reach, engagement, amplification, changes in public discourse, or institutional weakening.

2.2 Existing Tools for Campaign Analysis

Research has developed along several methodological lines, with a primary focus on the automated detection of falsified content. Numerous systems have emerged based on natural language processing (NLP) and machine learning, typically trained to detect fake or misleading information using annotated corpora [33]. Drawing on computational linguistics, sentiment analysis, and epistemic discourse modeling approaches [22], these tools effectively assess the veracity and rhetorical strategies of individual texts. Yet, they often rely on static and decontextualized perspectives, overlooking the relational and temporal patterns that characterize coordinated disinformation.

To address these limitations, a second line of work has focused on propagation dynamics. This behavioral perspective builds on techniques from graph theory and dynamic modeling of social networks [21] to identify patterns such as synchronized sharing or artificial amplification. It uses metrics such as centrality, clustering, and temporal bursts to detect anomalies. For example, retweet graphs or reply chains can reveal astroturfing or coordinated inauthentic behavior [19], reframing disinformation as a collective, temporally anchored phenomenon rather than an isolated anomaly.

Some tools aim to integrate these two analytical dimensions to offer a more holistic view of information operations. Hoaxy, visualizes the spread of URLs on Twitter over time, distinguishing between verified and unverified sources [24]. Although its content classification remains relatively basic, its value lies in the temporal and network mapping it enables, which supports both real-time monitoring and retrospective analysis. The botometer, developed by Indiana University, evaluates the likelihood that a given account is automated by analyzing more than a thousand features related to content, timing, sentiment, and network relations [30]. It is grounded in behavioral heuristics and probabilistic modeling, offering an operational means of assessing the ecosystem of amplifiers in a given campaign. Cyabra, a commercial platform, builds upon this approach by combining linguistic analysis, bot detection, and community detection. It allows analysts to track narratives, identify influence groups and evaluate manipulation strategies used in polarized online environments [16].

The growing adoption of these tools highlights their practical utility in countering influence operations at scale. Nevertheless, current solutions still fail to capture the full complexity of contemporary campaigns. Their analytical scope is typically restricted to a subset of the six dimensions defined above. In the absence of a canonical data model, outputs are generated in incompatible proprietary formats that hinder the necessary interoperability of these tools. In addition, most systems examine individual pieces of false content in isolation, rather than the coordinated sequence of information attacks that typifies a genuine campaign. Such operations are orchestrated by both human and automated actors, including states, organized groups, intermediaries, bots, trolls, and influence relays, who leverage digital platforms and media channels tailored to the sociodemographic profiles of their targets, and who deploy their actions over time in line with strategic objectives and tactical considerations. Without a holistic perspective, the analyses remain fragmented, and practitioners must consolidate the results manually and almost invariably *post hoc.*

Finally, the growing reliance on opaque machine learning models raises concerns about interpretability. Although effective in terms of performance, these black-box systems do not explain how they arrive at their conclusions. In critical contexts where traceability and justification are essential, such opacity undermines trust and accountability [2].

2.3 The Added Value of Conceptual Data Models

To overcome the limitations identified above, conceptual data models (CDMs) offer a promising solution. A conceptual model is a formal abstraction that organizes the relevant entities within a domain, along with their attributes and relationships. It facilitates the analysis, communication, and algorithmic implementation of complex phenomena. CDMs enable the structuring of domain knowledge in an intelligible, reproducible, and actionable form, particularly within hybrid architectures that combine symbolic and statistical approaches. As a result, several studies have explored the use of CDMs to enhance explainability, semantic structuring, and interoperability.

A growing body of work on explainable artificial intelligence (XAI) seeks to make algorithmic decisions transparent and interpretable [2]. Some approaches deliver local post hoc explanations with techniques such as LIME, SHAP, or attention-based visualization [18]. Others pursue intrinsic interpretability by structuring inputs according to semantic or linguistic criteria [3]. However, these methods are typically applied to individual items—an article, a tweet—and thus struggle to justify decisions that depend on multiple, interacting viewpoints. The difficulty is even greater when considering the complex and global structure of coordinated campaigns. To bridge this gap, several studies advocate the use of conceptual data models. Varela et al. present a model that coherently organizes intentions, sources, contexts, and dissemination channels, with an emphasis on information risk management [7]. Similarly, [5] highlights the value of a shared formalism that connects the symbolic and statistical components of an AI system, thereby enhancing the interpretability and traceability of its decisions.

Moreover, several studies emphasize the usefulness of CDMs as interoperability hubs between systems and tools. By providing a structured and shared foundation, CDMs enable better integration of heterogeneous resources, as demonstrated in the context of knowledge graphs applied to AI [29]. In addition, CDMs can guide the identification of relevant variables (features) for classification or prediction tasks. In contexts where semantic relationships are crucial, their use contributes to guiding the feature engineering process [25].

The ability of CDMs to structure multiscale knowledge, link disparate entities, and foster interpretability makes them particularly suitable tools for analyzing informational phenomena. In the context of disinformation campaign analysis, their capacity to formally represent the relationships between intentions, contexts, actors, targets, and content provides a particularly relevant means of understanding the overall logic at play.

3 Conceptual Model for Analyzing Disinformation Campaigns

To address the limitations of existing tools outlined in Sect. 2.2, we introduce a conceptual model grounded in the definitions and characterizations of disinformation campaigns presented in Sect. 2.1. We state the objectives of the model and describe its design, which is organized into three complementary facets. The subsequent sections develop the model by detailing each facet in turn.

3.1 Purpose and Design Process of the Conceptual Model

In this work, we posit that, consistent with current practice, analysts must use multiple, potentially heterogeneous tools to study disinformation campaigns, including platforms to monitor social media activity, detect fake news, and characterize disinformation operations. The primary role of the proposed conceptual model is to act as a *data hub* that interfaces with this full suite of analytical tools. It can also guide tool development by identifying relevant variables (features) for classification and prediction tasks, and by improving the explainability of deep learning algorithms through techniques such as Concept Bottleneck Models [14].

The information system instantiated from this model must support early detection and comprehensive characterization of disinformation campaigns. Part of the data should be ingested automatically via export or streaming mechanisms (e.g., from tools for network-activity analysis and for detecting or characterizing fake news), while other data will be entered by analysts using purpose-built interfaces for the study of disinformation operations.

To determine which concepts to include in the model—and to establish consistent terminology—we reviewed the literature on propagation-graph analysis [21], fake-news characterization and detection [1,32], and the previously cited DISARM and MITRE frameworks. We then systematically evaluated early versions of the model against real-world disinformation campaigns documented by institutional sources such as VIGINUM [31] and research organizations such as Graphika [11]—including well-known operations like Doppelganger [9]—to assess and validate its completeness, expressiveness and consistency.

Of the six dimensions identified in Sect. 2.1, we organized the model into three compartments: (i) the disseminated information, (ii) the activity of the accounts and channels involved in dissemination and (iii) the strategic orchestration of the operation. This choice not only reflects both the literature and the current segmentation of the tools market, but also aligns with the perspectives of domain experts (journalists and military personnel) whom we interviewed, thereby enhancing its acceptability to the target end users. We deliberately favored parsimony, aiming for a concise structure and, in particular, avoiding overly deep inheritance hierarchies. These decisions make the model easier to understand, reuse, and maintain.

In the following sections, we present each compartment of the model; common classes (highlighted in orange) connect the three submodels.

3.2 The Campaign Content Model

The Campaign Content Model (Fig. 1) structures each unit of information as a self-contained and interpretable object. The combination of these units enables the detection of recurring or coordinated patterns across the content of the disinformation campaign.

The pivot concept of the model is the **NewsItem** entity. It represents any kind of narrative and can be characterized by two associated types: **NewsType** and **ContentType**. These types allow for fine-grained identification of the narrative, specifying how it was published and the manipulation method used. **NewsNarrative** represents the general narrative idea conveyed by the news. The time and date of publication are also recorded.

A second core concept is **Actor**. Depending on its role in a news item, an actor can be (i) the author of the news, (ii) an authoritative figure cited to enhance credibility, or (iii) another entity mentioned in the narrative, such as a target, witness, or adversary. An actor can be a single person or an organization.

A further part of this model describes the intrinsic content of the **NewsItem**, shown in blue in the figure. A news item addresses themes (**Topic**) that refer to events (**Event**) occurring at a specific moment (**TemporalEntity**). It may also specify particular places (**Location**). Narratives usually convey information designed to provoke an emotion in the reader, characterized by its type and intensity. Lastly, the dissemination format is captured by the **MediaAsset** entity, which specifies whether the message is delivered as text, image, or video, an important element for analyzing emotional impact and virality strategies.

This submodel addresses several dimensions identified in Sect. 2.1: the narrative deployed, timing of actions, actors involved, and manipulation techniques.

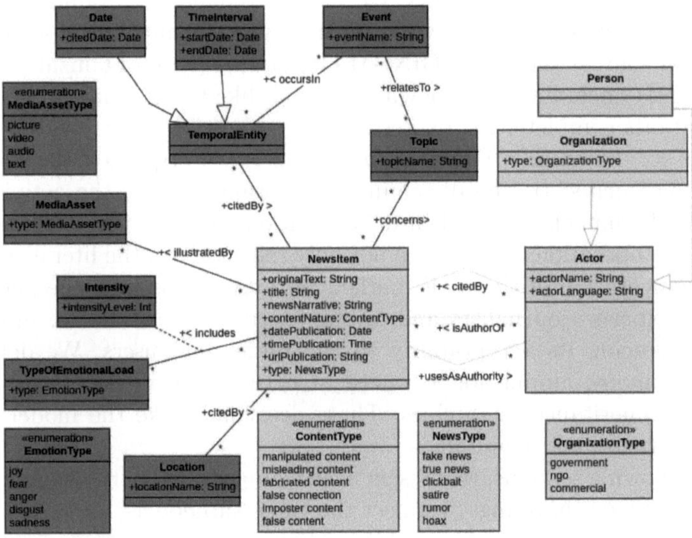

Fig. 1. Campaign Content conceptual model.

3.3 Account Behavioral Activity Model

The second submodel (Fig. 2) models the dissemination dynamics of news and the involved accounts. It enables the representation of publication dynamics, interaction patterns, and community-based relays. It provides a finer-grained characterization of the actors involved and the dissemination vectors, and helps identify targeted audiences. These are key elements in detecting coordinated or artificial behaviors.

Entities highlighted in orange, already introduced, ensure continuity and coherence across the submodels. This model relies primarily on the entities shown in cyan, which are specific to behavioral dynamics.

Account represents an actor's social media account. It is characterized by a set of properties useful for profiling the account(creation date, number of followers, and followings). Based on these properties, it can be typed by an **AccountType**. The owner's photo can also be analyzed by an image analyzer, and an **AuthenticityPictureType** can be assigned.

A **Publication** is made by an **Account**. It corresponds to an instance of content dissemination(**NewsItem**) by that account, at a given moment and within a specific linguistic context. Each publication is associated with the social interactions that accompany its dissemination.

The **Group** class groups accounts that share similar characteristics or objectives, while **Theme** identifies the topics they are associated with. These elements facilitate the detection of ideological clusters and targeted segmentation strategies. Finally, the dissemination strategy is specified through the **Media** class, defined by its type (**MediaType**) and reputation (**ReputationType**). Digital media refer to online outlets such as news websites, blogs, or video platforms, while social media designate interactive platforms centered on user exchanges, such as X, Facebook or Instagram. This distinction enables a more accurate identification of multivector approaches and differentiated relays depending on the target audience.

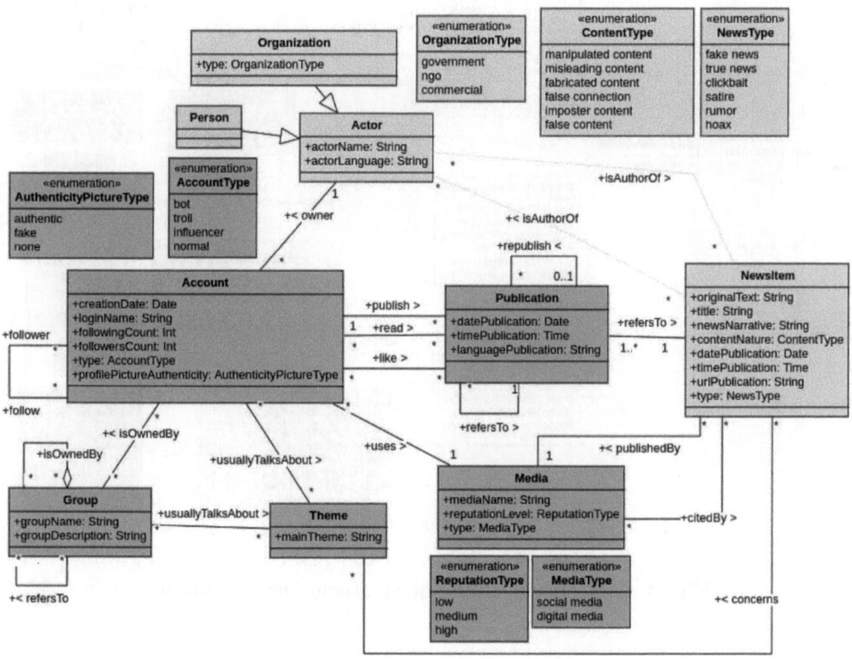

Fig. 2. Conceptual Model of Account Behavioral Activity.

3.4 Strategic Orchestration Model

The third submodel (Fig. 3) provides the strategic dimension of disinformation campaigns. It links content and observed behaviors to a hierarchical description built around objectives, targets, and contexts. This modeling draws on military and geopolitical frameworks, notably the DISARM framework [28] and studies produced by the RAND Corporation [12]. Campaigns are driven by strategic narratives, aimed at specific goals, and embedded in coordinated timelines. The model distinguishes three nested levels: the **DisinformationCampaign** defines long-term strategic goals; the **DisinformationOperation** adapts those goals to specific contexts; the **TacticalAction** implements them through concrete actions. This representation reflects the organization observed in real-world cases. A case documented by VIGINUM [31], shows how a consistent strategic objective is deployed through multiple coordinated waves. **Context** anchors each action in a specific setting, whether specific (**ElementaryContext**) or broader (**CompositeContext**). **Actor** captures the strategic leaders, operational agents, and content authors, highlighting delegation chains, and coordination mechanisms.

This submodel complements the previous two by offering a perspective on campaign orchestration. It integrates content and behavioral signals into a unified strategic interpretation and incorporates impact indicators.

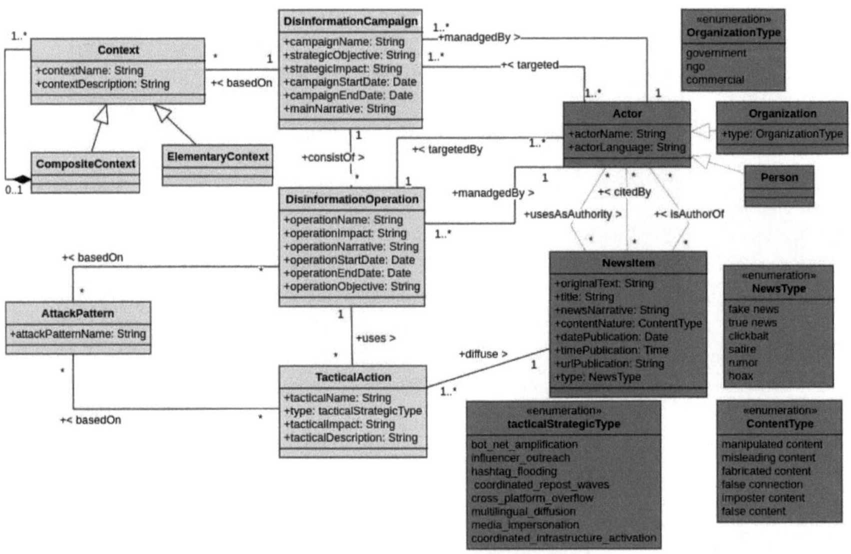

Fig. 3. Conceptual Model of Strategic Orchestration.

4 Deploying the Conceptual Model : an Illustration

In this section, we evaluate the model's fitness for purpose by demonstrating how it supports the analysis of a real-world, emerging disinformation campaign. Section 4.1 introduces the case study. Then, we begin with the message content (Sect. 4.2), proceed to dissemination behaviors (Sect. 4.3) and conclude by synthesizing the strategic objectives (Sect. 4.4). This workflow enables us to reconstruct the operation's overarching logic.

4.1 Case Study: the Reliable Recent News Disinformation Campaign

The Reliable Recent News (RRN) campaign was attributed to a pro-Russian network by **VIGINUM** in July 2023 [31]. The case study is based on two representative articles published online:

- Article (1): entitled *"CAESAR or How France is Responsible for War Crimes"*, it was published on June 25, 2022 [23], on *rrn.world*. It alleges that French CAESAR artillery systems were used to commit war crimes in the Donbass.
- Article (2): the second article [4], *"There is almost no grain left in Ukraine"*, was published on July 01, 2022, on *avisindependent.eu*, suggesting that humanitarian grain export operations are used to covertly transport weapons, implicating several Western countries.

At the time of their publication, the content distributed through websites appeared fragmented, without immediately revealing any coordinated logic. Some of these items may have been flagged as suspicious by automated systems, but lacked a clear understanding of their deeper connections or strategic coherence. Next, we will show how structuring the universe of data available via the CDM enhances the analytical capabilities of such a campaign. It took more than a year for the Viginum report to be published. This delay highlights the need for an analysis support tool such as the one proposed by our model.

4.2 Analysis of Narrative Contents

Figure 4 illustrates the description of Article (1) using the Campaign Content model. Although the content refers to real events, the arrangement of information, the absence of verification, and the direct attribution of blame to France without supporting evidence raise concerns about the reliability of the message.

The **newsNarrative** attribute reveals an accusatory framing portraying France as complicit in civilian attacks, emotionally reinforced through references to casualties and bombings. The **usedAsAuthority** field shows reliance on official figures to lend legitimacy, while geographical markers (e.g., Donetsk, France) situate the message within an international context.

This structured interpretation shows that the message does not merely rely on factual distortion. Rather, it mobilizes emotion, selective credibility, and political

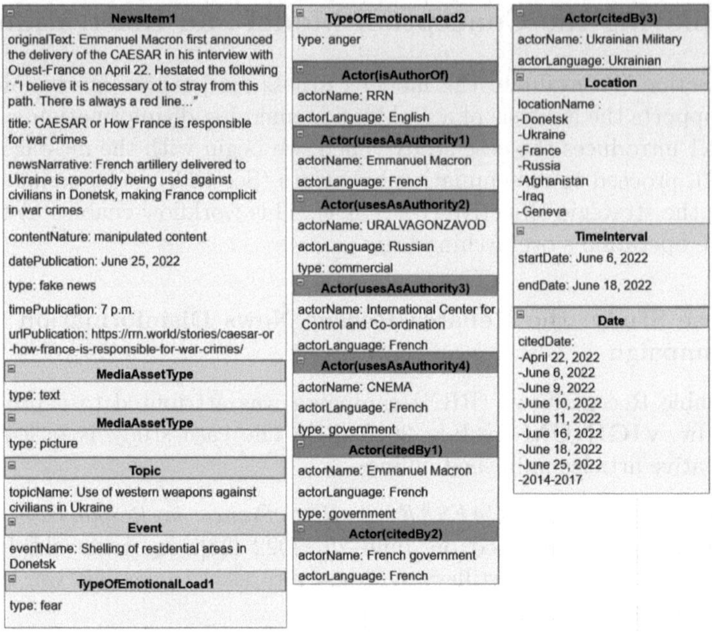

Fig. 4. Content analysis of Article(1).

framing to construct a persuasive narrative. The model enables a clearer understanding of the internal mechanics of manipulation by exposing the rhetorical and affective strategies embedded in the message.

Figure 5 presents the modeling of Article (2). The article discusses the export of Ukrainian grain through maritime corridors established as part of international humanitarian agreements. However, the message introduces a conspiratorial twist, suggesting that these shipments are being used to covertly transport weapons, allegedly involving France, Romania, and the UK.

Structured through the conceptual model, this message displays a narrative (**newsNarrative**) that reframes a humanitarian operation as a cover for military intervention. The emotional strategy is based on the simultaneous activation of **fear** and **disgust**, both aimed at discrediting Western involvement. The **usesAsAuthority** field shows that the message seeks validation through references to figures such as Mediapart and British advisers, giving the narrative a veneer of investigative credibility. Geopolitical references (Ukraine, Odessa, France, UK) set the message in a context of international collusion and deceit.

The structured representation highlights how the article constructs a deceptive message by blending factual elements with insinuations and emotionally charged framings. This semantic modeling provides insight into the persuasive mechanics of the message and allows a clearer interpretation of its intent to erode trust in humanitarian and diplomatic efforts.

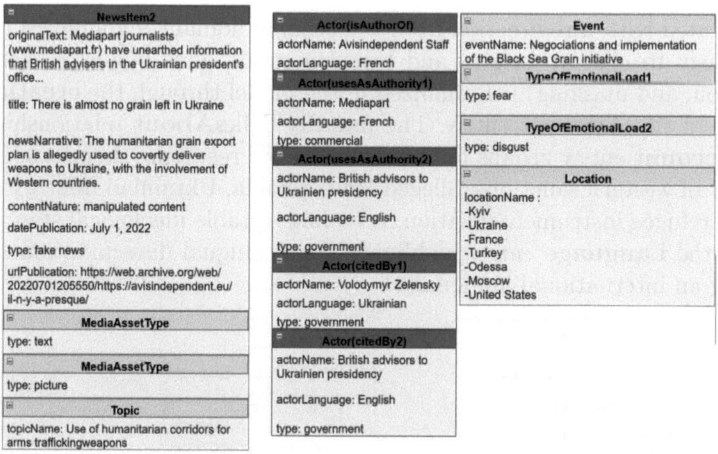

Fig. 5. Content analysis of Article(2).

The modeling of the two articles reveals deep structural parallels, suggesting a coordinated rhetorical strategy. Both employ accusatory narratives implicating France (either through direct military involvement or covert support) and cite similar authority figures like French politicians and investigative media. Their narratives unfold within a broad geopolitical context that involves Ukraine, France, and other Western powers. Emotionally, both messages strategically evoke fear (amplified by anger in one case and disgust in the other) to foster distrust toward Western involvement. These emotional frames are not incidental, but deliberately align with the underlying intentions of the narratives.

This representation reveals the persuasive mechanisms within each message and highlights recurring patterns across different contents. By applying a systematic structure, the model enables an interpretable and reproducible analysis, transforms subjective impressions into comparable attributes, and improves the explainability of disinformation strategies. However, the significance of these semantic patterns becomes fully apparent only when considered along with their dissemination. To assess whether messages are the result of isolated efforts or a coordinated strategy, it is essential to analyze their propagation. Examining the behavior of the accounts that relay them is therefore an important step.

4.3 Analysis of Dissemination Behavior

We analyze here Article (1) and (2) using the account behavior activity model.

The analysis of the domain registration date shows that `rrussianews[.]com` was created on 10 March 2022 from Russia, under the full name "Reliable Russian News" (see Fig. 6). This designation and its geographic origin immediately suggest an alignment with Russian informational interests. The site presents itself as an independent media outlet disseminating "verified information", with a particular focus on the war in Ukraine. On June 6, 2022, the domain "rrn[.]world" was activated with a redirection from the original domain, signalling a rebranding strategy to obscure origins and broaden reach. This sequence (activation, redirection, and masking) is formalized in the model through the **creationDate** attribute of the **Account** entity. The **usuallyTalksAbout** relationship linked to the **Account** entity groups publications around recurring themes, such as the inefficacy of western sanctions, alleged Russophobia, Ukrainian military extremism, and refugee instrumentalization, revealing a stable ideological stance. Additionally, the **Language** entity highlights a multilingual dissemination strategy, targeting an international audience.

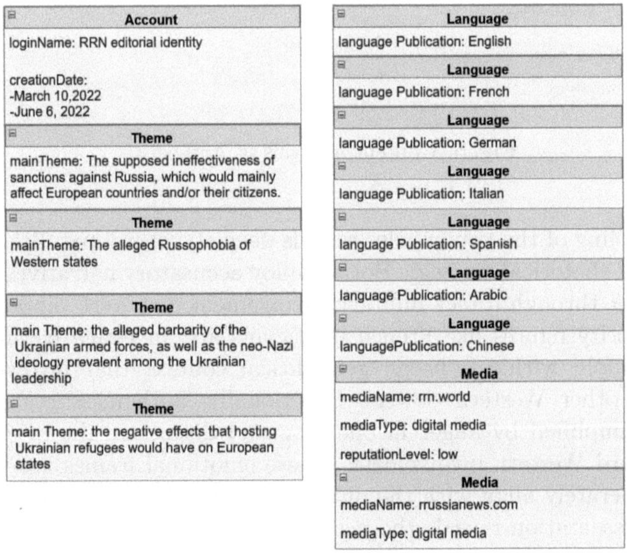

Fig. 6. Behavioural Analysis of Article(1).

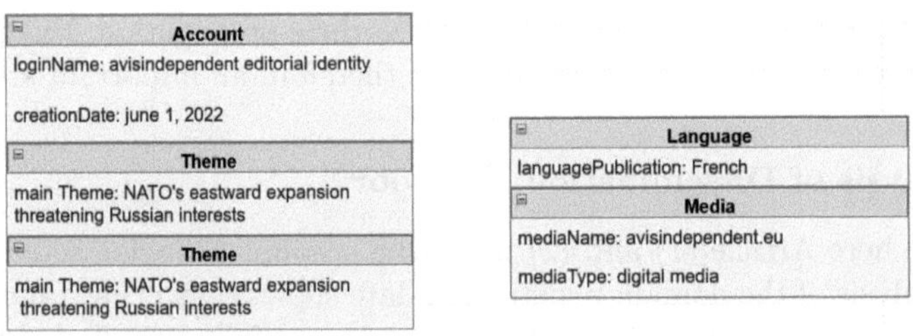

Fig. 7. Behavioural analysis of Article(2).

In Fig. 7, the model enables the identification of an infrastructure activated in an opportunistic context. The **creationDate** attribute indicates that the domain "avisindependent.eu" was registered on June 1, 2022. The publication of a polarizing article a few days later aligns this activation with a targeted informational sequence. The name of the publishing account, "La France Indépendante", represented by the **loginName** attribute, mimics the conventions of institutional French media. This semantic choice fosters false legitimacy, supported by an editorial line that seeks to appear independent. The exclusive use of French, indicated by the **language** attribute, reflects a deliberate strategy of cultural and linguistic targeting. The **usuallyTalksAbout** attribute reveals a coherent ideological position: denouncing NATO, defending Russian culture, and criticizing Western interventions. Combined with a low **reputationLevel** and editorial opacity, this suggests a media outlet designed to disseminate contested content outside of institutional oversight. Although identifiers of relay accounts are unavailable, weak signals from the model suggest organized dissemination through inauthentic accounts, hinting at a coordinated propagation infrastructure beyond initial publications.

By jointly structuring content and account activity, the model uncovers recurring dissemination patterns, revealing content embedded within strategic networks of ideologically aligned accounts, sometimes created or repurposed to serve this goal. The integration of semantic and activity models thus facilitates the identification of coordinated strategies, marking a first step toward reconstructing a broader campaign with defined objectives, targets, and resources.

4.4 Reconstructing Strategic Logic

The joint modeling of content and account activity related to the two analyzed articles reveals a coordinated tactical action.

Figure 8 highlights the following elements concerning Example(1): (i) the domain `rrussianews[.]com` was registered in March 2022, followed by the launch and redirection to `rrn[.]world` in June, indicating an effort to obscure its Russian origin; (ii) the article was published in seven languages, targeting an international audience; (iii) the narrative, built on partial facts and selective quotations, aims to delegitimize French arms deliveries to Ukraine and provoke indignation among French-speaking readers; (iv) the lack of legal notices and an anonymous editorial identity support the hypothesis of a non-institutional disinformation outlet; (v) these components are linked within the model through the **AttackPattern** and **TacticalAction** attributes.

Figure 9 highlights the following elements concerning Example(2): (i) the domain `avisindependent.eu`, registered on July 1, 2022, mimics French press design, illustrating typosquatting and impersonation; (ii) the exclusive use of French reflects targeted linguistic outreach; (iii) the narrative reframes humanitarian deliveries as covert arms shipments tied to the war in Ukraine; (iv) the

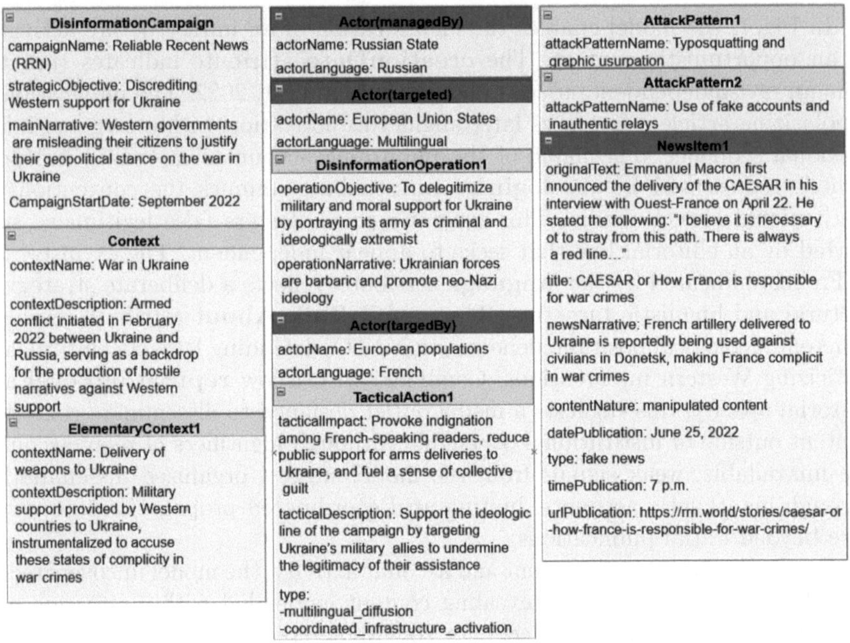

Fig. 8. Strategic Orchestration analysis of Article(1).

sender name, `La France Indépendante`, exploits national legitimacy cues; (v) the **usuallyTalksAbout** relationship formalized its ideological alignment with Example(1). The alignment between the two cases, through shared attack vectors, linguistic targeting, and editorial opacity, indicates that both items stem from the same **TacticalAction**. This action serves a larger **strategic objective**, namely to undermine Western support for Ukraine.

The conceptual model aggregates these seemingly isolated signals into a coherent dynamic. It provides an explanatory framework that not only supports documentation but also facilitates comparison, attribution, and anticipation of information operations in sensitive geopolitical contexts. The case study shows that, using of the model, it is possible to: (i) enrich the knowledge of each informational action with new information, (ii) detect disinformation campaigns from several distinct informational actions with no apparent connection between them, and (iii) provide explanatory elements on the justification for identifying these disinformation campaigns. This is one of the main advantages of the model over other approaches that could have identified the same informational attack but without being able to provide details on how the detection was carried out.

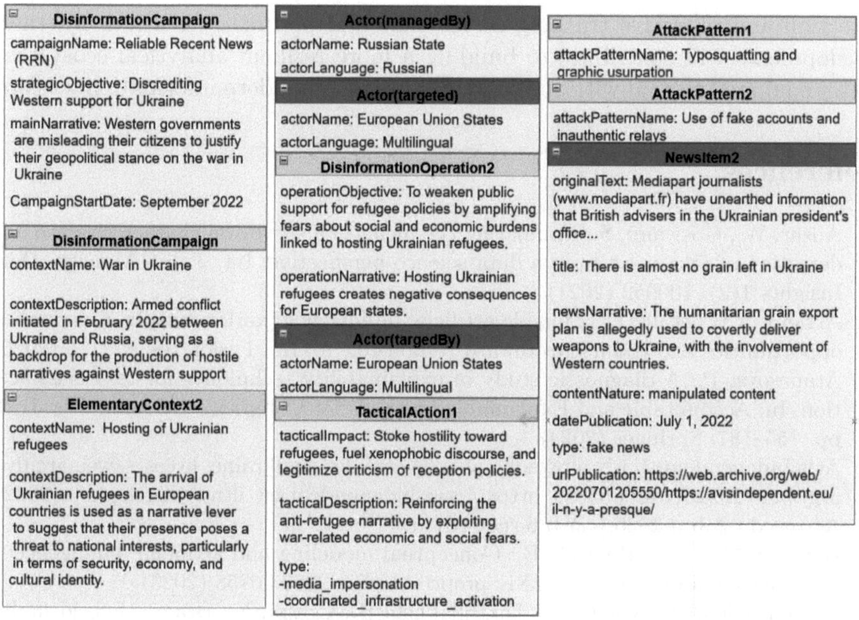

Fig. 9. Strategic Orchestration analysis of Article(2).

5 Conclusion and Perspectives

We have presented several challenges such as incompleteness, interoperability, and explainability that limit current tools for analyzing disinformation campaigns. We demonstrated the value of a Conceptual Data Model (CDM) that unifies the informational, behavioral, and strategic dimensions of disinformation, thereby supporting both analytical rigor and human comprehension. The usefulness of the CDM was illustrated through a case study on the RRN campaign, which showcased the model's ability to aggregate weak and dispersed signals and reveal their underlying coherence and strategic alignment.

An improvement of the model would be to separate the objective description of observed facts from their analytical interpretation, thus allowing multiple perspectives to be applied to the same dataset and supporting temporality and subjectivity modeling as introduced by Cesar Gonzalez-Perez [10]. An other direction is the design of hybrid AI systems that embed the CDM as an intermediate layer between raw data and high-level interpretation. It would combine the pattern recognition capabilities of machine learning with the transparency and formal structure of model-based reasoning. Within this architecture, the CDM can serve both as an explanatory scaffold and as a principled guide for feature extraction, enabling AI decisions that are genuinely interpretable and auditable.

Finally, constructing a curated repository of CDM-annotated campaigns would enable advanced applications such as patterns identification, community detection and narrative tracking across time and platforms. Collectively, these developments will contribute to building a more resilient analytical ecosystem, better equipped to deal with the evolving threats of modern information warfare.

References

1. Ansar, W., Goswami, S.: Combating the menace: a survey on characterization and detection of fake news from a data science perspective. Int. J. Inf. Manage. Data Insights **1**(2), 100052 (2021)
2. Arrieta, A.B., et al.: Explainable artificial intelligence (xai): concepts, taxonomies, opportunities and challenges toward responsible ai. Inf. Fusion **58**, 82–115 (2020)
3. Atanasova, P.: A diagnostic study of explainability techniques for text classification. In: Accountable and Explainable Methods for Complex Reasoning over Text, pp. 155–187. Springer (2024)
4. Avis Independent: Il n'y a presque plus de céréales en ukraine. https://web.archive.org/web/20220701205550/, https://avisindependent.eu/il-ny-a-presque/ (2022), Accessed 02 Jun 2025, via Internet Archive
5. Bork, D., Ali, S.J., Roelens, B.: Conceptual modeling and artificial intelligence: a systematic mapping study. arXiv preprint arXiv:2303.06758 (2023)
6. Chalehchaleh, R., Salehi, M., Farahbakhsh, R., Crespi, N.: Brag: a hybrid multi-feature framework for fake news detection on social media. Soc. Netw. Anal. Min. **14**(1), 35 (2024)
7. Varela da Costa, J., Bogea Gomes, S., Mira da Silva, M.: Fake news: a conceptual model for risk management. Hum. Soc. Sci. Commun. **11**(1), 1–11 (2024)
8. Do Nascimento, I.J.B., et al.: Infodemics and health misinformation: a systematic review of reviews. Bull. World Health Organ. **100**(9), 544 (2022)
9. EU DisinfoLab: Doppelgänger: Russian information operation impersonates western media outlets. Technical Report, Graphika, September 2022, https://www.disinfo.eu/wp-content/uploads/2022/09/Doppelganger-1.pdf, Accessed 17 Jun 2023
10. Gonzalez-Perez, C.: Conceptual modelling of temporality and subjectivity as cross-cutting concerns. Softw. Syst. Model. 1–16 (2024)
11. Graphika: Spamouflage goes to the beach: pro-chinese influence operation targets france with disinformation campaigns. Technical Report, Graphika (2023), https://public-assets.graphika.com/reports/graphika_report_spamouflage.pdf, Accessed 21 May 2024
12. Helmus, T.C., et l.: Russian social media influence: understanding Russian propaganda in Eastern Europe. Rand Corporation (2018)
13. Hu, L., Wei, S., Zhao, Z., Wu, B.: Deep learning for fake news detection: a comprehensive survey. AI Open **3**, 133–155 (2022)
14. Koh, P.W., et al.: Concept bottleneck models. In: International Conference on Machine Learning, pp. 5338–5348. PMLR (2020)
15. Lakzaei, B., Haghir Chehreghani, M., Bagheri, A.: Disinformation detection using graph neural networks: a survey. Artif. Intell. Rev. **57**(3), 52 (2024)
16. Lazer, D.M., et al.: The science of fake news. Science **359**(6380), 1094–1096 (2018)
17. Lin, H.: Developing responses to cyber-enabled information warfare and influence operations. Lawfare (2023)
18. Lundberg, S.M., Lee, S.I.: A unified approach to interpreting model predictions. In: Advances in Neural Information Processing Systems, vol. 30 (2017)

19. Mannocci, L., Mazza, M., Monreale, A., Tesconi, M., Cresci, S.: Detection and characterization of coordinated online behavior: a survey. arXiv preprint arXiv:2408.01257 (2024)
20. NATO: Media (dis)information security: information warfare. https://www.nato.int/cps/en/natohq/topics_219728.htm (2020), Accessed 12 Apr 2024
21. Phan, H.T., Nguyen, N.T., Hwang, D.: Fake news detection: a survey of graph neural network methods. Appl. Soft Comput. 110235 (2023)
22. Rashkin, H., Choi, E., Jang, J.Y., Volkova, S., Choi, Y.: Truth of varying shades: analyzing language in fake news and political fact-checking. In: Proceedings of the 2017 Conference on Empirical Methods in Natural Language Processing, pp. 2931–2937 (2017)
23. RRN World: Caesar, or how france is responsible for war crimes. https://web.archive.org/web/20220820064248/, https://rrn.world/stories/caesar-or-how-france-is-responsible-for-war-crimes/ (2022). Accessed 02 Jun 2025, via Internet Archive
24. Shao, C., Ciampaglia, G.L., Flammini, A., Menczer, F.: Hoaxy: a platform for tracking online misinformation. In: Proceedings of the 25th International Conference Companion on World Wide Web, pp. 745–750 (2016)
25. Sikelis, K., Tsekouras, G.E., Kotis, K.: Ontology-based feature selection: a survey. Future Internet **13**(6), 158 (2021)
26. Starbird, K., Arif, A., Wilson, T.: Disinformation as collaborative work: surfacing the participatory nature of strategic information operations. Proc. ACM Hum.-Comput. Interact. **3**(CSCW), 1–26 (2019)
27. Strom, B.E., Applebaum, A., Miller, D.P., Nickels, K.C., Pennington, A.G., Thomas, C.B.: Mitre att&ck: design and philosophy. MITRE Corporation, Technical Report (2018)
28. Terp, S.J., Breuer, P.: Disarm: a framework for analysis of disinformation campaigns. In: 2022 IEEE Conference on Cognitive and Computational Aspects of Situation Management (CogSIMA), pp. 1–8. IEEE (2022)
29. Tiddi, I., Schlobach, S.: Knowledge graphs as tools for explainable machine learning: a survey. Artif. Intell. **302**, 103627 (2022)
30. Vargas, L., Emami, P., Traynor, P.: On the detection of disinformation campaign activity with network analysis. In: Proceedings of the 2020 ACM SIGSAC Conference on Cloud Computing Security Workshop, pp. 133–146 (2020)
31. VIGINUM: Rrn: a complex and persistent information manipulation campaign. https://www.sgdsn.gouv.fr/files/files/Publications/20230719_NP_VIGINUM_RAPPORT-CAMPAGNE-RRN_EN.pdf, July 2023, Accessed 13 Aug 2025
32. Zhang, X., Ghorbani, A.A.: An overview of online fake news: characterization, detection, and discussion. Inf. Process. Manage. **57**(2), 102025 (2020)
33. Zhou, X., Zafarani, R.: A survey of fake news: fundamental theories, detection methods, and opportunities. ACM Comput. Surv. (CSUR) **53**(5), 1–40 (2020)

Ontology for Personalized Recipe Recommendations Supporting Sustainability, Personal Preferences, and Health Restrictions

Donika Xhani(✉) and Renata Guizzardi

Industrial Engineering and Business Information Systems, Department of High-Tech Business and Entrepreneurship, Faculty of Behavioural, Management and Social Sciences, University of Twente, 7522 NB, Enschede, The Netherlands
d.xhani@utwente.nl

Abstract. Many people consume food without having enough information about its nutritional value, environmental impact, or how it aligns with their personal preferences, health, and sustainability goals. With increasing concerns about human health and sustainability, there is a growing need for tools that help individuals make better-informed food choices. This paper introduces the SustainHealthyFood ontology to be used as a reference model for sustainable and healthy food consumption. The ontology serves two key purposes: (1) helping users make informed decisions by providing insights into food nutrients and Eco-Scores, enabling them to assess both health and environmental impact; and (2) facilitating personalized food recommendations, such as recipe suggestions, tailored to individual preferences, personal attributes, dietary needs, health conditions, and goals. The SustainHealthyFood ontology consists of four OntoUML conceptual models focusing on: (1) Food Nutrition, (2) Health Status and Diet, (3) Environmental Sustainability, and (4) Explainable Recommendations. The operational ontology is implemented in OWL, with instances populated from existing datasets in the domains of food and environmental sustainability. For ontology testing, SPARQL queries are used to assess whether the ontology meets the competency questions. This paper describes and evaluates the SustainHealthyFood ontology, presents related work, and discusses benefits, limitations, and future work.

Keywords: ontology · food · health · environmental sustainability · recommendation

1 Introduction

In today's fast-paced world, many people struggle to maintain a balanced diet, leading to widespread issues of malnutrition and poor food quality. Some overconsume ultra-processed foods, increasing their risk of obesity and chronic diseases, while others face nutrient deficiencies due to unbalanced eating habits. In 2022, an estimated 37 million children (5.6%) under five years of age were overweight, while 148.1 million (22. 3%) suffered stunting, which is poor nutrition during early development that can have long-term health consequences [1]. Malnutrition remains one of the most pressing global

D. Bork et al. (Eds.): ER 2025, LNCS 16189, pp. 376–392, 2026.
https://doi.org/10.1007/978-3-032-08623-5_20

health challenges [2,3], contributing to severe conditions such as anemia, vitamin deficiencies, and other diet-related illnesses. A major reason behind this issue is the lack of awareness and accessible information on proper nutrition. Many individuals are uncertain about which foods to prioritize or avoid based on their health conditions, leading to dietary choices, which may be influenced by a range of biological, emotional, or socio-economic factors [4]. Beyond personal health, there is also limited public awareness of the environmental impact of food consumption. Without clear information on the sustainability scores of different food products, consumers often make choices that contribute to larger ecological footprints without realizing it. Addressing these gaps requires more intelligent and personalized systems to guide people toward healthier and more sustainable eating habits.

Information systems play a crucial role in tackling malnutrition and improving dietary awareness by systematically collecting, analyzing, and sharing nutrition-related data. These systems also enable the development of recommender systems that provide nutritional advice, suggest recipes, and help users make better food choices. Various approaches have been used to build these systems, including traditional methods such as content-based filtering, collaborative filtering, and hybrid models, as well as more advanced techniques such as the Retrieval-Augmented Generation (RAG) approach. RAG combines retrieval-based and generative methods using Large Language Models (LLMs), allowing for more dynamic and context-aware recommendations [5].

However, most existing recommender systems struggle with two key challenges: explainability and personalization. Users often receive recommendations without understanding why certain foods or recipes are suggested, making it difficult to trust or follow the advice. Additionally, many systems fail to consider personal factors such as dietary preferences, cultural background, or specific health conditions [6]. Ontologies can significantly enhance both explainability and personalization in food recommender systems. By incorporating domain knowledge and intelligent reasoning, ontology-based systems can generate more meaningful and user-centric recommendations [7,8]. For example, instead of simply suggesting a recipe, an ontology-based system can give this kind of explanation: "This recipe is high in iron because it includes beef and spinach, which can help with iron deficiency". This kind of common-sense reasoning makes dietary recommendations more informative and actionable [9].

The goal of this paper is to introduce the SustainHealthyFood ontology, designed to integrate knowledge from three key domains: food, health, and sustainability. This ontology consists of four conceptual models done in OntoUML[1] language, which reveal the semantics regarding (1) Food Nutrition, (2) Health Status and Diet, (3) Environmental Sustainability, and (4) Explainable Recommendations. The operational ontology is created in Protégé, and the instances are added by using RDFlib[2] in Python.

This paper is structured as follows: Sect. 2 discusses related work. Section 3 presents the methodology behind this work, ontology requirements, and the conceptual models.

[1] OntoUML is an ontology-driven conceptual modelling language, which is based on the Unified Foundational Ontology (UFO). More information can be found here: https://ontouml.readthedocs.io/en/latest/index.html.

[2] RDFlib is a Python library for working with RDF format. More information can be found here: https://rdflib.readthedocs.io/en/stable/.

Section 4 describes the implementation of the operational ontology, and the ontology rules. Section 5 describes ontology testing by using SPARQL queries, Sect. 6 gives an example of how to apply the ontology, and finally, Sect. 7 discusses the contributions, limitations, and future work.

2 Related Work

Several studies use ontologies to standardize food- and health-related data, showcasing the potential of semantic technologies in these domains. However, many of these efforts exhibit limitations in their underlying conceptual models, focusing narrowly on specific domain components while neglecting inter-domain relationships and well-founded semantics.

For example, seminal efforts in the food domain such as the *FoodOn*[3] and the *WhatToMakeOntology*[4] ontologies, provide foundational food modeling and include biological processes. However, these ontologies primarily focus on domain-specific taxonomies without addressing personalization or interconnections with health and sustainability. In contrast, the SustainHealthyFood ontology employs a rigorous conceptual modeling approach in OntoUML, capturing inter-domain relationships and supporting user-specific reasoning.

In the health-related domain, ontologies such as the *Ontology of Dietary Recommendations* (ODR) [10], which assists individuals dealing with obesity, the *Alzheimer Disease Ontology* (ADO) [11], and the *Coronavirus Infectious Disease Ontology* (CIDO) [12] provide valuable domain-specific coverage. However, these ontologies lack integration with detailed nutritional modeling or the environmental impact of consumed food.

A more integrative approach is found in the *Food Explanation Ontology* (FEO) [13], which aims to provide human-understandable explanations for food recommendations. FEO supports various types of explanations, such as *Contextual* (why a user should consume a specific food), *Contrastive* (why one food is recommended over another), and *Counterfactual* (what would happen if an ingredient is changed). While FEO captures aspects like food seasonality, it does not include sufficient detail on the nutritional profiles of foods.

A notable effort that bridges multiple domains is the *Nutrition & Activity* (NAct) ontology [14], designed to support healthy lifestyle recommendations. NAct models relationships among food, health conditions, and user activity levels using OWL. Despite its broad scope, NAct lacks conceptual models, instantiated individuals, and reasoning mechanisms, making it operationally limited.

To the best of our knowledge, no existing work combines a unified conceptual framework that seamlessly integrates food nutrition, health, dietary restrictions, and environmental sustainability. The SustainHealthyFood ontology addresses this gap by employing a methodologically sound approach to conceptual modeling and operationalization, aligning with the principles of well-founded semantics, inter-domain reasoning, and actionable recommendations. While many of its concepts and relations coincide

[3] https://foodon.org.

[4] http://purl.org/heals/food.

with existing ontologies, enabling potential ontology alignment for interoperability, no available model provided the necessary coverage, motivating the development of a new ontology.

3 Ontology Design

3.1 SustainHealthyFood Ontology Requirements

The Sustainable Healthy Food (SustainHealthyFood) Ontology is designed by following the Systematic Approach for Building Ontology (SABiO) methodology [15]. This methodology follows a structured process divided into five key phases: (1) defining the purpose and gathering requirements, (2) ontology capture and formalization, (3) design, (4) implementation, and (5) testing. The initial phase focuses on establishing the ontology's purpose and identifying its requirements. These requirements are categorized into two types: non-functional requirements, which define qualitative attributes or characteristics of the ontology (e.g., ontology consistency, scalability, reusability), and functional requirements, which are framed as Competency Questions (CQs) to guide the ontology's scope and capabilities. The SustainHealthyFood ontology aims (1) to provide a structured representation of the relationships between food nutrition, health constraints and diet, and the environmental impact of consumed food, and (2) to identify foods and dietary patterns that are both healthy and environmentally sustainable.

The ontology is designed to support a range of practical applications, particularly in the areas of personalized diet or recipe recommendations and sustainability assessment. It enables the recommendations of personalized food items or recipes that account for not only individual nutritional needs but also environmental sustainability. For example, it can be used to suggest smoothie recipes tailored to the needs of sport athletes or to recommend lower-carbon, nutrient-dense food alternatives to everyday consumers. Additionally, it helps identify seasonal and local food options that can contribute to reducing the environmental impact of food consumption. On the sustainability front, the ontology facilitates the evaluation of key environmental indicators such as carbon footprint, water usage, and land use across various food items and dietary patterns. It also supports the identification of foods that are both nutrient-dense and environmentally friendly, encouraging informed choices that benefit both human health and the planet.

Table 1 shows the CQs of the SustainHealthyFood ontology which are categorized as Environmental Sustainability of Food Choices, Food and Nutrition (considering Health), Health State, Recipe, and User Evaluation. It is worth mentioning that expert knowledge has been implicitly embedded in the formulation of the competency questions and in the design of the conceptual models of the ontology, as this work is part of a broader work package that involves collaboration with health professionals, hospitals, and producers.

3.2 SustainHealthyFood Ontology Conceptual Models

The conceptual model on Food Nutrition (Fig. 1) describes the *food groups*, *food nutrients*, *food data properties*, besides the *person's data properties* and *daily intake levels*. FOODGROUP is specialized into subkinds such as DAIRY, FRUITS, VEGETABLES,

Table 1. Competency Questions of the SustainHealthyFood ontology

• **Environmental Sustainability of Food Choices**
CQ1: Which sustainability aspects are related to food consumption?
CQ2: What is the environmental (eco) score of a specific food or ingredient?
CQ3: What is the carbon footprint of a specific food item?
CQ4: Which food products have the lowest eutrophication footprint?
CQ5: Which local and seasonal food options are available for a given region and time of year?
• **Food and Nutrition (considering Health)**
CQ6: What is the health (nutrient) score of a specific food?
CQ7: What is the micronutrient profile (key micronutrients) of the (consumed) food?
CQ8: What is the macronutrient profile (key macronutrients) of the (consumed) food?
CQ9: Which foods are rich in protein but low in fat?
CQ10: What is a better (healthier) alternative for a specific food based on a health state?
CQ11: What are the recommended daily intake levels for specific nutrients based on the user's profile (i.e., age, sex, and activity level)?
• **Health State**
CQ12: Which health states lead to dietary restrictions?
CQ13: What food should be avoided if a person has specific dietary restrictions or health state?
CQ14: What food can be consumed in a certain amount if a person has specific dietary restrictions or a health state?
CQ15: Which food group is not suitable for individuals with specific dietary restrictions (e.g., vegan, vegetarian)?
• **Recipe**
CQ16: What are the ingredients of a recipe?
CQ17: How much of a certain ingredient is contained in a recipe?
CQ18: What is a recipe that does not contain any ingredients related to a specific dietary restriction?
CQ19: Which recipe has the best combination of ingredients a person with a particular health condition should consume?
CQ20: What is a recipe that includes ingredients that should be avoided in a dietary restriction?
• **User Evaluation**
CQ21: Which recipes are most liked by people?
CQ22: Which ingredients are contained in recipes that are liked by people?
CQ23: Which ingredients are contained in recipes that are not liked by people?
CQ24: Which recipe has a similar set of ingredients to a user's preferred recipe?

MEAT, GRAINS, BEVERAGES, etc., based on the food categories of NEVO[5] [16]. A NUTRIENT can be a MACRONUTRIENT or a MICRONUTRIENT. Macronutrients are nutrients that the human body requires in large amounts and are classified as PROTEIN, FAT, CARBOHYDRATE, FIBER, and WATER [17]. Carbohydrates and fats contribute to

[5] NEVO is the Dutch Food Composition Database and it contains data on the composition of foods. More information on NEVO can be found here: https://www.rivm.nl/en/dutch-food-composition-database.

the amount of energy, while proteins help build body cells and tissues [17]. Finally, micronutrients are required in smaller quantities and are categorized as VITAMIN and MINERAL [17].

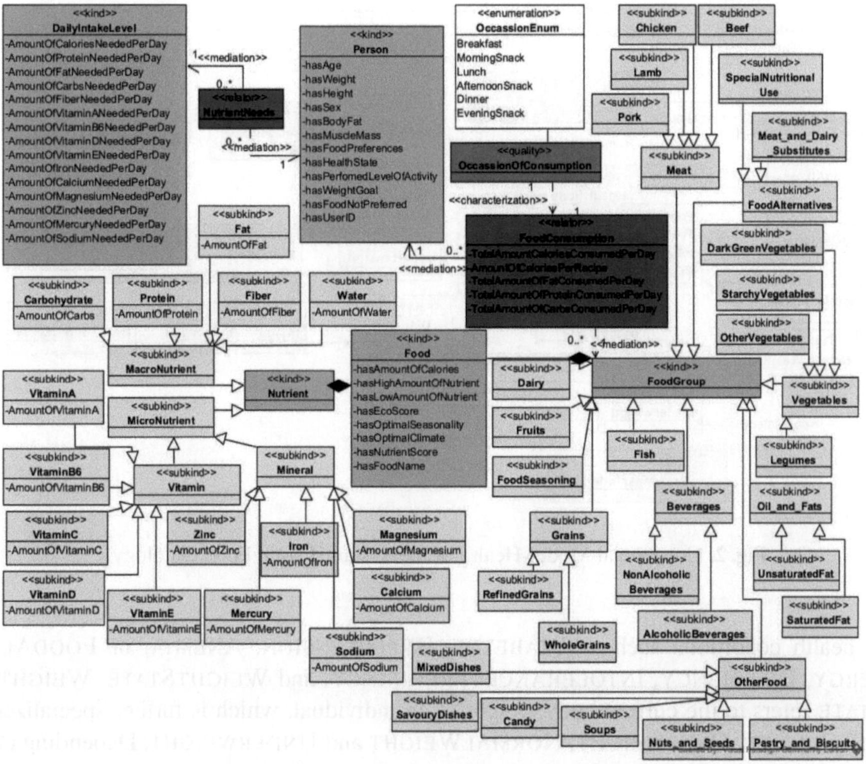

Fig. 1. Conceptual Model-Food Nutrition of the SustainHealthyFood Ontology

FOODGROUP is composed of FOOD, which refers to a specific food item (e.g., salmon, orange, rice) with its respective data properties[6] such as: amount of calories, high amount of nutrients, low amount of nutrients, eco score, etc. PERSON is a sortal type that has characteristics such as: AGE, WEIGHT, HEIGHT, FOOD PREFERENCES, etc. Each PERSON may have one or more NUTRIENT NEEDS which are related to the DAILYINTAKELEVEL. The DAILYINTAKELEVEL prescribes the recommended amount of calories, macronutrients, and micronutrients that a person should consume per day according to his/her characteristics.

The conceptual model on Health (Fig. 2) describes the different kinds of diets that a person may or must follow depending on his/her health state. HEALTHSTATE refers

[6] At the current SustainHealthyFood development stage, not all concepts are reified. The core concepts are reified while supporting ones are represented as properties.

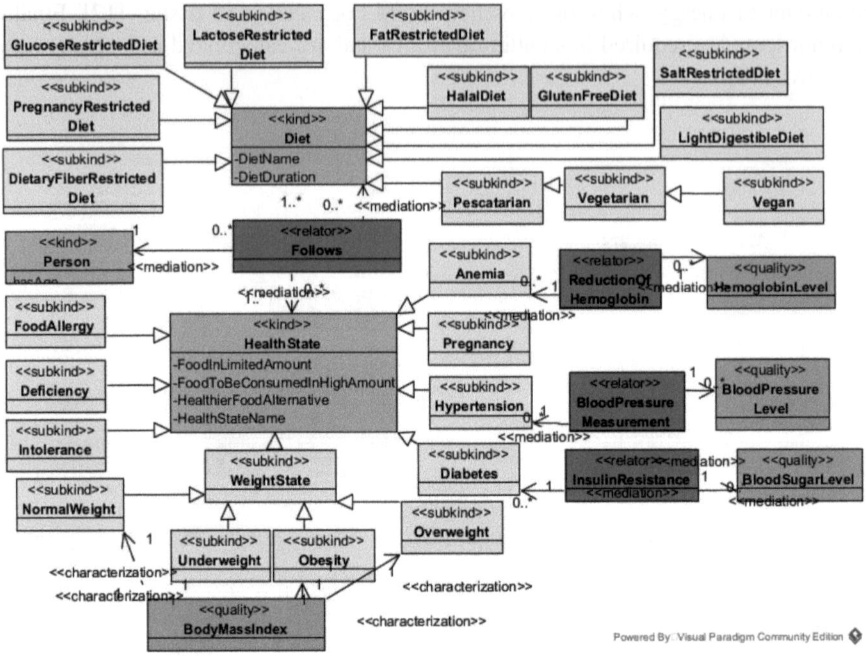

Fig. 2. Conceptual Model-Health of the SustainHealthyFood Ontology

to health conditions such as DIABETES, HYPERTENSION, ANEMIA, or FOODALLERGY, DEFICIENCY, INTOLERANCE, PREGNANCY, and WEIGHTSTATE. WEIGHTSTATE refers to the current body weight of an individual, which is further specialized into OBESITY, OVERWEIGHT, NORMALWEIGHT and UNDERWEIGHT. Depending on the person's health state, some food may be restricted, limited, not recommended, or highly recommended. For example, a *pregnant woman* should not consume any alcoholic beverages (*not recommended*), while foods high in potassium such as cantaloupe, mangoes, and bananas are *recommended*. DIET refers to a specific type of diet, such as GLUCOSERESTRICTEDDIET or LACTOSERESTRICTEDDIET or a preferred dietary choice such as the PESCATARIAN, VEGETARIAN, or VEGAN diet. A person may follow zero or more diets, depending on his/her needs and preferences.

The conceptual model for Environmental Sustainability (Fig. 3) illustrates that each FOOD item is associated with an ECOSCORE, which serves as an indicator of its ENVIRONMENTALSUSTAINABILITY. Environmental sustainability in this study refers to the impact that food production and consumption have on natural resources and ecosystems. It can be assessed through several key indicators, including GREENHOUSEGASEMISSIONS, WATERUSE, LANDUSE, and EUTROPHICATION. Eutrophication refers to a form of water pollution caused by disruptions in nitrogen and phosphorus cycles, which can lead to the degradation of aquatic ecosystems.

The conceptual model on Explainable Recommendation (Fig. 4) describes that each RECOMMENDATION takes an INPUT from a PERSON. In this case, the user inputs

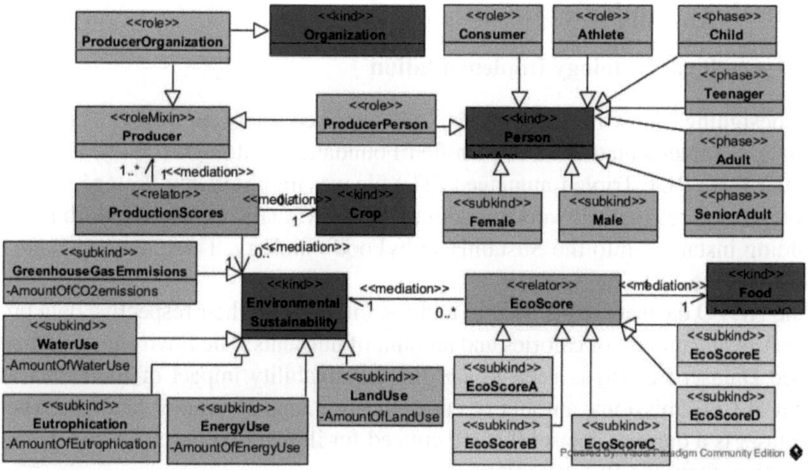

Fig. 3. Conceptual Model-Environmental Sustainability of the SustainHealthyFood Ontology

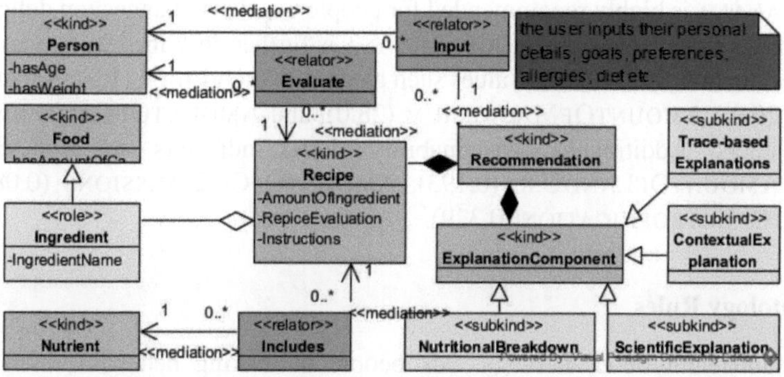

Fig. 4. Conceptual Model-Explainable Recommendation of the SustainHealthyFood Ontology

his/her personal details, goals, preferences, health status, etc. The RECOMMENDATION is composed of a RECIPE and an EXPLANATIONCOMPONENT. RECIPE prescribes the use of INGREDIENTS and offers some instructions. The EXPLANATIONCOMPONENT explains the output of the recommender. These explanations contain a NUTRITIONALBREAKDOWN of the recipe, listing the amount of calories, macronutrients and micronutrients of the recipe, and three other types of explanations: Scientific, Contextual and Trace-based. According to the Food Explanation Ontology (FEO) [13], SCIENTIFICEXPLANATION indicates which are the sources where the explanation is based, CONTEXTUALEXPLANATION explains why these foods are recommended to the user, while TRACE-BASEDEXPLANATION shows which steps led to that specific recommendation.

4 Ontology Implementation

4.1 Operational Ontology Implementation

After designing the OntoUML CMs, we exported them to gUFO[7], which is a lightweight implementation of the Unified Foundation Ontology (UFO), using OWL. Next, the Terse RDF Triple Language (TTL) file was imported into Protégé. In parallel, as Protégé requires manual work for adding the individuals, we used RDFlib in Python for adding instances into the SustainHealthyFood ontology. Three datasets were used for this purpose.

The NEVO dataset [16] is used to add food items with their respective data properties such as the amount of calories and amount of nutrients. The Environmental Impacts of Food Dataset by [18] is used to add the sustainability impact of food such as the amount of CO_2emissions, amount of eutrophication, and amount of land use. The Person dataset is a dummy dataset that we created for illustration purposes and it contains information about the PERSON class.

Figure 5 shows some individuals in the FRUITS subclass within the FOODGROUP class, and as an example, the data properties of a FOOD_BANANA individual per 100 g[8]. FOOD_BANANA is highly recommended for people who have magnesium deficiency as it contains 28 g of magnesium. FOOD_BANANA is further described using various data properties, including nutritional values such as AMOUNTOFFIBER (1.9), AMOUNTOFCARBS (20.0), AMOUNTOFMAGNESIUM (28.0), and AMOUNTOFCALORIES (92.0), among others. Additionally, sustainability-related indicators are also captured, such as AMOUNTOFLANDUSE (0.193), AMOUNTOFCO2EMISSIONS (0.086), and AMOUNTOFEUTROPHICATION (0.329).

4.2 Ontology Rules

The SustainHealthyFood ontology aids people in making better-informed choices towards what food they should or not consume, what food is highly recommended based on their health state, what food can be consumed in a limited amount based on their state, or what are better (healthier) alternatives. The rules of the SustainHealthyFood ontology are added by using RDFlib in Python. A summary of the rules in Description Logic (DL) is given in Table 2.

For instance, only a Female PERSON can have the PREGNANT HEALTH STATE. ALCOHOLICBEVERAGES are not recommended for her, food high in mercury such as SWORDFISH, TUNA, or COFFEE are food to be consumed in limited amounts, while food such as COOKEDMEAT, HERBALTEA, LEANBEEF can be consumed in high

[7] For the export, Visual Paradigm and the gUFO function provided at the OntoUML plugin is used.

[8] When implementing the ontology in Protégé, certain design decisions were necessary to adapt the ontology's conceptual models (CMs) to a less expressive language such as OWL. Consequently, some differences arise between the CMs of the ontology and its implemented version. For instance, Fig. 5 shows that individuals are also associated with their respective FOODGROUP while retaining the properties of FOOD. This is because the individuals were first added under FOOD and subsequently categorized into their respective FOODGROUP.

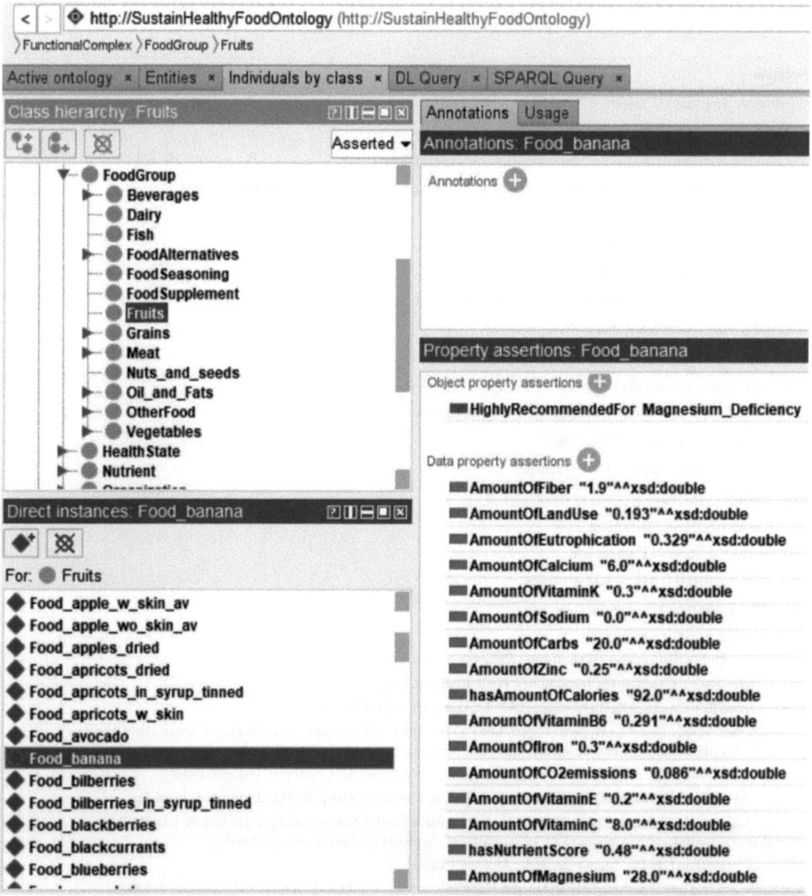

Fig. 5. Individuals of the 'Fruits' Class in the SustainHealthyFood Ontology

amounts. Other rules comply with the dietary preferences of the user, such as Meat and Fish products are not recommended if a person is Vegetarian, or Meat, Fish, Dairy, MixedDishes, Pastry_and_Biscuits, and SavoryDishes are not recommended if a person is Vegan.

Other rules define what foods are or not recommended based on a person's health state. For example, Dairy products are not recommended to LactoseIntolerant people or to people that follow the LactoseResctrictedDiet. HighIronFood are recommended to people with Anemia. Moreover, we also defined rules about RestrictedFood based on food allergies, or HighlyRecommended food for food deficiencies. For example, foods containing nuts (e.g., walnuts, pecans, etc.) are restricted if the person has treenut_allergy.

The recommended daily intake levels can be calculated based on the person's age, height, Body Mass Index (BMI), sex, activity level, and weight goal. In this study, these levels are calculated using the guidelines by WHO [19], FAO [20], and the Schofield

Table 2. Summary of SustainHealthyFood Ontology Rules (DL Notation)

DL Notation
$\exists \text{hasHealthState.Pregnancy} \sqsubseteq \text{hasSex} = \text{"Female"}$
$\text{AlcoholicBeverages} \sqsubseteq \forall \text{notRecommendedFor.Pregnancy}$
$\text{Dairy} \sqsubseteq \forall \text{notRecommendedFor.}(\text{LactoseIntolerant} \sqcup \text{LactoseRestrictedDiet})$
$\text{Dairy} \sqcup \text{Meat} \sqcup \text{Fish} \sqcup \text{MixedDishes} \sqcup \text{Pastry\_and\_Biscuits} \sqcup \text{SavouryDishes} \sqsubseteq \forall \text{notRecommendedFor.Vegan}$
$\text{Meat} \sqcup \text{Fish} \sqsubseteq \forall \text{notRecommendedFor.Vegetarian}$
$\text{Meat} \sqsubseteq \forall \text{notRecommendedFor.Pescatarian}$
$\text{PorkMeat} \sqsubseteq \forall \text{notRecommendedFor.HalalDiet}$
$\text{HighFiberFood} \sqsubseteq \forall \text{notRecommendedFor.DietaryFiberRestrictedDiet}$
$\text{HighFatFood} \sqsubseteq \forall \text{notRecommendedFor.FatRestrictedDiet}$
$\text{HighSaltFood} \sqsubseteq \forall \text{notRecommendedFor.SaltRestrictedDiet}$
$\text{HighIronFood} \sqsubseteq \forall \text{recommendedFor.Anemia}$
$\text{HighSugarFood} \sqcup \text{HighCarbFood} \sqsubseteq \forall \text{notRecommendedFor.Diabetes}$
$\text{Person} \sqcap (\text{hasAge} \geq 0 \sqcap \text{hasAge} \leq 12) \rightarrow \text{Child}$
$\text{Person} \sqcap (\text{hasAge} \geq 13 \sqcap \text{hasAge} \leq 17) \rightarrow \text{Teenager}$
$\text{Person} \sqcap (\text{hasAge} \geq 18 \sqcap \text{hasAge} \leq 64) \rightarrow \text{Adult}$
$\text{Person} \sqcap (\text{hasAge} \geq 65) \rightarrow \text{SeniorAdult}$
$\text{Person} \sqcap (\text{hasBMI} < 18.5) \rightarrow \text{Underweight}$
$\text{Person} \sqcap (18.5 \leq \text{hasBMI} < 25) \rightarrow \text{NormalWeight}$
$\text{Person} \sqcap (25 \leq \text{hasBMI} < 30) \rightarrow \text{Overweight}$
$\text{Person} \sqcap (\text{hasBMI} \geq 30) \rightarrow \text{Obesity}$
$\text{Diabetes} \sqsubseteq \forall \text{FoodInLimitedAmount.}\{\text{WhiteBread, WhiteRice, Pastries, SugaryCereal, Sugar, Sweet, Candy, Soda, Juice, Butter, Fried, FastFood, Chips, Cookies, Cake}\}$
$\text{Diabetes} \sqsubseteq \forall \text{FoodToBeConsumedInHighAmount.}\{\text{WholeGrains, BrownRice, Quinoa, Oats, Berries, Apple, Pear, Citrus, GreekYogurt, LowFatDairy, OliveOil, Avocado, Nuts, Hummus, Seeds, DarkChocolate}\}$
$\text{Pregnancy} \sqsubseteq \forall \text{FoodInLimitedAmount.}\{\text{RawMeat, RawFish, UnpasteurizedDairy, DeliMeat, Sushi, Swordfish, Shark, Tuna, Coffee, EnergyDrink, Cola, SoftCheese, Brie, FastFood, ProcessedMeat}\}$
$\text{Pregnancy} \sqsubseteq \forall \text{FoodToBeConsumedInHighAmount.}\{\text{CookedMeat, PasteurizedDairy, WellCookedEggs, Salmon, Sardines, Trout, DecafCoffee, HerbalTea, HardCheese, Cheddar, Mozzarella, Spinach, Lentils, LeanBeef}\}$
$\text{Hypertension} \sqsubseteq \forall \text{FoodInLimitedAmount.}\{\text{Salt, ProcessedFood, CannedFood, SnackFood, FastFood, FriedFood, Butter, Margarine, Soda, Alcohol, Pickles}\}$
$\text{Hypertension} \sqsubseteq \forall \text{FoodToBeConsumedInHighAmount.}\{\text{LowSodiumFood, FreshFood, NoSaltFood, OliveOil, Avocado, Nuts, WholeFruit, DarkChocolate, Water, HerbalTea, LeafyGreens, Beets, BellPeppers}\}$
$\text{Peanut} \sqsubseteq \forall \text{RestrictedFood.Peanut\_Allergy}$

equation [21]. The Schofield equation calculates the Total Daily Energy Expenditure (TDEE), which refers to the AmountOfCaloriesNeededPerDay, by multiplying a person's Basal Metabolic Rate (BMR) with his/her physical activity level factor (e.g., for sedentary activity the factor is 1.3, for moderate is 1.7, etc.). If a person's weight goal is to lose weight, then the TDEE will have a deficit of 500 kcal per day compared to normal, while if the goal is to gain weight then the TDEE will have a surplus of 500 kcal. A summary of the daily recommended nutritional requirements for adult males and females based on activity level (sedentary, moderate, or active) is given in Table 3.

The nutrient score of food is defined based on the Nutrient Rich Food (NRF) index [22]. NRF index ranks foods based on nutrient density, encouraging 9 essential nutrients (e.g., protein, fiber, vitamins, and minerals) while limiting 3 less desirable ones (saturated fat, added sugar, and sodium). The NRF9.3 algorithm determines the score by adding the percentage daily values of beneficial nutrients and subtracting the per-

Table 3. Daily Recommended Nutritional Requirements Based on WHO Guidelines

Nutrient	Unit	Sedentary Adult (Male/Female)	Moderate Activity (Male/Female)	Active (Male/Female)
Calories	kcal	2,000–2,500/1,800–2,000	2,500–2,800/2,000–2,200	3,000+/2,400+
Protein	g	56/46	76/66	100+/80+
Fat	g	60–70	70–80	80–100
Carbohydrates	g	250–300	300–350	350–400
Fiber	g	30–38/25–28	38+/28+	40+/30+
Vitamin A	mcg	900/700	1,000/800	1,200/900
Vitamin B6	mg	1.3–1.7	1.7–2.0	2.0+
Vitamin D	mcg	15	15–20	20+
Vitamin E	mg	15	15–20	20+
Iron	mg	8/18	10/18	15+
Calcium	mg	1,000	1,200	1,200+
Magnesium	mg	400/310	420/320	450+
Zinc	mg	11/8	12/9	13+
Sodium	mg	≤2,000	≤2,000	≤2,000

centage maximum recommended values of nutrients that should be limited, without applying any weight to the individual components.

A higher NRF score indicates a more nutrient-dense and health-promoting food, while a lower or negative score suggests poorer nutritional quality. Scores higher than 10 reflect *very healthy* foods such as leafy greens and legumes, while scores between 5 and 9 are *healthy*, including whole grains and lean proteins. A score between 0 to 4 suggests *moderate* quality, as seen in eggs or fruit juices. Foods scoring -1 to -5 are *less healthy*, and those below -5 are considered *unhealthy*, such as fast food and sugary drinks. For example, in the case of FOOD_BANANA (Fig. 5), the nutrient score of 0.48[9] suggests that the limiting nutrients slightly outweigh the beneficial ones on a per-calorie basis, though the food may still offer specific benefits (e.g., it is HighlyRecommended-For MAGNESIUM_DEFICIENCY).

5 Ontology Testing

Ontology validation typically consists of verifying if the developed ontology is able to respond to the competency questions created as ontology requirements. In this study, SustainHealthyFood ontology is validated using SPARQL queries to answer the competency questions given in Table 1.

For example, to answer CQ6 about the nutrient score of a specific food item, CQ7 about the micronutrients, and CQ8 about the macronutrients of a food item, we formulated the SPARQL code shown in Fig. 6. This query retrieves the nutrient composition of FOOD_AVOCADO. All the nutrients are per 100 g of product.

[9] The real calculation of the nutrient score of banana may be higher as in the used dataset there was no information regarding some micronutrients such as vitamin A or potassium.

```
PREFIX shfo: <http://SustainHealthyFoodOntology#>
PREFIX xsd: <http://www.w3.org/2001/XMLSchema#>
SELECT ?property
       (REPLACE(STR(xsd:decimal(?value)), "^(\\d+)$", "$1.0") AS ?formattedValue)
WHERE {
  shfo:Food_avocado ?property ?value .
  FILTER (
    ?property IN (
      # Macronutrients
      shfo:AmountOfProtein,shfo:AmountOfCarbs,shfo:AmountOfFat,
      shfo:AmountOfFiber, shfo:AmountOfSugar,shfo:hasAmountOfCalories,
      # Micronutrients
      shfo:AmountOfCalcium,shfo:AmountOfIron,shfo:AmountOfMagnesium,
      shfo:AmountOfZinc,shfo:AmountOfVitaminA,shfo:AmountOfVitaminB6,
      shfo:AmountOfVitaminD,shfo:AmountOfVitaminE,
      # Nutrient Score
      shfo:hasNutrientScore))}
```

Table | Response | Visualization | 10 results in 6.009 seconds

property	formattedValue
shfo:AmountOfCalcium	15.0
shfo:AmountOfFiber	3.1
shfo:AmountOfIron	0.5
shfo:AmountOfMagnesium	26.0
shfo:AmountOfProtein	2.0
shfo:AmountOfVitaminB6	0.32
shfo:AmountOfVitaminE	2.7
shfo:AmountOfZinc	0.6
shfo:hasAmountOfCalories	186.0
shfo:hasNutrientScore	0.24

Fig. 6. SPARQL Result for Obtaining Nutrients of *Food_avocado* in SustainHealthyFood Ontology

To give another example, the SPARQL query in Fig. 7, referring to CQ13, shows which food is restricted for a PEANUT_ALLERGY. The output of the other SPARQL queries can be found in the github page[10]. In addition, SPARQL queries can be used to check whether the ontology rules (see Table 2) are implemented correctly. For example, the rule: Peanut $\sqsubseteq \forall$RestrictedFood.Peanut_Allergy is covered by the SPARQL output in Fig. 7.

6 Ontology Application

This section discusses why and how we intend to apply the SustainHealthyFood ontology to support a RAG-based Food/Recipe Recommender or Question/Answering (QA) system. The RAG framework comprises three key processes: retrieval, augmentation,

[10] The github repository contains the OWL ontology, the conceptual models in OntoUML, the Appendix with the SPARQL queries, and the full list of ontology rules. This is the link: https://github.com/DonikaXhani/SustainHealthyFood_Ontology/tree/main.

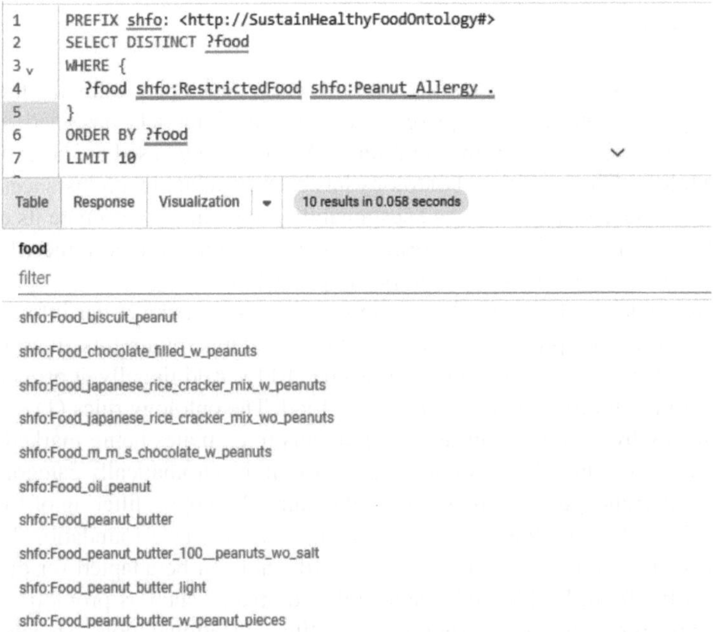

Fig. 7. SPARQL Result for Restricted Food for *Peanut_Allergy* in SustainHealthyFood Ontology.

and generation [23]. In a recipe recommender context, retrieval extracts relevant data from a vector database, such as ChromaDB. Augmentation customizes recommendations by incorporating user-specific parameters, including demographic features, allergens, and preferences. Finally, generation produces a recipe featuring an ingredient list, preparation steps, and explanations based on the augmented context.

While RAG-based systems can generate extensive recipe collections, they often lack semantic understanding, leading to misinterpretation and mishandling of ingredients. For instance, if a user specifies lactose intolerance, the system may fail to infer that lactose is present in dairy products. Similarly, specifying a nut allergy might not prevent the inclusion of all nuts, such as almonds, cashews, and walnuts.

Integrating a domain ontology, like the SustainHealthyFood ontology, mitigates these issues by providing structured, machine-readable knowledge. The ontology enables semantic reasoning, such as linking allergens to ingredients, and context-aware filtering, such as excluding nuts for nut-free recipes.

Incorporating the SustainHealthyFood ontology into a RAG-based system influences all three processes. During retrieval, the ontology enables semantic query expansion by linking related terms. For example, a query for "lactose-free" could retrieve items tagged "dairy-free" or "non-dairy" through ontology relationships. In augmentation, the ontology adds semantic enrichment to retrieved documents, offering detailed knowledge like ingredient hierarchies and allergen relationships for more accurate data. During generation, the ontology indirectly ensures recipes adhere to semantic rules, producing outputs aligned with user constraints.

7 Conclusions

This paper presents the *SustainHealthyFood* ontology, developed following the SABiO methodology. The ontology comprises four conceptual models designed using the OntoUML language, as well as an operational OWL ontology based on the gUFO foundational ontology. The operational ontology has been populated with instances sourced from existing datasets in the food and sustainability domains. To evaluate its effectiveness, a set of SPARQL queries was formulated and executed to determine whether the ontology successfully addresses its competency questions.

The SustainHealthyFood ontology empowers users to make better-informed decisions, by providing comprehensive information on food macronutrients, micronutrients, overall nutrient score, and amount of calories per 100 g. Additionally, it provides information regarding the environmental impact of food. The ontology rules (1) ensure logical consistency by preventing invalid assignments (e.g., males being marked as pregnant), (2) enhance semantic reasoning (e.g., a person is automatically categorized as a CHILD or a different age phase based on his/her age, (3) support filtering of food based on a person's health and dietary restrictions, and (4) serve as a foundational basis for a recommender system. This ontology is versatile and can be adapted for diverse use cases across the food, health, and sustainability domains, such as promoting sustainable food choices during grocery shopping, creating educational tools to teach nutrition and sustainability in schools, and powering smart kitchen appliances to suggest recipes based on available ingredients.

A key limitation of this work lies in the availability of environmental sustainability data. Only one dataset was identified that includes relevant indicators such as carbon emissions, land use, and eutrophication levels, and even this was limited to approximately 40 food items. Another limitation is the lack of expert validation for the outputs generated via SPARQL queries. In particular, the food recommendations and nutrient profiles could not be reviewed or verified by professional nutritionists or dietitians, which limits the evaluation of their accuracy and practical relevance.

Additionally, the current version of the SustainHealthyFood ontology does not yet address competency questions related to recipe generation or user-specific evaluation. In the (recommender) system, the ratings of user will be used to determine how much a food is liked. In subsequent versions, we plan to align the ontology with established health and food standards to enhance semantic interoperability. For example, mapping to the SNOMED CT[11], which is widely used for representing medical terminology, will further enrich the ontology's expressiveness and utility. As a case in point, the class FISH_ALLERGY, defined as a subclass of FOODALLERGY, could be aligned with the SNOMED CT concept *Allergy to fish* (SNOMED CT: 417532002). This alignment also enables the integration of more granular, domain-specific concepts from SNOMED CT, such as *Allergy to fish oil* (SNOMED CT: 294968004), thereby supporting more precise and clinically relevant reasoning.

Our future research agenda also includes the integration of the SustainHealthyFood ontology into a Retrieval-Augmented Generation (RAG) framework for the development of a knowledge-aware food recommender system. Recipe generation will be facil-

[11] https://bioportal.bioontology.org/ontologies/SNOMEDCT.

itated by a RAG architecture incorporating a Large Language Model (LLM), specifically LLaMA 3.2. By aligning structured semantic knowledge from the ontology with user-specific parameters (e.g., dietary preferences, nutritional goals, and allergen constraints), the system aims to synthesize novel, nutritionally appropriate recipes tailored to individual profiles. The incorporation of ontological domain knowledge is expected to substantially enhance the contextual relevance, explainability, and accuracy of the generated recommendations by mitigating hallucinations commonly observed in LLM outputs. For example, the SustainHealthyFood ontology enforces semantic precision by explicitly defining which foods are suitable for specific health conditions, such as diabetes, dietary regimes, and nutritional contexts.

Furthermore, we aim to validate the system's outputs, including food and recipe suggestions, through user studies involving individuals with diverse profiles in terms of age, dietary restrictions, and health status. Validation will also include consultations with professional nutritionists and dietitians to assess the nutritional accuracy and real-world applicability of the recommendations.

References

1. World Health Organization: Levels and trends in child malnutrition child malnutrition: UNICEF/WHO/World Bank Group Joint Child Malnutrition Estimates: Key findings of the 2023 edition (2023)
2. Ahmed, M.H., Vasas, D., Hassan, A., Molnár, J.: The impact of functional food in prevention of malnutrition. PharmaNutrition **1**(19), 100288 (2022)
3. Saunders, J., Smith, T.: Malnutrition: causes and consequences. Clin. Med. **10**(6), 624 (2010)
4. Leng, G., Adan, R.A.H., Belot, M., Brunstrom, J.M., Graaf, K., Dickson, S.L., et al.: The determinants of food choice. Proc. Nutr. Soc. **76**(3), 316–27 (2017)
5. Di Palma, D.: Retrieval-augmented recommender system: enhancing recommender systems with large language models. In: Proceedings of the 17th ACM Conference on Recommender Systems. Singapore, pp. 1369–1373. ACM (2023). https://dl.acm.org/doi/10.1145/3604915.3608889
6. Sedrakyan, G., Gavai, A., van Hillegersberg, J.: Design implications towards human-centric semantic recommenders for sustainable food consumption. In: Sales, T.P., Araújo, J., Borbinha, J., Guizzardi, G. (eds.) Advances in Conceptual Modeling. LNCS, pp. 312–28. Springer Nature Switzerland, Cham (2023)
7. Confalonieri, R., Weyde, T., Besold, T.R., Prado, M., Martín, F.: Using ontologies to enhance human understandability of global post-hoc explanations of black-box models. Artif. Intell. **296**, 103471 (2021)
8. Donadello, I., Dragoni, M.: SeXAI: a semantic explainable artificial intelligence framework. In: Baldoni, M., Bandini, S., (eds.) AIxIA 2020 – Advances in Artificial Intelligence. LNCS, vol. 12414. Springer International Publishing, Cham, pp. 51–66 (2021). https://link.springer.com/10.1007/978-3-030-77091-4_4
9. Confalonieri, R., Guizzardi, G.: On the multiple roles of ontologies in explainable AI arXiv (2023). http://arxiv.org/abs/2311.04778
10. Mckensy-Sambola, D., Rodríguez-García, M.Á., García-Sánchez, F., Valencia-García, R.: Ontology-based nutritional recommender system. Appl. Sci. **12**(1), 143 (2022)
11. Malhotra, A., Younesi, E., Gündel, M., Müller, B., Heneka, M.T., Hofmann-Apitius, M.: ADO: a disease ontology representing the domain knowledge specific to Alzheimer's disease. Alzheimer's Dementia **10**(2), 238–46 (2014)

12. He, Y., et al.: CIDO, a community-based ontology for coronavirus disease knowledge and data integration, sharing, and analysis. Sci. data **7**(1), 181 (2020)
13. Padhiar, I., Seneviratne, O., Chari, S., Gruen, D., McGuinness, D.L.: Semantic modeling for food recommendation explanations (2021). http://arxiv.org/abs/2105.01269
14. Tsatsou, D., Lalama, E., Wilson-Barnes, S., Hart, K., Cornelissen, V., Buys, R., et al.: NAct: The Nutrition & Activity Ontology for Healthy Living (2021)
15. Falbo, R.A.: SABiO: systematic approach for building ontologies. In: Proceedings 1st Joint Workshop ONTO.COM/ODISE. CEUR Workshop Proceedings. CEUR-WS.org, vol. 1301, pp. 1–14 (2014). https://ceur-ws.org/Vol-1301/ontocomodise2014_2.pdf
16. Rijksinstituut voor Volksgezondheid en Milieu (RIVM): NEVO online, version 2023/8.0. Bilthoven: RIVM. https://www.rivm.nl/en/dutch-food-composition-database
17. Taşğın, E.: Macronutrients and micronutrients in nutrition. Int. J. Innov. Res. Rev. **1**(1), 10–5 (2017)
18. Poore, J., Nemecek, T.: Reducing food's environmental impacts through producers and consumers. Science **360**(6392), 987–992 (2018). https://doi.org/10.1126/science.aaq0216
19. World Health Organization: Healthy diet - fact sheet (2025). https://www.who.int/news-room/fact-sheets/detail/healthy-diet
20. Food and Agriculture Organization of the United Nations: Food-based dietary guidelines – Netherlands. https://www.fao.org/nutrition/education/food-dietary-guidelines/regions/countries/netherlands/en/
21. Schofield, W.N.: Predicting basal metabolic rate, new standards and review of previous work. Hum. Nutr. Clin. Nutr. **1**(39), 5–41 (1985)
22. Drewnowski, A.: Defining nutrient density: development and validation of the nutrient rich foods index. J. Am. College Nutr. (2009). https://www.tandfonline.com/doi/abs/10.1080/07315724.2009.10718106
23. Fan, W., Ding, Y., Ning, L., Wang, S., Li, H., Yin, D., et al.: A survey on RAG meeting LLMs: towards retrieval-augmented large language models. In: Proceedings of the 30th ACM SIGKDD Conference on Knowledge Discovery and Data Mining. New York, NY, USA: Association for Computing Machinery, pp. 6491–501. KDD (2024). https://dl.acm.org/doi/10.1145/3637528.3671470

OntoInsight - A Metric-Guided Tool for Ontology Quality Evaluation with LLM-Powered Recommendations

Daksh Sammi[1], Lakshay Bhushan[1(✉)], Raghava Mutharaju[1], and Cogan Shimizu[2]

[1] IIIT-Delhi, Delhi, India
{daksh21459,lakshay21397,raghava.mutharaju}@iiitd.ac.in
[2] Wright State University, Fairborn, USA
cogan.shimizu@wright.edu

Abstract. Ontologies are foundational to conceptual modeling and semantic systems across diverse domains, yet evaluating and improving their quality remains a complex challenge. Existing tools often focus on syntactic correctness or complex metric reporting, lacking actionable and interpretable feedback, which is not very intuitive. We present an ontology quality evaluation tool, named *OntoInsight*, that caters to different types of users, from beginners to advanced, with custom recommendations, basic (simple suggestions), and advanced (involving deep technical insights) recommendations. It can handle ontologies of varying size with full ontology evaluation and modular evaluation (useful for large and complex ontologies). The pipeline automates all the stages in the tool, from metric computation (via frameworks such as OQuaRE) and seed-term-based modularization to controlled natural language (CNL) translation and targeted prompt generation for Large Language Models (LLMs). The user has the freedom to configure their own LLM API key and choose the type of evaluation and suggestions they want, according to their needs and expertise. The source code of OntoInsight is available under Apache 2.0 license at https://github.com/kracr/onto-insight.

Keywords: Quality Paradigms and Metrics · AI-Assisted Modeling · Empirical Evaluation · Ontology Quality · Modularization · Controlled Natural Language · Large Language Models · Computational Tool

1 Introduction

Ontologies are an important aspect of conceptual modeling and semantic applications that enable structured knowledge to be represented for areas such as healthcare, biology, logistics, and e-commerce. How well an ontology performs, however, is contingent on its quality. Ontologies that are poorly developed will lead to vague interpretation, reasoning inconsistency, and less reusability. Although multiple ontology quality assessment frameworks have emerged, including metric-based approaches such as OQuaRE [1], semiotic-metric suite [3], and OntoQA [2],

D. Bork et al. (Eds.): ER 2025, LNCS 16189, pp. 393–411, 2026.
https://doi.org/10.1007/978-3-032-08623-5_21

no particular tool has been developed to offer interpretable, modular, and actionable feedback. These shortcomings become even more pronounced as ontologies scale in complexity and size. Present tools are either non-functional, unable to handle ontologies of larger sizes, or complex to understand in terms of usage and output. Their non-actionable feedback makes them less intuitive and more complicated to use for all types of users. In this paper, we present a hybrid analysis technique that combines empirical ontology measures with the generation capability of Large Language Models (LLMs). The tool accommodates the entire ontology and targeted modular testing for better scalability and contextual appropriateness. There are two independent recommendation modes, Basic (for end-users) and Advanced (for ontology engineers), offering tiered feedback for users with different levels of expertise. Our modularization mode isolates problem areas through seed-term-based extraction. Here, instead of evaluating an ontology solely in its entirety, we extract submodules around seed terms associated with the worst-scoring metrics. These modules are converted from OWL Syntax into Controlled Natural Language to enhance interpretability and prompt efficiency. This helps in generating targeted improvement suggestions through LLM prompts. The goal is to provide a diagnostic assessment of quality and actionable repair strategies grounded in best ontology design practices. The modular evaluation ensures focused diagnosis and promotes local quality improvements that scale to global impact, particularly helpful in large and complex ontologies. OntoInsight's architecture consists of several interconnected components that handle different aspects of ontology processing and analysis. The system can be accessed through either a command-line interface or a REST API.

2 Background and Related Work

2.1 Background

Ontology evaluation is a critical step in ensuring that ontologies are both **correct** (faithfully representing the intended domain) and **high-quality** (well-structured, reusable, and maintainable). Traditionally, evaluation has been framed along two axes [18]:

- **Verification:** Assessing whether the ontology has been constructed correctly according to formal rules and design principles.
- **Validation:** Assessing whether the ontology captures the intended conceptualization of the domain and meets user/application needs.

These perspectives have led to a variety of evaluation frameworks, methods, and tools, each addressing different aspects of ontology quality and correctness.

Established Evaluation Methods and Levels. These perspectives have led to diverse evaluation frameworks. Traditional approaches include: (1) **Gold standard comparison** against reference ontologies, (2) **Application-based assessment** using competency questions, (3) **Data-driven evaluation** against real-world datasets, and (4) **Manual expert review** for identifying logical/semantic issues. Evaluation is structured across three interdependent levels: **syntactic/structural** (language compliance, hierarchies), **lexical/semantic** (terminology, conceptual clarity), and **contextual** (application fit, interoperability) [18].

Empirical Approaches to Ontology Evaluation: In recent years, there has been a marked shift towards *empirical evaluation methodologies* in ontology engineering. This evolution is driven by the need for **objective, quantitative, and repeatable assessments** of ontology quality, beyond traditional manual or application-based reviews. Empirical evaluation provides measurable indicators that help capture the **structural soundness, functional richness, semantic clarity, semantic correctness, precision, and accuracy** of an ontology. Common metrics such as *relationship richness* [1], *attribute richness* [1], *depth of inheritance*, *semantic score* [14], *interpretability score* [14], and *class coupling* have become instrumental in analyzing design orientation (horizontal vs. vertical), annotation density, modular cohesion, and reuse potential. To address this need, multiple empirical frameworks have emerged, notably **OQuaRE** [1],**OntoQA** [2], and semiotic-based models. These frameworks offer structured approaches for mapping quality characteristics to quantifiable metrics, often inspired by established software quality standards (e.g., ISO/IEC 25010). While these frameworks have brought structure and rigor to ontology evaluation, most existing tools suffer from one or more of the following limitations:

- Lack of interpretability of metric outputs for general users
- Absence of actionable suggestions grounded in metric scores
- Inability to scale to large or modularized ontologies
- Poor integration with modern AI-based reasoning or assistance systems

2.2 Related Work

Several tools have emerged to operationalize quantitative empirical metrics. OntoMetrics [4] is a readily available web-based application that gives counts of object properties, class axioms, and annotations to give a structural overview. However, it does not offer more advanced semantic diagnostics or repair recommendations. OWLET [11], a Protégé plugin, applies precision and recall-based measures to assess classification performance, though its compatibility with recent OWL API versions remains limited. Delta [13] is a web-based platform that combines metric analysis with graphical visualizations, but instability in module dependencies has impeded its practical usability. Similarly, RePOSE [7] offers abductive reasoning for debugging subclass hierarchies and mappings but faces interoperability issues with OWL serialization formats. IRI_Debug [10] enables ontologists to validate their ontology's IRIs against standard reference ontologies to assess concept and property reuse. It supports ontology selection for comparison and evaluates the alignment and reusability of terms. While useful for assessing IRI-level compliance, it lacks broader metric-based evaluation and does not generate improvement suggestions. OntoKeeper [14] applies semiotic theory to assess ontologies across syntactic, semantic, pragmatic, and social dimensions, but its limited data access and lack of modular evaluation reduce its practical appeal. Tools like OOPS! [12] support anti-pattern detection and SHACL constraint validation but do not provide suggestions grounded in empirical metrics. NEOntometrics [9] is a recent web-based tool supporting empirical ontology evaluation using frameworks like OQuaRE and OntoQA. It excels in version-tracking for Git repositories, offering metric trend visualization and GraphQL API access. However, it focuses exclusively on metric reporting—providing no actionable improvement suggestions—and lacks support for large ontologies (>25MB), multi-user access, or automated modular evaluation.

3 Methodology

Among several ontology evaluation frameworks, such as OntoQA [2] and semiotic metrics [3], we selected the OQuaRE [1] framework as the starting point for our tool due to its comprehensive, empirically grounded structure and alignment with the ISO/IEC 25010 quality model. OQuaRE evaluates ontologies using 16 metrics and 24 sub-characteristics mapped to 9 key characteristics, which are structural, functional adequacy, compatibility, transferability, operability, maintainability, quality in use, performance efficiency, and reliability, offering a balanced assessment of both structure and semantics. A simplified brief description of the metrics, sub-characteristics, and characteristics can be found in Tables 1, 2, and 3.

While we acknowledge the strengths of other frameworks and plan to support them in future versions, OQuaRE [1] provided a scalable and extensible foundation.

3.1 Interpretation of OQuaRE Framework

Despite its holistic scope, OQuaRE [1] suffers from unclear thresholds for metric interpretation and lacks an overall ontology quality score, complicating comparative evaluation. To address OQuaRE's limitations, we:

- Developed a **standardized 5-point scaling system** for metrics (Table 4) and sub-characteristics under `metrics/` directory (repository[1])
- Created **simplified glossaries** for all metrics, sub-characteristics, and characteristics (Tables 1, 2, and 3)
- Built a **structured interpretation layer** mapping metrics to ISO/IEC 25010 via machine-readable CSVs

[1] https://github.com/kracr/onto-insight/.

Table 1. OQuARE Metrics: Codes, Terms, and Simplified Meanings

Metric Code	Term	Simplified Meaning
AROnto	Property Binding	Average domain axioms per class (defines how well properties are linked to classes)
ANOnto	Annotation Richness	Average annotations per class (shows richness of metadata)
CBOnto	Coupling	Average superclasses per non-root class (measures coupling/dependency)
CROnto	Class Population	Average instances per class (shows how populated each class is)
DITOnto	Hierarchy Depth	Maximum depth from root to leaf class (hierarchy depth)
INROnto	Relationship Density	Average object properties per class (relationship richness)
NACOnto	Ancestral Depth	Average ancestor classes per leaf (inheritance depth)
NOCOnto	Child Breadth	Average child classes per class (hierarchical spread)
NOMOnto	Property Variety	Average number of properties per class (functional richness)
LCOMOnto	Cohesion Loss	Lack of cohesion (measures how scattered the connections are)
RFCOnto	Property Usage	Average usage of properties per class (interaction level)
RROnto	Link Expressiveness	Ratio of relationships to total axioms (expressiveness of links)
TMOnto	Multi-Inheritance	Average number of superclasses per class (multi-inheritance level)
WMCOnto	Schema Density	Average datatype/object properties and subclasses per class (schema richness)
PROnto	Linkable Elements	Linkable elements based on domain axioms (connectivity potential)
POnto	Ancestral Breadth	Superclasses per class (hierarchical ancestry)

- **Metric-Axiom Dependency Grouping.** To isolate the effect of specific ontology elements, we grouped OQuaRE metrics by their dependency on OWL axiom types (Table 5). This allowed precise, targeted perturbation for fair evaluation.

While drawing inspiration from Reiz and Sandkuhl's harmonization principles [8], our interpretation layer represents a novel implementation with significant extensions. Our structured interpretation layer comprises 10 machine-readable CSV files:

- **Glossaries**: Plain-language definitions for metrics, sub-characteristics, and characteristics (`Simplified_Metrics.csv`, `Simplified_SubChars.csv`, `characterstics.csv`)
- **Scaling Parameters**: 5-point thresholds and computational formulas (`Metrics_1-5.csv`, `SubChars_1-5.csv`)
- **Hierarchical Mappings**: ISO/IEC 25010 relationships and quality dimension connections (`char_subchar_rel.csv`, `framework_metrics_descriptions.csv`)
- **Core Specifications**: Metric and characteristic metadata with extended documentation (`characteristics_desciptions.csv`, `subcharacteristic_descriptions.csv`, `Subchars_formulas.csv`)

Table 2. Ontology Sub-Characteristics: Codes, Terms, and Simplified Meanings

Sub-Characteristic	Term	Simplified Meaning
Formal Relations Support	Relation Formality	Ontology supports formal relations beyond taxonomy
Redundancy	Non-Redundancy	All knowledge items are informative (no duplication)
Tangledness	Inheritance Simplicity	Multi-inheritance is minimized
Cohesion	Class Cohesion	Classes are strongly related
Controlled Vocabulary	Term Uniformity	Heterogeneity of terms is avoided
Schema & Value Reconciliation	Interoperability	Provides a common data model for interoperability
Consistent Search & Query	Query Support	Ontology structure guides search/query
Knowledge Acquisition	Knowledge Capturing	Capability to represent acquired knowledge (instances)
Clustering	Term Grouping	Annotations enable grouping of terms
Similarity	Comparability	Components can be compared for similarity
Indexing & Linking	Indexability	Classes serve as indexes for retrieval
Result Representation	Output Analysis	Can analyze complex results
Guidance	Domain Guidance	Guides specification of domain knowledge
Decision Trees	Decision Support	Supports building decision trees
Knowledge Reuse	Reusability	Ontology can be used to build other ontologies
Inference	Inference Capability	Enables using reasoners to infer new knowledge
Replaceability	Ontology Replacement	Can replace another ontology for same task
Adaptability	Adaptability	Can be adapted to different environments
Learnability	Learnability	Users can easily learn the ontology
Modularity	Component Separation	Ontology is divided into independent components
Reusability	Reuse in Others	Parts of the ontology can be reused in others
Analyzability	Issue Diagnosability	Ontology can be diagnosed for issues
Changeability	Modifiability	Ontology can be easily modified
Modification Stability	Stability on Change	Avoiding unexpected effects of changes

Table 3. Ontology Quality Characteristics and Their Descriptions

Characteristic	Description
Structural	It evaluates the connections within an ontology and the attributes of the graph
Functional Adequacy	Describes the capability to provide concrete functions
Compatibility	Ability of two or more components to exchange information and/or perform functions in a shared environment
Transferability	Degree to which software can be transferred from one environment to another
Operability	Effort needed to use the ontology by stated or implied users
Maintainability	Capability of ontologies to be modified for changing environments, requirements, or specifications
Quality in Use	Extent to which a product, used by specific users, meets their needs in a given context
Performance Efficiency	Relationship between software performance and resource consumption under stated conditions
Reliability	Maintaining performance levels under the stated conditions

Stored in the `metrics` directory of our repository(see footnote 1), these files are parsed at runtime to provide consistent thresholds, computational logic, and quality mappings. The end-to-end process flows through the sequential stages shown in Fig. 1.

Format Validation and Conversion. The system begins by validating the input ontology format and converting it to a standardized OWL/XML format if necessary.

Table 4. OQuARE Metrics and Their Rating Scales: 5 means "exceeding expectations or best quality", 3 means "minimally acceptable", and 1 means "not acceptable or worst quality."

Metric	5 (Best)	4	3	2	1 (Worst)
ANOnto	> 0.8	0.6−0.8	0.4−0.6	0.2−0.4	< 0.2
AROnto	> 0.8	0.6−0.8	0.4−0.6	0.2−0.4	< 0.2
CBOnto	1−3	3−6	6−8	8−12	> 12
CROnto	> 0.8	0.6−0.8	0.4−0.6	0.2−0.4	< 0.2
DITOnto	1−2	2−4	4−6	6−8	> 8
INROnto	> 0.8	0.6−0.8	0.4−0.6	0.2−0.4	< 0.2
NACOnto	1−2	2−4	4−6	6−8	> 8
NOCOnto	1−2	2−4	4−6	6−8	> 8
NOMOnto	≤ 2	2−4	4−6	6−8	> 8
LCOMOnto	≤ 2	2−4	4−6	6−8	> 8
RFCOnto	1−3	3−6	6−8	8−12	> 12
RROnto	> 0.8	0.6−0.8	0.4−0.6	0.2−0.4	< 0.2
TMOnto	1−2	2−4	4−6	6−8	> 8
WMCOnto	1−2	2−4	4−6	6−8	> 8
PROnto	> 0.8	0.6−0.8	0.4−0.6	0.2−0.4	< 0.2
POnto	> 0.8	0.6−0.8	0.4−0.6	0.2−0.4	< 0.2

Metric Computation and Problem Identification. The system invokes a Java-based calculation engine to compute 16 OQuaRE [1]-based metrics for the ontology(as shown in Table 1). These metrics are stored in a JSON file for further analysis.

Seed Term Selection. Seed terms are central concepts (classes or properties) identified as contributors to low-scoring metrics (e.g., AROnto, CROnto, RFCOnto). These are extracted based on predefined logic for each metric - e.g., classes without instances for CROnto or properties lacking domains for AROnto. By targeting these entities, the system focuses evaluation on the ontology's most deficient components. Seed terms serve dual roles:

1. Input for **ROBOT-based modularization** [6]
2. Semantic anchors for **LLM prompt engineering**

This approach enables localized quality improvement while maintaining global context.

Metric-Driven Modularization. To efficiently handle large or domain-diverse ontologies, OntoInsight offers modular evaluation. Instead of analyzing the entire ontology, we isolate and evaluate focused subgraphs (modules), centered around identified *seed terms*. This approach is triggered when metrics indicate structural deficiencies (e.g., CBOnto > 12 or WMCOnto > 8), prioritizing localized repair over global analysis. This not only reduces computational overhead but also

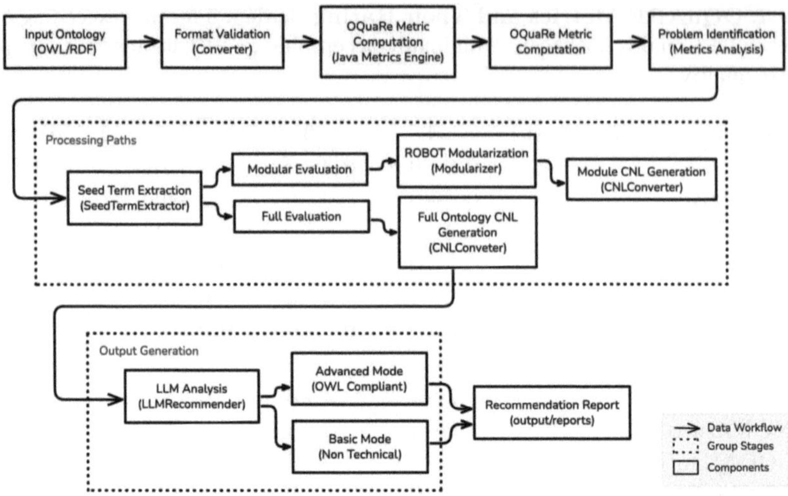

Fig. 1. Processing Pipelines. Solid arrows indicate the flow of processing between stages. Dashed boxes group related stages into **Processing Paths** and **Output Generation**. Solid rectangles denote individual modules and tools within the pipeline.

Table 5. OQuaRE Metric Grouping by OWL Axiom Type

Axiom Type	**Dependent Metrics**
Class Axioms	CBOnto, DITOnto, INROnto, LCOMOnto, NACOnto, NOCOnto, NOMOnto, POnto, PROnto, RFCOnto, RROnto, TMOnto, WMCOnto
Object Property Axioms	AROnto, NOMOnto, PROnto, RFCOnto, RROnto, WMCOnto
Data Property Axioms	AROnto, NOMOnto, PROnto, RFCOnto, RROnto, WMCOnto
Individual Axioms	CROnto, NOMOnto
Annotation Axioms	ANOnto

increases interpretability by narrowing the LLM's focus to local problem areas. The modularization workflow, implemented in `module_extractor.py`, consists of three validated stages:

1. **Problem Metric Identification**: Automatically select the worst-performing metric(s) by comparing scores against "1 (Worst)" thresholds in `oquare_metrics.csv`
2. **Seed Term Extraction**: Retrieve associated concepts from JSON files using metric-specific heuristics. For instance:
   - Low **AROnto**: Properties lacking domain definitions
   - Low **CROnto**: Classes without instances
   - Low **RFCOnto**: Underutilized properties (usage $<$ threshold)

3. **Axiom-Preserving Extraction**: Execute ROBOT [6] with TOP method: `robot extract -method TOP -term-file <seeds> -output module.owl`

ROBOT [6] **Extraction Methods:**

- **TOP (default)**: Preserves superclass hierarchy *above* seed terms
- **BOTTOM**: Captures subclasses *below* seed terms (suitable for leaf-node issues)
- **STAR**: Includes neighboring classes/properties (ideal for relationship density)

We default to TOP for its balance of context preservation and computational efficiency. This method optimally captures hierarchical deficiencies identified by metrics like DITOnto and NACOnto. For non-hierarchical issues, users can override via CLI parameters. This methodology delivers three empirically validated benefits:

- **Interpretability Enhancement**: significant reduction in CNL content enables focused LLM analysis
- **Scalability Guarantee**: Processes large ontologies like SNOMED CT [16] (more than 375k classes) in a much shorter time (<15 min)
- **Prompt Efficiency**: Reduces average token count versus full-ontology evaluation

After extraction, metrics are recomputed within modules to generate localized recommendations grounded in quantitative deficiencies. This precision targeting ensures suggestions directly address the root causes of quality degradation.

Choosing CNL for LLM Context. Raw OWL syntax (e.g., RDF/XML, Functional, Manchester, etc.) is verbose (high token count), cannot represent general class axioms, and is ill-suited for direct LLM interpretation. To overcome this, we translate ontology structures into Controlled Natural Language (CNL)—a simplified, human-readable textual format. The CNL follows linguistic templates like "Class A is a subclass of Class B" and "Property P links Class X to Class Y." This translation improves prompt clarity, reduces hallucination, and helps LLMs generate more relevant suggestions. CNL is produced for both full ontologies and extracted modules, ensuring contextual adaptability in downstream tasks. This approach is supported by recent work showing the value of CNL verbalization in ontology learning tasks [19]. CNL can reliably verbalize common OWL constructs, including:

- **Class relations:** subsumption, equivalence, disjointness.
- **Property characteristics:** functional, transitive, symmetric/asymmetric, etc.
- **Domain and range:** specifications for object and data properties.

- **Restrictions:** existential, universal, and compact cardinality restrictions.
- **Assertions:** simple class memberships and property assertions.

However, not all logical entailments are practically verbalizable. Challenging constructs include property chains, complex role inclusions, keys, deeply nested boolean expressions, and datatype facets. Attempting to verbalize all entailments would yield redundant or unreadable output (e.g., transitive closure expansions). We therefore adopt a pragmatic policy to verbalize asserted axioms where clear templates exist, and selectively include salient inferences that aid understanding without introducing noise. This ensures correctness, conciseness, and human-oriented brevity.

Implementation. The CNL is generated via our in-repo verbalizer (`src/verbalizer/*`), which traverses the asserted RDF graph, matches axioms to linguistic templates, and produces sentences. For example, an `subClassOf` edge becomes "X is a type of Y," while `disjointWith` axioms aggregate into "X is different from Y and Z." Optional paraphrasing is gated by policy, ensuring readability improvements without altering semantics. When template coverage is incomplete, fallback methods (e.g., ROBOT [6] export or label/comment extraction) generate minimal descriptions to preserve context.

Benefits for LLM Prompting. By design, CNL verbalization yields inputs that are:

- **Readable:** human-friendly statements reflecting OWL structures.
- **Scoped:** produced per ontology module, aligning with modularization.
- **Token-efficient:** avoiding verbose OWL syntax and limiting redundancy.

3.2 System Architecture and Implementation

The architecture combines robust ontology parsing, modularization, and evaluation with advanced prompt engineering to provide interpretable feedback for ontologists. The system supports both command-line and RESTful interfaces and is fully containerized for portability and reproducibility.

Core Components and Their Integration. The core architecture consists of loosely coupled components organized into four layers: application, processing, external services, and infrastructure (shown in Fig. 2). The modular design allows independent improvements to each component while supporting both interactive and programmatic usage via CLI and REST APIs.

- **Application Layer:** Users interact via a CLI (run.sh) or REST API (api.py), specifying the ontology file, evaluation type (`FULL`/`MOD`) and mode (`BASIC`/`ADVANCED`).
- **Processing Layer:**
  - Format Converter: Standardizes the ontology into OWL/XML format.
  - Metrics Engine: A Java-based module computes 16 OQuaRE [1] metrics and 24 sub-characteristics using the OWL API.

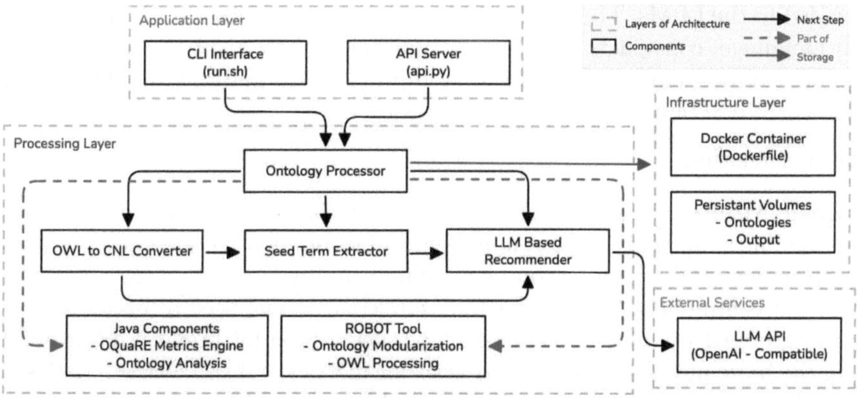

Fig. 2. OntoInsight Architecture. Dashed boxes represent layers of architecture. Solid rectangles denote system components and tools. Arrows indicate **Next Step** (black), **Part of** (dashed green), and **Storage** (red).

- Seed Term Extractor: Identifies concepts linked to low-quality metrics to guide modularization.
- Ontology Modularizer: Uses the ROBOT [6] tool to extract focused sub-graphs centered around seed terms.
- CNL Generator: Converts OWL axioms into CNL for LLM input.
- Recommender Module: LLM prompts and processes to model responses for basic or advanced modes.

– **External Services:** An OpenAI-compatible LLM API is used to generate improvement suggestions.
– **Infrastructure:** The entire system is Dockerized with persistent volumes for input ontologies and output results.

OntoInsight takes as input the ontology to be evaluated along with the configuration of the evaluation process. Along with the recommendations, OntoInsight provides the metrics as the output.

Command Line Interface (CLI). The CLI is the primary entry point for local use. It orchestrates the entire pipeline, including validation, metric computation, modularization, CNL generation, and LLM-based recommendation.

REST API. For remote and programmatic access, OntoInsight exposes a REST API mirroring the CLI's functionality. It supports endpoints to evaluate the ontology. The API enables easy integration with web dashboards, CI/CD pipelines, or external ontology platforms.

LLM Integration. A core innovation of OntoInsight lies in its use of LLMs for recommendation generation. The temperature of LLMs is set to 0.1 to minimize hallucinations and reduce variances. As context, the metric and framework description CSVs, all quality scores, and the top five worst-performing metrics are provided to the LLMs. The pipeline prepares ontology content in Controlled Natural Language, constructs detailed prompts tailored for the basic and advanced recommendation modes, sends structured prompts to the LLM, and formats the response into actionable feedback.

Prompt Design

- **Basic Mode**: In the basic mode[2], the prompt is designed with an objective of providing simple, actionable, non-technical recommendations so that any user can understand where the ontology stands and what to do next. The LLM's output is limited to 2048 tokens to ensure conciseness. Seed terms are selected and grouped by metrics, capped at five per metric for brevity. Additionally, in the basic mode, simplified glossaries for metrics and sub-characteristics are used to provide recommendations entirely in natural language. The prompt is structured with the following constraints.
  - **System role:** Defined as an "Ontology Assistant" targeting simplicity and actionability.
  - **Output format:** Required Markdown sections enforce consistency:
    * Overview
    * Key Strengths
    * Areas for Improvement
    * Simple Recommendations with Why/How
    * Next Steps
  - **Schema design:** Discourages jargon and focuses on explicit, easy steps.

  This strategy is adopted because
  - Grounding with scores and worst metrics ties suggestions to weak areas.
  - Seed terms anchor advice to ontology-specific concepts, reducing generality.
  - Simplified glossaries lower cognitive load and reduce user confusion.
  - Deterministic settings and fixed sections ensure consistency.
- **Advanced Mode**: In the advanced mode[3], the prompt is designed with an objective of delivering technically rigorous, metric-grounded recommendations suitable for ontology engineers, including metric semantics, sub-characteristic impacts, and implementation roadmaps. The maximum token size limit is increased to 4096 in this mode to allow detailed analysis. Full list of seed terms by metrics are provided as context to LLM to support deeper cross-referencing. Detailed context is provided to the LLM with simplified glossaries, framework metric descriptions, formulas, ranges, and characteristic-subcharacteristic relationships. Quality scores, top highest metrics (strengths), lowest sub-characteristics, and auto-selected worst metrics for focus are used as quantitative signals. We designed the prompt structure and constraints as follows.

[2] Prompts for the basic mode are available at https://github.com/kracr/onto-insight/blob/main/src/basic_recom.py.

[3] Prompts for the advanced mode available at https://github.com/kracr/onto-insight/blob/main/src/adv_recom.py.

- **System role:** Defined as an "Advanced Ontology Engineering Specialist."
- **Output format:** Required Markdown sections include
  * Comprehensive Assessment
  * Per-dimension analyses (Structural, Functional, Semantic)
  * Critical Metrics Improvement Plan (for each selected metric: explanation, impact, seed terms, detailed steps, expected improvement)
  * Implementation Roadmap (Immediate / Medium / Long-term)
- **Traceability:** Sections enforce linkage from data to recommendations and ensure explicit expected improvements.

This strategy is adopted because

- Metric formulas and ranges contextualize scores, guiding the model to explain root causes and impacts.
- Seed terms ensure ontology-specific advice, limiting hallucinated fixes.
- Separation by dimensions mirrors evaluation theory and enhances clarity.
- Deterministic controls and schema enable consistency.

Configuration: `'AI_API_KEY'`, `'AI_URL'`, and `'MODEL_NAME'` are managed through an `.env` (configuration) file, supporting flexibility across deployment environments and models. The default integration targets any OpenAI-compatible endpoint.

4 Tool Evaluation and Testing

To assess the effectiveness and generalizability of OntoInsight across ontologies of varying size and structural complexity, we adopted two complementary evaluation strategies: (1) a systematic *perturbation-based testing* framework and (2) a *user study* to capture experiential insights from real users. Together, these methods provide both empirical and experiential validation of the system. They also simulate real-world challenges such as incomplete modeling, thereby demonstrating OntoInsight's robustness in practical settings. This testing approach is inspired by a similar ontology evaluation work using OQuaRE metrics [17] that emphasizes version-control-based analysis of evolving ontologies. It has been demonstrated that ontology engineers often employ version-control-driven testing, where every real-world addition or deletion perturbs the ontology and requires re-evaluation.

4.1 Perturbation-Based Testing with Use Case

To evaluate whether OntoInsight can detect and explain quality deterioration in large and complex ontologies, we applied a perturbation-based testing protocol to the gene ontology (`go.owl`). This ontology was chosen due to its scale and widespread adoption in biomedical informatics, making it a representative case for complex real-world settings.

Perturbation Protocol. We introduced controlled degradation by randomly removing 10% of axioms across all categories (classes, properties, individuals, and

Table 6. Metrics affected by 10% perturbation of `go.owl`

Metric (Axiom Type)	Original	Perturbed	Interpretation
ANOnto	5.95	1.93	Severe annotation loss
DITOnto	13.0	12.0	Slightly shallower hierarchy
INROnto	1.41	1.04	Weaker subclass relations
LCOMOnto	3.61	3.95	Reduced cohesion
NACOnto	1.17	0.98	Fewer descriptions
NOCOnto	1.56	1.22	Reduced branching
NOMOnto	0.18	0.04	Major operation loss
POnto	1.23	1.00	Fewer properties
RFCOnto	5811	513	Reference collapse
RROnto	0.11	0.03	Fewer outgoing links
WMCOnto	1.59	1.09	Method richness loss
Modularity Score	2.95	2.26	Weaker modules
Reusability/Analyzability/Testability	∼5800	∼530	Structural degradation

annotations). OQuaRE metrics were recomputed on both the original and perturbed versions, and OntoInsight was used to generate recommendation reports. The original and perturbed metric scores along with the interpretations are shown in Table 6. The goal is to assess whether the system correctly captured the metric drop and translated them into actionable improvement suggestions.

Impacted Quality Characteristics. Using Table 5's grouping:

- **Annotation Axioms** → ANOnto, NACOnto decline: weaker *controlled vocabulary* and reduced *guidance.*
- **Class Axioms** → INROnto, LCOMOnto, NOCOnto, NOMOnto, DITOnto shifts: reduced *maintainability* and *functional adequacy.*
- **Property Axioms** → RFCOnto, RROnto, POnto drops: weaker *interoperability* and *inference support.*
- **Composite Scores** → modularity and reusability decline: lower *quality in use.*

Seed Term Extraction. To further support modular evaluation, OntoInsight identified key seed terms in the perturbed ontology for focused analysis. These included: `GO_0016891` (appearing across AR, CR, and RR), `GO_0015599` (DIT), and `GO_0030704` (RFC). These seed terms were used to isolate modules for targeted recommendation.

Recommendations on Perturbed Ontology for Full Basic Mode. OntoInsight's basic report highlighted organizational weaknesses and structural overload:

Areas for Improvement:
- Weak property-class connectivity (AROnto = 0, RFCOnto collapse).
- Missing real-world examples (CROnto = 0).

- Overly deep hierarchy (DITOnto = 12).

Simple Recommendations:
- Add properties (e.g., `has_function`, `related_to`) to improve connectivity.
- Populate classes with 3–5 example instances.
- Flatten overly deep class hierarchies by merging similar subclasses.

Recommendations on Perturbed Ontology for Modularized Basic Mode. The modular analysis produced more fine-grained suggestions centered on seed terms:

Areas for Improvement:
- Reliance on only "is-a" relationships (formalRelationsSupport = 0).
- Empty classes with no biological examples (CROnto = 0).
- Focus on `GO_0016891` affecting AR, CR, and RR(Duplicacy).

Simple Recommendations:
- Add richer relation types (`part_of`, `participates_in`).
- Introduce concrete examples (e.g., insect-specific vitelline formation).
- Merge or clarify duplicate terms to avoid redundancy.

Overall Results: Both modes pointed to missing properties, absent real-world instances, and structural complexity. At the same time, the full report emphasized hierarchy depth and overall annotation loss, while the modular report focused on duplicate terms and module-level relation gaps. The consistency across modes demonstrated robustness, while their differences showed that modularization helped uncover finer, term-level issues not visible in the global view. Perturbation caused measurable declines in annotation coverage, cohesion, property connectivity, and modularity. OntoInsight was able to successfully map these drops to higher-level quality characteristics and produce concrete, ontology-specific recommendations.

4.2 User Study

To complement perturbation-based testing and reference validation, we conducted a structured user study to assess OntoInsight's usability, interpretability, and impact on ontology engineering practice. The study involved eight participants, drawn from both professional and academic backgrounds. Raw anonymized survey results[4] and some reports[5] are available in our repository.

Participant Demographics. Participants included ontology engineers (12.5%), Semantic Web researchers (12.5%), and students with a technical background (75%). In terms of experience, 50% had less than one year in ontology evaluation, 25% had 1–3 years, and the remaining 25% reported 3–10 years of experience. This distribution ensured representation from both novice and intermediate practitioners, reflecting the diverse audience of ontology tools.

[4] https://github.com/kracr/onto-insight/blob/main/user_study_responses.csv.
[5] https://github.com/kracr/onto-insight/blob/main/recommendation_reports.pdf.

Study Design. Participants were asked to do the following.

1. Select an ontology of their choice.
2. Run OntoInsight in either the Basic or Advanced recommendation mode, with options for full ontology or modular evaluation.
3. Review the automatically generated reports.
4. Complete a structured questionnaire (5-point Likert scale) on clarity, usefulness, modularization, interpretability, and ontology improvement outcomes.

Quantitative Findings. Overall, participants rated OntoInsight positively, particularly on interpretability and recommendation clarity. Table 7 summarizes the mean scores across dimensions.

Table 7. User Study Ratings across Quality Dimensions (n=8)

Survey Dimension	Mean Rating (/5)
Relevance of suggestions	3.88
Clarity of explanations	4.00
Context sufficiency	3.75
Helpfulness of modularization	3.38
Improved understanding of ontology quality	3.88
Awareness of OQuaRE or similar frameworks	3.00
Clarity of seed-term selection	3.75
Readability of Basic report	4.75
Depth of Advanced report	3.71
Effectiveness in improving ontology	4.00

Results indicate that the Basic mode was highly effective for readability (4.75), while the Advanced mode was valued for technical depth (3.71). Suggestions were consistently judged as actionable (4.0), with multiple participants noting that they successfully applied recommendations to target specific degraded metrics.

Qualitative Findings. Participants provided detailed written feedback, which we summarize as follows.

Features Valued. Participants highlighted three main strengths: (i) modular evaluation for isolating problems, (ii) report generation with actionable suggestions, and (iii) comprehensive multi-dimensional analysis of ontology quality.

Preferred Interface. Most participants preferred a web-based application. Reasons included accessibility, iterative testing, and better potential for visualization. One respondent noted alignment with the SAMOD [20] methodology, suggesting that web-based modular testing could enhance iterative ontology development.

Requests for Improvement. Feedback converged around the following.

- Providing raw metric counts alongside ratios for transparency.
- Explaining how seed-term modularization is performed, not only why terms are selected.
- Allowing customization of evaluation focus (e.g., prioritizing annotations vs. connectivity).
- Comparative results across LLMs, with stability indicators such as variance across runs.
- Extending reports to include inferred axioms.

Overall Assessment. The user study shows OntoInsight balances interpretability and technical rigor. Basic mode was preferred for readability, while Advanced mode was valued by experienced users for diagnostic depth. Modularization received mixed quantitative ratings but was praised in qualitative feedback when seed terms were relevant. Importantly, participants rated the tool positively on its ability to **support metric-driven improvements**, with an average score of **4.0/5** on "the suggestions helped me improve my ontology effectively." For complete details, including the verbatim comments, we direct readers to the raw responses in the repository[6].

4.3 Limitations

Despite its contributions, the present study has several limitations.

- **Structural Reliance.** The framework currently focuses on structural OQuaRE metrics. While this ensures reproducibility and comparability, it cannot guarantee semantic adequacy. An ontology may score well structurally yet misrepresent domain knowledge—analogous to a building that is structurally sound but aesthetically flawed.
- **Empirical Scope.** Our user study was modest in scale (8 participants) and centered on ontology engineers and students. Broader validation across larger and more diverse user groups, including domain scientists, is needed to fully establish interpretability and usability.
- **Scalability and Efficiency.** Although the tool produced concise outputs via token-capped prompts (2048/4096 tokens), more systematic benchmarks are required to validate prompt efficiency and scaling across very large ontologies.
- **Semantic Trade-offs.** By grounding recommendations in structural deviations, OntoInsight assumes "function follows form." This limits direct evaluation of semantic truth but provides a necessary first step toward deeper semantic assessment.
- **LLM Dependency.** While OntoInsight is designed to be LLM-agnostic(low quality metrics are always targeted in recommendations), the interpretability of recommendations vary by model.

6 https://github.com/kracr/onto-insight/blob/main/user_study_responses.csv.

– **Hallucination Risk.** Despite prompt templating and modularization, LLM outputs may occasionally introduce hallucinated recommendations or omit relevant improvements. Although these risks are partially mitigated by grounding outputs in metric values, absolute reliability cannot be guaranteed.

5 Conclusion and Future Work

OntoInsight addresses a long-standing gap in ontology evaluation which is that while existing frameworks provide quantitative and quality metrics, they rarely translate these into actionable, human-readable recommendations. By combining empirical measures with the generative capabilities of LLMs, OntoInsight provides an end-to-end pipeline, from modularization by metric to Controlled Natural Language generation and explainable LLM-facilitated feedback. OntoInsight is highly dependable, LLM-independent, and contextually versatile across ontologies of different complexities. The system balances interpretability (Basic mode) with diagnostic depth (Advanced mode), addressing both novice and expert needs. Our evaluation through perturbation testing and a user study demonstrates that OntoInsight produces actionable, metric-grounded recommendations rather than generic advice. This positions the tool as a bridge between quantitative ontology metrics and qualitative improvement strategies. OntoInsight's source code is available under Apache 2.0 license at https://github.com/kracr/onto-insight.

We plan to integrate advanced evaluation metrics, including the *semantic score* [14], *interpretability score* [14], OntoQA [2], and semiotic measures [3], to capture semantic quality. OntoInsight can be aligned with agile ontology engineering practices such as SAMOD [20], reflecting feedback from our user study. We also plan to explore the reciprocal synergy between LLMs and ontologies, where ontologies enhance LLM reliability in retrieval-augmented generation (RAG) while benefiting from LLM interpretability. Finally, a community-facing web platform with visualization support will be developed to enable iterative and practical use.

Acknowledgements. The authors acknowledge the partial support of the Infosys Centre for Artificial Intelligence (CAI), IIIT-Delhi, in this work.

References

1. Duque-Ramos, A., Fernandez-Breis, J., Stevens, R., Aussenac-Gilles, N.: OQuaRE: A SQuaRE-based approach for evaluating the quality of ontologies. J. Res. Pract. Inf. Technol. **43**, 159–176 (2011)
2. Tartir, S., Arpinar, I.B., Moore, M., Sheth, A.P., Aleman-Meza, B.: OntoQA: metric-based ontology quality analysis (2005)
3. Burton-Jones, A., Storey, V.C., Sugumaran, V., Ahluwalia, P.: A semiotic metrics suite for assessing the quality of ontologies. Data Knowl. Eng. **55**(1), 84–102 (2005). https://doi.org/10.1016/j.datak.2004.11.010

4. Tartir, S., Arpinar, I.B.: OntoQA: metric-based ontology quality analysis. In: IEEE International Conference on Semantic Computing, pp. 45–52 (2007)
5. Knublauch, H., Fergerson, R.W., Noy, N.F., Musen, M.A.: The Protégé OWL plugin: an open development environment for semantic web applications. In: International Semantic Web Conference, pp. 229–243. Springer (2004)
6. Jackson, R.C., Balhoff, J.P., Douglass, E., et al.: ROBOT: a tool for automating ontology workflows. BMC Bioinf. **20**, 407 (2019). https://doi.org/10.1186/s12859-019-3002-3
7. Dragisic, Z., Li, Y., Lambrix, P.: RepOSE-CTab-A Protégé plugin for completing ontologies. In: Proceedings of the Sixth International Workshop on the Visualization and Interaction for Ontologies and Linked Data co-located with the 20th International Semantic Web Conference (ISWC 2021), Virtual Conference, 2021 (CEUR Workshop Proceedings), vol. 3023, pp. 56–62. CEUR-WS. org (2021)
8. Reiz, A., Sandkuhl, K.: Harmonizing the OQuaRE quality framework. In: International Conference on Enterprise Information Systems (2022)
9. Reiz, A., Sandkuhl, K.: NEOntometrics: a flexible and scalable software for calculating ontology metrics. In: SEMANTiCS (Posters & Demos) (2022)
10. Lama, V., Patel, A., Debnath, N.C., Jain, S.: IRI_Debug: an ontology evaluation tool. New Gen. Comput. **42**(1), 177–197 (2024). https://doi.org/10.1007/s00354-024-00246-5
11. Lampoltshammer, T., Heistracher, T.: Ontology evaluation with Protégé using OWLET. Infocommun. J. **VI**, 12–17 (2014)
12. Poveda-Villalón, M., Gómez-Pérez, A., Suárez-Figueroa, M.C.: Oops!(ontology pitfall scanner!): an on-line tool for ontology evaluation. IJSWIS **10**(2), 7–34 (2014)
13. Kondylakis, H., et al.: Delta: a modular ontology evaluation system. Information **12**(8), 301 (2021). https://doi.org/10.3390/info12080301
14. Amith, M., et al.: Architecture and usability of OntoKeeper, an ontology evaluation tool. BMC Med. Inform. Decis. Mak. **19**, 1–18 (2019)
15. Gene Ontology Consortium: The gene ontology resource: 20 years and still GOing strong. Nucleic Acids Res. **47**(D1), D330–D338 (2019)
16. El-Sappagh, S., Franda, F., Ali, F., Kwak, K.S.: SNOMED CT standard ontology based on the ontology for general medical science. BMC Med. Inform. Decis. Mak. **18**, 1–19 (2018)
17. Ison, J., et al.: EDAM: an ontology of bioinformatics operations, types of data and identifiers, topics and formats. Bioinformatics **29**(10), 1325–1332 (2013). https://doi.org/10.1093/bioinformatics/btt113
18. Wilson, R.S.I., Goonetillake, J.S., Indika, W.A., Ginige, A.: A conceptual model for ontology quality assessment: a systematic review. Semantic Web **14**(6), 1051–1097 (2023)
19. Zaitoun, A., Sagi, T., Peleg, M.: Generating ontology-learning training-data through verbalization. In: Proceedings of the AAAI Symposium Series, vol. 4, issue 1, pp. 233–241 (2024). https://doi.org/10.1609/aaaiss.v4i1.31797
20. Peroni, S.: SAMOD: an agile methodology for the development of ontologies. In: Proceedings of the 13th OWL: Experiences and Directions Workshop and 5th OWL reasoner evaluation workshop (OWLED-ORE 2016), pp. 1–14 (2016)

Towards Automating the Life Cycle Management of Digital Twins

Gwendal Beaumont[1,2(✉)], Antoine Beugnard[1], Salvador Martínez[1], Christelle Urtado[2], and Sylvain Vauttier[2]

[1] IMT Atlantique, Lab-STICC, UMR 6285, Brest, France
{gwendal.beaumont,antoine.beugnard,salvador.martinez}@imt-atlantique.fr
[2] EuroMov Digital Health in Motion, Univ. Montpellier and IMT Mines Ales, Ales, France
{christelle.urtado,sylvain.vauttier}@mines-ales.fr

Abstract. Digital Twins (DTs) are key to Industry 4.0 and IoT systems. By definition, as virtual counterparts of a Physical Object (PO), they have to be kept up-to-date with the PO at a fast pace, leading to multiple reconfigurations, reconnections and redeployments throughout their lifetime. On the one hand, there is a growing interest around DT platforms and DT modeling languages from both academia and industry. However, systematic operational methodologies and practical tools for managing DTs resources and life cycle are more scarce. This paper identifies the need for a domain-agnostic solution to systematically manage the DT life cycle. On the other hand, *GitOps* provides principles and concrete actionable tools, such as CI/CD pipelines, declarative cluster state and version control, to manage software architectures that needs to: (1) be redeployed swiftly without interruptions and, (2) be versioned. By combining the static Digital Twin Definition Language and the GitOps framework, a new way of *automating life cycle management of DTs* at runtime is proposed in this paper. A conceptualization of core DT life cycle operations at runtime such as `connect`, `synchronize`, or `configure` and a similar work on generic GitOps operations is provided. Then, a mapping from DT to generic GitOps operations is proposed. Finally, a proof-of-concept involving a Fischertechnik Training Factory 4.0 as a use-case is presented.

Keywords: Digital Twin · Model-Driven Engineering · DevOps · GitOps

1 Introduction

Coined by Grieves [9], the term 'Digital Twins' (DTs) defines virtual clones of '*something*'. This 'something', or *Physical Object* (PO), can be anything ranging from an industrial supply chain to humans [7]. One of the most common ways to picture a DT is to decompose it in three parts: a PO, a Digital Object and a Data Flow linking them together [16]. The pair of physical and digital objects

D. Bork et al. (Eds.): ER 2025, LNCS 16189, pp. 412–430, 2026.
https://doi.org/10.1007/978-3-032-08623-5_22

is considered a DT if, and only if, the Data Flow between them is automated. Many alternative definitions, such as the 5D model by Tao et al., exist [7,33]. DTs purpose is to maintain one or several models up-to-date by mirroring the PO. In a perfect scenario, they can also be used to carry out actions on the PO. This continuous synchronization between the DT and its physical system entails multiple (re)configurations, (re)connections and (re)deployments during the lifetime of the DT [1].

Many recent contributions focus on architectures and frameworks to improve the engineering (description, implementation, and federation) of DTs [11,17, 19,31]. This comprises not only academic works but also mature open-source frameworks such as Eclipse's Vortolang[1] and Microsoft's Digital Twin Definition Language (DTDL)[2] which are both popular options for describing DTs. While these solutions are suitable for the static description of DTs [27], they are not tailored to: *i)* the dynamic description of the aforementioned recurrent DT life cycle operations and, *ii)* the management of different configurations of DTs [22].

As DTs are model-centric [13], there is a growing interest in applying Model-Driven Engineering tools and techniques as a mean to deal with their sheer complexity, such as in their description and management [25]. However, in their recent systematic mapping study, Lehner et al. highlight that most MDE contributions primarily focused on the implementation life cycle of the DT, leaving a gap at the operational phase [19].

GitOps is an operational framework that combines Git version control with DevOps [2,21] best practices to automate the deployment, scaling, and management of applications. The advantages of using Git as the operation center include: *i)* strong integration with a wide range of tools and services such as continuous integration and continuous deployment (CI/CD) pipelines, *ii)* version control and code histories, and *iii)* efficient handling of large, complex projects using branching strategies.

In order to improve the management of recurrent DTs life cycle operations, this paper proposes an approach to integrate DevOps practices into the life cycle management of DTs, leveraging MDE and GitOps. To achieve this goal, a definition of the DT life cycle operations is presented. Then, a vendor-independent conceptual model of GitOps is developed. Subsequently, an approach, combining elements from DTDL, GitOps and DT life cycle operations is presented. Using these elements as inputs, a process to generate GitOps artifacts that can be executed and manipulated is presented. Finally, a mapping between life cycle operations and GitOps elements is proposed.

The remainder of the paper is structured as follows. Section 2, gives an overview of DT modeling languages, the lacks in dynamic description of DTs of these languages and how MDE, through DTDL and GitOps, can be a solution in solving this issue. Section 3 presents DTs life cycle operations. Section 4 proposes a conceptual model of GitOps crafted as an abstraction of popular tools. Section 5 presents an approach to enable the systematic description of

---

1 https://eclipse.dev/vorto/.
2 https://github.com/Azure/opendigitaltwins-dtdl.

DTs life cycle operations by mapping them to GitOps elements. Section 6 gives a proof-of-concept implementation of the approach over a Fischertechnik Training Factory 4.0. Section 7 discusses related work and limitations of the approach. Section 8 concludes the paper.

2 Background

This section introduces DT modeling languages and more specifically the Digital Twin Definition Language. It also introduces GitOps.

2.1 Digital Twin Modeling and DTDL

Many DT modeling languages have been proposed [7,19,27,28,32]. These languages have mostly been employed for the structural modeling of DTs. Among them, DTDL [12], defined by Microsoft, is a popular open-source standard for describing DTs of different kinds (assets, IoT systems, environments, etc.) in the form of JSON-LD files. DTDL models can be created by hand, or using a graphical user interface with the Azure Digital Twins (ADT) web-service. While it proposes functionalities which are common to other languages, it notably differentiates itself by providing the means to represent Relations and Composition between DTs [30]. A fully featured proprietary platform allows one to instantiate the models, connect the DTs to actual devices and telemetry.

DTDL is made up of a set of classes that are used to structurally describe DTs. The central class, `Interface`, which is used to describe any DT, is complemented by five classes enabling the description of telemetry data, properties, commands, relationships and components. Each DTDL element has an identifier, a Digital Twin Model Identifier (DTMI), in the form of `<scheme> : <path> ; <version>`. Also, DTDL uses Internationalized Resource Identifiers (IRIs) to refer to DTDL language elements (*e.g.*, names) and model-defined elements (*e.g.*, schemas). In DTDL, a distinction is made between `Component` and `Relationship`. While the former describes components that are part of the Interface, the latter describes links between DTs, thus enabling graphs of DTs. [27]. Figure 1 presents an excerpt of the DTDL version 4 metamodel, inspired from Jacoby and Usländer [12].

Although DTDL offers the possibility to finely describe any DT, its approach is mainly static and lacks dynamic elements to fully answer the continuous redeployment, reconnections and reconfiguration matter of the DT.

2.2 GitOps, a Relative of DevOps

DevOps enables the continuous life cycle management of a software by improving the collaboration between development (Dev) and operational (Ops) teams. Over the years, it has proven to be successful in regular software applications and is now making its way to Cyber-Physical Systems (CPS) and more recently,

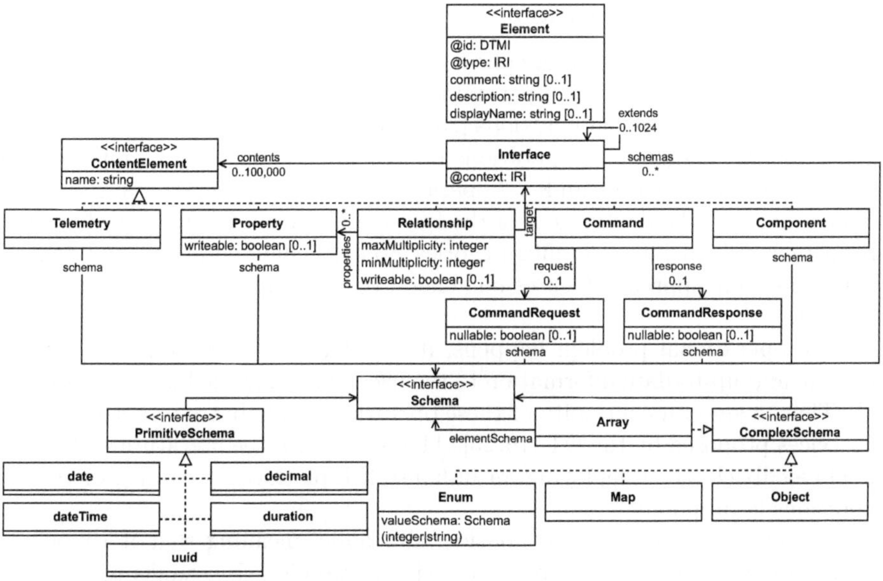

Fig. 1. Digital Twin Definition Language version 4 metamodel (excerpt), inspired from Jacoby et al. [12]

DTs [11,15]. It enables a better management of complex systems (*e.g.*, DT) and better integration of different components of such systems.

GitOps is a software development and deployment strategy centered around Git, a version control system, as the *source of truth*. Its main goals are to provide better efficiency, reliability and traceability compared to traditional software development strategies. These goals can be achieved thanks to a declarative description of the infrastructure and a process to make the environment match the declared infrastructure, mainly through orchestrators [34]. In a few words, GitOps is a way of implementing CI/CD pipelines for applications. The benefits of using GitOps include: faster deployment life cycles, easy declarative configuration, configuration drift detection, fast error recovery, and better stability and reliability [20,34].

3 Digital Twin Life Cycle

This section describes the DT life cycle at runtime and a running example. First, *core* DT life cycle operations and a simple DT life cycle are proposed. Then, a running example featuring the `connect` operation is presented to illustrate the approach. This operation, specific to the DT, involves not only a software connection to endpoints but also a physical connection to the PO and the sensors.

3.1 DT Life Cycle Operations

This work focuses on the *Operate* phase of the DevOps strategy [24] by establishing more tailored DT-specific operations. Research on the merging of DTs and DevOps exhibits plenty of operations [25]. For this paper, operations are categorized into two categories: *i)* operations related to the PO, *e.g.*, the replacement of a machine in a factory and, *ii)* operations related to the DT as a software application, *e.g.*, the deployment of the DT to a platform. Operations of type *ii)* are further refined into two subcategories: tool-specific operations and general operations. Our approach focuses on general operations related to the life cycle of the DT.

If an operational problem happens, it is unlikely that the DT will provide accurate and up-to-date information to the user, removing the benefits of using a DT. Thus, a smooth continuity of these operations contributes to better quality of services proposed by the DT [19,25]. Thanks to both the literature and experiments feedback when deploying an in-house DT platform, a catalog of general operations is proposed.

Each of these operations is considered atomic, meaning that it cannot be further decomposed, and is applied to a single, atomic DT. Thanks to the composition capabilities in DTDL, if an operation is applied to a composite DT, we expect this operation to propagate to each DT composing the main DT. In the best case scenario, the operation should only redeploy the modified atomic DT.

These operations compose *DT 'core' life cycle management operations* and form a basis for our approach. A representation of the succession of these operations as a state-machine diagram is depicted in Fig. 2.

In this diagram, each life cycle operation appears as a transition and each target state is named `{operation}-ed`. The only exceptions are the In-Sync and Out-of-Sync states which are inside the `Connected` state. This is because the DT can transition from being In-Sync or Out-of-Sync when the connection is established to the PO [25]. While the `synchronize` operation allows to enter the In-Sync state, the transition to Out-of-Sync happens through *events* such as an evolution of the PO or a drift from the DT.

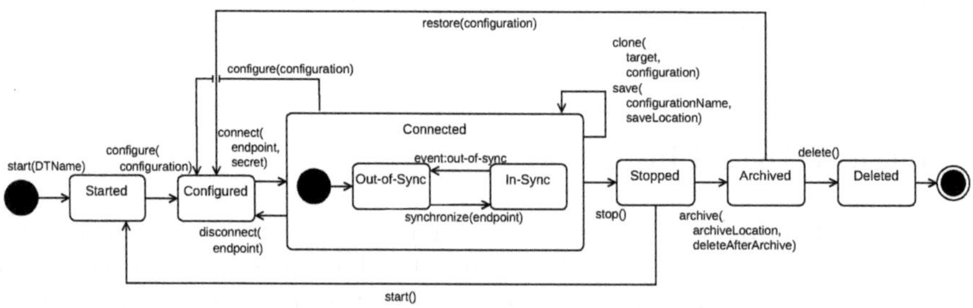

Fig. 2. Simple DT life cycle as a state-machine

A detailed definition of each operation is given below:

- `start(DTName: String)` scaffolds the DT [31]. None of the parameters or variables of the DT are set yet. The `DTName` permits to identify the DT. This operation always happens first. At this stage, the only possible action is to `configure` the DT.
- `configure(configuration: Configuration)` takes the DT provided by the `start` operation and configures specific variables of the DT [1,13,25,31]. A `Configuration`, which is a specific state of the DT (*e.g.*, parameters, tools, physical structure) at a given time, provides the necessary information to be initialized. This operation is available for the first time after a `start` operation and may be triggered at any time while the DT is connected, causing a reconfiguration. If the DT is in a twinning phase (see below), it will disconnect. The next possible operation is `connect`.
- `connect(endpoint: URI, secret: Secret (optional))` connects the DT to the PO by means of an endpoint, represented by a URI, and authentication secrets if necessary [31]. It connects the DT to a particular sensor or component of the PO. Once the connection is established, the DT enters a connected state in which the *twinning*, *i.e.*, the process of maintaining the representation of the PO up-to-date, happens. A `connect` operation usually happens after a `configure` operation since the latter automatically disconnects the DT when applied. The next possible operations are `save`, `clone`, `synchronize` and `stop`.
- `disconnect(endpoint: Endpoint (optional))`: disconnects an endpoint (if specified) or the entire DT from the PO [31]. Once applied, the DT no longer receives real-time data from the PO, thus the *twinning* process stops. This operation only applies if the DT is connected. If not, nothing happens and / or an error can be raised. Afterward, it is possible to `connect` again to the PO.
- `synchronize(endpoint: Endpoint (optional))`: applies in case of a desynchronization with the PO (the latest available data can not be pulled by the DT) [25,31]. This operation only happens if at least one connection to a sensor (or the whole PO) is established. A synchronize operation can be triggered to force a reconnection. At this stage, the possible operations are: `clone`, `configure`, `save`, and `stop`.
- `clone(target: DT, configuration: Configuration (default: latest))`: clones this DT to a new target DT. More specifically, it copies all the data and models into a new target DT based on a given configuration. It clones the latest configuration by default. This operation is applied as long as a configuration of the DT exists. What's more, it does not change the state of the current DT. The next possible operations depend on the current state of the DT.
- `save(configurationName: string, saveLocation: string)`: saves the current configuration of the DT [31] using `configurationName` as the name of the configuration and `saveLocation` as a save path. This operation does not change the state of the DT and can be applied as long as the DT has been configured at least once and is not deleted. The next available operations depend on the current state of the DT.

- `stop()` stops the DT, thus disconnecting from the PO and de-configuring the DT [13,31]. From now on, new knowledge (data, knowledge) can be added to the DT but not in real-time. This state can serve maintenance or upgrade purposes. This operation can be applied if the DT is configured and connected to the PO. A restart of the DT is possible thanks to the `start` operation.
- `archive(archiveLocation: string, deleteAfterArchive: boolean (optional))` puts the repository containing the data of the DT into a read-only mode [25]. No further knowledge (models, data, configurations) can be modified after this [25]. A `deleteAfterArchive` option allows to immediately `delete` the DT after it has been archived. `archive` can only happen after a `stop` operation. The possible operations after this are `restore` and `delete`.
- `restore(configuration: Configuration (default: latest))` undoes the `archive` operation, putting the DT repository into read-write mode [25]. Connections and configurations of the DT are re-enabled. This operation necessitates to specify a version to restore to. By default, it uses the latest known configuration. Possible operation after this one is `connect`.
- `delete()` deletes all the data related to the DT (repository, data, models, connections...) [13,25]. It can only happen after the DT has been archived and is irreversible. No further operation can be applied after this one.

3.2 Running Example

An example of the `connect` operation is given below using a Fischertechnik Factory 4.0. This training model of a real-world factory, helps us illustrating how GitOps and DTDL could facilitate the connection to the PO. This example is based on the Sorting Line based on color Detection (SLD) module of the factory. An instantiation of this module can be found in Fig. 3.

The traditional way of connecting the SLD module to a telemetry tool (in this case MQTT Broker) is to *hand-write* scripts using the information provided by the DTDL model. This task can be tedious, requiring to go back and forth between the script and the model. Furthermore, if a change happens physically or within the DTDL model, the coder needs to manually change the script, which is not instant and can lead to errors.

However, a direct integration of DTDL elements within GitOps could help us alleviate such risks. Indeed, when the DT of the module performs the `connect` operation, if a process could automatically retrieve the information from the DTDL model, then the time needed to update the information on the running would be much lower. This could also reduce the risks of typing errors.

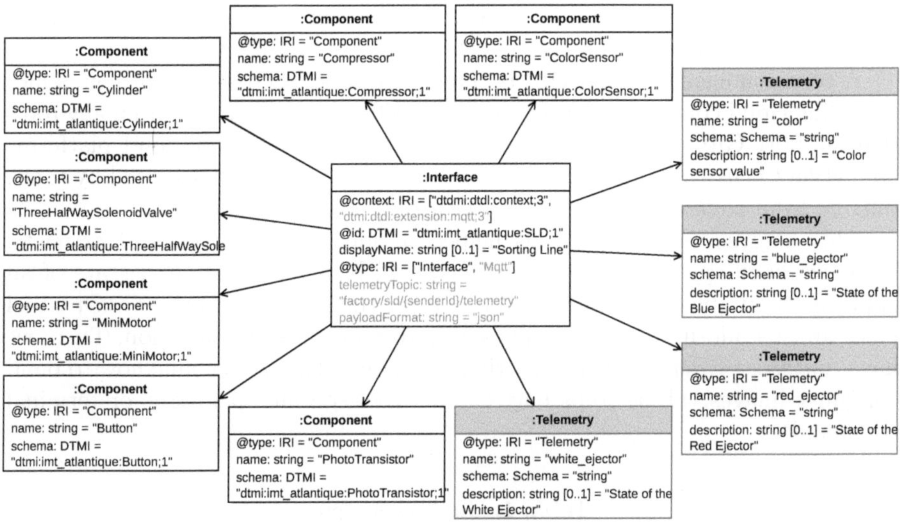

Fig. 3. Instantiation of the Sorting Line based on color Detection (SLD) module of the Fischertechnik Factory 4.0. Connection-related elements are represented in red. (Color figure online)

4 GitOps Conceptual Modeling

This section covers the conceptual modeling of GitOps. First, we extract GitOps concepts by analyzing popular tools. Then, we present a conceptual model, leveraging the concepts we extracted.

4.1 Extraction of GitOps Concepts

This paper proposes to establish a direct link between *a)* DT life cycle operations and *b)* GitOps elements. Thus, a unified model is required to achieve abstraction across different tools. As GitOps definition is not formal [34], we propose to extract a conceptual model by analyzing GitOps tools: ArgoCD[3], Flux[4] and Jenkins X[5]. These tools are regarded as the most common and popular tools to setup GitOps environments [10].

Table 1 gathers common concepts observed in the different tools. The main element is the *GitOps platform* as it is what we are conceptualizing. A simple definition of a GitOps platform can be: tool set that automates infrastructure and software application deployment by using Git as the source-of-truth. This means that in case of conflicts or errors, Git is the source of what we trust. The two main components of Git are *Git repositories* and *Git operations*. The former

[3] https://argo-cd.readthedocs.io/.
[4] https://fluxcd.io/.
[5] https://jenkins-x.io/.

refers to the hosts that store the software applications, while the latter refers to the operations performed on those hosts.

A common element of GitOps is *cloud providers.* These represent companies providing cloud computing services through different *tools.* There are many tools that support GitOps workflows today. Another component of cloud platforms are *artifact registries.* These hosts different kinds of *artifacts* produced by tools, ranging from *container images* to *packages*, *CI/CD pipelines*, etc.

This analysis of GitOps tools helped us identify other types of artifacts. First, we have *app configuration artifacts* which define the desired state of an application. If the application deviates from the desired state, a GitOps tool picks up this information and applies fixes to remediate the situation. Then, we have *container image recipes* consisting in a series of steps to define how to build container images. These steps may contain tool-specific operations or terminal commands.

Table 1. GitOps concepts

Concept	Description
GitOps platform	This represents the GitOps platform we are modeling
Git repository	The main element of GitOps which hosts software files.
Git operations	Set of operations which can be performed on the Git repository.
Cloud provider	Company that deliver cloud computing services. These services are provided by tools hosted on the platform.
Tool	Software application which provides a service. They can be provided by cloud providers or standalone (self-hosted).
Artifact registry	Centralized repository which hosts artifacts of different kinds (container images, packages, CD/CI pipelines, etc.)
CI/CD Pipelines	Series of steps which should deliver new software. Usually stored in JSON or YAML files.
App configurations	Define the configuration of a software application.
Orchestrator manifest	Piece of code which declares the desired state of a cluster.
Container Image Recipe	Series of steps which define how to build a new container image.
Container Image	Lightweight, standalone and executable software package which contains everything needed to run an application.

4.2 GitOps Conceptual Model

Figure 4 gathers the concepts identified in Sect. 4.1 as a GitOps conceptual model. The center piece of the figure is the GitOps platform. A platform has a name and an optional description. First, one or many *Git Repositories* compose the platform. Each repository has a name and can have a description. A remote URL locates the repository on the network. Different branches, one of which is the default branch, compose Git repositories. Visibility can be set using keywords as *Public* (everyone can access), *Internal* (limited to some groups of users) or *Private* (only the owner and designated users can access).

Another main component of the Git tool is *Git Operations*. Identified main Git operations are *Commit* to locally save changes to the code, *Push* to send one or many commits to the Git repository, *Fetch* to check for changes on the repository, *Pull* to retrieve changes pushed to the repository, *Diff* to show changes between two versions of the code and *Merge* to join multiple development histories together.

A GitOps platform can also be linked to one or many *Cloud Providers*. Tools, which can be provided by a cloud provider or as standalone, self-hosted applications are also part of the GitOps platform. Different kinds of tools are identified, an *Orchestrator* orchestrates application clusters, an *Operator* operates the different GitOps operations, a *SyncTool* detects changes in the code, a *Database* stores data and a *DiffTool* detects the differences between the desired state and the actual state of the application.

CI/CD Pipelines play a key role within GitOps platforms. These pipelines have a name and are stored as files at given file locations. Different *Parameters* and a set of *Stages*, or jobs, to produce different artifacts compose these pipelines. At least one *Step* composes a job.

Finally, an *Artifact Registry* is identified by a name, an URL and a type to restrict the type of artifacts they can host. An *Artifact* has a name, a URI to access the artifact and it can have a description. Different types of artifacts are identified. *Orchestrator Manifests* which are composed of at least one *Orchestrator Object* and *Container Image Recipes* which can build *Container Images* artifacts based on a set of *Image Recipe Instructions*.

5 GitOps Artifacts Generation Process

This section focuses on the description of the process to generate tangible GitOps artifacts and the mapping between previously described DT operations and GitOps elements for the systematic life cycle management of DTs.

5.1 Approach Description

This paper envisions a process which takes DTDL models, Git repositories containing the GitOps environment parameters, and the extracted GitOps model as inputs to generate GitOps artifacts tailored to the GitOps platform as outputs. To achieve such goal, the proposed process decomposes into multiple steps pictured in Fig. 5.

First Step. Involves that a DT Modeler produces DTDL models. The correct filling of the DTDL models is crucial to ensure that the generated artifacts will

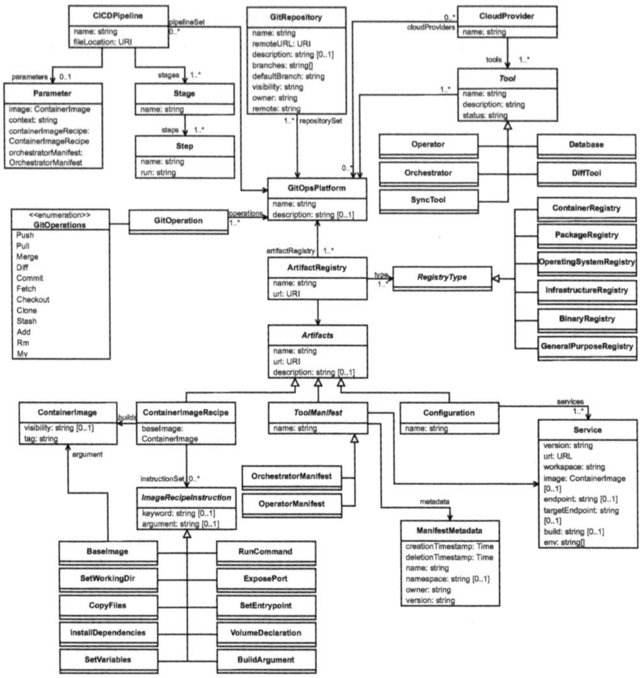

Fig. 4. Model of GitOps

be usable. To craft the DTDL models, the DT modeler uses both the PO and the Git repositories containing the code to execute the DT. Once the models are finished, they get pushed to a Git repository. Good practices to produce DTDL models include the use of already existing industry-standard DTDL ontologies, the crafting of one interface per file and the validation of models.

Second Step. Simultaneously or asynchronously, a DevOps/GitOps engineer defines a GitOps infrastructure for the DT. This involves to choose one or many GitOps tools. This produces artifacts such as infrastructure specification and tool configuration which are pushed to the GitOps repository.

Third Step. The third step is an instantiation phase and necessitates the first and second steps to be complete. In this step, an actor takes the DTDL models and the set up GitOps platform to manually instantiate a GitOps model (presented in Sect. 4.2) using the mapping proposed below. For the `connect` operation, the actor fills the identified GitOps elements in the model using the `Telemetry` and `MQTT` DTDL elements and the tools `Configuration`.

Fourth Step. Using the GitOps model instances crafted in the previous step, GitOps artifacts adapted to the platform get generated. These tailored artifacts, ranging from CI/CD pipelines to GitOps configuration files and manifests, can be pushed to the GitOps platform in order to be executed.

Ideally, this process does not regenerate every artifacts each time an update is made to the DT or the GitOps platform. Only the updated parts are regenerated, *e.g.*, for a connect operation, if an endpoint changes, only the parts related to that endpoint are regenerated. This should speed up the generation process and the deployment of new changes on the DT.

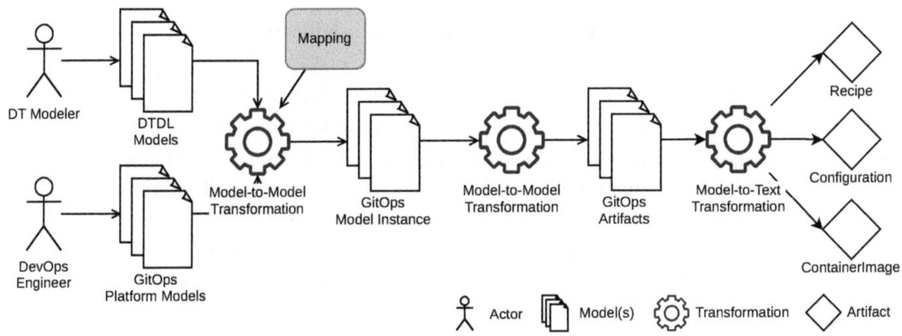

Fig. 5. Generation process from DTDL models and a GitOps configuration to platform-specific artifacts

5.2 DTDL and GitOps to Life Cycle Mapping

We establish a mapping between DT life cycle operations and DTDL and GitOps elements. This mapping is done manually, from experiments feedback.

The mapping is represented in Table 2. Each row shows which DTDL and GitOps elements can be associated with a given life cycle operation. While DTDL elements act as source of information for the generation process, GitOps elements of this mapping include both input elements and outputs elements. The mapping is not one-to-one, multiple elements from one set may correspond to multiple elements in the other.

As an example, in the `connect` operation, `Telemetry` and `MQTT` elements both contribute to set information about the endpoint we want to connect to. For GitOps elements, the `Git Repository` provides missing information in DTDL models such as tool-specification, workspaces and remote URLs.

6 Proof of Concept: Fischertechnik Factory Use Case

As a mean of demonstration of feasibility of the approach, this paper proposes a proof of concept involving the `connect` operation and a Fischertechnik Training Factory 4.0.

The Fischertechnik Factory 4.0 [29] is a small training factory designed to simulate modern industrial processes, focusing on the principles of Industry 4.0.

Table 2. Mapping between DT life cycle operations, DTDL and GitOps

Operation	DTDL element	GitOps element
start	Interface	GitRepository, GitOperations (clone), Operator, Orchestrator, CICDPipeline, AppConfiguration
configure	Interface, Property, Component	Operator, Orchestrator, CICDPipeline, ContainerImage, ToolManifest, AppConfiguration
connect	Telemetry, MQTT	ContainerImageRecipe, ContainerImage, ToolManifest, AppConfiguration
disconnect	Telemetry, MQTT	ToolManifest, AppConfiguration
synchronize	Telemetry, MQTT	GitRepository, GitOperations (fetch, pull)
clone	Interface, Telemetry, Property, Relationship, Command, Component, MQTT	GitRepository, GitOperations (fetch, pull, clone, commit), ContainerImage, ToolManifest, AppConfiguration, Database
save	Interface, Telemetry, Property, Relationship, Command, Component, MQTT	GitRepository, GitOperations (add, commit, push), ToolManifest, Database, CICDPipeline
stop	Interface	GitRepository, GitOperations (mv, add, commit, push), Operator, Orchestrator, ToolManifest, AppConfiguration
archive	Interface	GitRepository, ToolManifest, CICDPipeline, ContainerImage
restore	Interface, Telemetry, Property, Relationship, Command, Component, MQTT	GitRepository, GitOperations (mv, add, commit, push), CICDPipeline, ToolManifest
delete	Interface	GitRepository, GitOperations (rm, commit, push)

It includes components like sensors, actuators, and control systems that allow users to build and program automated production lines.

For this use case, we use our running example, the `connect` operation which can be summarized to: setup an MQTT Broker and connect (subscribe) to the right topic. Then, our approach should enable us to: gather the necessary MQTT parameters from the DTDL model and gather information from the GitOps configuration to craft a GitOps instance of the proposed model. A handmade deployment of the `connect` operation reveals that expected artifacts are an orchestrator manifest, a container image recipe, a container image and a CI/CD pipeline.

First Step. A scoped-down, but sufficient for this paper, DTDL model of the factory is handcrafted. We start by using the physical structure of the factory, *i.e.*, we declare each factory module as a DT in separate JSON files and also declare a main 'Fischertechnik Factory' DT which is composed of each module. The physical description in DTDL ends by describing each component for each module. Then, we use the software components at our hand to refine the DTDL model by adding MQTT connections and annotations. The model then get instantiated using an EMF model of DTDL. The crafted DTDL models can be found on the dedicated repository[6].

Second Step. Concurrently, we setup, by hand, a GitOps platform on a machine using the ArgoCD operator and the Kubernetes[7] orchestrator. This produces configuration files for both ArgoCD and Kubernetes. This GitOps platform is then used as input to fill a GitOps platform EMF model.

Third Step. We then instantiate identified GitOps elements in the mapping. This means handcrafting a `GitRepository`, a `Configuration` and a `Container ImageRecipe` objects (blue in Fig. 6). To create these elements, we use both DTDL elements, mostly MQTT elements within the `Interface` and `Telemetry` and GitOps elements extracted from configuration files.

Fourth Step. The GitOps elements instantiated in the third step are used to generate artifacts useful to perform the `connect` operation using Acceleo Model-to-Text transformations. These artifacts include an `OrchestratorManifest`, an `OperatorManifest` and a `ContainerImage`.

Application of the approach used the elements depicted in Fig. 6. To make sure that the generated artifacts make sense, we compared them to the ones we handcrafted and found that they correspond closely syntactically and semantically.

7 Related Work and Discussion

In recent years, many different approaches to model DTs have been proposed in the literature [3,19,23,26,27]. We center our discussion on contributions specially focused on the modeling and management of DTs life cycle.

Kamburjan et al., describe an automatic method for self-adaptation on DTs to address shifts between life cycle phases in a PO [13]. They propose declarative life cycle stages expressed by using the Manchester OWN Syntax. Our work targets the DTs operational life cycle and thus may be seen as complementary to theirs. More similar to our work, Lehner et al. [18] propose a reference architecture to take advantage of the principles of MDE to connect models crafted at design times with running systems [18]. It proposes to use model repositories as artifacts from the design phase and to connect them to running systems and use them as a source of information. Our work differentiates from Lehner's proposed architecture, by focusing on automating DTs life cycle operations by generating and orchestrating GitOps artifacts.

DevOps and life cycle management have also been studied from the Cyber Physical Systems perspective [5,8,18]. Koren et al. [14] showcase the DevOps4CPPS framework, spotlighting the use of microservices and GitOps in a CPPS environment. Furthermore, Aissat et al. [1] introduce JuNo-OPS, a DevOps framework establishing guidelines on using DevOps for DTs. Based on

[6] https://github.com/labsticc-p4s/er2025-proof_of_concept.
[7] https://kubernetes.io/.

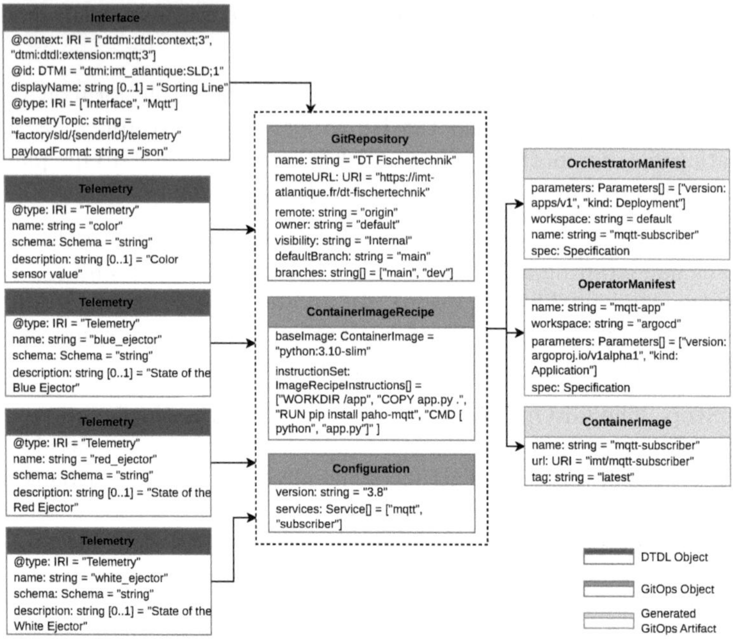

Fig. 6. Implementation of the *connect* operation on the SLD module of the Fischertechnik Factory 4.0 (simplified).

their experiment, they showcase the difficulties of collaboration between domain and non-domain experts (*e.g.*, git training). Our work takes inspiration from these efforts, but focuses on the particularities of the DT life cycle.

Recent works from Talasila et al. [31] and Dalibor et al. [6] center their attention on platforms for running DTs. Their platforms allow users to describe DTs life cycle operations through scripts. Our approach aims at the automatic generation and management of such scripts leveraging GitOps.

Finally, and focused on modeling the DevOps process and platform, Colantoni et al. [4] propose a framework, Dev-Ops-ML, which allows users to model DevOps platforms and engineering processes, but do not deal directly with DTs nor GitOps.

Thus, while this paper capitalizes on previous work, it differentiates itself by shifting the focus from the development part of DevOps to the operational part. For instance, we have not seen solutions in the literature putting a clear focus on the life cycle operations of the DT at runtime. Generally, this part has been, at best, handled in an *ad hoc* manner. The idea of combining an existing DT modeling language with a DevOps operational framework like GitOps is original. We believe that the benefits of using a framework centered around Git and DevOps principles match the needs of DTs w.r.t. the management of their life cycle. While the initial setup and the general maintenance of a GitOps platform introduce complexity to the system, the automation of life cycle processes frees up useful time to engineers which they could allocate towards other parts of the DTs such as services.

8 Conclusion and Future Work

In this paper, we have presented a model-driven approach for the life cycle management of DTs. Our approach is based on the combination of a DT description language and GitOps. It includes the definition of a novel GitOps metamodel and the corresponding mapping between a DT description, a number of high level DT life cycle operations and GitOps operations and artifacts. A proof of concept demonstrating the feasibility of the approach has been presented as well.

In future work, we plan to both extend our approach to include additional operations and to work on the granularity of the ones presented here. Indeed the operations presented here refer to the DT as a whole, and not to parts of it (*e.g.*, we may want to disconnect just some part of a given DT). Furthermore, we intend to study DT configuration management, *i.e.*, manage different versions of a DT using Git branching strategies. Besides, we plan to study a DTDL extension (*e.g.*, by including life cycle operation annotations) which may facilitate the mapping of language elements in our approach. Additionally, we intend to extend the evaluation to larger and more complex DTs in order to evaluate the scalability and generalizability of our approach.

Finally, while Fig. 2 proposes baseline DT operations, further investigations will focus on the customization and modularity of this approach to further align with DevOps principles.

Acknowledgments. Gwendal Beaumont's Ph.D. is funded by the Futur, ruptures & impacts program by Fondation Mines-Télécom and the TSN CARNOT institute. Authors thank Région Bretagne for the CPER Industrie du Futur 2021-2027 grant, and the ANR (French National Research Agency) MODES JCJC project n° ANR-23-CE25-0011-01 as well for partially funding this research.

Disclosure of Interests. The authors have no competing interests to declare that are relevant to the content of this article.

References

1. Aissat, S., Beaulieu, J., Bordeleau, F., Gascon-Samson, J., Poirier, E., Motamedi, A.: JuNo-OPS: a DevOps framework for the engineering of digital twins for built assets. In: Proceedings of the ACM/IEEE 27th International Conference on Model Driven Engineering Languages and Systems, pp. 496–506. MODELS Companion '24, Association for Computing Machinery, Linz, Austria (2024). https://doi.org/10.1145/3652620.3688266
2. Beetz, F., Harrer, S.: GitOps: the evolution of DevOps? IEEE Softw. **39**(4), 70–75 (2022). https://doi.org/10.1109/MS.2021.3119106

3. Bordeleau, F., Combemale, B., Eramo, R., Brand, M.V.D., Wimmer, M.: Towards model-driven digital twin engineering: current opportunities and future challenges. In: Systems Modelling and Management, pp. 43–54. Springer (2020). https://doi.org/10.1007/978-3-030-58167-1_4
4. Colantoni, A., Berardinelli, L., Wimmer, M.: DevOpsML: towards modeling DevOps processes and platforms. In: Proceedings of the 23rd ACM/IEEE International Conference on Model Driven Engineering Languages and Systems: Companion Proceedings, pp. 1–10. MODELS '20, Association for Computing Machinery, New York, NY, USA (2020). https://doi.org/10.1145/3417990.3420203
5. Combemale, B., Wimmer, M.: Towards a model-based DevOps for cyber-physical systems. In: Bruel, J.M., Mazzara, M., Meyer, B. (eds.) Software Engineering Aspects of Continuous Development and New Paradigms of Software Production and Deployment, pp. 84–94. Springer, Cham (2020). https://doi.org/10.1007/978-3-030-39306-9_6
6. Dalibor, M., et al.: Generating customized low-code development platforms for digital twins. J. Comput. Lang. **70**, 101117 (2022). https://doi.org/10.1016/j.cola.2022.101117
7. Dalibor, M., et al.: A cross-domain systematic mapping study on software engineering for digital twins. J. Syst. Softw. **193**, 111361 (2022). https://doi.org/10.1016/j.jss.2022.111361
8. Dobaj, J., Riel, A., Macher, G., Egretzberger, M.: Towards DevOps for cyber-physical systems (CPSs): resilient self-adaptive software for sustainable human-centric smart CPS facilitated by digital twins. Machines **11**(10), 973 (2023). https://doi.org/10.3390/machines11100973
9. Grieves, M.: Product Lifecycle Management: Driving the Next Generation of Lean Thinking. McGraw-Hill, New York (2006)
10. Gupta, S., Bhatia, M., Memoria, M., Manani, P.: Prevalence of GitOps, DevOps in fast CI/CD cycles. In: 2022 International Conference on Machine Learning, Big Data, Cloud and Parallel Computing (COM-IT-CON), vol. 1, pp. 589–596 (2022). https://doi.org/10.1109/COM-IT-CON54601.2022.9850786
11. Hugues, J., Hristosov, A., Hudak, J.J., Yankel, J.: TwinOps - DevOps meets model-based engineering and digital twins for the engineering of CPS. In: Proceedings of the 23rd ACM/IEEE International Conference on Model Driven Engineering Languages and Systems: Companion Proceedings, pp. 1–5. MODELS '20, Association for Computing Machinery, New York, NY, USA (2020). https://doi.org/10.1145/3417990.3421446
12. Jacoby, M., Usländer, T.: Digital twin and internet of things–current standards landscape. Appl. Sci. **10**(18), 6519 (2020). https://doi.org/10.3390/app10186519
13. Kamburjan, E., Bencomo, N., Tarifa, S.L.T., Johnsen, E.B.: Declarative lifecycle management in digital twins. In: Proceedings of the ACM/IEEE 27th International Conference on Model Driven Engineering Languages and Systems, pp. 353–363. MODELS Companion '24, Association for Computing Machinery, Linz, Austria (2024). https://doi.org/10.1145/3652620.3688248
14. Koren, I., Rinker, F., Meixner, K., Kröger, M., Zeng, M.: Implementing DevOps practices in CPPS using microservices and GitOps. In: 2023 IEEE 28th International Conference on Emerging Technologies and Factory Automation (ETFA), pp. 1–4 (2023). https://doi.org/10.1109/ETFA54631.2023.10275433
15. Koren, I., Rinker, F., Meixner, K., Matevska, J., Walter, J.: Challenges and opportunities of DevOps in cyber-physical production systems engineering. In: 2023 IEEE 6th International Conference on Industrial Cyber-Physical Systems (ICPS), pp. 1–6 (2023). https://doi.org/10.1109/ICPS58381.2023.10128073

16. Kritzinger, W., Karner, M., Traar, G., Henjes, J., Sihn, W.: Digital twin in manufacturing: a categorical literature review and classification. IFAC-PapersOnLine **51**(11), 1016–1022 (2018). https://doi.org/10.1016/j.ifacol.2018.08.474
17. Lee, A., Manrique Negrin, D.A., Cleophas, L.: Evaluating open-source tools for heterogeneous model-based digital twin development: a microbrewery case study. In: 2024 Annual Modeling and Simulation Conference (ANNSIM), pp. 1–13 (2024). https://doi.org/10.23919/ANNSIM61499.2024.10732658
18. Lehner, D., Wolny, S., Mazak-Huemer, A., Wimmer, M.: Towards a reference architecture for leveraging model repositories for digital twins. In: 2020 25th IEEE International Conference on Emerging Technologies and Factory Automation (ETFA), vol. 1, pp. 1077–1080 (2020). https://doi.org/10.1109/ETFA46521.2020.9212109
19. Lehner, D., et al.: Model-driven engineering for digital twins: a systematic mapping study. Softw. Syst. Model. (2025). https://doi.org/10.1007/s10270-025-01264-7
20. Limoncelli, T.A.: GitOps: a path to more self-service IT: IaC + PR = GitOps. Queue **16**(3), 13–26 (2018). https://doi.org/10.1145/3236386.3237207
21. Linsbauer, S., Hark, R., Koziolek, H., Eskandani, N.: Runtime orchestration of distributed control system services with TOSCA, kubernetes, and GitOps. In: 2024 IEEE 21st International Conference on Software Architecture Companion (ICSA-C), pp. 40–47 (2024). https://doi.org/10.1109/ICSA-C63560.2024.00013
22. Lu, H., Yue, T., Ali, S.: Pattern-based interactive configuration derivation for cyber-physical system product lines. ACM Trans. Cyber-Phys. Syst. **4**(4), 44:1-44:24 (2020). https://doi.org/10.1145/3389397
23. Maree, J.M.J., Kruger, K., Basson, A.H.: A digital twin architecture for the provisioning, management, and monitoring of heterogenous IoT devices. In: Proceedings of the ACM/IEEE 27th International Conference on Model Driven Engineering Languages and Systems, pp. 442–452. MODELS Companion '24, Association for Computing Machinery, Linz, Austria (2024). https://doi.org/10.1145/3652620.3688258
24. Mejía Miranda, J., Muñoz, M., Rocha, A., Hernández Pérez, Y., Avila-George, H. (eds.): New Perspectives in Software Engineering. No. 1135 in Studies in Computational Intelligence, 1st edn. Springer, Cham (2024). https://doi.org/10.1007/978-3-031-50590-4
25. Michael, J., et al.: Model-driven engineering for digital twins: opportunities and challenges. Syst. Eng. J. (2025)
26. Negrin, D.A.M., Cleophas, L., Van Den Brand, M.: Using Ptolemy II as a framework for virtual entity integration and orchestration in digital twins. In: 2021 ACM/IEEE International Conference on Model Driven Engineering Languages and Systems Companion (MODELS-C), pp. 233–236 (2021). https://doi.org/10.1109/MODELS-C53483.2021.00041
27. Pfeiffer, J., Lehner, D., Wortmann, A., Wimmer, M.: Modeling capabilities of digital twin platforms - old wine in new bottles? J. Object Technol. **21**(3), 3:1 (2022). https://doi.org/10.5381/jot.2022.21.3.a10
28. Qi, Q., et al.: Enabling technologies and tools for digital twin. J. Manuf. Syst. **58**, 3–21 (2021). https://doi.org/10.1016/j.jmsy.2019.10.001
29. Sala, R., Pirola, F., Pezzotta, G.: On the development of the digital shadow of the Fischertechnik training factory industry 4.0: an educational perspective. Procedia Comput. Sci. **217**, 640–649 (2023). https://doi.org/10.1016/j.procs.2022.12.260
30. Schmidt, C., Volz, F., Stojanovic, L., Sutschet, G.: Increasing interoperability between digital twin standards and specifications: transformation of DTDL to AAS. Sensors **23**(18), 7742 (2023). https://doi.org/10.3390/s23187742

31. Talasila, P., Gomes, C., Mikkelsen, P.H., Arboleda, S.G., Kamburjan, E., Larsen, P.G.: Digital twin as a service (DTaaS): a platform for digital twin developers and users. In: 2023 IEEE Smart World Congress (SWC), pp. 1–8 (2023). https://doi.org/10.1109/SWC57546.2023.10448890
32. Tao, F., Xiao, B., Qi, Q., Cheng, J., Ji, P.: Digital twin modeling. J. Manuf. Syst. **64**, 372–389 (2022). https://doi.org/10.1016/j.jmsy.2022.06.015
33. Tao, F., Zhang, H., Liu, A., Nee, A.Y.C.: Digital twin in industry: state-of-the-art. IEEE Trans. Ind. Inf. **15**(4), 2405–2415 (2019). https://doi.org/10.1109/TII.2018.2873186
34. Weaveworks: GitOps—Operations by Pull Request (2018). https://medium.com/weaveworks/gitops-operations-by-pull-request-14e8b659b058

Author Index

D. Bork et al. (Eds.): ER 2025, LNCS 16189, pp. 431–432, 2026.
https://doi.org/10.1007/978-3-032-08623-5

MIX
Papier aus verantwortungsvollen Quellen
Paper from responsible sources
FSC® C105338

If you have any concerns about our products,
you can contact us on
ProductSafety@springernature.com

In case Publisher is established outside the EU,
the EU authorized representative is:
Springer Nature Customer Service Center GmbH
Europaplatz 3, 69115 Heidelberg, Germany

Printed by Libri Plureos GmbH
in Hamburg, Germany